Belgium & Luxembourg

THIS EDITION WRITTEN AND RESEARCHED BY

Helena Smith, Andy Symington, Donna Wheeler

PLAN YOUR TRIP

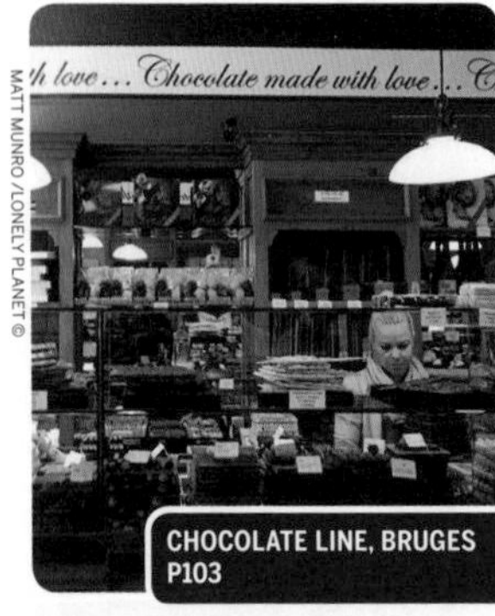

CHOCOLATE LINE, BRUGES P103

MATT MUNRO /LONELY PLANET ©

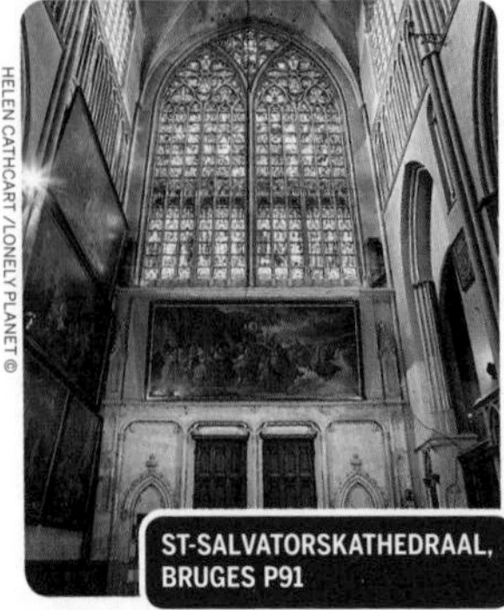
ST-SALVATORSKATHEDRAAL, BRUGES P91

HELEN CATHCART /LONELY PLANET ©

ON THE ROAD

Contents

UNDERSTAND

SURVIVAL GUIDE

SPECIAL FEATURES

Welcome to Belgium & Luxembourg

Fabulously historic yet flush with the shock of the new, these compact, gentle and decidedly multilingual little countries are packed with great, big, wonderful surprises.

Unexpected Riches

Belgium's exquisite medieval towns are home to a bounty of Unesco sites, but there are many other attractions, including happening big cities, caves, kayaking, industrial locations and sandy North Sea beaches. The region was a crucible of European painting and has remained astonishingly creative ever since. Revel in the strange, affecting beauty of the Flemish Primitives, the voluptuousness of Rubens, the sinuous curves of art nouveau and the country's great contemporary scene. Popular culture is also a hoot: comic strips and fashion have dedicated museums, and Belgium's carnivals are some of the world's weirdest and wildest.

Battle Scars

Belgium's cities and fields bear the scars of centuries of invasion, siege, conquest, assimilation and resilience. Site of some of the most brutal conflicts of modern history, the country draws visitors looking to understand, remember and mourn. The battlefield where Wellington defeated Napoleon at Waterloo, the many towns and frontlines of WWI, as well as the less commemorated, but no less significant, WWII sites – all have museums and memorials that sensitively honour the dead and keep their stories alive.

Town & Country

Belgium is both tiny and a place of distinct contrasts. The historic 'art' cities of Flanders seduce visitors with medieval belfries, magical market squares and step-gabled houses overlooking pretty urban canals, all interspersed with superb museums and galleries. And they're all close together, seamlessly interconnected by regular public transport. Head south and much of Wallonia is profoundly rural: impressive caves, castles and bucolic valleys to explore and lots of outdoor fun to be had in the wooded hills. Luxembourg falls somewhere between the two, its small but sophisticated capital encircled by magnificent castles and pretty hill villages.

Chips, Chocolate & Beer

Pack your elastic-waisted pants. Belgians serve up a remarkable range of edible specialities, including the world's most luscious chocolate. Jumbo mussels in a briney, winey broth are served with crispy, twice-fried *frites*. Then, of course, there's the beer. Brewing is an almost mystical art in Belgium and many ales are still created in the traditional manner: in monasteries. Meanwhile, Luxembourg has the world's highest number of Michelin stars per capita and keeps all comers in a celebratory mood with an ever-flowing supply of local Moselle bubbly.

Why I Love Belgium & Luxembourg

By Donna Wheeler, Writer

My childhood bedroom in Sydney was decorated with postcards of Van Eyck Madonnas, but it wasn't until a couple of decades later, during one of Europe's coldest winters, that infatuation turned to love. My first impression of Antwerp was one of sheer wonder, the guildhalls of Grote Markt glinting as snow fell at the Christmas markets, and the dimmed, richly cosy interiors of the Rubenshuis and the Museum Plantin-Moretus. This sense of quiet magic has accompanied each subsequent visit, whether it's to galleries or gigs in Ghent or for family time in a 17th-century farmhouse.

For more about our writers, see page 320

Above: Grand Place (p38), Brussels

Belgium & Luxembourg

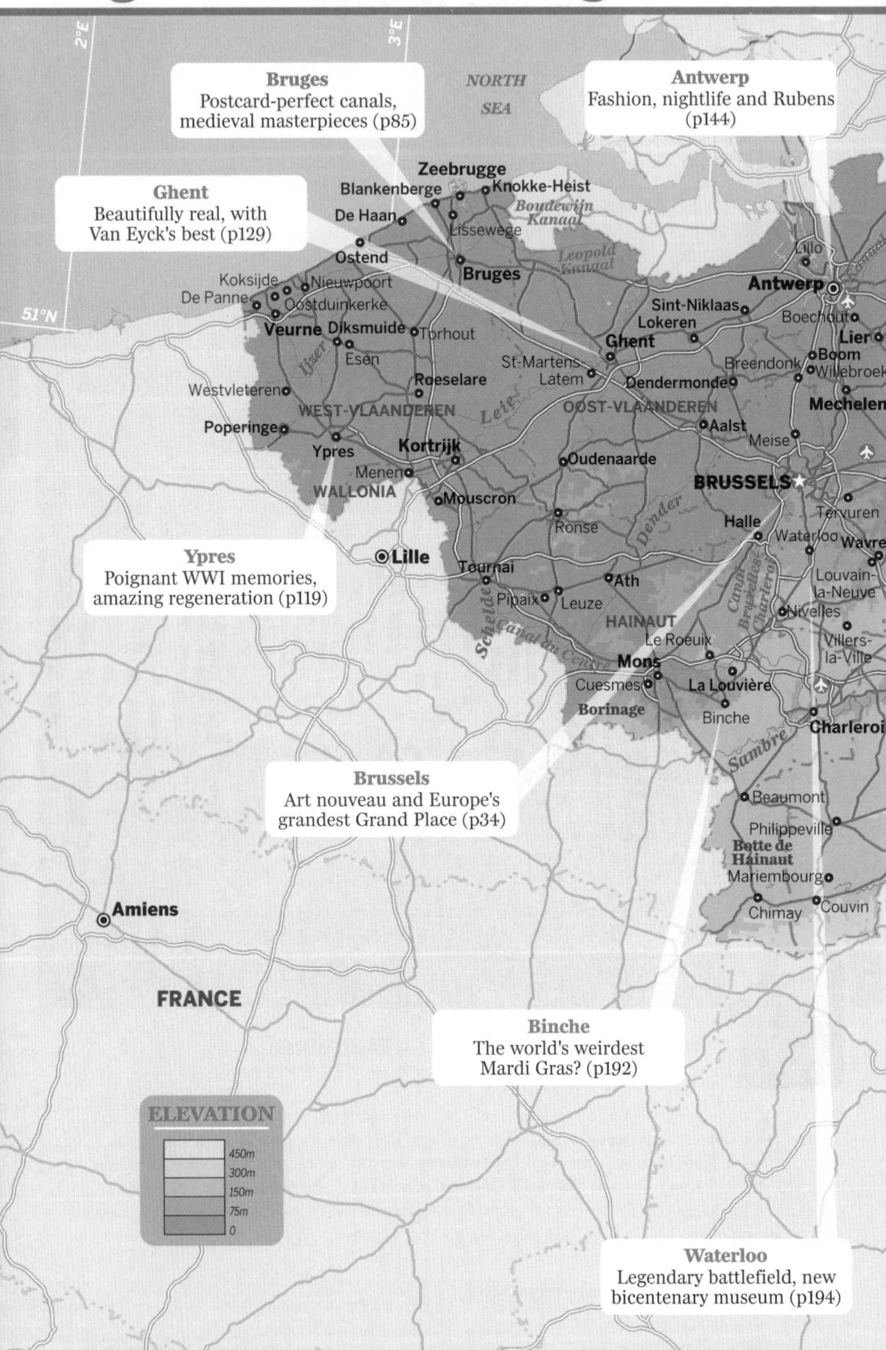

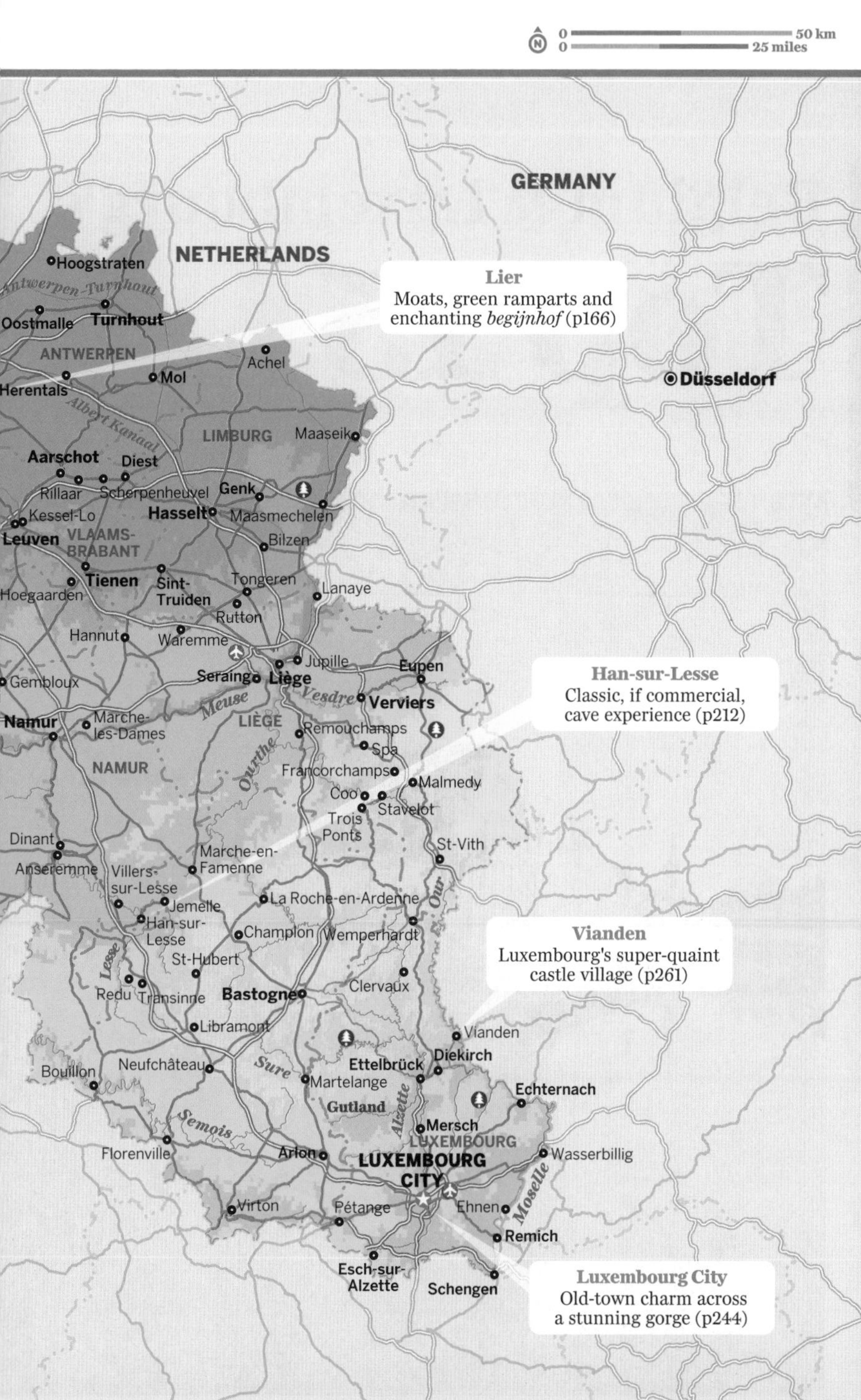

0
50 km
0
25 miles
GERMANY
NETHERLANDS
Lier
Moats, green ramparts and enchanting *begijnhof* (p166)
Hoogstraten
Antwerpen-Turnhout
Oostmalle
Turnhout
ANTWERPEN
Achel
Herentals
Mol
Düsseldorf
Albert Kanaal
LIMBURG
Maaseik
Aarschot
Diest
Rillaar
Scherpenheuvel
Genk
Kessel-Lo
Hasselt
Maasmechelen
Leuven
VLAAMS-BRABANT
Bilzen
Tienen
Sint-Truiden
Tongeren
Hoegaarden
Lanaye
Rutton
Hannut
Waremme
Jupille
Eupen
Gembloux
Seraing
Liège
Vesdre
Verviers
Han-sur-Lesse
Classic, if commercial, cave experience (p212)
Meuse
Namur
Marche-les-Dames
LIÈGE
Remouchamps
Spa
NAMUR
Ourthe
Francorchamps
Malmedy
Coo
Stavelot
Trois Ponts
Dinant
St-Vith
Marche-en-Famenne
Anseremme
Villers-sur-Lesse
Jemelle
La Roche-en-Ardenne
Our
Han-sur-Lesse
Champlon
Wemperhardt
Vianden
Luxembourg's super-quaint castle village (p261)
Lesse
St-Hubert
Redu
Transinne
Bastogne
Clervaux
Libramont
Vianden
Diekirch
Bouillon
Neufchâteau
Sure
Ettelbrück
Martelange
Echternach
Gutland
Alzette
Semois
Mersch
LUXEMBOURG
Florenville
Arlon
LUXEMBOURG CITY
Wasserbillig
Moselle
Virton
Pétange
Ehnen
Remich
Esch-sur-Alzette
Schengen
Luxembourg City
Old-town charm across a stunning gorge (p244)

Belgium & Luxembourg's Top 15

1

Bruges

1 Laced with canals and full of evocative step-gabled houses, Bruges (p85) is the ultimate picture-postcard tourist destination. Of course, that's all too well known and the city is often overrun, but come midweek in February and you may have it largely to yourself. Year round you can escape the crowds and carriage rides by dipping into some of Bruges' majestic art collections. The Groeningemuseum is hard to beat, offering a potted history of Belgian art, with an outstanding selection of works by the Flemish Primitives. Medieval houses, Bruges

Brussels' Grand Place

2 Brussels' heart beats in the Grand Place (p38) – the most theatrically beautiful medieval square in Europe. It is ringed by gold-trimmed, gabled guild-houses and flanked by the 15th-century Gothic town hall. The cobblestones were laid in the 12th century, when the square was used as a marketplace; the names of the surrounding lanes evoke herbs, cheese and poultry. And indeed the Grand Place still hosts a flower market, as well as Christmas stalls, concerts and – every two years – a dazzlingly colourful 'carpet' of flower petals. Flower market, Grand Place, Brussels

ANDREA THOMPSON PHOTOGRAPHY / GETTY IMAGES ©

2

EURASIA PRESS / GETTY IMAGES ©

KRIS PANNECOUCKE / GETTY IMAGES ©

Carnival Capers

3 If your neighbours' idea of a good time is to dress up in barrel costumes jingling with little bells, don spooky masks and ostrich-feather hats and then go throwing oranges at passers-by, you might wonder about their sanity. Then again you might just be living in Binche. That's the town whose unique Mardi Gras carnival (p192) has long been so indulgent it gave the English language the term 'binge'. Belgium's carnival season stretches way beyond Shrove Tuesday with other unique twists, especially in Stavelot and Aalst. Carnaval de Binche

Flemish Primitives

4 Western representational art was transformed in the 15th century by a group of Bruges-based painters whose mastery of oil paints allowed them to simulate reality and paint faces that expressed real emotional states. Flanders' burgeoning economy meant that the time was ripe for wealthy, mercantile sponsors to commission secular works, as well as religious works full of hidden messages... does Ghent's *Mystic Lamb* altarpiece (p133) really hold secret clues to a mysterious Jesus legacy? *The Adoration of the Mystic Lamb* by Jan van Eyck

Luxembourg City

5 No, it's not just banks and Eurocrats. Wealthy Luxembourg City (p244) is one of Europe's most underestimated capitals, with a fine range of museums and galleries and a brilliant dining scene. But most impressive is the town centre's spectacular setting, straddling a deep-cut river gorge whose defences were the settlement's original raison d'être. Come on a summer weekend when accommodation prices drop, the streets are often full of music and there's an ample flow of inexpensive local bubbly.

5

HAYKAL / GETTY IMAGES ©

Chocolate

6 In 1857 Swiss confectioner Jean Neuhaus opened a 'medicinal sweet shop' in Brussels' glorious Galeries St-Hubert (p43) – it's still there. But it was in 1912 that Neuhaus' son was credited with creating that most Belgian of morsels, the praline, by filling a chocolate shell with flavoured centres. Belgian chocolates remain world beaters due to the local insistence on 100% cocoa butter, and every town has its selection of *chocolatier* shops, hushed, hallowed temples where glove-handed assistants patiently load up ballotin boxes with your individual selection.

MATT MUNRO / LONELY PLANET ©

Chocolate display at Chocolate Line (p103), Bruges

Castles

7 From French-style châteaux to Crusader-era ruins, Belgium is overloaded with spectacular castles. Antwerp and Ghent both retain dinky medieval ones right in their city centres. And Namur, like Huy and Dinant, is dominated by a massive fortress citadel that retained military importance well into the 20th century. Probably nowhere has a better set of atmospheric castles than rural Luxembourg. Larochette, Bourscheid and Beaufort are all magnificent ruins, while Vianden's brooding masterpiece (p261) is the focal point of one of the Grand Duchy's most delightful country getaways. Gravensteen (p132), Ghent

Belfries & Begijnhoven

8 When Unesco contemplated Belgium's magnificent range of medieval architecture, it was clearly too overwhelming to decide what should go on the World Heritage list. So a whole range was selected. This includes 33 belfries (church-like clock towers built as symbols of civic freedoms); Tournai, Bruges and St-Truiden have fine examples. Also included were around 20 beautiful *begijnhoven,* enclosed urban villages that were a form of 'convent lite' (p166). It's hard to beat those of Diest, Turnhout, Lier and Kortrijk. Belfort (p87), Bruges

7

THOMAS DEKIERE / SHUTTERSTOCK ©

8

ALEXANDER SPATARI / GETTY IMAGES ©

9

HELEN CATHCART / LONELY PLANET ©

10

HAVANA1234 / GETTY IMAGES ©

Belgian Beer

9 Ordering in a classic hop-draped Belgian pub requires you to trawl through a menu that might have 200 choices. Each brew is served in its own special, occasionally outlandish, glass. Exports of Hoegaarden, Leffe and Stella Artois have introduced mainstream Belgian brewing (p283) into bars worldwide, but what really excites are the abbey-brewed Trappists, locally crafted dark ales, crisp golden triples and so much more. Go easy – many are over 8% alcohol. For the adventurous there's a range of sharp, spontaneously fermented lambics, often made more palatable by blending or by flavouring with soft fruit.

Flanders Fields

10 Flanders Fields, once known for potato and hop production, became synonymous with death in the wake of the trench warfare of WWI. The area around Ypres (p119) remains dotted with manicured graveyards where white memorial crosses movingly bear silent witness in seemingly endless rows. Museums vividly evoke the context and conditions for everyday soldiers, and the central squares of Diksmuide and Ypres, both rebuilt, are wonders in themselves.

LYNNE MCPEAKE / GETTY IMAGES ©

ALEXANDER KLEIN/AFP / GETTY IMAGES ©

ARTERRA PICTURE LIBRARY / ALAMY STOCK PHOTO ©

Art Nouveau

11 Swirls, curlicues and architectural daring: don't leave Brussels without exploring some of its art nouveau marvels. When star architect Victor Horta designed his own house, he combined technological innovation with high artistry to create a stunning and poetic art nouveau masterpiece. Across town, the elongated, exuberant Old England Building (p48) houses the marvellous Musée des Instruments de Musique. But there's plenty more beyond Brussels, with many stained-glass and curved-wood masterpieces in Antwerp's Zurenborg and 't Zuid districts. Rue du Lac 6 (p57), Brussels

Antwerp Art & Fashion

12 Fashion-forward Antwerp (p144) has it all. Its skyline is still dominated by one of the lowlands' most magnificent stone steeples and its medieval house-museums are stuffed with works by its most famous 17th-century resident, Pieter Paul Rubens. That said, it's also a dynamic modern city with state-of-the-art museums, vibrant nightlife and an edgy design scene: it's hard to think of anywhere else in the world with so many big-name boutiques, designer consignment shops and *brocante* dealers packed into a compact city centre.

Museums of Remembrance

13 The 100th anniversary of WWI's opening fire in 2014 and the bicentenary of the battle of Waterloo in 2015 saw the opening of a handful of state-of-the-art museums around Belgium. The Mons Memorial Museum explores the city's experience of both world wars, getting the balance just right between military history and personal testimony; indulging in a little toy-soldier fantasy at Waterloo can now be done in totally revamped surrounds (p194); and Belgium's WWII history, including the Battle of the Bulge, is tackled in a marvellous modern museum in Bastogne. Bastogne War Museum (p239)

Art Cities

14 If you love the medieval appeal of Bruges but want to be a little more original, a great choice is Ghent (p129). This historic city has its share of canalside splendour but also has a great arts scene and a grittier charm that many visitors find refreshing. Or try Mechelen (p168). It's overloaded with splendid churches, and the grand central square is graced with a fanciful town-hall complex that's only topped for sheer flamboyance by the statue-festooned equivalent in Leuven, Belgium's ancient university city. Waterfront town houses, Ghent

Caves of the Ardennes

15 You don't need to be a daring speleologist to explore some of northern Europe's most awesome cave systems, hollowed out beneath the rolling countryside of the Belgian Ardennes. The best known, at Han-sur-Lesse (p212), even starts with a train ride, while at Remouchamps you float part of the way on an underground river. On cave credentials only, though, Hotton and Rochefort really impress. Once you're caved out, there's gentle kayaking amid pretty valleys and grey-stone villages and plenty more castles to visit. Grottes de Han (p212)

14

15

Need to Know

For more information, see Survival Guide (p291)

Currency
Euro (€)

Languages
Dutch in Flanders, French in Wallonia, both in Brussels, German in the Eastern Cantons. Letzeburgesch, French and German in Luxembourg.

Visas
EU citizens can stay indefinitely; many other nationals can enter visa free for up to 90 days.

Money
Credit cards are widely accepted. ATMs are very prevalent.

Mobile Phones
Roaming charges for EU phones are low or non-existent. With an unlocked phone, local SIM cards are cheap and have good packages available.

Time
Central European Time (GMT/UTC plus one hour)

When to Go

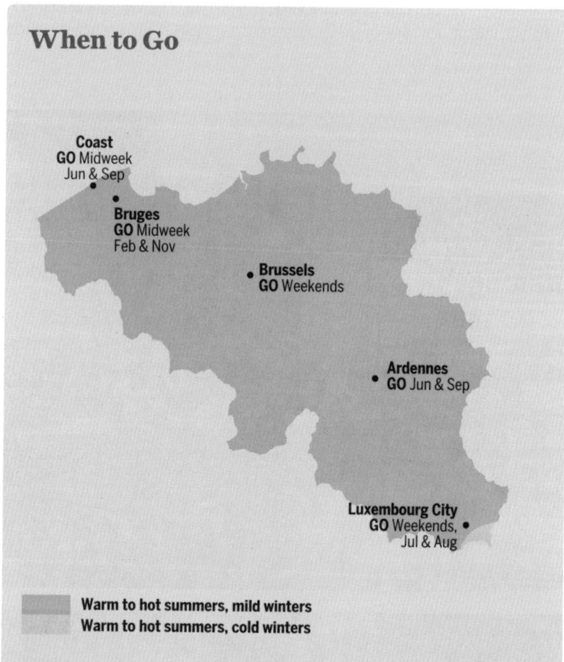

High Season (Jul & Aug)

- Warm weather, many outdoor activities and festivals
- Hotels get overloaded in the Ardennes, Bruges and coastal towns but are cheaper in Brussels and Luxembourg City

Shoulder (May, Jun & Sep)

- Pleasant weather is reasonably likely
- Crowds thinner, prices might fall slightly but most tourist facilities still open
- Rush-hour traffic jams return

Low Season (Oct–Mar)

- Weather often cold and wet
- Hotels cheaper, but some attractions close
- From the start of Lent there are numerous superbly colourful carnivals

Useful Websites

Visit Wallonia (www.belgiumtheplaceto.be) Tourism website for Wallonia and Brussels.

Visit Flanders (www.visitflanders.com) Tourist information on Flanders.

Visit Luxembourg (www.visitluxembourg.com) Excellent tourist information on the Grand Duchy.

Lonely Planet (www.lonelyplanet.com/belgium; www.lonelyplanet.com/luxembourg) Destination information, hotel bookings, traveller forum and more.

SNCB & CFL (www.belgianrail.be; www.cfl.lu) Trains in Belgium and Luxembourg respectively.

Important Numbers

Emergency	☎112
Country code Belgium/Luxembourg	☎32/352
International access code	☎00
Police in Belgium	☎101
Police in Luxembourg	☎113

Exchange Rates

Australia	A$1	€0.62
Canada	C$1	€0.66
Japan	¥100	€0.72
New Zealand	NZ$1	€0.57
UK	UK£1	€1.37
US	US$1	€0.87

For current exchange rates see www.xe.com.

Daily Costs

Budget: Less than €100

- Dorm bed including breakfast: €20–25
- Daily meal special: €9–14
- Train ticket: €10
- Museum entry: €6–12
- A beer: €2–4
- Short-hop city bike hire: €2

Midrange: €100–200

- Double room at B&B or midrange hotel: €70–120
- Midweek lunch special: €10–15
- Car hire per day: €15–20
- Two-course meal with wine for two: €80–110

Top End: More than €250

- Double room at better hotel or top B&B: €150–200
- Cocktails and mixed drinks: €10–20
- Degustation meal with wine for two: €180–350

Opening Hours

Many sights close on Monday. Restaurants normally close one full day per week. Opening hours for shops, bars and cafes vary widely.

Banks 8.30am–3.30pm or later Monday to Friday, some also Saturday morning

Bars 10am–1am, but hours very flexible

Restaurants noon–2.30pm and 7pm–9.30pm

Shops 10am–6.30pm Monday to Saturday, sometimes closed for an hour at lunchtime

Arriving in Belgium

Brussels Airport (p79) Several trains an hour to central Brussels (€8.50, 20 minutes), and two to Leuven (€8.80, 15 minutes), 4.40am to 12.30am.

Bruxelles-Midi Train Station (p79) Take any east-bound train to Bruxelles-Central station (three minutes, 4.45am to 12.15am) rather than walking into central Brussels.

Charleroi ('Brussels-South') Airport (p198) Two or three coaches (p198) per hour take 70 minutes to go to Brussels (around €14, 7.50am to midnight). Flibco (www.flibco.com) offers connections to Luxembourg, Bruges and Ghent. Bus A runs between the airport and Charleroi-Sud train station (€5, 20 minutes, free with train ticket, purchase bus-rail combo ticket at airport).

Getting Around

With short distances and good public transport, Belgium and Luxembourg are easy to get around.

Train Comprehensive network in Belgium and some service in Luxembourg, with reasonable prices.

Car An easy option for travel at your own pace, though regular traffic jams on Belgian motorways can be frustrating.

Bus Useful for accessing rural destinations or places where the train station is out of town.

For much more on **getting around**, see p299

First Time Belgium & Luxembourg

For more information, see Survival Guide (p291)

Checklist

- Check the validity of your passport and whether you need a visa
- Plan your itinerary carefully around festivals, events and to have weekends/weekdays where accommodation is business/tourism oriented
- Make necessary accommodation and restaurant bookings
- Download offline city maps for your smartphone
- Print out boarding passes and hire-car receipts
- Organise travel insurance
- Check airline baggage restrictions

What to Pack

- Passport with at least six months' validity.
- A thirst for great beer
- Two-pin adaptor plug for Europe
- A USB hub or multi-plug if you have to charge lots of gadgets
- A dual-SIM or spare phone so you can buy a local SIM card
- A phrasebook
- Padlock for hostel lockers
- Drivers' licence

Top Tips for Your Trip

- You can save a lot of money on accommodation by visiting tourist towns midweek and larger cities at weekends.
- Take smaller country roads whenever you can: distances are short anyway, and you'll make the most of the countries' charming scenery.
- Be aware that Belgian beers can pack quite a punch – they are often double the strength of international lager-style beer.
- A range of bike-hire options make the train/bike combination an appealing way of visiting the region.
- Budget extra travel time for traffic jams – roadworks and accidents frequently clog up major routes.

What to Wear

Antwerp is a major fashion centre, yet even in its upmarket boutiques you can see the Belgian love of understatement. In a male business context, a blazer and smart slacks are likely to be more appropriate than a tailored suit, which might be considered stuffy. Smart casual is the norm for going out to restaurants. It's worth bringing heavy clothes in winter when things can feel much colder than the temperature suggests due to the pervading damp. Similarly, summers can feel surprisingly hotter due to frequent humidity.

Sleeping

It's worth booking accommodation ahead in summer, and also in spring at popular tourist destinations. Cities can fill up midweek at any time with conferences and festivals. See p292 for more accommodation information.

- **Hotels** From converted palaces to functional boxes, and everything in between.
- **Hostels** Decent network in Belgium, excellent in Luxembourg. Often block-booked in both countries.
- **B&B** A wide range, called by a variety of names, ranging from the boutique to the homestyle.
- **Rural** Belgium has plenty of options, ranging from farmstays to whole houses for rent by the day or week.
- **Campsites** A good network, with many open all year.

Saving Money

➡ Using a debit or credit card to withdraw money at ATMs is often the cheapest method of accessing cash, but check what your home bank will charge you: it may be better to withdraw large amounts each time.

➡ Travel-specific credit cards can be pre-loaded with holiday cash and are often the cheapest way of spending abroad.

➡ Many towns have passes which will save you money if you are a heavy sightseer.

➡ Many restaurants – even the posh ones – have weekday lunchtime specials that offer great value, so if you're on a budget, make this your main meal of the day.

Bargaining

Gentle haggling is common in markets; in all other instances you're expected to pay the stated price.

Tipping

Personnel receive living wages and tipping is not required for taxis, restaurants, hairdressers or bars, though it won't be refused and some locals round up a bill. If service was quite exceptional, you could show appreciation (up to 10%). In a few tourist-oriented locations, unaware foreigners regularly leave disproportionate tips, leading to a certain expectation from staff. Similarly, airport taxis may hint (or even state outright) that a tip is appropriate. But that's a gentle scam. Don't be bullied.

SANTIAGO URQUIJO / GETTY IMAGES ©

Villo! rental bicycles (p80), Brussels

Language

Especially in Flanders it's almost embarrassing to try Dutch on locals if they speak English – which many will speak as well as you. But it's still polite to know some basic Dutch greetings...and of course the term *'pintje'* for ordering beer. In Wallonia, a grasp of French will prove more important. If you learnt French in France, be prepared for a few little differences.

Etiquette

➡ **Say hello, wave goodbye** Entering a shop or arriving at a cash desk, it's polite to offer a cheery greeting to staff. And as you leave say thank you and 'good day'/'good evening' (in French using the specific terms *bonne journée/bon soirée*).

➡ **Giving gifts** When visiting someone's home it's appropriate to bring wine, flowers or chocolates – choose the brand carefully!

➡ **Liberal or conservative?** Local ideas about political correctness might not match your own. Don't jump too quickly to conclusions. A light-hearted approach to serious issues is common, and underneath, many attitudes are very liberal.

➡ **Kissing** Traditionally Belgians welcome good friends with three kisses on alternating cheeks. But knowing when that's appropriate confuses even the locals.

If You Like...

Castles

Castles might not be the first things that jump to mind when you imagine Belgium and Luxembourg. Yet both little nations are remarkably over-endowed with them. From grand châteaux to rugged stone ruins, there's a site for all tastes. See www.chateaubelgique.com for lesser-known alternatives.

Belœil (p189) **and Modave** (p223) These indulgent châteaux compete as candidates for the title 'Belgian Versailles', each lavishly furnished and set in fine manicured grounds.

Horst (p177), **Beersel** (p82), **Lavaux-Ste-Anne** (p214) **and Jehay** (p223) As pretty as they come if you want moated beauties.

Bourscheid (p260), **Beaufort** (p259), **La Roche-en-Ardenne** (p219) **and Crusader classic Bouillon** (p215) Archetypal classics in the medieval ruin genre.

Namur (p205), **Huy** (p223) **and Dinant** (p211) Vast, latter-day citadel-fortresses whose structures are functional and brooding but unquestionably impressive for their sheer power and scale.

Château de la Poste A splendid castle you can sleep in (p211).

Bourglinster Fine château dining (p256)

Industrial Heritage

Belgium has often been at the forefront of European technological advances. Inspired visitor attractions bring alive everything from medieval Mosan metalwork to 21st-century wind energy.

Blégny Mine Go underground to have your senses bombarded with the sights and sounds of a 20th-century coal mine (p231).

Museum Plantin-Moretus The world's oldest surviving printing works is a work of art in itself (p145).

Seraing Still creating the Belgian glassware that took the world by storm a century ago (p231).

Turnhout Discover the huge scale of machines required to make playing cards (p165).

Le Bois du Cazier Climb a slag heap in archetypal post-industrial Charleroi (p198).

Tienen A museum that sprinkles endless imagination on the sugar industry (p178).

Canals of the Borinage Remarkable ship-lifts, old and new (p196).

Verviers (p233), **Oudenaarde** (p127), **Kortrijk** (p126) **and Comines** (p124) Fascinating textile museums.

Antwerp Port Ugly, vibrant and thrillingly vast (p144).

War & Peace

Ever since real-life cousins of Asterix tried to blow raspberries at the Roman legions, Belgium has been getting in the middle of other people's wars. While nothing will ever assuage the carnage and destruction of times past, the countless historical battlefields are a compelling attraction for tourists, veterans' families and fancily dressed fantasy warriors.

Waterloo The site of the gory battle that finally stopped Napoleon's advance can be viewed from atop a lion-topped mound, or venture underground for the film-driven bicentennial museum (p194).

Ypres Salient Restored WWI trenches, resurrected townscapes and contemplative graveyards dot 'Flanders Fields', now sorrowfully synonymous with blood and poppies (p121).

Kortrijk Triumphantly commemorated, the 1302 'Golden Spurs' battlefield is where Flemish townsfolk turned the tables on the dastardly French. Or did they? (p125).

Ardennes Hitler's devastating last-gasp counter-attack of Christmas 1944 is still a vivid memory in Bastogne, Diekirch and La Roche-en-Ardenne (p240).

Ostend Well-explained 20th-century wartime sea defences (p110).

Hamm General Patton, along with scores of his troops, is buried at this moving US Military Cemetery, just west of Luxembourg City (p249).

Outdoors Action

Getting soaked is not a challenge here, a Belgian might quip. Wet weather gear requirements aside, there are loads of totally worth-it and well-organised outdoor pursuits whether there's a gentle drizzle or brilliant sun.

Bouillon (p215) **and La Roche** (p218) Attractive centres from which to kayak some of the prettiest rivers of southern Belgium.

Coo (p238) **and Durbuy** (p220) Of all the Ardennes outdoor-sports getaways, these tiny villages are the best equipped for drop-in visitors with a huge range of options.

The Coast Sea swimming is an option on Belgium's sandy coastline, but would be so much lovelier were it warmer (and not marred by abysmal apartment towers along some stretches) (p106).

Skiing The Ardennes has a short window of skiing opportunity, including the cross-country trails of the misty Hautes Fagnes (p235).

L'Eau de Heure Belgium's forested lakeland is a rare piece of wilderness and activity-rich (p200).

Belfries & Begijnhoven

Oh yes, Bruges is gorgeous. But it's by no means the only place with a magical medieval centre and pretty urban canals. Another 16 Flemish towns have beautiful *begijnhoven* (enclosed semireligious subvillages) with special gems at Diest, Kortrijk and Turnhout. And over 30 Belgian cities have historic belfry towers that are Unesco-listed.

Ghent Challenges Bruges for canalside scenery, has three *begijnhoven* and a city-centre castle that once tried to intimidate the rebellious townsfolk (p129).

Lier Compact, canal-ringed beauty with a fanciful clock tower (p167).

Tournai Belgium's oldest belfry, a beautiful main square and superb Romanesque cathedral (p183).

Mechelen Belgium's religious capital is overloaded with fine churches (p168).

Ypres The Ieper Lakenhalle (cloth hall) is arguably Belgium's most glorious single building, yet astonishingly it is a post-WWI rebuild (p119).

Cave Systems

Beneath the limestone Ardennes, several spectacular caverns and underground waterways have been made accessible for the non-speleologically adept. Guided visits each tell similar tales of stalactite spaghetti and carbonate concretions, but visually each experience has its own particular attraction. Dress for temperatures of around 10°C; it feels cold in summer but can be warm on a snowy day.

Grotte de Lorette Walking distance from appealing Rochefort, Lorette is remarkable for its great depth. Lots of steps (p212).

Grottes de Hotton Fewer visitors than most, yet superb for grottoes and its fabulously vertical subterranean chasm (p220).

Grottes de Han Some of Belgium's greatest stalactites are easy to visit with comparatively little effort. The experience is unself-consciously commercial and the caves get very busy with summer tour groups, but there's a fun train ride and many other family attractions nearby (p212).

Grottes du Remouchamps The interior lacks much in the way of stalagmite spectacle but the tour ends with a memorable underground river ride (p239).

Month by Month

TOP EVENTS

Binche Carnival, February

Le Doudou, May/June

Waterloo Battle Re-enactment, June

Luxembourg Jazz & Blues Rallye, July

Heritage Days, September

The truly extraordinary wealth of festivals in Belgium and Luxembourg takes many visitors quite by surprise, especially the bizarre Lenten/Carnival pageants.

January

Days are short, cold and often grey, so as the New Year hangovers wear off, Belgians need January's sales to drag them out of their houses.

Ski Time

Belgium has neither Alpine mountains nor ski resorts, but when enough snow falls in the Ardennes, the perilous E411 fills with day-tripping skiers making a bee-line for the Haute Fagnes. (p236)

February

Some years frigid and damp, others sparkling if cold. Early February is one time you might have beautiful Bruges largely to yourself...until the start of the Carnival holiday that is.

Carnival

The orange-lobbing Gilles lead one of the world's oddest Carnivals in Binche (p192) on Shrove Tuesday (Mardi Gras), a day that might fall in February or March. The Sunday before that, Malmédy's Carnival climaxes with the parade of the masked *Haguètes* and next day Eupen's Rosenmontag is joyously colourful.

March

March could host a late Carnival or an early Easter. Either way there's still bound to be plenty of pageantry and Lenten shenanigans.

Burning of Winter

The Spirit of Winter is ceremonially cremated on the first Sunday of Lent, both with bonfires in Belgian village fields and with cruciform fires on hillsides across Luxembourg where the day's called *Buergsonndeg*. Bouge near Namur has the biggest, most folkloric conflagration.

Laetare

Sinister Pinocchio-like *Blanc Moussis* stuff confetti down women's clothes, dangle smelly dried herrings in people's hair and beat bystanders with dried pigs' bladders. It's all part of Stavelot's unique Laetare carnival (www.laetare-stavelot.be; p237), held on the fourth Saturday of Lent.

Ars Musica

A respected festival of contemporary classical music (www.arsmusica.be) held from mid-March at various Brussels venues.

April

Spring springs forth with a day of practical jokes – in Belgium the classic prank is to slap an April Fish, unnoticed, onto someone's back. At Easter children seek out eggs in their gardens, deposited there not by Easter bunnies but by the 'Bells of Rome'.

Penitents' Procession

After dusk on Good Friday, Lessines turns off the city lights as eerie figures in monks habits and medieval conical hoods parade moodily around town carrying flaming torches. The procession dates back to 1475.

Ronde van Flanders

Flanders' most imporatant cycling race, the one-day classic Ronde van Vlaanderen (Tour of Flanders; www.rvv.be) starts in Bruges and culminates in Oudenaarde.

Serres Royales

The glorious royal greenhouses at Laeken (p58) are open to the public for 10 days in late April.

May

May starts with old-fashioned chivalry as Belgian men present female friends or colleagues with a delicate sprig of Lily of the Valley.

Hanswijk Procession

Part religious tableau, part medieval pageant, the Sunday before Ascension see thousands dress up to thank the Virgin Mary for sparing Mechelen from the plague back in 1272.

Zinneke Parade

Thoroughly contemporary one-day multicultural parade held every two years, designed to bridge social divides and expose Brussels' zanier side (www.zinneke.org).

Heilig-Bloedprocessie

On Ascension Day, Bruges' biggest folklore event (www.holyblood.com) sees the parading around town of an enormously revered reliquary supposedly containing a few drops of Christ's blood. Book for a grandstand seat on the Markt.

Sprinprozession

Echternach pilgrims celebrate the town's Anglo-Saxon founding father with handkerchief dances on Whit Tuesday morning in late May. (p258)

Brussels Jazz Marathon

Three fabulous evenings of free, nonstop jazz, blues and zydeco concerts on the last weekend of the month, on stages and in pubs all over Brussels (www.brusselsjazzmarathon.be).

Le Doudou

On Trinity Sunday (p191), a golden 'coach' of relics has been paraded through town, Mons goes completely nuts as St George fights the dragon on the Grand Place.

June

A great travelling month with long, long days and mild weather.

Kattenfestival

Ypres cat festival has furry feline toys flung about while giant cats parade through the street. It's held every third year (next in 2018) on the second Sunday of June.

Waterloo Battle Re-enactments

Waterloo anniversary celebrations of the battle often include re-enactments, where over a thousand costumed 'soldiers' recreate scenes from the classic 1815 battle. This annual event may be disrupted by ongoing works in the Waterloo area.

Luxembourg National Day

Fireworks and an all-night party in Luxembourg City on 22 June are followed by a military parade on 23 June.

Couleur Café

Three-day festival of world-music concerts, workshops and ethnic-dining opportunities attracts over 75,000 people to Brussels' Tour & Taxis complex (www.couleurcafe.be) at the end of June.

July

Schools close and Belgians begin their lengthy holidays: suddenly beach and Ardennes hotels are full. Across the region it's party time with a smorgasbord of summer festivals.

Wiltz Festival

Impressive month-long theatre, jazz and music festival in the château grounds at Wiltz (www.festivalwiltz.online.lu).

Ommegang

It costs nothing to watch Brussels' biggest medieval-style procession (www.ommegang.be) wind around town from the Sablon.

But book tickets ahead to witness the lavish finale on the illuminated Grand Place. First Thursday of July.

Rock Werchter

The four-day Belgian equivalent of Glastonbury or Roskilde rocks fields north of Leuven (www.rockwerchter.be).

Les Francofolies

The first week of July, Spa hosts one of Belgium's biggest French-language cultural festivals (www.francofolies.be), notable for attracting some of the biggest names in *chanson*.

Tomorrowland

Tomorrowland is the world's largest annual electronic music festival, held annually in the appropriately named town of Boom, 16km south of Antwerp.

De Gentse Feesten

This fabulously raucous 10-day festival (www.gentsefeesten.be) transforms the heart of Ghent into a youthful party of music and street theatre, with packed streets and merry drinking.

Luxembourg Jazz & Blues Rallye

The Grund and Clausen areas of Luxembourg City party all night to a fine array of free concerts (www.bluesjazzrallye.lu).

Boetprocessie

Held in Veurne since 1644, this solemn street parade (www.boetprocessie.be) sees hundreds of biblically costumed players illustrate 40 scenes from Jesus' life, death and Resurrection interspersed with masked 'penitents' in brown monk-style robes, some carrying heavy wooden crosses. Last Sunday of July.

August

Peak summer season.

Festival Musica Antiqua

Weeklong festival of medieval music (www.mafestival.be) in Bruges in the first week of August.

La Nuit du Livre

All night book-fest in Redu accompanied by music and midnight fireworks. Held first Saturday of August.

Folk Dranouter

One of Europe's most important folk-music festivals (www.folkdranouter.be) held on the first weekend of August at Dranouter, a small town 12km southwest of Ypres.

Meyboom

On 9 August this merrily low-key Brussels' folkloric procession (www.meyboom.be) ends with the planting of a 'tree of joy', as has happened since 1308. Symbolically the tree must be erected before 5pm to ensure the rights of the ancient guilds.

St-Rochus-Verlichting

In Aarschot, electric lamps are extinguished from dusk to midnight on 15 August, replaced by flickering lines of candles along window sills and footpaths and accompanied by folk dances and brass bands.

Festival Outremeuse

A week of raucously drunken celebrations in Liège's 'Republic of Outremeuse' (www.tchantches.eu; p227) culminates on 15 August when sermons are read in full Walloon dialect, then everyone gets tipsy on *pékèt* (Walloon gin). Expect fire crackers, puppet shows, traditional dances, a folkloric procession of giants and vast, possibly unruly, crowds.

Golden Tree Pageant

Every five years in mid-/late August, Bruges lays on this grandiose procession (www.goudenboomstoet.be) celebrating the 1468 marriage of Charles the Bold to Margaret of York. Next in 2017.

Giants' Procession

On August's fourth weekend, Ath holds a series of parades featuring enormous Unesco-listed models with biblical and folkloric connections. One such giant, Goliath (Gouyasse), has his trousers 'burnt' on Friday night, gets married on Saturday, then fights David.

September

Belgians go back to work and those depressingly snail-paced rush-hour traffic jams re-materialise on the Brussels ring road. Weather is often lovely while accommodation in rural getaways is not so overstretched.

Belgian Grand Prix

Formula 1 comes to Spa-Francorchamps (www.belgium-grand-prix.com; p232) in late August/early September; expect full occupancy at virtually every hotel in eastern Wallonia.

Heritage Days

The second weekend of September sees Flanders' Open Monumentendag (www.openmonumenten.be) and Wallonia's Journées du Patrimoine (www.journeesdupatrimoine.be). Both open a selection of monuments to the public, many of which are not otherwise accessible. A week later Brussels follows suit.

Combat de l'Échasse d'Or

On the third Sunday of September, Namur's weeklong Fêtes de Wallonie (www.fetesdewallonie.be) culminates in this jousting competition between two teams of stilt-walkers dressed in medieval garb.

October

As temperatures cool, days get shorter and trees develop a pretty autumnal blush, many a restaurant finds space on its menu for boar, venison and other forms of game.

Nocturne des Coteaux

Liège comes alive at dusk on the first Saturday of October with 20,000 candles forming beautiful patterns on the city's vertiginous stairway, Montagne de Bueren.

Hasseltse Jeneverfeesten

The most celebrated moment in Hasselt's famous gin festival (www.jeneverfeesten.be) comes at 4.30pm when the little Borrelmanneke Fountain briefly pours forth *jenever* (gin) instead of water. Third weekend of October.

Klapstukfestival

Leuven's international contemporary dance festival (www.stuk.be) lasts throughout October.

November

Christmas markets begin making the rounds of many a town square. These typically come with nativity scenes that sometimes have living characters rather than mannequins... right down to the baby Jesus in the manger.

All Saints' Day

The first of November (Allerheiligen/Toussaint) is the day that Belgian familes take flowers to the graves of deceased relatives.

December

Belgian kids get presents twice over, not just on 24/25 December, but also on 6 December from red-coated, bushy-bearded Sinterklaas/St-Nicholas. He's accompanied by club-wielding Zwarte Piet (Black Peter, though usually now called 'Peter') from whom 'bad children' get nothing but a token thwack. A speciality for the day is fancily shaped *speculaas/speculoos* (cinnamon-flavoured gingerbread).

Itineraries

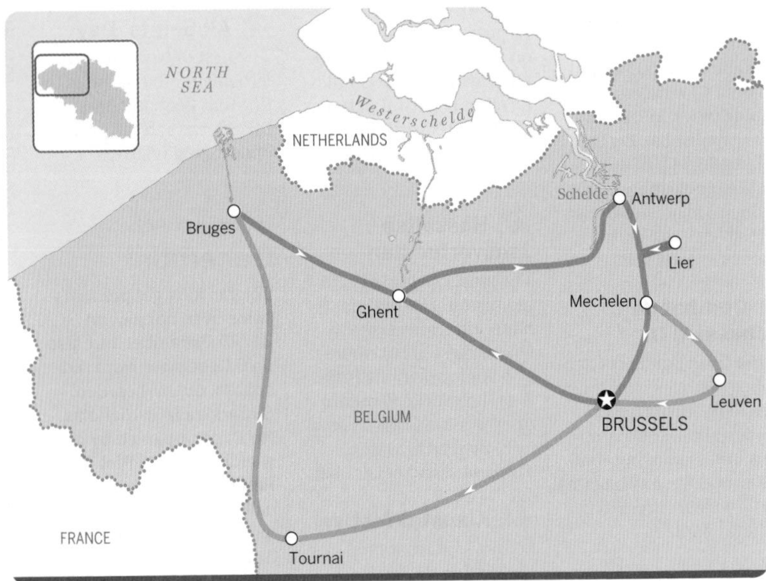

Historic Cities

Four of northern Europe's most memorable historic cities are so handily close together that an hour's train ride is enough to get between any of them. So you *could* just about glimpse them all in a long weekend. However, even one week wouldn't really do them full justice. Take as long as you can. To save on midrange accommodation costs, arrange your trip to sleep in Brussels at the weekend and Bruges midweek.

EU capital, **Brussels**, has a Grand Place that's one of the world's most beautiful squares. Explore seductive chocolate shops, wonderful *cafés,* great galleries, fine museums and art nouveau buildings. And don't miss the unique 1958 Atomium.

Medieval architecture and endless canalside charm make beautiful **Bruges** one of Europe's most romantic getaways. Less tourist-oriented, grittier yet somehow more satisfying, is magical **Ghent**, whose intimate medieval core is complemented by a lively student vibe and some wonderful museums. Larger **Antwerp** is an eclectic port city whose historical credentials are balanced by its vibrant nightlife, *café* culture and cutting-edge designer fashions. If time allows, there are numerous appealing add-on options: **Leuven**, **Lier**, **Tournai**, or **Mechelen**.

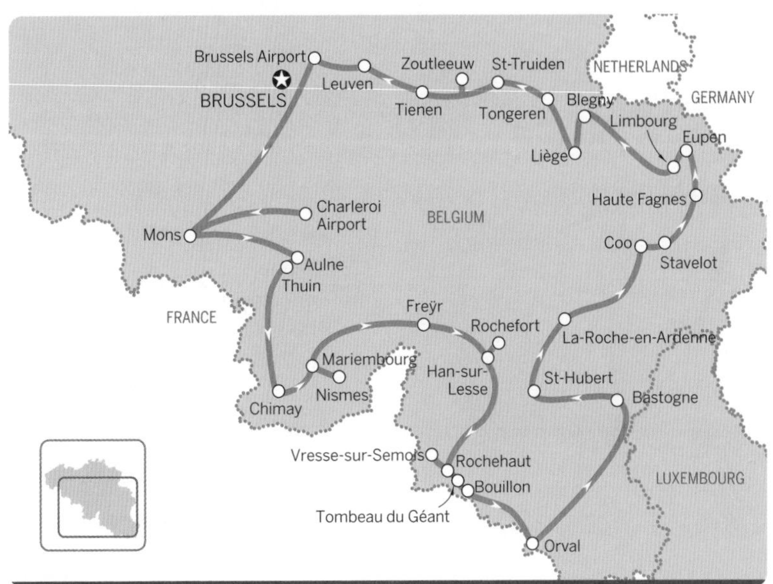

2 WEEKS Dawdling the Back Roads

If you want to drive around some of Belgium's more off-beat and rural corners, try this trip. It starts and ends in Brussels or Charleroi Airport, where you can pick up a rental car. It takes in some of the most charming countryside of the Ardennes and eastern Flanders.

Head first to **Mons**, which now has a serious portfolio of excellent museums thanks to its year as Capital of Culture. Then drive down to beer-famed **Chimay** for two nights, taking in **Aulne** abbey ruins and **Thuin** on the way. Tootle along the pretty lanes to **Mariembourg** and **Nismes**, possibly taking the steam train. Visit the splendid gardens of **Freÿr** and the fabulous caves at **Han-sur-Lesse** or less commercial **Rochefort**, which has some fine local accommodation. From there drive down to **Bouillon** with its Crusader castle, and kayak along some of Belgium's prettiest stretches of wooded valley around **Vresse-sur-Semois**. Follow the lovely Semois Valley in both directions enjoying the panoramas at **Rochehaut** and **Tombeau du Géant**. Visit the golden stone ruins of **Orval's** monastery and its modern brewery *café* to taste the monks' legendary beer. Head northeast to visit the excellent war museum at **Bastogne**, then cut across through thick forests via **St-Hubert** to **La Roche-en-Ardenne**. Famed for its carnival, attractive **Stavelot** makes a good base for a few nights and a range of outdoor activities (organised at nearby **Coo**), and a day hike on the **Haute Fagnes**. Stop for coffee and pastries in **Eupen**, Belgium's only really Germanic city, and explore the attractive country lanes, not missing delightful little **Limbourg**. Nip up the motorway to visit **Blegny**, descending into Belgium's last accessible coal mine, then, for a dose of big-city action, drop by **Liège** with its lively riverside vibe, top eating scene and boisterous nightlife. Next, it's a quieter visit to appealing **Tongeren**, Belgium's 'oldest' town, then drive the Roman road to underrated **St-Truiden** with random wanders off into the pretty Haspengouw area. Don't miss the remarkable church in **Zoutleeuw** and drop into **Tienen** to see the sugar museum. Spend your last night in lively student city **Leuven**.

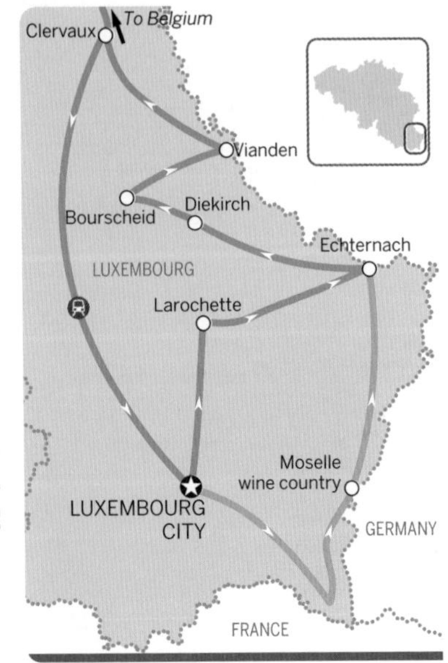

Loveable Luxembourg

Little Luxembourg makes an unexpectedly complete destination. Accommodation prices in Luxembourg City fall dramatically at weekends. Midweek is better for the rural castle villages with fewer Dutch bikers on the country lanes.

Arrive in **Luxembourg City** on Friday afternoon, making the most of the city's decent range of nightlife options and free weekend on-street parking. On Saturday buy a two-day Luxembourg Card if you're planning to see all of the main museums, or just stroll the remarkable city ramparts and gorges. On Monday head for **Echternach**, perhaps going via **Larochette** or through **Moselle wine country**. Hike in the attractive Müllerthal micro-canyons then head to **Diekirch** for the best Ardennes battle museum around. By bus it's a bit of a fiddle, but consider visiting **Bourscheid** to admire the Grand Duchy's impressive castle ruin. Head to charming **Vianden**, the most convenient rural getaway, whose restored fortress looms above the charming little town. Take the bus to pretty **Clervaux** and continue by train to Coo or Liege in Belgium or return to Luxembourg City.

Belgian Beer Tour

In Belgium you can be a complete boozehound but look very cultured as you tour medieval monasteries and historic towns, trying a drop of the local brew out of politeness along the way.

Start your pilgrimage in **Brussels**, where you can pay your respects at L'Arbre d'Or, the venerable brewers' guild on the Grand Place, before learning about lambics at Cantillon Brewery. Next head north to **Mechelen's** legendary Het Anker.

Then head to western Flanders, Belgium's hop-growing country, stopping at **Diksmuide** to sip an Oerbier, then tasting the fabled **Westvleteren** 12 Trappist at Abdij Sint-Sixtus and a St-Bernardus Tripel in **Watou**.

Head southeast to Dubuisson at **Pipaix** and visit the charming nearby steam brewery. The enticingly rural Botte du Hainaut is home to the legendary **Chimay** Trappist beer, and the Fagnes brewery at **Mariembourg** is a good lunch stop.

Belgium's deep southeast holds lovely **Orval's** brewery-monastery. On your way back north, drop by the rural hamlet of **Achouffe** for La Chouffe's magnificent offerings. Heading back to Brussels, stop for a glass of **Hoegaarden's** famous white beer.

Plan Your Trip

Travel with Children

From spooky rambles through candlelit castles to high-tech space simulators to splashing about on beaches and rivers, Belgium and Luxembourg have plenty to thrill and inspire beyond the sheer magic of their historic chocolate-box old cityscapes.

Children's Highlights

Theme Parks

Very helpfully, several of Belgium's best theme parks have been installed near enough to other major sites so that one parent might slope off to enjoy a different kind of attraction while the rest of the family is busily soaking up the fun rides.

- **L'Eau de Heure** (p200) Natura Parc is a great addition to this already activity-filled area.
- **Plopsaland** (p115) The biggest theme park on the coast is tucked back off the beach strip at De Panne.
- **Plopsa Coo** (p239) Brilliantly named and very handily located to entertain the younger kids while teenagers have a choice of more full-on adrenaline sporting activities available across the road at Coo Adventure (p238).

Educational Attractions

The difference between educational attractions and theme parks is increasingly blurred as the best install simulators and full-sense experiences. Many museums are designed in large part with children in mind, and include interactive activities and workshops. It's well worth looking at the websites of the various museums or sights before going as some activities might operate only on certain days of the week. Naturally many will be in local languages, but are often tactile and intuitive, so an

Best Regions for Kids

The Ardennes

The wide range of summer sports activities goes well beyond the archetypal kayaking weekend, offering something for kids of all ages with Durbuy and Coo especially well set up.

Bruges

For any age Bruges is enchanting, but if the kids are tiring of history they might still get excited by museums of chips and chocolate.

The Coast

Even if it's too cold to swim they can still ride *kwistax* (pedal carts) along the prom and visit the craziest sandcastles they're likely to have seen.

Ghent

Magical townscapes are inspiring while plenty of interactive museums have activities for youngsters.

Antwerp

The city is very much a grownups town, but the zoo (p149) and Aquatopia (p149) will keep little ones engrossed; city museums cater well for tweens and teens adore the shopping.

Müllerthal

Hiking the Müllerthal trail through Luxenbourg's Little Switzerland; no mighty mountains but some mighty impressive castles to retreat to in case it rains.

adventurous child is likely to enjoy them, and most leaders speak excellent English. Even non-child-specific museums tend to have a toddlers' zone equipped with relevant play activities.

➡ **Technopolis** (p171) Mechelen's cutting-edge science-experience museum.

➡ **Euro Space Center** (p214) A major interactive experience, but awkward to reach without a car.

➡ **Earth Explorer** (p110) Ostend's equivalent lets rip with earthquakes and storms, then tries to explain them. Very obliging English-speaking staff are on hand to guide the baffled.

➡ **Bakkerijmuseum** (p116) Veurne's underrated delight has a weekly bake-in.

Outdoor Excitement

➡ **Château de Bouillon** (p215) This wonderfully evocative Crusader ruin is likely to inspire young minds; the birds-of-prey show is memorable. The site is all the more special if you visit on a summer's night by the light of burning torches.

➡ **Han-sur-Lesse** (p212) Younger kids might find the cave visit a little long, but there's the fun of starting out by train. With the 'safari' and various other minor attractions, it all adds up to a fine day out.

➡ **Durbuy** (p220) Belgium's smallest 'town' is brilliantly set up with activities to keep the whole family active, while a few kilometres away in Barvaux there's also the fun of the great cornfield labyrinth.

➡ **Mini Europe** (p59) Confuse the kids' sense of scale by visiting a whole series of Europe's monuments in miniature while overhead towers the Atomium (p58) – a vastly oversized representation of iron's atomic crystal lattice.

Planning

Entrance Fees

For most attractions, there are discounted children's tickets for those 12 years old or under, though occasionally eligibility is judged by height. Many top attractions across Flanders have a €1 entry rate for young people over 12 but under 26, which can make a big difference if you're planning to see a number of museums.

Accommodation

Hotels don't usually charge for toddlers, while many will provide an extra bed for children for around €15 (variable). A great idea for bigger families is to rent a *gite* for a week to use as a base for visiting one region. If you've got a car, the compact nature of Belgium and Luxembourg means that driving times are rarely painful.

Eating

All restaurants are free of smoking (though foodless cafes in Luxembourg aren't). Many midrange restaurants and especially brasseries have a small selection of simpler dishes (burger, pasta, meatballs, chicken-in-apple) or smaller portions for children, typically priced around €10. A fair proportion of eateries across all categories have high chairs for youngsters, but it's worth calling ahead to check availability.

Babies

Baby cots are available on request in many B&Bs, hotels and even some hostels, but it's worth reserving ahead as most places stock only one or two. Nappy-changing facilities are patchily available: try the female toilets at branches of hamburger chain Quick if you're stuck. Breastfeeding in public is acceptable, though not commonly seen.

Transport

When travelling by car, children under 1.35m must travel in a child's safety seat. Most car-rental firms have such safety seats for hire if you book well ahead. Theoretically taxis should provide a seat if you book in advance.

Train travel in Belgium is free for under-12s after 9am when accompanied by an adult. Families with three or more children can get 50% discounts with a Famille Nombreuse discount card (€5 per month, passport photos required).

Further Information

Family Guide is a remarkably detailed resource book for Luxembourg, suggesting around 700 activities, trips and contacts. It's available online from Maison Moderne (www.maisonmoderne.lu).

Lonely Planet's *Travel with Children* offers plenty of useful advice.

Regions at a Glance

Brussels

Architecture
Beer
Music

Art Nouveau Trail

Victor Horta was Brussels' master architect, his buildings characteristically austere from the outside, but light-filled symphonies of curved wood and stained glass within. Take a neighbourhood walk to find other gorgeously ornamented art nouveau houses.

Spontaneous Success

Brussels' unique contribution to brewing is the spontaneously fermented lambic. But if that's too off-the-wall for your taste buds, the capital's opulent old *cafés* and hip new minimalist bars are sure to offer something that will wow your senses.

Jazz Heaven

Brussels is mad about jazz. The Jazz Marathon weekend is held in May, but year-round you can enjoy great live music in venues from basement bars to sit-down restaurants and jazz clubs.

p34

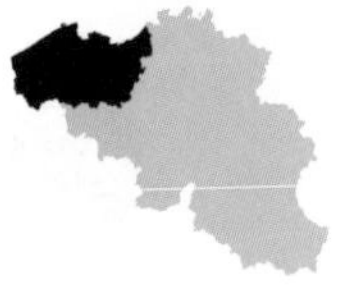

Bruges & Western Flanders

Medieval Towns
Beer
Battlefields

Step-Gabled Delights

Whether prettily preserved like Bruges, reconstructed like Diksmuide and Ypres, or a vibrant mixture like Ghent, there are few places in Northern Europe that thrust so much medieval-style architecture in your face.

Heavenly Hops

The hops that flavour virtually all great Belgian beers are cultivated around Poperinge, an area which is, not surprisingly, the epicentre of great local brewing and home to the almost mystical Trappist wonder, Westvleteren 12.

Flanders Fields

WWI cemeteries are movingly beautiful throughout the region, with battlefield tours, war museums and trench sites around Ypres, whose whole centre was rebuilt after the war.

p83

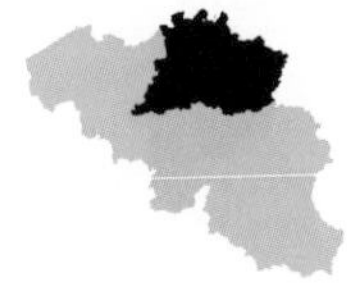

Antwerp & Eastern Flanders

Architecture
Beer
Galleries

Beguiling Buildings

For architectural inspiration compare the *begijnhoven* of Diest, Lier and Turnhout, cathedrals at Antwerp and Mechelen, belfries of Hoogstraten and Tienen, and city halls of Leuven, Mechelen and Zoutleeuw.

Rainbow of Ales

Westmalle and Achel are this region's Trappists, but Het Anker's Mechelen-brewed range is arguably as fine. Hoegaarden makes the classic White Beer.

Rubens and More

Antwerp and Mechelen's galleries and churches are bristling with Rubens. But for cutting-edge contemporary you won't beat, the Verbeke Foundation is where life and art are one.

p142

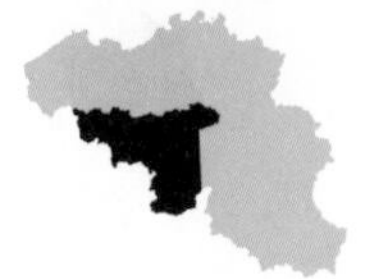

Western Wallonia

Museums
Festivals
Landscapes

Napoleon to Tintin

New museums have enlivened the region in recent years, from a hatful of Capital of Culture projects in Mons to Waterloo's revamped displays for the battle's bicentenary, and the sweet Hergé exhibition in Louvain-la-Neuve.

Carnival Capers

Who needs Rio when you have Binche for the original 'binge-ing' Carnival; watch George re-slay the Dragon at Mons and follow spooky pointy-hatted penitents parade through the torch-lit streets of Lessines.

In the Botte

The gently rolling countryside has particular charm when you get into the Botte du Hainaut with a series of attractive villages to visit and the glorious beers of Chimay to sip.

p182

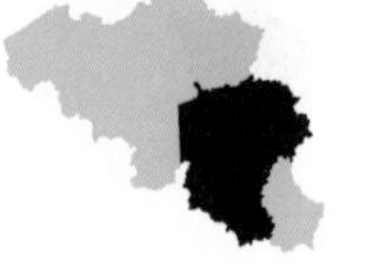

The Ardennes

Landscapes
Castles
Caves

Hilly Highs

The Ardennes aren't rugged mountains, and skiing is only possible a few weekends each winter, but gentle delights of expansive forests and Hautes Fagnes moorlands offer plenty of attractions for hikers, and kayakers can paddle on a series of pretty rivers.

Fortify Yourself

From the medieval ruins of Bouillon and La Roche, to the latter-day fortresses of Namur and Huy, via splendid châteaux like Modave and moated beauties like Jehay, the Ardennes has a castle for all seasons.

Cavern Country

Han, Rochefort or Hotton? In relatively close proximity lie three of Northern Europe's most impressive cave systems. Each is different so if you have time, try them all!

p203

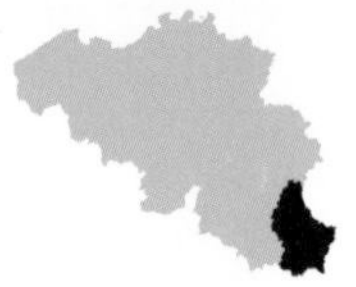

Luxembourg

City
Castles
Wine

Capital Class

One of Europe's more underrated capitals, Luxembourg City has a gloriously dramatic clifftop-and-valley setting and backs up the scenic impact with interesting museums, great dining and a lively bar scene.

Fortress Fiesta

The nation is studded with spectacular castles, often picturesquely set in idyllic wooded countryside. Looming Vianden contrasts brilliantly with ruined Bourscheid or Beaufort. Hollenfels castle houses a hostel, while Bourglinster's hosts two fabulous restaurants.

Bubbling Over

Sipping fine fizzy wines amid the immaculately groomed hillside vineyards of the Moselle Valley is all the more enjoyable with the region's handy bicycle-rental scheme.

p242

On the Road

Brussels

POP 1,200,000

Includes ➡

Best Places to Eat

- L'Ogenblik (p65)
- Soul Food (p67)
- L'Idiot du Village (p67)
- Saint-Boniface (p68)
- Stirwen (p67)

Best Places to Stay

- Chambres en Ville (p63)
- Maison Noble (p63)
- Chambres d'Hôtes du Vaudeville (p61)
- Hôtel Métropole (p62)
- The Captaincy Guesthouse (p63)

Why Go?

Belgium's fascinating capital, and the administrative capital of the EU, Brussels is historic yet hip, bureaucratic yet bizarre, self-confident yet unshowy, and multicultural to its roots. These contrasts are multilayered - Francophone alongside Flemish, and Eurocrats cheek-by-jowl with immigrants. And all this plays out in a cityscape that swings from majestic to quirky to rundown and back again. Organic art nouveau facades face off against 1960s concrete disgraces, and regal 19th-century mansions contrast with the brutal glass of the EU's Gotham City. This whole maelstrom swirls out from Brussels' medieval core, where the Grand Place is surely one of the world's most beautiful squares.

One constant is the enviable quality of everyday life, with a *café*/bar scene that could keep you drunk for years. But Brussels doesn't go out of its way to impress. The citizens' humorous, deadpan outlook on life is often just as surreal as the canvases of one-time resident Magritte.

Driving Distances

	Brussels	Antwerp	Liège	Bruges	Arlon
Antwerp	47				
Liège	90	115			
Bruges	115	113	205		
Arlon	187	236	140	283	
Ostend	140	138	230	25	300

History

According to legend, St-Géry built a chapel on a swampy Senne (Zenne) River island back in AD 695. A settlement that grew around it had become known as Bruocsella (from *bruoc,* marsh, and *sella,* dwelling) by 979 when Charles, Duke of Lorraine, moved here from Cambrai. He built a fort on St-Géry island amid flowering irises, which have since become the city's symbol. By 1100 Bruocsella was a walled settlement and capital of the Duchy of Brabant. In 1355 the Count of Flanders invaded and seized Brussels. However, a year later Brussels citizens, led by Everard 't Serclaes, ejected the Flemish. 't Serclaes went on to become a prominent local leader fighting for ever more civic privileges, a stance that finally saw him assassinated in 1388. This caused a furore in Brussels, whose townsfolk blamed the lord of Gaasbeek and took revenge by burning down his castle. Today, an anachronistic statue of 't Serclaes' corpse (at Grand Place 8) is still considered a potent source of luck.

Booming Brussels

Meanwhile, the cloth trade was booming. By the 15th century, prosperous markets filled the streets around the Grand Place, selling products for which some are still named: Rue au Beurre (Butter St), Rue des Bouchers (Butchers' St) etc. The city's increasingly wealthy merchant guilds established their headquarters on the Grand Place, where medieval tournaments and public executions took place in the shadow of a towering Hôtel de Ville.

From 1519 Brussels came to international prominence as capital of Charles Quint's vast Habsburg Empire. But Charles' future successor, the fanatically Catholic Philip II of Spain, was unimpressed with the lowlanders' brewing Protestantism. His Spanish Inquisition resulted in thousands of executions, including those of anti-Spanish Counts Egmont and Hoorn in front of the Maison du Roi.

The City Under Siege

In 1695, Louis XIV's French army under Marshal De Villeroy bombarded Brussels for 36 hours, hoping to divert Dutch attention from its attempts to regain Namur. This was truly catastrophic. Around 4000 houses were destroyed, around a third of the city was reduced to rubble and damage is thought to have been in the order of €5 billion in today's terms. The Grand Place was virtually obliterated, though miraculously the Hôtel de Ville survived relatively intact. And within five years most of the square's guildhalls were rebuilt, making them even more impressive than they'd been before.

Austrian rule in the 18th century fostered urban development, with the construction of grand squares such as Place Royale. Many of the Upper Town's architectural gems were built during this time and in the brief eras of French and Dutch rule that followed. In 1830 Brussels proved the unlikely starting point of the curious 1830 'operatic' revolt that led Belgium to entirely unexpected independence.

The Congo & Postwar Brussels

In the early 1800s Brussels was home to around 100,000 people. However, the city grew enormously in both population and stature during the next century, greatly funded by Wallonia's industrial revolution along with King Léopold II's plunder of the Congo. While an estimated 10 million people were killed in the Congo, Brussels lavished on itself some of Europe's finest belle époque and art nouveau buildings.

Unlike much of the country, Brussels survived both world wars comparatively unscathed. The city underlined a new era of postwar optimism by hosting the 1958 World's Fair in the shadow of the Atomium. Brussels' growth was further boosted when it became the headquarters of NATO and the EEC (later EU). However, in the city's pursuit of progress and modernism, much fine architecture was torn down to make way for mediocre concrete office buildings, a form of architectural vandalism that's now widely known as Brusselisation. A stint as Cultural Capital of Europe in 2000 finally gave the city the push it needed to start properly protecting heritage buildings and sprucing up neglected neighbourhoods.

Sights

The medieval grandeur of the Grand Place has an immediate wow factor that rarely fails to impress, and numerous excellent museums lie further afield. But much of the fun in Brussels is found simply by wandering the streets, enjoying the bizarre mismatch of building styles, spotting quirky architectural details and dropping regularly into fabulous *cafés* (bars) en route.

Grand Place, Bourse & Around

From the spectacular historic centrepiece of the Grand Place, there's lots to explore in the cobbled streets of the Îlot Sacré (once an island in the Senne), around the neoclassical

Brussels Highlights

1 Drinking a few beers in situ, and pondering the question of whether the gorgeous **Grand Place** (p38) is indeed Europe's most beautiful square

2 Taking in the work of old masters and surrealists at the **Musées Royaux des Beaux-Arts** (p48), with its **Musée Magritte annexe** (p48)

3 Lounging in **cafés ancient and modern** (p139), including an inspiring selection of art nouveau classics scattered around the Bourse

4 Joining the city's many jazz fans at the **Music Village** (p74), one of an array of venerable live-music venues

5 Visiting the wonderful **Old England Building** (p48) – one of Brussels' many art nouveau masterpieces – which houses a mesmerising music museum

6 Hunting for bric-a-brac bargains at the **Place de Jeu-de-Balle flea market** (p78) in the earthy Marolles district

7 Discovering Congolese Brussels in the **Matongé district** (p57)

8 Marvelling at the extraordinary riches lurking in the vast **Musée du Cinquantenaire** (p54)

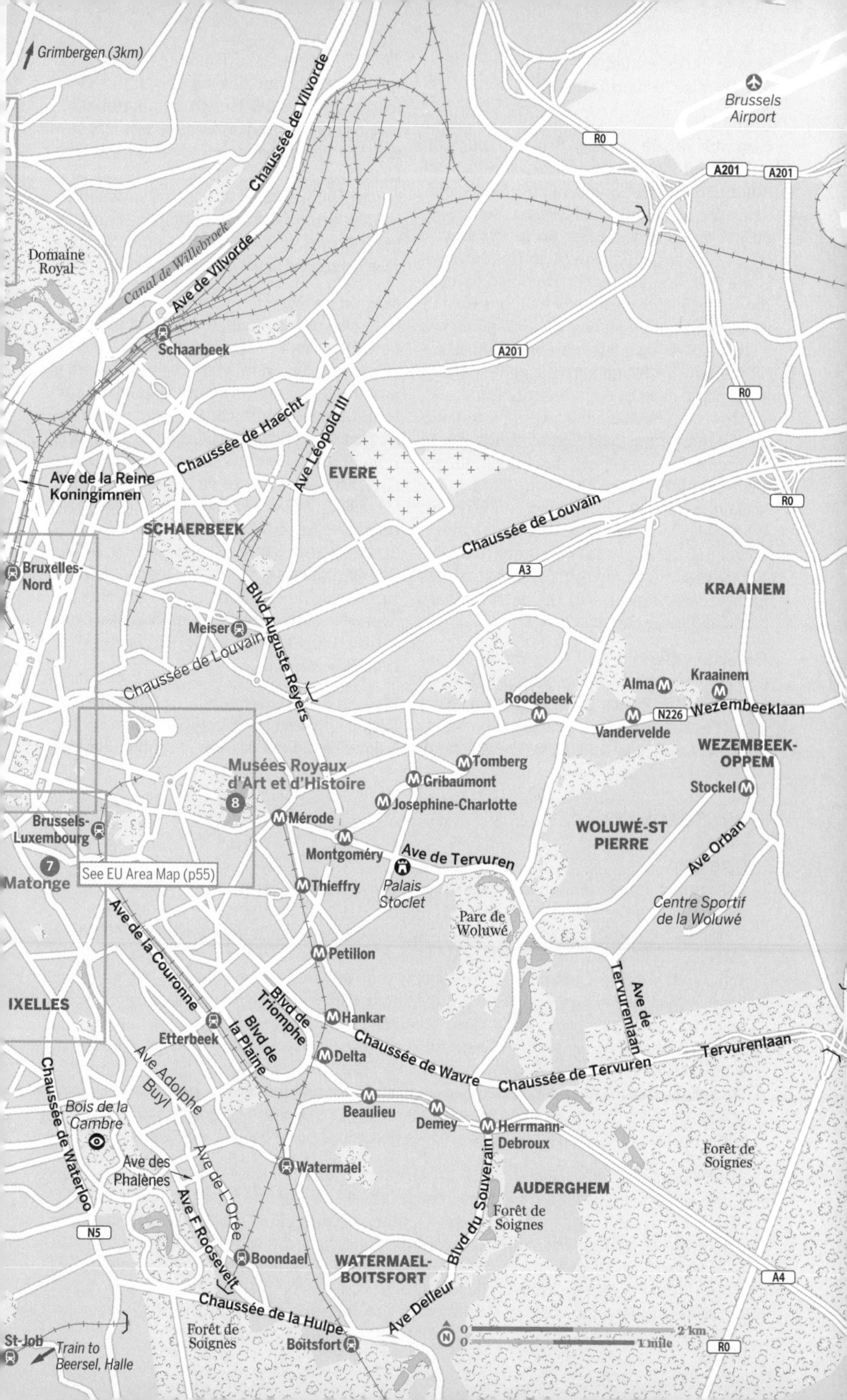
Grimbergen (3km)
Brussels Airport
R0
A201
A201
Chaussée de Vilvorde
Domaine Royal
Canal de Willebroek
Ave de Vilvorde
Schaarbeek
A201
R0
Chaussée de Haecht
Ave Léopold III
EVERE
Ave de la Reine Koningimnen
R0
Chaussée de Louvain
SCHAERBEEK
A3
Bruxelles-Nord
KRAAINEM
Blvd Auguste Reyers
Meiser
Chaussée de Louvain
Alma
Kraainem
Roodebeek
N226
Wezembeeklaan
Vandervelde
WEZEMBEEK-OPPEM
Musées Royaux d'Art et d'Histoire
Tomberg
Gribaumont
Stockel
8
Josephine-Charlotte
Mérode
WOLUWÉ-ST PIERRE
Brussels-Luxembourg
Montgoméry
Ave de Tervuren
Ave Orban
7
See EU Area Map (p55)
Matonge
Thieffry
Palais Stoclet
Centre Sportif de la Woluwé
Parc de Woluwé
Ave de la Couronne
Petillon
Ave de Tervurenlaan
IXELLES
Blvd de Triomphe
Hankar
Etterbeek
Blvd de la Plaine
Chaussée de Wavre
Tervurenlaan
Delta
Chaussée de Tervuren
Chaussée de Waterloo
Ave Adolphe Buyl
Beaulieu
Demey
Herrmann-Debroux
Bois de la Cambre
Forêt de Soignes
Ave des Phalènes
Ave de L'Orée
Watermael
Blvd du Souverain
AUDERGHEM
Ave F Roosevelt
Forêt de Soignes
N5
Boondael
WATERMAEL-BOITSFORT
A4
Chaussée de la Hulpe
Ave Delleur
Forêt de Soignes
0 2 km
0 1 mile
St-Job
Train to Beersel, Halle
Boitsfort
R0

Bourse (stock exchange) and in revitalised St-Géry, also formerly an island.

Grand Place SQUARE
(Map p40; Ⓜ Gare Centrale) Brussels' magnificent Grand Place is one of the world's most unforgettable urban ensembles. Oddly hidden, the enclosed cobblestone square is only revealed as you enter on foot from one of six narrow side alleys: Rue des Harengs is the best first approach. The focal point is the spired 15th-century city hall, but each of the antique guildhalls (mostly 1697–1705) has a charm of its own. Most are unashamed exhibitionists, with fine baroque gables, gilded statues and elaborate guild symbols.

Alive with classic *cafés,* the square takes on different auras at different times. Try to visit more than once, and don't miss looking again at night, when the scene is magically (and tastefully) illuminated. On Monday, Wednesday and Friday mornings there's a flower market and at various other times the square might host anything from Christmas fairs to rock concerts to the extraordinary biennial 'flower carpet'.

Hôtel de Ville HISTORIC BUILDING
(City Hall; Map p40; ☎ visitors office 02-279 43 47; guided tours €5; ⏰ tours 3pm Wed year-round, 10am & 2pm Sun Apr-Sep; Ⓜ Gare Centrale) Laboriously built between 1444 and 1480, the splendid, slightly asymmetrical Hôtel de Ville was almost the only building on the Grand Place to escape the 1695 French bombardment – ironic considering it was their primary target. The creamy stone facade is replete with Gothic gargoyles and reliefs. Its intricate tower soars 96m, topped by a gilded statue of St-Michel, Brussels' patron saint. For 45-minute guided tours, go to the tourist office 40 minutes before the departure time to buy tickets.

Maison du Roi HISTORIC BUILDING
(Map p40; Grand Place; Ⓜ Gare Centrale) This fanciful feast of neo-Gothic arches, verdigris statues and mini-spires is bigger, darker and nearly 200 years younger than the surrounding guildhalls. Once a medieval bread market, the current masterpiece is an 1873 rebuild and nowadays houses the **Brussels City Museum** (Musée de la Ville de Bruxelles; Map p40; ☎ 02-279 43 50; www.museedelavilledebruxelles.be; adult/concession/BrusselsCard €4/3/free; ⏰ 10am-5pm Tue-Sun, to 8pm Thu; Ⓜ Gare Centrale, 🚋 Bourse), whose old maps, architectural relics and paintings give a historical overview of the city. Don't miss Pieter Bruegel the Elder's 1567 *Cortège de Noces* (Wedding Procession).

Maison des Boulangers HISTORIC BUILDING
(Map p40; Grand Place 1; Ⓜ Gare Centrale) The bakers' guildhall is now the cafe Le Roy

BRUSSELS IN...

One Day

Gape in wonder at the **Grand Place**, Brussels' gorgeous central square. Discover that the **Manneken Pis** is much smaller than you'd imagined, then stroll through the **Galeries St-Hubert** en route to finding his 'squatting sister', the **Jeanneke Pis**. Marvel at the colourful scene that is the **Rue des Bouchers**, then move on for a seafood lunch in the convivial **Ste-Catherine** area. Window shop up Rue Antoine Dansaert, exploring the compact, quirky **Fashion District**, then grab a drink in **Le Cirio** or one of the other fabulous classic *cafés* around the **Bourse**. Admire the cityscape as well as the musical instruments at the majestic **Old England Building**, nip across the road to the **Musée Magritte**, then have a drink in the eccentric **La Fleur en Papier Doré**, where Magritte himself used to booze. Have a pita snack in the art nouveau *café* **Perroquet** or head straight to lively **Délirium Café** to sample a range of fine Belgian beers, then tune in to some live jazz at **L'Archiduc**. Quickly realise that you should have stayed a week.

One Week

Buy a 72-hour BrusselsCard for three intense prepaid days of brilliant museums. With card in hand, don't miss the **Musée des Sciences Naturelles**, the **Cinquantenaire museums** or avant-garde **Wiels**. Once the card has expired, discover lambic beers at the **Cantillon Brewery** or **De Lambiek**, visit the unique **Atomium**, peruse the comic-strip murals and discover the restaurants, cultural complexities and art-nouveau houses of **Ixelles**, and bus it out to the **Waterloo Battlefield**. And all the while, never stop drinking your way through our list of inspirational *cafés*. *Santé!*

d'Espagne. The gilded bronze bust above the door is bakers' patron St-Aubert.

La Brouette HISTORIC BUILDING
(The Wheelbarrow; Map p40; Grand Place 2; Ⓜ Gare Centrale) The grease-makers' guildhall has faint gold wheelbarrows above the door. The statue of St-Gilles (the grease-makers' patron) was added in 1912.

Le Sac HISTORIC BUILDING
(The Bag; Map p40; Grand Place 4; Ⓜ Gare Centrale) Perhaps as you'd expect, the cabinet-makers' guildhall is incredibly ornate. It takes its name from the sign above the door.

La Louve HISTORIC BUILDING
(The She-Wolf; Map p40; Grand Place 5; Ⓜ Gare Centrale) The archers' guildhall features a golden phoenix rising from the ashes, which signifies the rebirth of the Grand Place after its bombardment by the French in 1695. It also has a relief depicting Romulus and Remus, hence its name.

Le Cornet HISTORIC BUILDING
(The Horn; Map p40; Grand Place 6; Ⓜ Gare Centrale) The boatmen's guildhall, befittingly, has a stern-shaped gable. Its name refers to the horn on its facade.

Le Renard HISTORIC BUILDING
(The Fox; Map p40; Grand Place 7; Ⓜ Gare Centrale) The haberdashers' guildhall has a statue of a fox above the door.

L'Étoile HISTORIC BUILDING
(The Star; Map p40; Grand Place 8; Ⓜ Gare Centrale) The square's smallest building, surmounted by a star, is where city hero Everard 't Serclaes died in 1388. A fairly contemporary 'tradition' claims you'll garner good luck by rubbing a 1902 brass statue of Everard's reclining corpse. The statue adorns the house's arcaded north wall in Rue Charles Buls, the road separating the house from the Hôtel de Ville. Also notice the lovely 1899 gilded art nouveau plaque dedicated to the city by its appreciative artists.

Le Cygne HISTORIC BUILDING
(The Swan; Map p40; Grand Place 9; Ⓜ Gare Centrale) The lovely butchers' guildhall, featuring a carved swan above the door, hosted Karl Marx in 1847. Ironically, it's now home to the square's finest upmarket restaurant (p65).

L'Arbre d'Or HISTORIC BUILDING
(The Golden Tree; Map p40; Grand Place 10; Ⓜ Gare Centrale) Notice the hop plants climbing columns here! At the former brewers' guildhall, which is still the Belgian brewers' headquarters, two atmospheric but small basement rooms house a cursory **Brewery Museum** (Map p40; www.belgianbrewers.be; Grand Place 10; adult/BrusselsCard €5/free; ⏲10am-5pm; Ⓜ Gare Centrale). Entry includes a beer, which can be supped amid barrels and delightfully antiquated wooden brewers' tools: with the BrusselsCard it's a great opportunity for a free drink. The building's name derives from the gold reliefs of branches around the pillars.

OTHER PISSERS

The Manneken Pis has a much younger little squatting 'sister', the 20th-century **Jeanneke Pis** (Map p40; www.jeannekepisofficial.be; Impasse de la Fidélité; Ⓜ Gare Centrale), and there's also **Zinneke** (Map p40; cnr Rue des Chartreux & Rue du Vieux Marché aux Grains; Ⓜ Bourse), a mongrel dog standing with cocked (if dry) leg as though to show his contempt for the surrounding Fashion District.

Dukes of Brabant Mansion HISTORIC BUILDING
(Map p40; Grand Place 13-19; Ⓜ Gare Centrale) Six 1698 houses sit behind this single palatial facade, reworked in 1882. Had the imperial governor had his way after 1695, the whole square would have looked rather like this.

Chaloupe d'Or HISTORIC BUILDING
(The Golden Boat; Map p40; Grand Place 24-25; Ⓜ Gare Centrale) The dressmakers' guildhall is now a particularly splendid grand cafe (p69) whose upper-storey rooms (when open) offer fine views across the square.

Le Pigeon HISTORIC BUILDING
(The Pigeon; Map p40; Grand Place 26-27; Ⓜ Gare Centrale) Victor Hugo lived here at the artists' guildhall during his exile from France in 1852.

Manneken Pis MONUMENT
(Map p40; cnr Rue de l'Étuve & Rue du Chêne; Ⓜ Gare Centrale) Rue Charles Buls – Brussels' most unashamedly touristy shopping street, lined with chocolate and trinket shops – leads the hordes three blocks from the Grand Place to the Manneken Pis. This fountain-statue of a little boy taking a leak is comically tiny and a perversely perfect national symbol for surreal Belgium. Most of the time the statue's nakedness is hidden beneath a costume relevant to an anniversary, national day or local event: his ever-growing wardrobe is partly displayed at the Maison du Roi.

Lower Town

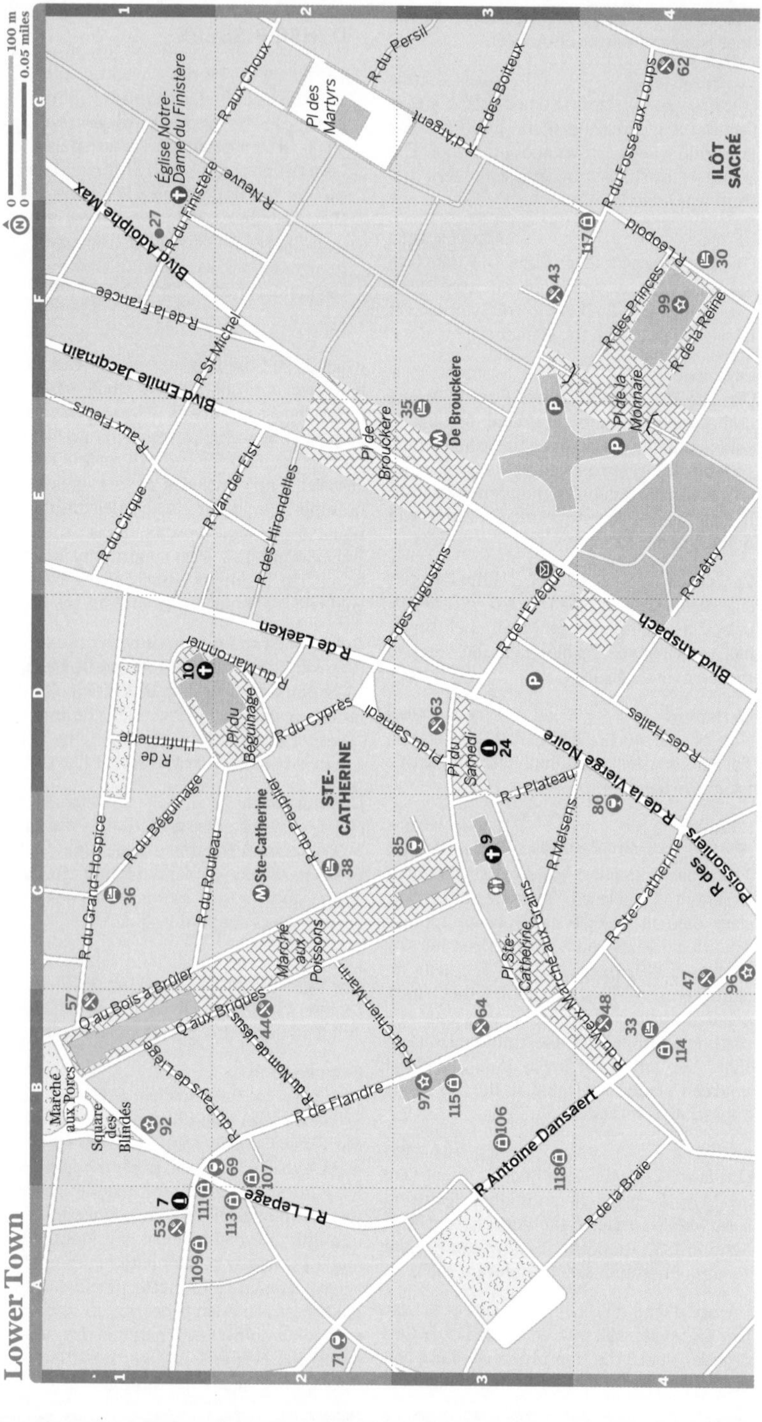

0 100 m
0 0.05 miles

A B C D E F G
1 2 3 4

Marché aux Pores
Square des Blindés
57
R du Grand-Hospice
36
Q au Bois à Brûler
R du Béguinage
R de l'Infirmerie
R du Cirque
R aux Fleurs
Blvd Emile Jacqmain
R de la Francée
Blvd Adolphe Max
27
Église Notre-Dame du Finistère
R du Finistère
53
7
92
109
111
113
69
107
R du Pays de Liège
Q aux Briques
R du Rouleau
10
Pl du Béguinage
R du Marronnier
R Van der Elst
R St Michel
R aux Choux
R Neuve
R du Nom de Jésus
44
Ste-Catherine
R des Hirondelles
R L Lepage
R de Flandre
Marché aux Poissons
R du Peuplier
R du Cyprès
R de Laeken
Pl des Martyrs
71
STE-CATHERINE
38
R du Chien Marin
Pl de Brouckère
R du Persil
85
R des Augustins
35
97
Pl du Samedi
63
De Brouckère
115
Pl du Samedi
R d'Argent
64
9
24
R des Boiteux
R Antoine Dansaert
106
Pl Ste-Catherine
R de l'Evêque
R du Vieux Marché aux Grains
R J Plateau
118
R Melsens
43
R de la Braie
48
80
117
R Ste-Catherine
R de la Vierge Noire
R des Halles
Pl de la Monnaie
R des Princes
R du Fossé aux Loups
33
Blvd Anspach
R Léopold
114
47
R Grétry
99
62
R des Poissoniers
R de la Reine
30
96
ILÔT SACRÉ

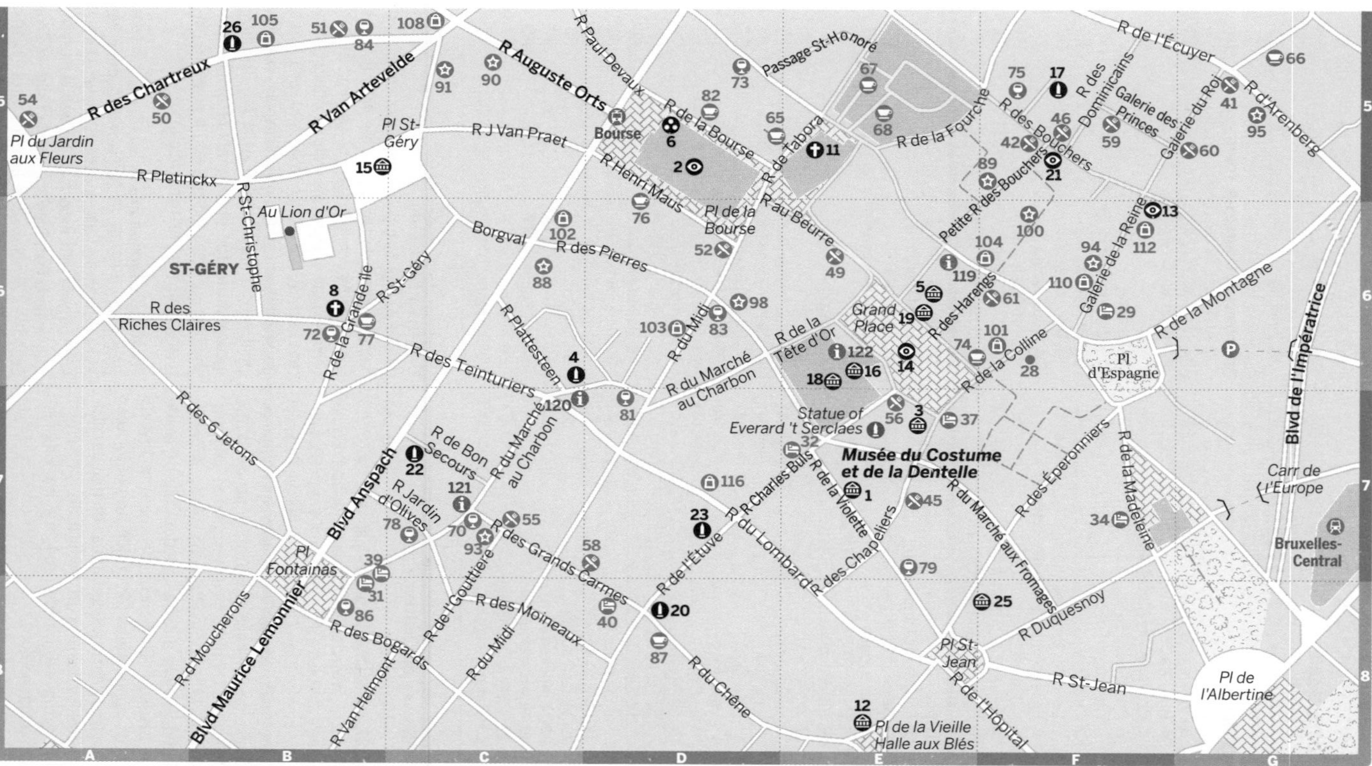
R des Chartreux
Pl du Jardin aux Fleurs
R Van Artevelde
R Auguste Orts
R Paul Devaux
Passage St-Honoré
R de l'Écuyer
R d'Arenberg
Galerie du Roi
Galerie des Princes
R des Dominicains
R des Bouchers
Petite R des Bouchers
R de la Fourche
R de Tabora
R de la Bourse
Bourse
Pl de la Bourse
R au Beurre
R Henri Maus
R J Van Praet
Pl St-Géry
R Pletinckx
R St-Christophe
Au Lion d'Or
ST-GÉRY
Borgval
R des Pierres
R St-Géry
R de la Grande Île
R des Riches Claires
R des Teinturiers
R Plattesteen
R du Midi
R du Marché au Charbon
R de la Tête d'Or
Grand Place
R des Harengs
R de la Colline
Galerie de la Reine
R de la Montagne
Pl d'Espagne
Blvd de l'Impératrice
Statue of Everard 't Serclaes
Musée du Costume et de la Dentelle
R Charles Buls
R de la Violette
R des Chapeliers
R du Lombard
R de l'Étuve
R du Marché aux Fromages
R des Éperonniers
R de la Madeleine
Carr de l'Europe
Bruxelles-Central
R des 6 Jetons
R de Bon Secours
Blvd Anspach
R Jardin d'Olives
R des Grands Carmes
R de l'Goutttière
R des Moineaux
Pl Fontainas
R d Moucherons
Blvd Maurice Lemonnier
R des Bogards
R Van Helmont
R du Chêne
R Duquesnoy
Pl St-Jean
R St-Jean
R de l'Hôpital
Pl de la Vieille Halle aux Blés
Pl de l'Albertine
A
B
C
D
E
F
G
5
6
7
8

Lower Town

Top Sights
1 Musée du Costume et de la Dentelle E7

Sights
2 Bourse D5
3 Brewery Museum E7
4 Broussaille C6
5 Brussels City Museum E6
6 Bruxella1238 ..... D5
Chaloupe d'Or ..... (see 14)
7 Cubitus A1
Dukes of Brabant Mansion ..... (see 14)
8 Église Notre-Dame des Riches Claires B6
9 Église Ste-Catherine C3
10 Église St-Jean-Baptiste au Béguinage D1
11 Église St-Nicolas E5
12 Fondation Jacques Brel E8
13 Galeries St-Hubert F6
14 Grand Place E6
15 Halles St-Géry B5
16 Hôtel de Ville E6
17 Jeanneke Pis F5
La Brouette ..... (see 14)
La Louve ..... (see 14)
L'Arbre d'Or ..... (see 14)
Le Cornet ..... (see 14)
Le Cygne ..... (see 14)
Le Pigeon ..... (see 14)
Le Renard ..... (see 14)
Le Sac ..... (see 14)
L'Étoile ..... (see 14)
18 Maison des Boulangers E6
19 Maison du Roi E6
20 Manneken Pis D8
21 Rue des Bouchers F5
22 Tibet & Duchâteau C7
23 Tintin D7
24 Tour Noire D3
25 Underpant Museum F8
26 Zinneke B5

Activities, Courses & Tours
27 Atelier de Recherche et d'Action Urbaines F1
28 Brussels City Tours F6

Sleeping
29 Chambres d'Hôtes du Vaudeville F6
30 Dominican F4
31 Downtown-BXL B8
32 Hôtel Amigo E7
33 Hotel Café Pacific B4
34 Hôtel Le Dixseptième F7
35 Hôtel Métropole E3
36 Hôtel Noga C1
37 Hotel Residence Le Quinze E7
38 Hôtel Welcome C2
39 La Casa-BXL B7
40 La Vieille Lanterne D8

Eating
41 Arcadi G5
42 Aux Armes de Bruxelles F5
43 Belga Queen Brussels F3
44 Bij den Boer B2
45 Brasserie de la Roue d'Or E7
46 Chez Léon F5
47 Comocomo C4
48 Cremerie De Linkebeek B4
49 Dandoy E6
50 Den Teepot A5
51 Fin de Siècle B5
52 Fritland D6
53 Henri A1
54 In't Spinnekopke A5
55 Kokob C7
56 La Maison du Cygne E7

★Musée du Costume et de la Dentelle — MUSEUM

(Costume & Lace Museum; Map p40; ☎02-213 44 50; www.museeducostumeetdeladentelle.be; Rue de la Violette 12; admission €4, with Brussels-Card free; ⏲10am-5pm Thu-Tue; Ⓜ Gare Centrale) Lace making has been one of Flanders' finest crafts since the 16th century. While *kloskant* (bobbin lace) originated in Bruges, *naaldkant* (needlepoint lace) was developed in Italy but was predominantly made in Brussels. This excellent museum reveals lace's applications for under- and outerwear over the centuries, as well as displaying other luxury textiles in beautifully presented changing exhibitions. Ask for an English-language booklet.

Underpant Museum — GALLERY

(Musée du Slip; Map p40; www.janbucquoy.be/janbucquoy/Musee_du_slip.html; Dolle Mol, Rue des Éperonniers 52; admission €1; ⏲2–6pm Sun; Ⓜ Gare Centrale) One of the city's weirder offerings, located upstairs from the Dolle Mol *café*. Not a museum in any real sense, it displays collages created by filmmaker and artist Jan Bucquoy, incorporating the underpants of Belgian celebs. The entrance fee gets you a postcard featuring your pant artwork of choice.

Fondation Jacques Brel — MUSEUM

(Map p40; ☎02-511 10 20; www.jacquesbrel.be; Place de la Vieille Halle aux Blés 11; adult/student €5/3.50, walk with audio guide €8, walk & museum €10; ⏲noon-6pm Tue-Sat, plus Mon Aug; Ⓜ Gare Centrale) *Chansonnier* Jacques Brel (1929–

57 La Marie-Joseph B1
58 Le Cercle des Voyageurs D7
59 L'Ogenblik F5
60 Mokafé G5
Ommegang Brasserie .... (see 56)
61 Osteria a l'Ombra F6
62 Sea Grill G4
63 Vismet D3
64 Viva M'Boma B3

Drinking & Nightlife

65 À la Bécasse D5
66 À la Mort Subite G5
67 A l'Image de Nostre-Dame E5
68 Au Bon Vieux Temps E5
69 Au Laboureur B2
70 Au Soleil C7
71 BarBeton A2
72 Booze'n'Blues B6
73 Celtica D5
74 Chaloupe d'Or E6
75 Délirium Café F5
76 Falstaff D6
77 Floreo B6
78 Fontainas Bar C7
79 Goupil le Fol E7
80 La Vilaine C4
81 Le Belgica D7
82 Le Cirio D5
83 Le Club D6
84 Le Greenwich B5
85 Madame Moustache C3
86 Moeder Lambic Fontainas B8
87 Poechenellekelder D8
Toone .... (see 100)

Entertainment

88 AB C6
89 Actor's Studio F5
90 Beursschouwburg C5
91 Bizon C5
92 Bronks Youth Theatre B1
93 Chez Maman C7
94 Cinéma Galeries F6
95 Cinema Nova G5
96 L'Archiduc C4
97 Maison de la Bellone B3
98 Music Village D6
99 Théâtre Royal de la Monnaie/Koninklijke Muntschouwburg F4
100 Théâtre Royal de Toone F6

Shopping

101 Boutique Tintin F6
102 Brüsel C6
103 Catherine D6
104 De Biertempel F6
105 Gabriele B5
106 Hoet B3
107 Just In Case B2
108 Kartell C5
109 Lowi A1
110 Manufacture Belge de Dentelles F6
111 Martin Margiela A1
112 Neuhaus F6
113 Outlet Privejoke A2
114 Passa Porta B4
115 Pimpinelle B3
116 Planète Chocolat D7
117 Sterling Books F4
118 Stijl B3

Information

Accessible Travel Info Point .... (see 119)
119 Flanders Info E6
120 Rainbow House C7
121 Tels Quels C7
122 Visit Brussels E6

78) made his debut in 1952 at a cabaret in his native Belgium and shot to fame in Paris, where he was a contemporary of Édith Piaf and co, though his songs continued to hark back to the bleak 'flat land' of his native country. This dedicated archive centre and museum, set up by his daughter, contains more than 100 hours of footage and another 100 of audio recordings, plus thousands of photographs and articles.

Dedicated fans can also take the audio walking tour.

Galeries St-Hubert ARCHITECTURE

(Map p40; www.galeries-saint-hubert.com; Ⓜ Gare Centrale) When opened in 1847 by King Léopold I, the glorious Galeries St-Hubert formed Europe's very first shopping arcade. Many enticing shops lie behind its neoclassical glassed-in arches flanked by marble pilasters. Several eclectic *cafés* spill tables onto the gallery terrace, safe from rain beneath the glass roof. The arcade is off Rue du Marché aux Herbes.

Rue des Bouchers STREET

(Map p40) Uniquely colourful Rue and Petite Rue des Bouchers are a pair of narrow alleys jam-packed with pavement tables, pyramids of lemons and iced displays of fish and crustaceans. It's all gloriously photogenic, but think twice before eating here, as the food standards are generally poor – an exception is the classic **Aux Armes de Bruxelles** (Map p40; 02-511 55 98; www.auxarmesdebruxelles.com; Rue des Bouchers 13; mains €19-57; noon-11.15pm Tue-Sun; Bourse, Ⓜ De Brouckère).

Don't miss peeping inside marionette theatre Toone (p75) and, nearby, into the wonderful, age-old biscuit shop **Dandoy** (Map p40; ☎02-511 03 26; www.maisondandoy.com; Rue au Beurre 31; ⊙9.30am-7pm Mon-Sat, 10.30am-7pm Sun; Bourse), full of splendid moulds for *speculaas/speculoos* (traditional spiced biscuit) figures.

Bourse BUILDING
(Map p40; Place de la Bourse; Bourse) The Bourse is Belgium's 1873 stock-exchange building. It's closed to visitors, but you can enjoy its grandiose neoclassical facade, brilliantly festooned with friezes and sculptures, reclining nudes, lunging horses and a multitude of allegorical figures. Some of the work is by Rodin, then a young apprentice sculptor.

Bruxella1238 ARCHAEOLOGICAL SITE
(Map p40; admission €4; ⊙tours in English 10.15am 1st Wed of month) Bruxella1238 is the scanty remains of a Franciscan convent that was bombarded into ruins in 1695. Most of the site is visible by peeping through the glass windows set into the pavement roughly outside Le Cirio cafe (p70).

Église St-Nicolas CHURCH
(Church of St-Nicolas; Map p40; Rue au Beurre 1; ⊙8am-6.30pm Mon-Fri, 9am-6pm Sat, 9am-7.30pm Sun; Bourse) Near the Bourse, this pint-sized church is as old as Brussels itself. What really makes it notable is its virtual invisibility – the exterior is almost totally encrusted with shops. Appropriately enough, it's dedicated to the patron saint of merchants.

Halles St-Géry HISTORIC BUILDING
(Map p40; www.hallessaintgery.be; Bourse) In 1881 this superb neo-Renaissance brick-and-wrought-iron meat market was built around a curious pyramidal monument-fountain (itself built to replace a medieval Gothic church demolished in 1799 by the anti-religious French regime). The monument marks 'kilometre zero' – the point from which all distances in Belgium are measured. The market lay derelict for much of the 1980s but has since been beautifully renovated and is now a combined bar-cafe, club and exhibition space.

Black steel gates beside the bistro Le Lion St-Géry lead into a private courtyard in which one branch of the mostly covered Senne River has been uncovered, along with a reconstructed historical mooring point. The stream is bridged by the vaulted 1811 brick, neo-Gothic Au Lion d'Or building. The courtyard also offers interesting views of the bulb-spired **Église Notre-Dame des Riches Claires** (Map p40; Bourse).

Ste-Catherine

It's hard to imagine today, but fishing boats once sailed up the now-invisible Senne River, mooring in the heart of Ste-Catherine, which was for centuries a major fish market. Although the river has been covered over since 1870, the area's reputation for fish persists and the main reason you're likely to visit is to choose from the numerous well-regarded seafood restaurants around Place Ste-Catherine.

Église Ste-Catherine CHURCH
(Map p40; Place Ste-Catherine; Ⓜ Ste-Catherine) Église Ste-Catherine must be one of the only religious buildings that positively encourages folks to urinate on its walls (there's a 'pissoir' on its northwestern flank). Inside is a black statue of the Virgin and Child that Protestants hurled into the Senne in 1744; the statue was found 'miraculously' floating on a chunk of turf. It's rarely open.

Église St-Jean-Baptiste au Béguinage CHURCH
(Map p40; Place du Béguinage; Ⓜ Ste-Catherine) This soaring 1657 Flemish baroque masterpiece was designed by Luc Fayd'Herbe, a student of Rubens. It's often cited as Belgium's most beautiful church and has become something of a temporary refuge and work space for asylum seekers.

Tour Noire TOWER
(Map p40; Place du Samedi; Ⓜ Ste-Catherine) Boxed in on three sides and incongruously dwarfed by the back of a Novotel Hotel, this is an ivy-draped remnant of Brussels' original city wall.

Pigeon Soldat Memorial MONUMENT
(Map p46; Ⓜ Ste-Catherine) This monument commemorates the carrier pigeons of WWI.

Cathedral Area

Cathédrale des Sts-Michel & Gudule CHURCH
(Map p46; www.cathedralisbruxellensis.be; Place Sainte-Gudule; admission free, treasury €1, crypt €3; ⊙7am-6pm Mon-Fri, 8.30am-6pm Sat, 2pm-6pm Sun; Ⓜ Gare Centrale) Host to coronations and royal weddings, Brussels' grand, twin-towered cathedral bears at least some resemblance to Paris' Notre Dame. Begun in 1226, construction took 300 years. Stained-glass windows flood the soaring nave with light, while col-

umn-saints brandish gilded tools. An enormous wooden pulpit by Antwerp artist Hendrik Verbruggen sees Adam and Eve driven out of Eden by skeletons. To climb the cathedral towers (€5, 10am on the second Saturday of each month), sign up a day or two ahead.

The treasury is open shorter hours and the crypt by appointment only.

National Bank of Belgium Museum MUSEUM
(Map p46; ☎02-221 22 06; www.nbbmuseum.be; Blvd de Berlaimont 3; ⏰10am-5pm Mon-Fri; Ⓜ Gare Centrale) FREE Unexpectedly absorbing, the National Bank Museum is far more than just a coin collection. Well-presented exhibits trace the very concept of money all the way from cowrie shells to credit cards.

Colonne du Congrès MONUMENT
(Map p46; Place du Congrès; Ⓜ Madou) Brussels' 25m-tall version of Nelson's Column is an 1850s monolith topped by a gilded statue of King Léopold I. It commemorates the Belgian constitution of 1831. The four female figures around its base represent the four constitutionally upheld freedoms of religion, association, education and the press. The last of these encouraged Victor Hugo, Karl Marx and others to visit Belgium back when such freedoms were much more restricted in other parts of Europe.

Between two bronze lions, an eternal flame honours Belgian victims of the two world wars.

Centre Belge de la Bande Dessinée MUSEUM
(Belgian Comic Strip Centre; Map p46; ☎02-219 19 80; www.comicscenter.net; Rue des Sables 20; adult/concession €10/6.50; ⏰10am-6pm Tue-Sun; Ⓜ Rogier) This centre offers a definitive overview of the country's vibrant comic-strip culture. Even if you're not excited by the 'ninth art', do peep inside the impressive 1906 art nouveau building, a Victor Horta classic with wrought-iron superstructure and a glass roof. You don't have to pay an entrance fee to enjoy the central hallway or to drink a coffee (€2.20) at the attached cafe.

Place Royale Area

A short stroll up the Mont des Arts steps from the Grand Place area, neoclassical Place Royale forms the heart of Brussels' regal Upper Town area. The square is flanked by museums and has a curious secret lurking beneath. North of the Palais Royal is a spacious formal park dotted with classical statues.

DISCOUNTS & FREEBIES

On the first Wednesday afternoon of each month, most of Brussels' major museums are free to enter. At other times the cheapest way to see a bunch of top sites is with the **BrusselsCard** (www.brusselscard.be; 24/48/72hr €22/29/35). The card gets you into 30 major museums and provides free city transport plus discounts for other attractions and some shops and restaurants. It's available through the tourist offices, STIB agencies and larger museums. Prepaying online saves €1. When picking your dates don't forget that most museums close Monday. The **Arsène50 office** (p79) at the tourist office offers heavily discounted tickets for cultural events.

Palais Royal PALACE
(Map p46; ☎02-551 20 20; www.monarchy.be; Place des Palais; ⏰10.30am-4.30pm Tue-Sun late Jul-early Sep; Ⓜ Parc) FREE These days Belgium's royal family lives at Laeken (p58), but this sturdy 19th-century palace remains its 'official' residence. One unique room has had its ceiling iridescently clad with the wing cases of 1.4 million Thai jewel beetles by conceptual artist Jan Fabre. You'll also see contemporary royal portraits. It's only open to visitors in summer.

Musée BELvue MUSEUM
(Map p46; ☎07-022 04 92; www.belvue.be; Place des Palais 7; adult/concession €6/5; ⏰9.30am-5pm Tue-Fri, 10am-6pm Sat & Sun; Ⓜ Parc) Take a chronological audio tour through the airy stuccoed interior of this former royal residence to explore Belgium's history from independence to today, brought to life by exhibits and film footage. Among the artefacts is the jacket worn by Albert I when he died in a climbing accident in 1934. In summer, the restaurant has tables in the pretty garden.

Coudenberg ARCHAEOLOGICAL SITE
(Map p46; www.coudenberg.com; adult/under 26/BrusselsCard €6/5/free; ⏰9.30am-5pm Tue-Fri, 10am-6pm Sat & Sun; Ⓜ Parc) Coudenberg Hill (now Place Royale) was the site of Brussels' original 12th-century castle. Over several centuries this was transformed into one of Europe's most elegant and powerful palaces, most notably as the 16th-century residence of Holy Roman Emperor Charles V. Around the palace, courtiers and nobles in turn built fine mansions. The vast complex was

Central Brussels

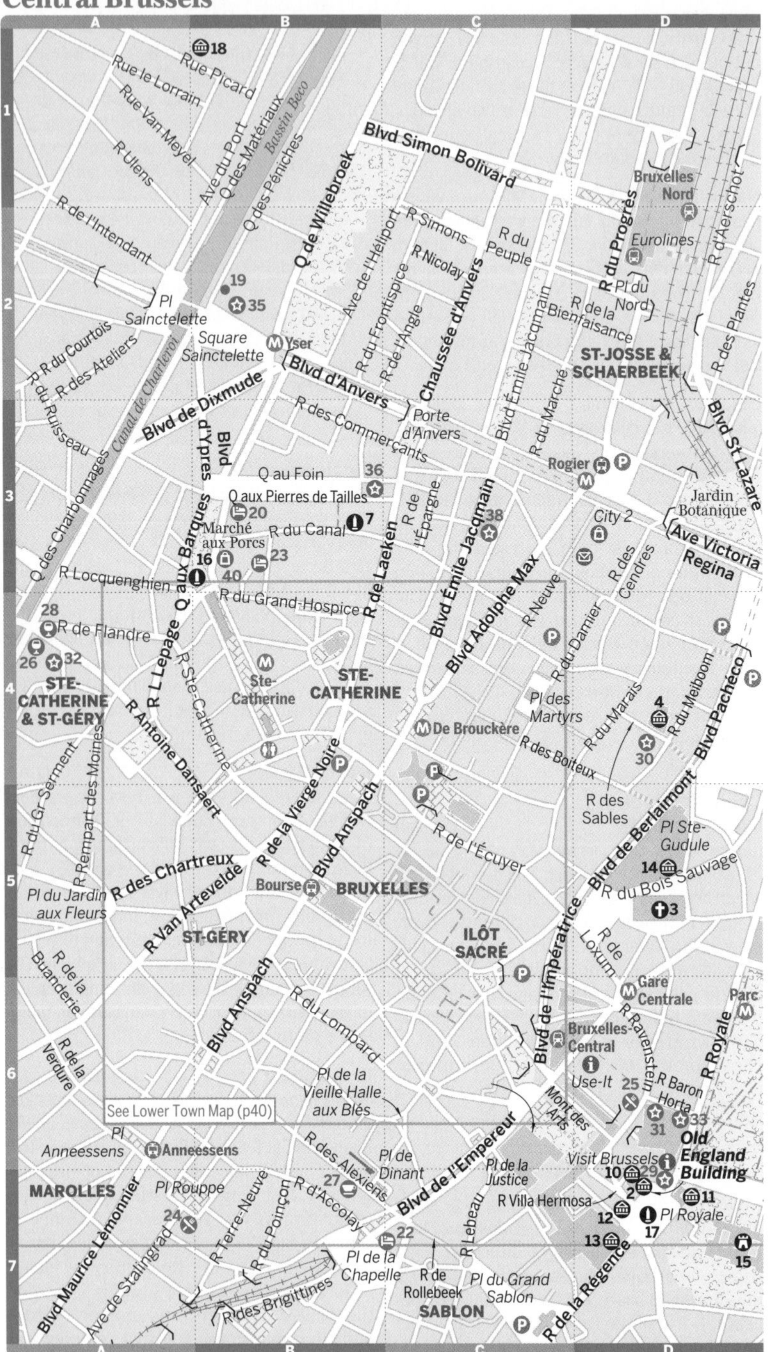

Central Brussels

Top Sights

1 De Ultieme Hallucinatie E2
2 Old England Building D7

Sights

3 Cathédrale des Sts-Michel & Gudule D5
4 Centre Belge de la Bande Dessinée D4
5 Colonne du Congrès E4
Coudenberg .... (see 11)
6 Église Ste-Marie E2
7 FC de Kampioenen B3
8 Halles de Schaerbeek F2
9 Maison Autrique F1
10 MIM D7
11 Musée BELvue D7
12 Musée Magritte D7
13 Musées Royaux des Beaux-Arts D7
14 National Bank of Belgium Museum D5
15 Palais Royal D7
16 Pigeon Soldat Memorial B3
17 Statue of Godefroid (Godefroy) de Bouillon D7
18 Tour & Taxis B1

Activities, Courses & Tours

19 Brussels by Water B2

Sleeping

20 Captaincy Guesthouse B3
21 Centre Vincent van Gogh E3
22 HI Hostel John Bruegel C7
23 Maison Noble B3

Eating

24 Comme Chez Soi A7
25 Laurent Gerbaud D6

Drinking & Nightlife

26 Bistro du Canal A4
27 La Fleur en Papier Doré B7
28 Walvis A4

Entertainment

29 Arsène50 .... D7
30 Art Base D4
31 BOZAR D6
32 Bravo A4
33 Cinematek D6
34 Cirque Royal E5
35 Kaaitheater B2
36 Koninklijke Vlaamse Schouwburg B3
37 Le Botanique E3
38 Théâtre National C3

Shopping

39 Mary E5
40 Micro Marché B3

See EU Area Map (p55)

See Marolles, Sablon & Ixelles Map (p50)

INSIDE INFORMATION

A great way of exploring a specific area or indulging in a passion for anything from *gueuze* beers to Belgian politics is to contact Brussels Greeters (www.brussels.greeters.be) two weeks before your trip. You fill in a simple online form and the coordinator sets you up with a local who will take you to relevant sights in the city, usually with stops for coffee and lunch along the way (trips take two to four hours). There is no charge for the service, and tips are not accepted.

destroyed in a catastrophic 1731 fire, but beneath street level the basic structure of the palace's long-hidden lower storeys remains.

Whole stretches of the medieval street layout are now discernible, though little atmosphere remains. The subterranean site is entered from Musée BELvue and you emerge near the Old England Building.

★Old England Building HISTORIC BUILDING
(Map p46; Rue Montagne de la Cour 2; Ⓜ Gare Centrale, Parc) This 1899 former department store is an art nouveau showpiece with a black facade aswirl with wrought iron and arched windows. The building contains the groundbreaking **music museum** (Musée des Instruments de Musique; Map p46; ☎02-545 01 30; www.mim.be; Rue Montagne de la Cour 2; adult/concession €8/6; ⏲9.30am-5pm Tue-Fri, 10am-5pm Sat & Sun; Ⓜ Gare Centrale, Parc), a celebration of music in all its forms, as well as a repository for more than 2000 historic instruments. The emphasis is very much on listening, with auditory experiences around every corner, from shepherds' bagpipes to Chinese carillons to harpsichords. Don't miss the rooftop *café* for a superb city panorama.

Musées Royaux des Beaux-Arts GALLERY
(Royal Museums of Fine Arts; Map p46; ☎02-508 32 11; www.fine-arts-museum.be; Rue de la Régence 3; adult/6-25yr/BrusselsCard €8/2/free, with Magritte Museum €13; ⏲10am-5pm Tue-Fri, 11am-6pm Sat & Sun; Ⓜ Gare Centrale, Parc) This prestigious museum incorporates the Musée d'Art Ancien (ancient art); the Musée d'Art Moderne (modern art), with works by surrealist Paul Delvaux and fauvist Rik Wouters; and the purpose-built Musée Magritte. The 15th-century Flemish Primitives are wonderfully represented in the Musée d'Art Ancien: there's Rogier Van der Weyden's *Pietà* with its hallucinatory sky, Hans Memling's refined portraits, and the richly textured *Madonna With Saints* by the Master of the Legend of St Lucy.

Pieter the Elder was the greatest of the Brueghel family of artists, whose humorous and tender scenes feature a wealth of lively rustic detail. The most famous example is *The Fall of Icarus,* where the hero's legs disappearing into the waves are overshadowed by the figure of an unconcerned ploughman and a jaunty ship. Inspired by Renaissance artists, Antwerp painter Peter Paul Rubens specialised in fleshy religious works, of which there are several colossal examples here. Look out, too, for Anthony van Dyck's contemplative human studies, Cornelis de Vos' charming family portrait, and works by Rembrandt and Frans Hals.

Musée Magritte MUSEUM
(Map p46; www.musee-magritte-museum.be; Place Royale; adult/under 26/BrusselsCard €8/2/free; ⏲10am-5pm Tue-Fri, 11am-6pm Sat & Sun; Ⓜ Gare Centrale, Parc) The beautifully presented Magritte Museum holds the world's largest collection of the surrealist pioneer's paintings and drawings. Watch his style develop from colourful Braque-style cubism in 1920 through a Dalí-esque phase and a late-1940s period of Kandinsky-like brushwork to his trademark bowler hats of the 1960s. Regular screenings of a 50-minute documentary provide insights into the artist's unconventionally conventional life.

Statue of Godefroid (Godefroy) de Bouillon STATUE
(Map p46; Ⓜ Gare Centrale, Parc) The bold equestrian statue at the centre of Place Royale depicts Godefroid (Godefroy) de Bouillon, the crusader knight who very briefly became the first European 'king' of Jerusalem in 1099.

Sablon & Marolles

The Sablon is a cobbled square whose *cafés,* antique shops and *chocolatiers* are typically frequented by the see-and-be-seen Brussels upper crust. Surrounding lanes sport plenty more intriguing antique shops and the square itself hosts a Sunday antique market.

Brussels' once resolutely working-class Marolles quarter has partly shed its proletarian image with a clutch of intimate restaurants and funky interior-design shops along the main streets, Rue Haute and Rue Blaes. Nonetheless, pockets of original Bruxellois character can still be found, notably around the Place du Jeu-de-Balle. At a few of the down-market *cafés* here you might overhear people speaking in the earthy Bruxellois dialect, and at least one stall still sells the traditional street food: snails. Note that, despite the name, Jeu-de-Balle (aka *balle-pelotte)* is no longer played here.

★Église Notre-Dame du Sablon CHURCH
(Map p50; Rue de la Régence; ⌚9am-6pm Mon-Fri, 10am-6pm Sat & Sun; Ⓜ Porte de Namur) The Sablon's large, flamboyantly Gothic church started life as the 1304 archers' guild chapel. A century later it had to be massively enlarged to cope with droves of pilgrims attracted by the supposed healing powers of its Madonna statue. The statue was procured in 1348 by means of an audacious theft from an Antwerp church – apparently by a vision-motivated husband-and-wife team in a rowing boat. It has long since gone, but a boat behind the pulpit commemorates the curious affair.

Église Notre-Dame de la Chapelle CHURCH
(Map p50; Place de la Chapelle; admission free, pamphlet €3; ⌚9am-7pm Jun-Sep, to 6pm Oct-May; Anneessens) Brussels' oldest surviving church now curiously incorporates the decapitated tower of the 1134 original as the central section of a bigger Gothic edifice. Behind the palm-tree pulpit, look on the wall above a carved confessional to find a small memorial to 'Petro Brevgello', ie artist Pieter Bruegel the Elder, who once lived in the nearby Marolles.

Recyclart ARTS CENTRE
(Map p50; 02-502 57 34; www.recyclart.be; Rue des Ursulines 25; Anneessens) This graffitied 'arts laboratory' in the old Chapelle station along Rue des Ursulines revitalised what was once an industrial wasteland. It now hosts art installations and theatre productions, cutting-edge gigs and parties with DJs, and has a daytime cafe; above is a skate park. Its mini magazine, available in bars across Brussels, lists current events.

Place du Petit Sablon PARK
(Map p50; Ⓜ Porte de Namur) About 200m uphill from Place du Grand Sablon, this charming little garden is ringed by 48 bronze statuettes representing the medieval guilds. Huddled on a fountain plinth like two actors from a Shakespearean drama are Counts Egmont and Hoorn, popular city leaders who

COMIC-STRIP MURALS

Over 40 comic-strip murals currently enliven alleys and thoroughfares throughout the old city centre, with more added year after year. These bright artworks are a great prompt to explore less-visited neighbourhoods. Some favourites:

Tibet & Duchateau (Map p40; Rue du Bon Secours 9; Bourse) Very effectively depicts a life-sized figure teetering towards a *trompe l'œil* window.

Josephine Baker (Map p50; Rue des Capucins 9; Ⓜ Porte de Hal) In one of the most distinctive Marolles murals, slinky chanteuse Josephine, with a leopard on a lead, shakes hands with a rotund monk. Behind, both in the mural and in real life, is the looming dome of the Palais de Justice. Baker performed in Brussels in the 1920s and '30s, and famously kept a leopard as a pet.

Tintin (Map p40; Rue de l'Étuve; Bourse) The most famous of Belgium's fictional characters.

Broussaille (Map p40; Rue du Marché au Charbon; Bourse) Depicts a young couple arm-in-arm. The original 1991 version showed a couple of very ambiguous sex that the neighbouring gay establishments used to promote the quarter. However, a 1999 repaint seemed to give the black-haired figure a more feminine hairstyle, earrings and (slightly) bigger breasts. Creeping homophobia or honest mistake? Nobody knows.

Peeping Policeman (Map p50; Rue Haute; Ⓜ Louise) This Hergé character uses the terrace end brilliantly for a little spying.

Manneken Pis Displaced (Map p40; Rue de Flandre; Ⓜ Ste-Catherine) A tetchy-looking Manneken Pis gazes up at his pediment, from which he has been displaced by a grinning, peeing bear.

FC de Kampioenen (Map p46; Rue du Canal; Ⓜ Ste-Catherine) This bright, dynamic mural features not a football club but a parade of characters based on a TV series that ran from 1990 to 2011. The show was turned into a comic strip by Hec Leemans in 1997.

Marolles, Sablon & Ixelles

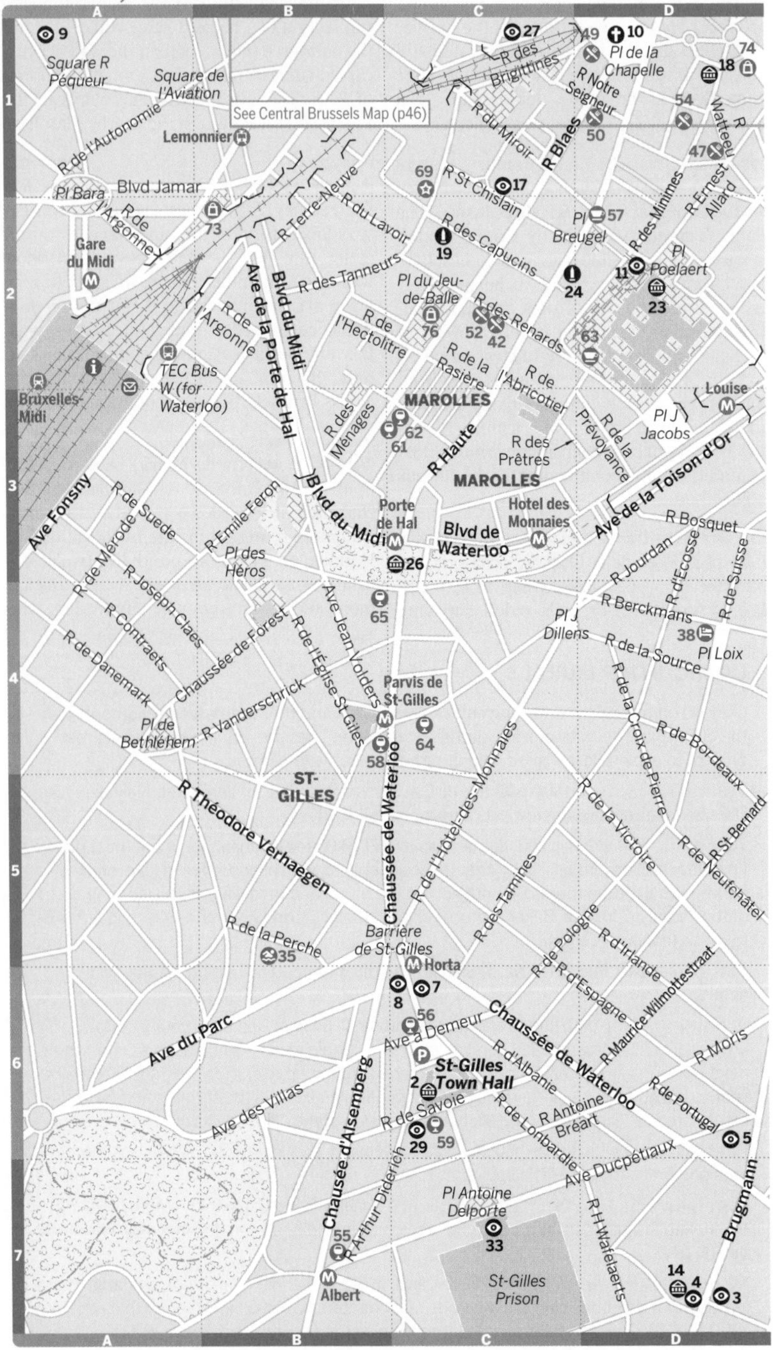

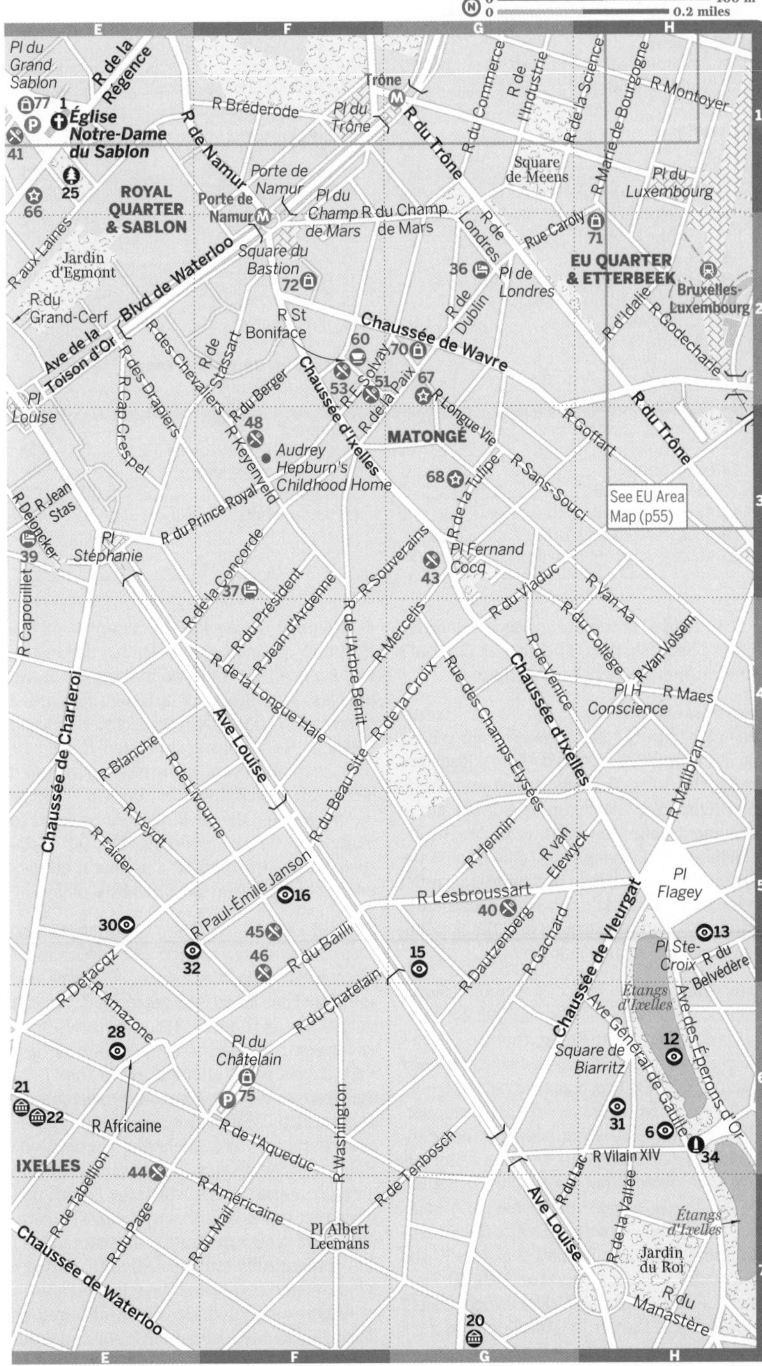

0 400 m
0 0.2 miles
Église Notre-Dame du Sablon
ROYAL QUARTER & SABLON
MATONGÉ
EU QUARTER & ETTERBEEK
IXELLES
Pl du Grand Sablon
R de la Régence
R Bréderode
Trône
Pl du Trône
R du Trône
R de Namur
Porte de Namur
Pl du Champ de Mars
R du Champ de Mars
Square du Bastion
Blvd de Waterloo
Jardin d'Egmont
R aux Laines
R du Grand-Cerf
Ave de la Toison d'Or
Pl Louise
R des Drapiers
R Cap Crespel
R des Chevaliers
R de Stassart
R St Boniface
R du Berger
R Keyenveld
Audrey Hepburn's Childhood Home
Chaussée d'Ixelles
Chaussée de Wavre
R E Solvay
R de la Paix
R Longue Vie
R du Commerce
R de l'Industrie
R de la Science
R Marie de Bourgogne
R Montoyer
Square de Meeus
Pl du Luxembourg
R de Londres
Pl de Londres
Rue Caroly
R de Dublin
Bruxelles-Luxembourg
R d'Idalie
R Godecharle
R Goffart
R Sans-Souci
R de la Tulipe
See EU Area Map (p55)
R Jean Stas
R Deloncker
Pl Stéphanie
R du Prince Royal
R de la Concorde
R du Président
R Jean d'Ardenne
R Souverains
Pl Fernand Cocq
R du Viaduc
R Van Aa
R du Collège
R Van Volsem
R Capouillet
R de l'Arbre Bénit
R Mercelis
R de la Croix
Rue des Champs Elysées
R de Venice
Pl H Conscience
R Maes
R de la Longue Haie
Ave Louise
Chaussée de Charleroi
R Blanche
R de Livourne
R Veydt
R Faider
R du Beau Site
R Malibran
R Hennin
R van Elewyck
Pl Flagey
R Paul-Émile Janson
R Lesbroussart
R Dautzenberg
R Gachard
Chaussée de Vleurgat
Pl Ste-Croix
R du Belvédère
R du Bailli
R Defacqz
R Amazone
R du Chatelain
Étangs d'Ixelles
Ave des Éperons d'Or
Ave Général de Gaulle
Square de Biarritz
Pl du Châtelain
R Africaine
R de l'Aqueduc
R Washington
R de Tenbosch
R Vilain XIV
R du Lac
R de la Vallée
R de Tabellion
R Américaine
R du Page
R du Mail
Pl Albert Leemans
Jardin du Roi
R du Manastère
Chaussée de Waterloo
E
F
G
H
1
2
3
4
5
6
7
1
77
41
25
66
72
60
70
53
51
67
36
71
48
68
39
37
43
16
30
45
46
32
15
40
13
28
12
21
22
75
31
6
34
44
20

Marolles, Sablon & Ixelles

Top Sights
1 Église Notre-Dame du Sablon ... E1
2 St-Gilles Town Hall ... C6

Sights
3 Ave Brugmann 30 ... D7
4 Ave Brugmann 55 ... D7
5 Ave Ducpétiaux 18–24 ... D6
6 Ave Général de Gaulle 38-39 ... H6
7 Ave Paul Dejaer 16 ... C6
8 Ave Paul Dejaer 9 ... C6
9 Cantillon Brewery ... A1
10 Église Notre-Dame de la Chapelle ... D1
11 Elevator ... D2
12 Étangs d'Ixelles ... H6
13 Flagey ... H5
14 Hôtel Hannon & Contretype Photographic Gallery ... D7
15 Hôtel Solvay ... G5
16 Hôtel Tassel ... F5
17 Jardin d'Enfants ... C1
18 Jewish Museum ... D1
19 Josephine Baker Mural ... C2
20 Musée Constantin Meunier ... G7
21 Musée d'Art Fantastique ... E6
22 Musée Horta ... E6
23 Palais de Justice ... D2
24 Peeping Policeman ... C2
25 Place du Petit Sablon ... E1
26 Porte de Hal ... C3
27 Recyclart ... C1
28 Rue Africaine 92 ... E6
29 Rue de Savoie 66 ... C6
30 Rue Defacqz 71 ... E5
31 Rue du Lac 6 ... H6
32 Rue Faider 83 ... E5
33 St-Gilles Prison ... C7
34 WWI Memorial ... H6

Activities, Courses & Tours
35 Piscine Victor Boin ... B5

Sleeping
36 Chambres en Ville ... G2
37 Hôtel Rembrandt ... F3
38 Pantone ... D4
39 Vintage Hotel ... E3

were beheaded in the Grand Place in 1568 for defying Spanish rule. The site of Egmont's grand former residence lies behind.

Jewish Museum MUSEUM

(Map p50; 02-512 19 63; www.new.mjb-jmb.org; Rue des Minimes 21; admission €8; 10am-5pm Tue-Sat; M Louise) The Jewish Museum hosts good temporary photography exhibits and a permanent collection relating to Jewish life in Belgium and beyond, with a section on the Holocaust. The museum was hit by a terrorist attack in 2014 that killed four people; there is stringent security on arrival and the building is protected by armed guards.

Palais de Justice HISTORIC BUILDING

(Map p50; Place Poelaert; M Louise, 92, 94) Larger than St Peter's in Rome, this 2.6-hectare complex of law courts was the world's biggest building when it was constructed (1866–83). While the labyrinthine complex is undoubtedly forbidding, it is not easy to secure. Indeed, in several high-profile cases criminals have absconded from its precincts. Behind the building a terrace offers wide panoramas over the Brussels rooftops, with the Atomium and Koekelberg Basilica the stars of the skyline show. A glass **elevator** (Map p50; Place Breugel, Rue de l'Epée; 7.30am-11.45pm) FREE leads down to the earthy Marolles district.

Designed to evoke the temples of the Egyptian pharaohs, the Palais de Justice was sited on the hill dominating the working-class Marolles as an intimidating symbol of law and order. When its architect, Joseph Poelaert, went insane and died during its construction, legends promptly suggested he'd been struck down by the witchcraft of the numerous Marolles residents evicted to make way for the building. The term *skieven* (twisted) *architekt* remains a characteristic insult in the old Bruxellois dialect.

Porte de Hal HISTORIC BUILDING

(Map p50; www.kmkg-mrah.be; Blvd du Midi; adult/concession/child/BrusselsCard €5/4/free/free; 9.30am-5pm Tue-Fri, 10am-5pm Sat & Sun, last entry 4.15pm; M Porte de Hal) For centuries Brussels was surrounded by a grand 8km fortress wall. It was partly demolished in the 1790s, then removed altogether on Napoleon's orders in 1810. Well, almost. In fact, a few isolated parts survived, including the Porte de Hal, one of the seven very imposing 14th-century gatehouse towers, which the French preserved for use as a military prison. The Porte de Hal was converted into a museum in 1847 and romantically embellished with statuary, windows and neo-Gothic turrets thereafter.

Today an audio guide leads you round its decent little city-history museum and exhi-

Eating
40 Chez Oki G5
41 Claire Fontaine E1
42 Het Warmwater C2
43 Imagin'Air G3
44 La Quincaillerie E6
45 La Tsampa F5
46 Le Framboisier F5
47 Le Perroquet D1
48 Les Brassins F3
49 Les Brigittines D1
50 L'Idiot du Village D1
51 L'Ultime Atome F2
52 Restobières C2
53 Saint-Boniface F2
54 Soul Food D1

Drinking & Nightlife
55 Bar du Matin B7
56 Brasserie de la Renaissance C6
57 Brasserie Ploegmans D2
58 Brasserie Verschueren B4
Café Belga .... (see 13)
59 Chez Moeder Lambic C6
60 Comptoir Florian F2
61 Fuse C3
62 La Démence C3
63 L'Inattendu D2
64 Maison du Peuple C4
65 Potemkine B4

Entertainment
66 Conservatoire Royal de Musique E1
Flagey .... (see 13)
67 Kuumba cultural centre G2
68 Sounds Jazz Club G3
69 Théâtre Les Tanneurs C1

Shopping
70 Africamäli G2
71 Crush Wine H2
72 Galerie d'Ixelles & Galerie de la Porte de Namur F2
73 Gare du Midi Market B2
74 Pierre Marcolini D1
75 Place du Châtelain Market F6
76 Place du Jeu-de-Balle Flea Market C2
77 Sablon Antiques Market E1

bition of armour, and you can climb to the 6th-storey battlements.

EU Area

Along the thundering thoroughfares Rue de la Loi and Rue Belliard, tragically bland office blocks are packed so close together they form dark concrete canyons. To the east, EU office buildings cut a brutally modern gash through a once attractive neighbourhood behind Bruxelles-Luxembourg station. But it's not all horror. The EU area also has lovely gardens, fountains and some fine early-20th-century houses, notably around Sq Marie-Louise.

★ **Musée des Sciences Naturelles** MUSEUM
(Map p55; 02-627 42 38; www.naturalsciences.be; Rue Vautier 29; adult/concession/child/BrusselsCard €7/6/4.50/free; 9.30am-5pm Tue-Fri, 10am-6pm Sat & Sun; 38 (direction Homborch, departs from next to Gare Centrale) to De Meeus on Rue du Luxembourg) Thought-provoking and highly interactive, this museum has far more than the usual selection of stuffed animals. But the undoubted highlight is a unique 'family' of iguanodons – 10m-high dinosaurs found in a Hainaut coal mine in 1878. A computer simulation shows the mudslide that might have covered them, sand-boxes allow you to play dino hunter, and multilingual videos give a wonderfully nuanced debate on recent palaeontology.

EU Parliament BUILDING
(Map p55; 02-284 34 57; www.europarl.europa.eu; Rue Wiertz 43; tours 10am & 3pm Mon-Thu, 10am Fri; 38 (direction Homborch, departs from next to Gare Centrale) to De Meeus on Rue du Luxembourg) FREE Inside this decidedly dated blue-glass building (completed only just over a decade ago) political junkies can sit in on a parliamentary session in the huge debating chamber known as the hemicycle, or tour it when parliament's not sitting. Tours (using multilingual headphones) start at the visitor centre, attached to the Paul-Henri Spaak section of the parliament.

Parc Léopold PARK
(Map p55; M Schuman) Steep-sloping Parc Léopold was Brussels Zoo until 1880 and now forms an unexpectedly pleasant oasis, hidden away just behind the EU Parliament.

Musée Antoine Wiertz MUSEUM
(Map p55; 02-648 17 18; Rue Vautier 62; 10am-noon & 1-5pm Tue-Fri, plus alternate weekends; 34, 80, Trône, Maelbeek) FREE If you're into the shocking or the nasty, this museum may appeal. Antoine Wiertz (1806–65) was a Brussels artist bent on painting giant religious canvases depicting hell and other frenzied subjects.

The building was Wiertz' home and studio and was also once the residence of noted Flemish writer Hendrik Conscience.

Berlaymont Building BUILDING

(Map p55; Rue de la Loi 200; Ⓜ Schuman) The European Commission, the EU's sprawling bureaucracy, centres on the vast, four-winged Berlaymont building. Built in 1967, it's striking but by no means beautiful, despite a billion-euro rebuild between 1991 and 2004 that removed asbestos-tainted construction materials. Information panels dotted around the building give insight into the history of this neighbourhood and Brussels' international role. The building is not open to the public.

Cinquantenaire & Around

The Cinquantenaire is a triumphal arch reminiscent of Paris' Arc de Triomphe. It was designed to celebrate Belgium's 50th anniversary ('*cinquantenaire*') in 1880 but took so long to build that by that date only a temporary plaster version was standing. The full beast wasn't completed until 1905. In summer, the arcade forms the curious backdrop to a drive-in cinema screen, while around it are several grand-scale museums.

Musée Royal de l'Armée et d'Histoire Militaire MUSEUM

(Royal Museum of the Armed Forces & of Military History; Map p55; ☎ 02-737 78 11; www.klm-mra.be; Parc du Cinquantenaire 3; ⏲ 10am-6pm Tue-Sun; Ⓜ Mérode) FREE One for military buffs, this museum houses an extensive array of weaponry, uniforms, vehicles, warships, paintings and documentation dating from the Middle Ages through to Belgian independence and the mid-20th century. You can climb to the top of the arch or take the lift for sweeping city views.

Autoworld MUSEUM

(Map p55; www.autoworld.be; Parc du Cinquantenaire; adult/BrusselsCard €9/free; ⏲ 10am-6pm Apr-Sep, to 5pm Oct-Mar; Ⓜ Mérode) Autoworld displays one of Europe's biggest ensembles of vintage and 20th-century cars. Among all the four-wheelers, notice the Harley Davidson the present king gave to Belgium's police force when he decided his biker days were over.

★ **Musée du Cinquantenaire** MUSEUM

(Map p55; ☎ 02-741 72 11; www.kmkg-mrah.be; Parc du Cinquantenaire 10; adult/child/BrusselsCard €5/€1.50/free; ⏲ 9.30am-5pm Tue-Fri, from 10am Sat & Sun; Ⓜ Mérode) This astonishingly rich collection ranges from ancient Egyptian sarcophagi to Meso-American masks to icons to wooden bicycles. Decide what you want to see before coming or the sheer scope can prove overwhelming. Visually attractive spaces include the medieval stone carvings set around a neo-Gothic cloister and the soaring Corinthian columns (convincing fibreglass props) that bring atmosphere to an original AD 420 mosaic from Roman Syria. Labelling is in French and Dutch, so the English-language audio guide (€3) is worth considering.

Maison Cauchie BUILDING

(Map p55; ☎ 02-733 8684; www.cauchie.be; Rue des Francs 5; adult/child €5/free; ⏲ 10am-1pm & 2-5.30pm 1st Sat & Sun of each month, plus 6-8.30pm most evenings May-Aug) Built in 1905, this stunning house was the home of architect and painter Paul Cauchie (1875–1952), and its *sgraffito* facade, adorned with graceful female figures, is one of the most beautiful in Brussels. It looks like a Klimt painting transformed into architecture. A petition saved the house from demolition in 1971 and since 1975 it has been a protected monument. If you can't time a visit to meet

BRUSSELS' ART NOUVEAU MASTERPIECES

Brussels excels in art-nouveau architecture. In the city centre, don't miss the **Old England Building** (p48) or the magnificent *café* **Falstaff** (p70). Many other top examples are scattered fairly widely, but there are decent concentrations of fine facades in St-Gilles and Ixelles, where a classic art nouveau house hosts a **museum** (p57) in the former home of maestro architect Victor Horta. Near the Cinquantenaire monument, the loveliest of all art nouveau town houses is the **Maison Cauchie**. In Schaerbeek **Maison Autrique** (p56) appeals to some Horta aficionados, while a drink at **De Ultieme Hallucinatie** (p56) offers marvellous art nouveau interiors. The famous **Palais Stoclet** (Ave de Tervuren 281), now Unesco listed, is not open to visitors.

Excellent **ARAU tours** (p60) can get you into some normally closed gems, including the **Hôtel Solvay** (Map p50; Ave Louise 224; Ⓜ Louise) and **Hôtel Van Eetvelde**, (p56) whose facades barely hint at the wonders within.

EU Area

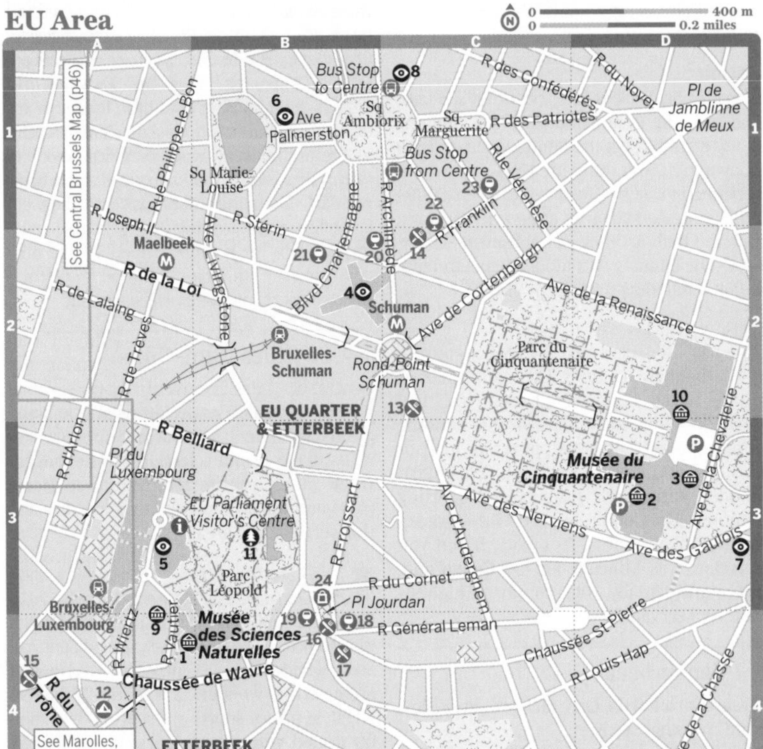

EU Area

Top Sights
1 Musée des Sciences Naturelles............ A4
2 Musée du Cinquantenaire D3

Sights
3 Autoworld D3
4 Berlaymont Building.............................. B2
5 EU Parliament A3
6 Hôtel Van Eetvelde B1
7 Maison Cauchie...................................... D3
8 Maison St-Cyr C1
9 Musée Antoine Wiertz........................... A4
10 Musée Royal de l'Armée et d'Histoire Militaire D2
11 Parc Léopold B3

Sleeping
12 Camping Bruxelles-Europe à Ciel Ouvert.. A4

Eating
13 Au Bain Marie..C2
14 L'Atelier Européen.....................................C2
15 L'Horloge du Sud.......................................A4
16 Maison Antoine..B4
17 Stirwen...B4

Drinking & Nightlife
18 Café de l'Autobus.......................................B4
19 Chez Bernard..B4
20 James Joyce B2
21 Kitty O'Shea's B2
22 Old Oak C1
23 Piola Libri... C1

Shopping
24 Place Jourdan Market.................................B3

the limited opening hours, the facade alone definitely warrants a visit.

Maison St-Cyr HOUSE

(Map p55; Sq Ambiorix 11; closed; Schuman) The haunting facade of this narrow building is an extravagance of knotted and twisted ironwork. It was built in 1903 for painter Léonard St-Cyr by Gustave Strauven (1878–1919), who worked as an apprentice to Horta and also built art nouveau houses in Schaerbeek. The building was hidden beneath renovation scaffolding during our visit.

Hôtel Van Eetvelde HOUSE

(Map p55; Ave Palmerston 2-4; Schuman) A great highlight of an ARAU tour (p60) is getting into the otherwise closed Hôtel Van Eetvelde. While the outside of this building is not Brussels' most gripping, its interior is a Horta masterpiece (built 1895–1901) studded with exotic timbers and sporting a central glass dome infused with African-inspired plant motifs. Its owner, Baron Van Eetvelde, was Minister for the Congo and, not coincidentally, the country's highest-paid civil servant.

Schaerbeek

The area around the Gare du Nord (Bruxelles-Nord) is rather seedy.

★ **De Ultieme Hallucinatie** BUILDING

(Map p46; www.ultiemehallucinatie.be; Rue Royale 316; 10.30am-2am Mon-Sat; 92, 93) This *café* is a classic town house refitted with art nouveau interiors in 1904. The front salon is truly marvellous, with original lamps, brass radiator covers and stained glass. The brasserie area (behind) that's publicly accessible is much less interesting, but buying a drink (beers start at €2.20) earns you a walk-through glimpse of the highlights.

Église Ste-Marie CHURCH

(Map p46; Place de la Reine; 92, 93) Looking east along Rue Royale, your gaze is unavoidably drawn to this very distinctive octagonal 19th-century church in neo-Byzantine style, replete with buttresses and a star-studded central cupola.

Halles de Schaerbeek ARTS CENTRE

(Map p46; 02-218 21 07; www.halles.be; Rue Royale Ste-Marie 22; 92, 93) This 1901 former food market is a great example of glass and wrought-iron industrial architecture that's been restored as a cultural centre and performance space.

Maison Autrique HISTORIC BUILDING

(Map p46; 02-215 66 00; www.autrique.be; Chaussée de Haecht 266; adult/senior/concession €6/4.30/3; noon-5.30pm Wed-Sun; 92, 93) Horta's 1893 house shows little luxury or extravagance but many design elements hint at the art nouveau wave that was about to sweep Brussels to architectural glory. It hosts regularly changing exhibitions and the website offers an interesting downloadable walking guide to the neighbourhood. At the time of writing the building was closed for restoration; check the website before visiting.

St-Gilles (Sint-Gillis)

Central St-Gilles has plenty of century-old houses. Although many are grimy and neglected and virtually none are open for visits, walking past a selection of fine facades whets your appetite for the Musée Horta (p57) and makes a pleasant way to discover this very eclectic area.

★ **St-Gilles Town Hall** HISTORIC BUILDING

(Maison Communale de St-Gilles; Map p50; 02-536 02 11; www.stgilles.irisnet.be; Place Maurice van Meenen; 8am-noon daily, plus 3-6pm Tue-Sun; Horta) One of Brussels' overlooked architectural wonders, a splendid Napoleon III–style palace sporting a soaring brick belfry dotted with gilt statuary: try to see the wedding hall ceiling, painted by Belgian symbolist artist Fernand Khnopff.

Ave Paul Dejaer 9 ARCHITECTURE

(Map p50; Ave Paul Dejaer 9; Horta) A colourfully refurbished art nouveau house.

Ave Paul Dejaer 16 ARCHITECTURE

(Map p50; Ave Paul Dejaer 16; Horta) A sadly abandoned former charcuterie store, inside which 'lives' a giant rooster fashioned out of spoons.

Rue de Savoie 66 ARCHITECTURE

(Map p50; Rue de Savoie 66; Horta) An art nouveau house.

St-Gilles Prison ARCHITECTURE

(Map p50; Ave Ducpétiaux; Albert) The crenellated white-stone facade of this prison imitates a Crusades-era fortress.

Hôtel Hannon & Contretype Photographic Gallery GALLERY, ARCHITECTURE

(Map p50; 02-538 42 20; www.contretype.org; Ave de la Jonction 1; admission €2.50; 11am-6pm Wed-Fri, 1-6pm Sat & Sun; 91, 92) If you're into photographic art you might want to catch an exhibition here. Even if you're not, it's worth stopping by for the splendid art nouveau building in which it's housed, Hôtel Hannon, designed in 1902 by Jules Brunfaut and graced by stone friezes and stained glass.

Ave Ducpétiaux 18–24 ARCHITECTURE
(Map p50; Ave Ducpétiaux 18–24; Ⓜ Horta) Home to fine archetypal art nouveau town houses.

Ave Brugmann 55 ARCHITECTURE
(Map p50; Ave Brugmann 55; 🚊91, 92) This building features archetypal art nouveau circular window-tops and little owls over the door.

Ave Brugmann 30 ARCHITECTURE
(Map p50; Ave Brugmann 30; 🚊91, 92) This building features a round-ended art deco tower apartment.

Ixelles (Elsene) & Matongé

Taking its name from a Kinshasa square, Matongé is home to Brussels' African community, though the compact area also encompasses a much wider ethnic mix. Like parts of Kinshasa, the architecture has its share of tired old 1960s concrete, but even the dreary **Galerie d'Ixelles** (Map p50; Ⓜ Porte de Namur) comes to life with African hairstylists, bars and a Congolese CD/DVDs outlet. The **Kuumba cultural centre** (Map p50; ☎02-503 57 30; www.kuumba.be; Rue de la Paix 35) organises tours of the district, plus excellent events featuring Congolese bands, dance workshops and food.

Musée Horta MUSEUM
(Map p50; ☎02-543 04 90; www.hortamuseum.be; Rue Américaine 25; adult/child €8/4; ⏲2-5.30pm Tue-Sun; Ⓜ Horta, 🚊91, 92) The typically austere exterior doesn't give much away, but Victor Horta's former home (designed and built 1898–1901) is an art nouveau jewel. The stairwell is the structural triumph of the house: follow the playful knots and curlicues of the banister, which become more exuberant as you ascend, ending at a tangle of swirls and glass lamps at the skylight, glazed with citrus-coloured and plain glass.

Floor mosaics, glittering stained glass and ceramic-brick walls reflect the light in the superbly harmonious dining room, rich with swirling American-ash furniture, glowing brass and a pink-and-orange colour scheme. Horta's daughter's room has a pretty winter garden, while you can only envy people who were invited to stay in the guest bedroom at the top of the house: the swirly brass door handle is a pleasure in itself.

Musée d'Art Fantastique MUSEUM
(Map p50; ☎0475-412 918; www.fantastic-museum.be; Rue Américaine 7; admission €7; ⏲2-5pm Sat & Sun May-Sep; Ⓜ Horta) In what seems an outwardly typical Ixelles town house, this museum hits you with jumbled rooms full of cyborg body parts, Terminator heads and vampire cocoons, then lets you electrocute a troll.

Flagey BUILDING
(Map p50; www.flagey.be; Place Flagey; 🚊81, 82) The marvellous 1938 'liner' building, Flagey, originally conceived as the national radio building, is now the centre of an up-and-coming nightlife area. With its distinctive round 'periscope' tower, it's an art deco classic that hosts a hip cafe, a cinema and various music venues.

Étangs d'Ixelles LAKE
(Ixelles Ponds; Map p50; 🚊81, 82) These two long, narrow freshwater ponds in Ixelles are flanked by many grand mansions.

WWI Memorial MONUMENT
(Map p50; 🚊81, 82) An artistic though modest tribute to the dead of WWI.

Ave Général de Gaulle 38-39 ARCHITECTURE
(Map p50; 🚊81, 82) Admire the crazy wrought-iron railings on this otherwise stern art nouveau private house.

Rue du Lac 6 ARCHITECTURE
(Map p50; 🚊81, 82) This slightly grubby 1904 private house has circular windows, super stained glass and a lovely 2nd-floor balcony.

Musée Constantin Meunier MUSEUM
(Map p50; ☎02-648 44 49; Rue de l'Abbaye 59; ⏲10am-noon & 1-5pm Tue-Fri; 🚊93, 94) FREE This intimate museum occupies an Ixelles town house that was the last home and studio of Brussels-born artist Constantin Meunier (1831–1905) and presents a substantial collection of his later works. Meunier is best known for emotive sculptures and social-realist paintings, including larger-than-life bronzes depicting muscular miners from Hainaut, dock workers from Antwerp and men reaping fields.

Rue Africaine 92 ARCHITECTURE
(Map p50; Rue Africaine 92; Ⓜ Horta) Art nouveau house with creamy tones, harmonious lines and a big circular window.

WORTH A TRIP

WIELS

Wiels (☎02-340 00 50; www.wiels.org; Ave Van Volxemlaan 354; adult/concession/BrusselsCard €8/5/free, Wed evening free; ⊙noon-6pm Wed-Sun; 🚊82) It's well off the usual tourist track in a run-down inner-city *commune*, but this converted brewery building located towards Bruxelles-Midi houses the capital's new centre for contemporary art and photography exhibitions. In the downstairs cafe the old tiled walls and vast copper vats have been retained.

Rue Defacqz 71 ARCHITECTURE
(Map p50; Rue Defacqz 71; Ⓜ Horta) An 1893 house designed by prominent art nouveau architect Paul Hankar (1859–1901) as his own studio.

Rue Faider 83 ARCHITECTURE
(Map p50; Rue Faider 83; Ⓜ Horta) Art nouveau house boasting beautiful, gilded *sgraffito* design at the top.

Uccle (Ukkel)

Uccle is an affluent, middle-class *commune,* though you'd hardly think so from a first glance at the graffiti-tagged station Uccle-Stalle.

Musée David et Alice van Buuren MUSEUM
(☎02-343 48 51; www.museumvanbuuren.com; Ave Léo Errera 41; adult/senior/student/child €10/8/5/free, garden only €5/4/2.50/free; ⊙2-5.30pm; 🚊23, 90) In a 1928 art deco showpiece house you'll find this exquisite museum, where five rooms are crammed with sublime furnishings, stained glass and top-quality paintings covering five centuries of art. Also notable are more than 30 works by van Buuren's talented symbolist protégé, van de Woestyne, and a Vincent van Gogh sketch for the latter's classic *Peeling Potatoes.*

Bois de la Cambre FOREST
(🚊92, 93) This extensive forest park forms Brussels' green lungs. It stretches from regal Ave Louise to the Forêt de Soignes, whose soaring beech trees then extend all the way to Waterloo. Established in 1862, the park has lawns, playgrounds, a 'pocket' theatre, a roller-skating rink and an island on an artificial lake, where the historic Chalet Robinson *café*-restaurant was recently rebuilt after a fire; take the €1 ferry across to the chalet to enjoy a swish lunch or an ice cream.

Heysel & Laeken

Domaine Royal HISTORIC BUILDING
(Royal Estate; Map p60; 🚌53 from Metro Bockstael) The Domain Royale contains a trio of palace-villas that are home to Belgium's ruling family. All are out of bounds to tourists, but two or three weeks a year (exact dates are announced each January) you can join the enthusiastic queues to visit the magnificent **Royal Greenhouses** (Serres Royales; Map p60; ☎02-551 2020; www.monarchy.be; Ave du Parc Royal 61; admission €2; ⊙late Apr-early May), designed in 1873 by Alphonse Balat (Horta's teacher). The construction was an engineering marvel of its day and the contents include many fabulous and rare tropical species.

Deceased Belgian royals are laid to rest in the crypt of the splendid, triple-spired stone church of Notre-Dame de Laeken.

Musées d'Extrême-Orient MUSEUM
(Map p60; ☎02-268 16 08; www.kmkg-mrah.be/museums-far-east; Ave Jules Van Praet 44; adult/concession/child/BrusselsCard €4/3/1.50/free, 1-4.45pm 1st Wed of month free; ⊙9.30am-4.30pm Tue-Fri, 10am-4.30pm Sat & Sun; 🚊4, 23 to Araucaria stop) A pair of East Asian pagodas form the key attractions here. Both are Léopold II leftovers, built in 1905 after the king had seen similar towers at the 1890 Paris World's Fair. An underpass leads from the ticket desk to the vermilion **Tour Japonaise** (Map p60; ☎02 268 16 08; Ave Jules Van Praet 44; admission €3, 1-4.45pm 1st Wed of month free; 🚊23, 52), fronted by a fabulous Japanese pavilion with occasional art nouveau flourishes, such as in the stained-glass windows. Inside the glittering **Pavillon Chinois** (Chinese Pavilion; Map p60; ☎02 268 16 08; Ave Jules Van Praet 44; admission €3, 1-4.45pm 1st Wed of month free; ⊙10am-4.45pm Tue-Sun; 🚊23, 52), the decor swings from gilded belle époque to Khajuraho Indian.

Both pagodas display priceless Asian decorative arts, while an easily overlooked Japanese art museum shows off swords, samurai armour and *ukiyo-e* painting.

Stretching west to the Atomium, the expansive Parc de Laeken is dotted with magnolia and mature chestnut trees.

Atomium MONUMENT, MUSEUM
(Map p60; www.atomium.be; Sq de l'Atomium; adult/student/BrusselsCard €11/8/9; ⊙10am-6pm; Ⓜ Heysel, 🚊51) The space-age Atomium looms 102m over north Brussels' suburbia,

resembling a steel alien from a '60s Hollywood movie. It consists of nine house-sized metallic balls linked by steel tube columns containing escalators and lifts. The balls are arranged like a school chemistry set to represent iron atoms in their crystal lattice…except these are 165 billion times bigger. It was built as a symbol of postwar progress for the 1958 World's Fair and became an architectural icon, receiving a makeover in 2006.

At night the spheres sparkle magically and, except during midsummer, the panorama-level restaurant reopens at 6.30pm, putting starched cloths on its functional tables and serving decent dinners with a view. Dinner guests don't pay the tower entrance fee, but reservations are essential.

Mini Europe AMUSEMENT PARK
(Map p60; www.minieurope.com; Ave de Bouchout 10; adult/child €14.50/10.80, with Atomium €23.60/15.80; ⏲10am-5pm Apr-Jun & Sep-Dec, 9.30am-8pm Jul & Aug; Ⓜ Heysel) Want to fool your friends that you saw all of Europe? Easy. Just photograph the dozens of 1:25-scale models of the continent's top monuments at Mini Europe. On certain midsummer Saturday nights it stays open till midnight, with firework displays at 10.30pm.

Palais du Centenaire PALACE
(Map p60) The distinctive 1930 art deco Palais du Centenaire features terraced tiers capped by statues.

Koekelberg, Molenbeek & Anderlecht

National Basilica CHURCH
(Basilique Nationale du Sacré-Cœur; ☎02-421 16 69; www.basilique.be; Parvis de la Basilique 1; ⏲9am-5pm May-Sep, 10am-4pm Oct-Apr; Ⓜ Elisabeth) Ghastly but gigantic, this is the world's fifth-largest church and the world's largest art deco building. When construction started in 1905 (to celebrate Belgium's 75th anniversary), a truly magnificent feast of neo-Gothic spires was planned. However, WWI left state finances impoverished, so a 1925 redesign shaved off most of the intricate details. The lumpy result, finally completed in 1969, has some attractive stained glass but is predominantly a white elephant of dull brown brick and green copperwork.

Take the lift (adult/BrusselsCard €4/2.40) to a 53m-high panorama balcony for sweeping views, including an interesting perspective on the Atomium.

Tour & Taxis HISTORIC BUILDING
(Map p46; ☎02-420 60 69; www.tour-taxis.com; Rue Picard 3; Ⓜ Ribaucourt) A postal sorting shed doesn't sound like an immediate tourist draw, but the Tour & Taxis complex is an architectural masterpiece, its 21st-century revamp creating a fine exhibition and commercial space in these Victorian warehouses and customs depots. It's all part of the ongoing gentrification of Brussels' run-down canal district, from where you can now take a variety of summer barge cruises (p61).

Erasmus House Museum MUSEUM
(☎02-521 13 83; www.erasmushouse.museum; Rue du Chapitre 31; admission €1.25; ⏲10am-5pm Tue-Sun, begijnhof closed noon-2pm, Church of St-Pierre & St-Guidon 9am-noon daily & 2-5.30pm Thu-Tue; Ⓜ St-Guidon) Anderlecht was still a country village when world-famous humanist Erasmus came to 'play at farming' in 1521. The lovely brick home where he stayed for five months is now an appealing something-of-everything museum tucked behind the nearby 16th-century Gothic Church of St-Pierre and St-Guidon. The museum is an unexpected little gem furnished with fine artworks including several Flemish Primitive paintings and containing some priceless manuscripts.

There's an attractive 'philosophy garden' behind the museum, and the modest entry fee also allows access to Belgium's smallest *begijnhof*.

The church has some original murals and was once a major pilgrimage site: right up until WWI, cart drivers and those suffering fits would arrive here to pray before the reliquary of 10th-century St-Guy (Guidon), the multitasked patron saint of cattle, workhorses, sheds and epileptics. The church's white-stone spire dominates the patchily attractive, *café*-ringed square Place de la Vaillance, where several 1920s buildings have pseudo-medieval facades.

Cantillon Brewery BREWERY
(Musée Bruxellois de la Gueuze; Map p50; ☎02-521 49 28; www.cantillon.be; Rue Gheude 56; admission €7; ⏲9am-5pm Mon-Fri, 10am-5pm Sat; Ⓜ Clemenceau) Beer lovers shouldn't miss this unique living brewery-museum. Atmospheric and family run, it's Brussels' last operating lambic brewery and still uses much of the original 19th-century equipment. After hearing a brief explanation, visitors take a self-guided tour, including the barrel rooms where the beers mature for up to three years in chestnut wine casks. The

Heysel & Laeken

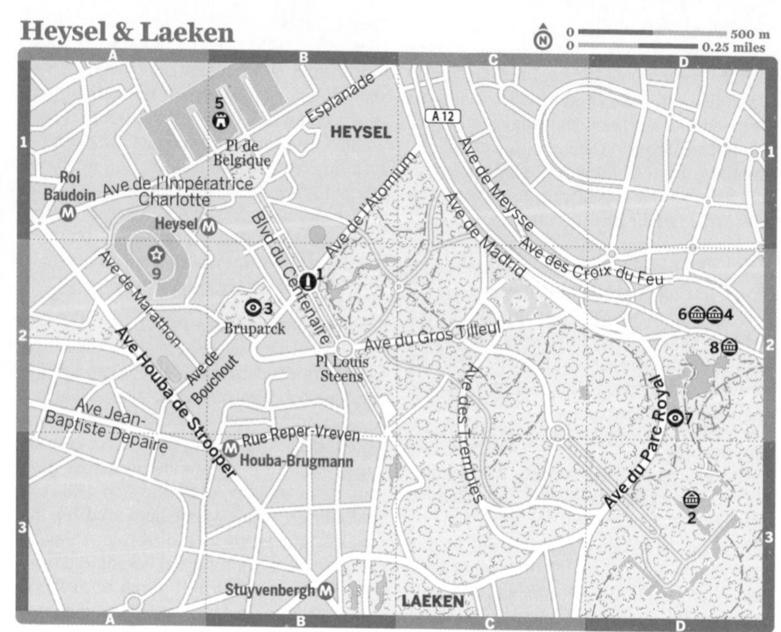

Heysel & Laeken

Sights

1	Atomium	B2
2	Domaine Royal	D3
3	Mini Europe	B2
4	Musées d'Extrême-Orient	D2
5	Palais du Centenaire	B1
6	Pavillon Chinois	D2
7	Royal Greenhouses	D2
8	Tour Japonaise	D2

Entertainment

9	Stade Roi Baudouin	A2

entry fee includes two taster glasses of Cantillon's startlingly acidic brews.

Expect plenty of cobwebs, as spiders are considered friends of lambic's spontaneous fermentation process, which occurs in winter in a vast, shallow copper tub in the attic room.

Tervuren

A 20-minute ride on tram 44 from Montgoméry metro station follows beautiful tree-lined Ave de Tervuren east past opulent embassy villas, the lovely parkland ponds of Woluwé and through the northern reaches of the leafy Forêt des Soignes. Sit on the right (south) side to spot the 1911 **Palais Stoclet**, whose radically geometric exterior is an early premonition of art deco: the architect was instructed to produce a Gesamtkunstwerk ('total work of art'). The building is closed to the public, but its dazzling interiors feature work by Klimt and Khnopff. Tervuren's unique **Africa Museum** is undergoing a major restoration, and won't reopen till 2017.

Activities

Piscine Victor Boin SWIMMING

(Map p50; ☎02-539 0615; www.stgilles.irisnet.be; Rue de la Perche 38; adult/child €3.50/2.50; ⊙noon-7pm Mon-Sat, from 2pm Wed; Ⓜ Horta) Covered art deco swimming pool in St-Gilles with a Turkish bath at the rear.

Tours

★**Atelier de Recherche et d'Action Urbaines** CULTURAL TOUR

(ARAU; Map p40; ☎02-219 33 45; www.arau.org; Blvd Adolphe Max 55; ⊙Apr–mid-Dec; Ⓜ De Brouckère) Get up close and personal with a wide variety of Brussels' architecture with this resident-run heritage-conservation group, which runs a program of coach tours (€19) and walking tours (€10) taking you into buildings that are often otherwise off-limits. Bookings can be made online through the Brussels tourist office.

Brussels City Tours TOUR
(Map p40; ☎02-513 77 44; www.brussels-city-tours.com; Grasmarkt 82; adult/concession/child €31/28/16; ⏰10am; Ⓜ Gare Centrale) These three-hour tours cover everything from the Atomium to the EU, and include some lovely art nouveau houses. You kick off with a walking tour of the Grand Place and are then transported by coach.

Brussels Bike Tours BICYCLE TOUR
(☎0484 89 89 36; www.brusselsbiketours.com; tour incl bicycle rental €25; ⏰10am & 2pm Apr-Oct) Many first-time visitors love this tour for the ride as well as the beer and *frites* stops along the way (food and drink cost extra). Tours start from the Grand Place and take 3½ hours; the maximum group size is 12. The outfit also offers chocolate and beer walking tours.

Brussels by Water BOAT TOUR
(Map p46; ☎02-201 10 50; www.brusselsbywater.be; Quai des Péniches 2b; trips from €10; Ⓜ Ribaucourt) Brussels' canals offer an interesting (if industrial) perspective of the capital.

Sleeping

Brussels has a vast range of accommodation. If you're on a short break, try to stay in the centre, ideally around the Grand Place or perhaps in nearby Ste-Catherine, which is less frenetic. Otherwise, areas like St-Gilles offer a more 'local' experience and the chance to explore some beautiful streets and squares. Brussels has a reasonable network of B&Bs, many listed and bookable through Bed & Brussels (www.bnb-brussels.be), or try sites like Airbnb (www.airbnb.com) and Wimdu (www.wimdu.co.uk).

There's a small, summer-only camping ground (p63) within the city; the nearest full camping grounds are much further afield in Wezembeek-Oppem and **Grimbergen** (☎0479 76 03 78; www.camping-grimbergen.webs.com; Veldkantstraat 64; per adult/tent/car €6/6/2; ⏰Apr-Oct).

Grand Place & Around

Centre Vincent van Gogh HOSTEL €
(Map p46; ☎02-217 01 58; www.chab.be; Rue Traversière 8; dm €21-24.50, s/tw/tr €35/58/87; @📶; Ⓜ Botanique) The lobby bar and pool-table verandah are unusually hip for a hostel, but rooms are less glamorous and, from some, reaching the toilets means crossing the garden courtyard. No membership is required, but you have to be under 35 unless in a group.

> **DON'T MISS**
>
> **GREEN BRUSSELS: PROMENADE VERTE**
>
> A great way to get off the beaten track in Brussels and discover the leafier fringes is to walk or cycle the **Promenade Verte** (www.promenade-verte.be), a 60km circuit divided into seven easy 5km to 10km sections. The route takes in the verdant Forêt de Soignes and surprisingly rustic parts of Uccle, as well as traversing more industrial landscapes.

HI Hostel John Bruegel HOSTEL €
(Map p46; ☎02-511 04 36; www.jeugdherbergen.be/brussel.htm; Rue du St-Esprit 2; dm/tw €27.20/63.30, youth €24.45/57.90; ⏰lockout 10am-2pm, curfew 1am-7am; @📶; Ⓜ Louise) Superbly central but somewhat institutional with limited communal space. The attic singles are a cut above singles at other hostels. Internet costs €2 per hour, lockers €1.50. There's a 10% discount for HI members. Free wi-fi.

★ **Chambres d'Hôtes du Vaudeville** B&B €€
(Map p40; ☎0471 47 38 37; www.theatreduvaudeville.be; Galerie de la Reine 11; d from €120; 📶; 🚇 Bruxelles Central) This classy B&B has an incredible location right within the gorgeous (if reverberant) Galeries St-Hubert. Delectable decor styles include African, modernist and 'Madame Loulou' (with 1920s nude sketches). Larger front rooms have claw-foot bathtubs and *galerie* views but can be noisy, with clatter that continues all night. Get keys via the art deco–influenced Café du Vaudeville, where breakfast is included.

Vaudeville's unique house beer is provided free in the minibar.

La Vieille Lanterne B&B €€
(Map p40; ☎02-512 74 94; www.lavieillelanterne.be; Rue des Grands Carmes 29; s/d/tr from €95/115/135; 📶; 🚇 Anneessens) Look out at the Manneken Pis from the window of room 5 in this neat, unsophisticated six-room B&B-style 'hotel', accessed by steep spiral stairs from an archetypal gift shop. Check in before 10pm. Free wi-fi.

Downtown-BXL B&B €€
(Map p40; ☎0475 29 07 21; www.downtownbxl.com; Rue du Marché au Charbon 118-120; r €99-109; 📶; 🚇 Anneessens) Near the capital's gay district, this B&B is superbly located if you're dancing the night away. From the communal breakfast table and help-yourself coffee bar, a clas-

HORTA'S CREATIONS

Victor Horta (1861–1947) was an architectural chameleon mostly remembered for his daring, light-suffused art nouveau buildings using trademark elements of wrought iron and glass. His once-celebrated Maison du Peuple was torn down in 1965, but surviving masterpieces include Rue Américaine 25, now the **Musée Horta** (p57), and Grand Magasin Waucquez, now the **Centre Belge de la Bande Dessinée** (p45), along with Horta's first truly art nouveau house, the 1893 **Hôtel Tassel** (Map p50; Rue Paul-Émile Janson 6; M Horta) and his first civic commission, the charming **Jardin d'Enfants** (Map p50; Rue St-Ghislain 40; M Porte de Hal) in the Marolles, which still functions as a schoolhouse.

Horta's WWI 'exile' in England and the USA marked a transition in styles – gone was sensuous art nouveau and in its place was his clean-cut, functional interpretation of art deco. From 1922 to 1928 Horta designed the bold but severe **BOZAR** (p74), while his last major work was the disappointing, rather drab post–art deco Bruxelles-Central train station.

sic staircase winds up to good-value rooms featuring zebra-striped cushions and Warhol Marilyn prints. One room features a round bed. Adjacent **Casa-BXL** (Map p40; ☎0475 29 07 21; www.downtownbxl.com; Rue du Marché au Charbon 16; €109-119; Anneessens) offers three rooms in a more Moroccan-Asian style.

Hotel Residence Le Quinze HOTEL **€€**
(Map p40; ☎02-546 09 10; www.hotel-le-quinze-grand-place.be; Grand Place 15; d from €98, with view €148; ; M Gare Centrale) With a unique location right on the fabulous Grand Place, Le Quinze offers recently revamped, budget-boutique-hotel decor. Views from the front rooms are truly breathtaking, but bear in mind that you'll also share the sounds of a square that remains alive with activity (and occasional full-scale rock concerts) till the wee hours.

★**Hôtel Métropole** HOTEL **€€€**
(Map p40; ☎02-217 23 00, reservations 02-214 2424; www.metropolehotel.com; Place de Brouckère 31; s/d/ste €330/360/500, weekend rates from €110; ; M De Brouckère) This 1895 showpiece has a jaw-droppingly sumptuous French Renaissance–style foyer with marble walls, coffered ceiling and beautifully etched stained-glass back windows. The *café* is indulgent and the bar (with frequent live music) features recently 'rediscovered' murals by a student of Horta. One of the lifts is an 1895 original.

Rooms have been redecorated in styles varying from art deco to 'Venetian Baroque' – slightly too colourful for some tastes. Much of the furniture is restored from 1930s originals.

★**Hôtel Le Dixseptième** BOUTIQUE HOTEL **€€€**
(Map p40; ☎02-517 17 17; www.ledixseptieme.be; Rue de la Madeleine 25; s/d/ste from €120/140/250, weekend from €120/120/200; ; Bruxelles Central) A hushed magnificence greets you in this alluring boutique hotel, partly occupying the former 17th-century residence of the Spanish ambassador. The coffee-cream breakfast room retains original cherub reliefs. Spacious executive suites come with four-poster beds. Across a tiny enclosed courtyard-garden in the cheaper rear section, the Creuz Suite has its bathroom tucked curiously into a 14th-century vaulted basement.

Lifts stop between floors, so you'll need to deal with some stairs.

Dominican BUSINESS HOTEL **€€€**
(Map p40; ☎02-203 08 08; www.thedominican.be; Rue Léopold 9; r weekday/weekend from €185/120; @; M De Brouckère) Combining classic elegance with understated modern chic, this excellent top-range palace occupies the site of a former abbey right behind La Monnaie. It's hard to beat for style and the location is wonderfully central, albeit in an area suffering from rather patchy architecture and atmosphere.

Hôtel Amigo HOTEL **€€€**
(Map p40; ☎02-547 47 47; www.roccofortehotels.com/hotels-and-resorts/hotel-amigo; Rue de l'Amigo 1-3; d weekend/summer/weekday from €180/200/320, ste from €1300; @; Bruxelles Central) Let faultlessly polite besuited staff usher you into central Brussels' top address. Behind a classical Flemish facade lies a stone-flagged reception area worn smooth by centuries of footsteps. Stylishly designed rooms have an airy and imaginative vibe, with art deco touches, surreal carved-'fruit' elements and art ranging from signed Goosens caricatures to Magritte prints and framed Tintin figurines.

Ste-Catherine & Around

★Captaincy Guesthouse HOSTEL €
(Map p46; ☎0496 59 93 79; www.thecaptaincybrussels.com; Quai à la Chaux 8; per person €34-50; Ⓜ Ste-Catherine) An idiosyncratic, warmly friendly venture, housed in a 17th-century mansion with a hip Ste-Catherine location and a mix of dorms (some mixed sex) and rooms. A generous €5 breakfast is served in the spacious living area. The wooden attic housing an en-suite four-bed female dorm has a fabulous boutique-hotel feel, and the attic double is a winner too.

Dorms have antique chests to lock your belongings in.

★Maison Noble B&B €€
(Map p46; ☎02-219 23 39; www.maison-noble.eu; Rue du Marcq 10; d from €139; @ 📶; Ⓜ Ste-Catherine) A stay at this refined four-room guesthouse starts with a welcome drink in the Flemish neo-Gothic lounge. It's backed by a gorgeous 1920s stained-glass panel and joined to a piano room. Guests are free to tickle the ivories, and occasional recitals are held featuring concert pianists. Rooms have rainforest showers, fine linens, and Brueghel prints over the beds.

While the target market is gay couples, the charming owners are hetero-friendly.

Hôtel Noga HOTEL €€
(Map p40; ☎02-218 67 63; www.nogahotel.com; Rue du Béguinage 38; weekday/weekend s from €95/65, d €130/85; @ 📶; Ⓜ Ste-Catherine) This very welcoming family hotel established in 1958 uses model yachts to give the lobby and piano room a certain nautical feel. Sepia photos of Belgian royalty, along with historic bellows, top hats and assorted random kitsch, lead up to variously decorated rooms that are neat and clean without particular luxury. Wi-fi is free for the first hour.

Hôtel Welcome BOUTIQUE HOTEL €€
(Map p40; ☎02-219 95 46; www.brusselshotel.travel; Rue du Peuplier 1; d €89-210; Ⓜ Ste-Catherine) The wooden-panelled reception area does nothing to prepare guests for the full-colour decor in each uniquely designed room transporting you to, say, Tahiti, Congo, Cuba or Zanzibar.

Hotel Café Pacific HOTEL €€
(Map p40; ☎02-213 00 80; www.hotelcafepacific.com; Rue Antoine Dansaert 57; s from €69; 📶; 🚇 Bourse) The hip design look here is all you'd expect from this Fashion District address, though the reception is just a desk attached to a revamped *café*. Most rooms come with high-powered showers and large but subtle black-and-white nudes above the bed. Fabrics by Mia Zia, toiletries by Bvlgari.

Ixelles & Ave Louise

Like everywhere in Brussels, this area's character can vary substantially from block to block, but overall it's one of the capital's most chic and lively inner suburbs.

Camping Bruxelles-Europe à Ciel Ouvert CAMPGROUND €
(Map p55; ☎02-640 79 67; http://cielouvertcamping.wordpress.com/about; Chaussée de Wavre 203; large tent/small tent/person €14/7/7; ⏱ reception 8am-11pm Jul & Aug; 🚆 Bruxelles-Luxembourg) The only campsite in central Brussels is a simple summer-only place hidden away in the garden of a spindle-spired church, Église du St-Sacrement. Rather ropy showers are available and campervans may park outside (€10 without hook-up).

★Pantone HOTEL €€
(Map p50; ☎02-541 48 98; pantonehotel.com; Place Loix 1; d from €62; Ⓜ Hotel des Monnaies) An eye-popping array of Pantone colours greets you here, from the turquoise pushbike at reception to moulded-plastic chairs to lime-green bedrooms – all with refreshing swaths of white too. Modern, stylish and functional, as well as surprisingly affordable.

★Chambres en Ville B&B €€
(Map p50; ☎02-512 92 90; www.chambresenville.be; Rue de Londres 19; s/d €80/100, 2 nights €140/180; 📶; Ⓜ Porte de Namur) Impressive B&B in an unmarked 19th-century town house featuring partly stripped wooden floors, high ceilings and large, tastefully appointed guestrooms. Furniture new and old

WEEKEND & SUMMER DEALS

With most of Brussels' accommodation scene aimed squarely at Eurocrats and business travellers, many mid- and upper-range hotels drop their rates dramatically at weekends and in summer. Double rooms with September midweek rates of €240 might cost as little as €69 in August. Shop around and check carefully for internet deals, especially on chain hotels.

combined with striking artwork and curiosities from all over the world (notably antique African statuettes) gives the place a unique character. A duplex top-floor studio is available (€1000 per month).

Hôtel Rembrandt GUESTHOUSE €€
(Map p50; 02-512 71 39; www.hotelrembrandt.be; Rue de la Concorde 42; s/d €74/95, without bathroom €54/75; ; Louise) A homely, friendly and good-value guesthouse just a block off Ave Louise. It's a jumble of ornaments, paintings and polished wooden furnishings. Rooms are well cared for, if a tad small. All have showers or baths, but the cheaper ones share toilets. Reception closes at 9pm.

Vintage Hotel HOTEL €€€
(Map p50; 02-533 99 80; www.vintagehotel.be; Rue Dejoncker 45; s/d €135/195; ; Louise) Stylish, modern option near Ave Louise but situated on a quiet courtyard, where a 1958 airstream caravan provides an urban 'glamping' experience – it's kitted out with bed, TV, shower and loo, a little table and a couple of chairs. In the converted mansion building, the focus is on 20th-century design in primary colours. Online discounts available.

Eating

The essential Brussels experience involves old-world restaurants where aproned waiters bustle across tiled floors and diners tuck into hearty Belgian cuisine in wood-panelled surroundings. But trendy minimalism has also swept the city, and there's no shortage of international food. As ever, *cafés* are generally cheaper and open longer than restaurants if atmosphere and price are more important to you than refinement and cuisine.

The cobbled streets around the Grand Place are the natural starting point, though be careful on the quaint but touristy Rue and Petite Rue des Bouchers. For fish and seafood (including the local speciality, mussels) Ste-Catherine's fish-market area is highly regarded. The streets around Place St-Géry offer a small line-up of great-value Asian eateries. The Marolles shelters several intimate and trendy options, while Matongé counterpoints cheap African and world cuisine with hip local fare on Rue St-Boniface. There's a lot more choice around Ixelles. Affluent locals tend to dine considerably further afield in middle-class areas such as Woluwé, Kraainem and Uccle or semi-rural escapes like Lasne and Linkebeek.

CHIP CHAMPS

Frying since 1948, **Maison Antoine** (Map p55; Place Jourdan; small chips from €2; 11.30am-1am Sun-Thu, to 2am Fri & Sat; Schuman) is a classic little *fritkot* (takeaway chip kiosk) whose reputation as 'Brussels' best' is self-perpetuating. 'Best' or not, its chips are certainly top notch and such is their popularity that *cafés* on the surrounding square (including beautifully wrought-iron-fronted L'Autobus) allow *frite* eaters to sit and snack so long as they buy a drink. Handily central **Fritland** (Map p40; Rue Henri Maus 49; 11am-1am Sun-Thu, 10am-3am Fri & Sat; Bourse) keeps frying till the wee hours.

Lower Town

★ **Arcadi** BRASSERIE €
(Map p40; 02-511 33 43; Rue d'Arenberg 1b; snacks from €5; 7am-11pm; Gare Centrale) The jars of preserves, beautiful cakes and fruit tarts of this classic and charming bistro entice plenty of Brussels residents, as do well-priced meals like lasagne and steak, all served nonstop by courteous staff. With a nice location on the edge of the Galeries St-Hubert, this is a great spot for an indulgent, creamy hot chocolate.

Mokafé CAFE €
(Map p40; 02-511 78 70; Galerie du Roi; waffles from €3; 7.30am-11.30pm; De Brouckère) Locals get their waffles in this old-fashioned cafe under the glass arch of the Galeries-St Hubert. It's a little time worn and dowdy inside, but wicker chairs in the beautiful arcade provide you with a view of passing shoppers.

Laurent Gerbaud CAFE €
(Map p46; 02-511 16 02; www.chocolatsgerbaud.be; Rue Ravenstein 2; snacks from €5; 7.30am-7.30pm; Parc) A bright and welcoming cafe with big picture windows that's perfect for lunch or a coffee if you're between museums. Don't leave without trying the wonderful chocolates, which count as healthy eating in the world of Belgian chocs – they have no alcohol, additives or added sugar. Friendly owner Laurent also runs chocolate-tasting and -making sessions.

Osteria a l'Ombra ITALIAN €€
(Map p40; Rue des Harengs 2; pasta €9-13, mains €11-16; noon-2.30pm & 6.30-11.30pm Mon-Sat;

Ⓜ Gare Centrale) Take a tiny, tile-walled 1920s shophouse. Keep the classic decor, wooden shelf-holders and cashier booth. Insert stools and a narrow communal table. Serve great fresh pasta and see if the customers finally communicate. Perhaps…at least with the farewell grappa.

Brasserie de la Roue d'Or BELGIAN €€
(Map p40; ☎02-514 25 54; Rue des Chapeliers 26; mains €15-28; ⏲noon-12.30am, closed Jul; Ⓜ Gare Centrale) Cosy in a cramped Parisian-bistro sort of way, this place serves excellent if somewhat pricey Belgian food. Wall murals and ceiling clouds pay homage to the city's surrealist artists.

Belga Queen Brussels BELGIAN €€
(Map p40; ☎02-217 21 87; www.belgaqueen.be; Rue du Fossé aux Loups 32; mains €16-25, weekday lunch €16; ⏲noon-2.30pm & 7pm-midnight; Ⓜ De Brouckère) Belgian cuisine given a chic, modern twist within a magnificent, if reverberant, 19th-century bank building. Classical stained-glass ceilings and marble columns are hidden behind an indecently hip oyster counter and wide-ranging beer and cocktail bar (open noon till late). In the former bank vaults beneath, there's a cigar lounge that morphs into a nightclub after 10pm Wednesday to Saturday.

Chez Léon BELGIAN €€
(Map p40; ☎02-513 04 26; www.chezleon.be; Rue des Bouchers 18; mains €15-27; ⏲11.30am-11pm; Ⓜ Gare Centrale) This long-time tourist favourite serves the original 'Mussels from Brussels', and makes a good place to try them if you don't mind that portions (mostly 850g) are somewhat small by Belgian standards. Rooms are spread over several gabled houses and decor varies from attractively classic to somewhat tacky depending on where you sit.

Kokob ETHIOPIAN €€
(Map p40; ☎02-511 19 50; www.kokob.be; Rue des Grands Carmes 10; menus per person from €20; ⏲6-11pm Mon-Thu, noon-3pm & 6-11pm Fri-Sun; 🚋Anneessens, Bourse) A warmly lit Ethiopian bar/restaurant/cultural centre at the bottom of Rue des Grands Carmes, where well-explained dishes are best shared, eaten from and with pancake-like *injera* – it's a place to visit in a group rather than on your own. Traditional coffee ceremonies are held on Wednesday evening and noon to 3pm Sunday.

★ **L'Ogenblik** FRENCH €€€
(Map p40; ☎02-511 61 51; www.ogenblik.be; Galerie des Princes 1; mains €23-29; ⏲noon-2.30pm & 7pm-midnight; 🚋Bourse) It may be only a stone's throw from Rue des Bouchers, but this timeless bistro with its lace curtains, resident cat, marble-topped tables and magnificent wrought-iron lamp feels a world away. They've been producing French classics here for more than 30 years, and the expertise shows. Worth the price for a special meal in the heart of town.

Sea Grill SEAFOOD €€€
(Map p40; ☎02-212 08 00; www.seagrill.be; Radisson SAS Royal Hotel Brussels, Rue du Fossé aux Loups 47; ⏲noon-2pm & 7-10pm, closed mid-Jul–mid-Aug; Ⓜ De Brouckère) You'd be hard pressed to find a more unlikely setting for Brussels' finest seafood than this '80s-styled place. But at the Michelin-starred Sea Grill, Yves Mattagne and his team create just that in the open kitchen. Try the Brittany lobster, crushed and extracted in an antique solid-silver lobster press (one of only four in the world) and prepared at your table.

Comme Chez Soi FRENCH €€€
(Map p46; www.commechezsoi.be; Place Rouppe 23; mains from €49; 🚋Anneessens) The name evokes cooking just like 'at home', but unless you have a personal chef crafting the likes of North Sea lobster salad with black truffles and potatoes, sole fillets with Riesling and shrimp mousseline or perhaps spicy lacquered pigeon breast with wild rice, it's nothing of the sort.

This is extraordinary food from master chef Pierre Wynants's son-in-law, Lionel Rigolet.

La Maison du Cygne BELGIAN €€€
(Map p40; ☎02-511 82 44; www.greatmomentsinbrussels.be; Rue Charles Buls 2; mains €38-65, menus from €65; ⏲noon-2pm & 7-10pm Mon-Fri, 7-10pm Sat; Ⓜ Gare Centrale) Gastronomic Belgo-French seasonal cuisine is served in this sophisticated restaurant on the 2nd floor of a classic 17th-century guildhall. Book way ahead to score one of the few tables with a Grand Place view. For something slightly less formal, try its 1st-floor **Ommegang Brasserie** (Map p40; www.greatmomentsinbrussels.be; mains €16-27; ⏲noon-2.30pm & 6.30-10.30pm Mon-Sat).

Ste-Catherine & Around

★ **Cremerie De Linkebeek** DELI €
(Map p40; ☎02-512 35 10; Rue du Vieux Marché aux Grains 4; ⏲9am-3pm Mon, to 6pm Tue-Sat; Ⓜ Ste-Catherine) Brussels' best *fromagerie* was established in 1902 and retains its

original glazed tiles. It still stocks a beguiling array of cheeses, which you can also try on crunchy baguettes with fresh salad, wrapped in blue-and-white-striped paper ready to take to a nearby bench.

Fin de Siècle BELGIAN €

(Map p40; Rue des Chartreux 9; mains €11.25-20; bar 4.30pm-1am, kitchen 6pm-12.30am; Bourse) From *carbonade* (beer-based hot pot) and *kriek* (cherry beer) chicken to mezzes and tandoori chicken, the food is as eclectic as the decor in this low-lit cult place. Tables are rough, music constant and ceilings purple. To quote the barman, 'there's no phone, no bookings, no sign on the door…we do everything to put people off but they still keep coming'.

Den Teepot VEGAN €

(Map p40; Rue des Chartreux 66; mains from €8; noon-2pm Mon-Sat; ; Bourse) Macrobiotic, veggie lunch place located above a mustard-yellow 'bio' shop. Bright decor with murals adorning the walls.

Viva M'Boma BELGIAN €

(Map p40; 02-512 15 93; Rue de Flandre 17; mains €12-19; noon-2.30pm & 7-10pm Thu-Sat, noon-2pm Mon & Tue; M Ste-Catherine) Hefty Belgian classics served in a long, narrow bistro entirely walled in gleaming white tiles like the butchers' shop it once was. Stuffed sheep's and pig's heads meet and greet.

★ **Henri** FUSION €€

(Map p40; 02-218 00 08; www.restohenri.be; Rue de Flandre 113; mains €16-20; noon-2pm Tue-Fri & 6-10pm Tue-Sat; M Ste-Catherine) In an airy white space on this street to watch, Henri concocts tangy fusion dishes such as tuna with ginger, soy and lime, artichokes with scampi, lime and olive tapenade, or Argentine fillet steak in parsley. There's an astute wine list, and staff who know their stuff.

Le Cercle des Voyageurs BRASSERIE €€

(Map p40; 02-514 39 49; www.lecercledesvoyageurs.com; Rue des Grands Carmes 18; mains €15-21; 11am-midnight; ; Bourse, Anneessens) Delightful bistro featuring globes, an antique-map ceiling and a travel library. If your date's late, flick through an old *National Geographic* in your colonial leather chair. The global brasserie food is pretty good, and there are documentary screenings and free live music: piano jazz on Tuesday and experimental on Thursday. Other gigs in the cave have a small entrance fee.

In't Spinnekopke BELGIAN €€

(Map p40; 02-511 86 95; www.spinnekopke.be; Place du Jardin aux Fleurs 1; mains €15-25; noon-2.30pm & 7-10.30pm Mon-Fri, 7-10.30pm Sat; Bourse) This age-old classic occupies an atmospheric 17th-century whitewashed cottage, with a summer terrace spilling onto the revamped square. Bruxellois specialities and meats cooked in beer-based sauces are authentic but hardly a bargain and some of the tables feel a tad cramped.

Vismet SEAFOOD €€

(Map p40; 02-218 85 45; www.levismet.be; Place Ste-Catherine 23; mains €17-26; noon-3pm & 7-10pm Tue-Sat; M Ste-Catherine) Vismet is popular and stylish in a simple, vaguely minimalist fashion, with rows of tiny bulb lamps and high-up mirrors like rectangular steersman's windows. Tables can feel slightly squashy, but quality is high and there's a daily changing shortlist of recommendations.

Bij den Boer SEAFOOD €€

(Map p40; 02-512 61 22; www.bijdenboer.com; Quai aux Briques 60; mains €15-28, menu €29.50; noon-2.30pm & 6-10.30pm Mon-Sat; M Ste-Catherine) Convivial favourite, with mirror-panelled walls, model yachts, sensible prices and a jolly ambience. The wine of the month is €20 a bottle.

Comocomo BASQUE €€

(Map p40; 02-503 03 30; www.comotapas.com; Rue Antoine Dansaert 19; 3/6/9 pintxos €9/15/20; noon-12.30pm & 7-11pm; M Ste-Catherine) *Pintxos* (the Basque version of tapas) snake past on an 80m-long conveyor belt. Colour codes include blue for fish, green for veggies, red for pork, and so on. It's all as cute and hip as you'd expect for this part of town.

La Marie-Joseph SEAFOOD €€€

(Map p40; 02-218 05 96; www.lamariejoseph.be; Quai au Bois à Brûler 47-49; mains €24-35; noon-3pm & 6.30-11pm Tue-Sun; M Ste-Catherine) Bright, modern art on whitewashed timber walls, simple tables including some terraced seating and a hushed air of mild formality. The fish meals get consistently good local reviews.

Sablon & Marolles

On the Sablon itself you'll often be paying a hefty premium for being seen in the 'right' place, though there are exceptions.

Walking distance from the centre, the Marolles' Rue Haute, Rue Blaes and some interconnecting lanes host an up-and-coming dining scene. It's worth strolling around, as new places open frequently. For really cheap food and drink from 5am till 5pm, try any *café* on Place du Jeu-de-Balle.

Le Perroquet CAFE €

(Map p50; Rue Watteeu 31; light meals €8-14; ⏲noon-1am; Ⓜ Porte de Namur) Perfect for a drink, but also good for a simple bite (salads and variations on croque-monsieurs), this art nouveau *café* with its stained glass, marble tables and timber panelling is an atmospheric, inexpensive stop in an area that's light on such places. Popular with expats.

Claire Fontaine DELI €

(Map p50; ☎02-512 24 10; Rue Ernest Allard 3; Ⓜ Porte de Namur) Just off Place du Grand Sablon, this is a tiny but atmospheric tile-floored *épicerie*, fragrant with spices and home-cooked dishes – there's a small kitchen at the back. It's perfect for a nutritious and filling take-out sandwich or quiche, or you can stock up on oils, wine and boxes of *pain d'épices* (spiced biscuits).

Het Warmwater CAFE €

(Map p50; www.hetwarmwater.be; Rue des Renards 25; snacks from €5; ⏲10am-6pm Thu-Sun; 🖉; Ⓜ Louise) Endearing and friendly little daytime cafe with stencilled teapots and art collages on the walls. The food – croque-monsieurs, salads, cheese and meat platters and quiches – is simple but satisfying.

★ **Soul Food** HEALTH FOOD €€

(Map p50; ☎02-513 52 13; www.soulresto.com; Rue de la Samaritaine 20; mains €15-22; ⏲7-10pm Wed-Sun; 🖉; Ⓜ Porte de Namur) With an intimate informal atmosphere, tiled floors and homey decor, Soul Food is a distinctly different dinner stop on the edge of the Marolles, ideal if Belgian food is beginning to weigh you down. The fusion food is organic and additive-free, and steers clear of butter and cream in favour of interesting oils, grains and seeds. Advance booking required.

Restobières BELGIAN €€

(Map p50; ☎02-502 72 51; www.restobieres.eu; Rue des Renards 9; mains €12-22, menus €18-38; ⏲noon-3pm & 7-11pm Tue-Sun; Ⓜ Louise) Beer-based twists on typical Belgian meals served in a delightful if slightly cramped restaurant. The walls are plastered with bottles, grinders and countless antique souvenir biscuit tins featuring Belgian royalty. Try the *carbonade* (beer-based hot pot) or *lapin aux pruneaux* (rabbit with prunes).

Les Brigittines FRENCH, BELGIAN €€

(Map p50; ☎02-512 68 91; www.lesbrigittines.com; Place de la Chapelle 5; mains €16-24; ⏲noon-2.30pm & 7-10.30pm Mon-Fri, noon-2.30pm & 7-11pm Sat; Ⓜ Louise) Offering grown-up eating in a muted belle époque dining room, Les Brigittines dishes up traditional French and Belgian food. Its classic (and very meaty) dishes include veal cheek, pigs' trotters and steak tartare. Staff are knowledgeable about local beer and artisanal wines, and can advise on pairing these with your food.

★ **L'Idiot du Village** BELGIAN €€€

(Map p50; ☎02-502 55 82; www.lidiotduvillage.be; Rue Notre Seigneur 19; mains around €30; ⏲noon-2pm & 7.30-11pm Mon-Fri; Ⓜ Louise) Booking ahead is essential to secure a table at this colourful, cosy restaurant, secluded on a little side street near the Place du Jeu-de-Balle flea market. Dishes are rich and aromatic and portions plentiful considering the cachet of the place.

EU Area

Capoue ICE CREAM €

(☎02-705 37 10; www.capoue.com; Ave des Celtes 36; ⏲noon-10pm; Ⓜ Mérode) Great ice cream in a dizzying variety of flavours, including *speculoos*, Belgium's trademark biscuit. It also serves frozen yoghurt and snacks.

L'Atelier Européen BELGIAN €€

(Map p55; ☎02-734 91 40; www.atelier-euro.be; Rue Franklin 28; mains €14-29; ⏲noon-2.30pm & 7-10.30pm Mon-Fri; Ⓜ Schuman) Tucked down an alley and fronted by a hedged courtyard, this former wine warehouse has a pared-back but sophisticated menu of meat and fish dishes, such as sautéed veal and grilled sea bass, with a couple (but only a couple) of offerings for vegetarians. Wine is given its due, with a well-chosen list and monthly specials.

Au Bain Marie ITALIAN €€

(Map p55; ☎02-280 48 88; Rue Breydel 46; mains from €13; ⏲noon-10pm Mon-Fri; Ⓜ Schuman) Dine among Eurocrats near EQ HQ. Despite the name, it's actually a casual and welcoming Italian restaurant. Sit outside on the terrace in summer.

★ **Stirwen** FRENCH €€€

(Map p55; ☎02-640 85 41; www.stirwen.be; Chaussée St-Pierre 15; mains €28-36; ⏲noon-midnight Mon-Fri; Ⓜ Schuman) This long-established Franco-Belgian restaurant is

LOCAL KNOWLEDGE

GAY & LESBIAN BRUSSELS

Brussels' compact but thriving Rainbow Quarter centres on Rue du Marché au Charbon. Here you'll find a dozen gay-oriented *cafés*, and two LGBT information centres/bars, the thriving and multilingual **Rainbow House** (Map p40; 02-503 59 90; www.rainbowhouse.be; Rue du Marché au Charbon 42; 6.30-10.30pm Wed-Sat; Anneessens) and Francophone **Tels Quels** (Map p40; 02-512 32 34; www.telsquels.be; Rue du Marché au Charbon 81; from 5pm Sun-Tue, Thu & Fri, from 2pm Wed & Sat; Anneessens), which runs telephone helpline **Telégal** (02-502 07 00; 8pm-midnight).

Belgian Gay & Lesbian Pride (www.pride.be; 1st Sat in May) culminates in this area with a vast-scale all-night party. The **Festival du Film Gay & Lesbien de Bruxelles** (www.fglb.org) runs for 10 days in late January, and Cinéma Nova runs occasional **Pink Screen weeks** (www.gdac.org).

La Démence (Map p50; www.lademence.com; Rue Blaes 208; M Porte de Hal), held at Fuse (p72), is a hugely popular gay rave that attracts men from all over Europe and beyond. It's only on once a month; check the website for dates. **Chez Maman** (Map p40; 02-502 86 96; www.chezmaman.be; Rue des Grands Carmes 12; from 10pm Fri & Sat; Anneessens) FREE is the capital's most beloved transvestite show, while ritzier **Le Club** (Map p40; 45 Rue des Pierres; 5pm-late; Bourse) also hosts transvestite nights and club nights. Try also established and stylish *café* **Le Belgica** (p71).

Handily central gay-friendly accommodation includes **Downtown-BXL** (p61), well placed for the nightlife area, and refined **Maison Noble** (p63), which is aimed more at couples and business folk.

popular with a discerning EU crowd. The decor is rather dark and conservative, but the classic and traditional French cooking is always reliable.

Matongé & St-Boniface

Very inexpensive African, Pakistani, South American, Italian and Franco-Belgian eateries are located side by side along Rue Longue Vie and are liberally scattered on Chaussée de Wavre. Meanwhile, one block southwest, St-Boniface is an island of decidedly trendier bistros and coffee shops.

★ Saint-Boniface — FRENCH, BASQUE €

(Map p50; 02-511 53 66; www.saintboniface.be; Rue St-Boniface 9; mains €12-17; noon-2.30pm & 7-10pm Mon-Fri; M Porte de Namur) Enchanting old-world restaurant near the eponymous church, featuring gingham tablecloths, walls jammed with framed pictures and authentic dishes from France's southwestern and Basque regions, notably *cassoulet*, Périgord duck, foie gras and *andouillette* (strongly flavoured tripe sausage – very much an acquired taste).

L'Horloge du Sud — AFRICAN €

(Map p55; www.horlogedusud.be; Rue du Trône 141; mains from €12; 11am-3pm & 6pm-midnight Mon-Fri, 6pm-midnight Sat; M Porte de Namur) A Matongé institution, the exterior here is distinguished by a large clock – hence the name. It has a Senegalese owner and serves all types of African food to a mixed crowd.

Imagin'Air — CAFE €

(Map p50; 02-511 33 31; Place Fernand Cocq 6; mains €9-17; 10am-10pm Mon-Sat, to 6pm Sun, closed Wed winter; ; M Porte de Namur) Adorable, organic-food 'Art Café' with exposed brick walls and one of Brussels' prettiest patio terraces, decked with plants and bonsai-sized trees. Short, handwritten menus change frequently and dishes can be made to order for those on gluten-free, lactose-free, vegetarian and vegan diets.

Les Brassins — BELGIAN €

(Map p50; 02-512 69 99; www.lesbrassins.be; Rue Keyenveld 36; mains €13.50-23; noon-midnight; M Louise) On a quiet, unpromising backstreet, this unpretentious brasserie is decorated with old enamel brewery adverts and serves reliable, well-priced Belgian home-cooked classics such as *carbonade* (beer-based hot pot), *filet américain* and *boulettes* (meatballs), accompanied by perfect *frites* (or *stoemp;* you choose) and washed down by an excellent range of Belgian beers. No credit cards.

L'Ultime Atome — BELGIAN €€

(Map p50; 02-513 13 67; www.ultimeatome.be; Rue St-Boniface 14; mains €11-19; 8.30am-1am

Mon-Fri, 10am-1am Sat & Sun; Ⓜ Porte de Namur) This cavernous brasserie has curious train-wheel decor enlivening the pale wooden panelling of an otherwise classic *café*. A youthful crowd keeps things buzzing day and night and the non-stop kitchen turns out great-value meals including cheesy endives, tajines and mussels (€17).

Ixelles & Ave Louise

La Tsampa VEGETARIAN €
(Map p50; ☎02-647 03 67; www.tsampa.be; Rue de Livourne 109; daily special €10; ⏲noon-7.30pm Mon-Fri, closed Aug; ✎; Ⓜ Louise) This vegetarian restaurant and organic delicatessen offers a choice of meals till 2.30pm, then salads, pies or set-dish plates till close. The hippyish decor is simple but appealing.

Le Framboisier ICE CREAM €
(Map p50; ☎02-647 51 44; Rue du Bailli 35; ⏲1-8pm; Ⓜ Louise) Imaginatively flavoured ice cream to take away or, in summer, eat in the garden. Sorbets, including some made from Cantillon beers, are the house specialities.

La Quincaillerie SEAFOOD €€
(Map p50; ☎02-533 98 33; www.quincaillerie.be; Rue du Page 45; mains €19-38; ⏲noon-2.30pm Mon-Sat, 7pm-midnight daily; Ⓜ Horta) A central Victorian stairway and station-style clock dominate this unique brasserie-restaurant. Wooden box-drawers, gleaming copperware and a green wrought-iron interior date from its days as an upmarket ironmonger's shop. Upper-level seating is a bit squashy but offers unusual views down upon other diners. Menus are multilingual and food standards reliable.

Chez Oki FRENCH, JAPANESE €€
(Map p50; ☎02-644 45 76; www.chez-oki.com; Rue Lesbroussart 62; lunch menu €9, mains €20-25, 3-/4-/5-course menu €30/39.50/49.50; ⏲noon-2pm Tue-Fri, 6.30-10pm Mon-Sat; 🚊81, 82) Modern minimalism wraps around an internal 'Zen garden' while French-Japanese fusion food works wonders on your plate. Hope that your *yeux fermés* (surprise) menu starts as ours did – with utterly divine foie-gras sushi drizzled with caramelised soya. Wow. Wines from €26.

Drinking & Nightlife

In most cities, tourists stop in *cafés* in between visiting the sights. Here the *cafés* are the sights: visiting a museum or two just gives your liver the necessary respite before another drink. Nearly every street in the city centre has at least one marvellously atmospheric *café*. Styles vary from showy art nouveau places and medieval survivors around the Bourse to hip and heaving options in St-Géry and Ixelles.

Grand Place & Around

Whether you're sitting on one of the incomparable open-air terraces or within a 17th-century guildhouse, drinking on the grandest of Grand Places is a delight, and the surrounding streets have plenty of tucked-away pubs.

★ **Goupil le Fol** BAR
(Map p40; ☎02-511 13 96; Rue de la Violette 22; ⏲9pm-5am; Ⓜ Gare Centrale) Overwhelming weirdness hits you as you acid-trip your way through this sensory overload of rambling passageways, ragged old sofas and inexplicable beverages mostly based on madly fruit-flavoured wines (no beer served). Unmissable.

La Fleur en Papier Doré CAFE
(Map p46; www.goudblommekeinpapier.be; Rue des Alexiens 53; ⏲11am-midnight Tue-Sat, to 7pm Sun; 🚊Bruxelles Central) The nicotine-stained walls of this tiny *café*, adored by artists and locals, are covered with writings, art and scribbles by Magritte and his surrealist pals, some of which were reputedly traded for free drinks. '*Ceci n'est pas un musée*', quips a sign on the door reminding visitors to buy a drink and not just look around.

Chaloupe d'Or CAFE
(Map p40; Grand Place 24; Ⓜ Gare Centrale) The 'secret' upstairs room is a particularly superb vantage point, though it's not always open. Not surprisingly, prices are steep, so if you're not here to soak up the special Grand Place ambience you can save up to 50% on drinks by walking just a block or two further.

Poechenellekelder CAFE
(Map p40; Rue du Chêne 5; 🚊Bruxelles Central) Despite facing Brussels' kitsch central, this is a surprisingly appealing *café* full of genuine old puppets. It offers a decent selection of fairly priced beers, including Oerbier and *gueuze* (a type of lambic beer) on tap.

Au Soleil BAR
(Map p40; ☎02-513 34 30; Rue du Marché au Charbon 86; ⏲10.30am-late; 🚊Bourse) This old clothes shop has been converted into a shabby-chic bar with good beats and

surprisingly inexpensive drinks given its status as a favourite for posers in shades.

Celtica BAR
(Map p40; www.celticpubs.com/celtica; Rue de Marché aux Poulets 55; Bourse) Lewd, loud, central and – most importantly – cheap: just €1 for a beer.

Bourse

Ah, the classics. If you do nothing else in Brussels, visit at least a couple of these close-packed yet easily overlooked gems. Each has its own unique character.

★Falstaff CAFE
(Map p40; www.lefalstaff.be; Rue Henri Maus 17; 10am-1am; Bourse) The interior of this *grand café* is an astonishing festival of century-old, art nouveau stained glass and fluidity designed by Horta disciple Houbion. A wide range of meals is available.

★Le Cirio CAFE
(Map p40; Rue de la Bourse 18; 10am-midnight; Bourse) This sumptuous 1886 *grand café* dazzles with polished brasswork and aproned waiters, yet prices aren't exorbitant and coiffured *mesdames* with small dogs still dilute the gaggles of tourists. The house speciality is a half-and-half mix of still and sparkling wines (€3.20).

A l'Image de Nostre-Dame CAFE
(Map p40; noon-midnight Mon-Fri, 3pm-1am Sat, 4-10.30pm Sun; Bourse) Down a tiny hidden alley from Rue du Marché aux Herbes 5, Nostre-Dame has an almost medieval feel but retains a genuine local vibe. Magical... except for the toilets.

Au Bon Vieux Temps CAFE
(Map p40; Impasse St-Michel; 11am-midnight; Bourse) Duck beneath the bishop, then tunnel through the centuries to this lushly panelled 1695 gem. You'll find lavish fireplaces, fascinating characters and even mythical Westvleteren 12 (€10!) on the beer menu.

À la Bécasse CAFE
(Map p40; www.alabecasse.com; Rue de Tabora 11; 11am-midnight, to 1am Fri & Sat; M Gare Centrale) Hidden almost invisibly down a body-wide alley-tunnel, the Bécasse has long rows of tables that give it a certain Bruegelesque quality, even though it's 'only' been operating since 1877. The unusual speciality is *panaché,* a jug of Timmermans lambic mixed with fruit beer or faro to make it more palatable. It's not to everyone's taste.

BRUSSELS' TOP DRINKING SPOTS FOR...

Bottled-beer choice Délirium Café (p70)

Cheap beer Celtica (p70)

Classic brown-cafe ambience À la Mort Subite (p70), La Fleur en Papier Doré (p69)

Draught-beer choice Moeder Lambic Fontainas (p71)

Eccentricity Goupil le Fol (p69)

Fin-de-siècle brilliance Falstaff (p70), Le Cirio (p70)

Hipsters and laptops Café Belga (p72), BarBeton (p71), Bar du Matin (p73)

Medieval atmosphere A l'Image de Nostre-Dame (p70)

Ornate interior at bargain prices Brasserie de la Renaissance (p72)

Reading Cercle des Voyageurs (p66), Floreo (p71)

Tea Comptoir Florian (p72)

Ilot Sacré

★Toone BAR
(Map p40; Petite Rue des Bouchers; beer from €2.50; noon-midnight Tue-Sun; M Gare Centrale) Home to Brussels' classic puppet theatre (p75); this irresistibly quaint and cosy timber-framed bar serves beers and basic snacks.

À la Mort Subite CAFE
(Map p40; 02-513 13 18; www.alamortsubite.com; Rue Montagne aux Herbes Potagères 7; 11am-1am Mon-Sat, noon-midnight Sun; M Gare Centrale) An absolute classic unchanged since 1928, with lined-up wooden tables, arched mirror panels and entertainingly brusque service.

Délirium Café PUB
(Map p40; www.deliriumcafe.be; Impasse de la Fidélité 4a; 10am-4am Mon-Sat, to 2am Sun; M Gare Centrale) The barrel tables, beer-tray ceilings and over 2000 world beers were already impressive. Now they've added a rum garden, a tap house and the Floris Bar (from 8pm), serving hundreds of *jenevers* (Dutch

gins), vodkas and absinthes. No wonder it's lively. Live music at 10.15pm

St-Géry & Ste-Catherine

Our listings can barely scratch the surface of all that's available within a few easy blocks.

Moeder Lambic Fontainas BEER HALL
(Map p40; www.moederlambic.com; Place Fontainas 8; 11am-1am Sun-Thu, to 2am Fri & Sat; Anneessens, Bourse) At the last count they were serving 46 artisanal beers here, in a contemporary rather than old-world setting: walls are bare brick and hung with photos, and booths are backed with concrete. They dish up great quiches and cheese and meat platters. The mood is upbeat and the music loud.

Bistro du Canal BAR
(Map p46; www.bistroducanal.be; Rue Antoine Dansaert 208; noon-11pm Mon-Fri; ; M Ste-Catherine) A swirling wrought-iron and glass canopy distinguishes this cute corner bar by the canal at the top end of Rue Antoine Dansaert; parquet floors and metal pendant lights complete the look.

Floreo CAFE
(Map p40; 02-514 39 05; Rue des Riches Claires 19; beer/coffee/shots/cocktails €1.80/1.90/4.50/6.50, wraps/mains €5.50/11.50; 11am-late; Bourse) Big windows and a 1920s/'30s charm make this intimate *café* a particularly relaxing place to read the newspapers (provided in several languages) by day. On weekend evenings things heat up around 10pm with a DJ perched on the wooden spiral stairs. There's also a soul-funk jam session on Thursday night around 9.30pm.

Le Greenwich PUB
(Map p40; 02-511 41 67; Rue des Chartreux 7; beer/coffee/wine from €2.10/2.10/3.50, croque/spaghetti €4/9; 11am-10pm; Bourse) At this high-ceilinged pub with belle-époque gilt woodwork a recent renovation has restored the gilt and glamour, but the soul – and the chess players who stayed for hours – seem to have left the building.

Fontainas Bar BAR
(Map p40; 02-503 31 12; Rue du Marché au Charbon 91; 10am-late Mon-Fri, 11am-late Sat & Sun; Bourse) The ripped black-vinyl seats, '60s tables and light fittings, and cracked tiles of this loud and ultratrendy bar provide the backdrop for locals reading newspapers by day, until the party cranks up again come nightfall.

BarBeton BAR
(Map p40; www.barbeton.be; Rue Antoine Dansaert 114; 8am-late; ; M Ste-Catherine) Typical of the new array of hip but relaxed Brussels bars, with a tiled floor and unpolished wood furnishings. It's good for an early breakfast, and there's a lavish €15 brunch on Sunday. Cocktail happy hour is 7pm to 8pm Thursday, there's an *aperitivo* buffet from 6pm to 8pm Friday and there are DJs from 10pm till late on Saturday.

La Vilaine CLUB
(Map p40; www.clublavilaine.be; Rue de la Vierge Noire 10; cover €8-12; 10pm-4am Wed-Sat; M De Brouckère) Brand-new club in an art deco building with a louche speakeasy vibe and leather armchairs. They play electronica and hip-hop to a young, fun crowd.

Au Laboureur PUB
(Map p40; Rue de Flandre 108; beer €1.60; 9.30am-10pm; M Ste-Catherine) Amid surrounding trendiness, this refreshingly unpretentious corner bar still attracts crusty beer-nursing locals with unfeasibly long moustaches. Hurry before it gentrifies.

Booze'n'Blues BAR
(Map p40; Rue des Riches Claires 20; beer from €2; 4pm-late; Bourse) Cramped and rough, Booze'n'Blues features a mannequin torso, an old juke box and an extended bar panelled like a choir stall. Unpredictable, entertainingly grouchy staff.

Le Belgica BAR
(Map p40; www.lebelgica.be; Rue du Marché au Charbon 32; 10pm-3am Thu-Sun; Bourse) DJs transform what looks like a 1920s traditional brown cafe into one of Brussels' most popular gay music pubs.

Madame Moustache CLUB
(Map p40; www.madamemoustache.be; Quai au Bois à Brûler 5-7; 9pm-4am Tue-Sun; M Ste-Catherine) Cute Ste-Catherine club with a retro, burlesque feel. It hosts funk all-nighters and swing nights, plus garage and DJ sets.

Marolles

Brasserie Ploegmans CAFE
(Map p50; www.ploegmans.be; Rue Haute 148; mains €13.50-18.50; noon-2.30pm Tue-Fri & 6-10pm Tue-Sat, closed Aug; M Louise) This classic local hostelry with old-fashioned mirror-panelled seats and 1927 chequerboard flooring is well regarded for its typical Bruxellois meals.

L'Inattendu CAFE
(Map p50; Rue de Wynants 13; beers €1.70-3, mains €8-15.50; ⏲9am-11pm Mon-Thu, to 5am Fri; Ⓜ Louise) As unexpected as the name suggests, this is one classic little wood-panelled *café*-bistro tourists have largely overlooked. Basic, traditional pub meals are served, including *stoemp* (€9.50) and *waterzooi* (cream-based stew; €12).

Fuse CLUB
(Map p50; www.fuse.be; Rue Blaes 208; cover €5-12; ⏲11pm-7am Sat; Ⓜ Porte de Hal) The Marolles club that 'invented' European techno still crams up to 2000 people onto its two dance floors. Once a month it also hosts epic gay night La Démence (p68).

EU Area

Each national group has its own Eurocrat hangout. On Thursday night the bars of Place du Luxembourg are especially packed with parliamentary aides on the razz before their three-day weekend. Irish pubs around the European Commission, including **Kitty O'Shea's** (Map p55; www.kittyosheas.eu; Blvd Charlemagne 42; ⏲noon-1am; Ⓜ Schuman), the **James Joyce** (Map p55; Rue Archimède 34; Ⓜ Schuman) and the down-to-earth **Old Oak** (Map p55; Rue Franklin 26; beers from €1.50; ⏲noon-2.30pm & 5-10pm Mon-Fri, 11am-10pm Sat, 11am-8pm Sun; Ⓜ Schuman) are also favourites.

Café de l'Autobus BAR
(Map p55; ☎02-230 63 16; Place Jourdan; Ⓜ Schuman) This old-timers' bar is opposite Maison Antoine, the city's most famous *friture*. The owners don't mind if you demolish a cone of *frites* while downing a beer or two. On Sunday it's a breather for vendors from the Place Jourdan food market.

Chez Bernard BAR
(Map p55; ☎02-231 10 73; Place Jourdan 47; ⏲11am-midnight; Ⓜ Schuman) At this old-fashioned, classic Belgian bar, beer is most definitely the main attraction. You can buy your chips from Maison Antoine, opposite, and sit down to tuck into them with a drink Chez Bernard.

Piola Libri BAR
(Map p55; ☎02-736 93 91; www.piolalibri.be; Rue Franklin 66; ⏲noon-8pm Mon-Fri, to 6pm Sat, closed Aug; 📶; Ⓜ Schuman) Italian Eurocrats relax after work on sofas, at pavement tables or in the tiny triangle of back garden and enjoy free tapas-style snacks with chilled white wines at this convivial bookshop-*café*-bar. It has an eclectic program of readings and DJ nights.

La Terrasse CAFE
(☎02-732 28 51; www.brasserielaterrasse.be; Ave des Celtes 1; beers €2.40-4.50, mains €9.90-18; ⏲8am-midnight Mon-Sat, 10am-midnight Sun; Ⓜ Mérode) Handy for the Cinquantenaire, this wood-panelled classic *café* has a tree-shaded terrace and makes an ideal refreshment stop after a hard day's museuming. Snacks, pancakes, ice creams, breakfasts (from €3.90) and decent pub meals are all available at various times. Try sampling the 'beer of the month'.

Ixelles, St-Gilles & Matongé

★**Café Belga** BAR
(Map p50; ☎02-640 3508; www.cafebelga.be; Place Flagey 18; ⏲8am-2am Sun-Thu, to 3am Fri & Sat; 🚌81, 82) This hip brasserie in a corner of the art-deco Flagey 'liner' building is mellow by day, but the beats grow ever louder towards closing time. There's live jazz on a Sunday twice a month (at 5pm).

★**Comptoir Florian** TEAHOUSE
(Map p50; ☎02-513 91 03; www.comptoirflorian.be; Rue St-Boniface 17; coffee/tea €2.50/4.50; ⏲11am-8pm Tue-Sat; Ⓜ Porte de Namur) Two tiny, super-cosy tasting rooms behind a tea-trading store offer six bean types for its coffees, and 200 teas, served in an eclectic range of pots. The teahouse has a classic curved-wood and tiled interior.

★**Chez Moeder Lambic** PUB
(Map p50; ☎02-539 14 19; www.moederlambic.com; Rue de Savoie 68; ⏲4pm-4am; Ⓜ Horta) An institution. Behind windows plastered with beer stickers, this tattered, quirky old brown cafe is the ultimate beer spot in Brussels. Sample some of its hundreds of brews while flipping through its collection of dog-eared comics.

★**Brasserie de la Renaissance** BAR
(Map p50; ☎02-534 82 60; Ave Paul Dejaer 39; ⏲9am-midnight; Ⓜ Horta) This *grand café* has a single, high-ceilinged room whose walls sport a ludicrously ornate load of gilt stucco tracery. Yet despite the grandeur, drinks are cheap and the food (Portuguese, Italian and Belgo-French) is an amazing bargain. The street terrace surveys St-Gilles' splendid town hall.

Brasserie Verschueren PUB
(Map p50; Parvis de St-Gilles 11-13; Ⓜ Parvis de St-Gilles) Characterful and enjoyably down-at-heel art nouveau *café*, with geometric floor

tiling, a handsome wooden bar, stained glass and vintage light fittings. Check out the score board with coloured slats representing Belgian football teams. Very affordable simple food is served.

Maison du Peuple BAR

(Map p50; www.maison-du-peuple.be; Parvis de St-Gilles 37A; 📶; Ⓜ Parvis de St-Gilles) A venerable 19th-century building facing out onto the market square of Parvis de St-Gilles. A combined *café,* bar and exhibition space, its scruffy-cool decor, with exposed light bulbs and bare-brick walls, marks it out as one of the hippest destinations in the area. Regular club nights.

Bar du Matin BAR

(Map p50; http://bardumatin.blogspot.com; Chaussée d'Alsemberg 172; Ⓜ Albert) The impeccably trendy Bar du Matin sits on a corner site, the noisy road screened by beech trees. There's a serious beer menu and pared-back '60s decor with a curved aluminium bar, pale-wood columns and softly flattering light. Gorgeous.

Potemkine CLUB

(Map p50; www.lepotemkine.be; Ave de la Porte de Hal 2-4; ⏲ 4pm-late Mon-Fri, 9.30am-late Sat & Sun; Ⓜ Porte de Hal) It serves a good Sunday brunch, but what you really come here for are the DJ sessions, electronica and live acoustic and jazz nights. There's arty, functional decor, and a log bench outside from where you can survey the medieval Porte de Hal.

☆ Entertainment

For extensive listings, check www.agenda.be, also available in print in English, Flemish and French. Otherwise see the English-language magazine *Bulletin* (www.xpats.com). For discounted tickets for arts, music and cinema, head to Arsène50 (p79).

Cinema

★ Cinéma Galeries CINEMA

(Map p40; ☎ 02-514 74 98; www.arenberg.be; Galerie de la Reine 26; 🚊 Bourse) Inside the graceful glassed-over Galeries St-Hubert, this art deco beauty concentrates on foreign and arthouse films. An authentic Brussels movie experience.

Cinematek CINEMA

(Map p46; ☎ 02-507 83 70; www.cinematheque.be; Rue Baron Horta 9; Ⓜ Gare Centrale) In a wing of the BOZAR cultural centre, the modern and stylish Cinematek includes a little museum where you can browse archives and memorabilia. The real highlight, though, is the program of silent films screened nearly

JACQUES BREL

Born in Schaerbeek in 1929, Belgium's greatest 20th-century singer started his career in 1952 in the Brussels cabaret La Rose Noire. The following year he headed to Paris, where he mixed with songwriters and fellow artists, including Édith Piaf. His first record was released in 1954 and he rapidly became an idol. His passionate, transcendent songs were performed with astounding intensity. As one fan described it, 'he sang like a boxer and usually lost a kilo during each performance'. The wide-ranging themes of his songs include love, spirituality, nostalgia, the hypocrisy of the bourgeoisie and beautiful evocations of Belgium's contradictions. Despite the latter, he was often thought of as French and became a 'French' film star in the late 1960s. In 1973 he quit performing to sail around the world. He spent the last two years of his life in the remote Marquesas Islands of French Polynesia, where he's now buried near French painter Paul Gauguin, having died of lung cancer in 1978.

Top five Brel songs:

'Bruxelles' Upbeat nostalgic favourite in which he somehow gets away with turning the capital into a verb (approximately translated as 'That was the time when Brussels Brusseled').

'Ne me Quitte Pas' The classic tear-jerker.

'Madeleine' Don't be fooled by the jolly banjo sound...waiting for a Brussels tram has never sounded so poignant.

'Le Plat Pays' Rain, fog and dismal Belgian landscapes are somehow rendered as poetic idylls.

'Les Flamands' Light-heartedly mocks the po-faced lifestyle of the Flemish, even though he is of Flemish descent.

BILINGUAL BRUSSELS

The 19 *communes* of the Brussels Capital Region (Brussels Hoofdstedelijk Gewest in Dutch, Région de Bruxelles-Capitale in French) comprise the only area in Belgium that's officially bilingual. Throughout Brussels – on buildings, train stations, road signs, you name it – there are two names for everything: one French, the other Dutch. That explains why certain Brussels street names look so flabbergastingly long. In fact, they're saying the same thing twice. For example, in 'Rue de l'Ecuyer Schildknaapstraat', both Rue de l'Ecuyer (French) and Schildknaapstraat (Dutch) mean Squire Street. Handily, the grammatical form of the two languages means that the French *rue/avenue* (street/avenue) always comes first, while the Dutch *straat/laan* is tacked onto the end. This allows for a space-saving trick when the core name doesn't need translating: a sign might end up reading something like 'Ave Maxlaan' (literally Ave Max Avenue). In the Marolles, street names even add a third version in Bruxellois (the city's traditional dialect).

every day at the cinema, with live piano accompaniment. There's also an impressive program of arthouse movies.

Actor's Studio CINEMA

(Map p40; ☎02-512 16 96; www.actorsstudio.cinenews.be; Petite Rue des Bouchers 16; Bourse) This intimate and tucked away three-screen cinema, a little hard to locate just off touristy Petite Rue des Bouchers, shows arthouse flicks as well as some mainstream reruns, and has a tiny bar. Try to catch a movie here – it's one of the city's indie treasures and the tickets are cheaper than in the big movie houses.

Cinema Nova CINEMA

(Map p40; ☎02-511 24 77; www.nova-cinema.org; Rue Arenberg 3; M Gare Centrale) The ultimate in alternative cinema, Nova shows off-beat international movies that are more thought-provoking than entertaining (subtitles will be French/Dutch), and there's a brilliantly rough student-style bar.

Live Music

★ **Music Village** JAZZ

(Map p40; ☎02-513 13 45; www.themusicvillage.com; Rue des Pierres 50; cover €7.50-20; from 7.30pm Wed-Sat; Bourse) Polished 100-seat jazz venue housed in two 17th-century buildings with dinner (not compulsory) available from 7pm and concerts starting at 8.30pm, 9pm at weekends. The performers squeeze onto a small podium that's visible from any seat. Bookings advised.

L'Archiduc JAZZ

(Map p40; ☎02-512 06 52; www.archiduc.net; Rue Antoine Dansaert 6; beer/wine/cocktails €2.50/3.60/8.50; 4pm-5am; Bourse) This intimate, split-level art deco bar has been playing jazz since 1937. It's an unusual two-tiered circular space that can get incredibly packed but remains convivial. You might need to ring the doorbell. Saturday concerts (5pm) are free; Sunday brings in international talent and admission charges vary.

BOZAR LIVE MUSIC

(Map p46; www.bozar.be; Palais des Beaux-Arts, Rue Ravenstein 23; M Gare Centrale) This celebrated classical-music space is home to the National Orchestra and Philharmonic Society. From the outside, the Horta-designed 1928 art deco building is bold rather than enticing, but Henri Le Bœuf Hall is considered to be one of the five best venues in the world for acoustic quality. BOZAR also hosts major art and science exhibitions.

Art Base LIVE MUSIC

(Map p46; ☎02-217 29 20; www.art-base.be; Rue des Sables 29; Fri & Sat; M Rogier) One of the best little venues in town for music fans with eclectic tastes. It resembles someone's living room, but the programming is first rate, and it's worth taking a punt on Greek *rebetiko*, Indian classical music, chamber concerts, Argentine guitar or whatever else is playing.

Flagey LIVE MUSIC

(Map p50; www.flagey.be; Place Flagey; 81, 82) Ixelles' stylish flagship venue in an art deco liner-esque building has several concert halls and an eclectic music policy.

Théâtre Royal de la Monnaie/ Koninklijke Muntschouwburg OPERA, DANCE

(Map p40; ☎02-229 13 72; www.lamonnaie.be; Place de la Monnaie; M De Brouckère) Belgium was born when an opera at this grand venue inspired the 1830 revolution. Nowadays it primarily mounts contemporary dance, and classic and new operas.

Beursschouwburg LIVE MUSIC
(Map p40; 02-513 82 90; www.beursschouwburg.be; Rue Auguste Orts 22; exhibition area 10am-6pm Mon-Sat, cafe 7.30pm-late Thu-Sun, closed summer; Bourse) Offers a diverse mix of contemporary music including rock, jazz, rap and disco. The *café* approximates to a free club late on weekend nights.

Sounds Jazz Club JAZZ
(Map p50; 02-512 92 50; www.soundsjazzclub.be; Rue de la Tulipe 28; 8pm-4am Mon-Sat; M Porte de Namur) An unassuming but immensely popular little Ixelles venue, Sounds has concerts most nights, styles varying from modern to big band to salsa. The website has links to artists' web pages. Cover charges vary and acts typically start around 10pm.

Jazz Station JAZZ
(02-733 13 78; www.jazzstation.be; Chaussée de Louvain 193a; exhibitions 11am-7pm Wed-Sat, concerts 6pm Sat & 8.30pm some weeknights; M Madou) An appealing venue in an 1885 former station. There are also exhibitions, a multimedia jazz archive and practice rooms, where you can listen in on musicians honing their art.

AB LIVE MUSIC
(Ancienne Belgique; Map p40; 02-548 24 00; www.abconcerts.be; Blvd Anspach 110; Bourse) The AB's two auditoriums are favourite venues for mid-level international rock bands and acts such as Jools Holland and Madeleine Peyroux, plus plenty of home-grown talent. The ticket office is located on Rue des Pierres. There's a good on-site bar-restaurant that opens at 6pm (bookings essential).

Bravo JAZZ
(Map p46; www.bravobxl.com; Rue d'Alost 7; 9am-midnight Mon & Tue, to 2am Wed & Fri-Sat, to 1am Thu, 10am-midnight Sun; M Ste-Catherine) The latest in Brussels' collection of hipster minimalist/industrial bars, Bravo has a downstairs jazz club with nightly and mostly free events.

Bizon BLUES
(Map p40; 02-502 46 99; www.cafebizon.com; Rue du Pont de la Carpe 7; 4pm-late, from 6pm Sat & Sun; Bourse) Happening little grunge bar in St-Géry featuring home-grown live blues, a range of beers and a selection of *jenevers* (gin-like drink). Located on a street of lively *café*-bars.

Cirque Royal THEATRE
(Map p46; 02-218 20 15; www.cirque-royal.org; Rue de l'Enseignement 81; M Madou) This converted indoor circus is now a venue for dance, operetta, classical and contemporary music.

Conservatoire Royal de Musique CLASSICAL MUSIC
(Royal Music Conservatory; Map p50; 02-511 0427; www.conservatoire.be; Rue de la Régence 30; M Porte de Namur) Classical-music venue.

Maison de la Bellone CONCERT VENUE
(Map p40; 02-513 33 33; www.bellone.be; Rue de Flandre 46; M Ste-Catherine) The glass-vaulted courtyard of this 18th-century stunner is used for occasional concerts.

Forest National LIVE MUSIC
(02-340 22 11; www.forestnational.be; Ave du Globe 36; 81) The city's temple for larger international gigs and local favourites.

Sport

Stade Roi Baudouin STADIUM
(Map p60; 02-479 36 54; www.prosportevent.be; Ave de Marathon 135; M Heysel) In Heysel the national stadium hosts major cycling races, athletics meetings and international football matches. For club matches Brussels', most famous football team is RSC Anderlecht.

Theatre

Touring international productions occasionally supplement the local-language scene with English-language performances. The theatre season runs September to June. Brussels has no resident classical ballet – that's in Antwerp – but innovative contemporary-dance companies stage occasional performances.

★ **Théâtre Royal de Toone** THEATRE
(Map p40; 02-511 7137; www.toone.be; Petite Rue des Bouchers 21; adult/child €10/7; variable, typically 8.30pm Thu & 4pm Sat; M Gare Centrale) Eight generations of the Toone family have staged classic puppet productions in the Bruxellois dialect at this endearing marionette theatre, a highlight of any visit to Brussels. Shows are aimed at adults, but kids love them too.

Théâtre Les Tanneurs THEATRE
(Map p50; 02-512 17 84; www.lestanneurs.be; Rue des Tanneurs 75; M Louise) Sitting on the edge of the Marolles, the theatre is known for dynamic drama and dance.

Le Botanique ARTS CENTRE
(Map p46; 02-218 79 35; Rue Royale 236; M Botanique) Cultural centre, exhibition hall and concert venue incorporating an 1826 glass verandah.

Rosas DANCE
(☎02-344 55 98; www.rosas.be) This Brussels-based company built around choreographer Anne Teresa De Keersmaeker strikes a winning balance between traditional and avant-garde dance. When not globetrotting it typically performs at La Monnaie (p74) or **Kaaitheater** (Map p46; ☎02-201 59 59; www.kaaitheater.be; Square Sainctelette 20; MYser).

Koninklijke Vlaamse Schouwburg THEATRE
(Map p46; ☎02-210 11 12; www.kvs.be; Rue de Laeken 146; MYser) Behind a restored Renaissance facade, the state-of-the-art Royal Flemish Theatre mounts edgy dance and theatre productions, occasionally in English.

Théâtre National THEATRE
(Map p46; ☎02-203 41 55; www.theatrenational.be; Blvd Émile Jacqmain 111-115; MRogier) The Francophone community's rectilinear glass theatre.

Bronks Youth Theatre THEATRE
(Map p40; ☎02-219 75 54; www.bronks.be; Marché aux Porcs 15; MSte-Catherine) Offers theatre, mime and workshops for toddlers and children most weekends.

Shopping

The splendid Galeries St-Hubert (p43), once frequented by Victor Hugo, feature swish chocolate and fashion stores in a calm, grand setting. Rue Antoine Dansaert is the nerve centre of Brussels' design and fashion quarter, the Sablon features antiques, and the Marolles district is full of quirky interior-design shops. Ave Louise is the setting for many up-market chain boutiques.

Place du Grand Sablon sports particularly chic shops, and others are dotted along Rue des Minimes, Rue Charles Hanssens and Rue Watteeu. For a more funky selection of less exclusive ornaments and retro ware, trawl the appealing shops of Rue Haute and Rue Blaes in the Marolles district.

Standard beers like Leffe, Hoegaarden, Chimay etc are usually cheaply available in supermarkets. But if you want rarer types without going to the brewery, there are specialist beer shops to help you. They'll also sell matching glasses for some, along with various other beer paraphernalia.

BRUXELLOIS

The old Marolles-Brussels dialect, Bruxellois, is a curious mixture of French, Dutch and Walloon with elements of Spanish and Yiddish thrown in. These days very few people beyond Place du Jeu-de-Balle actually speak the full dialect. Nonetheless, certain Bruxellois words are used, consciously or otherwise, to punctuate local French, whether for comic effect or because no better words exist. Classic examples that hint at the playful Bruxellois character:

- *blèter* – to snivel, complain
- *in stoemelings* – sneakily, on the quiet
- *papzak* – fatso
- *zatlap* – habitual drunkard
- *zieverair* – time-waster, idiot
- *zieverer* – to mess around

Grand Place, Bourse & Around

Manufacture Belge de Dentelles CRAFTS
(Map p40; ☎02-511 44 77; www.mbd.be; Galerie de la Reine 6-8; ⌚9.30am-6pm Mon-Sat, 10am-4pm Sun; MGare Centrale) Excellent stock of antique lace, and staff who love the stuff.

De Biertempel DRINK
(Map p40; ☎02-502 19 06; Rue du Marché aux Herbes 56b; ⌚9.30am-7pm; Bourse) As its name states, this shop is a temple to beer, stocking upwards of 700 brews along with matching glasses and other booze-related merchandise. For more ordinary beers and for bulk purchases, make like the locals and go to the supermarket.

Brüsel BOOKS
(Map p40; www.brusel.com; Blvd Anspach 100; ⌚10.30am-6.30pm Mon-Sat, from noon Sun; Bourse) Chic comic-book shop named after a book by one of Belgium's best-known contemporary comic artists, François Schuiten. Comics with English translations available.

Boutique Tintin BOOKS
(Map p40; ☎02-514 51 52; en.tintin.com; Rue de la Colline 13; ⌚10am-6pm Mon-Sat, 11am-5pm Sun; ; MGare Centrale) No prizes for guessing the star of this comic shop, which stocks albums galore and cute merchandise.

Sterling Books BOOKS
(Map p40; ☎02-223 62 23; www.sterlingbooks.be; Rue du Fossé aux Loups 38; ⌚10am-7pm Mon-Sat, noon-6.30pm Sun; MDe Brouckère) English-language bookshop with comfy sofas and a kids' play area.

TOP CHOCOLATE SHOPS

Pierre Marcolini (Map p50; ☎02-512 43 14; www.marcolini.be; Rue des Minimes 1; chocolate per kilogram €70; ⏱10am-7pm Sun-Thu, to 6pm Fri & Sat; Ⓜ Porte de Namur) Rare chocolate beans, experimental flavours (eg tea) and designer black-box packaging make Marcolini's pralines Belgium's trendiest and most expensive.

Mary (Map p46; ☎02-217 45 00; www.mary.be; Rue Royale 73; chocolate per kilogram €58; ⏱10am-6pm Mon-Sat; Ⓜ Madou) Supplies pralines to Belgium's royals plus the odd US president.

Neuhaus (Map p40; ☎02-512 63 59; www.neuhaus.be; Galerie de la Reine 25; chocolate per kilogram €52; ⏱10am-8pm Mon-Sat, to 7pm Sun; Ⓜ Gare Centrale) Belgium's original – established in 1857. This stunning flagship shop has stained-glass windows and sumptuous displays.

Planète Chocolat (Map p40; ☎02-511 07 55; www.planetechocolat.be; Rue du Lombard 24; chocolate per kilogram €50; ⏱11am-6pm Mon & Sun, 10.30am-6.30pm Tue-Sat; 🚊 Bourse) Both moulds and chocolates are made on-site. At 4pm Saturday and Sunday there are praline-making demonstrations explaining chocolate's development, culminating in a chance for visitors to create their own chocolates.

Ste-Catherine

★ **Gabriele** VINTAGE

(Map p40; ☎02-512 67 43; www.gabrielevintage.com; Rue des Chartreux 27; ⏱1-7pm Mon & Tue, 11am-7pm Wed-Sat; 🚊 Bourse) For amazing vintage finds, try eccentric, elegant Gabriele. There's a gorgeous jumble of cocktail dresses, hats, Chinese shawls and accessories; only original clothes from the '20s to the '80s are stocked.

Martin Margiela FASHION

(Map p40; www.maisonmargiela.com; Rue de Flandre 114; ⏱11am-7pm Mon-Sat; Ⓜ Ste-Catherine) Margiela is often tagged the unofficial seventh member of a group of designers known as the Antwerp Six (he graduated from Antwerp's fashion academy in 1980). Shoes, accessories and men's and women's body-skimming fashions in understated colours are artfully arranged in this white-on-white boutique.

Passa Porta BOOKS

(Map p40; www.passaporta.be; Rue Antoine Dansaert 46; ⏱11am-7pm Tue-Sat, noon-6pm Sun; 🚊 Bourse) This stylish bookshop located down an alley has a small but classy English-language section. Look out for the leaflet listing literary events, many of which are hosted in English.

Micro Marché HANDICRAFTS

(Map p46; www.micromarche.com; Quai à la Houille 9; ⏱4-9pm Fri, 11am-7pm Sat & Sun; Ⓜ Ste-Catherine) You'll find alternative and affordable handmade crafts at boho Micro Marché, which adjoins the convivial Traveller's Café.

Just In Case CLOTHING

(Map p40; www.justincase.be; Rue Léon Lepage 63; ⏱11am-7pm Tue-Sat; Ⓜ Ste-Catherine) Poetic and feminine garments inspired by the past, with vintage-style shapes in dazzling colours: electric blue, coral and orange.

Pimpinelle HOMEWARES

(Map p40; www.pimpinelle.be; Rue de Flandre 57; ⏱11am-6.30pm Thu-Sat, closed Aug; Ⓜ Ste-Catherine) This cute boutique sells pale ceramics and utilitarian tin plates, plus cake tins, pots and pans and scales. It also runs cookery workshops in the attractively tiled back room.

Catherine FOOD

(Map p40; ☎02-512 75 64; Rue du Midi 23; ⏱9am-6pm Mon-Sat; 🚊 Bourse) A traditional and welcoming grocery in the heart of town, specialising in artisanal cheeses, several of them organic. You'll also find cured meats and condiments – all the perfect basis of a simple supper if you're self-catering.

Stijl FASHION

(Map p40; www.stijl.be; Rue Antoine Dansaert 74; Ⓜ Ste-Catherine) A top address, Stilj is well stocked with Antwerp Six classic designer-ware (Ann Demeulemeester, Dries Van Noten) but also features up-to-the-minute designers including Haider Ackermann, Gustavo Lins (www.gustavolins.com) and Raf Simons. It's a hip place but not unduly daunting to enter and, unlike in many such

WORTH A TRIP

FASHION DISTRICT

You don't have to be a fashion hound to enjoy the quirky facades, shops and idiosyncrasies of this compact area that neatly divides St-Géry and Ste-Catherine. Heading northwest from the Bourse, you'll pass the magnificent wrought-iron frontage of the Beursschouwburg (p75), a cultural centre built in 1885 as a grand brasserie. A block north, check out the flamboyant lamps and translucent plastic chairs displayed in the **Kartell furniture shop** (Map p40; Rue Antoine Dansaert 2; Bourse). Veer west here on Rue des Chartreux to admire the art nouveau ironwork over the entrance to classic *café* Le Greenwich (p71) and admire the vintage bounty of clothes store Gabriele (p77). Look out for a typically Brussels-style piece of street humour, the statue of cocked-legged dog Zinneke ('Mongrel'). Heading west up Rue Antoine Dansaert towards the canal, you'll see increasing numbers of Moroccan shops and cafes among chichi boutiques and such cutting-edge bars as BarBeton (p71) and **Walvis** (Map p46; 02-219 95 32; www.cafewalvis.be; Rue Antoine Dansaert; 11am-2am Mon-Thu & Sun, to 4am Fri & Sat; M Ste-Catherine). On the eastern side of the street, **Hoet** (Map p40; www.optiekhoet-brussel.be; Antoine Dansaert 97; M Ste-Catherine) is a designer-eyewear specialist with an extraordinary line in silver filigree eyeshades. Look up to admire the shop's Parisian-style gables, and glance back to the upper facade of the outwardly uninspired KBC bank building to notice an unexpected frieze of bananas. Along Rue Léon Lepage, you'll find a cluster of fashion stores, including bargain-hunters' **Outlet Privejoke** (Map p40; Rue Léon Lepage 30; 2pm-7pm Wed-Sun; M Ste-Catherine) and feminine but edgy Just In Case (p77).

boutiques, prices are clearly labelled. Has fashion for men and women.

Lowi FASHION, ACCESSORIES

(Map p40; www.lowi.be; Rue de Flandre 124; 11am-6.30pm Tue-Sat; M Ste-Catherine) Idiosyncratic fashion and accessories are the order of the day at Lowi, including covetable ceramic and porcelain jewellery.

Ixelles, Sablon & Marolles

★Place du Jeu-de-Balle Flea Market MARKET

(Map p50; Place du Jeu-de-Balle; 7am-2pm; M Porte de Hal, Lemonnier) The quintessential Marolles experience is haggling at this chaotic flea market, established in 1919. Weekends see it at its liveliest, but for the best bargains, head here early morning midweek.

Sablon Antiques Market MARKET

(Map p50; www.sablon-antiques-market.com; Place du Grand Sablon; 9am-6pm Sat, to 2pm Sun; M Porte de Namur) Over 100 vendors fill this stately square on weekends, selling crockery, crystal, jewellery, furniture, 18th-century Breton Faïence (pottery) and other relics of bygone eras. Prices generally reflect the high quality of the goods for sale.

★Place du Châtelain Market MARKET

(Map p50; Place du Châtelain; afternoon Wed; M Louise) Fabulous food stalls cluster around an elongated, leafy square at this market. Cheese, charcuterie, fresh fruit and veg, seasonal fodder – truffles, mushrooms, berries and so on – a Middle Eastern food van, Turkish bread, vats of Congolese stew, a wine bar and cake stalls: it's a true foodie heaven, well worth a special trip.

Gare du Midi Market MARKET

(Map p50; Gare du Midi; 6am-1pm Sun; M Gare du Midi) Said to be the biggest market in Europe, this sprawl of colourful stalls next to the railway lines has an international flavour, with exotic North African and Mediterranean spices, cheeses, meats, clothing, leather goods and everything else under the sun.

Its food stands, selling bites like Moroccan crêpes with cheese, honey and vegetables along with mint tea, are a favourite with clubbers winding down from Saturday night.

Africamäli ACCESSORIES

(Map p50; 02-503 00 74; Chaussée de Wavre 83; M Porte de Namur) A community project – the name means 'African treasures' in Swahili – selling fair traded and ethical jewellery, accessories and homewares from sub-Saharan Africa.

EU Quarter

Crush Wine WINE

(Map p50; 02-502 66 97; www.crushwine.be; Rue Caroly 39; 11am-7pm Mon-Fri plus 1 Sat per month; Ⓜ Trône) Wondrous cellar stocking over 190 Australian wines (the most comprehensive selection in Europe). Look out for rare drops from Tasmania and deliberate over dozens of Margaret River reds. There are daily tastings and tapas and regular wine events; call ahead for the schedule of Saturday openings.

Place Jourdan Market MARKET
(Map p55; Place Jourdan; ⏱7am-2pm Sun; Ⓜ Schuman) Place Jourdan hosts a small Sunday-morning market selling food and clothes.

Information

INTERNET ACCESS

There's free wi-fi at the Use-It office, the Le Cercle des Voyageurs (p66), Maison du Peuple (p73) and many other *cafés*: note that while wi-fi signs aren't often displayed, many *cafés* and bars do offer it, so be sure to ask.

MEDICAL SERVICES

Community Help Service (☎02-648 40 14; www.chsbelgium.org; ⏱24hr) English-speaking crisis helpline. Can also help find English-speaking doctors, dentists and other health professionals.

Hôpital St-Pierre (☎02-535 31 11; www.stpierre-bru.be; Rue Haute 290-322; ⏱emergency 24hr, consultation 8am-5pm; Ⓜ Louise) Central hospital offering emergency assistance.

MONEY

ATMs and exchange facilities are found near the Bourse, at Bruxelles-Midi station and Brussels Airport.

POST

Post Office (Map p50; Gare du Midi, Ave Fonsny 1e; ⏱7am-7pm Mon-Fri, 10am-3pm Sat; Ⓜ Gare du Midi, Ⓡ Bruxelles-Midi)

Post Office (Map p40; Blvd Anspach 1; ⏱8am-6pm Mon-Fri, 10.30am-4.30pm Sat; Ⓜ De Brouckère)

Post Office (Map p46; City 2 Shopping Centre, Rue Neuve; ⏱9.30am-6.30pm Mon-Fri, 10am-1pm Sat; Ⓜ Rogier)

TOURIST INFORMATION

BIP (Map p46; ☎02-548 04 58; http://bip.brussels; Rue Royale 2-4; ⏱10am-6pm; Ⓜ Parc) Official Brussels-region tourist office. Hotel bookings and lots of information.

Espace Wallonie-Bruxelles (☎02-504 02 00, 02-725 52 75; www.belgique-tourisme.be; Arrivals Hall, Brussels Airport; ⏱8am-9pm) Information on Brussels and Wallonia.

Flanders Info (Map p40; ☎02-504 03 90; www.visitflanders.com; Rue du Marché aux Herbes 61; ⏱9am-6pm Mon-Sat, 10am-5pm Sun; 📶; 🚋 Bourse) Flanders information. Free wi-fi.

Use-It (Map p46; ☎02-218 39 06; http://use-it.travel/cities/detail/brussels; Galerie Ravenstein 17; ⏱10am-6.30pm Mon-Sat; 📶; Ⓜ Gare Central) Meeting place for young travellers, with free coffee and tea and a list of live-music events written up by the door. It does a free alternative city tour at 2pm on Monday, with an emphasis on social history and nightlife. The printed material is first rate, with a quirky city map, a guide for wheelchair users and a beer pamphlet.

Visit Brussels (Map p40; ☎02-513 89 40; http://visitbrussels.be; Hôtel de Ville, Grand Place; ⏱9am-6pm; 🚋 Bourse) Visit Brussels has stacks of city-specific information as well as handy fold-out guides (independently researched) to the best shops, restaurants and pubs in town. The Rue Royale (Map p46; ☎02-513 89 40; rue Royale 2; ⏱9am-6pm Mon-Fri, 10am-6pm Sat-Sun; Ⓜ Parc) office is much less crowded than the Grand Place one. Here you'll also find the Arsène50 (Map p46; ☎02-512 57 45; www.arsene50.be; ⏱12.30-5.30pm Tue-Sat; Ⓜ Parc) desk, which provides great discounts for cultural events.

Getting There & Away

AIR

Brussels Airport (BRU; www.brusselsairport.be) is 14km northeast of Brussels. There are ATMs on most levels and for stamps there's a post point in the Louis Delhaize grocery. The arrivals hall (Level 2) has currency exchange, car-rental agencies and tourist information. The bus terminus and luggage lockers are on Level 0, the train station on Level 1.

BUS

Eurolines (Map p46; ☎02-274 13 50; www.eurolines.be; Rue du Progrès 80; ⏱5.45am-8.45pm; 🚋 Gare du Nord) operates services to London, Amsterdam, Paris and other international destinations from Bruxelles-Nord.

CAR

Major car-rental companies have offices at Gare du Midi and Brussels Airport, but rentals from their downtown premises usually cost less.

Avis (☎02-537 12 80; www.avis.be; Rue Américaine 145; 🚋93, 94)

Budget (☎02-646 51 30; www.budget.be; Hotel Bristol, Ave Louise 91; 🚋93, 94)

TRAIN

Bruxelles-Midi (Gare du Midi; luggage office per article per day €2.50, luggage lockers per 24hr small/large €3/4; ⌚ luggage office 6am-9pm; Ⓜ Gare du Midi, 🚉 Bruxelles-Midi) is the main station for international connections: the Eurostar, TGV and Thalys high-speed trains (with prebooking compulsory) only stop here. Most other mainline trains stop in quick succession at Bruxelles-Midi, **Bruxelles-Central** (Gare Centrale) and, except for Amsterdam trains, also at **Bruxelles-Nord** (Gare du Nord). Information offices at all three stations open early morning to late evening. For all enquiries, consult www.b-rail.be or call ☎ 02-555 25 55.

The following fares (one way, 2nd class) are for standard trains from Bruxelles-Central:

DESTINATION	FARE (€)	DURATION (MIN)	FREQUENCY (PER HR)
Antwerp	7.30	35-49	5
Binche	9.40	59	1
Bruges	14.10	62	2
Charleroi	9.40	60	2
Ghent	8.90	36	2
Hasselt	12.80	75	2
Kortrijk	12.80	69	1
Leuven	5.30	24-36	4
Liège	14.80	60-80	2
Luxembourg City	37.80	180	1
Mechelen	4.50	15-28	2
Mons	9.40	55	2
Namur	8.90	62	2
Nivelles	5.70	30	2
Ostend	16.80	75	1
Tournai	12.80	61-73	2
Ypres	17.50	105	1

ℹ Getting Around

TO/FROM THE AIRPORT

Airport City Express (tickets €5.60; ⌚ 5.30am-12.20am) trains run four times hourly between Brussels Airport and the city's three main train stations, Bruxelles-Nord (15 minutes), Bruxelles-Central (€8.50, 20 minutes) and Bruxelles-Midi (25 minutes). Express bus 12 links the airport to Bruxelles-Luxembourg via Nato HQ and Schuman metro station (prepurchased/bought aboard €3/4). It should take around 30 minutes, but allow much more time at rush hour. After 8pm at weekends, the slower route 21 is substituted. See www.stib.be for the rather complex timetables. An airport taxi to central Brussels costs around €38 (some accept credit cards), but once you're stuck in rush-hour traffic you'll probably wish you'd taken the train.

BICYCLE

Intolerant drivers, slippery cobblestones and tram tracks combine to make Brussels a cyclist's nightmare. However, a network of bike paths (separated from the traffic) and bike lanes (usually painted red and marked with white lines) is being introduced, and bicycles may legally take certain (marked) one-way streets in the wrong direction: convenient but hazardous, as few car drivers realise that this is the case. Bicycles can be carried on the metro and trams except during rush hour (7am to 9am and 4pm to 6.30pm), once you've purchased a one-year bike pass (€15).

Rental

Villo! (☎ 078-05 11 10; en.villo.be; subscription day/week €1.60/7.65) is a system of 180 automated stations for short-term bicycle rental (30/60/90/120 minutes free/€0.50/1/1.50/2). First you need a subscription (day/week/year €1.60/7.65/32.60), then charges accumulate and are debited from your credit/bank card. When making stops the idea is to return the bike to the nearest station and take a new one when continuing. Failure to return the bicycle or to follow the rules could cost you €150. Read the website carefully for details and a station-finder map (note that only major stations issue subscriptions).

For longer bike hires, try **FietsPunt/Point-Velo** (www.recyclo.org; Carrefour de l'Europe 2; per 1/3 days €7.50/15; ⌚ 7am-7pm Mon-Fri; 🚉 Bruxelles-Central), which is also a cycle-repair shop. You'll need ID and credit card or a €150 deposit. The shop is somewhat hidden: look left as you leave Bruxelles-Central station via the daytime-only Madeleine exit. Another rental option is **Maison des Cyclistes** (☎ 02-502 73 55; www.provelo.be; Rue de Londres 15; ⌚ noon-6pm Mon-Fri, 10am-6pm Sat & Sun Apr-Oct; Ⓜ Trone), which also offers tours.

ROLLERBLADES

Belgium is perhaps unique in having special road rules for 'rollers' (those on rollerblades or rollerskates). On Friday evenings from June to September certain major city streets give temporary right of way to rollers from 7pm (see www.belgiumrollers.com).

CAR

The slightest hiccup on either ring road brings traffic to a halt, especially on Friday afternoons. Brussels-Mobilty (www.bruxellesmobilite.irisnet.be) maps real-time congestion problems.

Street parking requires meter payment when signs say *betalend parkeren/stationnement payant* (usually 9am to 1pm and 2pm to 7pm Monday to Saturday).

PUBLIC TRANSPORT

Brussels' integrated bus-tram-metro system is operated by **STIB/MIVB** (☎02-515 20 00; www.stib.be; Rue de l'Évêque 2; ⏰10am-6pm Mon-Sat). Public transport runs from about 6am to midnight, after which it's taxi only except on Friday/Saturday and Saturday/Sunday nights, when 17 Noctis night-bus routes (€3 single) operate twice hourly from midnight to 3am, most starting from Place de Brouckère.

Tickets & Passes

Tickets are valid for one hour and are sold at metro stations, at STIB/MIVB kiosks, newsagents and on buses and trams. Single-/five-/10-journey STIB/MIVB tickets cost €2.10/8/14 including transfers. Unlimited one-day passes cost €6. Note that airport buses are excluded and slightly higher 'jump' fares apply if you want to connect to city routes operated by De Lijn (Flanders bus), TEC (Wallonia bus) or SNCB/NMBS (rail). Children under six travel free.

Tickets must be validated, before travel, in machines located at the entrance to metro platforms or inside buses and trams. Tickets without validation incur fines of €55. Random checks are made.

Brussels International sells one-day passes and **BrusselsCards** (p45).

Metro

Metro stations are marked with a white 'M' on a blue background. Lines 1A (northwest–southeast) and 1B (northeast–southwest) share the same central stretch including useful stops at Bruxelles-Central, Ste-Catherine and Schuman (for the EU area). Line 2 basically follows the Petit Ring. Don't expect London-style frequency: trains only run every 10 to 15 minutes. While you wait there's often artwork to peruse. Highlights:

Bourse Paul Delvaux' *Nos vieux trams bruxellois* depicts old trams in the capital.

Horta Relics from Horta's Maison du Peuple have been integrated into the foyer.

Porte de Hal Old trams and futuristic vehicles merge in scenes mirroring the comic strips of artist François Schuiten.

Stockel Features life-size murals of Tintin and pals.

Tram, Premetro & Bus

The vast web of bus and tram transport has no central hub, so grab a free STIB/MIVB transport map before going too far. Underground *premetro* trams link Brussels-Nord and Brussels-Midi via the Bourse, travelling beneath the boulevard known consecutively as Adolphe Max/Anspach/Maurice Lemonnier.

TAXI

Official taxis (typically black or white) charge €2.40 pick-up plus €1.80/2.70 per kilometre within/outside the Brussels region. There's a €2 surcharge between 10pm and 6am. Waiting costs €30 per hour. Taxes and tips are officially included in the meter price, so you should ignore requests for extra service charges. Taxis wait near the three central train stations, outside Hôtel Amigo, near the Grand Place and at Place Stéphanie on Ave Louise. Website www.bruxellesmobilite.irisnet.be/articles/taxi/ou-trouver-un-taxi lists other ranks and taxi operators including **Taxis Bleus** (☎02-268 00 00; www.taxisbleus.be) and **Taxis Verts** (☎02-349 49 49; www.taxisverts.be). Cabbies have a reputation for aggressive, fast driving, but if you're seriously dissatisfied you can report them toll-free on ☎0800-94001 – the receipt, which they must legally print for you, should have their four-digit taxi ID.

AROUND BRUSSELS

South of Brussels

Forêt de Soignes

Forêt de Soignes FOREST

(Zoniënwoud; www.foret-de-soignes.be) This vast suburban forest about a 40-minute drive from Brussels is a botanical cathedral of glorious towering beech trees. Many were planted by proto-Belgium's 18th-century Austrian rulers, with oaks added by the French to provide timber for future naval ships. By the time those trees had matured, however, shipbuilders preferred metal, so the trees went uncut. Today the result is a delightful regional park with hundreds of kilometres of cycle, horse and walking paths.

Tucked into the forest fringes are arboreta at Tervuren and Groenendaal.

Jean Massart Experimental Garden GARDENS

(www.ulb.ac.be/musees/jmassart; ⏰9am-5pm Mon-Fri) FREE This 5-hectare garden in the Forêt de Soignes has themed zones: medicinal, evolutionary and so on.

Rouge Cloître ARTS CENTRE

(www.rouge-cloitre.be) The Rouge Cloître, an arts centre occupying a 14th-century abbey in the Forêt de Soignes, offers a playground suitable for kids up to about 12.

Southwest of Brussels

Beersel

Kasteel van Beersel CASTLE

(☎02-359 16 46; Lotsestraat; adult/concession €3/1.50; ⏲10am-noon & 2-6pm Tue-Sun Mar–mid-Nov, Sat & Sun only winter, closed Jan) The 1310 Kasteel van Beersel is the closest medieval castle to Brussels. And from outside it's a beauty. The picture-perfect brick towers, rebuilt in 1498, are topped off with 17th-century roofs and rise proudly above a tree-ringed moat. However, it's an empty shell, the building having been used as a cotton factory in the 19th century.

The castle is handily close to the west Brussels ring motorway (junction 19). By train from Brussels, you'll need to change at Halle, from which services run three times an hour to Beersel station, adjacent to the castle. Halle's interesting historic centre is worth a quick look while you're in transit.

Alsemberg

De Lambiek MUSEUM

(☎02-359 16 36; www.beersel.be; Gemeenveldstraat 1, Alsemberg; admission €3; ⏲11am-5pm Fri-Sun & Wed) For fans of the Brussels area's trademark *gueuze* and lambic beers there's a sparkling new showpiece attraction. De Lambiek explains the beers' qualities and production methods, then allows a tasting of a range of local speciality brews that can prove hard to find anywhere else. Alsemberg is a 40-minute drive from Brussels. By public transport, take a train to Halle and then change to a bus for Alsemberg.

Gaasbeek

Kasteel van Gaasbeek CASTLE

(www.kasteelvangaasbeek.be; adult/senior/under 26 €7/5/1; ⏲10am-6pm Tue-Sun Apr–early-Nov, last admission 5pm) One of the finest rural castles within striking distance of Brussels, the Kasteel van Gaasbeek is set in an extensive 17th-century park. Originally built to guard the medieval Brabant–Flanders border, this was the castle that angry Brussels folk burnt down in response to the 1388 murder of Everard 't Serclaes. In 1565, Gaasbeek was briefly home to Count Egmond before he was executed by the Spanish. Elements of each era are visible.

The building is furnished inside, romantically crenellated outside and looks quite different when viewed from different angles – though the majority of the structure is the result of an extensive 1897 renovation.

The castle is 14km southwest of central Brussels. Take bus 142 from Erasmus metro station.

North of Brussels

Nationale Plantentuin Van België

Nationale Plantentuin Van België GARDENS

(National Botanic Garden; ☎02-260 09 20; www.botanicgarden.be; Domein van Boechout; adult/senior/concession €7/6/3.50; ⏲9.30am-6.30pm mid-Mar–mid-Oct, last entry 5pm, 9.30am-5pm winter, last entry 4.30pm) Belgium's National Botanic Garden is a 93-hectare park located in the village of Meise, 12km north of Brussels. It's based around two lakes and includes the Kasteel van Boechout, a moated castle that Léopold II gave to his sister, Princess Charlotte, after her own at Tervuren burnt down in 1879.

Of the 18,000 plant species, the park's most prized orchids, carnivorous plants and famous giant Amazonian water lilies are housed in the 1966 Plantenpaleis (Plant Palace), a series of 13 connecting greenhouses.

Other highlights are the outdoor medicinal garden and a small 1864 greenhouse shaped like a king's crown. That was built in by Balat, Horta's teacher and the architect responsible for the Serres Royales. The 18th-century orangery has been converted into a cafe and shop.

From Brussels, De Lijn buses 250/251 run every 15 minutes from Bruxelles-Nord (35 minutes) via Bockstael metro station (20 minutes).

Grimbergen

Briefly its own principality (in the 18th century), Grimbergen is about an hour's drive from Brussels – just 2km north of Brussels' ring road at junction 7. It's worth a brief detour if you're driving by, to drink in one of its two watermill cafes and to admire the central Sint-Servaasbasiliek, an 1128 abbey-church that was majestically rebuilt after 1660 with one of Belgium's most breathtaking baroque-rococo interiors.

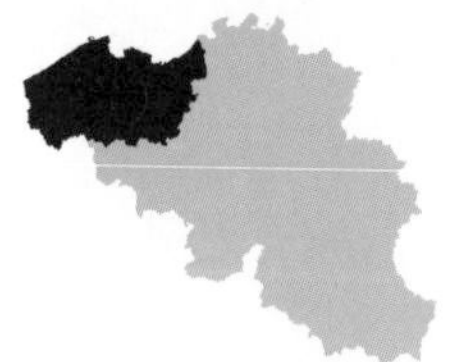

Bruges & Western Flanders

LANGUAGE: DUTCH

Includes ➡

Why Go?

The smallest of towns in this region feature fabulous medieval city centres, complete with belfries and *begijnhoven*. Bruges and Ghent top the bill, but even lesser-known places such as Oudenaarde and Veurne retain wonderfully picturesque town squares. Ypres and Diksmuide are charming, too, and all the more extraordinary for having been meticulously rebuilt following WWI. Scars and souvenirs of the Great War remain poignant attractions in the surrounding countryside, which also grows hops for some of Belgium's trademark beers. Western Flanders is not a place of spectacular scenery, but Belgians love this region for its extensive sandy beaches, which provide relief from the sombre sight of battlefields.

Best Places to Eat

- De Stove (p99)
- In 't Nieuwe Museum (p100)
- Restaurant Pegasus (p118)
- Den Gouden Harynck (p100)
- House of Eliott (p138)

Best Places to Stay

- St-Niklaas B&B (p96)
- Guesthouse Nuit Blanche (p97)
- Steenhuyse (p128)
- Main Street Hotel (p121)
- Uppelink (p136)

Driving Distances

	Poperinge	Kortrijk	Ypres	Ghent
Kortrijk	42			
Ypres	12	28		
Ghent	92	48	76	
Bruges	83	44	57	55

Bruges & Western Flanders Highlights

1. Exploring the impossibly picturesque canals, cobbled alleys and windmills of beautiful **Bruges** (p85)
2. Lingering among salient reminders of WWI around **Ypres** (p121)
3. Adoring the **Mystic Lamb** (p133) in Ghent
4. Drinking in centuries' old pubs as wonderful Westvleteren and Pannepot battle it out for best **beer**
5. Bunkering down at the WWII sea defences west of **Ostend** (p108)
6. Taking a bucolic canalside cycle ride to **Damme** and beyond (p105)
7. Wandering around little **Veurne**, which survived two wars and features a magnificent medieval market square (p115)

BRUGES (BRUGGE)

POP 117,000

If you set out to design a fairy-tale medieval town, it would be hard to improve on central Bruges (Brugge in Dutch). Picturesque cobbled lanes and dreamy canals link photogenic market squares lined with soaring towers, historic churches and old whitewashed almshouses. And there's plenty of it. The only downside is that everyone knows. That means that there's a constant crush of tourists in the centre, especially through the summer months. So to really enjoy Bruges stay overnight (day trippers miss the fabulous evening floodlighting) and try to visit midweek (avoiding floods of weekend visitors). There's a special charm in spring when daffodils carpet the tranquil courtyard of the historic *begijnhof* retreat, or in winter (except Christmas) when you can have the magnificent, if icy, town almost to yourself.

History

The fortress around which Bruges grew was originally constructed by Baldwin Iron Arm, first Count of Flanders, just beyond the head of a long sea channel called the Zwin. As with other Flemish cities, Bruges' medieval prosperity came from trading and manufacturing textiles from high-quality English wool. Trade came via the Zwin and a linking waterway from nearby Damme village. Thirteenth-century traders meeting at the Bruges house of a certain Van de Burse (Vlamingenstraat 35) were the first to formalise stock trading, and to this day stock exchanges are still called *bourses* in many languages. By 1301 Bruges' citizens were already so wealthy that French King Philip the Fair's wife, Joanna of Navarre, claimed: 'I thought I alone was queen, but I see that I have 600 rivals here'.

Despite occasional rebellions, Bruges' zenith came in the 14th century. As a key member of the Hanseatic League (a powerful association of northern European trading cities), international trading houses set up shop here, and ships laden with exotic goods from all over Europe and beyond docked at the Minnewater.

Prosperity continued under the dukes of Burgundy, especially Philip the Good (r 1419–67), who arrived in 1430 to marry Isabella of Portugal. Bruges grew fat and at one point the population ballooned to 200,000, double that of London. Flemish art blossomed and the city's artists, known misleadingly as the Flemish Primitives, perfected paintings that were anything but primitive.

However, the guildsmen's relationships with their distant overlords was tense. A dynastic conflict between the French and Hapsburg empires in 1482 caused rising taxes and restrictions of the guildsmen's privileges. This in turn sparked a decade of disastrous revolts. At one point in 1488, presumptuous Bruges townsmen even dared to imprison the Hapsburg heir, Maximilian of Austria, for four months on a site that's now the Craenenburg Café (Markt 16). The Hapsburgs took furious retributions, with Bruges forced to demolish its city walls. While on paper the 'Liberty of Bruges' remained as a powerful autonomous district, traders sensed the city's coming demise. The Hanseatic League moved from Bruges to Antwerp and many merchants followed. But most devastating of all, the Zwin gradually silted up so Bruges lost all access to the sea. Despite attempts to build another canal, the city's economic lifeline was gone and the town was left full of abandoned houses, deserted streets and empty canals. Bruges slept for 400 years.

The city slowly emerged from its slumber in the early 19th century as war-tourists passed through en route to the Waterloo battlefield. In 1892 Belgian writer and poet Georges Rodenbach published *Bruges-la-Morte* (Bruges the Dead), a novel that beguilingly described the town's forlorn air and alerted well-heeled tourists to its preserved charm. Curious, wealthy visitors brought much-needed money into Bruges, and ever since the town has worked hard at renovations and embellishments to maintain its reputation as one of the world's most perfectly preserved medieval time capsules.

Antique Bruges escaped both world wars relatively unscathed and now lives largely off tourism. However, beyond the cute central area, greater Bruges includes a newer sprawl where vibrant manufacturing industries produce glass, electrical goods and chemicals, much of it exported via the 20th-century port of Zeebrugge ('Sea Bruges') to which Bruges has been linked since 1907 by the Boudewijnkanaal (Baudouin canal).

Sights

Old-town Bruges is neatly encased by an oval-shaped moat that follows the city's medieval fortifications. Though the walls are gone, four of the nine 14th-century gates still stand. The city centre is an ambler's dream, its sights sprinkled within leisurely

Bruges

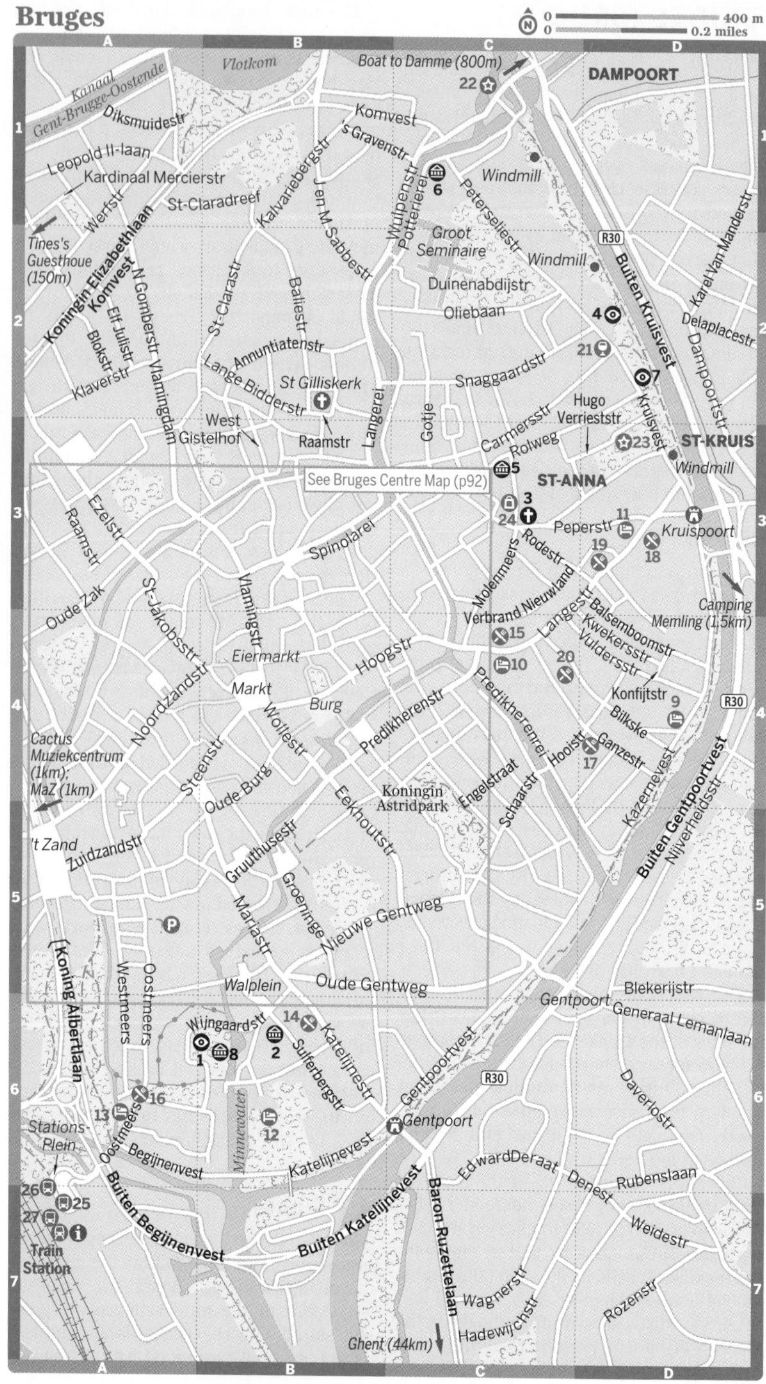

Boat to Damme (800m)
DAMPOORT
ST-KRUIS
ST-ANNA
See Bruges Centre Map (p92)
Tines's Guesthoue (150m)
Cactus Muziekcentrum (1km); MaZ (1km)
Camping Memling (1,5km)
Ghent (44km)
Train Station

Bruges

Sights

1	Begijnhof	B6
2	Godshuis de Vos	B6
3	Jeruzalemkerk	C3
	Kantcentrum	(see 3)
4	Koeleweimolen	D2
5	Museum voor Volkskunde	C3
6	OLV-ter-Potterie	C1
7	St Janshuismolen	D2
8	't Begijnhuisje	B6

Sleeping

9	B&B Degraeve	D4
10	B&B Yasmine	C4
11	Bauhaus	D3
12	Hotel Egmond	B6
13	't Keizershof	A6

Eating

14	De Bron	B6
15	De Karmeliet	C4
16	De Stoepa	A6
	De Zwarte Kat	(see 5)
17	In 't Nieuwe Museum	D4
18	Pro Deo	D3
19	Sans Cravate	D3
20	't Ganzespel	C4

Drinking & Nightlife

21	De Windmolen	D2

Entertainment

22	Du Phare	C1
	Entrenous	(see 11)
23	Vinkenzettingen	D3

Shopping

24	't Apostelientje	C3

Transport

25	Bus Station	A7
26	Bus to City Centre	A7
27	De Lijn Office	A7

walking distance of its compact centre. The train station sits about 1.5km south of the central square (Markt); buses shuttle regularly between the two, but it's a lovely walk via Minnewater.

Markt

Flanked by medieval-style step-gabled buildings, this splendid open market square is Bruges' nerve centre. Horse-drawn carriages clatter between open-air restaurants and camera-clicking tourists, all watched over by a verdigris-green statue of Pieter De Coninck and Jan Breydel, the leaders of the Bruges Matins (p89).

Belfort HISTORIC BUILDING

(Belfry; Map p92; adult/child €8/5; 9.30am-5pm, last tickets 4.15pm) Towering 83m above the square like a gigantic medieval rocket is the fabulous 13th-century belfort. There's relatively little to see inside, but it's worth the mildly claustrophobic 366-step climb for the fine views. Look out through wide-gauge chicken wire for panoramas across the spires and red-tiled rooftops towards the wind turbines and giant cranes of Zeebrugge. Visitor numbers are limited to 70 at once, which can cause queues at peak times.

The belfry's 47-bell carillon is still played manually on a changing schedule (typically Wednesdays and weekends). Timings are posted on a signboard in front of the 13th-century **Hallen** (Map p92; former market halls) FREE, which host occasional exhibitions and fairs.

Historium MUSEUM

(Map p92; 050 27 03 11; www.historium.be; Markt; adult/child €12.50/7.50; 10am-6pm) The Historium occupies a neo-Gothic building on the northern side of the Markt. Taking visitors back to 1435, it is a multimedia experience, claiming to be more medieval movie than museum. The 'immersive' one-hour audio and video tour aims to take you back to medieval Bruges: a fictional love story gives narrative structure, and you can nose around Van Eyck's studio, among other pseudo-historic experiences.

It's a little light on facts, so for many it will be a diversion from the real sights of the city – perhaps best for entertaining kids on a rainy day.

Burg

One short block east of the Markt, the less theatrical but still enchanting Burg has been Bruges' administrative hub for centuries. It also hosted the St-Donatian Cathedral till 1799, when it was torn down by anti-religious zealots. A modern addition is the mildly baffling **Toyo Ito pavilion** (Map p92), a geometric contemporary artwork at the square's tree-filled centre. With your back to it you can admire the southern flank of the Burg, incorporating three superb interlinked facades which glow with gilded detail.

DISCOUNT CARDS

If you're visiting more than a couple of sights, invest in a **Bruges City Card** (http://bezoekers.brugge.be/bruggecitycard; 48/72hr €46/49), which gives entry to all the main city museums, plus various attractions including private ventures such as Choco-Story (p95) and De Halve Maan brewery (p91). You'll also score a canal boat ride (which shouldn't be missed, however cheesy it may seem), as well as discounts on bicycle rental, concerts, films and theatre.

Brugse Vrije HISTORIC BUILDING

(Map p92; Burg 11a; ⏲9.30am-noon & 1.30-4.30pm) FREE Most eye-catching with its early baroque gabling, gilt highlights and golden statuettes, this was once the palace of the 'Liberty of Bruges', the large autonomous territory and administrative body that ruled from Bruges (1121–1794). Much of the building is still used for city offices, but you can visit the former aldermen's room, the **Renaissancezaal**, to admire its remarkable 1531 carved chimney piece.

Above a black marble fireplace and alabaster frieze, an incredibly detailed oak carving depicts a sword-waving Emperor Charles V. Charles is flanked by his grandfathers, Ferdinand of Aragon and Maximilian of Austria, both of whom sport extremely flattering codpieces.

Stadhuis HISTORIC BUILDING

(City Hall; Map p92; Burg 12) FREE The beautiful 1420 stadhuis features a fanciful facade that's second only to Leuven's for exquisitely turreted Gothic excess. Inside, an audio guide explains numerous portraits in somewhat excessive detail before leading you upstairs to the astonishing **Gotische Zaal** (Gothic Hall). Few rooms anywhere achieve such a jaw-dropping first impression as this dazzling hall with its polychrome ceiling, hanging vaults, romantically historic murals and upper frieze of gilt figures.

The exterior is smothered with replica statues of the counts and countesses of Flanders, the originals having been torn down in 1792 by French soldiers.

Heilig-Bloedbasiliek CHURCH

(Basilica of the Holy Blood; Map p92; www.holyblood.com; Burg 5; admission €2; ⏲9.30am-noon & 2-5pm, closed Wed afternoons mid-Nov–Mar) The stadhuis's western end morphs into the strangely invisible Heilig-Bloedbasiliek. The basilica takes its name from a phial supposedly containing a few drops of Christ's blood that was brought here after the 12th-century Crusades. The right-hand door leads upstairs to a colourfully adorned chapel where the relic is hidden behind a flamboyant silver tabernacle and brought out for pious veneration at 2pm daily.

Also upstairs is the basilica's one-room treasury, where you'll see the jewel-studded reliquary in which the phial is mounted on Ascension Day for Bruges' biggest annual parade, the Heilig-Bloedprocessie. Downstairs, entered via a different door, is the basilica's contrasting bare-stone 12th-century Romanesque chapel, a meditative place that's almost devoid of decoration.

Central Canal Area

A cute passageway (Blinde Ezelstraat, 'blind donkey street') burrows out of the Burg and crosses the very picturesque canal: don't forget to look behind you!

Vismarkt MARKET

(Map p92; ⏲7am-1pm Tue-Fri) The stone slabs of the colonnaded 1821 fish market still accommodate fish stalls most mornings, along with trinket sellers later in the day. Several seafood restaurants here back onto pretty Huidenvettersplein, where archetypal Bruges buildings include the old tanners' guildhouse.

Canal View CANAL

(Map p92; www.360cities.net/image/rozenhoedkaai-brugge) Don't miss the superb canal view from outside 't Klein Venetie cafe. With the belfry towering above a perfect canal-fronted gaggle of medieval house-fronts, the view is lovely any time, but it's especially compelling at dusk as the floodlights come on. From here, canalside Dijver leads southwest towards Bruges' foremost city museums.

★Groeningemuseum GALLERY

(Map p92; www.brugge.be; Dijver 12; adult/concession €8/6; ⏲9.30am-5pm Tue-Sun) Bruges' most celebrated art gallery boasts an astonishingly rich collection whose strengths are in superb Flemish Primitive and Renaissance works, depicting the conspicuous wealth of the city with glitteringly realistic artistry. In room 2 are meditative works including Jan Van Eyck's 1436 radiant masterpiece *Madonna with Canon George Van der Paele* (1436) and the *Madonna* by the Master of the Embroidered Foliage, where the rich fabric of the Madonna's robe meets the 'real' foliage at her feet with exquisite detail.

Gruesomely gory scenes include a live flaying in Gerard David's *Judgement of Cambyses* (1498; room 1) and the multiple tortures of St George (room 3). Visions of the city surface again in the Townscapes and Landscapes room, with picturesque scenes by Jan Anton Garemijn, as well as Auguste van de Steene's austere view of the market square. Later artistic genres also get a look in, including a typically androgynous figure by superstar symbolist Fernand Khnopff, plus a surrealist canvas each from Magritte and Delvaux. Flemish Expressionist works from the 1920s show the influence of cubism and German expressionism on Flemish artists – most striking are Constant Permeke's earth-coloured depictions of peasant life in *Pap Eaters* and *The Angelus*.

Arentshuis ART GALLERY

(Map p92; Dijver 16; adult/concession/child €4/3/free; ⌚9.30am-5pm Tue-Sun) With your Groeningemuseum ticket, admission is free to this stately 18th-century patrician house displaying the powerful paintings and dark-hued etchings of Frank Brangwyn (1867–1956), a Bruges-born artist of Welsh parentage. His images of WWI – he was an official war artist – are particularly powerful.

Gruuthuse MUSEUM

(Map p92; Dijver 17; adult/concession €8/6; ⌚9.30am-5pm Tue-Sun) The museum takes its name from the flower and herb mixture *(gruut)* that used to flavour beer before the cultivation of hops. The romantic heraldic entrance in a courtyard of ivy-covered walls and dreaming spires is arguably more interesting than the rambling, somewhat unsatisfying decorative-arts exhibits within. The unusual view from the upstairs oratory window into the treasury-apse of the Onze-Lieve-Vrouwekerk is worth a look.

Hof Arents PARK

(Map p92; ⌚7am-10pm Apr-Sep, to 9pm Oct-Mar) FREE Behind the Arentshuis, Hof Arents is a charming little park where a hump-backed pedestrian bridge, **St-Bonifaciusbrug**, crosses the canal for idyllic views. Generally nicknamed Lovers' Bridge, it's where many a Bruges citizen steals their first kiss. Privileged guests staying at the Guesthouse Nuit Blanche (p97) get the romantic moonlit scene all to themselves once the park has closed.

Onze-Lieve-Vrouwekerk CHURCH

(Church of Our Lady; Map p92; Mariastraat; ⌚9.30am-4.50pm Mon-Sat, 1.30-4.50pm Sun) This large, somewhat sober 13th-century church sports an enormous tower that's currently 'wrapped' for extensive renovation. Inside, it's best known for Michelangelo's serenely contemplative 1504 *Madonna and Child* statue, the only such work by Michelangelo to leave Italy during the artist's lifetime; look out also for the *Adoration of the Shepherds* by Pieter Pourbus.

In the church's apse, the treasury section displays some splendid 15th- and 16th-century artworks plus the fine stone-and-bronze tombs of Charles the Bold (Karel de Stoute) and his daughter, Mary of Burgundy, whose pivotal marriage dragged the Low Countries into the Hapsburg empire, with far-reaching consequences.

★**Museum St-Janshospitaal** MUSEUM

(Memlingmuseum; Map p92; Mariastraat 38; adult/concession/child €8/€6/free; ⌚9.30am-5pm Tue-Sun) In the restored chapel of a 12th-century hospital building with superb timber beamwork, this museum shows various torturous-looking medical implements, hospital sedan chairs and a gruesome 1679 painting of an anatomy class. But it is much better known for six masterpieces by 15th-century artist Hans Memling, including the enchanting reliquary of St Ursula. This gilded oak reliquary looks

THE BRUGES MATINS, 1302

The precocious wealth and independent-mindedness of Bruges' medieval guildsmen brought political tensions with their French overlords. In 1302, when guildsmen refused to pay a new round of taxes, the French sent in a 2000-strong army to garrison the town. Undeterred, Pieter De Coninck, dean of the Guild of Weavers, and Jan Breydel, dean of the Guild of Butchers, led a revolt that would go down in Flanders' history books as the 'Bruges Matins' (Brugse Metten). Early in the morning on 18 May, guildsmen crept into town and murdered anyone who could not correctly pronounce the hard-to-say Dutch phrase *'schild en vriend'* (shield and friend). This revolt sparked a widespread Flemish rebellion. A short-term Flemish victory six weeks later at the Battle of the Golden Spurs (p126) near Kortrijk gave medieval Flanders a very short-lived moment of independence.

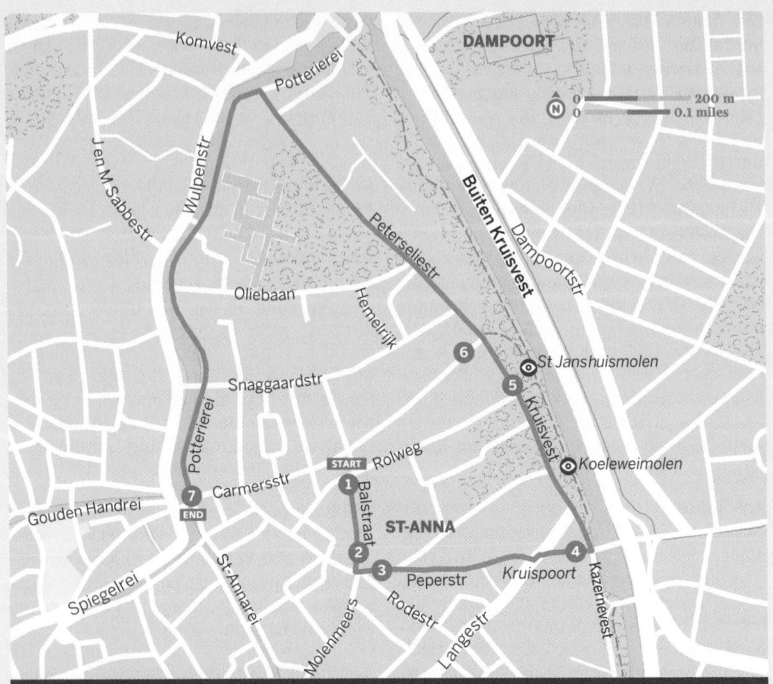

City Walk
St-Anna Windmills

START MUSEUM VOOR VOLKSKUNDE
END POTTERIEREI
LENGTH 2.5KM; ONE HOUR

The district of St-Anna provides a delightful breather away from central Bruges, as well as an insight into the industrious past of the district.

The appealing 1 **Museum voor Volkskunde** (p95) presents visitors with 18 themed tableaux illustrating Flemish life in times gone by (a 1930s sweetshop, a hatter's workshop etc). It's set in an attractive *godshuis* (almshouse); the old-style museum *café*, De Zwarte Kat, charges just €1.25 for a beer.

Once you locate the scenic backstreets of Bruges you'll find there's scarcely a soul in sight. Take a wander up Balstraat to quaint little 2 **'t Apostelientje** (p103). The delicate garments and gifts on sale are made from beautiful and authentic lace, handmade by two sisters and their mother; the husband of one of the sisters makes the wooden bobbins.

Past the dramatic Jeruzalemkerk, the 3 **Kantcentrum** (p95) displays a collection of lace in a row of interlinked old cottages. The centre's main attraction is that (afternoons only) you can watch bobbin lace being made by informal gatherings of experienced lace-makers and their students.

The fortified gate-tower 4 **Kruispoort** (on Langestraat) is an impressive isolated remnant of the former city wall. From the 13th century through to the 19th century, Bruges' ramparts were graced with 5 **molens** (windmills); ambling along the canal bounding the eastern side of the city takes you through pretty parkland past Bruges' four remaining examples. You can visit two of the four, which still grind cereals into flour today: 18th-century St Janshuismolen and the Koeleweimolen.

Take a break at quaint corner 6 **De Windmolen** (p101), with a sunny terrace overlooking one of the St-Anna windmills. It's mainly patronised by locals, and offers a good low-key location to sample the local brews. Wind your way back to the centre by heading north up Peterseliestraat and then heading left along scenic 7 **Potterierei**, where statues of the Madonna adorn every corner.

like a mini Gothic cathedral, painted with scenes from the life of St Ursula, including highly realistic Cologne cityscapes.

The devout Ursula was a Breton princess betrothed to a pagan prince. She agreed to marry him on the condition she could make a pilgrimage to Rome (via Cologne) with 11,000 virgins, but all were murdered on the return journey by the king of the Huns, along with Ursula and her betrothed. The largest of the Memlings on display is the triptych of St John the Baptist and St John the Evangelist, commissioned by the hospital church as its altarpiece. Look out for St Catherine (with spinning wheel) and St Barbara, both seated at the feet of the Virgin. The artist's secular portrayals are just as engrossing as the devotional work, and include the delicate *Portrait of a Young Woman* (1480), in which the subject's hands rest on the painted frame of her portrait.

Your ticket also allows visits to the hospital's restored 17th-century *apotheek* (pharmacy), accessed by an easily missed rear door.

St-Salvatorskathedraal CATHEDRAL
(Map p92; Steenstraat; ⏲2-5.45pm Mon, 9am-noon & 2-5.45pm Tue-Fri, 9am-noon & 2-3.30pm Sat & Sun) Stacked sub-towers top the massive central tower of 13th-century St-Saviour's Cathedral. In daylight the construction looks somewhat dour, but once floodlit at night, it takes on a mesmerising fascination. The cathedral's interior is vastly high but feels oddly plain despite a selection of antique tapestries. Beneath the tower, a glass floor reveals some painted graves, and there's a passingly interesting **treasury** (Map p92; Steenstraat; adult/child €2/1; ⏲2-5pm Sun-Fri) displaying 15th-century brasses and a 1559 triptych by Dirk Bouts.

Walplein

Brouwerij De Halve Maan BREWERY
(Map p92; ☎050 33 26 97; www.halvemaan.be; Walplein 26; ⏲10.30am-6pm, closed mid-Jan) Founded in 1856, though there has been a brewery on the site since 1564, this is the last family *brouwerij* (brewhouse) in central Bruges. Multilingual 45-minute **guided visits** (tours €8; ⏲11am-4pm, to 5pm Sat) depart on the hour. They include a tasting but can sometimes be rather crowded. Alternatively you can simply sip one of their excellent Brugse Zot (Bruges Fool, 7%) or Straffe Hendrik (Strong Henry, 9%) beers in the appealing brewery *café*.

Diamantmuseum MUSEUM
(Diamond Museum; Map p92; ☎050 34 20 56; www.diamondmuseum.be; Katelijnestraat 43; adult/senior/student €8/7/7, combined ticket with Choco-Story €14; ⏲10.30am-5.30pm) While Antwerp is now the centre of the diamond industry, the idea of polishing the stones with diamond 'dust' was originally pioneered in Bruges. This is the theme developed by this slick museum, which also displays a lumpy, greenish 252-carat raw diamond and explains how the catchphrase 'Diamonds are Forever' started as a De Beers marketing campaign. Diamond-polishing demonstrations (12.15pm and 3.15pm) cost €3 extra.

Godshuizen HISTORIC BUILDINGS
Several attractive *godshuizen* (almshouses) include the 1713 **Godshuis de Vos** (Map p86; Noordstraat 2-8), 1654 **Godshuis OLV Zeven Weeën** (Map p92; Driekroezenstraat 2-6) and 1330 **Rooms Convent** (Map p92; Mariastraat 9-21). For the most spacious little oases of calm, push the green door and relax in **Godshuis St-Jozef & De Meulenaere** (Map p92; Nieuwe Gentweg 24).

Begijnhof Area

Known in English as the 'Lake of Love', the charming green park around the Minnewater really does give this area a romantic quality. In Bruges' medieval heyday, this is where ships from far afield would unload their cargoes of wool, wine, spices and silks.

Begijnhof BEGIJNHOF
(Map p86; Wijngaardstraat; ⏲6.30am-6.30pm) FREE Bruges' delightful *begijnhof* originally dates from the 13th century. Although the last *begijn* has long since passed away, today residents of the pretty, whitewashed garden complex include a convent of Benedictine nuns. Despite the hoards of summer tourists, the *begijnhof* remains a remarkably tranquil haven. In spring, a carpet of daffodils adds to the quaintness of the scene. Outside the 1776 gateway bridge lies a tempting, if predictably tourist-priced, array of terraced restaurants, lace shops and waffle peddlers.

't Begijnhuisje MUSEUM
(Map p86; Begijnhof, Wijngaardstraat; adult/senior/child €2/€1.50/€1; ⏲10am-5pm Mon-Sat, 2.30-5pm Sun) Just inside the main entrance of the *begijnhof*, this is a charming 17th-century house now converted into an endearing little four-room museum. In the rustic kitchen with its blue and white Delft tiles you'll see a Louvain stove which extends into the room from the hearth so that people can sit around it. The sitting room displays black Chantilly lace, while the

Bruges Centre

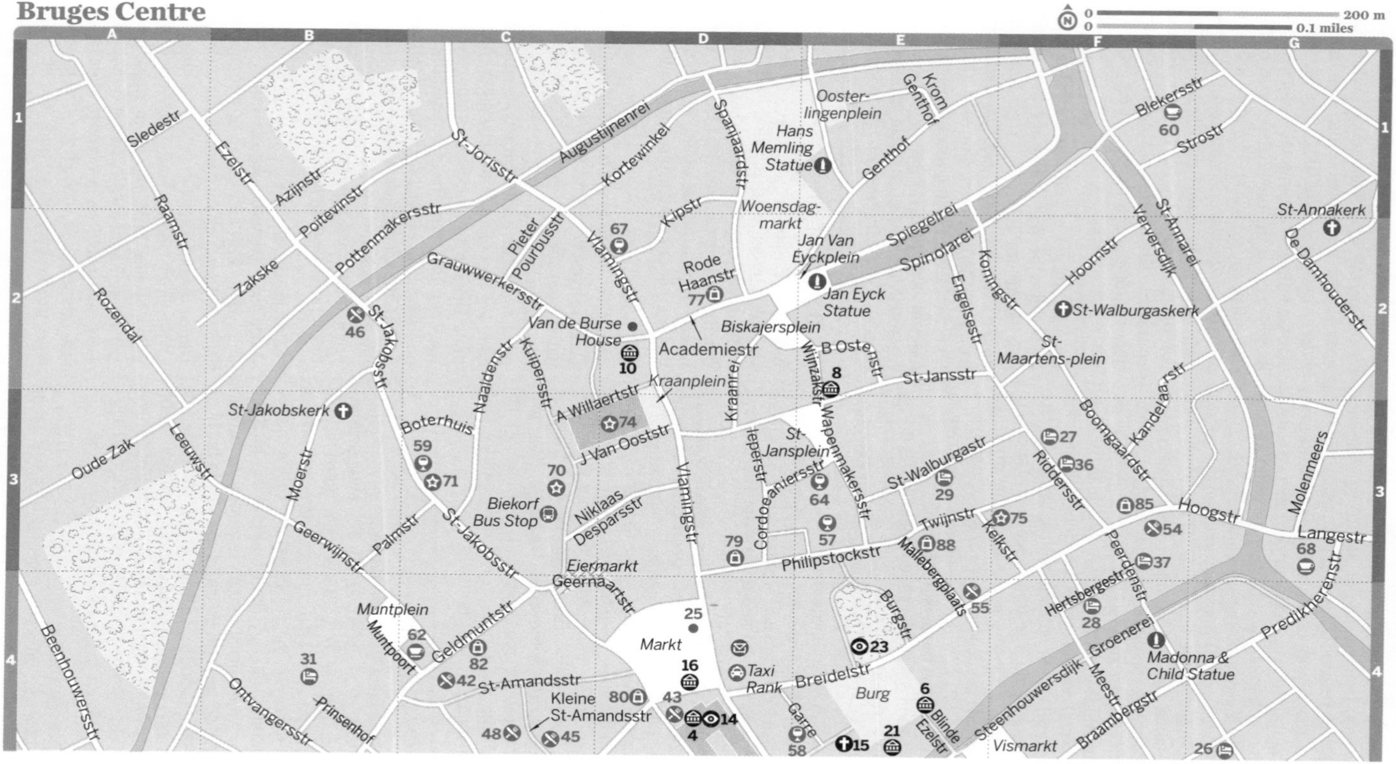

0 — 200 m
0 — 0.1 miles

St-Annakerk
De Damhouderstr
Molenmeers
Langestr
Predikherenstr
68
Stroostr
Blekersstr
60
St-Annarei
Verversdijk
Kandelaarstr
Hoogstr
54
37
85
Boomgaardstr
Hoornstr
St-Walburgaskerk
St-Maartens-plein
27
36
Riddersstr
Peerdenstr
Hertsbergestr
28
Groenerei
Madonna & Child Statue
26
Meestr
Braambergstr
Koningstr
Engelsestr
St-Jansstr
St-Walburgastr
29
75
Kelkstr
Twijnstr
88
55
Mallebergplaats
Steenhouwersdijk
Vismarkt
Krom Genthof
Genthof
Spiegelrei
Spinolarei
Jan Van Eyckplein
Jan Eyck Statue
B-Ostenstr
8
Wapenmakersstr
Burgstr
23
6
Blinde Ezelstr
21
Burg
15
Oosterlingenplein
Hans Memling Statue
Woensdagmarkt
Biskajersplein
Wijnzakstr
St-Jansplein
Cordoeaniersstr
64
57
Philipstockstr
Breidelstr
Garre
58
Spanjaardstr
Rode Haanstr
77
Academiestr
Kraanrei
Ieperstr
79
Taxi Rank
14
Kipstr
Kraanplein
Vlamingstr
25
16
4
43
Markt
Kortewinkel
Augustijnenrei
67
Vlamingstr
10
Van de Burse House
74
A Willaertstr
J Van Ooststr
Desparsstr
Niklaas
Eiermarkt
Geernaartstr
80
St-Amandsstr
Kleine St-Amandsstr
45
Pieter Pourbusstr
Grauwwerkersstr
Kuipersstr
70
Biekorf Bus Stop
Naaldenstr
St-Jorisstr
Boterhuis
59
71
St-Jakobsstr
Geldmuntstr
82
42
St-Amandsstr
48
Pottenmakersstr
St-Jakobsstr
46
Palmstr
Muntplein
Muntpoort
62
Potteriinstr
Azijnstr
St-Jakobskerk
Moerstr
Geerwijnstr
31
Prinsenhof
Zakske
Ezelstr
Ontvangersstr
Sledestr
Raamstr
Leeuwstr
Rozendal
Oude Zak
Beenhouwersstr

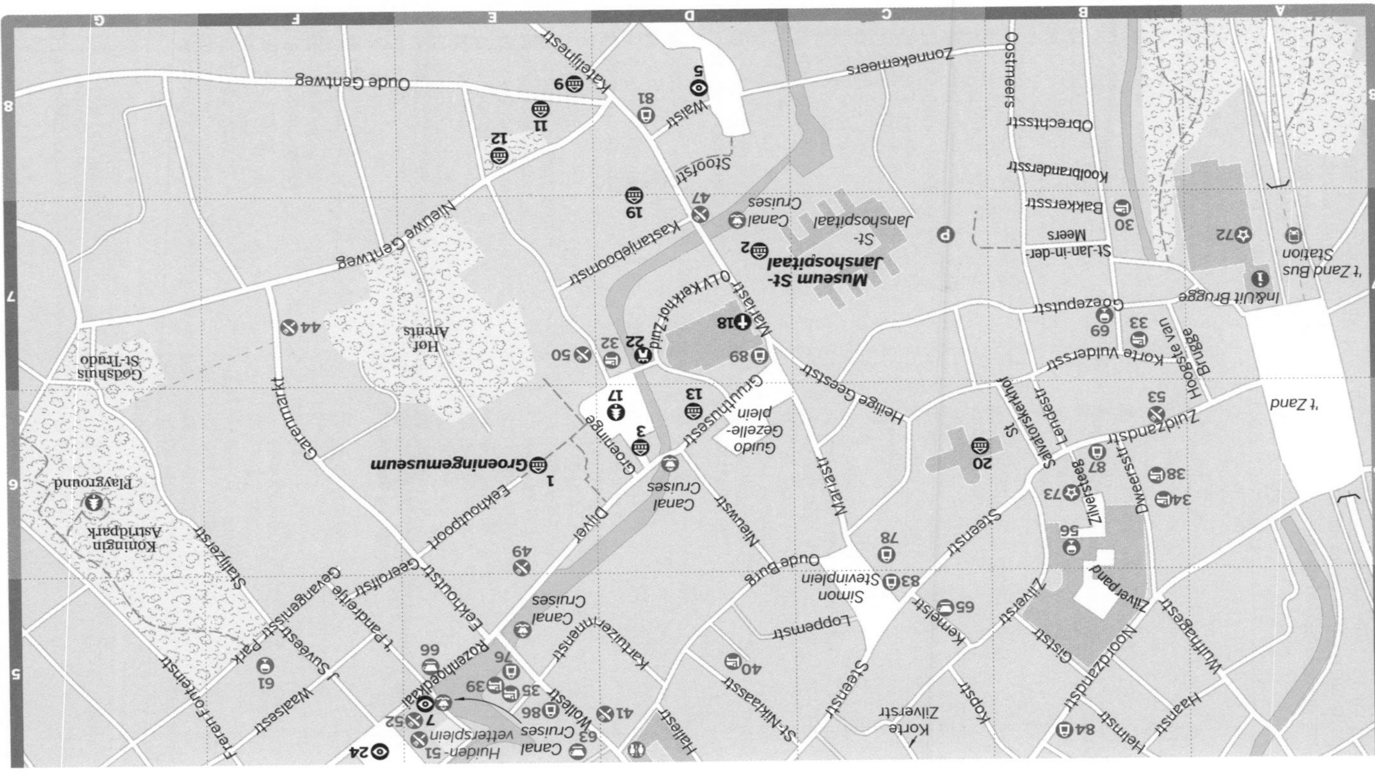
Groeningemuseum
Museum St-Janshospitaal
St-Janshospitaal
Koningin Astridpark
Playground
Godshuis St-Trudo
Hof Arents
Guido Gezelle-plein
Simon Stevinplein
Huiden-vetterspein
Canal Cruises
'Zand
't Zand Bus Station
In&Uit Brugge
Zilverpand
Garenmarkt
Eekhoutpoort
Eekhoutstr
Geerolfstr
Gevangenisstr
Park
Stalijzerstr
Freren Fonteinstr
Waalsestr
J Suvéestr
't Pandreitje
Rozenhoedkaai
Wollestr
Kartuizerinnenstr
Dijver
Groeninge
Gruuthusestr
Nieuwstr
Oude Burg
Hallestr
St-Niklaasstr
Loppemstr
Steenstr
Mariastr
Heilige Geeststr
OLV-Kerkhof-Zuid
Kastanjeboomstr
Nieuwe Gentweg
Oude Gentweg
Katelijnestr
Walstr
Stoofstr
Zonnekemeers
Ostmeers
Obrechtsstr
Koolbrandersstr
Bakkersstr
St-Jan-in-der-Meers
Goezeputstr
Korte Vuldersstr
Hoogste van Brugge
Zuidzandstr
Lendestr
St Salvatorskerkhof
Dweersstr
Zilversteeg
Zilverstr
Gistsr
Noordzandstr
Wulfhagestr
Haanstr
Helmstr
Kopstr
Korte Zilverstr
Kemelstr

Bruges Centre

austere bedroom has a portrait showing a traditional *begijn* costume.

The dining room features a simple wooden cupboard which served as a pantry, china store and pull-out dining table; beyond the house is a simple stone cloister with a well.

't Zand

This oversized square is part bus station, part bleakly paved promenade lined by hotels and restaurants. Its latter-day fountain featuring cyclists and lumpy nudes looks more appealing when floodlit at night. The dominant building is the vast red Concertgebouw (p102), a concert hall and art space opened in 2002 to celebrate Bruges' year-long stint as the European City of Culture. Views from the 7th-floor Sound Factory are magnificent, though partly interrupted by vertical struts.

Choco-Story MUSEUM
(Map p92; www.choco-story.be; Wijnzakstraat 2, on Sint-Jansplein; adult/child €8/5, combined ticket with Diamantmuseum €14; ⏲10am-5pm) A highly absorbing chocolate museum tracing the cocoa bean back to its role as an Aztec currency. Learn about choco-history, watch a video on cocoa production and sample a praline that's made as you watch (last demonstration 4.45pm).

Frietmuseum MUSEUM
(Map p92; ☎050 34 01 50; www.frietmuseum.be; Vlamingstraat 33; adult/concession/child €7/6/5; ⏲10am-5pm, closed Christmas–mid-Jan) Follows the history of the potato from ancient Inca gravesites to the Belgian fryer. The entry fee includes a discount token for the basement **frituur** (Frietmuseum; frituur fries €2; ⏲ 11am-3pm) that immodestly claims to fry the world's ultimate chips.

St-Anna & Dampoort Quarters

Charming canalscapes, street scenes and a few minor sights make the centre's little-visited northeastern corner a fine place for random wandering, perhaps en route to the Damme paddle-steamer.

OLV-ter-Potterie MUSEUM
(Map p86; Potterierei 79; adult/concession €4/3; ⏲9.30am-12.30pm & 1.30-5pm) Admission to this small historical church-hospital complex is free with a St-Janshospitaal museum ticket. Ring the bell to gain entry and you'll find fine 15th- to 16th-century art. The lushly baroque church section houses the reliquary of St-Idesbaldus and a polychrome wooden relief of Mary breastfeeding baby Jesus. In more prudish later centuries, the Virgin's nipple received a lacy camouflage, rendering the scene bizarrely impractical.

Jeruzalemkerk CHURCH
(Map p86; Peperstraat 1; adult/child €2.50/1.50; ⏲10am-5pm Mon-Sat) In western St-Anna is one of Bruges' oddest churches, the 15th-century structure built by the Adornes family. Supposedly based upon Jerusalem's Church of the Holy Sepulchre, it's a macabre monument with a gruesome altarpiece covered in skull motifs and an effigy of Christ's corpse tucked away in the rear mini-chapel. The black-marble tomb of Anselm Adornes contains only his heart, presumably all that could be carried back to Bruges after he was murdered in Scotland in 1483.

Buy tickets at nearby Kantcentrum.

Kantcentrum MUSEUM
(Lace Centre; Map p86; http://kantcentrum.eu; Balstraat 16; adult/child €5/4; ⏲10am-5pm) The Kantcentrum displays a collection of lace in a row of interlinked old cottages. The centre's main attraction is that in the afternoons (2pm to 5pm) you can watch bobbin lace being made by informal gatherings of experienced lace-makers and their students who gather to chat and work here. Once you've seen how mind-bendingly fiddly the process is, you'll swiftly understand why handmade lace is so very expensive; a small piece costs €10.

Museum voor Volkskunde MUSEUM
(Museum of Folklore; Map p86; Balstraat 43; adult/concession €4/3; ⏲9.30am-5pm Tue-Sun) The appealing Museum voor Volkskunde presents visitors with 18 themed tableaux illustrating Flemish life in times gone by (a 1930s sweetshop, a hatter's workshop, a traditional kitchen etc). It's a static affair, but the setting is an attractive *godshuis,* and the time-warp museum *café,* **De Zwarte Kat** (Map p86; Balstraat 43; ⏲closed 11.45am-2pm), charges just €1.25 for a beer. Temporary exhibits upstairs are often worth a look, and

IN BRUGES

'Maybe that's what hell is – the entire rest of eternity spent in Bruges...' The city hit the big screen when the 2008 Sundance Film Festival premiered the action-comedy, *In Bruges*. Written and directed by Irish playwright Martin McDonagh, it stars Colin Farrell and Brendan Gleeson, who play hit men ordered by their boss (Ralph Fiennes) to hide out in Bruges during the pre-Christmas frenzy. The tagline 'shoot first, sightsee later' gives you an idea of the plot – made more bizarre by encounters with a string of surreal Felliniesque characters. It's peppered with hilariously obscene, aggressive and un-PC invective about the quaintly pretty city which, to their credit, the people of Bruges seem to find as funny as everyone else.

traditional candies are made here every first and third Thursday of the month.

Activities

Cycling

For picturesque cycling routes follow rural canals beyond Damme. Oostkerke (9km from Bruges' Dampoort) makes a good short run, or head for pretty Sluis just across the Dutch border (15km via canal banks). For simple routes like these, use the detailed *Bruges Surroundings* map (available free from Snuffel and Bauhaus hostels). For more complex routes, the tourist office sells the *5x Bike Around Bruges* map-guide (€1.50).

Tours

Canal Tours

Taking a **canal tour** (adult/child €7.60/3.40; ⏲10am-6pm Mar–mid-Nov) is a must. Yep, it's touristy, but what isn't in Bruges? Viewing the city from the water gives it a totally different feel than on land. Cruise down Spiegelrei towards Jan Van Eyckplein and it's possible to imagine Venetian merchants entering the city centuries ago and meeting under the slender turret of the Poortersloge building up ahead. Boats depart roughly every 20 minutes from jetties south of the Burg, including Rozenhoedkaai and Dijver, and tours last 30 minutes. Expect queues in summer.

There's also a **paddle-steamer** (adult/child one way €7.50/6, return €10.50/8.50; ⏲10am-5pm Easter–mid-Oct) to Damme.

Horse-Drawn Carriage Rides

Carriage tours (€44 for up to five people) depart from the Markt and take 35 minutes, including a pit stop at the *begijnhof*. In summer, aim to jump on board between 6pm and 7pm when most day trippers have left town and Bruges' buildings glow golden in the sun's late rays. Horses appear well cared for.

Minibus Tours

City Tour BUS TOUR
(Map p92; www.citytour.be; adult/child €16/9.50; ⏲10am-sunset) Runs hourly 50-minute don-your-headphones city tours plus some two-hour trips to Damme. Tours start from the Markt; pay on board.

Quasimodo BUS TOUR
(☎050 37 04 70; www.quasimodo.be; under/over 26 €55/65) Quasimodo runs minibus Triple Treat tours which visit a selection of castles plus the fascinating WWII coastal defences near Ostend. Its Flanders Fields tour visits the Ypres Salient.

Festivals & Events

Highlights include the Holy Blood procession Heilig-Bloedprocessie (www.holyblood.com) and the roughly five-yearly Golden Tree pageant (held next in August 2017).

Sleeping

Almost all options can get seriously overbooked from Easter to October and over Christmas. Things get especially tough at weekends when two-night minimum stays are often required. Many cheaper B&Bs charge around €10 per room less if you stay more than one night.

Central Canal Area

Passage Bruges HOSTEL €
(Map p92; ☎050 34 02 32; www.passagebruges.com; Dweersstraat 26-28; dm/tw/tr €25/50/75) Located above an invitingly old-fashioned cafe-restaurant is a recently renovated hostel; the next door building houses spartan but large and well-priced hotel rooms.

Hostel Lybeer HOSTEL €
(Map p92; ☎050 33 43 55; www.hostellybeer.com; Korte Vuldersstraat 31; dm from €16, s/d without bathroom €28/50; @📶) The Lybeer traditionally had plenty of tatty edges, but is now in the process of renovation. It's handily central in a typical Bruges terraced house and has a large and convivial sitting and dining room.

★**St-Niklaas B&B** B&B €€
(Map p92; ☎050 61 03 08; www.sintnik.be; St-Niklaasstraat 18; s €100-130, d €120-150; 📶) Room 1 has a claw-foot bath and antique glass panel, but it's the other two rooms' remarkable Pisa-like belfry views that make this welcoming B&B so special and popular.

★**B&B Dieltiens** B&B €€
(Map p92; ☎050 33 42 94; www.bedandbreakfastbruges.be; Waalsestraat 40; s €60-80, d €70-90, tr €90-100) Old and new art fills this lovingly restored classical mansion, which remains an appealingly real home run by charming musician hosts. Superbly central yet quiet. It also operates a holiday flat (from €75 per night) nearby in a 17th-century house.

Baert B&B B&B €€
(Map p92; ☎050 33 05 30; www.bedandbreakfastbrugge.be; Westmeers 28; s/d €80/90) In a 1613 former stable this is one of very few places in Bruges where you'll get a private canalside terrace (flower-decked, though not on the loveliest canal section). Floral rooms have

bathrooms across the landing; bathrobes are provided. A big breakfast spread is served in a glass verandah, and extras include a welcome drink and a pack of chocolates.

Hotel Bourgoensch Hof HOTEL €€
(Map p92; ☎050 33 16 45; www.belforthotels.com; Wollestraat 39; standard/canal-view from €125/150) Historic hotel with one of the most spectacular canal views in Bruges. The decor is a little dated and bland, but the central location is hard to beat.

Hotel Bla Bla HOTEL €€
(Map p92; ☎050 33 90 14; www.hotelblabla.com; Dweersstraat 24; s €85-95, d €95-105, tr €130; 📶) A shuttered and step-gabled building given an elegant makeover, with parquet floors, modern art works and soothingly pale rooms. Excellent buffet breakfast included.

B&B Gheeraert B&B €€
(Map p92; ☎050 33 56 27, 0473 76 32 99; www.bb-bruges.be; Riddersstraat 9; s/d/tr €75/85/95; @📶) At the top of a steep spiral staircase, three bright, lofty rooms with whitewashed walls, art prints and polished wood floors share a plain lounge and computer room. Two-night minimum.

B&B Setola B&B €€
(Map p92; ☎050 33 49 77; www.bedandbreakfast-bruges.com; St-Walburgastraat 12; s/d/tr €65/75/105; 📶) Pleasant and very central, with three neat and attractive pine-floored rooms arranged around a guest kitchen. The Orange Room has A-frame beams and two ladder-accessible extra beds.

B&B Yasmine B&B €€
(Map p86; ☎050 68 70 32; www.gallery-yasmine.be; Langestraat 30-32; s/d €75/95) This is a self-styled gallery and B&B, and while you might want to forgo the artworks, the amazing location, budget prices and warm welcome make this a winner. The super-generous breakfast includes pancakes.

Hotel Patritius HOTEL €€
(Map p92; ☎050 33 84 54; www.hotelpatritius.be; Riddersstraat 11; d €70-150, tr €134-175, q €160-240; P📶) Enter this proud 1830s town house through the carriageway and past a bar-lounge. Up the historic spiral staircase, 16 guest rooms vary in size and style, some with exposed beams, others mildly chintzy and some renovated in bolder style (albeit with oddly kitschy dog portraiture). Despite relatively modest prices, there's a decent breakfast and pretty garden, but parking costs extra.

★**Guesthouse Nuit Blanche** B&B €€€
(Map p92; ☎0494 40 04 47; www.bb-nuitblanche.com; Groeninge 2; d €175-195) Pay what you like, nowhere else in Bruges can get you a more romantic location than this fabulous B&B, which started life as a 15th-century tannery. It oozes history, retaining original Gothic fireplaces, stained-glass roundels and some historic furniture, while bathrooms and beds are luxury-hotel standard.

Room rates cover the bottle of bubbly in your minibar. Drink it in the fabulous canalside garden or on 'Lovers' Bridge' in Hof Arents (p89), to which the guesthouse has a unique private entrance.

★**B&B Huyze Hertsberge** B&B €€€
(Map p92; ☎050 33 35 42; www.bruges-bedandbreakfast.be; Hertsbergestraat 8; d €155-170) Very spacious and oozing good taste, this late-17th-century house has a gorgeous period salon decked with antiques and sepia photos of the charming owner's great-great-grandparents (who first moved in here in 1901). The four guest rooms are comfortably grand, each with at least partial views of the tranquil little canalside garden.

★**Number 11** B&B €€€
(Map p92; ☎050 33 06 75; www.number11.be; Peerdenstraat 11; d €165-245; 📶) Featuring the distinctive ceramic works of Martine Bossuyt, this artistic, top-notch B&B, with logoed linens and pralines on the pillow, feels more like an intimate boutique hotel. There's a private salon and courtyard garden for the handful of guests.

Relais Bourgondisch Cruyce BOUTIQUE HOTEL €€€
(Map p92; ☎050 33 79 26; www.relaisbourgondischcruyce.be; Wollestraat 41-47; d €195-420) This luxurious little boutique hotel occupies a unique part-timbered medieval house that's been tastefully updated and graced with art, antiques, Persian carpets and fresh orchids. A special delight is relaxing in the canalside lounge while drooling tourists cruise past on their barge tours.

Most of the 16 rooms are somewhat small but full of designer fittings, including top-quality Vispring beds, Ralph Lauren fabrics and (in some) Philippe Starck bathrooms.

Dukes' Palace LUXURY HOTEL €€€
(Map p92; ☎050 44 78 88; www.hoteldukespalace.com; Prinsenhof 8; d €295-498; P📶🏊) Imposingly tall with a Disney-esque turret, this large-scale five-star hotel partly occupies the

Prinsenhof building, Bruges' 15th-century royal palace and the place where Phillip III of Burgundy created the chivalric Order of the Golden Fleece in 1430. It was massively rebuilt in 2008 – some guest rooms retain historical elements though, and the decor creates a timeless feel.

St-Anna

Bauhaus HOSTEL €
(Map p86; ☎050 34 10 93; www.bauhaus.be; Langestraat 145; hostel dm/tw €16/50, hotel s/d €16/50, 2-4 person apt per weekend from €240; @ wifi) One of Belgium's most popular hangouts for young travellers, this backpacker 'village' incorporates a hostel, apartments, a nightclub, internet cafe and a little chill-out room that's well hidden behind the reception and laundrette section at Langestraat 145. Simple and slightly cramped dorms are operated with key cards; hotel-section double rooms have private shower cubicles; bike hire is also available.

Take bus 6 or 16 from the train station.

B&B Degraeve B&B €€
(Map p86; ☎050 34 57 11; www.bedandbreakfastmarjandegraeve.be; Kazernevest 32; s/d/tr €50/65/100; closed Feb) Two remarkably eccentric guest rooms with shared musical bathrooms are overloaded with religious trinkets and doll parts. Draped in artificial flowers, the house has a pleasant if slightly out-of-centre location. Bicycle rental costs €6 per day. Try the homemade sweet apple wine (free tasting) and beer (€2).

Begijnhof Area

't Keizershof HOTEL €
(Map p86; ☎050 33 87 28; www.hotelkeizershof.be; Oostermeers 126; s €35-47, d €47; P wifi) Remarkably tasteful and well kept for this price, the seven simple rooms with shared bathrooms are above a former brasserie-cafe decorated with old radios (now used as the breakfast room). Free parking.

Hotel Egmond HOTEL €€
(Map p86; ☎050 34 14 45; www.egmond.be; Minnewater 15; s €89-125, d €98-140; P wifi) First impressions are truly exciting: a peaceful Minnewater park location, a classic step-gabled facade and ancient fireplaces in a medieval-styled lobby. Sadly, the guest rooms are an anticlimax, ranging from bland to dowdy.

North of the Centre

Tine's Guesthouse GUESTHOUSE €€
(☎050 34 50 18; users.telenet.be/nico.van.dale; Zwaluwenstraat 11; s/d €60/70; P wifi) Offers freshly decorated rooms and use of a kitchen, lounge room, top billiard table and small patio, while the 'suite' has a roof terrace. Special pluses here are Tine's effervescent hospitality, the great breakfast (including homemade pastries), free lunch packet, free bicycle hire and station pick-up – very helpful given the somewhat out-of-centre location. There's free street parking.

East of the Centre

Camping Memling CAMPGROUND €
(☎050 35 58 45; www.campingmemling.be; Veltemweg 109; sites/caravan €20/32; year-round; wifi) Quiet camping ground in St-Kruis where pitch prices assume two adults. Get off bus 11 at Vossensteert and walk back 400m towards Bruges.

Eating

From cosy *estaminets* (taverns) to first-class restaurants, Bruges has all bases covered.

Markt

Chip Vans FAST FOOD €
(Map p92; Markt; chips from €2.25; 10am-3am) Takeaway *frites* (chips) and hot dogs (from €3) sold from two green vans on the Markt.

Central Canal Area

Den Gouden Karpel SEAFOOD €
(Map p92; ☎050 33 33 89; www.dengoudenkarpel.be; Vismarkt 9-11; mains from €4; 11am-6pm Tue-Sat) Takeaway or eat in, this sleek little *café*/bar is a great location for a jumpingly fresh seafood lunch, right by the fish market. Crab sandwiches, smoked salmon salads, shrimp croquettes and oysters are on the menu.

Est Wijnbar TAPAS €
(Map p92; ☎050 33 38 39; www.wijnbarest.be; Braambergstraat 7; mains €10-14, tapas €4-10; 4pm-midnight Fri-Mon; ♪) This attractive little wine bar – the building dates back to 1637 – is a pleasantly informal supper spot, with raclette, pasta, snacks and salads on the menu, and tasty desserts. It's especially lively on Sunday nights, when you can catch live jazz, blues and occasionally other musical styles from 8.30pm.

Merveilleux Tearoom CAFE
(Map p92; ☎050 61 02 09; www.merveilleux.eu; Muntpoort 8; high tea €11, mains €15-24; ⏰10am-6pm) Elegant marble-floored tearoom on a cobbled passage near the Markt. Coffee comes with a dainty homemade biscuit and sometimes a little glass of strawberry ice cream or chocolate mousse. Pretty cakes and tea are on offer too.

Gran Kaffee De Passage BISTRO €
(Map p92; ☎050 34 02 32; www.passagebruges.com; Dweersstraat 26-28; mains €10-16.50; ⏰5-11pm Tue-Thu & Sun, noon-11pm Fri & Sat) A mix of regulars and travellers staying at the adjoining hostel, Passage, give this candle-lit, alternative art deco–styled bistro one of the best atmospheres in town. Its menu of hearty traditional dishes, such as *stoverij* (local meat in beer sauce), as well as filling tofu creations, is a bargain.

De Proeverie CAFE €
(Map p92; ☎050 33 08 87; www.deproeverie.be; Katelijnstraat 5-6; snacks from €5; ⏰9.30am-6pm) A chintzy but appealing tearoom serving a variety of teas, gloopy hot chocolate, milk-shakes and indulgent homemade sweets including crème brûlée, chocolate mousse and *merveilleux* cake. Coffee comes with generous goodies on the side.

★**De Stove** INTERNATIONAL €€
(Map p92; ☎050 33 78 35; www.restaurantdestove.be; Kleine St-Amandsstraat 4; mains €19-34, menu without/with wine €49/67; ⏰noon-1.30pm Sat & Sun, 7-9pm Fri-Tue) Just 20 seats keep this gem intimate. Fish caught daily is the house speciality, but the monthly changing menu also includes the likes of wild boar fillet on oyster mushrooms. Everything, from the bread to the ice cream, is homemade. Despite perennially rave reviews, this calm, one-room, family restaurant remains friendly, reliable and inventive, without a hint of tourist-tweeness.

★**Christophe** BISTRO €€
(Map p92; ☎050 34 48 92; www.christophe-brugge.be; Garenmarkt 34; mains €19-29; ⏰6pm-1am Thu-Mon) A cool late-night bistro with marble table tops and a decent range of Flemish staples including fresh Zeebrugge shrimps. An excellent late-nighter.

Den Dyjver BELGIAN €€
(Map p92; ☎050 33 60 69; www.dyver.be; Dijver 5; mains €17-32, tasting menu €49; ⏰noon-2pm & 6.30-9.30pm Fri-Mon) Den Dyjver is a pioneer of fine beer cuisine where you match the brew you drink with the one the chef used to create the sauce on your plate. But this is no pub: beers come in wine glasses served on starched table cloths in an atmosphere of Burgundian grandeur. The lunch menu includes *amuse-bouche,* nibbles and coffee.

LATE NIGHT, EARLY MORNING

If your stomach demands more than just chips or a kebab after 11pm, try the effortlessly elegant, open-kitchened restaurant **Christophe** (☎050 34 48 92; www.christophe-brugge.be; Garenmarkt 34; mains €17-30; ⏰6pm-1am Thu-Mon), which serves until 1am. Or, before 3am, you could tuck into typical Flemish fare at the cosily historic **'t Gulden Vlies** (Map p92; ☎050 33 47 09; www.tguldenvlies.be; Mallebergplaats 17; mains €14.50-25; ⏰7pm-3am Wed-Sun).

Most of the restaurants that line the Markt offer breakfasts with a view from €7, but check carefully what's included before sitting down. If you just want coffee and a croissant, the cheapest deal is at chain bakery **Panos** (Map p92; Zuidzandstraat 29; coffee/croissant €1.80/1.10; ⏰7am-6.30pm Mon-Sat, 11am-6.30pm Sun) whose Zuidzandstraat branch has plenty of seating upstairs and, unlike most other bakeries, no extra charge for eating in.

De Bottelier MEDITERRANEAN €€
(Map p92; ☎050 33 18 60; www.debottelier.com; St-Jakobsstraat 63; mains from €16; ⏰noon-10pm Tue-Fri, 7-10pm Sat) Decorated with hats and old clocks, this adorable little restaurant sits above a wine shop overlooking a delightful handkerchief of canalside garden. Pasta/veggie dishes cost from €9/13.50. Diners are predominantly local. Reservations are wise.

De Belegde Boterham BRASSERIE €€
(Map p92; ☎050 34 91 31; www.debelegdeboterham.be; Kleine St-Amandsstraat 5; mains from €12; ⏰noon-4pm Mon-Sat) Duck the tourist crowds at this popular lunch spot for well-heeled locals. The monochrome boutique styling is a bit formal, but it's a friendly place and the food – soups, sandwiches and large salads – is excellent, with fresh ingredients and tasty dressings. Good coffee, too.

Ryad INDIAN, MOROCCAN €€
(Map p92; ☎050 33 13 55; Hoogstraat 32; mains €18-24, lunch menu €10.50; ⏰noon-2.30pm & 6-10.30pm Thu-Mon) Indian curries supplement the usual couscous and tajines offered

by this atmospheric Moroccan restaurant that's heavily perfumed with incense. Upstairs is a cosy cushioned 'Berber' tea lounge.

Chagall BELGIAN €€

(Map p92; ☎050 33 61 12; www.restaurantchagall.be; St-Amandsstraat 40; mains €10-22; ⏰closed Wed) Chequered olive banquettes, candles, shelves cluttered with knick-knacks and an upright piano make you feel like you're dining in a family home. Seafood, such as several variations on eel, is Chagall's forte, but it also does daily meat specials and good deals on two- and three-course menus.

Bistro Arthies BISTRO €€

(Map p92; ☎050 33 43 13; www.arthies.com; Wollestraat 10; mains & mussels from €17; ⏰noon-10pm Wed-Mon) Managed by Arthies, an interior designer who looks like a dashingly Gothic Billy Connolly. He uses a projected clock, giant black flower bowls and stylishly wacky lamps to create an ambience that's eccentric yet fashion-conscious. There's an all-day, €18 three-course menu.

★**Den Gouden Harynck** INTERNATIONAL €€€

(Map p92; ☎050 33 76 37; www.dengoudenharynck.be; Groeninge 25; mains €38-46, set lunch menu €45, midweek dinner €60, surprise menu €89; ⏰noon-1.30pm & 7-9pm Tue-Fri, 7-9pm Sat) Behind an ivy-clad facade, this uncluttered Michelin-starred restaurant garners consistent praise and won't hurt the purse quite as severely as certain better-known competitors. A lovely location: both central and secluded; exquisite dishes might include noisettes of venison topped with lardo and quince puree or seed-crusted fillet of bream.

St-Anna

't Ganzespel BELGIAN €

(Map p86; ☎050 33 12 33; www.ganzespel.be; Ganzenstraat 37; mains from €9.50; ⏰6-10pm Fri-Sun) Providing a truly intimate eating experience in a lovely old gabled building, the owner serves classic Belgian dishes such as meatballs and *kalfsblanket* (veal in a creamy sauce), as well as pasta dishes. Upstairs are three idiosyncratic B&B guest rooms (double €55 to €85), one with a musical shower.

★**Pro Deo** BELGIAN €€

(Map p86; ☎050 33 73 55; www.bistroprodeo.be; Langestraat 161; mains €19-28; ⏰11.45am-1.45pm & 6-9.30pm Tue-Fri, 6-10pm Sat) A snug and romantic restaurant in a 16th-century whitewashed gabled building. The owner couple bring a personal touch, and serve up superb Belgian dishes such as *stoofvlees* (traditional stew).

★**In 't Nieuwe Museum** CAFE €€

(Map p86; ☎050 33 12 22; Hooistraat 42; mains €16-22; ⏰noon-2pm & 6-10pm Thu-Tue, closed lunch Sat) So called because of the museum-like collection of brewery plaques, money boxes and other mementos of *café* life adorning the walls, this family-owned local favourite serves five kinds of *dagschotel* (dish of the day) for lunch (€7 to €12.50), and succulent meat cooked on a 17th-century open fire in the evenings.

Specials include veggie burgers, eel dishes, ribs, steaks and creamy *vispannetje* (fish casserole).

De Karmeliet INTERNATIONAL €€€

(Map p86; ☎050 33 82 59; www.dekarmeliet.be; Langestraat 19; mains from €70, menus from €85; ⏰noon-1.30pm & 7-9.30pm Tue-Sat) Chef Geert Van Hecke's intricate combinations, such as stuffed courgette with poached quail eggs, caviar, king crab and mousseline champagne, have earned him a trio of Michelin stars. The setting is slightly austere, but gourmands will be too busy swooning to notice. Lunch is slightly easier on your wallet. Book well ahead, especially for weekends.

Sans Cravate FRENCH €€€

(Map p86; ☎050 67 83 10; www.sanscravate.be; Langestraat 159; mains €38-42, menus €58-89; ⏰noon-2pm Tue-Fri, 7-9.30pm Tue-Sat) Bare brick walls, a modernistic fireplace and striking contemporary modern ceramics form a stage for this open-kitchened 'cooking theatre' that prides itself on its gastronomic French cuisine and fresh ingredients.

Begijnhof Area

De Bron VEGETARIAN €

(Map p86; ☎050 33 45 26; Katelijnestraat 82; snacks from €5; ⏰11.45am-2pm Mon-Fri; 🌿) By the time this glass-roofed restaurant's doors open, a queue has usually formed outside, full of diners keen to get vegetarian fare direct from *de bron* (the source). Dishes are available in small, medium and large, and there are some delicious soups, such as pumpkin. Vegans are catered for on request.

De Stoepa BISTRO €€

(Map p86; ☎050 33 04 54; www.stoepa.be; Oostmeers 124; ⏰noon-2pm & 6pm-midnight Tue-Sat, noon-3pm & 6-11pm Sun) A gem of a place in a peaceful residential setting with a slightly hippy/Buddhist feel. Oriental statues, terracotta-coloured walls, a metal stove and wooden floors and furniture give a homey but stylish feel. Best of all though is the leafy terrace garden. Tuck into the upmarket bistro-style food.

Drinking & Nightlife

Tempting terraces line the Markt, while for canal views it's hard to beat the seats outside *cafés* **'t Klein Venetie** (Map p92; Braambergstraat 1) or **Uilenspiegel** (Map p92; Langestraat 2-4). If it's cold, a cosy place for canal-view beers is the semi-medieval-styled *café* within the Hotel Bourgoensch Hof. And if you want a big night out, head for the clubs and bars of Kuipersstraat.

't Brugs Beertje CAFE
(Map p92; www.brugsbeertje.be; Kemelstraat 5; 4pm-midnight Mon, Thu & Sun, to 1am Fri & Sat) Legendary throughout Bruges, Belgium and beyond for its hundreds of Belgian brews, this cosy *bruin café* (brown cafe) is filled with old advertising posters and locals who are part of the furniture. It's one of those perfect beer-bars with smoke-yellowed walls, enamel signs, hop-sprig ceilings and knowledgeable staff to help you choose from a book full of brews.

Herberg Vlissinghe CAFE
(Map p92; 050 34 37 37; www.cafevlissinghe.be; Blekerstraat 2; 11am-10pm Wed & Thu, to midnight Fri & Sat, to 7pm Sun) Luminaries have frequented Bruges' oldest pub for 500 years; local legend has it that Rubens once painted an imitation coin on the table here and then did a runner. The interior is gorgeously preserved with wood panelling and a wood-burning stove, but in summer the best seats are in the shady garden where you can play boules.

Nice snacks (€4.50) such as croques, soup and cheese and meat platters.

De Garre PUB
(Map p92; 050 34 10 29; www.degarre.be; Garre 1; noon-midnight Mon-Thu, to 1am Fri & Sat) Try their very own and fabulous Garre draught beer, which comes with a thick floral head in a glass that's almost a brandy balloon; they'll only serve you three of these due to the head-spinning 11% alcohol percentage. The hidden two-floor *estaminet* (tavern) also stocks dozens of other fine Belgian brews, including remarkable Struise Pannepot (€3.50).

Rose Red BAR
(Map p92; 050 33 90 51; www.cordoeanier.be/en/rosered.php; Cordoeaniersstraat 16; 11am-11pm Tue-Sun) Outstanding beers from 50 of the best breweries in Belgium, served by charming and informative staff in this pink-hued and rose-scattered bar. It keeps five to six beers on tap and 150 bottles, or you can taste four beers for €10. Snack on tapas-style dishes, including cheese produced by the Trappist monks of Chimay (from €3.50).

De Republiek PUB
(Map p92; www.derepubliek.be; St-Jakobsstraat 36; 11am-late) Set around a courtyard comprising characterful brick buildings, this big buzzing space is super-popular with Brugelingen (Bruges locals). DJs hit the decks on Friday and Saturday nights and there's a range of well-priced meals, including vegetarian options, available until midnight, plus a long cocktail list.

De Windmolen PUB
(Map p86; 050 33 97 39; Carmersstraat 135; beer/snacks/pasta from €1.80/4.50/8.50; 10am-late Mon-Thu, to 3am Fri & Sun) Quaint corner *café* with a sunny terrace overlooking one of the St-Anna windmills.

Cambrinus PUB
(Map p92; 050 33 23 28; www.cambrinus.eu; Philipstockstraat 19; 11am-11pm Sun-Thu, to late Fri & Sat) Hundreds of varieties of beer are available at this 17th-century sculpture-adorned brasserie-pub, as well as traditional Belgian and Italian inspired snacks and meals.

't Poatersgat PUB
(Map p92; www.poatersgat.com; Vlaamingstraat 82; 5pm-late) Look carefully for the concealed hole in the wall and follow the staircase down into this cross-vaulted cellar glowing with ethereal white lights and flickering candles. 't Poatersgat (which means 'the Monk's Hole' in the local dialect) has 120 Belgian beers on the menu, including a smashing selection of Trappists.

Cafédraal BAR
(Map p92; 050 34 08 45; www.cafedraal.be; Zilverstraat 38; beer/wine/cocktails from €2.80/5/10; 6pm-1am Tue-Thu, to 3am Fri & Sat) Attached to an upmarket seafood restaurant (mains €25 to €48), this remarkable cocktail bar is enclosed by beech hedges and red-brick-gabled buildings, and displays bottles in gilt 'holy' niches. Suavely classy.

L'Estaminet PUB
(Map p92; 050 33 09 16; Park 5; beer/snacks/pasta from €1.80/6/8; 11.30am-11pm Tue-Sun, 4-11pm Thu) With its dark timber beams, low lighting, convivial clatter and park setting, L'Estaminet scarcely seems to have changed since it opened in 1900. It's primarily a

drinking spot, but also serves time-honoured dishes such as spaghetti bolognaise with a baked cheese crust (€10). Summer sees its loyal local following flow out onto the front terrace.

Vintage BAR
(Map p92; ☎050 34 30 63; www.thevintage.be; Westmeers 13; ⌚11am-1am Mon, Tue & Thu, to 2am Fri & Sat, noon-1am Sun) Unusually hip for Bruges, with a '60s/'70s vibe and a vintage Vespa hanging from the roof. The sunny terrace is a nice spot for a Jupiler, and the theme parties can be raucous.

Opus Latino CAFE
(Map p92; ☎050 33 97 46; Burg 15; beer/snacks/tapas from €2.20/8.50/6; ⌚11am-11pm Thu-Tue) Modernist *café* with weather-worn terrace tables right at the waterside – where a canal dead-ends beside a Buddha-head fountain. Access is via the easily missed shopping passage that links Wollestraat to Burg, emerging near the Basilica of the Holy Blood. Serves tapas, as well as more substantial snacks.

☆ Entertainment

You can hear low-key jazz and blues every Sunday night from 8pm at the loveable Est Wijnbar (p98).

Cultuurcentrum Brugge (☎info 050 44 30 40, tickets 050 44 30 60; www.ccbrugge.be) coordinates theatrical and concert events at several venues, including the majestic 1869 theatre **Koninklijke Stadsschouwburg** (Map p92; ☎050 44 30 60; Vlamingstraat 29), out-of-centre **MaZ** (Magdalenastraat 27) and experimental little **Biekorf Theaterzaal** (Map p92; Kuipersstraat 3) in the public-library complex.

Concertgebouw CONCERT HALL
(Map p92; ☎050 47 69 99; www.concertgebouw.be; 't Zand 34; tickets from €10) Bruges' stunning 21st-century concert hall is the work of architects Paul Robbrecht and Hilde Daem and takes its design cues from the city's three famous towers and red bricks. Theatre, classical music and dance are regularly staged. The tourist office is situated at street level.

★ **Retsin's Lucifernum** CLUB
(Map p92; ☎0476 35 06 51; www.lucifernum.be; Twijnstraat 6-8; admission incl drink €10; ⌚8-11pm Sun) A former Masonic lodge owned by a self-proclaimed vampire: ring the bell on a Sunday night, pass the voodoo temple and hope you're invited inside where an otherworldly candlelit bar may be serving potent rum cocktails and serenading you with live Latin music. Or maybe not. It's always a surprise. Don't miss the graves in the tropical garden.

In case you're wondering, the permanent scaffolding is an artwork – and a thorn in the side of the local council.

Cinema Lumière CINEMA
(Map p92; ☎050 34 34 65; www.lumiere.be; St-Jakobsstraat 36) Just a couple of blocks back from the Markt, this art-house cinema screens a well-chosen program of foreign films in their original languages and is home to the Cinema Novo Film Festival.

Du Phare LIVE MUSIC
(Map p86; ☎050 34 35 90; www.duphare.be; Sasplein 2; ⌚kitchen 11.30am-3pm & 6pm-midnight, bar 11.30am-late, closed Tue) Tucked into the remains of one of Bruges' original town gates, this off-the-beaten-track tavern serves up huge portions of couscous (and offers free bread, a rarity in Belgium). But Du Phare is best known for its live blues and jazz sessions – check the website for dates. Bus 4 stops out the front.

Entrenous CLUB
(Map p86; ☎050 34 10 93; www.bauhauszaal.be; Langestraat 145; ⌚10pm-late Fri & Sat) A real nightclub in the centre of the city. A very youthful crowd packs out the DJ nights, gigs and after parties.

Cactus Muziekcentrum LIVE MUSIC
(☎050 33 20 14; www.cactusmusic.be; Magdalenastraat 27) Though small, this is the city's top venue for contemporary and world music, both live bands and international DJs. It also organises festivals including July's **Cactus Music Festival** (www.cactusfestival.be), held in the Minnewater park at the southern edge of the old city.

Vinkenzettingen LIVE PERFORMANCE
(Map p86; www.avibo.be; Hugo Verrieststraat) There's no set schedule, but one place you might witness the eccentric (if hardly exciting) 'traditional sport' of finch singing is along Hugo Verrieststraat, early on summer Sunday mornings. Dating from the late 16th century, the idea is to find which caged chaffinch, within a wooden box, can chirrup more times in an hour than its competitor.

Only a specific 'susk-WEET' sound is acceptable, with some potty *vinkeniers* (finch fanciers) claiming that birds from Wallonia can't pronounce correct Flemish!

WORTH A TRIP

CASTLES AROUND BRUGES

There are several attractive castles right on Bruges' doorstep. Moated Kasteel Tillegem, 7km southwest of the city, is now used as district offices and is set in the extensive public parkland of Domaine Tillegembos. Also accessed off Torhoutsteenweg (the N32 road leading south) in Sint-Michiels, the 1904 **Kasteel Tudor** (www.conquistador.be; Zeeweg 147) is backed by the beech woods of Domein Beisbroek, part of the 42km Bossenroute cycle loop. In an outbuilding, the little-heralded **Mary Tudor Tavern** (Domein Beisbroek; lunch €12; ⌚11am-7pm Wed-Sun) makes a decent refreshment stop if cycling past. **Kasteel van Loppem** (☎050 82 22 45; www.kasteelvanloppem.be; Steenbrugsestraat 26; adult/child €4/1; ⌚10am-noon & 2-6pm Tue-Sun Jul & Aug, 2-5pm Wed, Sat & Sun Apr-Oct) is a mid-19th-century brick castle-mansion which had its moment of fame at the end of WWI when it was briefly home to the Belgian king and the command centre for the Belgian army. Kasteel van Loppem is accessed by the first lane to the left after the southbound N309 passes beneath the E40 highway. At the entrance of the grounds is a small **labyrinth** (Doolhof; admission €1.25; ⌚2-6pm Sat & Sun Apr-Oct; 🚌72, 74).

Joey's Café LIVE MUSIC
(Map p92; ☎050 34 12 64; Zuidzandstraat 16A; ⌚11.30am-late Mon-Sat) These days Joey's is run by Stevie, who performs with local band Cajun Moon; consequently, this dark, intimate bar is a gathering spot for Bruges' musos. You can sometimes catch live music here (call to check dates) or chill out with a creamy Stevie cocktail or Joey's Tripel any time.

Shopping

The main shopping thoroughfares are Steenstraat and Geldmuntstraat/Noordzandstraat, along with linking pedestrianised Zilverpand. There are morning markets on Wednesdays (Markt) and Saturdays ('t Zand).

Several shops offer a vast array of Belgian beers and their associated glasses to take away. Compare prices carefully and remember that 'standard' brews like Leffe or Chimay will generally be far cheaper in supermarkets.

★'t Apostelientje HANDICRAFTS
(Map p86; www.apostelientje.be; Balstraat 11; ⌚1-5pm Tue, 9.30am-12.15pm & 1.15-5pm Wed-Sat, 10am-1pm Sun) Bruges overflows with lace vendors, but this sweet little 'museum shop' is well off the normal tourist trail. The delicate garments and gifts on sale are made from beautiful and authentic lace, handmade by two sisters and their mother; the husband of one of the sisters makes the wooden bobbins. An unusual opportunity to buy the real Bruges deal lace-wise.

★Diksmuids Boterhuis FOOD
(Map p92; www.diksmuidsboterhuis.be; Geldmuntstraat 23; ⌚10am-12.30pm & 2-6.30pm) This gorgeously traditional grocery is now surrounded by mainstream boutiques but has been here since 1933. Decked out with red and white gingham flounces and featuring a ceiling hung with sausages, it purveys cheeses, honey, cold meat and mustard.

Bacchus Cornelius FOOD & DRINK
(Map p92; www.bacchuscornelius.com; Academiestraat 17; ⌚1-6.30pm) There's a cornucopia of 450 beers and rare *gueuzes* (type of lambic beer), as well as *jenevers* (gin) and liqueurs flavoured with elderflower, cranberries and cherries. Ask the shop owner if you can try her home-brewed silky smooth *jenever*, made with real chocolate. The two pianos are there for shoppers to play, and an open fire in winter adds to the cosy vibe.

The adjoining chocolate shop is run by the owner's husband.

Chocolate Line FOOD
(Map p92; www.thechocolateline.be; Simon Stevinplein 19; per kg €50; ⌚10am-6pm) Bruges has 50 chocolate shops, but just five where chocolates are handmade on the premises. Of those, the Chocolate Line is the brightest and best. Wildly experimental flavours by 'shock-o-latier' Dominique Persoone include bitter Coca-Cola, Cuban cigar, wasabi and black olive, tomato and basil; it also sells pots of chocolate body paint (complete with a brush).

Dille & Kamille HOMEWARES
(Map p92; ☎050 34 11 80; www.dille-kamille.com; Simon Stevinplein 17–18) A great homeware store, with the covetable kitchenware, crockery and fabrics grouped by colour. You'll find gadgets you never knew you wanted, alongside all sorts of jars, bowls, cutlery, organic tea towels, soaps, sieves and scales. Remarkably cheap given the quality.

Rombaux MUSIC
(Map p92; ☎050 33 25 75; www.rombaux.be; Mallebergplaats 13; ⏰2-6.30pm Mon, 10am-12.30pm & 2-6.30pm Tue-Fri, 10am-6pm Sat) Here since 1920, this large, family-run music shop specialises in classical music, jazz, world music, folk and Flemish music, and is the kind of place where you can browse for hours. It also sells sheet music and accoustic guitars.

L'Heroine FASHION
(Map p92; www.lheroine.be; Noordzandstraat 32; ⏰10.30am-6pm Mon-Sat) The cool concrete exterior of L'Heroine stands out among the chains. Here you'll find established Belgian designers Dries Van Noten and Ann Demeulemeester as well as young talents including Christian Wijnants. It stocks beautiful silk print dresses, asymmetrical tailoring and sumptuous scarves and drapes – staff can help you combine pieces for a strong, idiosyncratic look.

De Biertempel FOOD & DRINK
(Map p92; ☎050 34 37 30; Philipstockstraat 7; ⏰10am-6pm) Beer specialist shop where you can even pick up a well-priced bottle of Westvleteren.

De Striep COMICS
(Map p92; ☎050 33 71 12; www.striepclub.be; Katelijnestraat 42; ⏰10am-12.30pm & 1.30-7pm Tue-Sat, 2-6pm Sun) Look for Thibaut Vandorselaer's wonderful illustrated guides at this colourful comic shop. There's also a comprehensive collection in Dutch, French and English. You'll find Bruges-set comics by the counter.

Zucchero FOOD
(Map p92; ☎050 33 39 62; www.confiserie-zucchero.be; Mariastraat 18; ⏰10am-6pm Tue-Sat, 11am-6pm Sun) A fabulous new sweet shop with eye-popping fuschia decor. It sells umpteen varieties of fudge and candies, plus ice cream to go. Check out the candy sticks being hand-chopped by the young owners.

2-Be FOOD & DRINK
(Map p92; www.2-be.biz; Wollestraat 53; ⏰10am-7pm) Vast range of Belgian products from beers to biscuits in a snazzy, central location, but prices can be exorbitant. Their 'beer wall' is worth a look, as is the wonderfully located canalside bar terrace, where 'monster' 3L draught beers (€19.50) are surely Belgium's biggest.

Mille-Fleurs HOMEWARES
(Map p92; ☎050 34 54 54; www.millefleurstapestries.com; Wollestraat 33) A cornucopia of Flemish tapestries machine-made near Wetteren. Worth a browse if you want to take a piece of Belgium home with you. It also sells throws, tapestry cushions, runners and doilies, and bags and purses.

Madam Mim FASHION, ANTIQUES
(Map p92; www.madammim.be; Hoogstraat 29; ⏰11am-6pm Wed-Mon) Quirky clothes handmade from vintage fabrics by shopowner Mim herself, as well as '60s crockery, cut glass, glorious hats and '70s kids' clothes. You can also pick up antique lace for a fraction of the cost it goes for elsewhere.

Olivier Strelli FASHION
(Map p92; ☎050 34 38 37; strelli.be; Zuidzandstraat 11/13; ⏰10am-6pm Mon-Sat) Belgium's best-known designer, who has an emphasis on colourful scarves, shoes and watches.

De Reyghere Reisboekhandel BOOKS
(Map p92; ☎050 33 34 03; www.reisboekhandel.be; Markt 13; ⏰9.30am-noon Tue-Sat & 2-6pm Mon-Sat) Well-stocked travel bookshop.

ℹ Information

INTERNET ACCESS

Bauhaus Cybercafe (Bauhaus Hostel, Langestraat 145; per hr €3; ⏰9am-10pm) Town's hippest internet cafe.

LAUNDRY

Wassalon (Ezelstraat 51) Washing and drying services.

LEFT LUGGAGE

Train Station Lockers (small/large per 24hr €3/4) Left-luggage facilities at the train station.

MEDICAL SERVICES

Akademisch Ziekenhuis St-Jan (☎050 45 21 11; Ruddershove 10) The city's main hospital has a 24-hour emergency unit.

Apotheek Soetaert (☎050 33 25 93; Vlamingstraat 17; ⏰9am-12.30pm & 2-6.30pm Mon-Sat, closed Wed afternoon) Charming olde-worlde pharmacy.

Doctors On Weekend Duty (☎050 36 40 10)

Pharmacists On Weekend Duty (☎050 40 61 62)

MONEY

There are ATMs at the post office, **Fortis Bank** (Simon Stevinplein 3) and **Europabank** (Vlamingstraat 13).

Fintro (Vlamingstraat 18; ⏰8.30am-4.45pm Mon-Fri, 9am-12.30pm & 2-4pm Sat) Offers better commission-free rates for cash than most competitors. Cashing travellers cheques incurs a €2.48 charge (up to €500).

POST

Post Office (Map p92; ☎050 33 14 11; Markt 5) Gorgeous building with spires, brick gables and a stone arcade.

TOURIST INFORMATION

There are two offices; both sell extensive €2 guide booklets and €0.50 city maps. They also stock the great map-guide Use-it (www.use-it.be), which offers useful, funky and friendly local tips on a decent map. It's free but you'll have to ask for it.

Tourist Information Counter (Map p86; Train Station; ⏲10am-5pm Mon-Fri, to 2pm Sat)

WEBSITES

Lonely Planet Bruges (www.lonelyplanet.com/belgium/flanders/bruges) For planning advice, author recommendations, traveller reviews and insider tips.

ℹ Getting There & Around

BICYCLE

B-Bike (☎0499 70 50 99; Zand Parking 26; per hr/day €4/12; ⏲10am-7pm Apr-Oct)

Rijwielhandel Erik Popelier (☎050 34 32 62; www.fietsenpopelier.be; Mariastraat 26; per hr/half-/full day €4/8/12, tandem €10/17/25; ⏲10am-6pm) Good bicycles for adults and kids; helmets for hire, free map, no deposit.

BUS

Eurolines (☎02-274 13 50; www.eurolines.be) has buses to London (around €30) departing at 5.30pm from the bus station, but tickets must be booked by phone, online or in Ghent. Eurolines has no Bruges ticket office, but **Flibco** (www.flibco.com) has an efficient service from Charleroi airport (€20 one way). For **city buses** (single/day-pass €1.60/6; ⏲5.30am-11pm) you'll save money purchasing tickets (single/day-pass €1.20/5) at the **De Lijn Office** (Map p86; www.delijn.be). Any bus marked 'Centrum' runs to the Markt. To return to the station, the best central stop is Biekorf.

CAR

Given central Bruges' nightmarish one-way system, the best idea for drivers is to use the large covered **car park** (Train station; per hr/24hr €0.50/2.50) beside the train station. Bargain fees here include a free return bus ticket to the centre for the car's driver and all passengers. Just show your parking ticket when boarding the bus. If you park elsewhere, be aware that non-metered street parking still requires you to set your parking disc (maximum stay four hours). Traffic wardens are merciless.

TAXI

Taxis wait on the Markt and in front of the train station. Otherwise phone ☎050 334 444 or ☎050 384 660.

TRAIN

Bruges' **train station** (☎050 30 24 24) is 1.5km south of the Markt. Twice-hourly trains run to Kortrijk (€7.70, fast/slow 38/51 minutes) and to Brussels (€14.10, 62 minutes) via Ghent (€6.50, 23 minutes). Hourly trains go to Antwerp (€14.80, 80 minutes), Knokke (€3.70, 20 minutes), Ostend (€4.10, 13 minutes) and Zeebrugge (€3, 13 minutes) via Lissewege.

For Ypres (Ieper), take the train to Roeselare then bus 95 via Langemark or 94 via Passendale, Tyne Cot and Zonnebeke, all places you're likely to want to see anyway.

Train Station Luggage Room (Train station; per half-/full day €6.50/9.50, deposit €12.50; ⏲7am-8pm) Must return same day.

Damme

POP 10,900

The historic inland-port village of Damme is so super-pretty that in summer it's all too often overwhelmed with cars, cyclists, walkers and boat-loads of day trippers jostling down the dead-straight 5km of road/canal from Bruges, the approach signalled by the scarlet sails of a working windmill. Drive or cycle another 2km east and you'll quickly leave some 90% of the tourist crowds behind. Then turn south where two canals meet and pick a random spot to admire the soaring rows of wind-warped poplars. Whether reflected in glass-still waters or fog-draped on a misty winter's morning, the scene is a magical, visual poem drawn straight from Jacques Brel.

Charming Damme village is little more than a single street plus a main square upon which the fine Gothic stadhuis is fronted by a statue of Jacob Van Maerlant, a 13th-century Flemish poet who lived and died in Damme. He's buried in the 13th-century **Onze Lieve Vrouwekerk** (Our Lady's Church; church/tower €0.50/1; ⏲2-5.30pm Tue-Sun May-Sep), which was vastly expanded in the village's heyday, only to be partially torn down when things started to wane.

Opposite the stadhuis, a restored patrician's house is home to the **tourist office** (☎050 28 86 10; www.toerismedamme.be; Jacob Van Maerlantstraat 3; ⏲9am-noon & 3-5pm Mon-Sat, 9am-noon & 2-5pm Sun) and the **Uilenspiegel Museum** (adult/concession/family €2.50/1.50/5; ⏲9am-noon & 3-5pm Mon-Sat, 9am-noon & 2-5pm Sun) recounting the stories of Uilenspiegel, a villain in German folklore but a jester and freedom fighter in Flemish literature.

Nearby, the **Museum Sint-Janshospitaal** (Kerkstraat 33; admission €1.50; ⏲2-6pm daily,

MAKING THE MOST OF THE COAST

The coast has swimming beaches right along its length, and almost all resorts will rent a curious selection of kids' buggies and go-cart-like *kwistax*. But there's a whole lot more if you know where to look. A useful starting point is website www.dekust.be, or use the quick reference list below.

Best for...

Art St-Idesbald (Delvaux), Ostend

Casinos Knokke, Ostend

Medieval townscapes Veurne, Nieuwpoort, Lissewege

Nudist beaches Bredene (Renbaan tram stop)

Old-world elegance De Haan, De Zoute

Horseback fishermen Oostduinkerke

Russian submarine Zeebrugge

Simulated storms Blankenberge Pier, Oostduinkerke

Theme park De Panne

Upmarket boutiques Knokke

Walking Het Zwin, de Panne

WWII sea defences Ostend

Yacht and boat trips Nieuwpoort

Save on Entrance Fees

Note that many entry fees can be reduced with little Vlanderen Passie cards that you'll see hanging on boards in information offices and some hotels. In some cases (like Ostend's Earth Explorer) you can even get two-for-one deals.

The Coastal Tram

De Kusttram (www.delijn.be) coastal trams trundle all the way along the Belgian coast from Knokke to De Panne/Adinkerke, departing every 15 minutes from 5.30am to 11pm. The full route takes just over two hours. Single tickets cost €1.80/3 for a short/long journey. A one-/three-/five-day pass costs €5/10/15, or €7/12/18 purchased aboard.

plus 11am-noon Tue-Thu, Sat & Sun) was founded in 1249 and in addition to being a museum, also houses over 60 elderly people as well as a small community of Augustine nuns. There are occasional organ concerts in the chapel, and the museum contains a fairly absorbing collection of ecclesiastical garments and paintings, Delftware, and glass and oak furniture.

Damme is full of *cafés* and eateries with outside seating, but you'll find other less tourist-swamped taverns and restaurants along surrounding canal tow-paths every kilometre or two. However, many go into semi-hibernation in winter.

The classic if somewhat overrated way to visit Damme is to take a lazy 35-minute canal trip on the Lamme Goedzak tourist paddle steamer (p96). It departs every two hours from Bruges' Noorweegse Kaai, reached by bus 4 from the Markt. Alternatively bus 43 (€2, 20 minutes) runs every two hours until 3.30pm, April to September only. Or you can cycle.

THE COAST

Virtually all of Belgium's 66km coastline is fronted with a superbly wide, hard-sand beach. However, while some remnant sand dunes survive, the coast is predominantly backed by a succession of bland, concrete-blighted resorts. De Haan, central Nieuwpoort and outer parts of wealthy Knokke-Heist are the only real exceptions. Every settlement offers a wide selection of accommodation, but heavy bookings mean finding a room can still be hard in summer. Out of season many towns feel deserted, but with its regular events and conventions, hub-town Ostend manages to keep a lively vibe year-round.

Knokke-Heist

POP 34,000

Knokke is the preferred summer destination for Belgium's bourgeoisie. It's a sprawling place with a renowned nightlife scene that caters to a rather insular clique. Architecturally, Knokke's monotonous central high-rises look far from elite, but there's a plenty of art galleries and swanky shops, while low-rise mansions extend for several kilometres through neighbouring Duinburgen and De Zoute. Within the **Casino Knokke** (☎050 63 05 05; www.grandcasnoknokke.be/; Zeedijk-Albertstrand 509) is an incredible 72m circular mural by René Magritte and a superb 1974 Paul Delvaux lit by one of Europe's biggest glass chandeliers. However, none of the above is visible to gamblers or visitors. Ask at the **tourist office** (☎050 63 03 80; www.knokke-heist.info; Zeedijk-Knokke 660; ⏰8.30am-6pm) if they plan a tour.

Het Zwin

Around 5km northeast of Knokke, Het Zwin was once one of the world's busiest waterways, connecting Bruges with the sea. Howevver, in medieval times the river silted up, devastating Bruges' economy. The marshy area is now a reserve, a tranquil region of polders, ponds, scrub forest and mudflats that blush purple with *zwinnebloem* (sea lavender). Migrating swans, ducks and reed geese arrive here seasonally and there are populations of eagle owls and storks. To peruse the area from a distance (for free), walk or cycle a thoroughly upgraded 2.8km circular walk that starts down the promenade from Knokke's Surfers' Paradise beach bar (accessed from the easternmost end of Zwinlaan then by walking up Appelzakstraat and turning right) and ends at the 'flying' hare statue. The park is only accessible on foot; park your car at Bronlaan.

To walk in parts of the reserve, rather than simply looking down on it from the dunes, visit the **Het Zwin Nature Park** (☎050 60 70 86; www.zwin.be; Graaf Leon Lippensdreef 8; adult/child €2/1; ⏰9am-5.30pm Easter-Sep, to 4.30pm Oct-Easter, closed Mon Sep-Jun, closed Dec). Rubber boots might prove useful if you've come for more than the 3pm stork-feeding 'show'. Chose '*luisterwandeling*' from the website download options for a guided walk (English available) for your MP3 player or hire an audio guide (€2.50). Bus 12/13 (hourly in summer) gets you here.

De Haan

POP 11,700

Prim and proper De Haan (Le Coq) is Belgium's most compact and engaging beach resort. Its most famous visitor, Albert Einstein, lived here for a few months after fleeing Hitler's Germany in 1933.

Several fanciful half-timbered hotels and a scattering of tasteful eateries, bakeries and shops form an appealing knot around a cottage-style former tram station that houses the **tourist office** (☎059 24 21 35; www.dehaan.be; Koninklijk Plein; ⏰9.30am-6.30pm Jul & Aug, 10am-noon & 2-5pm Apr-Jun & Sep-Oct, Sat & Sun only Nov-Mar). Leopoldlaan leads 600m north to the beach, passing big bike-rental shop **Fietsen Andre** (www.fietsenandre.be; Leopoldlaan 9; bicycle per day/week/month €13/35/70, 1-/2-/3-/4-person kwistax per hr €5/10/15/20; ⏰9am-6pm) and **La Pontinière**, a distinctive circular park. East of the park, Normandiëlaan leads west to an area of indulgent mansions, some whitewashed and thatched, in lanes that undulate gently through what were once wild dunes.

When originally built in the late 19th century, the palatial town hall/police station at the northern edge of La Pontinière was De Haan's main seafront resort hotel. A century's land reclamation means that the beach now starts 300m further north with a promenade raised high enough above the sands that sea views are not hidden by all the beach huts as they are at other Belgian resorts. If it's too cold to stay outside, get a drink from the modest Strand Hotel and watch the sun set into the sea from its glassed-in terrace (beer from €2.30).

A new watersports centre is under construction at the eastern end of the promenade. De Haan is accessible form Knokke on the coastal tram (day pass €5, one hour).

Sleeping

La Tourelle B&B €€

(☎059 23 34 54; www.latourelle.be; Vondellaan 4; s/d/tr from €65/82/125; ⏰Feb-Nov; 📶) Just behind the town hall, this adorable family

WHY THE COCK?

According to local legend, De Haan (meaning 'The Rooster'), got its name because it had no lighthouse and in fog the fishermen used the sound of crowing cocks to work out where the shore was.

house-hotel occupies a pale, turreted mansion dating back to around 1912. Fully upgraded decor feels like Laura Ashley gone sailing. Rooms aren't large but they cram in contemporary four-poster beds, trestle tables and bow-tied lamps. There's a good free breakfast spread and day-round help-yourself coffee, plus a little roof-terrace sun deck.

Book well ahead to get the tower room (*torenkamer*, €98).

Manoir Carpe Diem HOTEL €€€
(☎059 23 32 20; www.manoircarpediem.com; Prins Karellaan 12; s/d/ste from €155/180/200; ⏱closed Jan–mid-Feb;) This cosy yet indulgent little hotel is set on top of a knoll, 400m back from the beach amid the finest local villas. Classical music, oil paintings, aged silverware, log fires and hunting prints create a welcoming atmosphere in the bar and lounge.

De Coqisserie GUESTHOUSE €€€
(☎059 43 00 43; www.decoqisserie.be; Koninklijke Baan 29; r/loft/apt from €120/165/185;) Very close to the beach, De Coqisserie is a stylish coffee-house restaurant with sleekly appointed new rooms and luxuriously modern apartments above. Save €15 if staying two nights or longer.

Zeebrugge

Initially built between 1895 and 1907, Zeebrugge's enormous artificial harbour had been in use less than a decade when Allied forces sank ships to block its entrance, thus preventing German naval use during WWI. Further bombed in WWII, the harbour finally reopened to sea traffic in 1957. The departure terminals for overnight P&O ferries to Hull are 2km north of Zeebrugge-Strandwijk tram stop, or 3km from Zeebrugge train station. It's an unpleasant walk. It's far better to arrive directly at the boat on the connecting bus from Bruges bus station.

Zeebrugge's play for the tourist euro is **Seafront** (www.seafront.be; adult/child €12.50/9; ⏱departs 7.30pm), whose main attractions are a parked Russian submarine and a lightship (sister to the one you'll see in Antwerp).

Lissewege

Though only 7km south of brutally functional Zeebrugge, the cute little village of Lissewege is a world away with its pretty whitewashed cottages and oversized brick church. Set in meadows 1.6km north of Lissewege, a sturdy 13th-century barn is the last remnant of the original Abdij Ter Doest, a once-powerful abbey ruined during the religious wars in 1569. Amid numerous sculptures, a smaller abbey farm, rebuilt in 1651, now hosts the very appealing **Hostellerie Hof Ter Doest** (☎050 54 40 82; www.terdoest.be; Ter Doeststraat 4; s/d €110/130), combining an excellent restaurant, six-room boutique hotel and apartment-sized lofts. Guests have use of a small hammam in the former stables and a sauna in a wheeled wagon facing the reed-filled canal outside. The village is accessible by regular buses from Zeebrugge (28 minutes). Bicycle hire is available.

Ostend (Oostende)

POP 69,000

Bustling Ostend (Oostende in Dutch, Ostende in French) is primarily a domestic seaside resort. Along its remarkably wide sandy beach is a spacious promenade surveyed by shoulder-to-shoulder tearooms with glassed-in terraces. But it's also rich in history. As a fortified port, it was ravaged by a four-year siege (1600 to 1604) as the last 'Belgian' city to refuse Spanish reconquest. Later it bloomed as one of Europe's most stylish seaside resorts. Most of that style was bombed into memories during WWII when German occupying forces (re)built the remarkable Atlantikwall sea defences that are today the town's most fascinating sight. In the postwar era, Ostend was rebuilt as a grid of entirely unaesthetic blocks, but its nightlife is accessible and its plethora of ho-hum hotels offer ample accommodation for any overspill from nearby Bruges.

Sights

The tourist office's **City Pass** (www.visitoostende.be/en/city-pass; 24-/48-/72hr/annual pass €12/15/20/25) gives free entry to eight main attractions but not Earth Explorer. Take at least the 48-hour version; seeing everything in one day is virtually impossible.

Central Ostend

Pier Area WATERFRONT
It's a pleasant diversion to watch squawking gulls scavenging from beam-netted sole-fishing boats as they unload behind the little **Fish Market** (Vistrap). The quayside road is backed with wall-to-wall fish restaurants, a tiny **Aquarium** (☎059 50 08 76; adult/child €2/1; ⏱10am-5:30pm) and two operators offering summer sea excursions.

Ensor Museum MUSEUM
(059 80 53 35; www.muzee.be/en/ensor; Vlaanderenstraat 27; adult/concession €2/1; 10am-noon & 2-5pm Wed-Mon) Pioneering expressionist painter James Ensor (1860–1945) lived and worked for almost 40 years in the house that forms this attractive little museum. Its ground floor is presented as a 19th-century souvenir shop, much as in Ensor's time. The cabinets full of crustacea, skulls, masks and bizarre fish grafted with demonic faces are elements that would appear in many an Ensor canvas. On the 2nd floor is a reproduction of his chaotic 1888 classic, *The Entry of Christ into Brussels.*

Stadsmuseum MUSEUM
(Langestraat 69; adult/concession/child €4/2/free; 10am-12.30pm & 2-6pm Wed-Mon) A house that hosted Napoleon in 1798 and Belgian royals (1834–1850) has been refitted as the city museum, put together with considerable imagination, but disjointed as an overall experience. The video montages, models of 'lost' buildings and the words of Queen Marie-Louise (who died here in 1850) create a sorrowful depiction of the city's lost glories.

Marien Ecologisch Centrum MUSEUM
(www.marinecocenter.be; Langestraat 99; 2-5pm Wed-Sun) FREE This educational operation has a little one-room collection of seashells and sand that you can examine under the microscope.

Museumschip Amandine MUSEUM
(059 23 43 01; www.museum-amandine.be; Vindictivelaan 35-Z; adult/child €4/2; 10am-5pm) The last Ostend trawler to have fished around Iceland (1970s) is brought to life for visitors with waxwork figures, videos and sound effects. Highlights include the fish-freezing room.

Statue of Marvin Gaye STATUE
(Kursaal) Soul superstar Marvin Gaye wrote his last hit 'Sexual Healing' in 1981 while living in Ostend. His residency is marked by a wildly tacky statue of the singer playing a golden piano. To see it, peep inside the convention centre of Ostend's bold 1950s landmark, the Kursaal, which also contains a gaudy **casino** (www.partouchecasinos.be; Kursaal; slots/table from 9am/3pm) (minimum age 21, passport/ID needed to enter).

Leopold II Statue STATUE
(Zeedijk) Most of the beachfront is overshadowed by 10-storey concrete buildings, but beside the very '50s Thermae Palace Hotel there's some respite where a neoclassical arcade is topped by a striking equestrian statue of Léopold II. Below him stands a fawning gaggle of European and African subjects.

WORTH A TRIP

THORNTON BANK

Looking across the harbour it's hard not to be intrigued by the the vast columns and sails stacked up on Zeewezendok. These are parts of gigantic wind turbines being slowly transported 30km out into the English Channel and erected to create the Thornton Bank offshore wind farm. The operating company C-Power has information boards near the Oosteroever miniferry jetty where you can also see a cross-section of the extraordinary undersea cable that will carry electricity from the wind turbines. Franlis (p111) organises boat trips out to see the wind farm at close quarters.

St-Petrus-&-Pauluskerk CHURCH
(Sint-Pietersstraat) This is Ostend's most striking historical building, with its beautifully ornate twin spires, rose window and a gloomy neo-Gothic interior. Despite its antique appearance, the church only dates from 1905. A stone 'bridge' behind the altar leads into the tiny crown-topped Praalgraf Louise-Marie, the 1859 tomb-chapel of Belgium's first queen, whose sad tale is told at the Stadsmuseum.

Despite its antique appearance, the rest of the building only dates from 1905; all that remains of far older churches that once stood in the same square is the 1729 St-Pieterstoren, a strangely detached octagonal tower.

Mu.Zee GALLERY
(059 50 81 18; www.muzee.be; Romestraat 11; adult/concession/under 26 €5/4/1; 10am-6pm Tue-Sun) Mu.Zee, Ostend's foremost gallery, features predominantly local artists. There's a significant collection by symbolist painter Léon Spilliaert (1881–1946) whose most brooding works are reminiscent of Munch.

Mercator MUSEUM
(www.zeilschip-mercator.be; Old Harbour; adult/child €4/2; 10am-5pm) This fully rigged, three-masted 1932 sailing ship was once used for Belgian navy training purposes and is now a nautical museum that hosts changing exhibitions.

Ostend (Oostende)

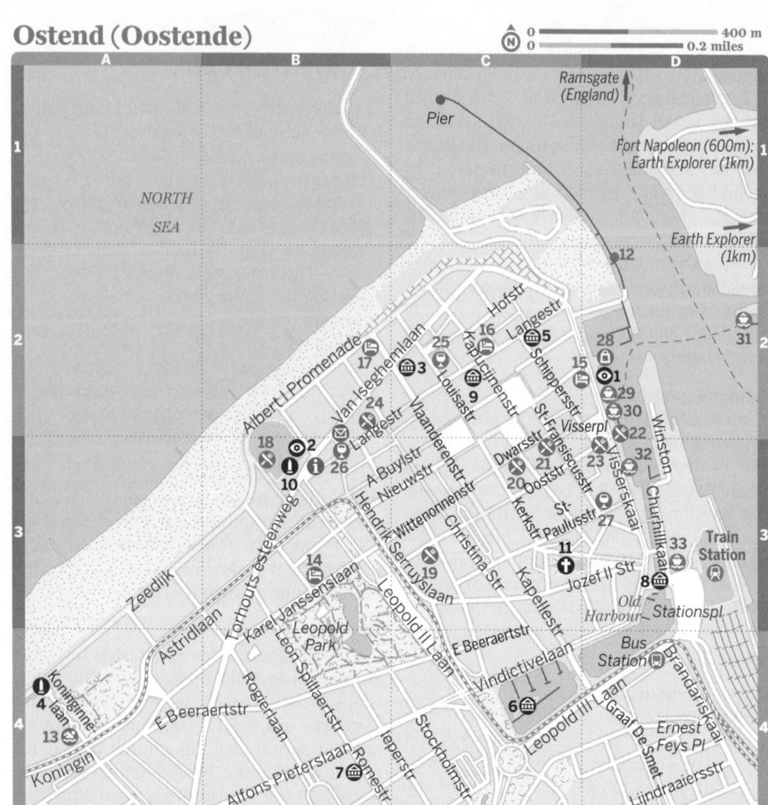

Oosteroever

If you've driven to Ostend, a money-saving tactic is to park for free in Oosteroever (the east side of the harbour), then use the passenger/bicycle **mini-ferry** (⏲6.30am-8.40pm Apr-Sep, 7.45am-6pm Oct-Mar) **FREE** that shuttles several times an hour across to the Aquarium jetty in the town centre. If coming from the centre, it's 10 minutes' walk from the ferry jetty to Fort Napoleon. Earth Explorer is 500m beyond that, near the Kusttram stop 'Duin en Zee'.

Fort Napoleon FORTRESS

(☎059 32 00 48; www.fortnapoleon.be; Vuurtorenweg; adult/senior/child €8/7/4; ⏲10am-6pm Wed-Sun Apr-Oct, 1-5pm Wed, Sat & Sun Nov-May) The impenetrable pentagon of Fort Napoleon is an unusually intact Napoleonic fortress dating from 1812, though there's comparatively little to see inside and the audio guide covers many of the same topics you'll have heard at the Atlantikwall. Drinking at the fortress *café* gets you decent glimpses without paying the entrance fee.

Earth Explorer SCIENCE MUSEUM

(☎059 70 59 59; www.explorado-oostende.be; Fortstraat 128b; adult/concession/child €14.95/12.95/11.95; ⏲10am-6pm Apr-Aug; 👪) Themed by the elements, this heavily interactive series of experiences is made to inspire primary-school age youngsters with awe for the forces that shape the earth. The most dramatic attractions are a walk-through earthquake and a volcano ride. When quiet, some sections close on hourly rotation. Look for half-price vouchers at hotels.

Domein Raversijde

Around 6km west of Ostend, the dunes and marshes of this extensive provincial reserve create a rare green gap between all the coast's apartment towers. If visiting both of the main

Ostend (Oostende)

Sights
1 Aquarium D2
2 Casino B3
3 Ensor Museum C2
4 Leopold II Statue A4
5 Marien Ecologisch Centrum C2
6 Mercator C4
7 Mu.Zee B4
8 Museumschip Amandine D3
9 Stadsmuseum C2
10 Statue of Marvin Gaye B3
11 St-Petrus-&-Pauluskerk C3

Activities, Courses & Tours
12 Franlis D2
13 Stedelijk Zwembad A4

Sleeping
14 De Hofkamers B3
15 De Mangerie C2
16 De Ploate C2
17 Hotel Die Prince B2

Eating
18 Aguadelmar B3
19 Belle du Jour C3
Bistro Beau-Site (see 17)
Den Artiest (see 16)
20 Di Vino C3
21 Finess C3
22 Kraampjes D2
Mosselbeurs (see 21)
23 't Zeezotje D3
24 Tao B2

Drinking & Nightlife
25 Café Botteltje C2
26 Lafayette Music Bar B3
27 't Kroegske D3

Shopping
28 Fish Market D2

Transport
29 Cross-Harbour Mini-Ferry D2
30 Harbour Mini-ferry D2
31 Harbour Mini-Ferry (Oosteroever) D2
32 Seastar D3
33 TransEuropa Ferries Ticket Desk D3

attractions, it's cheaper to buy the three-site combination ticket (adult/concession €9.75/8.10), which also throws in the Memorial Prins Karel, a minor house museum commemorating King Leopold II's brother, Charles. Charles had been regent following WWII, then in 1950 retired to this remarkably modest basket-weaver's cottage. It was by giving his Raversijde Royal Estate to the provincial government that Charles saved this fascinating area from coastal developers.

By public transport, take the Kusttram to 'Domein Raversijde', reach the Atlantikwall via wooden steps leading south up the duneside then follow the signs (around 150m). A footpath between the marshes takes around 10 minutes on to Walraversijde, from which you can take bus 6 back to Ostend. By car the only parking is at Walraversijde.

Bring waterproofs and walking shoes.

★ Atlantikwall HISTORIC BUILDING

(www.atlantikwall.co.uk; adult/concession €6.50/5.40; 10am-5pm Apr-early Nov, last entry 4pm) The gripping Atlantikwall is a remarkably extensive complex of WWI and WWII bunkers, gun emplacements and linking brick tunnels created by occupying German forces. Most bunkers are furnished and 'manned' by waxwork figures, and there's a detailed audio-guide explanation (albeit sometimes overly concerned with gun calibres). This is one of Belgium's best and most underrated war sites, but you'll need good weather, around two hours and reasonable fitness to make the most of the 2km walking circuit.

Walraversijde MUSEUM

(Nieuwpoortsteenweg 636; adult/concession €6.50/5.40; 2-5pm Mon-Fri, 10.30am-6pm Sat & Sun Apr-early Nov, 10am-6pm daily Jul & Aug, last entry 4pm) Once a vibrant fishing village, Walraversijde disappeared entirely following the strife of 1600 to 1604, leaving mere foundations. Today the archaeological site is enhanced by four convincingly rebuilt and furnished thatched houses, while an audio guide tells the village's history through the voices of a series of well-acted 1465 characters. An interactive museum then makes sense of why the village died out.

Activities

Franlis BOAT TOUR

(059 70 62 94; www.franlis.be; Langestraat 122/1; office 9am-noon & 2-5pm Mon-Fri) Offers a variety of out-and-back sea cruises.

Stedelijk Zwembad SWIMMING

(059 50 38 38; www.oostende.be/zwembad; Koninginnelaan 1; adult/child €3.50/2.25; 9am-5pm, longer hours in summer) A full-sized indoor swimming pool.

Sleeping

Ostend groans under the weight of hotels, with a row along Visserskaai and dozens of big, bland, fair-priced options in the central blocks around De Ploate youth hostel. Remarkably few are actually on the seafront. Some hotels close from December to March, while most charge higher rates in summer or at weekends.

De Ploate HOSTEL €
(☎059 80 52 97; www.vjh.be; Langestraat 82; dm from €27, d from €63; ⊗closed Oct–mid-Mar) This HI hostel is smart and minimal as well as being superbly central.

De Hofkamers HOTEL €€
(☎059 70 63 49; www.dehofkamers.be; IJzerstraat 5; s/d €70/99) Model yachts and dozens of teddies create a welcoming reception and lounge; rooms are all different but play on romantic pseudo-antique themes, some with four-poster beds. All have safe, fridge and kettle. There's a four-lounger roof terrace, but be aware that any claims of 'sea view' mean craning your neck and looking north down a tunnel of other hotels.

Breakfast (included) is relatively lavish.

Hotel Die Prince HOTEL €€
(☎059 70 65 07; www.hoteloostende.eu; Albert I Promenade 41; with/without sea view €108/88; ⓦ) Die Prince is one of the rare hotels with a beach view. Prices here are modest and the public areas rather swish. Room decor is functional, but little two-seat desks allow you to wave-gaze from your window. Breakfast included.

De Mangerie HOTEL €€
(☎059 70 18 27; www.mangerie.info; Visserskaai 36; d/ste €75/115, luxury d/tr/q €95/115/125) With dark-wood floors, fine linen and comfy sitting areas, the Mangerie's four spacious guest rooms continue the suave designer themes of their tempting fish restaurant downstairs (mains €20 to €25).

Eating

Tearoom restaurants covering a wide range of styles and prices stand side-by-side along the promenade west of the Kursaal. There are plenty more seafood restaurants along Visserkaai. Market day is Thursday.

't Zeezotje BRASSERIE €
(www.zeezotje.be; Bonenstraat; meals €9-24; ⊗10am-midnight, kitchen noon-11.45pm) Floor-to-ceiling glass and masses of outdoor seating including an easily missed upper-floor balcony draw in tourist diners, as do the English language menus, good prices and late-serving kitchen. Pizza and pasta are supplemented by a selection of seafood options. Try the Vispannetje, a trio of different fish fillets topped with melted cheese, mini-shrimps and a creamy light-curry sauce.

Bistro Beau-Site CAFE €
(☎0486 77 45 74; Albert I Promenade 39; pasta €13-18, sandwiches €5.50-9.50; ⊗11am-7pm Wed, Thu & Mon, noon-late Sat & Sun) Atmosphere-wise it's a

MARVIN GAYE IN OSTEND

'There are plenty of places I'd probably rather be, but I probably need to be here.'

Of all the towns in all the world...the story of how soul superstar and sex god Marvin Gaye came to Ostend in February 1981 is a curious one.

The tale of self-imposed exile in a one-horse seaside town is told in Richard Olivier's documentary *Marvin Gaye: Transit Ostend*. Promoter Freddy Cousaert met Gaye in London at a low in the singer's life – he was drugged, divorcing and losing it. Cousaert invited Gaye and his son for an open-ended visit to Belgium, partly so that Cousaert himself could stage a comeback concert for Gaye at the Kursaal. The visit ended up lasting two years.

Relocated to the somewhat bleak Belgian beaches, Gaye, who had attempted suicide by cocaine overdose in Hawaii two years earlier, spent time running along the sand, playing basketball and boxing in a briefly successful pitch at clean living. The singer also claimed to have eased up on the lovin' here – despite the fact that this is where the classic 'Sexual Healing' was written.

Gaye played his one-off comeback gig at the Kursaal in 1982; it was poorly attended but brilliant. The venue in turn commissioned an unflattering though glitzy bronze statue of the singer at his piano, which still sits in the lobby.

Within two years of Gaye leaving Ostend for Los Angeles he was dead. He was shot by his own father at the age of 44, having apparently goaded him into murder in a state of cocaine-fuelled paranoia. Unlikely as it seems, Ostend gave Gaye a last period of calm and creativity before the tragic storm that ended his life, and he gave the world 'Sexual Healing'.

class apart from anything else on the seafront. This small arty cafe has art-deco touches, a communal farmhouse table, jazz tinkling on the stereo and art books to peruse. Upstairs are window seats with great beach views.

Di Vino BISTRO €
(☎0473 87 12 97; Wittenonnenstraat 2; mains €12.50-17; ⊙11.45am-2pm & 6.30-10pm Wed-Sun Sep-Jun, daily Jul & Aug) Intimate candlelit wine-bistro with bottles and corks for decor, rustic furniture and a €9.50 lunch deal (one plate plus coffee).

Kraampjes SEAFOOD €
(promenade above Visserskaai; ⊙9.30am-dusk, seasonal) Several wagon-stalls sell smoked and cooked fish, pre-fried calamari rings, little tubs of grey shrimps and plastic bowls of steaming hot *wulloks* (whelks/sea snails) available *natuur* (in salty broth) or *pikant* (spicy).

Belle du Jour CAFE €€
(Aartshertoginnestraat 5; mains €15-27; ⊙noon-9pm) Ostend isn't known for its trendiness, but this little cafe with its pared-back decor, mosaic floor and old school furniture hits the mark. The menu features Italian influences and plenty of seafood; the Belle du Jour cocktail will set you back $8.

Finess FRENCH, GASTRONOMIC €€
(☎0489 32 99 20; www.restaurantfiness.be; Dwarsstraat 9; 1-/2-/3-/4-/5-course meal €24/36/48/60/72; ⊙noon-2pm Tue-Sun, 6.30-9.30pm Wed-Sun) Crockery cascades artistically off the wall in this intimate one-room restaurant with open kitchen. Forget standard starter/main differences – here the nouveau-cuisine menu is undivided and you simply take any dishes you fancy in any order.

Den Artiest BRASSERIE, BARBECUE €€
(☎059 80 88 89; www.artiest.be; Kapucijnenstraat 13; meals €14-24; ⊙5pm-2am, kitchen 7pm-midnight) Informal brasserie with tables multi-layered in an original fashion around a high central space. Long brass-tube lamps and fun knick-knacks provide atmosphere, while ultra-generous meals are barbecued in front of you in the central hearth. Recommended for drinks only, too. Occasional live music.

Tao INTERNATIONAL €€
(☎059 43 83 73; www.tao-oostende.be; Langestraat 24; mains €17.50-26; ⊙5.30-11pm, bar from 4pm) Despite the pink carrots at the street terrace, this is a fashion-conscious lounge-restaurant whose kitchen covers a gamut of culinary possibilities from Thai to Mexican.

Mosselbeurs SEAFOOD €€
(☎059 80 73 10; www.facebook.com/pages/De-Mosselbeurs; Dwarsstraat 10; mussels €22-28; ⊙noon-2pm & 6-10pm Wed-Sun) The decor, wrapped around a central spiral stairway, is stylish, except for the tacky silver mussel shells twinkling on some wall surfaces. Is the gratuitous meat-slicer displayed in the corner a veiled threat to those who don't pay their bill?

Aguadelmar EUROPEAN €€€
(☎059 29 50 52; www.ostendqueen.be; Kursaal; pancakes from €3.50, mains €26-42; ⊙noon-9.30pm) This business-casual restaurant has walls imaginatively mosaiced with mussel-shells, and the arc of its raised terrace surveys the western beaches. If you can't afford the upmarket food (scallop risotto, lobster with asparagus or duck in peanut sauce), come between 3pm and 6pm for pancakes and coffee (from €3.50), or later for cocktails (€7 to €10).

Drinking & Entertainment

A series of great and varied *cafés* and pubs lead north from the Kursaal on Langestraat and Van Iseghemlaan, and on several of the connecting lanes. Den Artiest (p113), Tao (p113) and Bistro Beau-Site (p112) are all great for drinks as well as food.

Café Botteltje PUB
(☎059 70 09 28; www.hotelmarion.be; Louisastraat 19; ⊙11.30am-1am or later Tue-Sun, 4.30pm-1am Mon) In a spacious *café* reminiscent of a British pub you'll find around 300 different beers, including a dozen on draught. Meals (noon to 2.30pm and 6pm to 10pm, mains €14 to €24) include a selection of beer-based recipes.

Lafayette Music Bar BAR
(www.laffayettemusicbar.be; Langestraat 12; beer/cocktails from €2/7.50; ⊙2pm-2am;) With the panelling of a traditional *café,* but the back-lit bottle racks of a fashion-conscious cocktail bar, Lafayette hits a fine balance between hip and friendly. The tubas and hanging hams add eccentricity, and conversation isn't quite drowned out by DJs whose tastes ranges from Parisian jazz to Barry White. Around 50 beers include the full sweep of Trappists.

Several other bars nearby are also lively until late.

't Kroegske BAR
(St-Paulusstraat 78; beer & coffee €1; ⊙11am-2pm & 6-11pm) There's a giant devil fish head on the roof of two old houses whose facades have been covered with lurid cartoons. Inside it's cramped and merrily tatty with bric-a-brac and a dangling two-eyed helix

hanging over the bar. Next door there's an art-packed smoking room.

Information

The main shopping thoroughfare is pedestrianised Kapellestraat.

Cyber Cafe (Koningsstraat 7; per hr €2; ⏲10am-11pm) Internet computers at the back of a tobacconist/bottleshop.

Goffin Exchange (St-Petrus & Paulusplein 19; ⏲9am-6pm Mon-Sat) Changes money without commission, but at far-from-generous rates.

Post Office (Van Iseghemlaan 52; ⏲9am-6pm Mon-Fri, 9am-12.30pm Sat)

Tourist Office (☎059 70 11 99; www.visitoostende.be; Monacoplein 2; ⏲10am-6pm Sep-Jun, 9am-7pm Jul & Aug) Copious maps and brochures, plus interesting themed tours based around Marvin Gaye or the perfume industry.

Getting There & Around

Air Ostend Airport (www.ost.aero), 6km west by bus 6, has summer charter flights on Jetairfly (www.jetairfly.com).

Bicycle Free one-day bicycle hire is available behind the train station and, in summer, beside the eastern jetty of the cross-harbour mini-ferry.

Buses For Diksmuide (route 53, 50 minutes) and Veurne, bus 68 (1¼ hours, hourly, not Sunday) leaves from the bus station and goes via Nieuwpoort and Oostduinkerke-dorp (for the fishery museum).

Kusttram Use for De Haan and Knokke. Buy bus/tram tickets at the bus terminal or Marie Joséplein tram stop.

Trains Run to Bruges (€3.90, 13 minutes) continuing to Kortrijk, Antwerp via Ghent or Liège via Brussels.

Nieuwpoort

These days Nieuwpoort is the coast's top sailing centre. But it is also a historic place, remembered for playing a key role in WWI. It was here that the German advance was thwarted by local partisans who opened (and repeatedly reopened) the sluice gates on the Noordvaart canal. This flooded (and kept flooding) the fields between the IJzer River and the railway, which essentially remained the front line for the rest of the war. The WWI bombardments devastated Nieuwpoort's historic townscape, but in the 1920s the medieval main square was rebuilt, including the former 1280 town hall, belfry and a sizeable church. Today, flanked by step-gabled houses, the scene looks lovely at dusk, thanks to tasteful floodlighting. By day, however, the overly neat brickwork lacks the apparent authenticity of similar reconstructions in Ypres or Diksmuide.

The historic main sluice gates are on the northeast approach to town where the bridge crosses the IJzer. Beside the site are a pair of memorials to the hundreds who died here in WWI, including a particularly ugly yellow-stone rotunda surrounding an equestrian Albert I statue.

Directly northwest of this point, an access road leads west from the N34 to the new yacht harbour, a memorable mass of masts overlooked by the panoramic **'t Vlaemsch Galjeon**. From this harbour **Zeilexcursies** (☎0474 97 95 25; www.zeilexcursies.be; per person €25) does two hour sail-rides (minimum six) at 12.30pm and 3.30pm. **AS** (☎0486 44 12 15; www.as-tian.com) and **Sailors Only** (☎058 23 26 73; www.sailorsonly.com; Albert I-laan 64G) offer yacht charters. In prevous years, **Seastar** (☎058 23 24 25; www.seastar.be; Orlenpromenade 2) has run river and sea trips, though currently most departures are dining cruises.

Oostduinkerke

The archetypal vision of Belgium's rural North Sea coast is of **paardevissers** (www.paardevissers.be), shrimp fishermen riding their stocky Brabant horses into the sea, dragging triangular nets through the low-tide shallows. These days shrimp catches are minimal, but the age-old tradition is maintained at Astridplein beach in Oostduinkerke-Bad. It's now a tourist spectacle that happens fewer than 30 times a year. That's mostly in July and August plus the last weekend of June when the town celebrates its annual *garnaalfeesten* (shrimp festival).

One of the shrimp fishermen moonlights as a barman serving unique, dark Peerdevisscher beer (€2.10) at **Estaminet de Peerdevisscher** (snacks €3-11.50, sandwiches €4.50-6; ⏲10am-8pm Tue-Sun), a wonderful old-time *café* 1.5km north of the beach in Oostduikerke's second centre, Oostduinkerke-dorp. The *café* is beside the entrance to **Navigo** (Nationaal Visserijmuseum; ☎058 51 24 68; www.visserijmuseum.be; Pastoor Schmitzstraat 5; adult/senior/youth €7/5/2; ⏲10am-6pm Tue-Fri, 2-6pm Sat & Sun), an interesting, state-of-the-art fishing museum. Visits walk you through a genuine 19th-century fisherman's cottage, teach about fish quotas and fishermen's superstitions, then send you and your audio guide beneath a 1930s fishing smack flanked by aquariums of fish. An accompanying soundtrack of waves and shrieking gulls builds up to a four-minute storm every half-hour. Veurne–Ostend bus 68 stops nearby.

Halfway between village and coast, **Sint-Niklaaskerk** is an extraordinary 1956 church whose bulky pale-brick tower has an almost medieval look, except for the massive 13m-high crucified Christ hanging on its east wall. Turn east 100m north of the church and continue 700m to find the modern, peacefully located **HI hostel De Peerdevisser** (Jeugdherberg; ☎058 51 26 49; www.peerdevisser.be; Duinparklaan 41; dm adult/under 26 €24.95/22.65, HI member €22.50/20.40, d €52.40-58.90).

St-Idesbald

Hidden in unexpectedly leafy suburbs, the **Delvaux Museum** (☎058 52 12 29; www.delvauxmuseum.com; Delvauxlaan 42; adult/concession €8/6; ⏲10.30am-5.30pm Tue-Sun Apr-Sep, Thu-Sun Oct-Dec, closed Jan-Mar) occupies a pretty whitewashed cottage that was home and studio to Paul Delvaux (1897–1994), one of Belgium's most famous surrealist artists. Delvaux' penchant for locomotives, skeletons and endless big-eyed nudes doesn't appeal to everyone, but there's something fascinating about his warped take on perspective and his dreamy evocations of the 'poetic subconscious'. This museum shows a wide range of his work, as well as family memorabilia and the numerous toy trains that decorated his studio. From the Koksijde/St-Idesbald tram stop, walk west along the main road towards De Panne, then follow signs inland and left – around 1km total. The museum has a delightful garden cafe.

De Panne & Adinkerke

POP 10,700

A busy beach resort, De Panne (www.depanne.be), started life as a fishing village set in a *panne* (hollow) among the dunes. It was here that King Léopold I, arriving from London, first set foot on Belgian territory in 1831. This event is commemorated by a massively framed royal statue that surveys the summer beer stalls and banal apartment towers on the beachfront directly north of De Panne Esplanade tram stop. In 1940 the sand dunes between De Panne and Dunkerque (Dunkirk, France) were the scene of the famous skin-of-their-teeth evacuation that saved a large part of the retreating WWII British army. West of De Panne's central strip, some of those grassy-topped dunes still survive, now forming part of a nature reserve for winter's migratory birds. The sand feels great underfoot, but westward coastal views are marred by the belching smokestacks of Dunkerque.

The train station called 'De Panne' is actually 3km inland at Adinkerke, with the Kusttram coastal-tram terminating next door. Less than 1km south of the station (and 600m north of the E40 motorway), Adinkerke's shops offer a last chance for chocoholic motorists heading to the channel ports or for bargain-hunting French smokers.

A Kusttram stop between Adinkerke and central De Panne serves **Plopsaland** (☎058 42 02 02; www.plopsa.be/plopsaland-de-panne/en; De Pannelaan 68; adult/child under 1m €35/10; ⏲hours vary), a major kids' theme park based around wonderfully named Belgian TV characters Wizzy, Woppy and Plop the gnome.

Veurne

POP 11,250

Delightful little Veurne has an architectural charm that trumps all of the coastal towns put together. Historic spires and towers peep above the picture-perfect Flemish gables that surround its super-quaint Grote Markt (central square). The view is especially magical at dusk when partly floodlit.

Sights

Belfort HISTORIC BUILDING

(Grote Markt; stadhuis tours adult/child €3/2; ⏲several stadhuis tours daily) Its 1628 octagonal belfort, a Unesco World Heritage site, rises behind the 17th-century former courthouse building. It now houses a helpful **tourist office** (☎058 33 55 31; www.veurne.be; Grote Markt 29; ⏲10am-noon & 1.30-5.30pm Apr-Sep, 10am-noon & 2-4pm Tue-Sun Oct-Mar, closed Sun mid-Nov–Mar) whose stadhuis tours offer the easiest way to peep inside the 1612 Flemish Renaissance–style town hall next door.

Spaans Paviljoen HISTORIC BUILDING

(Oosterstraat 2) The gabled 1615 Vleeshuis sits at Grote Markt 1; the 15th-century Spaans Paviljoen (Spanish Pavilion) was Veurne's town hall before being commandeered as a garrison for Spanish officers during Hapsburg rule.

St-Walburgakerk CHURCH

Veurne's main church is the delicately spired St-Walburgakerk, a spacious, heavily buttressed affair containing much-revered relics. The skull of St-Walburga is contained in a reliquary facing the entrance. A wooden fragment that was supposedly once part of Jesus' original cross is not displayed, but the story of its arrival here is the subject of local legends.

In an attractive small park behind, the Citerne is a strange crouched brick building converted into WWII barracks from the abandoned remnants of the 14th-century west portal.

St-Niklaaskerk CHURCH
(Appelmarkt; tower €1.50; ⌚10-11.45am & 2-4.45pm mid-Jun–mid-Sep) Behind the Grote Markt's southeast corner, St-Niklaaskerk has a bulky 13th-century tower that you can climb for good summer views and a small exhibit on bell-ringing.

Bakkerijmuseum MUSEUM
(Bakery Museum; ☎058 31 38 97; www.bakkerijmuseum.be; Albert I-laan 2; adult/senior/child €5/3.50/2; ⌚10am-5pm Mon-Thu, 2-5pm Sat & Sun) Near the motorway junction, 2km south of central Veurne, a classical 17th-century farmstead houses this delightful museum comprehensively examining baking from grain production to *speculaas* moulding. There's also a chocolate statue and barns of milling machines. Come in summer or holiday Tuesdays to see the baking demonstrations.

Sleeping

★ **Auberge de Klasse** B&B €€
(☎0479 76 55 13; www.aubergedeklasse.be; Astridlaan 3; d €130-150; ⌚from 4pm; 📶) This luxurious three-room B&B retains more of its 18th-century structure than you'd guess from the outside, albeit heaped with soft furnishings and filled with the delight of the owners for their courtyard garden.

Old House BOUTIQUE HOTEL €€
(☎058 31 19 31; www.theoldhouse.be; Zwarte Nonnenstraat 8; s/d/q €50/90/180; P) Creamy paintwork, indulgently oversized showers, splendid linen and gentle modernism turn this classically styled 1770 mansion into what's labelled a B&B but is more a beguiling boutique hotel. The salon-lounge features toy owls and a stuffed peacock, and there's an appealing front garden area. It's a short stroll through the park west of St-Walburgakerk.

Be aware that the very cheapest singles are narrow and cramped.

't Kasteel en 't Koetshuys B&B €€
(☎058 31 53 72; www.kasteelenkoetshuys.be; Lindendreef 5; s/d €108/115; 📶) This delightful 1907 red-brick mansion features high ceilings, old marble fireplaces and stripped floorboards, creating a lovely blend of classic and modern, all immaculately kept. Some rooms share one bathroom between two, and there's an extra charge for the sauna. It's three blocks south of Grote Markt.

Eating & Drinking

If offered the local speciality 'Potjesvlees', be aware that this is not a stew but a cold mixture of rabbit, chicken and veal meat in jelly, often presented in the jar. Coffee in this region is very often served with a free thimble of thick local *advocaat*. Use a spoon! Several inviting *cafés* ring the main square; the two options below are just off the square.

Grill de Vette Os STEAK €€
(☎058 31 31 10; www.grilldevetteos.be; Zuidstraat 1; mains €19-27; ⌚noon-2.30pm & 6pm-2am Fri-Tue) Old timbers, jugs, buckets, saints and so much more are crammed into this atmospheric carnivore's lair.

't Hof van de Hemel BISTRO €€
(www.thofvandehemel.be; Noordstraat 13; mains €10-17; ⌚9.30am-9pm Tue-Sat) Three ages of unplastered brick encompass what was once Veurne's narrowest alley but now a spruced-up teahouse-cafe with wooden beams and brick arches. Beerwise, the highlight is St-Bernardus Triple on tap. Food is relatively inexpensive if not especially refined.

Getting There & Around

Veurne's extravagantly spired little train station is 600m east of Grote Markt via Ooststraat. Trains leave twice hourly for De Panne (€2, six minutes) and Ghent (€12.10, 65 minutes) via Diksmuide (€3.10, 11 minutes). Hourly bus 68 goes to Oostduinkerke-dorp, Nieuwpoort and Ostend. Bus 50 runs to Ypres via Lo and Oostvleteren up to seven times daily.

Wim's Bike Center (☎058 31 22 09; www.wimsbikecenter.be; Pannenstraat 35; per day €8.70; ⌚9am-noon & 1.30pm-6pm Tue-Sat) Rents out bicycles.

Around Veurne

This pan-flat agricultural area of canal-diced potato- and corn-fields isn't dramatic, but back lanes are peaceful and several keyed bicycle routes mesh with the widely available Westhoek cycling guide-map (€6).

For a pleasant ride, head first for the pretty two-street village of **Wulveringem** with its spooky slate-towered church, curious statue-carving studio and late-16th-century **Kasteel Beauvoorde** (☎058 29 92 29; www.kasteelbeauvoorde.be; adult/child €8/6;

⌚2-5.30pm Thu-Sun Mar-Oct, daily Jul & Aug), a moated four-storey mansion-castle with intact, fully furnished interiors.

Then wind through tiny but historic **Lo**, with its pixie-esque twin-spired city gate, vastly oversized church and attractive Unesco-listed little brick belfry-tower attached to a photogenic 1566 former town hall that's now a hotel-restaurant. Lo's famous biscuit factory offers self-guided tours.

From Lo continue to Dijksmuide or backtrack to Oostvleteren and delve into 'beer country'.

Diksmuide

POP 16,300

Like Ypres, Diksmuide was painstakingly restored after total obliteration in WWI. Though used as a large car park, the resurrected Grote Markt (main square) offers an impressive array of traditionally styled brick gables, two inexpensive hotels, several terraced cafes and a romantically towered **city hall**. Set directly behind, the truly vast **church** (⌚9am-6pm) has a particularly fine rose window. The tulip-turreted Boterhalle hosts a **tourist office** (☎051 51 91 46; http://toerisme.diksmuide.be; Grote Markt 28; ⌚10am-noon & 2-5pm).

Pleasure boats are moored attractively at the river port 1km west. Directly beyond rises the unique 1950 **Ijzertoren** (☎051 50 02 86; www.ijzertoren.org; IJzerdijk 49; adult/senior/under 26 €7/5/1; ⌚10am-5pm, to 6pm Apr-Sep). Built of drab, purple-brown brick and topped with power station–style windows, this colossal 84m-high 'peace' tower is at once crushingly ugly and mesmerisingly fascinating. It's set behind the shattered ruins of a 1930 original, whose mysterious sabotage in 1946 remains controversial. The tower is probably Flanders' foremost nationalist symbol. Its 22 floors house a very expansive museum related to WWI and Flemish emancipation. There's no fee if you just want to walk up to the tower's base, starting through a WWI-style sandbag passage and crossing an over-pond passerelle.

Served at some Diksmuide hostelries you'll find Oerbier, a highly rated stealthy dark ale. It's brewed 3km east by **De Dolle Brouwers** (☎051 50 27 81; www.oerbier.be; Roeselarestraat 12B; tour €5; ⌚cafe 2-7pm Sat & Sun) in Esen village, 100m south of Esen's powerfully oversized church. At weekends, the brilliantly colourful little brewery *café* serves the stuff on draught and there's a 2pm tour in English on Sundays.

BEER COUNTRY

Westvleteren

If you're driving from Veurne to Ypres, a post-mill at Oostvleteren's main crossroads marks the turn to Westvleteren. However, the mythical Westvleteren Trappist beer actually comes from the isolated **Abdij Sint-Sixtus** (www.sintsixtus.be; St Sixtus Abbey; ⌚closed to visitors), some 4km further southwest via a web of tiny lanes. The architecturally unremarkable abbey is closed to visitors, but the abbey *café,* **In de Vrede** (www.indevrede.be; Donkerstraat 13; ⌚10am-8pm Sat-Wed) is the only place in the world where you can be (virtually) sure of tasting the incomparable Westvleteren 12°, often cited as Belgium's greatest beer. That doesn't mean that you can take bottles away, however. Purchasing a case is only possible by reserving an appointment using the abbey's infamously overloaded **'beerphone'** (☎high toll 070 21 00 45), preferably calling on the dot of 9am Monday morning. You'll need to give your car number plate and agree a pick-up time (weekday afternoons only, no credit cards!).

Woesten

Woesten is a forgettable town on the main Ypres–Veurne road, but the banal-looking **Deca Brewery** (www.decabrouwerij.be; Elverdingestraat 4; ⌚shop 9.30am-noon & 1-6pm Tue-Fri, 1-4.30pm Sat) here is one of the only places you're likely to be able to buy takeaway beers by respected local boutique-brewer, Struise.

Watou

POP 2000

Best known for its **St-Bernardus beers** (www.sintbernardus.be), brewed at the southern outskirts of town, little Watou has a pleasant central square dominated by a fine spired church. Here **Het Wethuys** (☎057 20 60 02; www.wethuys.be; Watouplein 2; s/d €75/100) is an historic if unpretentious *café* with B&B rooms. It serves St-Bernardus Triple on draught and a selection of local meals including *Hoppegaletten* – large cheese-filled pancakes where the batter is made from hops – and its own house beer, 8% Yedeghemsche Tripel (€3.50).

The network of quiet lanes and tracks in the Poperinge–Watou–Westvletteren triangle offer some particularly fine cycling.

Poperinge

POP 20,000

For centuries the Poperinge area has produced the quality hops required for Belgium's beer industry. During WWI Poperinge was just out of German artillery range so it became a posting and R&R station for Allied soldiers heading to or from the Ypres Salient. English troops, remembering it for its entertainments and prostitutes, referred to the town fondly as 'Pops'.

Sights

A €10 combi-ticket covers both the Hopmuseum and Talbot House.

National Hopmuseum MUSEUM
(057 33 79 22; www.hopmuseum.be; Gasthuisstraat 71; adult/under 26 €6/2.50; 10am-6pm Tue-Fri, 2-6pm Sat, 10am-noon & 2-6pm Sun, closed Dec-Feb) Once the municipal hops weighing- and storehouse, the 19th-century Stadsschaal now houses the distinctive smelling museum, where you'll learn more about hops than you'd ever want to know. The simple attached *café* serves several local brews and was once home to Dirk Frimout, Belgium's first astronaut.

Talbot House MUSEUM
(057 33 32 28; www.talbothouse.be; Gasthuisstraat 43; adult/senior/youth €8/7/5; 10am-5.30pm Tue-Sun) This is an unusually light-hearted WWI attraction. Reverend Philip 'Tubby' Clayton set up the Everyman's Club here in 1915 to offer rest and recreation for WWI soldiers regardless of rank. The main 1790 town house has barely changed since. The garden is a charming oasis, and visits start with a modest exhibition accessed from Pottestraat where photos, quotes and videos remind visitors of Tubby's sharp gallows humour. End the visit with a free cup of English-style tea in the kitchen.

You can can stay the night in one of the simple guest rooms (single/double €43/78) with shared bathrooms (bookings advised).

Death Cell MEMORIAL
(Guido Gezellestraat 1; 9am-5pm) FREE 'Good old Pops' also had a more sinister side...as a place of execution for wartime deserters. Hidden behind a red door in the north side of the stadhuis you can still see the chilling original shooting post and the stone-walled death cell where deserters spent their last night. Brochures available in the cell explain in some detail the era's injustices, accompanied by a soundscape telling of the 1917 execution of 17-year-old soldier Herbert Morris.

Sint-Janskerk CHURCH
(Sintjanskruisstraat; 7.30am-7pm) The imposing Sint-Janskerk's 'miraculous' little Virgin-and-child statuette reputedly brought a still-born child to life in 1479.

Sleeping & Eating

There are numerous cafes plus five simple hotels around the Grote Markt.

Hotel Amfora HOTEL €€
(057 33 94 05; www.hotelamfora.be; Grote Markt 36; d/ste from €83;) Behind the traditional step-gabled frontage, the bar-restaurant is equally traditional but the rooms have been upgraded in a muted modern style.

Hotel Recour BOUTIQUE HOTEL €€€
(057 33 57 25; www.pegasusrecour.be; Guido Gezellestraat 7; d from €140;) The main 18th-century house has a luxurious lounge and eight romantic individually themed rooms, most featuring nostalgic colour combinations, chandeliers, four-poster beds and Jacuzzi baths. A metal walkway above the garden lawn leads to another seven contrastingly modern rooms, each adopting the style of a classic 20th-century designer.

Around 100m east in a separate building, the somewhat cheaper *gastenkamers* are approached by a doorless lift but the rooms here are excellent too, with exposed brick walls and beams. One has a roof terrace.

★ **Restaurant Pegasus** RESTAURANT €€
(057 33 57 25; www.pegasusrecour.be; Guido Gezellestraat 7; mains €32-39; 8am-11pm Tue-Sat) The Hotel Recour's Restaurant Pegasus is a very upmarket affair. Those under 60 might feel out of place, but the food is very creative, and while mains are presented as nouveau cuisine, extra sides are provided for those who secretly prefer old-cuisine Belgian-size portions.

Information

Tourist Office (057 34 66 76; www.toerismepoperinge.be; Grote Markt 1; 9am-noon & 1-5pm Mon-Fri, to 4pm Sat & Sun, closed Sun Oct-Mar) The tourist office is on the almost attractive main square in the basement of the romantic neo-Gothic stadhuis, built 1911.

Getting There & Away

Poperinge–Ypres takes eight minutes by train (€2.30), or 18 minutes by bus 60, both hourly.

You'll need to book ahead (☎ 059 56 52 56) for the eccentrically routed Belbus 69 to Westvleteren, Woesten or Oostvleteren.

Ypres (Ieper)

POP 35,100

Only the hardest of hearts are unmoved by historic Ypres (Ieper in Dutch). In the Middle Ages it was an important cloth town, ranking alongside Bruges and Ghent. In WWI some 300,000 Allied soldiers died in the 'Salient', a bow-shaped bulge that formed the front line around town. Ypres remained unoccupied by German forces, but was utterly flattened by bombardment. Incredibly, after the war, the beautiful medieval core was convincingly rebuilt and the restored Ypres Lakenhalle is today one of the most spectacular buildings in Belgium. Most tourism still revolves around WWI and related themes, and the Salient remains dotted with cemeteries, memorials, bunkers and war museums.

Sights

Lakenhalle HISTORIC BUILDING

(Cloth Hall; Map p120; Grote Markt 34) Dominating the Grote Markt, the enormous reconstructed Lakenhalle is one of Belgium's most impressive buildings. Its 70m-high belfry has the vague appearance of a medieval Big Ben. The original version was completed in 1304 beside the Ieperslee, a river that, now covered over, once allowed ships to sail right up to the Lakenhalle to unload their cargoes of wool. These were stored beneath the high gables of the 1st floor, where you'll find the unmissable In Flanders Fields museum.

To climb the Lakenhalle Tower pay an extra €2 when entering that museum to have the electronic bracelet suitably charged to get you through the barrier. Appended to the Lakenhalle's eastern end, the working stadhuis was reconstructed in 1969, partly to the original 1619 design.

★In Flanders Fields MUSEUM

(Map p120; www.inflandersfields.be; Lakenhalle, Grote Markt 34; adult/under 26/child €9/5/4; ⏲10am-6pm Apr–mid-Nov, to 5pm Tue-Sun mid-Nov–Mar) No museum gives a more balanced yet moving and user-friendly introduction to WWI history. It's a multisensory experience combining soundscapes, videos, well-chosen exhibits and interactive learning stations at which you 'become' a character and follow his/her progress through the wartime period. An electronic 'identity' bracelet activates certain displays.

Menin Gate MEMORIAL

(Menenpoort; Map p120) A block east of Grote Markt, the famous Menin Gate is a huge stone gateway straddling the main road at the city moat. It's inscribed with the names of 54,896 'lost' British and Commonwealth WWI troops whose bodies were never found.

Last Post MEMORIAL

(Map p120; www.lastpost.be; ⏲8pm) At 8pm daily, traffic through the Menin Gate is halted while buglers sound the *Last Post* in remembrance of the WWI dead, a moving tradition started in 1928. Every evening the scene is different, possibly accompanied by pipers, troops of cadets or maybe a military band.

Ramparts HISTORIC SITE

(Map p120) Ypres is unusual in that it has retained extensive sections of its Vaubanesque city fortifications. These sturdy brick-faced walls line the town's southeastern moat and

TICKET SAVVY

Keep your In Flanders Fields ticket! It also gets you free entrance to three other pleasant if otherwise missable minor museums:

Stedelijk Museum (Map p120; www.stedelijk.nl; Ieperleestraat 31; adult/student/child €15/7.50/free; ⏲10am-12.30pm & 2-5pm Tue-Sun Nov-May, to 6pm Apr-Oct) This decent little gallery is set in a three-storey 1555 almshouse complex. Exhibitions change regularly but usually feature 19th-century paintings.

Belle Almshouse (Map p120; Rijselstraat 38; admission €2.50; ⏲10am-12.30pm & 2-6pm Tue-Sun Apr-Oct) A single small chapel room featuring some unexpectedly high-quality medieval art, mostly religious.

Onderwijsmuseum (Map p120; Gustave de Stuerstraat 6a; admission €2.50; ⏲10am-12.30pm & 2-5pm Tue-Sun Nov-May, to 6pm Apr-Oct) The history of Flemish education is presented in the large former St-Niklaas church, including some entertaining exhibits on sex education.

Ypres (Ieper)

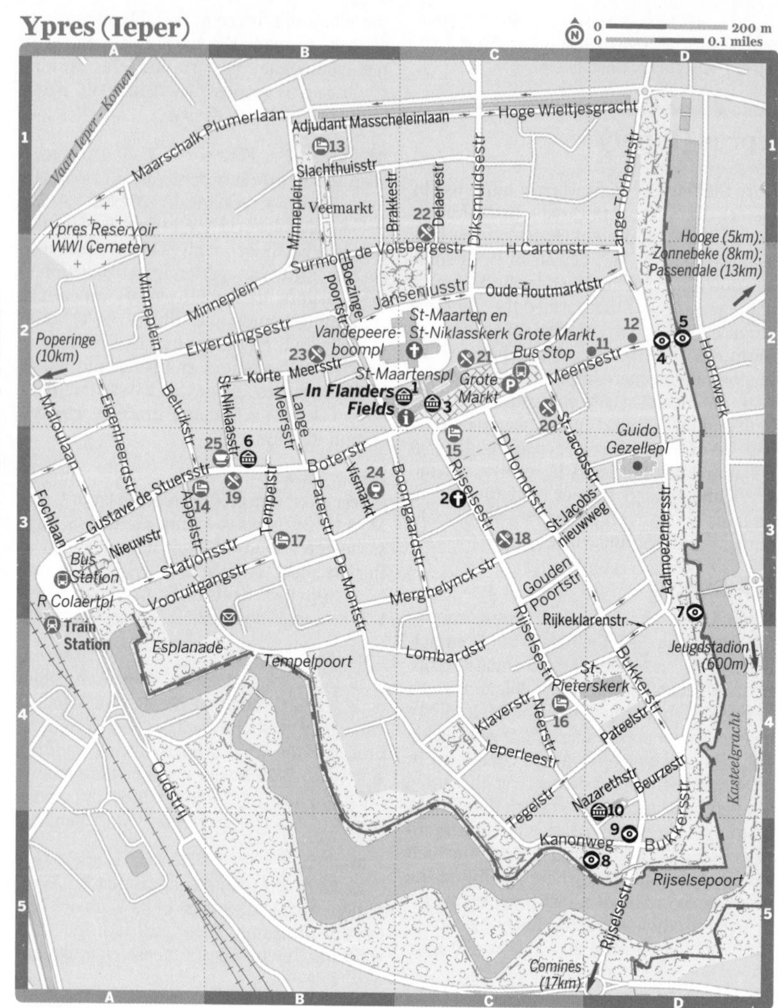

are topped by pleasant gardens. The tourist office's free *Ramparts Route* leaflet introduces a dozen of its historic fortifications, but most visitors simply stroll casually from the Menin Gate to the medieval **Rijselpoort** (Lille Gate; Map p120), just beyond which the **Ramparts Cemetery** (Map p120) is one of Ypres most attractive military graveyards.

Tours

A range of popular half-day tours of WWI Ypres Salient sites are available through two specialist bookshop-agencies, which also sell a range of WWI-related literature and battlefield souvenirs. Ideally book ahead.

British Grenadier BUS TOUR
(Map p120; ☎057 21 46 57; www.salienttours.be; Meensestraat 5; short/long tour €30/38; ⏱10am-2pm & 2.30-5pm) Two Ypres tours are available – the 2½-hour option takes in Hill 60, the Caterpillar Crater and the German Bayernwald trench complex, while the standard four-hour tour covers every site on the Salient.

Over the Top BUS TOUR
(Map p120; ☎0472 34 87 47; www.overthetoptours.be; Meensestraat 41; tours €40; ⏱tours 9am-1pm, 2.30-5.30pm & 7.30-8.30pm) A WWI specialist bookshop towards the Menin Gate offering twice-daily, half-day guided minibus tours of

Ypres (Ieper)

the Ypres Salient. The north salient tour is in the morning, the south in the afternoon.

Festival

Kattenstoet STREET CARNIVAL

(Cat Parade; www.kattenstoet.be; 13 May 2018) Every three years Ypres' classic feline fiesta sees parading giants and the throwing of cats from the Lakenhall tower. Toy ones these days, but before 1817 they were real!

Sleeping

Jeugdstadion CAMPGROUND €

(Map p123; 057 21 72 82; www.jeugdstadion.be; Bolwerkstraat 1; per tent/adult/child €3/4/2.50; mid-Mar–Oct) Camping ground and youth centre 900m southeast of the town centre.

Ariane Hotel HOTEL €€

(Map p120; 057 21 82 18; www.ariane.be; Slachthuisstraat 58; s/d from €89/109; P) This peaceful, professionally managed, large hotel has a designer feel to the rooms and popular restaurant, while wartime memorabilia dots the spacious common areas.

B&B Ter Thuyne B&B €€

(Map p120; 057 36 00 42; www.terthuyne.be; Gustave de Stuersstraat 19; d €95; @) Three comfortable rooms that are luminously bright and scrupulously clean, but not overly fashion-conscious.

Hotel Regina HOTEL €€

(Map p120; 057 21 88 88; www.hotelregina.be; Grote Markt 45; d €99;) Location, location, location. You can forgive the sometimes dated decor to be right on the central square overlooking the Lakenhalle. Friendly staff, decent food.

Kasteelhof 't Hooghe HOTEL €€

(Map p123; 057 46 87 58; www.hotelkasteelhofthooghe.be; Meenseweg 481, Hooghe; s/d/tr/q €65/85/115/140) If you're driving, this out-of-town mock-Tudor-styled hotel is a great choice with genuine WWI trenches in the gardens. It is ideally located for the kids to be first in at Park Bellewaerde (p124), directly behind. It is about 3km west on the N8.

Yoaké B&B B&B €€

(Map p120; 057 20 35 14; www.yoake-ieper.be/bedhome.htm; Tempelstraat 35; d €90;) Smart two-room B&B attached to a hip wellness centre.

★ **Main Street Hotel** GUESTHOUSE €€€

(Map p120; 057 46 96 33; www.mainstreet-hotel.be; Rijselsestraat 136; d €180-260;) Jumbling funky eccentricity with historical twists and luxurious comfort, this is a one-off that simply oozes character. The smallest room is designed like a mad professor's experiment, the breakfast room has a Tiffany glass ceiling…and so it goes on!

Eating

The Grote Markt hosts a Saturday morning market (so don't park there on Friday night).

't Leedvermaak BISTRO €

(Map p120; 057 21 63 85; Korte Meersstraat 2; mains €7-17; 11.30am-1.30pm & 6-11pm Tue-Sun) Low-key theatrically themed bistro serving fair-priced pasta, veggie dishes and tapas.

Henk Bakery BAKERY €
(Map p120; ☎057 20 14 17; Sint-Jacobsstraat 2; ⏰6.45am-6pm Tue-Fri, 5.45am-7pm Sat, 5.45am-4pm Sun) Fresh bread, pastries, croques and fancy patisserie goods to take away. Try the amazing and filling *broodpudding* (bread pudding), just 40c.

★ **De Ruyffelaer** FLEMISH €€
(Map p120; ☎057 36 60 06; www.deruyffelaer.be; Gustave de Stuersstraat 9; mains €15-21, menus €26-34; ⏰11.30am-3.30pm Sun, 5.30-9.30pm Thu-Sun) Traditional local dishes served in an adorable, wood-panelled interior with old chequerboard floors and a *brocante* decor, including dried flowers, old radios and antique biscuit tins.

Souvenir FRENCH, BELGIAN €€
(Map p120; ☎057 36 06 06; www.souvenir-restaurant.be; Surmont de Volsbergestraat 12; menus €38-78; ⏰noon-3.30pm & 6-10pm, closed Tue) Fish, steak or seafood served with beautifully pared-back minimalist style in a century-old town house. The emphasis is on seasonal and local produce

In 't Klein Stadhuis PUB FOOD €€
(Map p120; www.inketkleinstadhuis.be; Grote Markt 32; snacks €8.50-14, mains €16-27; ⏰11am-midnight, kitchen to 10.30pm) Tucked away in a quirkily decorated historic guildhall beside the stadhuis, this split-level *café* serves gigantic, good-value meals, including some beer-based recipes.

De Ecurie FRENCH, BELGIAN €€
(Map p120; ☎057 36 03 67; www.deecurie.be; A Merghelynckstraat 1a; mains from €18, lunch €13.50; ⏰11am-2pm & 6-10pm Tue-Sat) An intimate former stable building that features antique brick floors and delicious Flemish food.

Drinking

There are several fine choices on Grote Markt.

De Vage Belofte PUB
(Map p120; www.facebook.com/devagebelofte; Vismarkt 3; ⏰4pm-late Tue-Sun) A piano hangs on the two-storey inner wall above a row of Champagne bottles; summer tables spill out across appealing Vismarkt, and DJs turn the tables on weekend nights.

't Binnenhuys CAFE
(Map p120; Gustave de Stuersstraat 8; coffee/beer €2.20/2, snacks from €7; ⏰9.30am-6.30pm Mon & Wed-Sat, 2-6pm Sun; 📶) One of Ypres' oldest houses, the 1772 Binnenhuys was rare in surviving WWI relatively intact. It's now an old-world home interiors shop, but tucked away in the rear sitting room and attractive back garden are tables for coffee and cake or a very relaxed beer.

Information

Tourist Office (Map p120; ☎057 23 92 20; www.toerismeieper.be; Lakenhalle; ⏰9am-6pm Mon-Fri, 10am-6pm Sat & Sun Apr–mid-Nov, to 5pm mid-Nov–Mar) Tourist office for Ypres and surrounds with an extensive bookshop.

AT THE CROSSROADS OF WAR

The Ypres Salient was formed by Allied attempts to repel the invading German army before it reached the strategic North Sea ports in northern France. The area's line of barely visible undulations provided enough extra elevation to make good vantage points and were prized military objectives. Hundreds of thousands of lives were lost in numerous bids to take these very modest ridges. Years of deadlocked trench warfare obliterated local villages and created a barren landscape of mud and despair. The first battle of Ypres in October and November 1914 set the lines of the Salient.

After that, both sides dug in and gained relatively little ground for the remainder of the war, despite three valiantly suicidal battles that followed. The most infamous of these came in spring 1915 when Germans around Langemark launched WWI's first poison-gas attack. It had devastating effects on the advancing Allied soldiers, and on the Germans themselves. On 31 July 1917, British forces launched a three-month offensive commonly remembered as the Battle of Passchendaele (Passendale), or the 'battle of the mud'. Fought in shocking weather on fields already liquidised by endless shelling, this horrifically futile episode killed or wounded over half a million men, all for a few kilometres of ground. And these modest Allied gains were lost again in April 1918.

The reconstruction of villages and replanting of trees took years, and even now farmers regularly plough up unexploded munitions. Today the pleasant farmland is patchworked with 170 cemeteries where rows of crosses stand in silent witness to all the wasted life.

Getting There & Away

BIKE

Hire bikes from **Hotel Ambrosia** (057 36 63 66; www.ambrosiahotel.be; D'Hondtstraat 54; standard/electric bike per day €12/25; 7.30am-7pm).

BUS

Most buses leave from the train station and also pick up in Grote Markt (check the direction carefully). For Bruges, take bus 94 or 95 to Roeselare, then swap to a train. Bus 20 to Diksmuide (50 minutes) runs five times daily.

TRAIN

Trains run at least hourly to the following destinations:

Brussels (1¾ hours)
Comines (nine minutes)
Kortrijk (30 minutes)
Oudenaarde (one hour)
Poperinge (seven minutes)

Ypres Salient

Flanders' WWI battlefields are famed for red poppies, both real and metaphorical. From 1914 the area suffered four years of senseless fighting during which thousands of soldiers and whole towns disappeared into a muddy, bloody quagmire. The fighting was fiercest in the 'Ypres Salient', a bulge in the Western Front where the world first saw poison-gas attacks, and thousands of diggers valiantly tunnelled underground to dynamite enemy trenches.

These days many local museums have collections of WWI memorabilia, and dozens of painstakingly maintained war graveyards bear sad witness with regimented ranks of headstones. Concrete bunkers, bomb craters and trench sites can be visited, but remember that in 1917 these would have been infinitely muddier and unshaded as virtually every tree had been shredded into matchwood by artillery fire. A few non-war attractions lighten the mood.

Ypres Salient

0 — 2 km
0 — 1 mile

A B
1 Poelkapelle N313 Roeselare (10km)
Langemark
Passendale (1.5km)
Boezinge
10 8
5 6 9
New Irish Farm Cemetery
Sint-Juliaan
N369 N313
Poperinge (7km)
N38
Zonnebeke
4
N8
See Ypres (Ieper) Map (p120)
A19
3 12
11
N8
Zillebeke 7 2
Geluveld
Hill 60 (1km)
Menen (12km)

Ypres Salient

Sights

1 Deutscher Soldatenfriedhof ... A1
2 Hill 62 Museum ... B2
3 Hooge Crater Museum ... B2
4 Kasteel Zonnebeke ... B2
Memorial Museum Passchendaele 1917 ... (see 4)
5 New Zealand Memorial ... B1
6 Oude Kaasmakerij ... B1
7 Sanctuary Wood British Cemetery ... B2
8 St Juliaan Memorial ... B1
9 Tyne Cot ... B1
10 Yorkshire Trench ... A1

Sleeping

11 Jeugdstadion ... A2
12 Kasteelhof 't Hooghe ... B2

North of Ypres

Deutscher Soldatenfriedhof CEMETERY
(Map p123) FREE The area's main German WWI cemetery is smaller than Tyne Cot but arguably more memorable, amid oak trees and trios of squat, mossy crosses. Some 44,000 corpses were grouped together here, up to 10 per granite grave slab, and four eerie silhouette statues survey the site. Entering takes you through a black concrete 'tunnel' that clanks and hisses with distant war sounds, while four short video montages commemorate the tragedy of war.

It's beyond the northern edge of Langemark on bus route 95.

Essex Farm Cemetery CEMETERY
(N369) FREE The enduring image of poppies as a symbol of wartime sacrifice comes from the famous poem *In Flanders Fields*. It was penned by Canadian doctor John McCrae in a concrete first-aid bunker that's now preserved at Essex Farm Cemetery. Rare bus 40 passes by.

Passendale & Zonnebeke

The 1917 battles around Passendale (then Passchendaele) left almost 500,000 casualties and made Passendale synonymous with wasted life. These days it's known much more positively for its cheese. Ypres–Roeselare bus 94 (roughly twice-hourly weekdays, five daily weekends) goes through Zonnebeke and passes within 600m of Tyne Cot.

Memorial Museum Passchendaele 1917 MUSEUM
(Map p123; www.passchendaele.be; Ieperstraat 5; admission €7.50; 9am-6pm Feb-Nov; 94) In central Zonnebeke village, **Kasteel Zonnebeke** (Map p123; www.zonnebeke.be) is a lake-fronted Normandy chalet-style mansion built in 1922 to replace a castle bombarded into rubble during WWI. It hosts a tourist office, cafe and particularly polished WWI museum charting local battle progressions with plenty of multilingual commentaries. The big attraction here is descending into its multiroom 'trench experience' with low-lit, wooden-clad subterranean bunk rooms and a soundtrack. Explanations are much more helpful here than in 'real' trenches elsewhere.

Tyne Cot CEMETERY
(Map p123; 24hr, visitor centre 9am-6pm Feb-Nov; 94) FREE Probably the most visited Salient site, this is the world's biggest British Commonwealth war cemetery, with 11,956 graves. A huge semicircular wall commemorates another 34,857 lost-in-action soldiers whose names wouldn't fit on Ypres' Menin Gate. The name Tyne Cot was coined by Northumberland Fusiliers who fancied that German bunkers on the hillside here looked like Tyneside cottages. Two such dumpy concrete bunkers sit amid the graves, with a third visible through the metal wreath beneath the white Cross of Sacrifice.

Oude Kaasmakerij MUSEUM
(Map p123; 051 77 70 05; www.deoudekaasmakerij.be; 's Graventafelstraat 48a, Passendale; without/with cheese-tasting €5/8; 10am-5pm Mar-Oct, closed some Mon mornings) This interactive, mildly interesting cheese museum compares old and new cheese-making techniques while a gratuitous naked Cleopatra takes a bath in plastic asses' milk. It's 1.2km west of Tyne Cot.

Hooge & Around

Ypres–Menen buses pass through Hooge.

Hooge Crater Museum MUSEUM
(Map p123; 057 468 446; www.hoogecrater.com; Meenseweg 467; adult/child €5/2; 10am-6pm Tue-Sat, 10am-9pm Sun) In a quaint repurposed chapel on the Ypres–Menen road (N8), this small but characterful two-room museum is entered between assorted WWI sandbags, rusty rail sections and field guns. Inside, uniformed mannequins, arms and assorted memorabilia are ranged in venerable old display cases around a life-sized model of a red Fokker triplane. The attached *café* is appealing.

Massive explosions detonated beneath German defences by British engineers created the crater for which it's named. That crater now forms a pretty pond 100m east in the gardens of Kasteelhof 't Hooghe, which also has some re-excavated trenches.

Park Bellewaerde AMUSEMENT PARK
(057 46 86 86; www.bellewaerdepark.be; Meenseweg 497; adult/child €31/26; 10am-6pm Jun-Aug, to 5pm Easter holidays & Wed-Sun May) High-adrenaline amusement park behind the Crater Museum. This could be the place to give the kids a break from WWI graveyards. Online discounts.

Hill 62 Museum MUSEUM
(Map p123; 057 46 63 73; Canadalaan 26; adult/child €10/5; 9.30am-6pm Apr-Aug) This gnome-fronted, surreally ordinary house displays a chaotic hotchpotch of WWI helmets, shoes, guns and harrowing photos, some in antiquated wooden stereoscopic viewers. The main attempted justification for the hefty entrance fee is a string of 'original trenches' in the woodland garden and the cross-pinned relic of a bombarded tree. It's between Sanctuary Wood British Cemetery and the Canadian Hill 62 memorial, 2km down a dead-end lane from Hooge bus stop.

Comines

The commune of Comines-Warneton (www.villedecomines-warneton.be) is an administrative curiosity, a detached enclave of Francophone Hainaut sandwiched between Flanders and France with Comines town cut in half by the Belgo-French border. On the French side the distinctive 1623 Comines Town Hall has a wildly bulbous Unesco-listed belfry tower, meticulously rebuilt after WWI. It faces the 1922–1938 St-Chrysole church, a compulsively hideous attempt at neo-Byzantine grandeur. Across the River Lys on on the Belgian side, the unexpectedly fascinating **Musée de la Rubanerie** (056 58 77 68; https://larubanerie.wordpress.com; rue des Arts

3; adult/child €3/1; ⏲9-11.30am & 1.30-4.30pm Tue-Fri, tour 3pm Sat & 10.30am Sun) celebrates the ribbon-making industry, Comines' economic mainstay since 1719. Its antique machinery still works but little English is spoken.

Comines station, 800m north, has hourly trains to Ypres (€2.50, nine minutes).

Kortrijk

POP 76,000

Prosperous Kortrijk (Courtrai in French) was founded as the Roman settlement of Cortoriacum. It grew wealthy as a flax and linen centre, but was severely bombed by the Allies during WWII. It retains a gorgeous *begijnhof* and an important historical resonance as the venue for Flanders' defining medieval battle.

Sights

Begijnhof BUILDING

(⏲7am-9pm) FREE Small but utterly delightful, Kortrijk's enclosed *begijnhof* is as charming a cluster of whitewashed old terraced houses as you could hope to find. Enter through a portal tucked behind Cafe Rouge, seek out the little **information centre** (Begijnhof 2; ⏲1-5pm Tue-Sun) and admire the 1682 turreted mansion at Begijnhof 27.

Grote Markt ARCHITECTURE

Kortrijk's curved central square is scarred by insensitive 20th-century constructions, but the slightly leaning, multispired brick **belfort** (belfry) provides an attractive focus, and the restored 1421 **Historisch Stadhuis** (former town hall) building has a fine, ornate facade dotted with stone mini-spires and niche statues.

St-Maartenskerk CHURCH

(St-Maartenskerkstraat; ⏲7am-5pm Mon-Fri, 10am-5pm Sat & Sun) The noble 83m tower that adds such finesse to the Kortrijk skyline belongs to this mostly 15th-century Gothic church, built on the site of St-Eloi's 7th-century chapel.

Onze Lieve Vrouwekerk CHURCH

(⏲7am-7pm Mon-Sat, 7am-6pm Sun) Echoing with wistful music, this church has a gilt sunburst altarpiece, heraldic panels in the 1373 St-Catherinekapel and features Van Dyck's 1631 painting *Kruisoprichting* (Raising of the Cross) in the left transept. Poet-priest Guido Gezelle was once pastor here (1872–1889).

Kortrijk 1302 MUSEUM

(☎056 27 78 50; www.kortrijk1302.be; Begijnhofpark; adult/concession/youth €6/4/1; ⏲10am-5pm Tue-Sun, to 6pm summer weekends) This modern 'experience' museum explains the background events surrounding the classic Battle of the Golden Spurs (p126), but despite an English-language audio guide (essential) and multiple video screens, it can feel disappointingly static and rather unsatisfying for non-Flemish visitors. The 14-minute movie climax offers the intriguing conclusion that the battle's importance has been overblown. How self-deprecatingly Belgian.

Broeltorens TOWER

(Broelbrug) This iconic pair of three-storey fortress towers guards a picturesque arched stone bridge across the River Leie in central Kortrijk. Last reminders of a long-gone medieval city wall, their machicolations and conical roofs look magical in night-time floodlights when the backdrop of mediocre apartments is less obvious.

PLANNING A VISIT

The sites are spread over a vast agricultural area that's scenically pleasant without being especially memorable. So your first chore is figuring out what you really want to see. Fine starting points are www.ypres-1917.com, www.wo1.be and www.inflandersfields.be or books from *Major & Mrs Holt's Concise Battlefield Guide* series (see www.guide-books.co.uk/ypres-leper.html), widely available in Ypres bookshops, which also organise guided tours. A car or tour makes visiting easy and reduces backtracking, but buses can get you close to the more famous sites.

If you had relatives killed in the fighting you might want to locate their grave or memorial. Ypres bookshops offer a search service or you can look for yourself online:

British and Commonwealth graves www.cwgc.org

American www.abmc.gov

French www.memoiredeshommes.sga.defense.gouv.fr

German www.volksbund.de

Broelmuseum GALLERY
(☎056 27 77 80; www.broelmuseum.be; Broelkaai 6; adult/concession/youth €3/2/free; ⊙10am-noon & 2-5pm Tue-Fri, 11am-5pm Sat & Sun) Highlights of this fine-art museum include Roelandt Savery's 1604 masterpiece *Plundering of a Village* and Emmanuel Viérin's semi-impressionist scenes of the Begijnhof. It occupies a classical river-facing 1785 mansion retaining Louis XVI gilt interiors and a notable orangery near the Broeltorens.

Texture MUSEUM
(www.texturekortrijk.be; Noordstraat 28; adult/concession/child €6/4/2; ⊙10am-6pm Tue-Sun May-Sep, to 5pm Oct-Apr) The Texture museum is located in an 1902 flax factory, and tells the story of the town's flax and linen industry; you'll also see a lovely collection of damasks and laces. The history of flax is told through individual accounts, and is surprisingly absorbing: you can touch and smell the fabric itself.

Sleeping

Kortrijk accommodation prices rise during trade expos in September, October, February and March.

★Hotel Messeyne HOTEL €€
(☎056 21 21 66; www.hotelmesseyne.be; Groeningestraat 17; s/d €120/135; @ 📶) A grand 1662 town house with beamed high ceilings and original fireplaces melds with stylishly contemporary decor, immaculate rooms and designer corridors imaginatively featuring cacti as art. There's a well-regarded restaurant (closed Sundays), free sauna, garden-facing fitness room and a darkly mysterious little bar-lounge.

Center Hotel HOTEL €€
(☎056 21 97 21; www.centerhotel.be; Graanmarkt 6; s/d/tr €75/85/110; 📶) Attractively modernised rooms at reasonable prices above a subtly fashionable bar with handy 24-hour reception. Breakfast €12.

Square Hotel HOTEL €€
(☎056 28 89 50; www.squarehotel.be; Groeningestraat 39; s/d/tr €90/100/110) Suave minimalism aimed at businessmen with relatively limited budgets. Spooky doll faces survey the breakfast area. Weekend discounts.

Eating

A range of tempting cafes line Grote Markt, with a couple more on Kapucijnenstr near the Broelmuseum.

Brasserie de Heeren van Groeninghe BRASSERIE €
(☎056 25 40 25; http://resto-deheerenvangroeninghe.be; Groeningestraat 36; snacks/pasta/mains from €4/11/14; ⊙10am-10pm Mon & Thu-Sun) Excellent-value meals are served in twinkling candlelight in a grand old mansion with high ceilings and original gilt decor. Reservations are wise, especially at weekends. The outdoor terrace is contrastingly bare, sandwiched between dull brick walls, but serves snacks and drinks all day, including bottled Quintine and draught Boon Kriek.

Teater Kaffee PUB FOOD €
(Schouwburgplein 6; waffles/snacks from €3.40/8.50; ⊙11am-8pm Mon-Sat, to 2pm Thu) Classic wood-panelled *café* with tulip lamps, Rodenbach beer on draught and inexpensive pub meals (cheese croquettes, fish-pan, baguette-sandwiches).

BATTLE OF THE GOLDEN SPURS

Flanders' French overlords were incensed by the Bruges Matins massacre of May 1302. Philip the Fair, the French king, promptly sent a well-equipped cavalry of aristocratic knights to seek retribution. Outside Kortrijk on 11 July this magnificent force met a ragged, lightly armed force of weavers, peasants and guild members from Bruges, Ypres, Ghent and Kortrijk. Expecting little from their lowly foes, the horseback knights failed to notice a cunningly laid trap. The Flemish townsfolk had previously disguised a boggy marsh with brushwood. Snared by the mud, the heavily armoured French were quickly immobilised and slaughtered, their golden spurs hacked off and displayed as trophies in Kortijk's Onze Lieve Vrowekerk (p125). It was the first time professional knights had ever been defeated by an amateur infantry and the event became a potent symbol of Flemish resistance. At least that's the way it's remembered thanks to Flanders' first great novel, *De Leeuw van Vlaanderen* (The Lion of Flanders), and 11 July is celebrated as Flanders' 'national' holiday.

The battlefield site is now Groeningheveld, a leafy park in relatively central Kortrijk marked by a 1906 pseudo-medieval gateway and the triumphant Groeninge Statue featuring a gilded woman unleashing the Flemish lion.

Café Rouge BRASSERIE €€
(☎056 25 86 03; www.caferouge.be; St-Maartenskerkhof 6a; snacks €10-15, mains €17-26; ⏰11am-9pm Tue-Sun, to 10pm Fri & Sat) This bistro's French-style shuttered facade contrasts with a bold, semi-minimalist interior, and the terrace fills a tree-lined pedestrianised square behind the Begijnhof. Great for drinks, meals or afternoon pancakes (from €4).

B'thoven STEAK €€
(☎056 22 55 42; Onze-Lieve-Vrouwstraat 8 ; mains €17-25; ⏰6.30-10pm Tue-Sun) Revelling in the cracked paintwork of this recycled old *café*, Ludwig busts sniff enviously at the range of ribs, steaks and fondues.

't Mouterijtje BRASSERIE €€
(☎056 20 14 14; www.mouterijtje.be; Kapucijnenstraat 25a; snacks €10-18, mains €14-24; ⏰5pm-midnight Fri-Tue) Convivially well lit, this spacious family-oriented brasserie retains lots of old bare brickwork, red steel beams and an undulating ceiling. There's a good range of beers, fish dishes and mussels, and the signature dish *côte-à-l'os* (rib roast).

Drinking

Gainsbar BAR
(http://gainsbar.org; Vlasmarkt; ⏰noon-1am Tue-Thu, 2pm-2am Fri-Sun) Beer specialist bar but with a youthful upbeat vibe. Organises occasional meet-the-brewer days and serves some rare gems, including occasional draught masterpieces from regional brewers Dupont and Struisse.

Staminee den Boulevard PUB
(denboulevard.wordpress.com; Groeningelaan 15; ⏰4.30pm-1am Thu-Mon) Flickering candles, crooning soft jazz and over 100 beers including draught Chimay Triple (€3.50). Tables spill onto the park opposite.

Viva Sara COFFEE
(www.vivasara.com; Grote Markt 33; ⏰8am-6.30pm Mon-Fri, 9am-6pm Sat) Kortrijk's leading coffee house plans a museum-like exhibition of their antique coffee-related contraptions.

Information

Centrale Bibliotheek (☎056 277 500; Leiestraat 30; ⏰10am-6.30pm Mon-Fri, 10am-4pm Sat; 📶) Library with free internet computers and wi-fi.

Tourist Office (www.toerismekortrijk.be; ⏰9am-5pm) Within Kortrijk 1302. Offers maps, brochures and bicycle rental.

Getting There & Around

BICYCLE HIRE

At **Mobiel** (☎056 24 99 10; www.mobiel.be; Pieter Tacklaan 57; per day city bike €12, electric €25, rickshaw incl driver €75; ⏰7am-6.50pm Mon-Fri, 10am-5.50pm Sat) you can hire a wide range of wheels – everything from city bikes to electric bikes to rickshaws (with or without driver).

TRAINS

Trains leave at least hourly for the following destinations

Bruges (fast/slow 40/53 minutes)
Brussels (one hour)
Ghent (20 minutes)
Lille, France (32 minutes)
Oudenaarde (20 minutes)
Tournai (Doornik, 32 minutes) Change in Mouscron (Moeskroen).
Veurne (52 minutes) Via Diksmuide (41 minutes), change in Lichtervelde.
Ypres (30 minutes)

Oudenaarde

POP 31,000

The little Flemish city of Oudenaarde (Audenarde in French) grew wealthy in the mid-16th century, local weavers having switched to tapestry making. Enormous Oudenaarde wall tapestries, filled with exquisite detail and luminous scenes of nature, nobility or religion, were in great demand by French and Spanish royalty. But by the end of the 18th century, wars had caused serious trouble and the industry all but disappeared.

Sights

Stadhuis TOWN HALL
Oudenaarde's impressive market square is dominated by a gorgeous 1536 town hall with a crown-topped central belfry-spire.

MOU MUSEUM
(www.mou-oudnaarde.be/; Stadhuis, Markt; adult/senior/student €6/5/1.50; ⏰10am-5.30pm Tue-Sun) Within the stadhuis, MOU displays collections of silverware and a dozen faded but priceless 16th-century Oudenaarde tapestries, along with a multimedia presentation on 1000 years of city history. Entry is through the tourist office.

Huis de Lalaing GALLERY
(Bourgondiëstraat 9; ⏰1.30-5pm Tue-Fri during exhibitions) This rococo-style historic mansion was reputedly the birthplace of Charles Quint's illegitimate daughter, Margaret

(Margaretha) of Palma, who later became governor of the Spanish Netherlands (1559–67). Today it hosts changing exhibits but is most interesting for its working tapestry design and repair workshops. Entrance is included in the MOU ticket price.

To get there from Grote Markt, walk southeast past the quaint 1499 Begijnhof (Achterburg) and cross the river via the lift bridge.

St-Walburgakerk CHURCH
(Sint-Walburgastraat; ⌚2.30-5pm Tue-Sun Jun-Sep, Tue, Thu & Sat only Easter-Oct) At the main square's western edge, this imposing church was cobbled together from a 13th-century chancel and a 15th-century Brabantine-Gothic tower. Inside are numerous paintings and tapestries. There are carillon concerts at 8.30pm Thursdays in July and August.

Centrum Ronde van Vlaanderen MUSEUM
(Tour of Flanders Reality Museum; ☎055 33 99 33; www.crvv.be; Markt 43; adult/concession/child €8/6/4; ⌚10am-6pm Tue-Sun) Facing the church's southern flank, this state-of-the-art museum lets cycling fans share the sensations and emotions of the classic Tour of Flanders bike race, which has its final stage in Oudenaarde.

PAM Ename MUSEUM
(www.pam-ov.be/ename; Lijnwaadmarkt 20, Ename; adult/concession €2.50/1.25; ⌚9.30am-5pm Tue-Sun) Ename is now a drab suburban village, 3km northeast of Oudenaade. But in AD 925 the site was one of three main defence posts along the border between pre-medieval France and Ottonian Germany (the others were Antwerp and Valenciennes). Later it was home to a vast abbey, reduced to scant remnants after the French Revolution. This history is imaginatively brought alive at PAM Ename using a 15-minute video and '1000-year feast' talking tableau. Next door is Ename's millennium-old stone church.

Sleeping & Eating

★ Steenhuyse GUESTHOUSE €€
(☎055 23 23 73; www.steenhuyse.info; Markt 37; s/d €95/120; 📶) A splendidly revamped 16th-century mansion has 21st-century Nordic-styled rooms with sun-drenched interiors, top-quality Philippe Starck fittings and performance (open to the room) bath areas. Champagne breakfasts are provided in the cafe area (€20 for non-guests, reservation required). Rates rise on weekends.

La Pomme d'Or BRASSERIE €€
(☎055 31 19 00; www.pommedor.be; Markt 62; mains €11-25, set menu €38; 📶) Tiffany-glass windows, wrought-iron lamps and 1930s decor create a welcoming feel to one of Oudenaarde's best value brasserie-cafes. Above, a free decanter of port awaits in the tastefully upgraded guest rooms (single/double €95/100).

Margaretha's INTERNATIONAL €€
(☎055 21 01 01; www.margarethas.be; Markt 40; mains €22-30, lunch/dinner menu €45/63; ⌚11.30am-2pm & 6.30-9pm Wed-Sun, closed lunch Sat) This top-notch if fiercely priced historical mansion-restaurant has royal connections, William Morris–style interiors, framed fabrics and a flurry of swords above the medieval fireplace. Seafood is a strong feature of the menu.

Getting There & Away

The station, 900m north of Markt via Nederstraat and Stationstraat, has trains at least hourly to Kortrijk (€3.90, 20 minutes), Ghent St-Pieters (€4.30, 28 minutes) and Brussels (€9, 50 minutes).

Geraardsbergen

POP 33,000

Known in French as Grammont, ancient Geraardsbergen has been a 'free city' since 1068. Unusually for Flanders, it's built on a distinctly sloping hillside and set with some beautiful rolling terrain nicknamed the Flemish Ardennes.

Sights

Manneken Pis STATUE
(Markt) Brussels isn't the only city in which a little boy statue relieves himself. Indeed many locals insist that Geraardsbergen's Manneken Pis is the 'original'. The gently dribbling fountain is in a corner of the main square fronting the turreted 1893 town hall, which adopts a medieval fantasy appearance when floodlit at night.

De Permanensje MUSEUM
(☎054 43 72 89; www.geraardsbergen.be; Markt; ⌚9am-noon & 1.30-4pm, closed some weekends) The tourist office within the town hall has a range of museum-like video introductions to the town's trades and traditions, push-and-sniff buttons to press and a selection of costumes for the Manneken.

Muur HILL

For cycle-racing enthusiasts the name Geraardsbergen is inextricably linked with the 'Muur' (Mur de Grammont in French), a steep cobbled rise that until 2011 formed a major highlight of the Tour of Flanders race. It's well signposted from behind the Markt and topped by the Oudenberg chapel.

Geraardsbergse Musea MUSEUM

(☎054 41 37 83; Kollegestraat 27; adult/child €1.25/0.75; ⏱2-5pm Tue-Sun Apr-Sep) This sweetly old-fashioned 'everything' museum has rooms celebrating matchboxes, cigars and Geraardsbergen's signature Chantilly black lace.

Sleeping & Eating

Casa Dodo B&B €€

(☎054 58 02 59; www.casadodo.be; Nieuwstraat 12/1; s/d €65/75, Fri-Sun €80/90) Choose a colour-themed room at this swish B&B over the station-area hotels for its friendly English-speaking welcome and bean-bag recliners. Book ahead to rent one of the bikes. From the Manneken Pis, walk 100m north, then 100m west. If you reach Molly Malone's Irish pub, you've gone too far.

't Hemelrijck PUB FOOD €

(www.taverne-hemelrijck.com; Oudenberg 2; beer/snacks/mains from €1.90/5/12.40; ⏱11am-10pm, closed Wed & Thu Oct-Mar) Work up an appetite by climbing almost to the summit of the Muur where this big, pleasant tavern serves great value pub food.

De Erfzonde PUB FOOD €

(☎054 41 78 87; www.de-erfzonde.be; Brugstraat 3; Mattentaart €1.50; ⏱8am-6pm Wed-Sun, 8.30am-1pm Mon) Just below the main square, this eclectic place has a zany mix of pots and saints and serves Geraardsbergen's signature *Mattentaart*, a light, semi-sweet curd-filled pastry.

Het Bruggenhuis PUB

(www.bruggenhuis.be; Majoor Van Lierdelaan 50; ⏱3-10pm Wed-Thu, 3pm-1am Fri-Sat, 2-10pm Sun) This picture-perfect rural *café* is just one small room that seems to have stepped straight out of an ethnographic museum. Seats spill out canalside with rural views along the towpath. It's a 2km walk/cycle down the Dender's western bank to Van Lierdebrug bridge. No food; occasional live jazz.

Getting There & Away

Trains run hourly to Lessines (€2, seven minutes), Ath (€3.40, 23 minutes), Ghent (€6.10, 50 minutes) and Brussels (€7.30, 80 minutes).

Ghent (Gent)

POP 247,500

Asking citizens of Ghent what they think of their city is a pointless exercise: you'll find only unanimous love. And with good reason. Ghent (www.visitgent.be) is one of Europe's greatest discoveries – small enough to feel cosy but big enough to stay vibrant. It has enough medieval frivolity to create a spectacle but retains a gritty industrial edge that keeps things 'real'. Tourists remain surprisingly thin on the ground, yet with its fabulous canalside architecture, wealth of quirky bars and some of Belgium's most fascinating museums, this is a city you really won't want to miss.

History

The seat of the Counts of Flanders, medieval Ghent (Gent/Gand in Dutch/French) was a great cloth town that grew to become medieval Europe's largest city after Paris and Constantinople. The hard-working townsfolk fought hard for their civil liberties, but were finally cowed in 1540 having enraged Ghent-born Holy Roman Emperor Charles V ('Keizer Karel', 'Charles Quint') by refusing to pay taxes to fund his military forays into France. He came down swiftly and heavily, abolishing the town's privileges and humiliating the guildsmen by making them walk around town wearing nooses around their necks. Ghent-folk are still nicknamed 'Stroppendragers' (rope pullers) to this day. This episode signalled the beginning of a long decline as the Low Countries' centre of gravity moved to Antwerp.

However, in the early 19th century, Ghent was the first town in Flanders to harness the Industrial Revolution. Many of its historical buildings were converted into flax- and cotton-processing mills and the city became known as the 'Manchester of the Continent'. These days, Ghent is Flanders' biggest university town, while its vast docks stretching for miles to the north provide its economic life-blood. Older dock areas Achterdok, Handelsdok and Houtdok are beginning a massive regeneration program.

Sights & Activities

The three-day **CityCard Gent** (www.visitgent.be; 48-/72-hour €25/30) gives free entrance to all of Ghent's top museums and monuments and allows unlimited travel on trams and city buses, plus a boat trip. It's excellent value. Buy one at participating museums, major bus offices or the tourist office.

Ghent

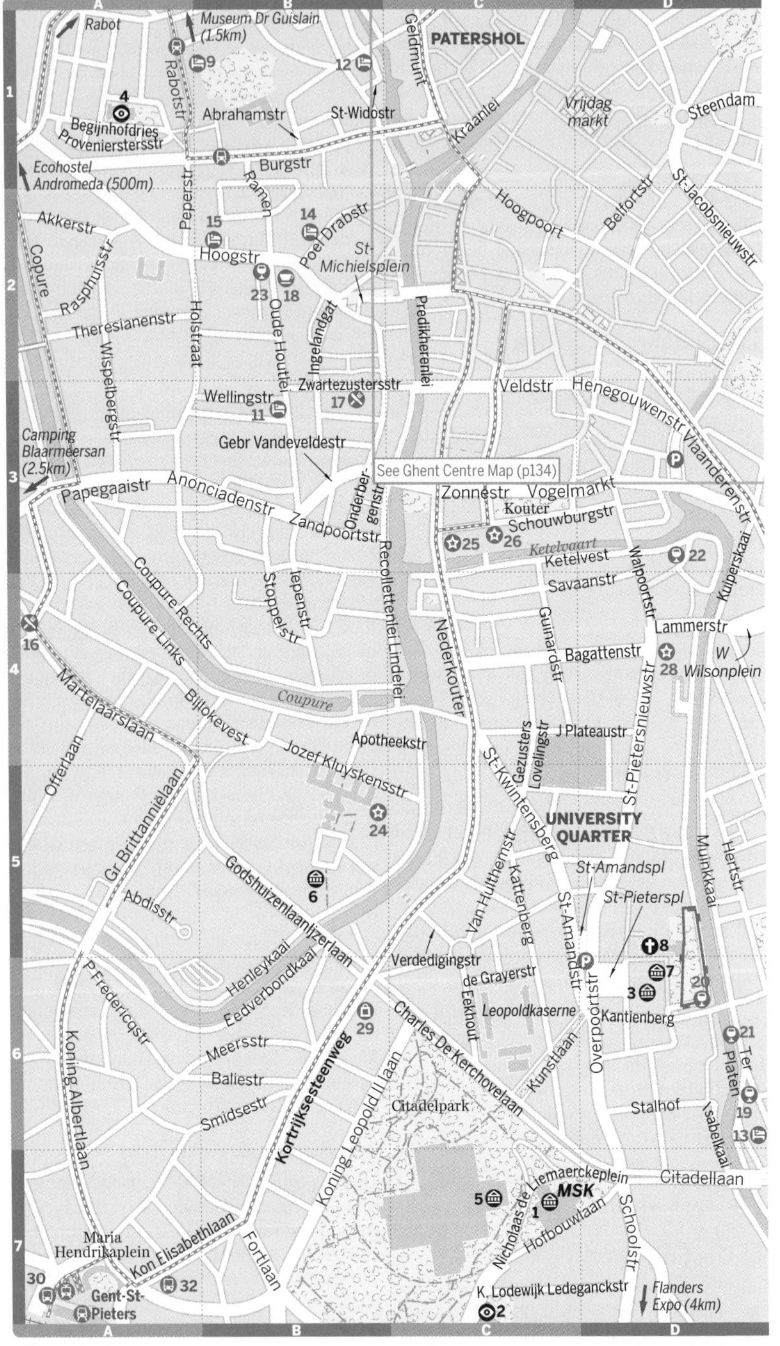

PATERSHOL
Rabot
Museum Dr Guislain (1.5km)
Geldmunt
Rabotstr
Abrahamstr
St-Widostr
Kraanlei
Vrijdag markt
Steendam
Begijnhofdries
Provenierstersstr
Burgstr
Ecohostel Andromeda (500m)
Peperstr
Ramen
Hoogpoort
Belfortstr
St-Jacobsnieuwstr
Akkerstr
Poel
Drabstr
Hoogstr
St-Michielsplein
Copure
Rasphuisstr
Oude Houtlei
Predikherenlei
Theresianenstr
Holstraat
Ingelandgat
Wispelbergstr
Zwartezustersstr
Veldstr
Henegouwenstr
Wellingstr
Gebr Vandeveldestr
Vlaanderenstr
Camping Blaarmeersan (2.5km)
See Ghent Centre Map (p134)
Papegaaistr
Anonciadenstr
Onderbergenstr
Zonnestr
Vogelmarkt
Kouter
Schouwburgstr
Zandpoortstr
Ketelvaart
Ketelvest
Walpoortstr
Kuiperskaai
Savaanstr
Coupure Rechts
Coupure Links
Stoppelstr
Iepenstr
Recollettenlei
Lindelei
Nederkouter
Guinardstr
Lammerstr
Bagattenstr
W Wilsonplein
Martelaarslaan
Coupure
Bijlokevest
Apotheekstr
Gezusters
Lovelingstr
J Plateaustr
St-Pietersnieuwstr
Offerlaan
Jozef Kluyskensstr
St-Kwintensberg
UNIVERSITY QUARTER
Gr Brittanniëlaan
Godshuizenlaan
Van-Hulthemstr
Kattenberg
St-Amandspl
Muinkkaai
Hertstr
Abdisstr
IJzerlaan
St-Amandstr
St-Pieterspl
Verdedigingstr
de Grayerstr
Henleykaai
Eedverbondkaai
P Fredericqstr
Leopoldkaserne
Overpoortstr
Kantienberg
Eekhout
Charles De Kerchovelaan
Kunstlaan
Koning Albertlaan
Meersstr
Baliestr
Smidsestr
Kortrijksesteenweg
Koning Leopold II laan
Citadelpark
Stalhof
Ter Platen
Isabelkaai
Nicholaas de Liemaerckeplein
MSK
Citadellaan
Hofbouwlaan
Schoolstr
Maria Hendrikaplein
Kon Elisabethlaan
Fortlaan
K. Lodewijk Ledeganckstr
Flanders Expo (4km)
Gent-St-Pieters
1
2
3
4
5
6
7
8
9
11
12
13
14
15
16
17
18
19
20
21
22
23
24
25
26
28
29
30
32
A
B
C
D

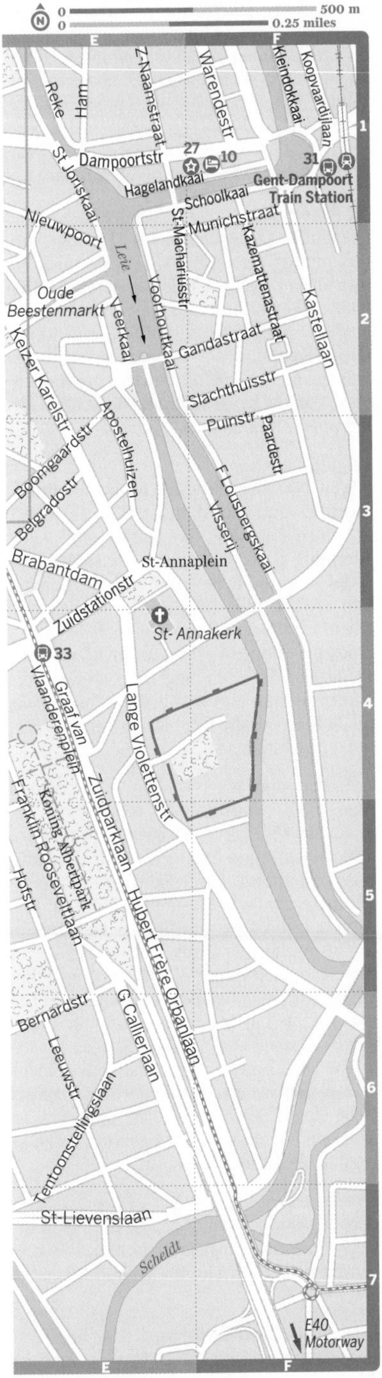

Ghent

Top Sights
1 MSK C7

Sights
2 Botanical Gardens C7
3 De Wereld van Kina D6
4 Oude Begijnhof A1
5 SMAK C7
6 STAM B5
7 St-Pietersabdij D6
8 St-Pieterskerk D5

Sleeping
9 Atlas B&B B1
10 Big Sleep F1
11 Chambres d'Hôtes Verhaegen B3
12 De Draecke B1
13 Engelen aan de Waterkant D6
14 Hotel Erasmus B2
15 Sandton Grand Hotel Reylof B2

Eating
16 Carte Blanche A4
17 't Oud Clooster B3

Drinking & Nightlife
18 Cafe Labath B2
19 De Brouwzaele D6
20 De Geus van Gent D6
21 De Planck D6
22 Gruut D3
23 Hotsy Totsy B2

Entertainment
24 De Bijloke B5
25 De Vlaamse Opera C3
26 Handelsbeurs C3
27 Muzikantenhuis F1
28 Vooruit D4

Shopping
29 Atlas & Zanzibar B6

Transport
30 De Lijn ticket kiosk A7
31 Eurolines Bus Departures F1
32 Eurolines Office A7
Gent-Dampoort Bus Station ..... (see 31)
33 Gent-Zuid Bus Station E4

Central Ghent

Ghent's magnificent medieval core comprises three interconnected squares, dominated by the towers and spires of the Belfort and two imposing, if dour, churches. Directly west, the canal is lined with medieval-styled buildings curving around to the pretty Patershol district.

St-Baafskathedraal CATHEDRAL

(Map p134; www.sintbaafskathedraal.be; St-Baafsplein; ⏲8.30am-6pm Apr-Oct, to 5pm Nov-Mar) St-Baafs cathedral's towering interior has some fine stained glass and an unusual combination of brick vaulting with stone tracery. A €0.20 leaflet guides you round the cathedral's numerous art treasures, including a big original Rubens opposite the stairway that leads down into the partly muralled crypts. However, most visitors come to see just one magnificent work – the Van Eycks' 1432 'Flemish Primitive' masterpiece, *The Adoration of the Mystic Lamb.*

It's kept in a special temperature-controlled, half-darkened chapel near the west entrance. If you don't want to queue to see the original, a photographic copy is displayed for free in side-chapel 30, the sixth on the right beside the altar.

Grasbrug VIEWPOINT

(Map p134) To admire Ghent's towers and gables at their most photogenic, stand just west of the little Grasbrug bridge at dusk. It's a truly gorgeous scene, though the appealing waterfront facades of Graslei aren't as old as they look – these 'medieval' warehouses and town houses were largely rebuilt to make Ghent look good for the 1913 World Fair. Canal trips depart from either end of the Grasbrug and nearby Vleeshuisbrug bridges.

Belfort HISTORIC BUILDING

(Map p134; www.belfortgent.be; Botermarkt; adult/concession/children €6/2/free; ⏲10am-5.30pm) Ghent's soaring, Unesco-listed, 14th-century belfry is topped by a large dragon. That's a weathervane not a fire breather and it's become something of a city mascot. You'll meet two previous dragon incarnations on the climb to the top (mostly by lift), but other than some bell-making exhibits, the real attraction is the view. Enter through the **Lakenhalle**, Ghent's cloth hall that was left half-built in 1445 and only completed in 1903.

The Belfort bells are played at carillon concerts at 11.30am Fridays and 11am on summer Sundays.

Gravensteen CASTLE

(Map p134; www.gravensteengent.be; St-Veerleplein; adult/concession/child €10/7.50/6; ⏲10am-6pm Apr-Oct, 9am-5pm Nov-Mar) The counts of Flanders' quintessential 12th-century stone castle comes complete with moat, turrets and arrow slits. It's all the more remarkable considering that during the 19th century the site was converted into a cotton mill. Meticulously restored since, the interior sports the odd suit of armour, a guillotine and torture devices. The relative lack of furnishings is compensated with a hand-held 45-minute movie guide, which sets a tongue-in-cheek historical costumed drama in the rooms, prison pit and battlements.

If you just want a photo of the castle, there's a great viewpoint on St-Widostraat.

★**Patershol** NEIGHBOURHOOD

(Map p134; www.patershol.be) Dotted with half-hidden restaurants, enchanting Patershol is a web of twisting cobbled lanes whose old-world houses were once home to leather tradesmen and to the Carmelite Fathers (Paters), hence the name. An aimless wander here is one of the city's great pleasures; the low key restaurants and bars make it a popular hangout for students.

Vrijdagmarkt NEIGHBOURHOOD

(Map p134) Once the city's forum for public meetings and executions, this large square is named for the Friday market (still held). Tempting *cafés* sit beneath step-gabled facades surveyed by a grand **statue of Jacob van Artevelde** (Map p134; Vrijdagmarkt), Ghent's 14th-century anti-French leader. A block west notice the 15th-century **Dulle Griet** (Map p134), a 5m-long red super-cannon whose 660mm bore and 250kg cannon balls made it one of the five biggest siege guns of the entire Middle Ages.

Huis van Alijn MUSEUM

(Map p134; www.huisvanalijn.be; Kraanlei 65; adult/child €6/2; ⏲11am-5.30pm Tue-Sat, 10am-5.30pm Sun) In a restored 1363 children's hospice complex, this delightful museum examines everyday life from the 1890s to 1970s. Although not all is in English, many exhibits are self-explanatory, including quaint recreated shop interiors, photos of wedding fashions, fun 1960s and '70s rooms, and the disarmingly moving collage of family home videos.

You can also try out the distinctive Ghent accent and see a traditional **Puppet Show** (adult €5; ⏲2.30pm Sat Sep-Jun), plus visit an atmospheric old-world *café* serving Trappist beers at old-world prices.

Werregarensteeg AREA

(Map p134; www.ghentizm.be) Graffiti is positively encouraged as an art form in this tiny central alley, known locally as Graffitistraatje.

Stadhuis CITY HALL

(Map p134; www.visitgent.be/en/town-hall; Botermarkt 1; tour €5; ⏲2.30pm Mon-Thu May-Sep)

Ghent's flamboyant city hall was started in 1519 but not finished till 1600, by which time it had transformed into a Renaissance-style palazzo. It's a prime spot for weddings, but tourist access is limited to one-hour guided visits starting from the tourist office. Don't confuse the Stadhuis with the controversial Stadshal, a brand new barnlike construction on nearby Bottermarkt.

Oude Begijnhof NEIGHBOURHOOD
(Map p130) Ghent has three widely separated *begijnhoven*. This is the most central but there's no remnant enclosing wall so it's just a pretty area of lanes around a church and green. The most photogenic alley is Proveniersterssstraat.

Design Museum MUSEUM
(Map p134; www.designmuseumgent.be; J Breydelstraat 5; adult/concession €8/6; ⏲10am-6pm Tue-Sun) A vast toilet-roll 'sculpture' humorously marks the back side of this museum, whose collection specialises in furnishings from baroque through art nouveau and 1970s psychedelic to 1990s furniture-as-art. It's hosted in an architecturally schizophrenic building that catapults you from the 18th century into the 21st, then drags you back again.

MIAT MUSEUM
(Museum voor Industriële Archeologie en Textiel; Map p134; www.miat.gent.be; Minnemeers 9; adult/youth €6/2; ⏲10am-6pm Tue-Sun) In a five-floor, 19th-century mill-factory building, this thought-provoking museum celebrates Ghent's history of textile production and examines the social effects of 250 years of industrialisation. A very extensive collection of heavy mechanical weaving equipment comes deafeningly alive on Tuesday or Thursday mornings around 10am; earplugs are provided. There are great city skyline views from the top floor.

Every second Sunday of the month a 35mm film is screened here at 5pm.

Canal Cruises BOAT TOUR
(adult/senior/child €7/6.50/4; ⏲10am-6pm Mar–mid Oct, weekends only in winter) Two companies using four names operate canal cruises starting from the Grasbrug or Vleeshuisbrug bridges. All depart several times hourly with frequency varying according to demand. They cover essentially the same three-pronged up-and-back route (40 minutes), but on fine days **De Gentenaer Rederij** (Map p134; ☎0473 48 10 36; www.rederijdegentenaer.be; Vleeshuisbrug) adds an extra 10 minutes along Ketelvaart and then tunnels under Francois Laurentplein to emerge briefly outside the Duivelsteen waterfront castle-house.

Greater Ghent

Museum Dr Guislain MUSEUM
(www.museumdrguislain.be; Jozef Guislainstraat 43; adult/youth €8/3; ⏲9am-5pm Tue-Fri, 1-5pm Sat & Sun; 🚊1) Hidden away in an 1857 neo-Gothic psychiatric hospital, this enthralling mental-health museum takes visitors on a trilingual, multicultural journey through the history of psychiatry, from gruesome Neolithic trepanning to contemporary brain scans via cage beds, straightjackets, shackles and phrenology. Dr D'Arsonval's extraordinary 1909 radiographic apparatus looks like a Dr Frankenstein creation. Tram 1 stops outside.

STAM MUSEUM
(Map p130; www.stamgent.be; Bijloke Complex; adult/concession €8/6; ⏲10am-6pm Tue-Sun; 🚊4) Shoehorned into a 17th-century former nunnery-hospital complex, this satisfying

ADORING THE MYSTIC LAMB

Completed in 1432 for a chapel of St- Baafskathedraal, the Van Eyck brothers' 20-panel altarpiece **The Adoration of the Mystic Lamb** (Het Lam Gods; http://vaneyck.kikirpa.be; St- Baafskathedraal; adult/child/audio guide €4/3/1.50; ⏲9.30am-4.45pm Mon-Sat, 1-4.30pm Sun, closes 3.45pm Nov-Mar) is one of the earliest major works of art ever undertaken using oil paints. It's had more than its fair share of adventures: it narrowly survived the Calvinists, was marched off to Paris during the French Revolution, and was grabbed by Germans during WWII who concealed it in an Austrian salt mine. The nudity of Adam and Eve on its outer panels so horrified Austria's Emperor Joseph II that he had them replaced with clothed versions. Today all but one of the original panels have been recovered. *De Rechtvaardige Rechters* (The Fair Judges) remains missing (replaced by a copy) following a 1934 theft, which is the subject of the investigative thriller *The Sacred Panel* published in 2010.

Note that until 2017, individual panels will be periodically removed from the cathedral for restoration, a job that will be performed in a special glass-sided workshop, visible to visitors at MSK (p135).

Ghent Centre

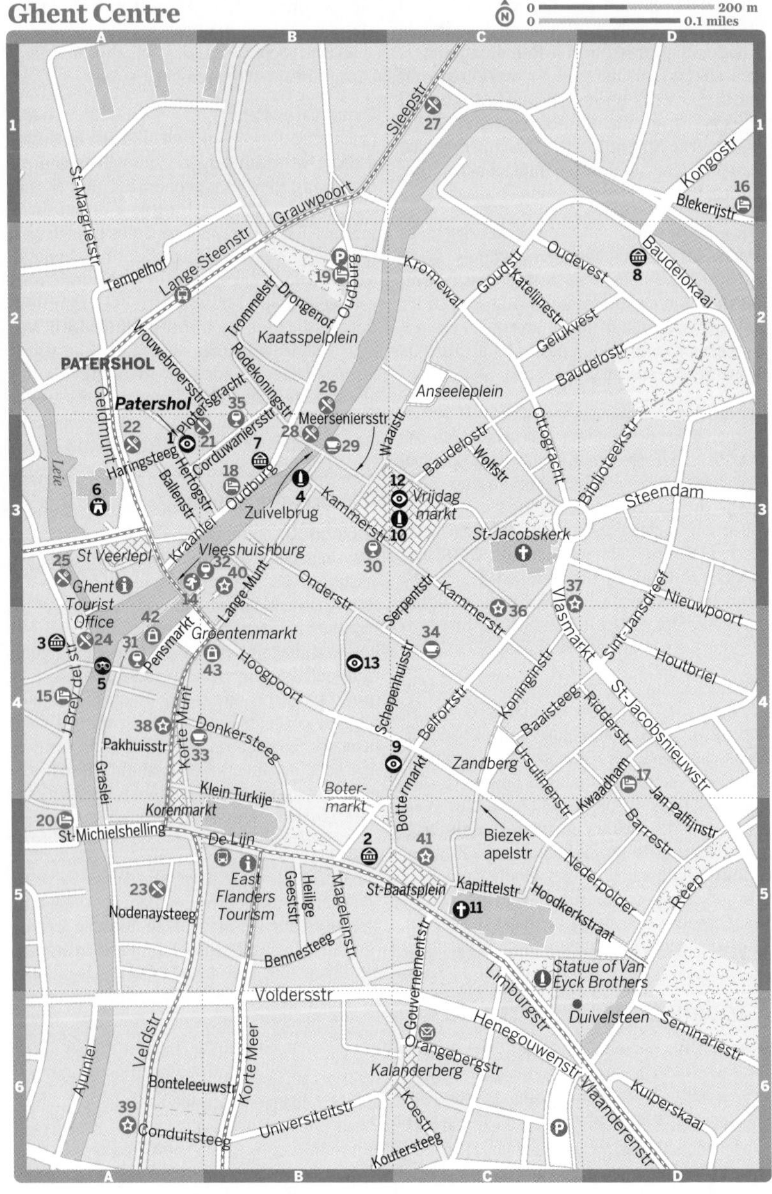

21st-century museum does a very thorough job of explaining Ghent's evolution over 70,000 years of history. A giant satellite image vividly illustrates the vast extent of the docks, and you could spend hours clicking between interactive map views of Ghent in different eras. City treaties and treasures are interspersed with choose-your-own film clips and a chance to peer into the future.

St-Pietersabdij HISTORIC BUILDING

(Map p130; www.sintpietersabdijgent.be; Alison tour €4, exhibitions adult/concession/child €6/

Ghent Centre

Top Sights
1 Patershol ... A3

Sights
2 Belfort ... B5
3 Design Museum ... A4
4 Dulle Griet ... B3
5 Grasbrug ... A4
6 Gravensteen ... A3
7 Huis van Alijn ... B3
8 MIAT ... D2
9 Stadhuis ... C4
10 Statue of Jacob van Artevelde ... C3
11 St-Baafskathedraal ... C5
12 Vrijdagmarkt ... C3
13 Werregarensteeg ... B4

Activities, Courses & Tours
14 De Gentenaer Rederij ... A3

Sleeping
15 Ghent Marriott ... A4
16 Hostel 47 ... D1
17 Hotel Flandria ... D4
18 Hotel Harmony ... B3
19 Simon Says ... B2
20 Uppelink ... A5

Eating
21 Amadeus ... B3
22 Avalon ... A3
23 Brasserie Pakhuis ... A5
24 Brooderie ... A4
25 House of Eliott ... A3
26 Panda ... B2
27 Pizza Gülhan ... C1
28 Soup Lounge ... B3

Drinking & Nightlife
29 Barista Zuivelbrug ... B3
30 Herberg de Dulle Griet ... B3
31 Het Spijker ... A4
32 Het Waterhuis aan de Bierkant ... B3
33 Mokabon ... A4
34 Pink Flamingo's ... C4
35 Rococo ... B3
't Dreupelkot ... (see 32)

Entertainment
36 Café Trefpunt ... C4
37 Charlatan ... C3
38 Damberd ... A4
39 FNAC ... A6
40 Hot Club de Gand ... B3
41 NT Gent Schouwburg ... C5

Shopping
42 Groot Vleeshuis ... A4
43 Tierenteyn-Verlent ... B4

4.50/free; ⏲10am-5pm Tue-Sun, last tour 4pm) Once the country's biggest abbey, St-Pieters was the original centre around which Ghent grew. Its fabulous wealth evaporated after French revolutionary armies confiscated all its properties, stripped its interiors and demolished the abbot's house. The impressively vast 1720 baroque-fronted **St-Pieterskerk** (Map p130) survived and the shell of the main monastery was later used as a military garrison. You can stroll for free among ruins, vines and apple trees in the abbey gardens.

Inside, the abbey's most impressive feature is the muralled roof of the monks' former refectory. That's point 15 in 'Alison', a handheld video tour designed as 90 minutes of tangential musings by a ghost monk guide in a medieval love triangle. If you're rushed, the key tracks are 2 to 4 (history) and 10 (the garden).

De Wereld van Kina MUSEUM

(Map p130; ☎09-244 73 73; www.dewereldvankina.be; St-Pietersplein 14; adult/concession/child €5/3.75/free; ⏲9am-4.30pm Mon-Fri, 2-5pm Sun; 👪) This mish-mash of a natural history museum is aimed primarily at school kids. Meet Pterygotus (a man-sized prehistoric lobster), walk through a human body with pounding heart, and get quizzed in the lively sex-education room. Press buttons to hear the songs of stuffed birds and find the model of Ghent as it looked in the 16th century.

★MSK GALLERY

(Museum voor Schone Kunsten; Map p130; ☎09-240 07 00; www.mskgent.be; Citadelpark; adult/youth €8/2; ⏲10am-6pm Tue-Sun) Styled like a Greek temple, this superb 1903 fine-art gallery introduces a veritable A–Z of great Belgian and Low Countries' painters from the 14th to mid-20th centuries. Highlights include a happy family of coffins by Magritte, Luminist canvases by Emile Claus, and Pieter Breughel the Younger's 1621 *Dorpsadvocaat* – a brilliant portrait of a village lawyer oozing with arrogance. English-language explanation cards are available in each room.

SMAK GALLERY

(Museum of Contemporary Art; Map p130; www.smak.be; Citadelpark; adult/youth €12/2, 10am-1pm Sun free; ⏲10am-6pm Tue-Sun; 🚌5) Ghent's highly regarded Museum of Contemporary

Art features regularly changing exhibitions of provocative, cutting-edge installations, which sometimes spill out right across the city.

Botanical Gardens GARDENS
(Map p130; Emile Clauslaan; ⏲glasshouses 9am-4.20pm Mon-Fri, 9-11.50am Sat & Sun) These pretty gardens' glasshouses contain an impressive collection of tropical plants and offer shivering winter travellers what's effectively a free sauna.

Festivals & Events

Gentse Feesten ARTS FESTIVAL
(www.gentsefeesten.be; ⏲Jul) During mid-July's raucous festival, the city's many squares become venues for a variety of street-theatre performances and there are big associated techno and jazz festivals. Those wanting a merrily boozy party atmosphere will love it. But consider avoiding Ghent at this time if you don't.

Gent Festival van Vlaanderen MUSIC FESTIVAL
(www.gentfestival.be; ⏲mid-Sep) As if the Gentse Feesten wasn't enough, there are dozens more concerts in September and a big fireworks display.

I Love Techno MUSIC FESTIVAL
(www.ilovetechnoeurope.com; Flanders Expo; ⏲2nd weekend Nov) One of Europe's biggest techno-music festivals has grown massively since 1995 when the first edition saw Daft Punk playing the Vooruit.

Sleeping

Ghent offers innovative accommodation in all budget ranges. Websites www.gent-accommodations.be and www.bedandbreakfast-gent.be help you judge availability in the city's numerous appealing B&Bs.

★**Uppelink** HOSTEL €
(Map p134; ☎09-279 44 77; www.hosteluppelink.com; Sint-Michielsplein 21; dm €19-35, s/tw €50/60) Within a classic step-gabled canalside house, the show-stopping attraction at this super-central new hostel is the unbeatable view of Ghent's main towers as seen from the breakfast room and from the biggest, cheapest dorms. Smaller rooms have little view, if any.

De Draecke HOSTEL €€
(Map p130; ☎09-233 70 50; www.jeugdherbergen.be/en/youth-hostels/city-hostels/gent-de-draeckewww.vjh.be; St-Widostraat 11; dm/tw €25/59, HI members save €3; @ 📶) Behind a pseudo-medieval facade facing a picturesque willow-lined central canal lies this slightly institutional modern HI hostel. Lockers cost €2 but the luggage room is free. No lockout.

Camping Blaarmeersen CAMPGROUND €
(☎09-266 81 60; www.gent.be/blaarmeersen; Zuiderlaan 12; campsite per adult/child/car/tent/caravan €6/3/3/6/6; ⏲Mar–mid-Oct) Camping ground in a recreational park 3.5km west of the centre.

★**Simon Says** GUESTHOUSE €€
(Map p134; ☎09-233 03 43; www.simon-says.be; Sluizeken 8; d from €110; 📶) Two fashionably styled guest rooms above an excellent coffee shop in a brightly coloured corner house with art-nouveau facade.

★**Engelen aan de Waterkant** B&B €€
(Map p130; ☎09-223 08 83; www.engelenaande-waterkant.be; Ter Platen 30; s/d €120/140) Two 'angel' rooms are an opportunity for the interior-designer owner to experiment and for guests to soak up the special atmosphere in a 1900 town house overlooking the tree-lined canal.

Big Sleep B&B €€
(Map p130; ☎0495 78 29 41, 09-233 43 52; www.bigsleep.be; Hagelandkaai 38; s €65-75, d €80-90; 📶) Friendly B&B whose three rooms have showers but shared toilets. The lovely high-ceilinged 1890 town house is decorated with souvenirs of world travels, while the quietest 'Green Room' has a swirling 1970s decor, hand-painted by a renowned local artist. It's handy for Gent-Dampoort station.

Hotel Erasmus HERITAGE HOTEL €€
(Map p130; ☎09-224 21 95; www.erasmushotel.be; Poel 25; small/large/luxury d from €99/120/150; ⏲reception 7am-10.30pm; 📶) A suit of armour guards the breakfast in this creaky 16th-century building whose 12 guest rooms have a mixture of old and antique furniture, giving it an atmospheric feeling of times gone by.

Atlas B&B B&B €€
(Map p130; ☎09-233 49 91; www.atlasbenb.be; Rabotstraat 40; s €63-78, d €79-99, tr €102-122; P @ 📶) This fine 1863 town house has gorgeous belle-epoque, art deco and art nouveau touches in a lounge featuring maps, globes and an honesty bar. Four very distinctive guest rooms are themed by continent.

A Place To Be B&B €€
(☎0495 15 47 42; Groot Begijnhof 91, Onze Lieve Vrowstraat; s/d from €53/63; 📶) A rare chance

to sleep within the walls of a *begijnhof*. The nicest of three homely rooms has its own kitchenette. St-Armandsberg *begijnhof* is around 500m east of Gent-Dampoort. Using the east gate off Schoolstraat, the B&B is the second doorway on the right, veering right near the little shrine-chapel. Check in before the *begijnhof* gates shut at night.

Hostel 47 HOSTEL €€
(Map p134; ☎0478 71 28 27; www.hostel47.com; Blekerijstraat 47-51; dm €26.50-29.50, d/tr €66/90; 📶) Unusually calm yet pretty central, this inviting hostel has revamped a high-ceilinged historic house with virginal white walls, spacious bunk rooms and designer fittings. Free lockers and cursory breakfast with Nespresso coffee; no bar.

Hotel Flandria HOTEL €€
(Map p134; ☎09-223 06 26; www.hotelflandria-gent.be; Barrestraat 3; s/d €60/70, without bathroom €45/57; @📶) Map-plastered walls beckon you into this helpfully central hotel. Rooms are mostly cramped and simple; some are better appointed than others. Attractive rooms 12 and 23 have shared bathrooms but appealing cathedral views. Good beds.

Ecohostel Andromeda HOSTEL €€
(☎0486 67 80 33; ecohostel.be; Bargiekaai 35; dm €22-24, d €65; ⌚reception 2-8pm; 📶; 🚊1) Sleep on a reed-sprouting 'recycled' barge with small, open-top conversation deck. The boat's canalside moorings are 600m northwest of Oude Begijnhof. Or from tram 1 stop Witte Kaproenenplein walk two minutes south between seven-storey apartment blocks on Alois Joosstraat. It's not in the most scenic part of the city. Organic breakfast included.

Sandton Grand Hotel Reylof HOTEL €€€
(Map p130; ☎09-235 40 70; www.sandton.eu/gent; Waaistraat 5; standard/deluxe/ste from €139/159/189; @📶🏊) Ghent's newest and biggest central hotel is the only one to offer an indoor swimming pool (albeit only 4m long). Publicity photos emphasise the palatial 18th-century reception building, but most of the 158 rooms are new with striking interior design, strong colours and lashings of modern art. Steep stairs lead to the hammam/sauna (no extra charge).

The showy champagne bar has a distinctly Las Vegas feel.

Hotel Harmony BOUTIQUE HOTEL €€€
(Map p134; ☎09-324 26 80; www.hotel-harmony.be; Kraanlei 37; s €140-210, d €155-230; 📶🏊) Luxuriously heaped pillows, fine linen, Miró-esque art and swish modern colours lie beneath the 18th-century beams of this old-meets-new beauty. Each of the 25 rooms has a coffee maker and even the smallest is amply sized, but shapes and views vary. Some have pastel nudes painted on the walls, others have Jacuzzis, and rooms 30 and 31 share a wonderful panorama of Ghent's spires.

Check Facebook for promotional deals.

Chambres d'Hôtes Verhaegen B&B €€€
(Map p130; ☎09-265 07 60; http://neooselonneo.be; Oude Houtlei 110; d €195-280; ⌚reception 2-6pm) This sumptuous 1770s urban palace retains original sections of 18th-century Chinese wallpaper, a dining room with romantic Austrian-era murals, a dazzling salon and a neatly manicured parterre garden. The five guest rooms combine well-placed modernist and retro touches with superb 'Paola's Room' named for the young Italian princess who stayed here long before becoming Belgium's present queen. Breakfast costs €18.

Ghent Marriott HOTEL €€€
(Map p134; ☎09-233 93 93; www.marriottghent.be; Korenlei 10; d from €159; 📶) Yes, it's an international chain complete with glass and steel atrium. But you'd never guess so from the traditional east facade that incorporates four medieval stone house fronts. Canal-view rooms (€50 extra) have superb waterfront panoramas. Look online for some good deals.

Eating

Cosy, upmarket restaurants in the delightful cobbled alleyways of Patershol cover most cuisines. Several eateries jostle for summer terrace space on Graslei's gorgeous canalside terrace; there's fast food around Korenmarkt and great-value Turkish options along Sleepstraat. Numerous vegetarian and organic choices feature on the tourist office's free Veggieplan Gent guide map.

Amadeus RIBS €
(Map p134; ☎09-225 13 85; www.amadeusspareribrestaurant.be; Plotersgracht 8/10; mains €13.75-18.75; ⌚6.30-11pm) All-you-can-eat spare ribs (€15.95) at four Ghent addresses, all within ancient buildings that are full of atmosphere, bustle and cheerful conversation.

't Oud Clooster TAVERNA €
(Map p130; ☎09-233 78 02; www.toudclooster.be; Zwartezusterstraat 5; mains €9-18; ⌚noon-2.30pm & 6-10.30pm Mon-Fri, noon-2.30pm & 5-10.30pm Sat, 5-10.30pm Sun) Mostly candlelit at night, this

atmospheric double-level 'pratcafe' is built into sections of what was long ago a nunnery, hence the sprinkling of religious statues and cherub lamp-holders. Well-priced *café* food is presented with unexpected style and the kitchen works until midnight. Try the original curry-cream Spaghetti Oud Clooster (€9).

Avalon VEGETARIAN €

(Map p134; ☎09-224 37 24; www.restaurantavalon.be; Geldmunt 32; mains €8-16; ⌚11.30am-2.30pm Tue-Sun; ✎) 'Live well and laugh often' is the Avalon's sage suggestion, backed up with copious, reliably delicious vegetarian and vegan lunches. Eat in the intriguing warren of little rooms or on a delightful tree-shaded rear terrace.

Soup Lounge CAFE €

(Map p134; www.souplounge.be; Zuivelbrug 4; small/large soup €4/5, sandwiches €2.80; ⌚10am-6pm) At this bright, central retro-'70s soup kitchen, each bowlful comes with add-your-own cheese and croutons, two rolls and a piece of fruit. Canal views are free.

Pizza Gülhan TURKISH €

(Map p134; Sleepstraat 70; pide from €5, grills €9-14, beer/cava/tea €1.80/3.20/1.25; ⌚11.30am-midnight Wed-Mon) Want to (over) fill your stomach for €5? It's possible at Gülhan, a large, mildly garish modern diner that's NOT a pizzeria, unless you count the groaning plate-loads of excellent garnished fresh pide as 'pizza'. It's often crowded with appreciative locals, both Flemish and Turkish.

Brooderie BAKERY €

(Map p134; ☎09-225 06 23; Jan Breydelstraat 8; mains €9-16; ⌚8am-6pm Tue-Sun) Rustic bakery and tearoom serving lunches, breakfasts, soups and savoury snacks. It also has simple, colourful B&B rooms with shared bathrooms (from €60).

Brasserie Pakhuis EUROPEAN, SEAFOOD €€

(Map p134; ☎09-223 55 55; www.pakhuis.be; Schuurkenstraat 4; mains €18-29, menu €45; ⌚noon-2.30pm & 6.30pm-midnight Mon-Sat, bar 11am-1am) This hip, if mildly ostentatious, modern brasserie-bar-restaurant is set in a magnificently restored former textile warehouse. It retains the original century-old wrought ironwork and an incredible roof. It's well worth popping inside, even if you only stop for a drink.

Panda VEGETARIAN €€

(Map p134; ☎09-225 07 86; Oudburg 38; mains €17-22; ⌚noon-2pm & 6.15-8.45pm Mon-Sat; ✎) Good veggie food set to classical music and served on linen at tables with fresh orchids. Three windows have canal views. The daily changing lunch plate presents a truly artistic palate of flavours, organic beers are available and there's a short wine list. By day enter through an organic food shop; at night seek out the side entrance passage.

★House of Eliott SEAFOOD €€€

(Map p134; ☎09-225 21 28; www.thehouseofeliott.be; J Breydelstraat 36; mains €36-50, menus €52-65; ⌚noon-2pm & 6-11pm Thu-Mon, closed Sep) Oozing pseudo-1920s charm, this gently camp canalside gem is full of flapper mannequins and sepia photos inspired by an old British TV series. The little balcony terrace perches just above the canal waters. Gastronomically, lobster dominates. Book well in advance.

Carte Blanche SEAFOOD €€€

(Map p130; ☎09-233 28 08; www.carte-blanchepw.be; Martelaarslaan 321; lunch menu €19, tasting menu €89.50; ⌚noon-2pm Mon-Thu, noon-2pm & 7-9.30pm Fri & Sat) Lobster is a big feature of the menu at this elegant but friendly restaurant. The dark-hued dining room feels very grown up, and the Flemish food is beautifully presented.

Drinking

Ghent's fabulous bar scene is endlessly inspiring, with more than 280 choices in the centre alone.

★'t Dreupelkot BAR

(Map p134; ☎09-224 21 20; www.dreupelkot.be; Groentenmarkt 12; ⌚4pm-late) A traditional *jenever* bar serving 100 Belgian concoctions – including the owner's home-made prune and raisin versions – and one north French. Traditionally *jenever* is made from grain and malt and packs a punch at 40% proof. The bare brick and tiled interior is warmly atmospheric.

Het Waterhuis aan de Bierkant PUB

(Map p134; www.waterhuisaandebierkant.be; Groentenmarkt 12; ⌚11am-1am) Sharing an enticing waterfront terrace, this photogenic classic beer pub has an interior draped in dried hops and three exclusive house beers amid the wide possible selection.

Hotsy Totsy JAZZ BAR

(Map p130; www.hotsytotsy.be; Hoogstraat 1; ⌚6pm-1am Mon-Fri, 8pm-2am Sat & Sun) A 1930s vamp pouts above the zinc of this classic artist's *café* with silver-floral wallpaper, black-

and-white film photos and free live jazz at 9pm most Thursdays (October to April). It was founded by the brothers of famous Flemish author Hugo Claus.

Pink Flamingo's CAFE, BAR
(Map p134; www.pinkflamingos.be; Onderstraat 55; ⏲noon-midnight Mon-Wed, noon-3am Thu-Sat, 2pm-midnight Sun) Lively kitsch-overloaded cafe-bar with Barbie lamps, 1970s wallpaper and ample plastic fruit.

Rococo BAR
(Map p134; Corduwaniersstraat 5; ⏲from 10pm) Lit only by candles, this classic late-night *café*-bar with carved wooden ceilings is an ideal place for cosy midnight conversations.

Herberg de Dulle Griet PUB
(Map p134; www.dullegriet.be; Vrijdagmarkt 50; ⏲noon-1am Tue-Sat, to 7pm Sun, 4.30pm-1am Mon) Heavy beams, a heraldic ceiling, barrel tables, lacy lampshades and the odd boar's head all add character to one of Ghent's best-known beer pubs.

De Planck PUB
(Map p130; www.deplanck.be; ⏲11.30am-11pm) Yes, palm trees grow in Ghent, albeit small ones on the deck of this appealing barge-*café*. Good-value snack meals supplement a choice of 150 beers, including its own, pleasantly hoppy 6.8% Planckske house beer.

Mokabon COFFEE
(Map p134; www.mokabon.be; Donkersteeg 35; ⏲8am-6pm Mon-Sat) In a graphic metaphor of globalisation, Ghent's classic old-world coffee shop is now hidden behind a brash new Starbucks. Its response? A bright new takeaway window beside the timewarp original. But it still serves old-school Belgian coffee with whipped cream.

Het Spijker PUB
(Map p134; ☎09-329 44 40; www.cafehetspijker.be; Pensmarkt 3; ⏲10am-5am) In winter, tongues of flame lick the entrance portal of this heavy-beamed stone *café*. The oldest building on Graslei (late 12th century), it was once the city grain store. Today it's a lively place that's usually the most central drinking spot to stay open really late.

De Geus van Gent BAR
(Map p130; ☎09-220 28 75; www.geuzenhuis.be; Kantienberg 9; ⏲4pm-late Mon-Thu, 7pm-late Fri-Sun) Congenial, multifaceted *café* with very eclectic decor and jazz jam nights during term-time Wednesdays (10pm).

De Brouwzaele BAR
(Map p130; Ter Platen 17; ⏲11am-2am) Local gents unwind with a newspaper, and grannies lunch on shrimp croquettes in this low-key classic *café* set in a triangular former brewery house. A giant copper brew-still is now the focal point of a very original hop-decked central bar serving Westmalle among many classic draught beers.

Barista Zuivelbrug COFFEE
(Map p134; www.mybarista.be; Meerseniersstraat 16; coffee €2.20-3.60, tarts €2.50-3.50; ⏲8am-6pm Tue-Fri, 9.30am-6pm Sat & Sun; 📶) Central coffee specialist in a 14th-century riverside house.

Cafe Labath COFFEE
(Map p130; www.cafelabath.be; Oude Houtlei 1; coffee €2-3.50, tea €2.70-2.90; ⏲8am-7pm Mon-Fri, 9am-7pm Sat, 10am-6pm Sun) Buzzing place for a fine coffee fix, 'organic' cava (€4.90) or various teas including Indian style *masala chai* and *verse muntthee* (fresh mint infusion).

Gruut BREWERY
(Map p130; ☎09-233 68 21; www.gruut.be; Grote Huidevettershoek 10; ⏲11am-1am) Ghent's brewery-pub serving excellent herb-infused brews.

☆ Entertainment

Dutch-language pamphlet-magazines *Week-Up* and *Zone 09 Magazine* are free from distribution boxes around town. Muziekclub Democrazy (www.democrazy.be) suggests an imaginative and varied network of clubs and events at various venues.

Live Music & Nightclubs

Most *cafés* don't charge entry fees for concerts, but might add a small supplement to listed drink prices.

Hot Club de Gand BAR
(Map p134; www.hotclubdegand.be; cnr Schuddevisstraatje & Groentenmarkt 15b; ⏲11.30am-late) Hidden down the tiny alley behind 't Dreupelkot *jenever* bar, this is a great place to seek out live acoustic music. Be it jazz, gypsy, blues or flamenco, there's likely to be a concert most term-time nights. Sometimes very late.

Charlatan BAR
(Map p134; www.charlatan.be; Vlasmarkt 9; ⏲7pm-late Tue-Sun during term) At perennial favourite Charlatan you might find live music in virtually any genre (from 10pm), sometimes with a cover charge. It generally opens long enough to leave you ready for breakfast. If not, others next door will.

WORTH A TRIP

AROUND GHENT

Greater Ghent peters out into woodlands and meadows in the upmarket suburban villages of Deurle and St-Martens-Latem. A century ago, this attractive area was home to several Symbolist and Expressionist artists, notably Gustave de Smet and Constant Permeke. Today the shady lanes are dotted with galleries and upmarket rural restaurants, ideal for casual exploration by car or bicycle. Behind St-Martens-Latem town hall/police station don't miss the huge sculpted torso that buries her head in the daisy-dotted watermeadow, mooning her bronze posterior at a particularly beautiful curve of river.

Castle fans will love the beauties at **Ooidonk** (09-282 2638; www.ooidonk.be; Ooidonkdreef 7; adult/concession/child €9/6/3, gardens only adult/child €2/0.50; castle 2-5.30pm Sat Jul & Aug, plus Sun Apr–mid-Sep, grounds 9am-6pm Tue-Sun), 3km beyond Deule, and at **Laarne** (www.slotvanlaarne.be; adult/senior/student/child €8/7/5/3; from 3pm Sun Easter-Sep, plus from 3pm Thu Jul & Aug), just east of Ghent.

Muzikantenhuis WORLD MUSIC

(Map p130; 0476 50 28 77; muzikantenhuis.be; Dampoortstraat 50; 6pm-2am Tue-Sun, concerts 9pm Thu-Sat) Ropes, horse harnesses and the sayings of Rumi give this very inexpensive *café* a slightly cheesy atmosphere, but the free traditional Turkish music concerts are the attraction. You might also find jazz and Latin styles.

Café Trefpunt LIVE MUSIC

(Map p134; 09-233 58 48; www.trefpuntvzw.be; Bij St-Jacobs 18; bar 5pm-late, concerts 9pm Mon Oct-Jul) On Monday evenings, when most other places close, Trefpunt has jam sessions or live concerts. Standards tend to be high as performers want to impress the owners, who also organise the Gentse Feesten (p136).

De Centrale WORLD MUSIC

(09-265 98 28; www.decentrale.be; Kraankindersstraat 2; 2pm-midnight) Multicultural centre offering an inspiring range of 'world' music concerts and dances (flamenco, Turkish, North African, Asian).

Damberd LIVE MUSIC

(Map p134; 09-329 53 37; www.damberd.be; Korenmarkt 19) Venerable old pub with live jazz on a Tuesday.

Culture Club CLUB

(09-233 09 46; www.cultureclub.be; Afrikalaan 174; Thu-Sat Oct-May) Once dubbed the 'world's hippest club'; themes and cover charges vary. It's roughly 1.5km north of Gent-Dampoort station via Koopvaardijlaan.

Flanders Expo CONCERT VENUE

(www.flandersexpo.be; Maaltekouter 1; 1) Though primarily for trade fairs, Flanders Expo also hosts occasional big-name rock concerts. It's at the southern terminus for tram 1, 4km beyond Gent-St-Pieters.

Performing Arts

Booking online is wise, though most websites are in Dutch.

Vooruit THEATRE

(Map p130; www.vooruit.be; St-Pietersnieuwstraat 23; 5) A visionary architectural premonition of art deco, the 1912 Vooruit building is a prominent venue for dance, rock concerts, film and visiting theatre companies. Its lively *café* also hosts occasional low-key free concerts and serves draught Moinette 'bio-beer'.

De Bijloke CLASSICAL MUSIC

(Map p130; www.debijloke.be; Jozef Kluyskensstraat 2) Good selection of classical music concerts on a site recycled from a historic abbey and hospital.

De Vlaamse Opera OPERA

(Map p130; www.vlaamseopera.be; Schouwburgstraat 3) Ghent's 1840 opera hall boasts horseshoe-shaped tiered balconies and elegant salons.

Handelsbeurs CONCERT VENUE

(Map p130; www.handelsbeurs.be; Kouter 29) Central concert hall for anything from classical music to Latin to blues.

NT Gent Schouwburg THEATRE

(Map p134; 09-225 01 01; www.ntgent.be; St-Baafsplein 17) Home to Ghent's premier theatre company. It also offers interesting 'open rehearsals' and workshops, but naturally almost everything's in Dutch. Its cafe-restaurant, de Foyer, has a great terrace overlooking the square.

FNAC BOOKING SERVICE
(Map p134; Veldstraat 88) Concert tickets are sold from this chain bookshop.

Shopping

South of Korenmarkt, tram-street Veldstraat sports standard department stores, while two blocks east Mageleinstraat and its offshoots are fashion hunting-grounds. Vlasmarkt is the location for the city's flea market (6am to 1pm Friday to Sunday).

Tierenteyn-Verlent FOOD
(Map p134; www.tierenteyn-verlent.be; Groentenmarkt 3; 9am-6pm Mon-Sat) Mustard makers since 1790, this museumlike shop also sells jams and spices.

Groot Vleeshuis FOOD
(Map p134; www.grootvleeshuis.be; Pensmarkt/Groentenmarkt 7; 10am-6pm Tue-Sun) This long medieval stone hall was built as a meat market and now acts as a promotion and tasting hall for regional agricultural produce. If you're passing by, consider strolling through beneath the hefty old wooden beams and dangling smoked hams.

Atlas & Zanzibar BOOKS
(Map p130; 09-220 87 99; www.atlaszanzibar.be; Kortrijksesteenweg 19; 10am-1pm & 2-6pm Mon-Sat) Ghent's best travel bookshop.

Information

Callshop (Sleepstraat 10; per hr €1.50; 10.30am-10pm Sat-Thu) Inexpensive internet and phone calls.

East Flanders Tourism (Map p134; 09-269 26 00; www.tov.be; St-Niklaasstraat 2; 9am-noon & 1.15-4.45pm Mon-Fri) Useful for cycling-route maps and information on the rural areas around Ghent. It's in the historic Metselaarshuis, a medieval house whose stepped-stone facade is topped with 20th-century bronze jester sculptures.

Ghent Tourist Office (Map p134; 09-266 56 60; www.visitgent.be; Oude Vismijn, St-Veerleplein 5; 9.30am-6.30pm mid-Mar–mid-Oct, to 4.30pm mid-Oct–mid-Mar) Very helpful for free maps and accommodation bookings.

Goffin Change (Henegouwenstraat 25; 9.15am-5.45pm Mon-Fri, 10am-4.30pm Sat) Exchanges cash and some travellers cheques.

Post Office (Map p134; Lange Kruisstraat 55; 9am-6pm Mon-Fri, 9am-3pm Sat) Main post office.

Rail@Net (Brabantdam 138; per hr €1.50; 9am-8pm Tue-Sun) Internet room above a grocery in Ghent's little red-light district.

Use-it (http://ghent.use-it.travel) Brilliantly opinionated, downloadable guide-maps. Available free in print form from hostels and tourist offices.

Getting There & Away

BUS

International There's a **Eurolines Office** (Map p130; 09-220 90 24; www.eurolines.be; Koningin Elisabethlaan 73; 8.30am-noon & 1.30-5.30pm Mon-Fri, 8.30am-noon Sat) near Gent-St-Pieters, but their buses (eg overnight to London at 11.35pm) depart from Gent-Dampoort bus stand.

Regional Some services start from Gent-Zuid bus station (Woodrow Wilsonplein); many more from various points around Gent-St-Pieters station.

TRAIN

Gent-Dampoort, 1km west of the old city, is the handiest station with useful trains to the following:

Antwerp (€9.40, fast/slow 42/64 minutes, three per hour)

Bruges (€6.50, 36 minutes, hourly)

Kortrijk (€6.90, 35 minutes, hourly).

Gent-St-Pieters, 2.5km south of centre and Ghent's main station, has more choices:

Bruges (€6.50 fast/slow 24/42 minutes, five per hour)

Brussels (€8.90, 36 minutes, twice hourly)

Kortrijk (€6.90, fast/slow 26/33 minutes)

Ostend (€9.40, fast/slow 38/55 minutes)

Oudenaarde (€4.50, 50 minutes)

Getting Around

BIKE HIRE

Biker (www.bikerfietsen.be; Steendam 16; per half-/full day €6.50/9; 9am-12.30pm & 1.30-6pm Tue-Sat)

Max Mobiel (www.max-mobiel.be; Vokselslaan 27; per day/week/month €9/25/30) Two minutes' walk south of Gent-St-Pieters station. Branch kiosk at Gent-Dampoort station.

TRAM & CITY BUS

Tickets are cheaper bought from machines, **De Lijn** (Map p134; www.delijn.be; Cataloniestraat 4; 10.15am-5pm Mon-Sat) or the **ticket kiosk** (Map p130; 7am-1.30pm & 2-7pm Mon-Fri) outside Gent-St-Pieters. Tram 1 runs from Gent-St-Pieters to and through the centre, passing walkably close to most major sites.

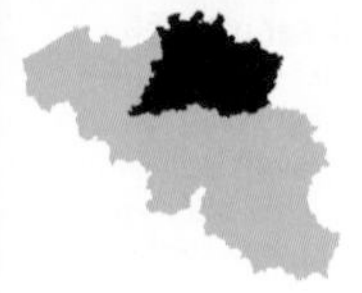

Antwerp & Eastern Flanders

LANGUAGE: DUTCH

Includes ➡

Best Places to Eat

- The Jane (p158)
- Bistro Bis (p181)
- Het Gebaar (p157)
- Il Cardinale (p172)

Best Places to Stay

- De Witte Lelie (p155)
- Rosier 10 (p153)
- Eburon Hotel (p181)
- Oude Brouwerei Keyser Carel (p174)

Why Go?

This region's undisputed centre is dynamic Antwerp, a historic port and diamond-trading city currently basking in a third golden age that has made it one of Europe's more unlikely design and music hubs. Flush with a globally significant fashion, drinking and clubbing scene it may be, but it also retains a small-city friendliness and ease.

Other historic cities on an even more intimate scale include resurgent, reinvented Mechelen, sweet little Lier and self-confident college town Leuven. Lier, Turnhout and lesser-known Diest have arguably Belgium's best *begijnhoven,* and loveable Tongeren claims to be Belgium's oldest settlement.

The towns of this region may be its main attraction, but the southeastern Haspengouw and Hageland do deliver some pretty, undulating hillsides green with orchards and even a few vineyards. And, as always, there are scattered castles to be found lurking in forgotten valleys and villages. Note that here 'Eastern Flanders' refers to the eastern half of today's Flanders region, not that of the historic Flanders county.

Driving Distances

	Antwerp	Tongeren	Turnhout	Mechelen
Tongeren	99			
Turnhout	40	82		
Mechelen	24	81	63	
Leuven	48	57	56	25

Antwerp & Eastern Flanders Highlights

1. Revelling in Rubens and shopping for avant-garde design in **Antwerp** (p144)
2. Marvelling at Leuven's ornate gothic **stadhuis** (p173)
3. Sweetening up at Tienen's sugary **Suikermuseum** (p178)
4. Being charmed by the historic *begijnhoven* in **Diest** (p177), **Lier** (p167) and **Turnhout** (p165)
5. Enjoying three towers for the price of one in magical **Sint-Truiden** (p180)
6. Tackling the 97m tower of Mechelen's **St-Romboutskathedraal** (p168)
7. Drinking in the white-beer experience of **Hoegaarden** (p179)

ANTWERP (ANTWERPEN)

POP 503,200

Belgium's second city and biggest port, Antwerp (Antwerpen/Anvers in Dutch/French) is the country's capital of cool, a powerful magnet for mode moguls, club queens, art lovers and diamond dealers. In the mid-16th century it was one of Europe's most important cities and home to baroque superstar painter Pieter Paul Rubens, as you'll be regularly reminded. Despite many historical travails thereafter and severe WWII bombing, the city retains an intriguing medieval heart with *café*-filled cobbled lanes, a riverside fortress and a truly impressive cathedral. Today Antwerp's top drawcards are its vibrant fashion and entertainment scene, along with its startling architectural and cultural contrasts.

History

A fort built here during Charlemagne's time (768–814) was visited by such noted Christian missionaries as St Amand and St Bavo before being destroyed by Vikings in 836. Antwerp's well-protected port on the wide Scheldt River (Schelde in Dutch, Escaut in French) really came into its own once the Zwin waterway silted up, destroying Bruges' economy and forcing traders to move east. In 1531 the world's first specially built stock exchange opened here and by 1555 Antwerp had become one of Europe's main trading, cultural and intellectual centres, with a population of around 100,000.

But prosperity was ruthlessly cut short when Protestants smashed the city's cathedral in 1566 (a period known as the 'Iconoclastic Fury'). Fanatically Catholic Spanish ruler Philip II sent troops to restore order, but 10 years later the unpaid garrison mutinied, themselves ransacking the city and massacring 8000 people (the 'Spanish Fury'). After further battles and sieges, Antwerp was finally incorporated into the Spanish Netherlands and force-fed Catholicism. Thousands of skilled workers (notably Protestants, Jews and foreigners) headed north to the relative safety of the United Provinces (today's Netherlands).

By 1589 Antwerp's population had more than halved to 42,000. Affluence passed progressively to Amsterdam, although Antwerp revived somewhat after 1609 with the Twelve Years' Truce between the United Provinces and the Spanish Netherlands. Once the city was no longer cut off from the rest of the world, its trade and arts flourished and its printing houses became known throughout Europe. The world's first newspaper, *Nieuwe Tydinghen,* was published here by Abraham Verhoeven in 1606.

Then the Treaty of Westphalia, which finally concluded the Dutch-Spanish wars in 1648, struck a massive blow by closing the Scheldt to all non-Dutch ships. Without its vital link to the sea, Antwerp was ruined. But Napoleon's arrival in 1797 changed all of that. The French rebuilt the docks, Antwerp got back on its feet, and by the late 19th century it had become the world's third-largest port after London and New York.

Antwerp was occupied by Germany in October 1914 after weeks of heavy bombardment and even aerial Zeppelin attacks.

PIETER PAUL RUBENS

Even if his signature plump nudes, muscular saints and gigantic ultra-Catholic religious canvases aren't your artistic cup of tea, it's hard to visit Antwerp without stumbling on at least a couple of attractions related to the city's superstar artist, Pieter Paul Rubens (1577–1640).

Rubens was born in Siegen, Germany, where his parents had temporarily fled to escape religious turmoil in Antwerp. They returned home a decade later, and by the age of 21 Rubens had become a master painter in Antwerp's Guild of St-Lukas. In 1600 he became court painter to the Duke of Mantua and travelled extensively in Italy and Spain, soaking up the rich Renaissance fashions in art and architecture. When his mother died in 1608, Rubens returned to Antwerp, built a city-centre house-studio (p146) and worked on huge religious canvases and portraits of European royalty. He was joined by contemporaries such as Anthony Van Dyck and Jacob Jordaens. The studio's output was staggering.

In the 1620s Rubens also took on diplomatic missions, including a visit to London, where he was knighted by Charles I.

For his family tomb, Rubens painted *Our Lady Surrounded by Saints,* which included portraits of his father, his wives, and himself in the role of St George. It's in a small chapel behind the high altar of the aristocratic, partly Gothic **St-Jacobskerk** (Map p150; Lange Nieuwstraat 73; adult/concession €3/2; ⏲2-5pm Mon-Sat Easter-Oct, 9am-noon Nov-Easter).

Around a million refugees left for the UK, France and the Netherlands, although most returned after 1918 to rebuild the city. In 1920 Antwerp hosted the Olympic Games and in 1928 construction began on Europe's first skyscraper, the 27-storey Torengebouw.

During WWII Antwerp's port again made it an obvious military target, as the city's architectural pattern attests. During German occupation around two-thirds of the Jewish population perished. The city's 20th-century regeneration has been a sometimes contradictory mixture of modern multiculturalism and backlash, but few places seem so optimistic and visionary in forging plans for a 21st-century future.

Sights & Activities

Grote Markt and Groenplaats are the twin hearts of old Antwerp. Around 1km east is magnificent Antwerpen-Centraal train station, and in between, Antwerp's major pedestrian shopping street, Meir/Leystraat, gloriously overendowed with statue-topped classical and rococo-style buildings. Just south of Centraal is the Diamant (diamond district); east are fashionable Zurenborg and edgy Borgerhout.

Heading south of Groenplaats, Nationalestraat runs into Sint-Andries, the fashionista hub, continuing down to Het Zuid ('t Zuid), a nightlife and museum zone. Around 800m north of Grote Markt, MAS museum is at the centre of a regenerated docklands area known as 't Eilandje (Little Island), with the busy Universiteitsbuurt and gradually gentrifying red-light district in between.

Old Antwerp

Several house-museums have priceless art collections and authentic period interiors. All are impressive and have their individual charm, but if you have time or energy for only one, make it the Plantin-Moretus house.

Grote Markt SQUARE

(Map p150) As with every great Flemish city, Antwerp's medieval heart is a classic Grote Markt (Market Sq). Here the triangular, pedestrianised space features the voluptuous, baroque **Brabo Fountain** (Grote Markt) depicting Antwerp's giant-killing, hand-throwing legend. Flanked on two sides by very photogenic guildhalls, the square is dominated by an impressive Italo-Flemish Renaissance-style **stadhuis** (Town Hall; Grote Markt), completed in 1565.

ANTWERP FREEBIES & DISCOUNTS

Most major city-run museums are free on the last Wednesday of each month – **This Is Antwerp** (http://thisisantwerp.be) lists these as well as other last-minute ticket deals on its calendar. The **Antwerp City Card** (1/2/3 days €25/32/37) will save you money if you want to visit a handful of the city's museums (and you will): it can be bought from Tourism Antwerp at Grote Markt or Centraal.

Onze-Lieve-Vrouwekathedraal CATHEDRAL

(Map p150; www.dekathedraal.be; Handschoenmarkt; adult/reduced €6/4; 10am-5pm Mon-Fri, to 3pm Sat, 1-4pm Sun) Belgium's finest Gothic cathedral was 169 years in the making (1352–1521). Wherever you wander in Antwerp, its gracious, 123m-high spire has a habit of popping unexpectedly into view and it rarely fails to prompt a gasp of awe. The sight is particularly well framed when looking up Pelgrimstraat in the afternoon light.

The cathedral's imposing interior sports late-baroque decorations, including four early Rubens canvases and, while the KMSKA gallery (p151) is closed, some of that collection's religious masterpieces. For a free glimpse down the nave, turn left on entry to the 'prayer' area, but do remain quiet. Guided tours at 11am.

★**Museum Plantin-Moretus** HISTORIC BUILDING

(Map p150; www.museumplantinmoretus.be; Vrijdag Markt 22; adult/reduced €8/6; 10am-5pm Tue-Sun) Giving a museum Unesco World Heritage status might seem odd – until you've seen this astonishing place. Once home to the world's first industrial printing works, it's been a museum since 1876. The medieval building and 1622 courtyard garden alone would be worth a visit, but the world's oldest printing press, priceless manuscripts and original type sets make for a giddy experience indeed. Other highlights include the 1640 library, a bookshop dating from 1700 and rooms lined with gilt leather.

The original interiors also feature a valuable painting collection, including work by family friend Rubens, and there are fascinating examples of books by Rubens' brother, illustrated by Pieter Paul and published by Moretus.

Antwerp

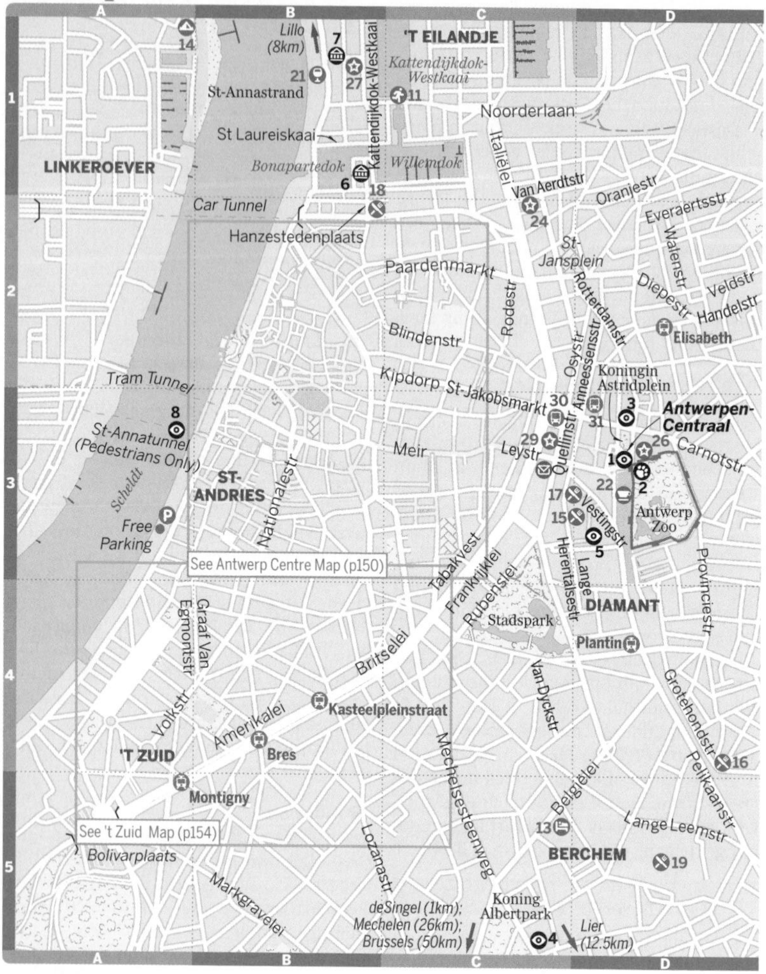

Rubenshuis MUSEUM

(Map p150; www.rubenshuis.be; Wapper 9-11; adult/reduced €8/6, audio guide €2; ⏲10am-5pm Tue-Sun) The 1611 building was built as home and studio by celebrated painter Pieter Paul Rubens. Rescued from ruins in 1937, and extensively and sensitively restored, the building is a delightfully indulgent one, with baroque portico, rear facade and exquisite formal garden. The furniture all dates from Rubens' era, although it's not part of the original decor. Fourteen Rubens canvases are displayed, along with some wonderful period ephemera, such as the metal frame of a ruff collar and a linen press.

Rubens highlights include intimate portraits of patron Nicolaas Rockox and fellow painter Anthony Van Dyck, along with a large-scale canvas of Eve glancing lustfully at Adam's fig-leaf.

Rockoxhuis MUSEUM

(Map p150; ☎03-201 92 50; www.rockoxhuis.be; Keizerstraat 10-12; adult/reduced €8/6; ⏲10am-5pm Tue-Sun) Nicolaas Rockoxhuis was a 17th-century Antwerp celeb: lawyer and *burgomaster* (city councillor), dedicated patron of the arts and humanist intellectual. His lovely house has a gem of a courtyard garden and, although most of Rockox' Rubens com-

missions are now in the hands of big-ticket institutions like the Prado and London's National Gallery, his collection gathered here contains works by Wildens, Van Dyck, Pieter Brueghel the Younger and, yes, Rubens.

While the KMSKA gallery (p151) is closed, many of its treasures are also on display here, including Jean Fouquet's striking c 1450s 'fashion-forward' Madonna and the sublime Jan van Eyck brush drawing on oak of St Barbara. This combined collection is entitled The Golden Cabinet, and works are hung closely together as they would have been in Rockox' time – fascinating in itself.

Antwerp

Top Sights

1 Antwerpen-Centraal D3

Sights

2 Antwerp Zoo D3
3 Aquatopia D3
4 De Koninck C5
De Vier Seizoenen .... (see 10)
5 Diamant D3
Les Mouettes .... (see 10)
6 MAS B1
7 Red Star Line Museum B1
8 Sint-Annatunnel A3
9 Sunflower House E5
10 Waterloostraat E5

Activities, Courses & Tours

11 Flandria Harbour Cruises C1

Sleeping

12 ABhostel E3
13 Boulevard Leopold C5
14 Camping De Molen A1

Eating

15 Aahaar D3
16 Dôme sur Mer D4
Domestic .... (see 16)
17 Empire Shopping Centre C3
18 Marcel B2
19 The Jane D5

Drinking & Nightlife

20 Bar Leon F3
21 Bocadero B1
22 Le Royal D3
23 Plaza Real E3

Entertainment

24 Boots C2
25 De Roma E3
26 Koningin Elisabethzaal D3
27 Theater 't Eilandje B1
28 Trix F3
29 Vlaamse Opera C3

Transport

30 Buses to Turnhout C3
31 Eurolines D3

St-Carolus-Borromeuskerk CHURCH

(Map p150; www.mkaweb.be/site/english/062.mv; Hendrik Conscienceplein 6; 10am-12.30pm & 2-5pm Mon-Sat) FREE Rubens turned interior designer as part of the team that created this superb 1621 baroque church. A wonder of its era, the overwhelming altarpiece was designed to allow vast canvases to be changed using a series of wire pulleys. In 1773 the church's original Rubens paintings

DON'T MISS

ART-NOUVEAU HIGHLIGHTS

Zurenborg

Residential Zurenborg's elegance stems from the fact that it was one of the few parts of Antwerp that were planned; its rich concentration of belle-époque, neoclassical and art-nouveau house facades all date from between 1894 and 1914. Delightfully, the wrought-iron balconies, bay windows, slate tiles, stained glass and mosaic work are often in service of a theme.

Waterloostraat (Map p146; 15 to Cuperus) Particularly rich mosaics celebrate the Battle of Waterloo at Nos 11 and 30.

De Vier Seizoenen (The Four Seasons; Map p146; cnr Waterloostraat & Generaal Van Merlenstraat; 15 to Cuperus) The four fine Joseph Bascourt houses on each corner of this intersection bear mosaics depicting the four seasons.

Sunflower House (Map p146; 50 Cogels Osylei; 15 to Cuperus) Possibly the the most individually exquisite of all, its characteristic organic forms and whiplash swirls are painted in white, black and gold; it's flanked by iris- and a tulip-themed houses.

Les Mouettes (The Seagulls; Map p146; Waterloostraat 39; 15 to Cuperus) Relatively modest by Zurenborg standards, but with a delightful central mosaic depicting seagulls and the Flemish coast.

't Zuid

While 't Zuid's streetscapes are far from cohesive, it has some stunning stand-alone masterpieces.

't Bootje (Map p154; cnr Schildersstraat & Plaatsnijdersstraat) Behind KMSKA, the eccentric 't Bootje has a corner balcony that resembles a boat's prow.

Help U Zelve (Steiner School; Map p154; Volkstraat 40) This is arguably the city's most arresting building. Built in 1901 by architects Van Asperen and Van Averbeke as the Socialist Party's headquarters, it's adorned with mosaics of rural workers – er, yes, naked workers – along with organic, sinuous wrought-ironwork and curved windows. It now houses a Rudolph Steiner school.

were whisked off to Vienna after the Jesuits were locally disbanded.

The magnificent carved confessionals were installed after a disastrous 1718 fire that ruined the nave, and they survived another fire in 2009.

Museum Mayer van den Bergh GALLERY
(Map p150; ☎03-232 42 37; www.museummayervandenbergh.be; Lange Gasthuisstraat 19; adult/reduced €8/6, with Rubenshuis €10/8; ⏰10am-5pm Tue-Sun) This 16th-century town house was actually constructed in 1904 and was one of the first museums in the world to be built around a single collection. Fritz Mayer van den Bergh's collection is indeed as rich as that of many a national gallery and includes Bruegel's brilliantly grotesque *Dulle Griet* (Mad Meg) as well as many notable paintings, sculptures, tapestries, drawings, jewellery and stained-glass windows.

Het Steen CASTLE
(Map p150; Steenplein) On a riverside knoll, Het Steen is a dinky but photogenic castle dating from 1200 and occupying the site of Antwerp's original Gallo-Roman settlement. Outside is a humorous **statue of Lange Wapper**, a tall folkloric 'peeping Tom' figure showing off his codpiece to two diminutive onlookers. Directly north, the misnamed **Maritime Park** is a long, open-sided wrought-iron shed displaying a historic barge collection. There is nothing to see inside the castle.

Scheldt Riverbank WATERFRONT
(Map p150) A raised southern promenade links Het Steen to St-Jansvliet, a tree-shaded square where a lift descends to the 572m-long **Sint-Annatunnel** (Map p146) FREE. This 1930s tunnel allows pedestrians and cyclists to cross beneath the river to the Linkeroever (Left Bank) – worth it for the beautiful original escalators and tilework in the tunnel and the novel city-skyline view on the other side.

Maagdenhuis GALLERY
(Map p150; ☎03-223 53 20; Lange Gasthuisstraat 33; adult/reduced €7/5; ⏰10am-5pm

Wed-Mon, 1-5pm Sat & Sun) Now a gallery of precious religious art, the Maagdenhuis was an orphanage and child refuge from 1553 to 1882 and also houses some fascinating objects from this time, including a collection of *majolica* (glazed ceramic) porridge bowls. Notice a few cut playing cards? They were snipped in half when girls were brought to the refuge by impoverished parents unable to feed them: one piece was retained by the parent and the other kept with the child as an identification token.

Paleis op de Meir PALACE

(Map p150; www.paleisopdemeir.be; Meir 50; tours €6; ⌚tours in Dutch 10am-2pm Sun) This palatial mid-18th-century building was used by Napoleon when he visited Antwerp in 1811 and later by the Belgian royal family. The most accessible sections are used by interior-design shop Flamant, a restaurant and chocolate shop Chocolate Line, whose walls maintain some remarkable original murals but otherwise lays on the tack. To visit the rest of the building you must join a tour.

Station Quarter

Around Antwerp's architecturally extraordinary main station is a highly multicultural area with a different atmosphere every few blocks. Sleazy peep shows rub shoulders with grand century-old buildings, a two-street Chinatown and the world's main diamond exchanges.

★Antwerpen-Centraal LANDMARK

(Map p146; Koningin Astridplein 27) With its neo-Gothic facade, vast main hall and splendidly proportioned dome, the 1905 Antwerpen-Centraal train station is one of the city's premier landmarks. It was rated by *Newsweek* as one of the world's five most beautiful stations. It's also very practical, the multilevel platforms having had a full 21st-century makeover.

Antwerp Zoo ZOO

(Map p146; ☎03-202 45 40; www.zooantwerpen.be; Koningin Astridplein 26; adult/reduced €22.50/17.50; ⌚10am-4.45pm winter, to 7pm summer; 👪) Splendid animal statues and striking big-cat mosaics welcome visitors to world-famous Antwerp Zoo. Although it's one of the world's oldest zoos (founded in 1843), enclosures in the 10-hectare site are state-of-the-art and the zoo's breeding program has an international reputation.

A fascinating reef environment has recently been added to the aquarium area, as part of a major overhaul. Popular new animal additions include a koala couple, Goonawarra and Guwara, who share a restored 1898 thatched-roof building with their antipodean friend Lily, a tree kangaroo.

Diamant AREA

(Diamond District; Map p146; www.awdc.be) An astounding 80% of the world's uncut diamonds are traded in Antwerp. Four dour exchange buildings lie along heavily guarded, pedestrianised Hoveniersstraat and Schupstraat, which are also home to Indian banks, specialist transportation companies, diamond 'boilers' and the industry's governing body, HRD Antwerp. Though now Indian dominated, historically the diamond business was mainly the domain of Orthodox Jews, whose black coats, broad-rimmed hats and long haircurls still remain a distinctive presence.

Aquatopia AQUARIUM

(Map p146; ☎03-205 07 50; www.aquatopia.be; Koningin Astridplein 7; adult/reduced €14.95/10; ⌚10am-6pm, last entry 5pm) Aquatopia is an extensive, child-friendly aquarium experience. Check out its jolly website for online family-ticket offers and save money with a Zoo-Aquatopia joint ticket.

North-Central Antwerp

Red Star Line Museum MUSEUM

(Map p146; ☎03-298 27 70; http://redstarline.be; Montevideostraat 3; adult/reduced €8/6; ⌚10am-5pm Tue-Sun, reservations required on weekends) Over two million passengers sailed from Antwerp on Red Star Line ships between 1873 and 1934, the great majority of these immigrants bound for America. The museum, housed in the very building where those many embarkations took place, is beautifully designed and extremely engaging, telling the story of individual journeys through photographs, recreations and objects, including some gorgeous period model ships. Even those a little beleaguered by contemporary museums' immersive narrative approach can't fail to be moved.

The observation tower has great views and is also a nod to the original chimney of the building, once a welcome landmark that guided passengers arriving at Antwerpen-Centraal station to the docks.

MAS MUSEUM

(Museum aan de Stroom; Map p146; www.mas.be; Hanzestedenplaats; adult/reduced €10/8;

Antwerp Centre

⌚10am-5pm Tue-Fri, to 6pm Sat & Sun) Opened in 2011, MAS is a 10-storey complex that redefines the idea of a museum-gallery. Floors are designed around big-idea themes using a barrage of media, from old master paintings through tribal artefacts to video installations.

Around half the building hosts special exhibitions, so if you're limited for time you can choose between these or the permanent collections. You don't need to pay the entry fee to take the succession of external escalators to MAS' open roof for a remarkable view across Antwerp, and three small free pavilions outside have exhibits on Antwerp's port, diamond and silver industries.

't Zuid

KMSKA GALLERY

(Map p154; www.kmska.be; Leopold de Waelplaats) KMSKA is one of Europe's finest art galleries, but it will be closed until the end of 2017 while it undergoes a total renovation. Elements of its superb collection of Belgian greats from Van Eyck to Wouters can be seen, however, at various regional exhibitions and at the Rockoxhuis (p146) and Onze-Lieve-Vrouwekathedraal (p145). From outside you can still admire the monumental 1890 building, a grandiose neoclassical masterpiece topped with winged charioteer statues.

MHKA GALLERY

(Map p154; ☎03-238 59 60; www.muhka.be; Leuvenstraat 32; adult/child €8/1; ⌚11am-6pm Tue-Sun, to 9pm Thu) MHKA is considered to be one of Belgium's best contemporary museums. Its collections and temporary exhibitions focus on work from the 1970s on and feature Belgian and international artists. Shows tend to the provocative.

FoMu MUSEUM

(FotoMuseum; Map p154; ☎03-242 93 00; www.fotomuseum.be; Waalsekaai 47; adult/child €8/3; ⌚10am-5pm Tue-Sun) The permanent collection gives a splendid potted history of photography (albeit mostly in Dutch), but there are also regularly changing exhibitions of no-holds-barred work by contemporary artists. As well as a shop and cafe, there is a fantastic cinema with many version-original (original-language) art-house films.

Justitiepaleis BUILDING

(Law Court; Map p154; Bolivarplaats; 🚋12 to Bolivarplaats) Antwerp's 21st-century law courts have a distinctive series of gleaming titanium 'sails'. Designed by Richard Rogers,

Antwerp Centre

Top Sights
1 Museum Plantin-Moretus ... B5

Sights
2 Brabo Fountain ... B3
Grote Markt ... (see 2)
3 Het Steen ... B3
4 Maagdenhuis ... D7
5 Maritime Park ... B2
6 Museum Mayer van den Bergh ... D6
7 Onze-Lieve-Vrouwekathedraal ... C4
8 Paleis op de Meir ... E5
9 Rockoxhuis ... D3
10 Rubenshuis ... E5
11 Scheldt Riverbank ... A4
12 Stadhuis ... B3
13 Statue of Lange Wapper ... B3
14 St-Carolus-Borromeuskerk ... D4
15 St-Jacobskerk ... F4

Activities, Courses & Tours
16 Antwerp By Bike ... B3
17 Flandria ... A3

Sleeping
18 A Place Antwerp ... B5
19 De Witte Lelie ... E3
20 Elzenveld Hotel ... D7
21 Enich Anders B&B ... B5
22 Hotel Julien ... D4
23 Hotel O ... B4
24 Hotel Scheldezicht ... A5
25 Hotel 't Sandt ... A4
26 Matelote Hotel ... B4
27 Pulcinella ... C6
28 Room National ... B5
29 Rosier 10 ... C7
30 Yellow Submarine ... D1

Eating
31 Arte ... B4
32 Chez Fred ... A7
33 De Groote Witte Arend ... B5
34 De Kleine Zavel ... A5
35 Het Gebaar ... E7
36 LOA ... B5
37 Nimman ... E2
38 Poule & Poulette ... A5
39 't Brantyser ... D3
40 Zuiderterras ... A5

Drinking & Nightlife
41 Baravin ... D3
42 Bierhuis Kulminator ... C7
43 Cafe Beveren ... A4
44 Café d'Anvers ... D1
45 Café Hessenhuis ... E1
46 De Duifkens ... E6
47 De Vagant ... B4
48 Normo ... D3
49 Private Bar ... C4
50 Red & Blue ... C1
51 Wijnbar Kloosterstraat 15 ... A6

Entertainment
52 De Muze ... C4
53 FNAC ... C4
54 Prospekta ... B3

Shopping
55 Art Partout ... A6
56 Fish & Chips ... C6
57 Het Modepaleis ... C5
58 Huis Boon ... C5
59 Rosier 41 ... D7
60 Verso ... D6
61 Viar ... A6

Information
62 Boekhandel 't Verschil ... D3
63 Tourism Antwerp ... C3

famous for the Centre Pompidou in Paris, the building is pleasant enough but failed to find the architectural cachet the city hoped for and there's little for visitors within.

Berchem

De Koninck BREWERY

(Map p146; www.dekoninck.be; Mechelsesteenweg 291; adult/reduced €12/10; ⏲10am-6pm Tue-Sun; 15 to Berchem De Merode) Antwerp's historic brewery – one of the few true city breweries left in Belgium – has recently been refurbished and is both a wonderful temple to the city's favourite drop and an evocative example of early-20th-century industrial architecture. Self-guided tours begin with interactive exhibitions on brewing, Belgian beer and Antwerp's beer specialities, then there's a 4m-high walkway that takes you over the working brewery hall.

Tastings are, naturally, part of the proceedings, and there's an attached shop selling beer, take-home signature *bolleke* (bowl) glasses and other beer souvenirs.

Tours

Flandria CRUISE

(Map p150; 03-231 31 00; www.flandria.nu; Steenplein 1; adult/concession €11/9; ⏲2pm & 4pm Tue-Sun) See the city skyline and river traffic with a 50-minute riverboat excursion on the Scheldt.

Antwerp By Bike BICYCLE TOUR
(Map p150; www.antwerpbybike.be; with/without bike rental €18/12; ⌚1.45pm Sat & Sun Jul-Sep) Three-hour weekend bicycle tours in Dutch or English starting from Steenplein. Check the website for details and to book.

Festivals & Events

Tomorrowland MUSIC
(⌚late July) World's largest electronic-music festival, held in Boom, 16km south of the city.

Borgerwood MUSIC
(www.borgerwood.be; ⌚late Jul) A new electronic-music festival held at Park Spoor Oost, on the far edge of hipster 'hood Borgerhout.

Museumnacht ART
(www.museumnacht.be; museums/museums & after-party €10/13; ⌚first Sat Aug) Over 20 of the city's museums stay open late, many staging special shows and performances; bus transport between venues is free and there is an all-night party on a boat once the museums close.

Linkerwoofer MUSIC
(www.linkerwoofer.be; ⌚early Aug) Family-friendly pop and indie fest in Linkeroever, with easy access by the Sint-Annatunnel.

Jazz Middelheim JAZZ
(www.jazzmiddelheim.be; ⌚mid-Aug) This four-day festival attracts huge crowds and is held in a handsomely landscaped suburban sculpture park 4km south of the centre.

Sleeping

Antwerp offers a staggering range of stylish, well-priced B&Bs. Many are listed on www.bedandbreakfast.eu. Central chain hotels include a Hilton with a lovely facade looking somewhere between a Parisian department store and a Budapest station. An Ibis Budget beyond the southeastern corner of Antwerpen-Centraal makes a good standby if you missed the last train. And the Park Inn fronting the zoo shares use of the nearby Radisson's swimming pool.

Centre

Pulcinella HOSTEL €
(Map p150; ☎03-234 03 14; www.jeugdherbergen.be; Bogaardeplein 1; dm/tw €27/32; @📶) This giant, tailor-made HI hostel is hard to beat for its Fashion District location and cool modernist decor. HI members and under-30s save €3; breakfast is included.

Hotel Scheldezicht HOTEL €€
(Map p150; ☎03-231 66 02; www.hotelscheldezicht.be; St-Jansvliet 12; s/d with shared bathroom from €50/70; ⌚reception 7am-10pm; 📶) This sweetly old-fashioned hotel has irregular floors and most rooms share toilets, but many rooms are spacious, the decor has been recently spruced up and the location is delightful.

Enich Anders B&B HOTEL €€
(Map p150; ☎0476 99 86 01; www.enich-anders.be; Leeuwenstraat 12; s/d/tr/q €62/64/76/88) Above the owner's small sculpture gallery; rooms are warm, clean and comfortable if not especially smart. Most have kitchenettes.

Rosier 10 B&B €€
(Map p150; ☎0489 27 99 99; www.rosier10.be; Rosier 10; s/d €110/120) There's a lovely warmth and grace to this contemporary B&B in a historic town house on quiet, central Rosier. Interior designer Roxanne's four spacious and comfortable rooms represent a moment of the day and match your circadian mood: morning, noon, evening and night. Each really does have a personality.

Breakfast is taken in the airy ground-floor room and Roxanne has great local knowledge. There are also kitchen-equipped apartments just along the street.

A Place Antwerp APARTMENT €€
(Map p150; ☎0473 73 56 50; http://aplaceantwerp.be; Vrijdagmarkt 1; ste/apt €130/150) Owner Karin has a good eye for vintage design and has filled this 1950s building with a collection of

HANDS UP FOR A LEGEND

It's said the name Antwerpen derives from a riverside mound *(aanwerp)* where archaeologists found remnants of a Gallo-Roman settlement. But legend offers a marketably colourful alternative starring a giant called Druon Antigoon. A fearsome extortionist, Druon controlled a bend of the Scheldt, forcing passing ship captains to pay a toll. However, the day was saved by Roman warrior Silvius Brabo, who killed the giant, chopped off his hand and chucked it in the river. The place of *hand werpen* (hand throwing) subsequently became Antwerpen. Today *Antwerpse handjes* (Antwerp hands) have become a virtual city trademark that turns up in all manner of guises, from de Koninck beer glasses to chocolates to souvenir jewellery.

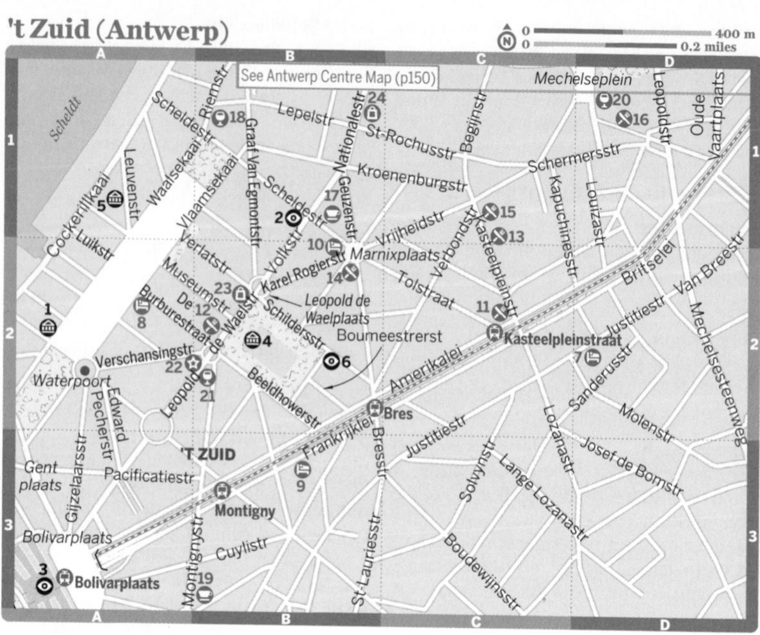

't Zuid (Antwerp)

Sights

1 FoMu A2
2 Help U Zelve B1
3 Justitiepaleis A3
4 KMSKA B2
5 MHKA A1
6 't Bootje B2

Sleeping

7 Bed, Bad & Brood D2
8 Glorius Inn A2
9 Hotel Rubenshof B3
10 SoulShow Suites & Studios B2

Eating

11 Ciro's C2
12 Civiltà del Bere B2
13 De Broers van Julienne C1
14 Fiskebar B2
15 Le John C1
L'Entrepôt du Congo .... (see 8)
16 Life Is Art D1

Drinking & Nightlife

17 Buchbar B1
Chatleroi .... (see 21)
18 De Vismijn B1
19 Kolonel Koffie B3
20 Korsåkov D1
21 Patine B2
Vitrin .... (see 10)

Entertainment

22 Café Hopper A2

Shopping

23 Ann Demeulemeester B2
24 Elsa B1

'60s and '70s pieces in an autumnal palette that's a comforting departure from Antwerp's usual monochromes. Two suites are large at 35 sq metres and two apartments are larger still – all are well equipped and have views over one of Antwerp's nicest squares.

Room National APARTMENT €€

(Map p150; ☎0475 23 47 03; www.roomnational.com; Nationalestraat 24; d/apt €95/135) Two suites and one room are spread over the upper floors of a 19th-century building. The subtly stylish apartment interiors mix vintage pieces like Jacobsen's 'ant chair' with marble fireplaces, painted floorboards and modern comforts like espresso machines and iMacs, and while the 'budget' room is small it's got a sneaky glamour to it.

Yellow Submarine B&B €€

(Map p150; ☎0475 59 59 83; www.yellowsubmarine.be; Falconplein 51; d with/without bathroom

€145/120; P 📶) From Antwerp's leading creative agency, Yellow Submarine has three slick, stylish rooms, two with big, circular baths. There's a nice buzz about the place – owner Elke goes all out and will happily bring breakfast to your room and cater for special diets. Lots of little extras include stocked minibars, espresso machines and free parking.

Hotel O HOTEL €€
(Map p150; ☎03-500 89 50; www.hotelokathedral.com; Handschoenmarkt 3; s/d €100/135) The immediate selling point here is an unbeatable location, staring across a square at the cathedral frontage. A little foyer bar lined with 1950s radios and audio equipment leads to midsize rooms with black and moody decor, giant Rubens reproductions spilling onto the ceilings, and baths in black-framed glass boxes.

Elzenveld Hotel HOTEL €€
(Map p150; ☎03-202 77 11; www.elzenveld.be; Lange Gasthuisstraat 45; s/d €80/100) Behind high walls and set among courtyard gardens and mature trees, this 34-room nonprofit hotel has bright, modern rooms in what was once a medieval hospital and monastery. It's well placed for a quick stroll to either the centre or the south, and for some respite from all that peace, the bars in the square out the front open late.

Ask at reception to see the surprisingly grand 1622 chapel, just off the entrance corridor.

Matelote Hotel BOUTIQUE HOTEL €€
(Map p150; ☎03-201 88 00; www.hotel-matelote.be; Haarstraat 11; d €120-160; @📶) In a 16th-century building on a pedestrianised old-city backstreet, the Matelote has 10 very contemporary rooms, some rather small, others with original beams and pebble-floored bathrooms. There's air-conditioning in the upper rooms.

★De Witte Lelie DESIGN HOTEL €€€
(Map p150; ☎03-226 19 66; www.dewittelelie.be; Keizerstraat 16-18; d €245-525; 📶) A trio of renovated 16th-century mansions houses 10 luxurious rooms at this elegant family-run hotel. Design choices are bold, mixing 20th-century pieces with grand original features and each of the rooms has a distinct look and layout. The public areas – two salons, a reading room, a pretty courtyard and a super-sexy private bar – are incredibly lavish considering the hotel's handful of guests.

The 'Flower' room, named for its wallpaper and curtains of gigantic graphic flowers, has an astonishingly large bathroom, with a wooden bath at its centre, a double shower in one corner and soaring white shuttered windows.

Hotel Julien BOUTIQUE HOTEL €€€
(Map p150; ☎03-229 06 00; www.hotel-julien.com; Korte Nieuwstraat 24; d €230; @📶) This discreet boutique mansion-hotel has an understated elegance. Rooms feature Carrara marble, underfloor heating, Moroccan plaster, DVD players and fresh orchids, while some also have exposed beams or old brick-tile floors. A wellness centre lies in the subterranean caverns, and the rooftop view is a well-kept secret.

Hotel 't Sandt BOUTIQUE HOTEL €€€
(Map p150; ☎03-232 93 90; www.hotel-sandt.be; Zand 17; s/d €190/210; P📶) Patterned marble, a grand piano lounge and a patio terrace are welcoming luxuries at this boutique hotel. Some rooms have period curiosities (beams, pulley wheels etc) and light neocolonial touches, while the cheaper 'duplex' rooms have wrought-iron stairs up to bed. Cheaper rates apply on weekends.

't Zuid, Diamant, Zurenborg & Borgerhout

ABhostel HOSTEL €
(Map p146; ☎0473 57 01 66; www.abhostel.com; Kattenberg 110; dm/tw €20/50; ⏰reception noon-3pm & 6-8pm; 📶; 🚊10, 24 to Drink) This adorable, brightly decorated and family-run hostel has lots of little added extras. Its Borgerhout setting is 20 minutes' walk east of Antwerpen-Centraal station. Across the street is the brilliantly unpretentious local pub **Plaza Real** (Map p146; http://plazareal.be/; Kattenberg 89; ⏰from 8pm Wed-Sun; 🚊10, 24 to Drink), owned by a member of Antwerp band dEUS, and there are lots of cheap ethnic eats nearby too.

Hotel Rubenshof HOTEL €
(Map p154; ☎03-237 07 89; www.rubenshof.be; Amerikalei 115-117; s/d/tr with bathroom €59/82/102, without bathroom €36/56/75; 🚊12 to Bresstraat) The large 1890s mansion has extraordinarily grand public spaces – breakfast is served in a fabulous art-nouveau dining room adjoining a partly gilded neo-rococo salon. By contrast, rooms here basic, but they're well sized, some are pleasingly quirky and they're all reasonably priced.

★Bed, Bad & Brood B&B €€
(Map p154; ☎03-248 15 39; www.bbantwerp.com; Justitiestraat 43; s/d/q €70/80/120, budget s/d €56/68; @) In a 1910, belle époque-era town house near the vast Gerechtshof

(former courthouse), this B&B impresses with authentic wooden floors, high ceilings and beautifully eclectic furniture. Rooms are remarkably spacious and comfortable for the price – all but the budget room have a bath, and the family room is a separate two-bedder tucked away up a mysterious little staircase.

Owners Koen and Marleen serve up a fresh and bountiful breakfast and are keen to help. Note that, apart from last-minute bookings, a two-night minimum applies.

Boulevard Leopold B&B €€
(Map p146; ☎0486 67 58 38; www.boulevard-leopold.be; Belgiëlei 135; d/apt €135/175) A fascinating evocation of Antwerp's 19th-century glory days in the heart of the Jewish district, this family-run B&B mixes a collection of curiosities, museum-worthy antiques, claw-foot baths and open fires with modern coffee machines and flatscreen TVs. Owner Martin makes magic here and is an ever-helpful host. There are three rooms and two apartments of varying sizes and moods.

Glorius Inn BOUTIQUE HOTEL €€
(Map p154; ☎03-237 06 13; www.theglorious.be; De Burburestraat 4; d €135) Up the stairs from an intimate Michelin-starred restaurant and wine bar, these three rooms are decorated in a romantic, maximalist style with huge, sexy bathrooms, four-poster beds and theatrical touches like birdcage canopies hanging from the lofty ceilings. Service is warm and, while there's no breakfast, there are espresso machines in the rooms and the neighbourhood is replete with cafes.

SoulShow Suites & Studios APARTMENT €€
(Map p154; ☎0471 28 57 16; www.soulsuites.com; Marnixplaats 15; apt €100-150;) Marnixplaats is 't Zuid locals' favourite square, making it lively but never oppressively so. These design-savvy studios and suites overlook the rather fabulous central statue from large windows or little balconies. At 40 sq metres, the studios are quite roomy, and they have basic kitchens; the suites are apartment sized and well equipped.

Linkeroever

Camping De Molen CAMPGROUND €
(Map p146; ☎03-219 81 79; www.camping-de-molen.be; Jachthavenweg 2; 2-person tents €16, caravans €28, 4-person huts €55; reception 5-8pm mid-Mar–mid-Oct; ; 36 to Gloriantlaan/Huygenstraat) Pleasantly sited camping ground across the Scheldt River, near Sint-Anna 'beach'.

Eating

Centre

Tempting, if unashamedly tourist-filled, options dot the streets around the cathedral's southern flank and the cobbled lanes around Hendrik Conscienceplein.

LOA INTERNATIONAL, FAST FOOD €
(Map p150; ☎03-291 64 85; www.loa.be; Hoogstaat 77; dishes €5-10; noon-10pm Wed-Thu, to midnight Fri & Sat, to 8pm Sun) International 'street food' – pad thai, Moroccan pancakes, tortillas, croquettes – are made with love and care in this bright cafe. There's complimentary mint tea to sip with your meal and front-row seats onto the square.

Poule & Poulette FAST FOOD €
(Map p150; ☎03-501 11 21; www.poulepoulette.com; Sint-Jansvliet 21; meals €15; 5-11pm Tue-Thu, noon-11pm Sat & Sun) At this cosy, casual place with rotisserie chickens cooking away up the back, you can order the birds in various sizes and with a large choice of sides. There's also broth, meatball and Thai chicken soups and a *waterzooï* (Flemish stew). Friendly staff are happy to make you up takeaway packs, too.

De Groote Witte Arend BELGIAN €€
(Map p150; ☎03-233 50 33; www.degrootewittearend.be; Reyndersstraat 18; mains €22; 10.30am-midnight, kitchen 11.30am-3pm & 5-10pm;) Retaining the Tuscan stone arcade of a 15th- and 17th-century convent building, as well as a little family chapel, this place combines the joys of a good beer bar with the satisfaction of well-cooked, sensibly priced Flemish home cuisine, notably *stoemp* (potato hash), *stoofvlees/carbonade* (beef, beer and onion stew) and huge portions of rabbit in rich Westmalle sauce.

Life Is Art BISTRO €€
(Map p154; www.lifeisart.be; Sint Jorispoort 21-23; mains €22; 5-10pm Thu-Sun) Two old shopfronts make up this convivial place on a lovely street. Food is simple and generous with choices that take in Flemish favourites – deer stew or tartare – along with lighter Mediterranean-style dishes such as grilled skate with capers. The attached wine bar is equally warm and welcoming.

Chez Fred BISTRO €€
(Map p150; ☎03-257 14 71; www.chezfred.be; Kloosterstraat 83; meals €16-22; 10am-1am) Join the *brocante* dealers and local families

for *moules-frites,* croquettes, steaks and stew at this always-open, always-busy place.

Zuiderterras EUROPEAN €€
(Map p150; ☎03-234 12 75; www.zuiderterras.be; Ernest van Dijckkaai 37; mains €22.50-33; ⊙9am-10pm) This landmark 1950s building provides river views through enormous plate-glass windows and from summer tables that fan out along the walkway. It's a superb place to be dazzled by sunset rays while ordering respectable, if somewhat predictable, modern standards. Bookings advised.

Arte ITALIAN €€
(Map p150; ☎03-226 29 70; Suikerrui 24; pasta & pizza €11.50-15.50, mains €16-26; ⊙noon-3pm & 6pm-midnight) Savour great Italian food and fresh wood-fired thin-crust pizza just a ravioli toss from the Grote Markt. Settle on the terrace with its cathedral views, or pick one of the crisply linen-topped tables in the glass-roofed rear section and watch the chefs at work.

't Brantyser EUROPEAN €€
(Map p150; ☎03-233 18 33; www.brantyser.be; Hendrik Conscienceplein 7; snacks €6-12.50, mains €17-26; ⊙11.15am-10pm) The cosy, double-level Brantyser gets the antique-clutter effect just right, while its enviable terrace surveys one of old Antwerp's most appealing pedestrian squares. Portions are generous.

★Het Gebaar BELGIAN €€€
(Map p150; ☎03-232 37 10; www.hetgebaar.be; Leopoldstraat 24; mains €35; ⊙noon-5.30pm) Chef Roger van Damme only does fancy and only does lunch. At the entrance to Antwerp's petite botanical gardens, the former gardener's house is a deeply romantic setting to write off an afternoon. The Flemish stew and tartares retain the essence of the original but use the best produce and are prettily presented. Highly theatrical desserts are a house speciality.

Nimman THAI €€€
(Map p150; www.sogoodnotnormal.com/nimman; Stadswaag 9/10; set menus €40-50; ⊙7-10pm Wed-Sun) A current darling of the neighbourhood's gentrifying army, Nimman is an airy and stylish contemporary-Thai place. There's no menu; rather, you are served a nightly selection of dishes. Reservations can only be made via the website.

De Kleine Zavel MEDITERRANEAN €€€
(Map p150; ☎03-231 96 91; www.kleinezavel.be; Stoofstraat 2; plates/menu €15/49; ⊙noon-2.30pm & 6-10.30pm Tue-Sun) The rough floorboards and wrought-iron chandeliers might suggest that this is another gleefully dishevelled Flemish bistro, but this fashion-set favourite offers an innovative menu of small dishes of mostly Mediterranean flavours that can be enjoyed individually or as a four-course menu.

't Eilandje

Marcel FRENCH €€
(Map p146; ☎03-336 33 02; www.restaurant-marcel.be; Van Schoonbekeplein 13; 3/4/5 courses €35/45/55; ⊙noon-1.30pm Mon-Fri, 7-9.30pm Mon-Sat) A dark and romantic 1920s dining room has been recreated in an old mission to seamen. A classic French menu, made with top-quality ingredients, keeps the local shipping magnates happy.

Station Quarter

Cheap dining is the thing north and east of Antwerpen-Centraal station: on the decidedly unglamorous Van Arteveldestraat alone you'll find African, Himalayan, Filipino, Thai and Indian *cafés* all within a block.

Aahaar INDIAN, VEGAN €
(Map p146; www.aahaar.com; Lange Herentalsestraat 23; buffet €10; ⊙noon-3pm & 5.30-9.30pm Mon-Fri, 1-9.30pm Sat & Sun; ✎) Unpretentious little place that's well known for its vegan/vegetarian Jain-Indian food. No menu, just an eat-all-you-like buffet with five mains, two sweets and rice.

Empire Shopping Centre FAST FOOD
(Map p146; Appelmansstraat 25; ⊙8am-6pm Mon-Sat) What looks like a shabby suburban mall keeps the diamond trade in equipment and repairs as well as feeding a huge number of them every lunchtime. Food outlets run the gamut of Thai, Vietnamese, shawarma, sushi, Lebanese and a kosher cafe – all no fuss but good quality.

't Zuid

Locals head to 't Zuid to dine, with restaurants lining Leopold de Waelplaats, Vlaamsekaai and Marnixplaats and fanning out through surrounding streets.

L'Entrepôt du Congo BISTRO, CAFE €
(Map p154; www.entrepotducongo.com; Vlaamsekaai 42; meals €5-20; ⊙7.30am-2am, kitchen to 10pm) As the name might suggest, dark marble tabletops, chequerboard floors, mirror panels and carved wooden beams on the high ceiling are all surveyed by a portrait of a young King Baudouin. The menu is extensive,

cheap and what Belgians might call 'plain': choose from omelettes, pasta and steak.

Ciro's BELGIAN €€
(Map p154; ☎03-238 49 67; www.ciros.be; Amerikalei 6; mains €17-26; ⏲11am-11pm Tue-Sun) An authentically nostalgic restaurant that dates back to 1962 and sports an almost untouched midcentury interior. The cuisine, too, is full of Flemish classics: smoked eel on toast, pot roast or the euphemistically dubbed 'Black Beauty' – horse fillet.

Fiskebar SEAFOOD €€
(Map p154; ☎03-257 13 57; http://fiskebar.be; Marnixplaats 12; mains €22-40; ⏲noon-10pm) Locals swear that Fiskebar serves Antwerp's best seafood, meaning there's always an almighty crush for tables in this bustling, fashionably dishevelled former fishmongers' shop. If you can't get a booking, try its oyster bar next door, which serves a more limited selection and works without reservations.

Civiltà del Bere ITALIAN, PIZZA €€
(Map p154; ☎03-257 56 60; www.civilatadelbere.be; De Burburestraat 43; ⏲noon-11pm Wed-Mon) Come here for bar-stool lunches, or dinners of various carpaccios or thin-crust pizza at this casual, stylish authentic Italian. Wine choices are interesting too.

Le John INTERNATIONAL €€
(Map p154; ☎03-289 92 25; www.lejohn.be; Kasteelpleinstraat 21; mains €18-26; ⏲6-10.30pm Mon-Sat) A whitewashed room and 1960s-style school chairs fill the shopfront of a landmark early-20th-century building just out of the main 't Zuid action. The short, monthly-changing menu presents an unpredictable mixture of styles, attractively presented and prepared in a glass-fronted show kitchen. There's a very cool, scruffily stylish bar upstairs.

De Broers van Julienne VEGETARIAN €€
(Map p154; ☎03-232 02 03; www.debroersvanjulienne.be; Kasteelpleinstraat 45; mains €9.50-18; ⏲noon-7pm Mon-Thu, to 10pm Fri & Sat; ☑) An upmarket vegetarian deli-cafe, with huge quiches and vegetable slices to take away from the deli section, or tables stretching back through a vine-draped verandah and onto a narrow sunny garden with bench chairs.

Zurenborg

Domestic CAFE, BAKERY €
(Map p146; ☎03-239 98 90; www.domeweb.be; Steenbokstraat 37; ⏲7.30am-6pm Mon-Sat, to 2.30pm Sun; 🚋9 to Zurenborg) Julien Burlat from the Dôme Sur Mer and its fine-dining original Dôme is one of Antwerp's best bakers. This marble-lined cafe is the perfect pit stop if you're exploring Zurenborg's architecturally stunning streets, with a wonderful range of breads, brioche, tarts and quiches to have by the evocative railway bridge or to take away.

Dôme sur Mer SEAFOOD €€
(Map p146; ☎03-281 74 33; www.domeweb.be; Arendstraat 1; mains €28, platters per person €45-75; ⏲noon-3pm & 7-10.30pm Mon-Fri, 7-10.30pm Sat; 🚋9 to Zurenborg) There's a quiet grandeur to this part of Antwerp, and this small, bright, elegant seafood place makes the most of its setting. There's a welcome flexibility to the menu, with large, decadent sharing platters, thoughtful and smartly presented mains, and a rather more impromptu selection of, say, oysters and calamari *a la plancha* (cooked on a griddle).

★The Jane INTERNATIONAL €€€
(Map p146; ☎03-808 44 65; http://hejaneantwerp.com; Site 't Groen Kwartier, Paradeplein 1; lunch menu €65, dinner 7/8 courses €85/100, bar plates €8-20; 🚋9 to Zurenborg) Fine dining meets rock 'n' roll at Antwerp's most dramatic restaurant, where architect Piet Boon has preserved the ceiling of an old military-hospital chapel in its decaying state and put an open kitchen where the altar once was. Michelin-starred chef Sergio Herman and his partner Nick Bril's degustation is a fabulous experience; you'll need to book online three months ahead.

Note (though it's unlikely you'll overlook it) the spiky 900kg chandelier specially commissioned to fill the chapel's ceiling void – it adds a little extra existential frisson for those sitting directly below. If you're not up for a full night of fine dining, or you miss out on a reservation, the stylish but casual upstairs bar space often has openings a few weeks out, and you can drop in any night after 10pm for expertly made cocktails.

Drinking & Nightlife

To sound like a local, ask for a *bolleke*. No, not an insult, but the nickname for a glass of De Koninck, Antwerp's favourite brown ale (literally, 'little bowl'). A less popular local classic is *elixir d'Anvers,* a saccharin-sweet, bright-yellow liqueur made in Antwerp since 1863 and reputed to aid digestion – Louis Pasteur awarded it a diploma in 1887.

From May to September, a number of summer bars open, some riverside, others in parks. This is Antwerp (thisisantwerp.be) lists the current crop, as does the tourist office.

At clubs, Thursday tends to be cheap or free for students.

City Centre

Baravin WINE BAR
(Map p150; ☎0474 22 75 86; Minderbroedersrui 31; ⏲3pm-1am Wed-Mon) Among the university quarter's rather raffish drinking holes, this wonderful wine bar combines 19th-century plasterwork, murals and parquetry with a gallery space, a cracking rock 'n' roll soundtrack and excellent French, Spanish and Italian wines by the glass. It might look rather pretty and prim, but they're known to kick on here.

De Vagant PUB
(Map p150; www.devagant.be; Reyndersstraat 25; ⏲11am-2am Mon-Fri, from noon Sat & Sun, bottle shop to 6pm) More than 200 *jenever* (similar to gin; €2.20 to €7.50) are served in this bare-boards local *café* or sold by the bottle across the road from its *slijterij* (bottle shop), which resembles an old-style pharmacy.

Bocadero CLUB
(Map p146; ☎03-231 92 65; www.bocadero.be; Rijnkaai 150; ⏲May-Sep) The largest of Antwerp's summer bars; after the daytime drinkers go home, this beach bunker morphs into an outdoor dance venue.

Private Bar COCKTAIL BAR
(Brasserie Appelmans; Map p150; ☎03-226 20 22; http://brasserieappelmans.be; Papenstraatje 1; ⏲5-11pm daily) While not exactly the city's best-kept secret, this bar at the very top of busy, bustling beer barn Appelmans has a dark, book-lined fitout and a certain mystique. Cocktails are the real deal – professionally made and interesting without too many gimmicks.

De Duifkens CAFE
(Map p150; Graanmarkt 5; ⏲10am-late Mon-Thu, from noon Fri-Sun) One of several classic cafes that spread summer seating onto the tree-shaded square at Graanmarkt, this one is particularly cosy and is decorated with photos of famous Belgian actors (some of them long-term patrons).

Cafe Beveren PUB
(Map p150; ☎0495 81 81 34; Vlasmarkt 2; ⏲1pm-3am) Port bar Cafe Beveren is the proud keeper of the city's last remaining 1930s Decap dance organ, a colourful specimen that belts out tunes at volume just when you least expect it. The jukebox's Dutch playlist fills the gaps and may break Shazam, but has all the boozy old regulars singing, dancing and spilling beer in unison.

Korsåkov BAR
(Map p154; Mechelseplein 21; ⏲10am-5am) One of Mechelseplein's trio of super-late (often early-morning) bars, Korsåkov has star-tiled floors, rambling back rooms and the best-looking crowd.

Bierhuis Kulminator PUB
(Map p150; ☎03-232 45 38; Vleminckveld 32; ⏲4pm-midnight Tue-Sat, from 8pm Mon) Classic beer pub boasting 800 mostly Belgian brews, including notably rare 'vintage' bottles laid down to mature for several years like fine wine.

Wijnbar Kloosterstraat 15 WINE BAR
(Map p150; Kloosterstraat 15; ⏲1-6pm Sat & Sun) Facing onto the courtyard of a 16th-century house, this is a ridiculously atmospheric spot for an afternoon glass of wine. In warm weather you can relax outside on one of the big sofas; otherwise, sit by the ancient panes of the window while the candles flicker.

Normo CAFE
(Map p150; www.normocoffee.com; Minderbroedersrui 30; ⏲10am-7pm Mon-Fri, to 6pm Sat) Attractively battered tiles, mismatched chairs and friendly bearded baristas make this a welcoming place to hang out. Coffee is as faultless as you'd expect from somewhere that roasts its own beans and supplies the best cafes in the city.

Red & Blue CLUB
(Map p150; www.redandblue.be; Lange Schipperskapelstraat 11; ⏲11pm-7am Thu-Sat; 🚊7) Great dance venue with decent-sized yet still intimate dance floor. It's most famous for its Saturday male-only gay night. There's also Thursday student night TGIT (www.thankgoditsthursday.be), Fridays are mixed and there's the occasional all-out '70s disco night.

Café d'Anvers CLUB
(Map p150; www.cafedanvers.com; Verversrui 15; ⏲11pm-7.30am Thu-Sat; 🚊7) Come late for wild nights at a 16th-century church in the red-light district. Tech house, deep house and progressive house in the main room, R & B and anything goes on the balcony; Thursday nights are studenty.

Station Quarter & Borgerhout

Le Royal CAFE
(Map p146; Antwerpen-Centraal Station; snacks from €3; ⌚7am-7.30pm Mon-Fri, 8am-7.30pm Sat & Sun) Take in the sumptuous 1905 giltwork, mirror-and-marble walls and 15m-high ceiling in this workaday but ever-majestic station buffet.

Bar Leon BAR
(Map p146; ☎0485 31 33 61; Reuzenstraat 23; ⌚noon-2am Mon-Sat, 10am-2am Sun; 🚊10 to Borgerhout De Roma) The ultimate local's local, this is for intrepid bar hounds or those looking for a spot to snack and drink before or after a gig at De Roma. It shape shifts its way through the day from early-evening catch-ups while the kids do their thing in the playground to late-night DJs and drinking when the young Borgerhout crew descends.

't Zuid

In addition to the options below, numerous terraced restaurants on Leopold de Waelplaats, western Waalsekaai and Marnixplaats all open late.

Vitrin WINE BAR, PUB
(Map p154; ☎0474 77 51 12; www.vitrin.eu; Marnixplaats 14; ⌚10am-1am) Beautiful big windows overlooking the giant Marnixplaats *Neptune* sculpture and a light, bright ply fitout make this a happy spot any time of day and in all weather – though it's particularly sweet when the sun's out and the terrace tables overflow with a hip, friendly young crowd.

Chatleroi BAR
(Map p154; Graaf van Hoornsestraat 2; ⌚noon-3am Sun-Wed, to 5am Thu-Sat; 📶) Grungier and friendlier than most in 't Zuid, and yes, in a good way, with eclectic musical taste and a deeply atmospheric interior.

De Vismijn PUB
(Map p154; ☎03-238 45 60; www.cafedevismijn.be; Riemstraat 20) Once the after-hours choice of workers from the former fish market, this brown pub has retained its soaring original frescoed ceilings, but the fishmongers have long gone.

Patine WINE BAR
(Map p154; ☎03-257 09 19; www.wijnbistropatine.be; Leopold de Waelstraat 1; ⌚7.30am-late Tue-Sun, from noon Mon) This appealing wisteria-fronted street-terrace bistro offers a huge wine list along with an all-day menu of pastries, quiches, pasta, salads, tapas and Flemish favourites.

Buchbar CAFE
(Map p154; www.buchbar.be; Scheldestraat 79; ⌚10am-7pm Thu-Tue, from 11am Sun) A cafe and bookshop that feels like a neighbourhood home away from home, with excellent coffee, good breakfast choices and, for later, natural wines and gin and rhubarb cocktails. The central bookshelves have a thoughtful collection of design books, novels in English, sweet stationery, and journals and magazines.

Don't forget to look up at the gorgeous pig- and sausage-themed tiles – a legacy from the original pre-WWII butcher's shop.

Kolonel Koffie CAFE
(Map p154; www.kolonelkoffie.be; Montignystraat 51; ⌚8am-6pm Mon-Sat) Boasting the sunniest terrace in Antwerp and a fantastic contemporary fitout, this cafe is the hub of the 'new Zuid', with lots of laptop action and lounging about on the smart vintage furniture. The coffee is some of the city's best, sandwiches are super stuffed and the cakes are homemade.

Entertainment

Extensive, if all in Dutch, *Week Up* (www.weekup.be) is available from tourist offices and many *cafés*.

Tickets for concerts, opera, theatre and dance performances can be bought from **FNAC** (Map p150; ☎0900 006 00; www.fnac.be; Grand Bazar, Beddenstraat 2) or **Prospekta** (Map p150; ☎03-203 95 86; www.prospekta.be; Grote Markt 13; ⌚10am-6pm Tue-Fri, noon-5pm Sat), which shares a guildhall with the tourist office.

Live Music

De Roma LIVE MUSIC
(Map p146; ☎03-235 04 90; www.deroma.be; Turnhoutsebaan 327; 🚊10, 24 to Drink) This classic 1928 cinema in the North African-meets-hipster Borgerhout has been meticulously restored by enthusiastic volunteers. As well as hosting big international acts it offers a program of film screenings.

Trix LIVE MUSIC
(Map p146; www.trixonline.be; Noordersingel 28-30; 🚌410-412 to Hof-ter-Lo) Great, slightly out-of-town venue with a calendar of alternative and up-and-coming bands, both international and local, plus DJ nights.

De Muze JAZZ
(Map p150; ☎03-226 01 26; http://jazzmuze.be; Melkmarkt 10; ⌚noon-4am) Intimate spaces fill

this three-level gabled *café* with good contemporary live jazz from 10pm Monday to Saturday (but not Wednesday or Thursday in summer).

Café Hopper JAZZ
(Map p154; ☎03-248 49 33; www.cafehopper.be; Leopold De Waelstraat 2; ⏲10am-2am) Free live jazz sessions most Sunday afternoons (4pm) and Monday evenings.

Theatre, Dance & Opera

deSingel PERFORMING ARTS
(☎03-248 28 28; www.desingel.be; Desguinlei 25) Two concert halls offering a highly innovative program of classical music, international theatre and modern dance. There's a well-respected, beautifully glamorous restaurant on the top floor that's open outside of performance times too.

Theater 't Eilandje DANCE
(Map p146; ☎03-234 34 38; www.balletvlaanderen.be; Kattendijkdok-Westkaai 16) The home base of the Royal Flanders Ballet.

Vlaamse Opera OPERA
(Map p146; ☎03-202 10 11; www.vlaamseopera.be; Frankrijklei 1) A stunning 1907 neo-baroque opera house with sumptuous marbled interior and a majestic facade that's sadly diminished by the 1960s monstrosity built next to it.

Koningin Elisabethzaal CONCERT VENUE
(Map p146; www.zalenvandezoo.be; Koningin Astridplein 23-24) Shows range from the Chippendales to Kodo drummers, Diana Kraal to the Flanders Philharmonic Orchestra (www.defilharmonie.be).

Shopping

Pedestrianised Meir is home to the chains and Belgian department store Inno. Many of Antwerp's antique shops are found on Steenhouwersvest, Schuttershofstraat, Komedieplaats and Leopoldstraat, while vintage dealers collect on Kloosterstraat and Sint-Jorispoort. Antwerp's great fashion retailers cluster in the Fashion District (p162). 't Zuid specialises in homewares and furniture.

Diamond and gold shops on Appelmansstraat, Vestingstraat and Hoveniersstraat are far from glitzy, but often offer retail prices that are typically around 30% below those of jewellers elsewhere. There are even more in the arcade fronting Antwerpen-Centraal on Pelikaanstraat.

Rosier 41 FASHION
(Map p150; ☎03-225 53 03; www.rosier41.be; Rosier 41; ⏲10.30am-6pm Mon-Sat) Some extraordinary bargains can be found here at one of the best of Antwerp's designer consignment shops. There's a focus on the Belgians, naturally, with a particularly large selection of Dries van Noten, though there's also a good range of French labels such as Lavin. Menswear is strong too.

Huis Boon ACCESSORIES
(Map p150; ☎03-232 33 87; www.glovesboon.be; Lombardenvest 2-4; ⏲10am-6pm Mon-Sat) In striking contrast to all the contemporary boutiques nearby, Boon is a traditional old-world glove shop established in 1884. Come and get hand fitted or just gawp at the exquisite interior.

GAY & LESBIAN ANTWERP

Antwerp's vibrant LGTB scene is widely diffused around town, with relevant places usually flying rainbow flags. Tourism Antwerp produces the useful multilingual map-guide *Gay Antwerpen* and other guides can be found at gay and lesbian bookshop-cafe **Boekhandel 't Verschil** (Map p150; www.verschil.be; Minderbroedersrui 33; ⏲11am-6pm Wed-Sat, 1-6pm Sun). In Zurenborg, **Het Roze Huis** (Map p146; ☎03-288 00 84; www.hetrozehuis.be; Draakplaats 1) is an umbrella organisation for LGTB groups and also a good source of information.

In a historic 16th-century warehouse, **Café Hessenhuis** (Map p150; ☎03-231 13 56; www.hessenhuis.com; Falconrui 53; ⏲10am-late) is a popular *café* whose cool, modern interior attracts a trendy mixed clientele by day but is exclusively for gay men at night. On Saturday Red & Blue (p159) hosts Antwerp's hottest club for gay men; it's friendly and unthreatening. **Boots** (Map p146; ☎03-231 34 83; www.the-boots.com; Van Aerdtstraat 22; ⏲10.30pm-late Fri & Sat), however, is for the hardcore, with rooms devoted to fulfilling almost every imaginable sexual fantasy. Its detailed dress code includes compulsory shoes for those otherwise arriving naked.

Antwerp Pride (www.antwerppride.eu; ⏲early Aug) incorporates the **Queer Arts Festival** (www.queerarts.be; ⏲early Aug).

DON'T MISS

FASHION DISTRICT

Antwerp's status as a global fashion leader dates from the late 1980s, when daring, provocative shows in London and Paris launched the reputations of half a dozen fashion graduates from Antwerp's Royal Academy.

Going on to be known as the Antwerp Six, the group's most commercially prominent figurehead is Dries Van Noten, whose colourful bohemian clothes sell worldwide. Conceptual artist–designer Walter Van Beirendonck has created outfits for rock stars and ballerinas, and merges wild and futuristic club-wear with postmodern ideas about everything from biotechnology to aliens. Ann Demeulemeester's timeless designs favour monochromes – black, more often than not.

Antwerp may seem far more sartorially laid-back than fashion heavyweights Paris or Milan, but it punches above its weight. In the space of just a few streets you'll find dozens of designer boutiques, along with a variety of streetwear, end-of-line discounters, upmarket vintage and designer consignment shops and more mainstream labels. Few places in the world have such a convenient and covetable concentration.

The tourist office has a fashion-walk directory pamphlet. Or simply stroll Nationalestraat, Lombardenvest, Huidevettersstraat and Schuttershofstraat, not missing Kammenstraat for streetwear and up-and-coming designers.

Fish & Chips FASHION
(Map p150; ☎03-227 08 24; www.fishandchips.be; Kammenstraat 36-38) Fish & Chips is an ever-popular streetwear purveyor with in-store DJs on Saturday afternoons and an upstairs exhibition space.

Het Modepaleis FASHION
(Map p150; www.driesvannoten.be; Nationalestraat 16; ⏲10am-6.30pm Mon-Sat) Dries Van Noten's beautiful Antwerp flagship store is located in a distinctive, 19th-century, domed triangular building in the heart of St Andries. It's worth a pilgrimage even if you're just window shopping.

Art Partout ARTS
(Map p150; www.artpartout.be; Kloosterstraat 30; ⏲1-6pm Fri-Sun) At this small gallery specialising in multiples (ie prints) you can see and acquire the work of Antwerp's own Luc Tuymans and Panamarenko. It also has a good selection of catalogues and limited-edition artists' books for sale.

Viar VINTAGE
(Map p150; ☎0497 57 57 69; www.viar.be; Kloosterstraat 65; ⏲2-6pm) Verlaine's loft-like place has been a Kloosterstraat fixture for over a decade and her dramatic displays of furniture and objects, many of them one-offs, as well as a stunning collection of rare vintage designer fashion, are well worth seeking out.

Elsa SHOES
(Map p154; ☎03-226 84 54; www.elsa-antwerp.be; Nationalestraat 147) Elsa Proost is a shoe designer by trade and, while you can occasionally find her small range here, she stocks the likes of United Nude, Costume National, Veronique Branquinho and a few new surprise designers each season. Shoe lovers, time your visit to coincide with the twice-yearly sales, when prices hover around the €100 mark.

Verso FASHION
(Map p150; ☎03-226 92 92; www.verso.com; Lange Gasthuisstraat 11; ⏲10am-6pm Mon-Sat) In an old bank building with a gorgeous stained-glass cupola, Verso offers designer wares, perfume and accessories. Attached is a dark and moody cocktail *café*.

Ann Demeulemeester FASHION
(Map p154; www.anndemeulemeester.be; Leopold de Waelplaats) Antwerp Six star Ann Demeulemeester's flagship store is a stunning fashion stage set; despite the sometimes conceptual nature of the clothes on display, staff are welcoming.

ℹ Information

There are left-luggage lockers at Antwerpen-Centraal Station.

Tourism Antwerp (Map p150; ☎03-232 01 03; www.visitantwerpen.be; Grote Markt 13; ⏲9am-5.45pm Mon-Sat, to 4.45pm Sun & holidays) Tourism Antwerp has a large, central office with helpful staff – pick up maps, buy tram/bus passes and book tickets here. There is also a booth on the ground floor of Antwerpen-Centraal station.

Getting There & Away

AIR

Antwerp Airport (ANR; www.antwerpairport.be) Tiny Antwerp Airport is 4km southeast of the city, accessible on bus 14 from Antwerpen-Berchem. The only scheduled flights to or via London are with CityJet; other flights mainly service Spanish cities, Hamburg or Berlin.

BUS

Eurolines (Map p146; ☎03-233 86 62; www.eurolines.com; Van Stralenstraat 8; ⊙9am-5.45pm Mon-Fri, to 3.15pm Sat) international buses start from near its office. Eastern European bus companies like **Ecolines** (Map p150; www.ecolines.net; Paardenmarkt 65) typically pick up and drop off at Borsbeekbrug near Antwerpen-Berchem. De Lijn (www.delijn.be) regional bus 410 to Turnhout via Westmalle starts from Franklin Rooseveltplaats. Buses for Lier and many other destinations start from Antwerpen-Berchem bus station, although trains are generally much faster.

TRAIN

The gorgeous main train station, **Antwerpen-Centraal** (Diamant), is an attraction in itself.

For Amsterdam there's a choice of two high-speed services: Fyra (1st/2nd class €62.80/31.40, 84 minutes) and Thalys (1st/2nd class €142/71, 71 minutes). Both go via Rotterdam and Schiphol Airport. To reach the Netherlands without reservations or high-speed supplements, take the hourly local service to Rosendaal (€9, 48 minutes), then change.

Domestic services:

DESTINATION	FARE (€)	DURATION (MIN)	FREQUENCY (PER HR)
Aarschot	6.50	fast/slow 36/48	2
Bruges	14.80	75	2
Brussels	7.30	35-49	5
Ghent-Dampoort	9.40	46	3
Hasselt	11.50	67	1
Leuven	7.30	fast/slow 42/63	4
Liège (Luik)	16.80	133 (quicker via Brussels)	1
Lier	2.90	17	5
Mechelen-Nekkerspoel	3.90	15	2
Ostende	18.20	100	1

Many trains also pick up from Antwerpen-Berchem station.

Getting Around

BICYCLE

Velo-Antwerpen (www.velo-antwerpen.be; Kievitplein 7; day/week membership €3.90/9; ⊙11am-5pm Mon-Thu, 9am-3pm Fri) Antwerp's extensive red-bike system works very smoothly, with thousands of bikes at over 100 stations. Membership can be purchased online with a credit (but not debit) card. Use the key code to release a bike, then return it at any other stand. Late fees start at 30 minutes and rise to €150 for 24 hours.

Stands are plentiful, but at times it can be hard to find a bike near the train station, or to drop one around KMSKA on a Saturday night. Pick up a map from the office beneath the train lines south of Antwerpen-Centraal.

Fietshaven (www.fietshaven.be; per day/2 days/week €13/19/42; ⊙9am-1pm & 3-6.30pm Mon-Fri, daily summer; last return 6.45pm) Bike rental at the basement level of Antwerpen-Centraal station.

CAR & MOTORCYCLE

Central parking 24-hour pay parking beneath Groenplaats.

Free parking Southern riverside quay, entered opposite Fortuinstraat, 800m south of Grote Markt. Also, when not used for festivities, the huge 't Zuid square between Vlaamsekaai and Waalsekaai has free parking.

PUBLIC TRANSPORT

The same tickets are valid for all buses, trams and *premetro* (underground trams), which mostly operate from about 5.30am to midnight.

Premetro trams 3, 5, 9 and 15 run underground from Diamant to Groenplaats and beneath the Scheldt River to Linkeroever. For 't Zuid, tram 4 runs from Groenplaats. Tram 24 heads to Borgerhout.

TAXI

Taxis wait at Groenplaats, outside Antwerpen-Centraal station and on Koningin Astridplein but are otherwise relatively hard to find. Book ahead for an **Antwerp Taxi** (☎03-238 38 38; www.antwerp-tax.be; €2.95 plus per kilometre €2). Between 10pm and 6am add €2.50 to all fares.

AROUND ANTWERP

Antwerp Port

★**Antwerp Port** PORT

(www.portofantwerp.com) Beautiful it ain't. But its sheer jaw-dropping scale makes driving through this historic port an unforgettable experience. It's the world's fourth-largest

OFF THE BEATEN TRACK

VERBEKE FOUNDATION

Verbeke Foundation (☎03-789 22 07; www.verbekefoundation.com; Westakker; adult/senior/student/child €8/7/6/free; ⏲11am-6pm Thu-Sun) This foundation, one of Europe's largest private initiatives for contemporary art, has a unique, boundary-pushing collection on a 12-hectare site that includes the warehouses of the former Verbeke transport agency. Much of the work here – installation, assemblage, eco and bio art that utilises living things – has an anarchic, unfinished quality, as does the foundation itself.

Take the A11 Antwerp–Bruges highway to junction 11, then from the northern exit roundabout follow 'Hellestraat/Koewacht' signs 600m further west.

port complex (Europe's second after Rotterdam) and a surreal industrial-age maze of cranes, loading yards, container stacks, docks, pipes, rail lines, warehouses and petrochemical refineries. These stretch to the Dutch border, all neatly spaced amid the remnants of grassy *polder* fields.

Flandria (Map p146; ☎03-231 31 00; www.flandria.nu; Kaai 14; short adult/concession €10.50/8.50, long €14.50/12; ⏲short/long depart 10.30am/2.30pm Tue-Sun Jul-Sep, Fri-Sun only Oct & Nov) offers short/long harbour cruises from 't Eilandje, going as far as Boudewijnsluis/Delwaidedok, respectively. The ticket booth opens half an hour before departure. No prebookings except for groups.

Lillo VILLAGE

(www.lillo-krabbevanger.be) When the vast Kanaldok (port extension) was built in the 1960s, seven villages were bulldozed to make space. Of most, just an isolated church tower or windmill remains. One exception is the two-street village of Lillo, population 40, which has been preserved within a Scheldt-side former star-fort. In extraordinary contrast to the light-industrial surroundings, Lillo's tiny village square comes quaintly to life with terraced cafes on sunny Sunday afternoons.

Antwerp to Ghent

The main city between Antwerp and Ghent is historic **Sint-Niklaas** (www.sintniklaas.be), where Belgium's largest Grote Markt features a baroque church dedicated (predictably enough) to St Nicholas, whose half-saint, half-Santa statue also adorns the square. By car from Antwerp, a more circuitous route takes you through **Bezel**, whose tall-steepled church is closely ringed by superb *café*-restaurants occupying picturesque traditional Flemish buildings. A crenellated gateway leads through to parkland, where the town's odd castle-mansion stands partly on stone stilts above its river moat.

Westmalle

Westmalle Abbey & Café Trappisten MONASTERY, BREWERY

(☎03-312 05 02; www.trappisten.be; Antwerpsesteenweg 487; ⏲10am-midnight, kitchen 11am-10pm) Despite its pleasant setting, surrounded by bucolic hiking trails, the monastic complex that produces Westmalle's famous Trappist beers looks more like a prison than an abbey – except that the walls are built to keep visitors out. At the abbey's own tavern, sample the two classic brews or have them mixed as a 'half-and-half' (€3.70). The complex is 2km southwest of Westmalle town beside the N12. Antwerp–Turnhout bus 410 stops outside twice hourly (at the Abdij stop).

Hoogstraten

POP 18,900

Forming a focus of the northbound N14 Malle–Breda road, Hoogstraten's fabulous **belfry** is an enormous 105m-tall red-brick edifice picked out with dots of white-stone detail. Originally dated 1556, it was dynamited by retreating WWII German troops in 1944. Photos in the attached **St-Katherinakerk** (Vrijheid; ⏲1-5pm Tue-Sun May-Sep) FREE document its meticulous reconstruction between 1950 and 1958. Next door the matching 1534 stadhuis (town hall) is also eye-catching and hosts a helpful **tourist office** (☎03-340 19 55; www.hoogstraten.be; Vrijheid 149; ⏲9am-noon & 1-4pm Mon-Fri Oct-Mar, plus from 10am Sat & Sun Apr-Sep). Further north lies the pretty little Unesco-listed *begijnhof* and **Laermolen** (www.laermolen.be; Molenstraat 21; ⏲tours by arrangement €50) FREE, a small 14th-century watermill in an idyllic location.

Turnhout

POP 41,000

Founded as an 11th-century hunting retreat for the Hertog (Duke) of Brabant, today

Turnhout doesn't offer quite the visual appeal of many other Flemish cities, but there's a good selection of museums and a lovely *begijnhof*. En route to the latter from the Grote Markt, catch a framed glimpse of Turnhout's impressive, moated castle, now used as the city courthouse.

Sights

The **tourist office** (☎014-44 33 55; www.tram41.be; Grote Markt 44; ⏰9am-4.30pm Mon-Fri, 1-4pm Sat & Sun) sells €10 discount combi-tickets saving you 50% should you wish to visit all four of Turnhout's main museums.

Turnhout Begijnhof RELIGIOUS SITE
(Begijnstraat 61; ⏰7am-10pm) FREE Hidden behind big wooden gates, one of Belgium's loveliest *begijnhoven* loops round a long, narrow garden set with grotto, church and religious statues. Its tiled brick houses have lanterns and matching shutters, and behind a sheep-mown lawn area is the excellent **Begijnhof Museum** (☎014-42 12 48; Begijnhof 56; adult/concession €5/3; ⏰2-5pm Tue-Sat, 11am-5pm Sun). Entering its perfectly preserved kitchen feels like you've walked straight into a Flemish Primitive painting. Turnhout's last *begijn* died in 2002 and the museum's many treasures are genuinely local.

Taxandria MUSEUM
(www.taxandriamuseum.be; Begijnenstraat 28; adult/concession €5/3; ⏰2-5pm Tue-Sat, 11am-5pm Sun) This historical museum sits behind a 18th-century brick facade and displays its collection in witty, thoughtful ways.

Speelkaartmuseum MUSEUM
(☎014-41 56 21; www.speelkaartenmuseum.be; Duivenstraat 18; adult/concession/under 18yr €5/3/free; ⏰10am-5pm Tue-Sat, 11am-5pm Sun) Celebrating Turnhout's role as the world's second-largest producer of playing cards, this museum displays a range of antique industrial machines used in card creation, including a vast steam-powered drive wheel.

Sleeping & Eating

Turnout City Hotel HOTEL €€
(☎014-82 02 02; www.turnhoutcity-hotel.be; Stationstraat 5; s/d €110/130, weekends €90/130; wi-fi) The best of three options around the train station, this unusual place was professionally converted from a railway depot. Tidy, well-appointed rooms have plug-in internet, kettle and free coffee and wine. Some overlook the rail tracks; others have open terraces at the streetside.

Priorij Corsendonk HISTORIC HOTEL €€
(☎014-46 28 00; www.priorij-corsendonk.be; Corsendonk 5; s/d €100/130; P wi-fi) Around 10-minute drive from Turnhout, just south of the E34, this is a great sleepover choice for those with a car. Simple, soothing rooms look over extensive private parkland in a 14th-century Augustinian priory.

Hotel Terminus HOTEL €€
(☎014-41 20 78; www.hotel-terminus.be; Grote Markt 72; s/d/tr from €56/78/114, s without toilet €50) Located above a busy cafe-restaurant on the main square's southwestern corner. Some rooms have creaky, uneven floors and tiny bathroom booths; others are more solid and have been reasonably well renovated. The lift saves you those steep, narrow steps and breakfast is included.

Cucina Marangon ITALIAN €€
(☎014-42 43 81; www.cucinamarangon.com; Patersstraat 9; mains €25, 3-course menu €45; ⏰11.30am-2pm, 6.30-9.30pm Tue-Fri, 6.30-9.30pm Sat) Simple, tasty Italian dishes that reference the Veneto are made with care and attention here. There's an attached shop where you can buy wine and other Italian products.

A MEDIEVAL BAARLES-UP

Belgian Baarle-Hertog (population 2590) and Dutch Baarle-Nassau effectively form one intermeshed town, but legally the **Baarle-Hertog** (http://baarledigitaal.org) consists of 22 miniature Belgian enclaves, within which are eight enclaves of the Netherlands. It's the world's messiest border-jigsaw. Nab the southernmost table on the Hotel Den Engel's terrace and sip a drink with one foot either side of the border.

The arrangement stems from a bizarre 1198 agreement in which the Duke of Breda (later Nassau) was given the village of Baarle but did not receive the surrounding farmland, which was jealously guarded by the Hertog (Duke) of Brabant for its valuable agricultural tax revenues.

Bus 460 runs from Turnhout to Baarle hourly. Dutch bus 132 (www.bba.nl) continues Baarle–Tilburg–Breda. By car there's a pleasantly rural lane from Hoogstraten.

Drinking & Nightlife

In den Spytighen Duvel PUB

(☎014-42 35 00; www.spytighenduvel.be; Otterstraat 99; ⏲2pm-1am Tue-Sun) Historic beamed ceilings, a central fireplace and games to play all add to the central attraction: a selection of some 160 beers.

't Convent CAFE

(☎014-70 00 33; Begijnhof 76; beer/coffee €2/2.10; ⏲9.30am-6.30pm Thu-Sun) Candles, board floors and an attractive garden tempt you into this archetypal *begijnhof* house for coffee, beer or ice cream.

Cafe Barzoen BAR

(⏲9am-1am Mon-Sat, 7am-8pm Sun) Part of a regional arts organisation, this cafe-bar opens for early-morning coffee and finishes with performances and DJs. There's a big terrace and playground for in between.

Getting There & Away

BUS

The following routes pick up at least hourly near both the station and the Grote Markt.

416, 417 and 410 To Antwerp-Groenplaats (60 to 80 minutes). Bus 410 runs via Westmalle (39 minutes).

430 To Hoogstraten

450 To Tilburg (Netherlands)

460 To Baarle-Hertog

TRAIN

Trains run twice hourly to Lier (€5.80, 32 minutes) and hourly to Antwerpen-Centraal (€7.30, 51 minutes). The station is 700m west of the Grote Markt along Merodelai.

Lier

POP 34,120

Another of Flanders' overlooked historical gems, compact Lier is ringed by a circular waterway and the Vesten, a walkable green rampart where the city walls once stood.

Sights & Activities

Archetypal pseudo-baroque facades line the Grote Markt, where a tall, elfin-spired 1369 belfry gives character to the refined stadhuis. In its basement an obliging **tourist office** (☎03-800 05 05; www.toerismelier.be; Grote

BEGIJNHOVEN & GODSHUIZEN

In the 12th century, large numbers of men from the Low Countries embarked on Crusades to the Holy Land and never returned. This, along with a widespread fracturing of rural communities, meant many single or widowed medieval women moved to the city seeking employment and security.

Often the only choice was to join a religious order, but getting into a convent required giving up one's worldly possessions and even one's name. A middle way, especially appealing to the well off and well educated, was to become a *begijn* (*béguine* in French). These lay sisters made Catholic vows including obedience and chastity but could maintain their assets. They lived in a self-contained *begijnhof* (*béguinage* in French): a cluster of houses built around a central garden and church, surrounded by a protective wall. Land (normally at the outskirts of town) was typically granted by a pious feudal lord, but once established these all-female communities were self-sufficient. Most had a farm and vegetable garden and derived supplementary income from lace making and from benefactors who would pay the *begijnen* to pray for them.

In the 16th century, Holland's growing Protestantism meant that most Dutch *begijnhoven* were swept away. In contrast, Spanish-ruled Flanders was gripped by a fervently Catholic counter-reformation that reshaped the *begijn* movement. Rebuilt *begijnhoven* became hospice-style institutions with vastly improved funding. From 1583 the Archbishop of Mechelen decreed a standardised rulebook and a nun-like 'uniform' for *begijnen*, who at one point composed almost 5% of Flanders' female population.

A century ago some 1500 *begijnen* still lived in Belgium; the last, Marcella Pattyn, died in 2013 after a life spent in Kortrijk's *begijnhof*, one of 14 on the Unesco World Heritage list. These are all beautifully preserved, albeit these days lived in by ordinary townsfolk.

Looking somewhat similar to *begijnhoven* but usually on a smaller scale are *godshuizen* (almshouses). Typically featuring red-brick or whitewashed shuttered cottages set around a tiny enclosed garden, these were built by merchant guilds for their members or by rich sponsors to provide shelter for the poor (and to save the sponsors' souls). Bruges has a remarkable 46 *godshuizen*.

Markt 57; ⏲9am-5pm Mon-Sat, to 4pm Sun, closed weekends & lunchtimes Nov-Mar) hands out free map-brochures and suggestions for walks.

★Lier Begijnhof RELIGIOUS SITE
Originally founded in 1258, this Unesco site is one of Belgium's prettiest 'street' *begijnhoven*, a small but picture-perfect grid of cobbled, gated lanes lined with archetypal houses and featuring the baroque-fronted 1671 **St-Margaretakerk**. The Wenzenstraat entrance is two short blocks southwest of Zimmerplein. The southern door leads out onto the riverbank walk.

★Stedelijk Museum GALLERY
(☎03-800 03 96; www.bruegelland.be; Florent Van Cauwenberghstraat 14; adult/reduced €4/3; ⏲10am-noon & 1-5pm Tue-Sun) This well-endowed provincial art gallery is always appealing, but it's a must-see while it hosts a long-term one-room Brueghel exhibition, taken in part from the collection of KMSKA (p151) during that Antwerp gallery's reconstruction.

Zimmertoren TOWER
(www.zimmertoren.be; Zimmerplein; adult/child €4/2; ⏲9am-noon & 1.30-5.30pm Tue-Sun) Lier's most iconic monument is the photogenic Zimmertoren, a partly 14th-century tower incorporating a fanciful 1930 timepiece that's eccentrically over-endowed with dials, zodiac signs and a globe on which the Congo remains forever Belgian. Figures on the south face perform bell-striking duties every hour.

Horology specialists can check out the mechanisms, slow-moving video explanations, and a pavilion displaying a second 1935 astronomical Wonder Clock. With 93 dials, the latter is undoubtedly super-clever but not so thrilling for nonspecialists.

Timmermans-Opsomerhuis MUSEUM
(☎03-800 03 94; Netelaan 4-6; adult/reduced €2/1; ⏲10am-noon & 1-5pm Tue-Sun; 👪) Works by renowned local artists include some fine pre-Raphaelite-style canvases by Isidore Opsomer (1878–1967), notably the 1900 painting of Jesus hanging out in Lier. Upstairs the museum's focus is on writer Felix Timmermans (1886–1947), whose 1916 novel *Pallieter* recast Lier folk as life-loving bohemians: they'd previously been dismissively nicknamed *schapekoppen* (sheep-heads) for their short-sighted medieval decision that the town should host a sheep market rather than Flanders' first great university.

St-Gummaruskerk CHURCH
(www.topalier.be/bezoeken; Kardinaal Mercierplein; presbytery €1.50; ⏲10am-noon & 2-5pm Tue-Sat, 2-5pm Mon & Sun Easter-Oct) Stand amid the flowerboxes of the Aragonstraat bridge and look southeast for a beautiful perspective on this huge, stone-buttressed Gothic church. It commemorates Lier's famously hen-pecked founder St-Gummarus, an 8th-century nobleman whose remains are contained in a grand 1682 silver reliquary.

Bootjevaren CRUISE
(www.bootjevareninlier.be; adult/child €3/2; ⏲2-6pm Sat & Sun Apr-Oct) A 40-minute cruise around Lier's canal ring.

Sleeping

The tourist office has a list of B&Bs, but almost all are outside the historic centre.

Best Western Plus Zimmerhof BOUTIQUE HOTEL €€
(☎03-490 03 90; www.zimmerhof.be; Begijnhofstraat 2; s/d €119/139) Converted from historic almshouses, the Lier outpost of this boutique chain offers modern rooms that retain the original building's pretty brick facade and the steep teak stairs. Decor includes paddle-plate lamps and misty B&W prints of the town, and the sweeping bar lies partly within what was once a prison gateway.

Hof van Aragon HOTEL €€
(☎03-491 08 00; www.hva.be; Aragonstraat 6; s/d €75/97; 📶) Once an orphanage, this small riverside hotel has medieval outer walls and elements of original beamwork (notably in rooms 20 and 21). It's quiet yet very central, making for a pleasant getaway.

Eating

The Grote Markt, Eikelstraat and Zimmerplein are lined with places to eat and drink, albeit most of them ho-hum. Bakeries sell Liers *vlaaike* (signature fat pastries made with syrup and cinnamon).

De Comeet EUROPEAN €€
(☎03-297 27 24; http://decomeet.be; Florent Van Cauwenberghstraat 18; wraps & tapas €4.50-9, mains €16-24.50; ⏲noon-11pm Wed-Sat, 5-10pm Wed-Sun Easter–mid-Oct, evening only winter) Gilt cherubs hold wooden beams, and a contemporary wrought-iron chandelier sits above the grand piano in this characterful eatery whose summer 'garden' retains the rubble of a demolished building, softened by creepers. Bookings recommended.

Annaloro ITALIAN €€€

(☎03-488 00 85; www.annaloro.be; Bril 17; mains €19-27; ⌚noon-2pm & 6-9.30pm Thu-Mon, closed lunch Sat) This intimate, upmarket Italian restaurant has a Sicilian slant, both in the cooking and in the baroque decor.

Drinking & Nightlife

De Mort BAR

(Café de Mort; www.demort.be; Grote Markt 28 b2; ⌚6pm-late) Atmospheric brown bar hidden in the alley signposted to Mister 100 Billiard Lounge.

Getting There & Away

Bus 90 runs from the Grote Markt to Antwerp-Berchem bus station. Buses 550 and 560 each head hourly to Mechelen (36 minutes). From the train station, 1km northeast of Grote Markt, trains run thrice hourly to Antwerp (20 minutes), and hourly to Diest (30 minutes), Leuven (44 minutes) via Aarschot (25 minutes), and Brussels (40 minutes) via Mechelen (16 minutes).

Mechelen

POP 82,300

With Belgium's foremost cathedral, a superb central square and a scattering of intriguing museums, Mechelen (Malines in French) is one of Flanders' most underrated historic cities. And, as the seat of Belgium's Catholic primate (the equivalent of an archbishop), it is overloaded with fine churches. It's true that baroque house fronts are all too often interspersed with banal postwar architecture and the canals generally lack Bruges' prettiness. But on summer weekends, when Bruges gets packed with tourists, surprisingly cool Mechelen offers a very attractive alternative, along with slashed room rates.

History

Converted to Christianity by 8th-century Irish evangelist St-Rombout, Mechelen became and has remained the country's religious capital. In 1473 Charles the Bold chose Mechelen as the administrative capital of his Burgundian Low Countries, a role maintained after his death by his widow, Margaret of York. Margaret's step-granddaughter Margaret (Margriet) of Austria (1480–1530) later developed Mechelen's court into one of the most glamorous of its day. Science, literature and the arts thrived, and elaborate buildings rose. When Margaret died, her ultrapowerful nephew Charles Quint moved the capital to Brussels. Mechelen's star faded, though the city regained the historical spotlight very briefly in May 1835 when continental Europe's first train arrived here.

Sights & Activities

West of Veemarkt (originally Mechelen's animal market), several fine churches face off along Keizerstraat. This part of town is good for a short sightseeing walk.

★St-Romboutskathedraal CATHEDRAL

(http://sintromboutstoren.mechelen.be; Grote Markt; ⌚1-6pm Mon-Fri, 10am-6pm Sat) FREE Dominating the central Grote Markt and indeed the whole city, this vast, robust cathedral features a Van Dyck crucifixion on the right as you enter and dozens more fine artworks below the stained glasswork of the apse.

But by far its most notable feature is the gobsmacking 15th-century tower, soaring 97m. Climbing it takes at least 40 minutes return (over 500 steps), for which the rewards are brilliant views from the new rooftop viewing platform. It's unsheltered, so avoid it in heavy rain, and consider booking ahead during major holidays, as space is limited. During the climb you'll see a human treadmill once used to bring up building materials, plus the impressive 49-bell carillon, which rings out across town during summer's hour-long carillon concerts.

Stadhuis HISTORIC BUILDING

(Grote Markt) Balancing the massive bulk of the cathedral across Mechelen's splendid Grote Markt is the contrastingly poetic stadhuis in all its devil-may-care stone flamboyance. Its architectural inventiveness stems from the fact that it's really three different buildings knocked together: a never-finished medieval belfry flanked by a 14th-century Cloth Hall and a 1911 neo-Gothic council hall built to a long-shelved 16th-century design.

Schepenhuis GALLERY, ARCHITECTURE

(www.rikwouters.be; Steenweg 1; adult/reduced €8/5; ⌚10am-5pm Mon, Tue & Thu-Sun) The Schepenhuis is a small castle fantasy that became the council-parliament for the Burgundian Netherlands from 1473. It is currently used as a gallery to display a major exhibition of works by celebrated Mechelen-born Fauvist painter-sculptor Rik Wouters. IJzerenleen, stretching south from here, is lined with a fine array of baroque house fronts.

Mechelen

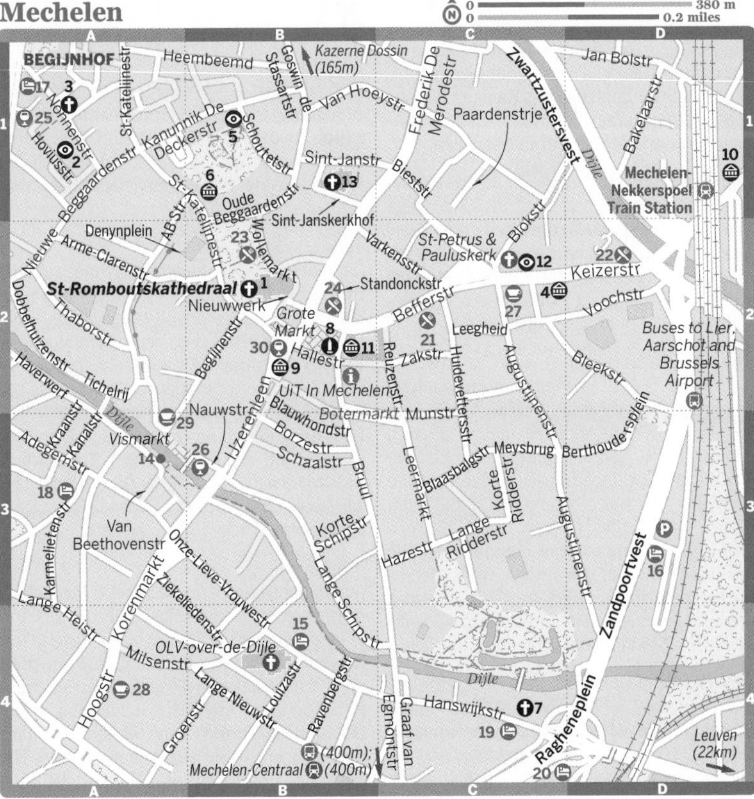

Mechelen

Top Sights

1 St-Romboutskathedraal B2

Sights

2 Begijnhof A1
3 Begijnhofkerk A1
4 Courthouse C2
5 De Wit Royal Manufacturers B1
6 Het Zotte Kunstkabinet B1
7 OLV-Hanswijkbasiliek C4
8 Op-Sinjoorke Statue B2
9 Schepenhuis B2
10 Speelgoedmuseum D1
11 Stadhuis B2
12 Stadsschouwburg C2
13 St-Janskerk B1
Tongerlo Refuge .... (see 5)

Activities, Courses & Tours

14 Boat Tours A3

Sleeping

15 Dusk till Dawn B4
16 Hostel De Zandpoort D3
17 Hotel Carolus A1
18 Martins Patershof A3
19 Muske Pitter C4
20 Patio Houses C4

Eating

21 Cosma Foodhouse C2
22 D'Afspraak D2
23 Il Cardinale B2
24 Sava B2

Drinking & Nightlife

25 Brouwerij Het Anker A1
26 De Gouden Vis B3
27 D'Hanekeef C2
28 Pelaton de Paris A4
29 Sister Bean A3
30 Unwined B2

Stadsschouwburg BUILDING
(Keizerstraat 3) The municipal theatre occupies the stone-fronted former palace of Margaret of York. The diplomatically brilliant sister of English king Richard III, she became the de facto dowager ruler of Burgundy's Low Countries from Mechelen.

Courthouse HISTORIC BUILDING
(⌚7.30am-6pm Mon-Fri, 9am-8pm Sat & Sun) FREE The city's step-gabled courthouse was Margaret of Austria's palace from 1506. Despite many subsequent alterations, it maintains a gorgeous courtyard garden where Charles Quint (p271) would have played as a boy.

Speelgoedmuseum MUSEUM
(☎015-55 70 75; www.speelgoedmuseum.be; Nekkerstraat 21; adult/child €8.50/6; ⌚10am-5pm Tue-Sun) With 7000 sq metres of toys, games, dolls, teddies and pastimes, the wonderful Speelgoedmuseum has lots to keep the kids busy. Meanwhile, adults can peruse the history of toys, walk inside a 'Bruegel' painting and get maudlin over the nostalgic range of playthings, from Meccano to Lego, toy soldiers to Airfix kits and working train sets. The museum backs onto Mechelen-Nekkerspoel train station.

OLV-Hanswijkbasiliek CHURCH
(Hanswijkstraat; ⌚1-4pm Tue-Sun) This dome-crowned three-wing basilica has an unusual circular interior, a superb *Paradise Lost* pulpit and brilliant 1690 carved confessionals. An octagonal floor stone commemorates the pope's 1985 visit. But its main treasure is the 'miraculous' Hanswijk Madonna statuette dating from 988, long an object of pilgrimage and still the centrepiece of Mechelen's greatest religious pageant.

St-Janskerk CHURCH
(Sint-Janstraat; ⌚1-4pm Tue-Sun) Built in white sandstone, the 15th-century Gothic church of the 'two Johns' (Baptist and Evangelist) has recently had its facade laboriously restored. Inside the church houses Rubens' *Adoration of the Magi*.

Tongerlo Refuge HOUSE
(Schoutestraat 7) In medieval times, abbots from wealthy monasteries would often travel to Mechelen to consult the primate (archbishop) and thus required city residences. Known as 'refuges', some such residences often became grand affairs. One such is the beautiful, brick-spired 1484 Tongerlo Refuge. Since 1889 it has been home to tapestry makers and repairers **De Wit Royal Manufacturers** (☎0475 52 29 05; www.dewit.be; adult/child €8/4; ⌚tours 10.30am-12.30pm Sat & by appointment 9am-3.30pm Thu-Sat).

Begijnhof AREA
(www.groot-begijnhof-mechelen.be) Mechelen's *begijnhof* is no longer classically distinct and is now an area of old-city lanes. Several are flower-strung and charming: the junction of Schrijnstraat and Twaalf-Apostelenstraat is particularly attractive, while the pretty Hoviusstraat frames a startlingly discordant rear view of the old Het Anker brewery. The splendid **Begijnhofkerk** (Nonenstraat; ⌚1-4pm Tue-Sun) is a baroque masterpiece with a God-the-father relief atop the front gable and an interior of particularly feminine decoration.

BEER & HISTORY

All around town *cafés* serve beers produced by celebrated local brewery Het Anker, many named with Mechelen's curious history in mind. Maneblusser, its sneakily drinkable, well-built 6.5% blond, literally means 'moon extinguisher'. That's been a self-mocking nickname for Mechelen townsfolk since 1687, when cloud-diffused moonlight above the cathedral tower was mistaken for a fire.

The famous Gouden Carolus brews commemorate the golden coinage of Charles Quint. Gouden Carolus 'Classic' is a rich 7.5% dark beer that has been declared the world's best. But there's also a sturdy 9% Tripel (cellar-aged blond) and the unique 8% Ambrio brown ale, loosely based on a 1433 recipe said to have been Charles' favourite tipple.

Slightly cloudy, with a mildly spiced acidic edge, Gouden Carolus Hopsinjoor is a hoppy pun on Op-Sinjoorke, a lewdly cackling folkloric anti-mascot whose reputation for wife-beating was traditionally punished by tossing him in the air during annual parades. The theft of the original 1647 mannequin was once the cause of conflict between Mechelen and Antwerp. There's a 'flying' **Op-Sinjoorke statue** outside the stadhuis.

Any of these beers can be tasted at Het Anker's recently revamped **Brouwerij Het Anker brasserie** (www.hetanker.be; Guido Gezellelaan 49; tours €8; ⌚tours hourly 11am-3pm Fri-Sun) along with varying seasonal specials.

Kazerne Dossin MUSEUM, MEMORIAL
(Jewish Museum of Deportation & Resistance; ☎015-29 06 60; www.kazernedossin.eu; Goswin de Stassartstraat 153; adult/reduced €10/4; ⏰9am-5pm Thu-Tue) The 18th-century Dossin Barracks were used by the Nazis as a WWII deportation centre, and 25,500 Jews and 352 Roma were sent to Auschwitz concentration camp from here in 28 convoys. Only 1400 returned. The complex has been preserved as a memorial and, across the road, there is a new, movingly austere museum building designed by celebrated Belgian architect bOb Van Reeth.

Het Zotte Kunstkabinet MUSEUM
(www.vliegendpeert.be; Sint-Katelijnestraat 22; admission/audio guide €5/1; ⏰1.30-5pm Wed & Sat) This small and suitably eccentric museum has some fun with the 'crazy' hell scenes and frolicking odd folk of 16th-century paintings by artists like Bruegel and Bosch.

Technopolis MUSEUM
(☎015-34 20 00; www.technopolis.be; Technologielaan; adult/child €16/12.50; ⏰9.30am-5pm; 👪) Designed for kids and teenagers but fascinating for those of all ages, one of Belgium's best science museums has dozens of hands-on activities to entertain and engage. The simulator rides are especially popular. It's 1.8km south of town at junction 10 (Mechelen-Zuid) of the E19 motorway, ideal if you're driving from Brussels to Antwerp. From Mechelen station take bus 282, which runs every half-hour on weekdays.

Fort Breendonk HISTORIC SITE
(☎03-886 75 25; www.breendonk.be; Brandstraat 57; adult/reduced €10/9; ⏰9.30am-5.30pm, last visit 4.30pm) Built in 1906 as an outlying defence post for Antwerp, Breendonk became a Nazi concentration camp in WWII. Visits take you through torture rooms, cells and dark, dank corridors accompanied by a two-hour audio guide relating harrowing personal accounts. Dress appropriately, as much of the visit is outside; even in high summer this place chills to the bone.

The fort is 12km west of Mechelen, just off the A12 Antwerp–Brussels highway at junction 7 in Willebroek.

Westbound bus 460 heads to Brussels' Gare du Nord (50 minutes) at 38 minutes past the hour on weekdays. Eastbound bus 260 from nearby Schalkstraat shuttles hourly to Willebroek train station (1.5km northeast), which is on the Leuven–Mechelen–St-Niklaas line.

Boat Tours CRUISE
(adult/child €6.50/4; ⏰1.30pm, 2.30pm, 3.30pm, 4.30pm & 5.30pm Tue-Sun Apr-Oct, Sat & Sun winter) Starting from Haverwerf, the *Malinska* takes passengers on 45-minute cruises along Mechelen's waterways.

Sleeping

Hostel De Zandpoort HOSTEL €
(☎015-27 85 39; www.mechelen-hostel.com; Zandpoortvest 70; dm/tw €24.95/58.90; ⏰check-in 5-10pm; P 📶) A spick-and-span modern youth hostel whose breeze-block-walled rooms all have decent private bathrooms. Bring your own towel and a padlock for the small safety lockers. Lockout 11am to 5pm. HI members and youth save €2 to €3.

Dusk Till Dawn B&B €€
(☎015-41 28 16; www.dusktilldawn.be; Onze-Lieve-Vrouwestraat 81; d €110-140) Turning the age-old silver handle rings the doorbell at this delightful two-room B&B in an 1870s town house once owned by the Lamot brewing barons. Subtle colours and discerning modern decor reign, while the bar-lounge adopts some art-nouveau touches. Guests can use the peaceful garden.

Martins Patershof BOUTIQUE HOTEL €€
(☎015-46 46 46; www.martinshotels.com; Karmelietenstraat 4; d €139; 📶) Fancy sleeping in a church? This one was originally part of a 1867 Franciscan monastery and it retains its rose window and religious mosaics. All but standard rooms maintain original design elements (some rather kitsch), from column tops to stained-glass windows. The meeting/breakfast room features the renovated altar.

Hotel Carolus HOTEL €€
(☎015-28 71 41; www.hetanker.be; Guido Gezellelaan 49; s/d €72/99; P 📶) Motel-style rooms in a partly creeper-covered house whose main draws are the summer terrace overlooking stacked beer casks in the historic Het Anker brewery. There's also an offer to get 'under the sheets with a brewer' – in fact, tours and tastings of the brewery. Heavy discounts apply over the weekend.

Muske Pitter GUESTHOUSE €€
(☎015-43 63 03; www.muskepitter.be; Hanswijkstraat 70; s/d €55/75) Comfortable rooms with either a terrace or nice architectural views are attached to a local tavern and handy for the main train station. New luxury rooms are bright white but also nicely simple. Breakfast included.

Patio Houses B&B €€€
(☎015-46 08 60; http://thepatiohouses.be; Hendrik Speecqvest 54; d €145; P 📶) A stylish, very personal B&B with beautiful terraces or spa baths for relaxing, helpful hosts and elegant rooms. Dinners around the large dining table can be arranged.

Eating

Mechelen's agricultural specialities include *witloof* (endives) and especially *asperges* (asparagus), prominent on restaurant menus mid-April to late June. For pittas and cheap takeaways look along Befferstraat, east of the Grote Markt.

★ **Il Cardinale** BURGERS €
(☎0468 21 00 91; www.ilcardinale.be; Sint-Romboutskerkhof 1; burger meals €14; ⏲noon-2pm & 5-10pm Mon-Fri & Sun, noon-10pm Sat) Belgian burger mania and a gently ironic reworking of the city's Catholic iconography meet at this friendly place, set in the shadow of the cathedral, with big windows facing a pretty patch of green. The burger menu continues the religious irreverence with a Godfather (mozzarella and pesto) and a Mary had a Little Lamb (lamb patty); the chips are notably good.

D'Afspraak BELGIAN €
(☎015-33 17 34; www.dafspraak.be; Keizerstraat 23; meals €6-20; ⏲11am-10pm Wed-Fri, 3-11pm Sat & Sun; 📶) Great-value pub food is served with unexpected aplomb in this traditional low-key *café* with high ceilings and a lamp fashioned from wine bottles. Good variety of beers available.

Sava TAPAS €€
(☎015-64 70 90; Grote Markt 13; tapas €4-10; ⏲9am-midnight) Right in the centre but tucked away from the tourist drag, Sava offers authentic, seasonal tapas dishes like spicy meatballs and whole anchovies. Plus there's cava (Spanish sparkling wine), good local beers and excellent people watching, especially as the night wears on and everyone in Mechelen seems to end up here.

Cosma Foodhouse INTERNATIONAL €€
(☎0477 23 48 43; Befferstraat 24; dishes €6-18; ⏲10.30am-6.30pm Mon-Wed, Fri & Sat, to 11pm Thu) Original beams and a lovely old staircase mix with a woody, contemporary fitout at this old bakery, where the owners have brought a 'London-style' bistro-meets-deli-meets-caterer concept to Mechelen. Dishes run the gamut of styles and can be eaten in the warm, welcoming space, or made up to take away for a picnic or a self-catering hotel dinner.

Drinking & Nightlife

The riverside quarter around Vismarkt/Nauwstraat is a compact but appealing nightlife zone, with a *café*-bar for virtually any taste along with a number of appealing little places around the Grote Markt.

De Gouden Vis PUB, BAR
(☎015-20 72 06; Nauwstraat 7; ⏲noon-4am) The bare boards of this age-old favourite have a pleasantly well-loved patina, the vine still threatens to break chunks out of the verandah and the rear riverside terrace catches afternoon sunshine before the serious drinking gets going.

D'Hanekeef CAFE, BAR
(☎015-20 78 46; Keizerstraat 8; ⏲9am-4am Mon-Sat, noon-3am Sun) Retaining its traditional patterned floor tiles and heavy wooden beams, Mechelen's 'oldest pub' is ideal for low-key beery conversations with newspaper-reading locals. The place started life as the chicken-farmers' exchange, hence all the cocks on the recently modernised walls.

Unwined WINE BAR
(☎015-41 81 85; http://unwined.be; Steenweg 22; ⏲6-11pm Mon, noon-midnight Wed-Sat, 11am-10pm Sun) Right under the cathedral's lofty tower, this stylish wine bar has lots of lounging spots out the back as well as a sunny courtyard. A great selection of wines by the glass can be sampled with Mediterranean-style nibbles, there's lots of interesting bottles to take away and there's a succinct list of proper grown-up cocktails.

Brunch, with bubbly of course, happens on Sunday between 11am and 3pm.

Sister Bean CAFE
(☎0496 12 86 30; http://sisterbean.be; Vismarkt 26; ⏲8.30am-6.30pm) Downstairs in this beautiful old corner building there's a bustling cafe with lounge chairs and outside tables in summer. The coffee is excellent and there's a neat breakfast or afternoon-tea menu of smoothies, juices, brownies and pancakes. Upstairs, lunch dishes such as noodles or quinoa salad are served in the large and light dining room.

If you can nab a table, there's a big Sunday-brunch buffet too.

Pelaton de Paris CAFE
(☎015-64 48 26; www.pelotondeparis.be; Hoogstraat 49; ⏲10am-6pm Wed-Sun) At this cyclist's dream cafe, you can relax with a beer

or a Baileys latte (yes, it's a latte spiked with Baileys) while a Belgian cycling aficionado looks over your bike. It's a little out of the centre, but you're on two wheels, right?

Information

Use-It (www.use-it.be) produces a brilliant free Mechelen guide-map that's available from the tourist office or the youth hostel or to download.

UiT In Mechelen (☎070 22 00 08; http://visit-mechelen.be; Hallestraat 2; ⏲10am-5pm Mon-Fri, 12.30-4pm Sun summer, to 4pm winter) Push-buttons light up attractions' locations on a city floor map, and upstairs there's an exhibit on local products. The website is comprehensive, there's an excellent free map and staff are very helpful.

Getting There & Around

From the bus station and adjoining Mechelen-Centraal train station, it's 1.3km to the Grote Markt (buses 1 to 5).

BICYCLE

Bicycle rental changes seasonally; the tourist office has a list online.

TRAIN

From Mechelen-Centraal, hourly trains run to Leuven (30 minutes) and to Turnhout (55 minutes) via Lier (15 minutes). Fast/slow trains take 15/28 minutes to Brussels and 17/33 minutes to Antwerp. Each runs up to three times hourly. Slow trains also stop in handier Mechelen-Nekkerspoel.

Leuven

POP 97,600

Lively Leuven (Louvain in French) is an ancient capital, a prominent brewing centre and Flanders' oldest university town. In term time, and even during holidays, some 25,000 students give the city an upbeat, creative air. The picturesque core is small enough that you could easily see the sights in a short day trip, but characterful pubs and good-value dining could keep you here for weeks.

Sights & Activities

Much of Leuven's historic townscape was obliterated in the world wars, but a few eye-catching baroque churches survive, including **St-Michelskerk** (Naamsestraat; ⏲1.30-4.30pm Tue-Sun) and **OLV-Ter-Koorts** (Vlamingenstraat).

Stadhuis ARCHITECTURE
(Grote Markt 9; tours €4; ⏲tours 3pm) Far and away Leuven's most iconic sight, the incredible 15th-century stadhuis is a late-Gothic architectural wedding cake flamboyantly overloaded with terraced turrets, fancy stonework and colourful flags. Added in the mid-19th century, a phenomenal 236 statues smother the exterior, each representing a prominent local scholar, artist or noble from the city's history. Somehow the stadhuis survived the numerous wars that devastated the rest of the town. A WWII bomb that scoured part of the facade miraculously failed to explode.

The interior is less dramatic but does feature a few sculptures by Constantin Meunier, who once had a workshop on Minderbroedersvest.

M Van Museum GALLERY
(☎016-22 69 09; www.mleuven.be; Leopold Vanderkelenstraat 28; adult/reduced €12/10; ⏲11am-6pm Fri-Tue, to 8pm Thu) Leuven's state-of-the-art gallery houses a priceless collection of mostly 15th- to 18th-century religious art along with contemporary works, and hosts high-profile exhibitions. An 'M' ticket allows free entrance to the *schatkamer* (treasury) of St-Pieterskerk.

St-Pieterskerk CHURCH
(Grote Markt; schatkamer adult/reduced €3/2, with M Van Museum 'M' ticket free; ⏲10am-4.30pm Mon-Sat, 11am-4.30pm Sun) The interior of this Brabantine-Gothic church (1425) is all about the elaborately carved stone rood screen and baroque wooden pulpit. In the *schatkamer* (treasury), don't miss the two priceless triptychs by Leuven-based Flemish Primitive artist Dirk Bouts, including the 1464–67 masterpiece *Het Laatste Avondmaal*, with Jesus' last supper set in a typical Flemish Gothic dining hall. The panels have been 'lost' several times, including during WWII, when Nazis carted them off and hid them in a salt mine.

The northwest facade's distinctly unfinished look came about as unstable subsoil forced builders to abandon a planned 170m-high tower.

Universiteitsbibliotheek ARCHITECTURE
(University Library; http://bib.kuleuven.be; Monseigneur Ladeuzeplein 21; tower €7; ⏲tower 10am-4.30pm Mon, Wed & Fri-Sun, from 1pm Tue & Thu) FREE Dominating Monseigneur Ladeuzeplein, this imposingly grand Flemish Renaissance-style palace features a soaring Scandinavian-style brick tower topped with a three-storey octagonal stone cupola. The library was convincingly rebuilt after WWI with the financial aid of 400 American universities, having been infamously put to the

torch in August 1914 during the *schrecklichkeit* (terror or 'hard measures') of the German occupation. It was then rebuilt a second time after WWII.

The public can visit at certain times during term, there's a summer program of exhibitions and the 300 steps of the the tower can be climbed year-round.

Stella Artois BREWERY

(www.breweryvisits.com; Vuurkruisenlaan; adult/reduced €8.50/7.50; ⏲9am-7.30pm Tue-Sat) There are two tour options at this world-famous, highly automated brewery. Book online at least two days ahead if possible: choose 'last minute' and find a slot according to the flagged language of the available tours. Alternatively, from May to October, 90-minute tours in English are available at 3.30pm on Saturday and Sunday, with tickets sold through the tourist office. The brewery is just off the main inner ring road around 800m northwest of the train station.

Sleeping

Most Leuven hotel prices fall at weekends.

Leuven City Hostel HOSTEL €

(☎016-84 30 33; www.leuvencityhostel.com; Ravenstraat 37; dm/d €23/54; ⏲reception 4-8pm; @ᯤ) This new hostel tucked away behind KUL comes with a comfy games lounge, a quality kitchen and a sweet little courtyard-garden area. There are no membership requirements, and breakfast and linen are included in the price.

Jeugdherbergen De Blauwput HOSTEL €

(☎016-63 90 62; www.leuven-hostel.com; Martelarenlaan 11a; dm/d €24.95/58.90, youth €22.65/54.90; @ᯤ) Relatively spacious dorm rooms have en-suite showers and toilets. There's an early-closing bar and internet access is available in the lounge. Access from town is via the underpass between the bus and train stations. Check in before 10pm. HI members save €3.

★Oude Brouwerei Keyser Carel B&B €€

(☎016-22 14 81; www.keysercarel.be; Lei 15; s/d €105/120) An inconspicuous facade hides this grand B&B, in a mansion whose oldest section dates from 1595. The best of three well-appointed rooms has a four-poster bed, a private sauna (extra charge) and views of the large family garden, which incorporates a 1940 wartime bunker and the most extensive surviving remnant of Leuven's 1120 city wall.

Casa Bollicine B&B €€

(☎0497 83 97 17; www.casabollicine.be; Parijsstraat 7; s/d €120/150; ᯤ) Black-and-white decor rules in this B&B's three stylishly appointed new guest rooms with high ceilings and show baths. They're accessed up steep stairs from a small, modernist snack bar right in the heart of Leuven's central entertainment district. The luxury breakfast includes salmon and sparkling wine. Breakfasts are hearty and generous.

Begijnhof Hotel HOTEL €€

(☎016-29 10 10; www.bchotel.be; Groot Begijnhof 15; d €105) Set among gardens in what was the town's *begijnhof*, this pretty if rather corporate hotel is a serene choice, especially out of term time, when there are few conferences and great rates.

Martin's Klooster Hotel HOTEL €€

(☎016-21 31 41; www.martins-hotels.com; Onze-Lieve-Vrouwstraat 22; d €95-250; @ᯤ) Central but peaceful, the Klooster is partly composed of a 16th-century building that was once home to Emperor Charles Quint's secretary and was later an Augustinian convent. A few suites may have antique brickwork, beams and simulated fires, but most rooms are in a modern annexe – comfortable but corporate.

Eating

Terrace cafes surround the stadhuis, and perpetually packed, casually stylish restaurants and bars spill tables onto a cosy flag-decked medieval alley called Muntstraat. For cheap Asian food, pizza and snacks, stroll pedestrianised Parijsstraat, Tiensestraat or Naamsestraat.

Domus PUB FOOD €

(☎016-20 14 49; www.domusleuven.be; Tiensestraat 8; snacks €6-8, mains €11-18; ⏲9am-1am Tue-Sun, kitchen to 10.30pm; ᯤ) Reminiscent of a rambling old-English country pub, this brewery-*café* has heavy beams and rough-plastered part-brick walls generously adorned with photos, paintings and assorted knick-knacks. It's great for sandwiches, fairly priced Flemish meals or one of its own brews: try Nostra Domus, a gentle but balanced 5.8% amber beer.

Burger Folie BURGERS €

(☎016-88 66 08; www.burgerfolie.be; Muntstraat 4; burgers €14-18; ⏲noon-2pm & 6-10pm Tue-Sat) Outside tables stretch to both sides of the street and two large whitewashed shopfronts fill up fast. Why the fuss? Burgers here are made from beef from the famous Belgian

Leuven

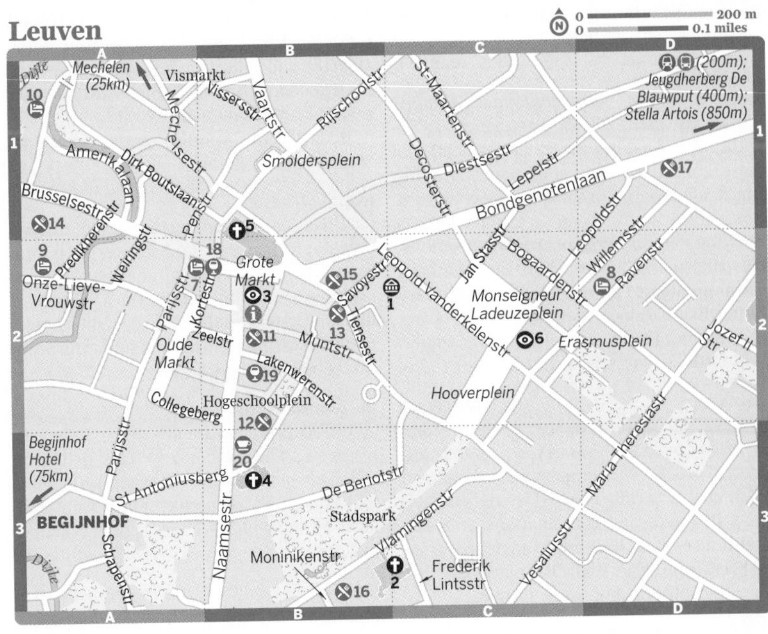

Leuven

Sights

1 M Van Museum C2
2 OLV-Ter-Koorts C3
3 Stadhuis B2
4 St-Michelskerk B3
5 St-Pieterskerk B1
6 Universiteitsbibliotheek C2

Sleeping

7 Casa Bollicine A2
8 Leuven City Hostel D2
9 Martin's Klooster Hotel A2
10 Oude Brouwerei Keyser Carel A1

Eating

11 Burger Folie B2
12 De Werf B2
13 Domus B2
14 Improvisio A1
15 La Divina Commedia B2
16 Lukemieke B3
17 Zarza D1

Drinking & Nightlife

18 Capital B2
19 De Blauwe Kater B2
20 Noir Koffiebar B3

producer Jos Theys, chips are cooked the traditional way – double-crisped in beef fat – and all sauces and relishes are house made.

La Divina Commedia ITALIAN €
(016-89 81 75; http://ladivinacommedia.be; Rector De Somerplein 15A; plates €8-12, pasta €14, takeaway pasta cups small/large €3/5; 9.30am-2.30pm & 5.30-9pm Mon-Sat) Bright, *molto*-authentic Italian wine bar that does morning croissants with jam and ricotta and, later, southern Italian–style plates to accompany its excellent all-Italian wine list. A takeaway window sends out pasta in a cup with a choice of *ragú*, pesto, four cheeses or salmon and zucchini.

Lukemieke VEGETARIAN €
(016-22 97 05; www.lukemieke.be; Vlamingenstraat 55; menus €14 & €12; noon-2pm & 6-8.30pm Mon-Fri;) This sweet vegetarian eatery with garden terrace is hidden in a pretty residential street facing Stadspark. The menu changes daily; add €2 for a glass of wine.

De Werf CAFE €
(016-23 73 14; www.dewerf-leuven.be; Hogeschoolplein 5; snacks €5-7, pasta & salads €11-15; 9am-midnight Mon-Fri) Road signs, lanterns and creeper-draped frontage on a tree-lined square and some organic ingredients add character to this otherwise back-to-basics

student favourite (yes, paper towel is used for serviettes).

Improvisio BISTRO €€
(☎016-20 76 46; www.improvisio.net; Brusselsestraat 63; mains €19-25, 3-course menu €47; ⏲11am-3pm & 6-10pm Tue-Fri, to 10pm Sat) On the other side of the canal-like Dijle, this smart, modern bistro occupies the courtyard of an 18th-century hospital complex that's now home to a number of arts organisations. It's particularly lovely when the weather's warm enough to sit outside. Contemporary dishes like haddock with quinoa and Asian greens are offered alongside well-prepared standards such as steaks and tartare.

Zarza BELGIAN €€€
(☎016-20 50 05; www.zarza.be; Bondgenotenlaan 92; mains €24-35, lunch menus €24-33, 4-/5-course dinner €54/62.50; ⏲11.45-3pm & 6.30pm-midnight) High-quality, locally sourced ingredients are used in interesting combinations at Zarza, and it also offers well-priced matched wines or beer (from €24). While the place is stylish, the atmosphere is not overly formal.

Drinking & Nightlife

The wall-to-wall *café*-bars on Oude Markt hum until the wee hours. Just pick the music and ambience that appeals. Domus and De Wiering are good drinking options if you want something a little more sedate. In season the tourist office operates a one-hour **beer history tour** (tour €2; ⏲11am Sun Apr-Oct).

★**Bar Stan** CAFE, BAR
(☎016-88 90 83; www.barstan.be; Constantin Meunierstraat 2; ⏲8am-midnight Mon-Fri, 10am-6pm Sun) Bar Stan is an airy, pot-plant-fringed hub of local life around 15 minutes' walk from the centre. Drink coffee with the early-morning laptop brigade, grab a burger (€11.50), quiche (€8.50) or salad (€14) come lunch, or hang around for the evening *spritzes* and natural wines. Staff members are a good info source for nightlife and other goings-on around town.

Book via the website for the occasional Saturday-night dinners.

Noir Koffiebar CAFE
(☎016-85 08 97; Naamsestraat 49; ⏲8.30am-6pm Mon-Fri, from 9am Sat & summer) A friendly and coffee-savvy crew churns out great espressos and flat whites on a Marzocco machine here, and there are delicious homemade cakes and pastries to scoff in the beautifully bohemian back room.

De Blauwe Kater BAR
(☎016-20 80 90; www.blauwekater.be; Hallengang 1; beers €2-4.50; ⏲7pm-2am) This delightful little jazz/blues bar serves around 100 beers and stages free live performances from 9pm most Monday nights in term time (October to June).

Capital BEER HALL
(www.thecapital.be; Grote Markt 14; ⏲noon-3am daily) Leuven's bars and pubs like to advertise how many beers they offer, with the average about 300 to 400. But the Capital – a relative newcomer despite looking as though it's been here for centuries – has upped the ante: 2000 brews on offer, with 20 or so on tap at any given time.

As you might imagine, the beer menu can take a while to wade through. Don't waste precious drinking time; ask the staff for suggestions.

ℹ Information

Tourist Office (☎016-20 30 20; www.visitleuven.be; Naamsestraat 1; ⏲10am-5pm Mon-Sat) Located around the side of the stadhuis. It produces a handy app called *Leuven Walk*.

THE KUL

Within a century of its founding in 1425, the Katholieke Universiteit van Leuven (KUL) had become one of Europe's most highly regarded universities. It attracted famous academics and free thinkers, such as cartographer Mercator, Renaissance scholar Desiderius Erasmus and father of anatomy Andreas Vesalius.

In response to suppression by French and Dutch rulers during the 18th and 19th centuries, the university became a bastion of Flemish Catholicism, and it has continued to foster Flemish identity in the last century.

As recently as the late 1960s, Flemish students protested the absence of lectures in their mother tongue. Violent riots in 1968 eventually forced the French-speaking faculties to leave Leuven and set up a separate Francophone campus in the purpose-built town of Louvain-la-Neuve, southeast of Brussels.

Leuven Leisure (016-43 81 44; www.leuven-leisure.com; Tiensestraat 5) 'Are you Leuven it yet?' is this group's slogan, and it'll share its infectious enthusiasm for the city via walks, beer tours, bike rides, raft and canoe trips, and other activities.

Getting There & Around

Leuven's **train station** (016-21 21 21) is 800m east of the Grote Markt by buses 1 or 2. Destinations include the following:

Antwerp (€7.90, fast/slow 50/65 minutes) Direct trains go via Lier or Brussels Airport but aren't always quicker than changing at Mechelen.

Brussels (€5.30, fast/slow 24/36 minutes, five times hourly)

Brussels Airport (€8.80, 16 minutes, twice hourly)

Diest (€5.30, fast/slow 24/32 minutes)

Liège (€10.80, fast/slow 34/54 minutes)

Mechelen (€4.50, fast/slow 22/29 minutes)

Public car-parking options, both free and paid, are detailed at www.leuven.be.

Leuven to Hasselt

Travelling by car, you could easily see this route's main sights in a day, but a better idea is to sleep in intriguing Diest, then return via Tongeren and Tienen.

Kasteel van Horst

Kasteel van Horst CASTLE

(016-62 33 45; www.kasteelvanhorst.be; Horststraat 28; adult/reduced €6/4, grounds free; 2-5pm Mon, Wed & Sun Apr-Oct) Ringed by a reflective moat, picture-perfect, medieval Kasteel van Horst enjoys a delightful rural setting. The lovely grounds are free to visit even when the interior is closed. Drawbridge-facing *café*-restaurant **Streekgasthof Wagenhuis** (016-62 35 84; www.hetwagenhuis.be; mains €22-30; 11.30am-11.30pm Wed-Mon) is great for a drink or afternoon ice cream, but the main courses are a little lacking in pizzazz given the prices charged. The castle is tucked away at the back of Sint-Pieters-Rode village, 7.5km south of Aarschot, so you'll need wheels and a good map to get here.

Scherpenheuvel

In the 14th century a wooden statue of the Virgin was attached to a solitary oak tree that had once been the centre of pagan worship. A boy who attempted to remove the statue was struck down with paralysis, a spiteful 'miracle' for which the spot became venerated. By 1609 a stream of pilgrims had funded a unique seven-sided baroque **basilica** (www.scherpenheuvel.be; 7.30am-7.30pm May-Aug, to 6.30pm Sep-Apr) whose domed exterior is distinctively dotted with gilded stars. Countless pilgrims still come to Scherpenheuvel from all over Belgium, particularly in May and on summer weekends, to pray for healing miracles and to pay homage to the minuscule Virgin statuette ensconced beneath a stylised tree-sculpture over the altarpiece.

An attractive circle of wooded parkland around the basilica features shedfuls of burning candles lit by the faithful. Albertusplein, the surrounding arc of road, is dotted with *cafés*, restaurants and seasonal hut-shops peddling all manner of religious trinkets. Out of season, try the shop **de Wildeman** (www.dewildeman.com; Albertusplein 1; 9am-6pm Mon-Thu, 9am-7pm Sat-Sun) to stock up on memorable Lourdes-style Catholic kitsch.

Scherpenheuvel is about 6km west of Diest, accessible by hourly Diest–Aarschot bus 35.

Diest

POP 23,260

From 1499 to 1794 the ancient town of Diest was a domain of the Orange-Nassau Princes, today's Dutch ruling family. The town retains a considerable scattering of fine old architecture, albeit much of it brutally interrupted by bland modernity. But what really makes Diest worth a stop is its wonderful 1252 *begijnhof*, arguably Belgium's most charming.

Sights

St-Sulpitius Church CHURCH

(Grote Markt; 2-5pm Tue-Sun Jul & Aug, Sat & Sun only mid-May–mid-Sep) St-Sulpitius Church is built in two discordantly different colours of stone. Lacking a substantial tower, its exterior seems oddly thrown together, but inside the nave is an impressive series of soaring Gothic vaults leading to a vast hanging crucifix over a magnificent apse full of angelic statuary.

St-Katharinabegijnhof RELIGIOUS SITE

Centred on a 14th-century church and sporting a few artists' studio-galleries, this picturesque village-within-a-village retains an aura that's spiritually authentic and well repays an idle wander. The site is entered through a splendid baroque portal at the eastern end of Begijnenstraat. That's a 10-minute stroll east of the Grote Markt, starting out along Koning Albertstraat.

Sleeping & Eating

Lodge HOTEL €€
(☎013-35 09 35; www.lodge-hotels.be; Refugiestraat 23; s/d €85/95; @) Diest's most charming hotel partly occupies a turreted stream-side mansion that was originally a medieval abbot's retreat. Peaceful yet central (just 200m north of the Grote Markt), the 20 rooms are attractively furnished and have an uncluttered elegance.

★**Gasthof 1618** BELGIAN €€
(☎013-67 77 80; www.gasthof1618.be; Kerkstraat 8; snacks €10-12, mains €20-27; ⏰11am-10pm Tue-Sun) At the heart of the *begijnhof* lies this suitably medieval-style hostelry whose high ceilings and manorial atmosphere feel all the more believable once the candles and central woodfire are lit. In summer, try the seasonal *Diestse kruidkoeck,* a pancake made with tansy (a herb known locally as *boerenwormkruid*), washed down with local Loterbol draught beer.

Information

Tourist Office (☎013-35 32 74; www.toerismediest.be; Albertstraat 16a; ⏰10am-noon & 1-5pm daily summer, Mon-Sat winter)

Getting There & Away

Brussels–Leuven–Tongeren and Antwerp–Lier–Liège trains (both hourly) stop in Diest, taking 11 minutes from Aarschot and 15 minutes from Hasselt. To find the Grote Markt (1.3km south), turn left out of the train station, veer right (crossing the Demer onto Weerstandplein), then continue down Statiestraat and Demerstraat.

Hasselt & Around

POP 74,590

Hasselt celebrates its fame as Belgium's unofficial *jenever* (gin) capital with a **gin festival** (www.jeneverfeesten.be; ⏰3rd weekend of Oct) and the **Nationaal Jenevermuseum** (☎011-23 98 60; www.jenevermuseum.be; Witte Nonnenstraat 19; adult/reduced €6/1; ⏰10am-5pm Tue-Sun summer, from 1pm Sat & Sun winter), housed in a beautifully restored, still-active 19th-century distillery. The highlight of the festival is when the town's little Borrelmanneke (barrel-carrying man) fountain is briefly re-plumbed to flow with *jenever.* It is on the Brussels–Leuven–Tongeren and Antwerp–Lier–Liège train routes.

Otherwise the region's main attraction is Bokrijk, a vast series of provincial parks and woodlands (open year-round, admission free) between Hasselt and Genk. These incorporate a splendid **arboretum** (⏰year-round) FREE and the 60-hectare **Bokrijk Openluchtmuseum** (☎011-26 53 00; www.bokrijk.be; adult/child €10/1; ⏰10am-6pm Tue-Sun Apr-Sep, daily Jul & Aug), one of Europe's largest open-air museums, offering a nostalgic look at Flanders' past with over 100 original old buildings reassembled here in 1958.

Genk–Hasselt trains (10 minutes, hourly) stop 500m south of Bokrijk Openluchtmuseum's southern entrance, but hourly bus 1 from Hasselt is more convenient (Monday to Saturday only). By car, it's better to park at the eastern entrance beside the 19th-century mansion-castle Kasteel Bokrijk.

Tienen

POP 32,000

Known as Belgium's sugar capital, Tienen (Tirlemont in French) has a liberal scattering of medieval buildings, including two spectacularly vast churches.

Sights

OLV-ten-Poelkerk CHURCH
(Grote Markt) OLV-ten-Poelkerk dominates the main square with a disproportionately tall (70m) white-stone 15th-century tower, capped by a 1654 baroque spire and fronted with empty statue niches.

Sint-Germanuskerk CHURCH
(Veemarkt) The partly 13th-century Sint-Germanuskerk sits on a rise directly above the town centre.

Suikermuseum MUSEUM
(☎016-80 56 66; www.erfgoedsitetienen.be; Grote Markt 6; adult/reduced €5/4; ⏰10am-5pm Tue-Sun, last entry 4pm) At one of Belgium's most inspired museums, the interactive, witty and surrealistically metaphorical presentations include a post-natal hospital ward for sugar beets, a cartoon encounter with Queen Bee and a 'painting' gallery with a talking Napoleon. Suddenly sugar lumps seem fascinating. Finish the visit in the attached cafe, where local apple cake marries well with Tienen's sour, unfiltered 'duck' beer, Tiense Kweiker Tripel.

Sleeping

★Carpe Diem B&B €€

(☎0489 77 81 88; www.bbcarpediem.be; Wolmarkt 5; s €75-105, d €90-120) Carpe Diem B&B has been lovingly converted from an antique shop, with hand-painted floors, lots of church statuary, and bath foam that comes in wine bottles. The most expensive room has an antique oak bed and a view of the Sint-Germanuskerk tower. The location is central and attractive, between Tienen's two main churches.

Information

Tourist Information Office (☎016-80 57 38; toerisme.tienen.be; ⏲10am-5pm Tue-Sun) In a solid 1846 militia house.

Hoegaarden

POP 6250

Home of the world-famous eponymous white beer, Hoegaarden was an autonomous county until feisty 10th-century Countess Alpaïdis cunningly ceded her lands to the prince-bishops of Liège. This made Hoegaarden a disconnected enclave surrounded by, but independent from, medieval Brabant. In the 18th century such enclaves enjoyed tax-free status, jump-starting dozens of breweries in Hoegaarden. After Liège's independence was quashed in 1795, Hoegaarden lost its tax advantage and the breweries progressively closed down, only reviving in the later 20th century. As a town, Hoegaarden has some banally glum areas, but the old centre does have a village feel.

Sights

Old Hoegaarden Brewery BREWERY

('t Wit Gebrow; ☎016-76 74 33; www.twitgebrouw.be; Stoopkensstraat 24; adult/child €6/free; ⏲10am-10pm Wed-Sun) The Old Hoegaarden Brewery has been converted into a slick, interactive museum experience celebrating the iconic white beer. Buy tickets from the attached 19th-century Kouterhof brasserie-restaurant (www.kouterhof.be) and return afterwards for two free beers (one to take away).

Sint-Gorgoniuskerk CHURCH

(www.gemeentehoegaarden.be; Houtmarkt; ⏲2-4pm Thu-Sun Jun-Sep) Belgium's 'largest Rococo church' rises from the town's cute central square. Finished in 1759, Sint-Gorgoniuskerk is more impressive inside than out and commemorates a Roman martyr whose relics were carried to Hoegaarden in 765.

Sleeping & Eating

★Klein Paradijs B&B €€

(☎016-76 64 70; www.kleinparadijs.be; Walestraat 2; s/d €80/85) Klein Paradijs is an adorable family B&B in a 360-year-old farmhouse that has been sensitively upgraded using clay-straw wall plaster and timber floorboards. Although it's just 50m from the church (direction Jodoigne/Geldenaken), the location feels idyllically rural.

Kapittelhuys CAFE €€

(www.kapittelhuys.be; Houtmarkt 1; mains €15-26; ⏲11.30am-9pm Thu-Tue) This 18th-century brick house fronts the beautiful Tuinen van Hoegaarden formal gardens and has a wisteria-shaded terrace that is a delight in summer. Croquettes, stews and other Belgian favourites share menu space with curries and salads, and it does pancakes and waffles several ways.

Drinking & Nightlife

Herberg-brouwerij Nieuwhuys BREWERY

(☎016-81 71 64; www.nieuwhuys.be; Ernest Ourystraat 2; beers €1.50-4, snacks €4-14; ⏲5pm-midnight Thu-Sat, plus 11am-10pm Sun summer) A 1636 brick house in central Hoegaarden has been converted into this brilliantly pitched, jazz-toned pub-*café* that produces its own mellow beer (Alpaïde stout) in a microbrewery that's partly visible through a glass plate in the floor.

Getting There & Away

Bus 360 (Tienen–Jodoigne/Geldenaken) departs from Zijdelingsestraat outside Tienen station, taking 15 minutes to Hoegaarden.

Zoutleeuw

POP 8100

Once one of Brabant's seven pre-eminent 'free-cities', sleepy little Zoutleeuw (Leau in French) followed the medieval cloth-making industry into decline from the 15th century. Despite terrible floods (1573), fires (1676), Spanish occupation (1578) and French looting (1701), two great historic structures have survived remarkably well. The **tourist office** (☎011-78 12 88; www.zoutleeuw.be; Grote Markt 11; ⏲10am-noon & 1.30-4pm Tue-Sun summer, 1.30-5pm Tue-Fri winter) lies within one: the intriguing composite Town Hall/Vleeshalle/Lakenhalle building, whose majestic pre-Raphaelite murals can be perused for free alongside occasional exhibitions.

Across the road, Zoutleeuw's main attraction is **St-Leonarduskerk** (☎011-78 11 07; Vleestraat; admission €2.50; ⊙10am-noon & 1.30-4.30pm Tue-Sun summer, 1.30-4.30pm Tue-Fri winter), topped with a fanciful tower reminiscent of a galleon's crow's nest. Miraculously, given Zoutleeuw's turbulent history, the interior of this huge Gothic church is the only significant example in all of Belgium to have escaped untouched from the religious turmoil and invasions of the 16th to 18th centuries. Its magnificent statuary thus offers a unique insight into pre-Iconoclastic church design.

Bus 23 from Tienen to Sint-Truiden runs hourly through Zoutleeuw.

Sint-Truiden

POP 39,750

A soaring trio of historical towers gives the extensive Grote Markt of Sint-Truiden (St-Trond in French) a fairy-tale feel that easily justifies an hour or two of your time. Famed for its fruit, the gently rolling Haspengouw area surrounding St-Truiden is attractive to explore by car and has become increasingly popular with local tourists since the TV drama *Katarakt* was filmed here.

Sights

Onze Lieve Vrouwekerk CHURCH
(Grote Markt; ⊙10am-5pm Mon-Fri, 2-5pm Sat & Sun) From the 7th century, the relics of local saint St Trudo made the town a major medieval pilgrimage centre. These relics are now housed in the treasury of this 1854 church.

Abdijtoren TOWER
(Diesterstraat 1; adult/concession €4/2; ⊙10am-6pm) The most significant remnant of the former St-Trudo Abbey, this unrefined seven-storey tower dates partly from the 11th century. You can survey the city from the rough metal viewing platform on top.

Sint-Agnesbegijnhof MUSEUM
Marred by several new constructions, the Sint-Agnesbegijnhof, 1km northeast of the centre via Plankstraat, is not an especially memorable *begijnhof,* but it's unique in that it has retained a *begijn* farmstead. The central, barnlike 1258 **Begijnhofkerk** (Begijnhof; ⊙10am-12.30pm & 1.30-5pm) FREE is renowned for a gruesome medieval fresco depicting St Agatha's martyrdom. While here, visit the **Festraets Studio** (☎011-68 87 52; Begijnhof 24; ⊙hourly 9.45am-3.45pm Tue-Fri except 12.45pm Tue-Fri, 2.45pm & 3.45pm only Sat & Sun, closed Oct-Mar) FREE, home to what is billed as the 'world's biggest astronomical clock' (6m high, weighing 4 tonnes).

Sleeping & Eating

Belle Vie LODGE €€
(☎011-68 70 38; www.belle-vie.be; Stationstraat 12; s/d €60/90) Four spacious and beautifully appointed, high-ceilinged rooms sit above a good-value restaurant in one of the town's predominantly art-nouveau streets. (Don't be put off by the lodge's severe brick facade.) It's 700m west of the Grote Markt (via Stapelstraat), just 150m southeast of the train station.

Nieuwscafe BRASSERIE €€
(☎011-70 28 50; www.nieuwscafe.be; Heilig Hartplein 5; mains €14-27; ⊙7am-1am Mon-Fri, 9am-6am Sat, 11.30am-11pm Sun; 📶) Just off the Grote Markt, tucked behind the main church, Nieuwscafe is a spacious, modern brasserie with giant halo lamps and walls decked in typewriters and Bombay Sapphire bottles. On offer are classic Flemish food, salads and 'wok' dishes.

Information

Tourist Office (☎011-70 18 18; www.toerisme-sint-truiden.be; Grote Markt; ⊙10am-12.30pm & 1-6pm) Inside the stadhuis.

Getting There & Away

Bus 23a runs to Tongeren; bus 23 goes to Tienen via Zoutleeuw.

Tongeren

POP 30,560

Proudly claiming to be Belgium's oldest town, likeable Tongeren (Tongres in French) was a prosperous 2nd-century Roman settlement on the Cologne–Bavay road. By the 4th century it had become one of the Low Countries' earliest Christian bishoprics, but in 1677 it was catastrophically torched by Louis XIV's French troops. Today the compact city is remarkable for retaining several sections of its Roman-era city walls and draws crowds to its Sunday antiques market.

Sights

Gallo-Roman Museum MUSEUM
(☎012-67 03 30; www.galloromeinsmuseum.be; Kielenstraat 15; adult/concession/youth €7/5/1; ⊙9am-5pm Tue-Fri, 10am-6pm Sat & Sun) In the town centre, the inventive modern Gallo-Roman Museum uses audio, video and mannequins as well as thousands of original

artefacts and archaeological discoveries to exemplify the way of life at the time of Tongeren's Roman heyday and thereafter.

Onze Lieve Vrouwebasiliek BASILICA
(Basilica of Our Lady; ☎012-21 33 24; www.basiliektongeren.be; Kloosterstraat 1; treasury €2; ⏲10am-noon & 1.30-5pm) The elegant Onze Lieve Vrouwebasiliek is a large, mostly 14th- to 16th-century church whose stone tower dominates Tongeren's neatly cafe-lined Grote Markt. The church marks the first place north of the Alps where the Virgin Mary is said to have been worshipped, and every seventh year in July a venerated 1479 walnut Madonna statue is piously paraded around town in the large-scale if very staid **Kroningsfeesten procession** (www.kroningsfeesten.be).

The basilica's rich treasury displays other valuable artefacts dating back to the 6th century.

Ambiorix Statue STATUE
The Grote Markt is surveyed by a muscular, moustachioed statue of Ambiorix, a local tribal chieftain who led a brief 54-BC revolt against Julius Caesar's Roman rule. Loosely represented by Beefix in the classic *Asterix* comics, Ambiorix had been largely forgotten by historians until the 1830s, when newly founded Belgium was in need of national heroes.

Tongeren Begijnhof RELIGIOUS SITE
(☎012-21 32 59; www.begijnhofmuseumtongeren.be; Onder de Linde 12; adult €4; ⏲10am-12.30pm & 1.30-5pm Tue-Sat, 11am-5pm Sun) Three blocks south and west of the basilica is a small web of pretty backstreets that once formed Tongeren's *begijnhof*. Here the **Beghina Museum** serves *béguine* beer (€2) and a small, picturesque canal leads towards the chunky 1379 **Moerenpoort**, a medieval city-gate tower.

Antiques Market MARKET
(⏲6am-1pm Sun) This is one of Belgium's best 'fleas', with a large number of *brocante* stalls and some serious antiques dealers. It takes place around Leopoldwal, Veemarkt, Maastrichterstraat, de Schiervelstraat, Clarissenstraat and Eburonenhal.

Sleeping & Eating

Begeinhof HOSTEL €
(☎012-39 13 70; www.vjh.be; St-Ursulastraat 1; dm HI member/nonmember €17.50/19; @📶) This youth hostel is a low-slung barn with functional six-bed dorms set behind a busy, fair-priced brasserie-*café;* prices are rock bottom and it's brilliantly located streamside in the *begijnhof* area.

★**Eburon Hotel** HOTEL €€
(☎012-23 01 99; http://eburonhotel.be; de Schiervelstraat 10; d €105; 📶) The dark beams of this former convent feature in the starkly beautiful, vast public spaces as well as in some of the jewel-toned contemporary rooms. The breakfast room commands a view of the basilica tower and there's a wine bar in the vaulted cellars.

★**Bistro Bis** INTERNATIONAL €€
(☎012-74 34 66; www.bistrobis.be; Hemelingenstraat 23; 3/4-courses €35/47; ⏲6.30-10pm Fri-Mon) Johan Haiverlain, former sous chef at the Michelin-starred Magis downstairs, has transformed Tongeren into a cool culinary destination with this 'no-nonsense' place. His young, bearded staff serves up dishes with Belgian, Mediterranean and Australian influences, well-chosen wines and old-school cocktails, all to a rock 'n' roll soundtrack.

Infirmerie BELGIAN €€
(☎012-44 10 44; www.infirmerie.be; St-Ursulastraat 11; mains €14-28, beer from €2; ⏲11.30am-10pm Wed-Sat, 9.30am-10pm Sun) Tucked away at the base of the *begijnhof,* Infirmerie is a relaxed modern brasserie incorporating elements of historic design from a 1701 building that had been a chapel before becoming the *begijns'* infirmary. The waterside terrace is especially appealing.

Information

Toerisme Tongeren (☎012-80 00 70; www.tongeren.be/toerisme; Via Julianus 2; ⏲8.30am-noon & 1-5pm weekdays, 9.30am-5pm weekends & holidays) In the Julianus shopping centre, part of the redeveloped 1660 Gasthuis Kapel complex.

Getting There & Away

The bus and train station is 400m west of the centre. Hourly trains depart for Hasselt (€4.30, 20 minutes), Liège-Palais (€4.40, 27 minutes) and Sint-Truiden (via Hasselt; €6.60, 45 minutes). Bus 23a runs directly to Sint-Truiden (35 minutes, hourly).

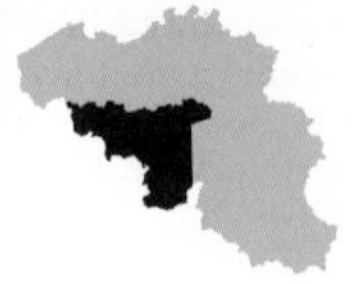

Western Wallonia

LANGUAGE: FRENCH

Includes ➡

Why Go?

With rolling farmland and small woods crowning the brows of low hills, the landscapes of Western Wallonia form idyllic Northern European perspectives. Yet the region's history is unbelievably turbulent: the area has been a battleground for millennia. Fine historic cities, notably Tournai and Mons, have loads to offer, especially since Mons' year as European Capital of Culture in 2015 endowed it with some striking new museums. Waterloo, where the future of Europe was forcefully debated, rejuvenated its museums and opened a smart new exhibition to mark the battle's bicentenary in the same year. Post-industrial cities such as Charleroi are yet to be similarly revitalised, but exploring this region's rural nooks, and discovering its notable beers, quirky corners and riotous festivals, is highly worthwhile.

Best Places to Eat

- La Bonne Auberge (p201)
- Le Cigalon (p197)
- La Petite Madeleine (p188)
- Vilaine Fille, Mauvais Garçon (p193)

Best Places to Stay

- Château Tromcourt (p201)
- Petit Chapitre (p202)
- B&B Mme Daniel (p186)
- Dream Hôtel (p192)
- Golf Hôtel de Falnuée (p199)

Driving Distances

	Waterloo	Mons	Tournai	Chimay
Mons	56			
Tournai	89	46		
Chimay	85	58	104	
Mariembourg	76	70	116	20

Tournai

POP 69,800

Enjoyable Tournai (tour-*nay,* Doornik in Dutch) has a memorable Grand Place and one of Belgium's finest cathedrals. Even by local standards, the city has been in the wars, occupied at various points by Romans, Franks, Normans, French, English, Spanish, Austrians, Dutch and Germans. Today it's a lovely place for casual strolling, with a lively bar and restaurant scene near the river.

History

Tournai grew to prominence as the Roman trading settlement of Tornacum, and was the original 5th-century capital of the Frankish Merovingian dynasty. Autonomous from France as of 1187, the city retains two towers (St-Georges and Prends-Garde) from the first 1202 city wall. In 1513 Tournai was conquered by Henry VIII of England – Thomas Wolsey, of *Wolf Hall* fame, was appointed bishop – before being sold back to France in 1519. Just two years later it was swallowed by the Habsburg Empire. Tournai found renewed wealth as a centre for, successively, tapestries, textiles and porcelain, but it was devastated by WWII bombing.

Sights

★Cathédrale Notre Dame CATHEDRAL

(www.cathedrale-tournai.be; Place de l'Évêché; 9am-6pm Mon-Fri, 9am-noon & 1-6pm Sat & Sun Apr-Oct, to 5pm Nov-Mar) FREE Dominating Tournai's skyline are the five spires of its remarkable cathedral, which survived WWII bombs only for a freak 1999 tornado to compromise its stability. It'll remain a vast building site until at least 2018; what you can see meanwhile depends on the restoration work. Despite the scaffolding, the interior remains a fascinating example of evolving architectural styles, from the magnificent Romanesque nave through a curious bridging transept into an early-Gothic choir whose soaring pillars bend disconcertingly.

The wood-panelled little Chapelle St-Louis is under restoration and its large canvases by Rubens and Jacob Jordaens are currently hidden, but there are some impressive pieces in the **treasury** (Cathédrale de Tournai; admission €2.50; 1-5.30pm Mon, 10am-5.30pm Tue-Fri, 1.30-5.30pm Sat, 1.30-4.30pm Sun), including a fabulous 'Last Judgement' *châsse* (casket), a chasuble worn by Thomas Becket and a 22m-long 1402 tapestry that culminates in the plague of Tournai.

★Grand Place SQUARE

Tournai's gorgeous triangular main square is ringed with cafes in fine gable-fronted guildhouses merrily flying guild banners. Kids play in 'dare-you' fountains beneath an axe-wielding statue of Princess d'Espinoy, the doomed heroine who led Tournai's eventually futile defence against a 1581 Spanish siege. The square's grandest building is the gilt-detailed **Halle-des-Draps** (Grand Place 57; exhibitions only), a former cloth hall whose brick-vaulted interior hosts occasional exhibitions.

Église St-Quentin CHURCH

(Grand Place 44; 9am-4pm Nov-Mar, to 6pm Apr-Oct) Église St-Quentin is a hefty Romanesque church with a 12th-century nave, posterior Gothic features and a striking red-tiled roof. When viewed from near here, the cathedral's classic cluster of five grey-stone towers seems to float ethereally above the Grand Place, especially at sunset or at night. Restored after heavy WWII damage, the interior is handsome in light-grey stone but lacks a bit of atmosphere.

Beffroi TOWER

(www.tournai.be; adult/child €2.10/1.10; 9.30am-12.30pm & 1.30-5.30pm Tue-Sun Apr-Oct, 9.30am-noon & 2-5pm Tue-Sat, 2-5pm Sun Nov-Mar) Belgium's oldest belfry is 72m high with a narrow 257-step spiral staircase that becomes even narrower higher up. There's a good multilingual display on the history and significance of belfries as symbols of civic liberties partway up, but otherwise the main attractions are the bells and the views, described by faded signboards. Ask at the tourist office about bell concerts, during which you can climb the tower to see the ringer at work.

Musée des Beaux-Arts GALLERY

(069-33 24 31; www.tournai.be; Enclos St-Martin 3; adult/child €2.60/2.10; 9.30am-12.30pm & 1.30-5.30pm Wed-Mon Apr-Oct, 9.30am-noon & 2-5pm Mon & Wed-Sat, 2-5pm Sun Nov-Mar) This airy gallery was designed by art-nouveau maestro Victor Horta. Though the interior and display halls are in need of a pep-up, it has a rich collection, including items by Tournai's best-known artist, the brilliant 15th-century Rogier Van der Weyden (Roger de la Pasture), works by Rubens, Jacob Jordaens, Manet and Monet, a beautiful Seurat seascape, and sketches by Van Gogh

Western Wallonia Highlights

1. Indulging in belated post-fight analysis at the modernised battlefield attractions of **Waterloo** (p194)
2. Exploring the wealth of museums at charismatic **Mons** (p190)
3. Observing how Romanesque transforms into Gothic in Tournai's iconic **cathedral** (p183)
4. Bingeing with the Gilles at the **Carnaval de Binche** (p192)
5. Halting time at evocative Cistercian abbey ruins at **Villers-la-Ville** (p197) and **Aulne** (p199)
6. Using **Chimay** (p202), famed for its legendary Trappist beer, as a base to explore the Botte du Hainaut
7. Delving into the world of Tintin and Snowy at the nostalgic **Musée Hergé** (p197)

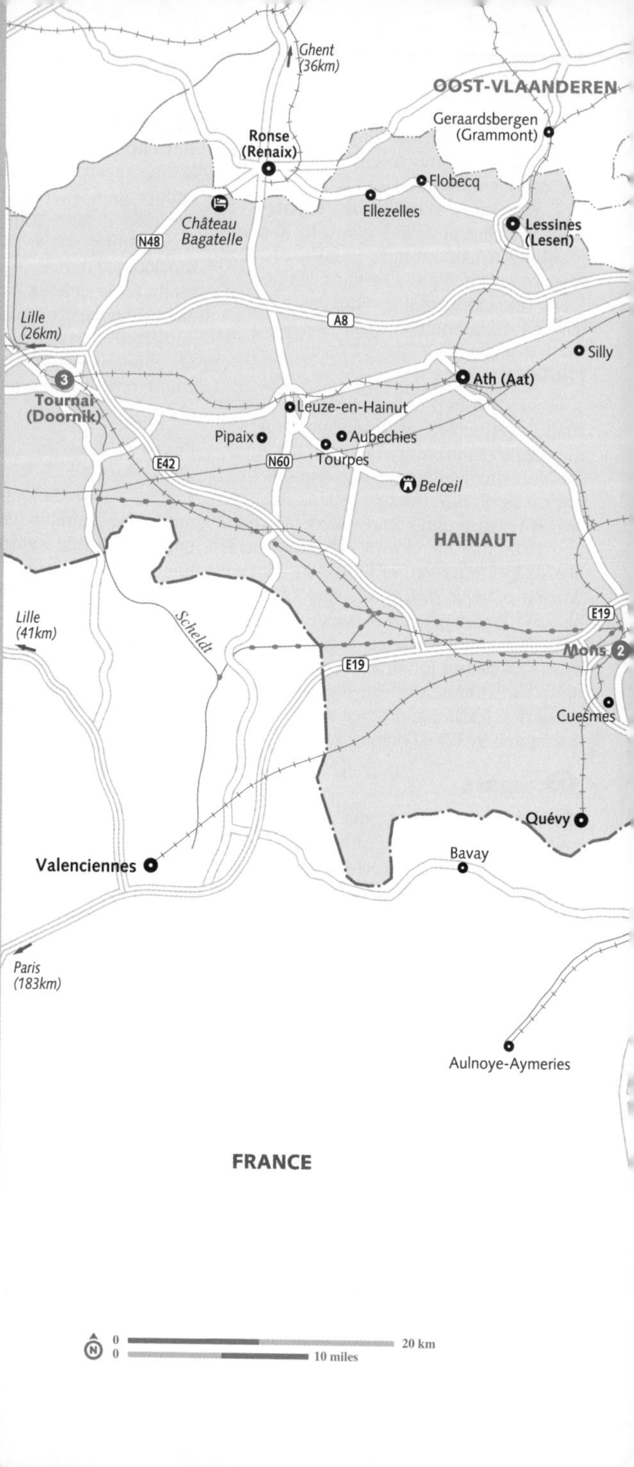

Ghent (36km)
OOST-VLAANDEREN
Geraardsbergen (Grammont)
Ronse (Renaix)
Flobecq
Ellezelles
Château Bagatelle
N48
Lessines (Lesen)
A8
Lille (26km)
Silly
3 Tournai (Doornik)
Ath (Aat)
Leuze-en-Hainut
Pipaix
Aubechies
Tourpes
E42
N60
Belœil
HAINAUT
Scheldt
Lille (41km)
E19
Mons 2
E19
Cuesmes
Quévy
Valenciennes
Bavay
Paris (183km)
Aulnoye-Aymeries
FRANCE

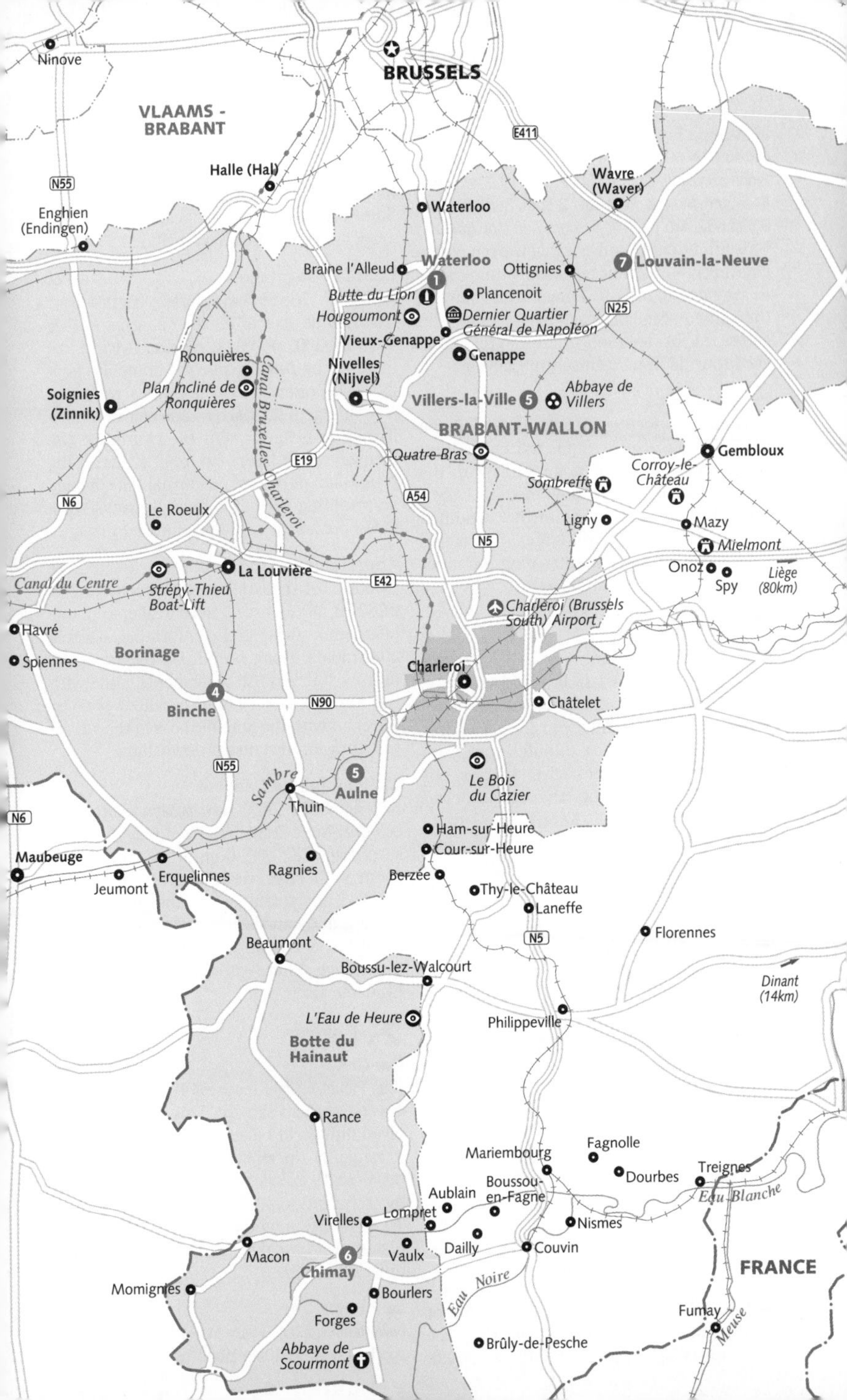

Ninove
BRUSSELS
VLAAMS - BRABANT
E411
Halle (Hal)
N55
Wavre (Waver)
Waterloo
Enghien (Endingen)
Braine l'Alleud
Waterloo
Ottignies
Louvain-la-Neuve
Butte du Lion
Plancenoit
N25
Hougoumont
Dernier Quartier Général de Napoléon
Vieux-Genappe
Genappe
Ronquières
Canal Bruxelles-Charleroi
Nivelles (Nijvel)
Soignies (Zinnik)
Plan Incliné de Ronquières
Abbaye de Villers
Villers-la-Ville
BRABANT-WALLON
Gembloux
Quatre Bras
E19
Corroy-le-Château
Sombreffe
N6
A54
Le Roeulx
Ligny
Mazy
N5
Mielmont
La Louvière
Onoz
Spy
Liège (80km)
Canal du Centre
Strépy-Thieu Boat-Lift
E42
Charleroi (Brussels South) Airport
Havré
Borinage
Spiennes
Charleroi
Binche
N90
Châtelet
N55
Aulne
Le Bois du Cazier
Sambre
Thuin
N6
Ham-sur-Heure
Maubeuge
Cour-sur-Heure
Erquelinnes
Ragnies
Jeumont
Berzée
Thy-le-Château
Laneffe
Florennes
N5
Beaumont
Boussu-lez-Walcourt
Dinant (14km)
L'Eau de Heure
Philippeville
Botte du Hainaut
Rance
Fagnolle
Mariembourg
Dourbes
Treignes
Aublain
Boussou-en-Fagne
Eau Blanche
Virelles
Lompret
Nismes
Macon
Vaulx
Dailly
Couvin
Chimay
FRANCE
Momignies
Bourlers
Eau Noire
Forges
Fumay
Meuse
Brûly-de-Pesche
Abbaye de Scourmont

and Toulouse-Lautrec. In the central atrium, a flying purple hippo gazes benevolently down on more classical sculptural forms.

Musée de Folklore MUSEUM
(069-22 40 69; www.tournai.be; Réduit des Sions 36; adult/child €2.60/2.10; 9.30am-noon & 2-5pm Mon & Wed-Sat, 2-5pm Sun Nov-Mar, 9.30am-12.30pm & 1.30-5.30pm Wed-Mon Apr-Oct) This is a loveable and sizeable warren of fascinating city-relevant relics and ethnographic artefacts. It's all in French, but many of the cameo scenes are self-explanatory, and across the 'bridge-room' there's a great model of Tournai in its 18th-century heyday.

Pont des Trous BRIDGE
This curious fortified bridge defended the city and was also used for toll collections. Blown up in WWII, it was rebuilt with the central arch larger to allow modern barges through. It is likely to be further modified at some point to let still larger river traffic pass, but it remains an intriguing reminder of Belgian defensive architecture.

Sleeping

Auberge de Jeunesse HOSTEL €
(069-21 61 36; www.lesaubergesdejeunesse.be; Rue St-Martin 64; dm/s/d incl breakfast €28/46/68;) In an historic former music college, this friendly place is just five minutes' walk from the Grand Place. Dorms have showers, but the shared toilets can get over-stretched when the hostel's full. Note that it's quite often booked out by groups. Significantly cheaper in summer and winter; €2 per person cheaper for under-26s; 10% discount for HI members.

★**B&B Mme Daniel** B&B €€
(0472 38 69 72; fdaniel@skynet.be; Rue des Soeurs Noires 35; s/d/tr €50/70/100;) Three art-filled rooms are available in this very homey 1673 stone house with flowerboxes and a charming little rear garden. Rooms are all very different in feel; the ground-floor room has garden access, the floral room is a dazzling visual overload, and the top-floor loft has a kitchenette and can sleep three. Homemade bread and jam make breakfast a treat.

The welcome is impeccable from Madame Daniel and loveable collie Dune and this is a really authentic Belgian experience. There's no sign; book ahead.

★**Hôtel d'Alcantara** HOTEL €€
(069-21 26 48; www.hotelalcantara.be; Rue des Bouchers St-Jacques 2; s €91-101, d €101-131;) Tournai's most appealing hotel has a regal northern facade, behind which is a beautifully realised boutique hotel. Well-modernised rooms, often with bold colour schemes, come in a variety of shapes and sizes. Rooms themed for musical styles have better bathrooms than the 'artist' rooms. Some are tucked into old beam-eaves. Pretty garden terrace. Breakfast included.

Château Bagatelle B&B €€
(069-66 33 35; www.chateau-bagatelle.com; Chaussée de Tournai 29, Arc-Wattripont; d/tr/q €100/110/120;) If you're driving, be tempted by this elegant yet homelike family castle offering two luxurious rooms in a building that's partly 12th century, albeit mainly 19th. Or rent the charming *gîte* cottage, which sleeps up to nine. It's on the N48, 19km northeast of Tournai. The owners are building further rooms. Breakfast €10. Often booked at weekends for weddings.

Appartement Studio Tournai APARTMENT €€
(069-23 51 27; Rue Marché au Jambon 12; s €55, d €60-80;) An excellent central option, this offers great value and comfortable, sizeable apartments: don't be put off by the steep, narrow stairway. All apartments come with full kitchen, big TV and excellent shower. Check in with the amiable boss in the attractive Tunisian restaurant downstairs.

La Chambre de Couvent B&B €€
(069-64 86 06; www.lachambreducouvent.be; Quai Notre Dame 6B12; s/d €65/75, 1-night supplement €10;) Comfortable homestay room with river view in the stylishly appointed apartment of an English-speaking former guide and teacher. Tiny roof terrace. Breakfast is an extra €6/12 for a quick/full experience. There's a supplementary room available also.

Eating

Eva Cosy CAFE €
(Rue Piquet 6; light meals €4-11; 8.30am-6pm Tue-Fri, 9am-6pm Sat;) This sensitively revived old-world bakery and teahouse offers a range of speciality teas but also wine, beer and excellent coffee accompanied by scrumptious 'traditional-recipe' cakes. There's also a good selection of savoury dishes, from breakfasts to salads, soups and open sandwiches.

Le Pinacle BISTRO €
(www.lepinacle.be; Vieux Marché aux Poteries 1; snacks €6-12; 10am-11pm;) The interior

Tournai

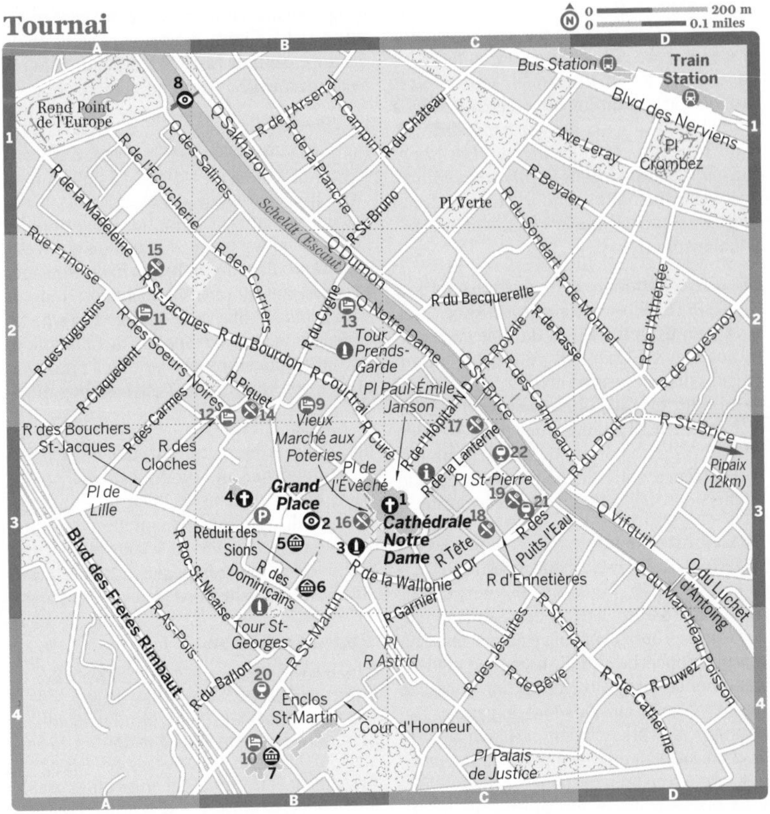

Tournai

Top Sights
1 Cathédrale Notre Dame C3
2 Grand Place B3

Sights
3 Beffroi B3
4 Église St-Quentin B3
5 Halle-des-Draps B3
6 Musée de Folklore B3
7 Musée des Beaux-Arts B4
8 Pont des Trous A1
Trésor de la Cathédrale .... (see 1)

Sleeping
9 Appartement Studio Tournai B2
10 Auberge de Jeunesse B4
11 B&B Mme Daniel A2
12 Hôtel d'Alcantara B2
13 La Chambre de Couvent B2

Eating
14 Eva Cosy B2
15 La Petite Madeleine A2
16 Le Pinacle B3
17 Le Quai Gourmet C3
18 L'Écurie d'Ennetières C3
19 L'Escaudoir C3

Drinking & Nightlife
20 Aux Amis Réunis B4
21 Cornwall C3
22 La Vie est Belge C3

is slightly bland, but Le Pinacle's enviable street terrace shares a quiet square with a breastfeeding Madonna and a view of the cathedral. The 'nonstop' kitchen produces sizeable *croques*, pancakes, pasta and the Belgian classic *chicons au gratin* (ham-wrapped endives in white sauce).

L'Escaudoir BELGIAN €€

(☎069-22 76 00; www.lescaudoir.com; Rue de la Triperie 3; mains €16-18; ⊙noon-2pm & 7-10pm Thu-Sat; 📶) 🍃 In two small, understated, casually elegant dining areas separated by a tight spiral staircase, this husband-and-wife team presents carefully prepared seasonal cuisine featuring lots of locally sourced produce. The changing menu features regional specialities as well as a few dishes of international inspiration.

L'Écurie d'Ennetières FRENCH, BELGIAN €€

(☎069-21 56 89; www.ecuriedennetieres.be; Ruelle d'Ennetières; mains €12-18, 3-course menu €27; ⊙noon-2pm & 7-10pm; 📶) Affordable Belgo-French cuisine is served in this high-ceilinged room with exposed-brick walls and a tribe of marionettes hanging from hefty wooden beams. It's not gourmet, but the classic bistro ambience, with gingham tablecloths and pitchers of wine, makes it a local favourite.

★**La Petite Madeleine** BELGIAN €€€

(☎069-84 01 87; www.lapetitemadeleine.be; Rue de la Madeleine 19; menus €30-65, mains €28-35; ⊙noon-2pm & 7-9pm Tue-Fri, 7-9pm Sat) Petite indeed in size, but flexing big culinary muscles, this place offers beautifully presented modern gastronomic fare, with more than a nod to the new Nordic cuisine's foraging ethos. The atmosphere is friendly and welcoming rather than intimidating or formal, so the stage is set for a top dining experience. Reasonably priced wine flights are available for all menus.

Le Quai Gourmet FRENCH €€€

(☎069-44 11 01; www.lequaigourmet.com; Quai du Marché au Poisson 8a; mains €25-36, menus €35-55; ⊙12.15pm sitting Thu, Fri & Sun, 7.15pm sitting Fri & Sat) The French food here is born of a gourmet imagination and served in an elegant setting: one of many revamped former shophouses on the river quay. There's a certain pernicketiness in play, but the food is faultless and exquisitely presented. Look out for seasonal special menus.

🍷 Drinking & Nightlife

Terrace *cafés* line the Grand Place, with more on Place St-Pierre and particularly around the riverside, where things stay lively later.

Cornwall PUB

(Rue des Puits l'Eau 14; ⊙noon-midnight Sun-Wed, to late Thu-Sat; 📶) This grungy pirate-haunt tavern is the sort of place Cornwall's legendary wreckers and smugglers would have called home. Great beer, a welcoming atmosphere and serious alternative cred make this Tournai's most interesting bar by some distance. Sounds range from Celtic neo-folk to death metal.

La Vie est Belge BAR

(www.lavieestbelge.be; Quai du Marché au Poisson 17; ⊙11am-midnight Mon-Thu, 11am-2am Fri, 2pm-2am Sat, 2pm-midnight Sun; 📶) On top of the usual beers and cocktails, this celebration of liquid Belgium pours Walloon *pékèts* (gin, sometimes flavoured), fruit-wine tasters and Belgian novelty drinks, including mojitos with *jenever* (like gin), Lambertus whisky, endive liqueur and *speculoos* (cinnamon-flavoured gingerbread) beer. You'll need long arms if you want to sit at the bar, though.

Aux Amis Réunis PUB

(Rue St-Martin 89; ⊙noon-last customer Mon-Sat) This archetypal old-time locals' pub dates from 1911. It retains its tiled floor, mirror-and-wood panelling, ceramic beer taps and pub game *jeu-de-fer,* in which players cue metal discs towards a series of pegs and gates. Decent-value food is also served.

ℹ Information

Office du Tourisme (☎069-22 20 45; www.visittournai.be; Place Paul-Émile Janson 1; ⊙9am-12.30pm & 1.15-6pm Mon-Fri, 10am-12.30pm & 1.15-6pm Sat & Sun Apr-Oct, to 5pm Mon-Sat, 1.15-5pm Sun Nov-Mar; 📶) Facing the cathedral, this excellent office offers great information, a couple of audiovisual presentations, exhibitions in a medieval cellar, tablets for internet access, free wi-fi and a shop with cute Tournai souvenirs. It also organises a program of guided tours of the town.

ℹ Getting There & Away

TRAIN

Tournai's train station is 900m northeast of the Grand Place. The following destinations are regularly served.

Brussels (€12.80, one hour)

Kortrijk (€5.30, 30 minutes) Via Mouscron.

Lille, France (€6.90, 25 minutes)

Mons (€7.30, 30 to 55 minutes)

BUS

TEC (www.infotec.be) buses serve a local network from the **bus station** by the train station.

Pipaix

The small village of Pipaix, 15km east of Tournai, has two very different breweries to experience.

Sights

★Brasserie à Vapeur BREWERY

(☎069-66 20 47; www.vapeur.com; Rue du Maréchal 1; Sun tour €6, Sat tour €5, incl lunch €35; ⊙brewery from 9am, tours 11am Sun Apr-Oct, 3pm last Sat of month) Started in 1785, this tiny affair is Belgium's last traditional steam-operated brewery. This wonderfully authentic family enterprise is best known for its Vapeur Cochonne, whose bare-breasted cartoon-pig labels were 'censored' for the US market. Sunday brewery tours include beer tasters. But, ideally, come on the last Saturday of each month to observe the brewery's whizzing flywheels and experience the sauna-like heat of the brewing process. Before the tour, pig out on a beer-influenced buffet lunch with endless ale. Book visits ahead.

Drinking & Nightlife

Brasserie Dubuisson BREWERY

(Trolls & Bush; ☎069-64 68 78; www.trolls-bush.be; Chaussée de Mons 32 (N50); ⊙11am-11pm Tue-Sun, kitchen noon-3pm & 6-10pm;) Wallonia's oldest brewery, Dubuisson sits on the N50 a couple of kilometres outside Pipaix. Its bar-brasserie offers several of its tasty beers on tap, of which the best-known are fresh, aromatic Cuvée des Trolls and sweet 12% Bush ambrée. Good-value meals, including tasty salads and pasta, make this a great pit stop. Brewery tours (€7) are at 3pm Saturday.

Getting There & Away

Both breweries can be reached from Tournai on TEC bus 95 (€3.20, 35 minutes, Monday to Friday only).

Aubechies

Aubechies is one of the region's prettiest villages.

Sights

Archeosite MUSEUM

(☎069-67 11 16; www.archeosite.be; Rue d'Abbaye 1; adult/child €9.50/3.50; ⊙9am-5pm Mon-Fri mid-Oct–mid-Apr, 9am-5pm Mon-Fri, 2-6pm Sun mid-Apr–Jun & Sep–mid-Oct, 9am-6pm Mon-Fri, 2-7pm Sat & Sun Jul & Aug) Archéosite is a recreated 'settlement' of ancient dwellings and workshops representing Neolithic, Bronze Age, Iron Age and Gallo-Roman eras. It's an interesting visit, with a very informative (French text) archaeological museum and an effort to present Roman buildings as they actually might have been. On summer Sundays, volunteer craftsmen in period costume often demonstrate cottage industries of times gone by.

WORTH A TRIP

GIANTS' FESTIVAL

The regionally important town of Ath is famous for its Ducasse (festival) on the fourth weekend of August. It features giant figures including Gouyasse (Goliath), whose wedding and battle with David are focal points of the Saturday. On the Sunday is a big procession.

You can learn more at the **Maison des Géants** (☎068-26 51 70; www.maisondesgeants.be; Rue de Pintamont 18; adult/child €6/5; ⊙10am-5pm Tue-Fri, to 6pm Jun-Sep, 2-6pm Sat & Sun, closed Sun Dec & Jan), in a mansion opposite the Église St-Julien near the Grand Place. While the giants' story is professionally told (in English by request), you're effectively locked into an hour-long series of multimedia presentations.

Ath's train station, 400m south of the Grand Place, is on the Brussels–Tournai line.

Eating

Taverne St-Géry PUB

(☎069-67 12 74; www.taverne-saint-gery.be; Place 2; ⊙6-11.30pm Fri, 5-11.30pm Sat, 10am-10pm Sun) Facing Aubechies' barrel-vaulted 1077 church, Taverne St-Géry is one of rural Belgium's most authentic village pubs. It's a whitewashed farm-style place whose interior walls incorporate Roman pottery finds and an original stable trough. Try the Dupont honey beer.

Getting There & Away

TEC bus 86a between Leuze-en-Hainaut (€3.20, 15 minutes) and Peruwelz (€3.20, 40 minutes) train stations stops in Aubechies twice, weekdays only. Other buses can get you within 20 minutes' walk – do a journey search on the TEC website (www.infotec.be).

Belœil

Château de Belœil CHATEAU

(☎069-68 94 26; www.chateaudebeloeil.com; Rue du Château 11; adult/child €9/4, gardens only €4/2; ⊙1-6pm daily Jul & Aug, 10am-6pm Sat & Sun only Apr-Jun & Sep) Sitting in an artificial lake within a vast manicured park, the Château de Belœil is a regal country palace-house, immodestly seeing itself as the Belgian Versailles. Inside it's packed with classical furniture and portraiture relevant to the princes 'de Ligne', whose scion, Eugène de Ligne (1804–80), turned down the chance to be Belgian king in 1831. An audio guide explains things in detail, but the interior somehow lacks majesty.

TEC bus 81 goes from the train station at Ath to Belœil (€3.20, 25 minutes) roughly hourly weekdays, less often on Saturday, and not at all on Sunday.

Lessines

POP 18,400

Birthplace of surrealist artist René Magritte, Lessines would be largely forgettable but for two outstanding attractions. One is the spooky penitents' procession on the night of Good Friday, which is one of Belgium's most memorable parades. The other is **Hôpital Notre-Dame à la Rose** (☎068-33 24 03; www.notredamealarose.com; Place Alix de Rosoit; adult/child €8.50/3.50; ⏲2-6.30pm Tue-Sun). Founded in 1242, it's Belgium's only medieval convent-farm-hospital complex to have survived reasonably intact. Laboriously restored, it demonstrates the development of medieval medicine from a beautiful herb garden via different hospices to historical medical implements. The collection of religious art includes a curious 16th-century painting showing Jesus with a female breast. There's a decent restaurant here for a pre-visit lunch.

Lessines is accessible by train from Ath (€2.50, 15 minutes, hourly weekdays, every two hours at weekends).

Enghien

POP 13,100

Behind the old-town core of charming Enghien (Edingen in Dutch) lies lovely **Parc d'Enghien** (www.enghien.be; admission free, audio guide €2; ⏲8am-8pm Apr-Oct, to 6pm Nov-Mar) FREE. Originally set out in the 17th century by the dukes of Arenberg, the park incorporates vast stands of woodland, fountains, statues, a tiny 'Chinese' pavilion, a topiary garden, a pond-side terrace *café* and the mansion-castle **Château Empain** (closed to the public). Views here are beautiful. By the park entrance, through the stone arch on the main square, is the **tourist office** (☎023 97 10 20; www.enghien-edingen.be; Park 5; ⏲10am-midday & 1-6pm Tue-Sun Apr-Sep, 10am-5pm Tue-Sun Oct-Mar), which can provide you with an audio guide. Central *cafés* serve excellent full-strength Double Enghien beer (www.silly-beer.com). That's brewed 9km west in humdrum Silly, worth driving through if only to photograph the town sign.

Enghien is a regular stop for trains between Brussels (€5.70, 30 minutes) and Kortrijk, Tournai and other destinations.

Mons

POP 93,400

With a characterful medieval centre climbing up a hill and a fine Grand Place, Mons (Bergen in Dutch) had a substantial facelift in 2015, when it was a European Capital of Culture. The legacy is a handful of entertaining modern museums that make Mons an excellent visit, with plenty to keep you busy for two or three days. One museum covers war in excellent fashion, while another celebrates the riotous Doudou festival, which stars St George, a dragon, St Waudru, devils and thousands of beery revellers.

History

Mons developed around the site of a Roman *castrum* (fortified camp). For centuries it was the capital of the powerful county of Hainaut, until 1436, when that was incorporated into the Duchy of Burgundy. To some Brits, Mons is remembered for the Angels of Mons, a legend that arose in 1914 based around a host of heavenly archers. Since 1967 Mons has been home to NATO command-operations headquarters, based 5km north of town.

Sights & Activities

★ **Mons Memorial Museum** MUSEUM
(☎065-40 53 12; www.monsmemorialmuseum.mons.be; Blvd Dolez 51; adult/child €9/2; ⏲10am-6pm Tue-Sun) A superb new museum, this extensive display mostly covers Mons' experience of the two world wars, though the constant sieges of this town's turbulent history are also mentioned. It gets the balance just right between military history, personal testimony of civilians and soldiers, and thought-provoking items on display. Some seriously good visuals make the to-and-fro (and stuck for years in the mud) of WWI instantly comprehensible, and there's an animated 3D film on the legend of the Angels of Mons.

Mons was the scene of the first British involvement in WWI, and its liberation coincided with the end of the conflict. In between, the city lived through a four-year German occupation, an experience it relived just 22 years later. The museum's strength is its focus on the human side of war, whether through soldiers' diaries or the day-to-day hardships of civilians. Poignant items are numerous, including a cross made by locals for a German and an English soldier buried together, and the tombstone of the last WWI soldier killed, two minutes before the armistice.

Musée du Doudou MUSEUM
(www.museedudoudou.mons.be; Jardin du Mayeur; adult/child €9/2; ⏲10am-6pm Tue-Sun) Head through the Hôtel de Ville on the Grand Place to reach this museum, dedicated to Mons' riotous Ducasse festival. All aspects of this curious event, as well as background on St George, Ste Waudru and dragons, are covered in entertaining interactive fashion, and there are interesting cultural musings on the festival's changing nature over time. At the audiovisual showing the climactic Lumeçon battle, you can almost smell the beer and sweat. There's audio content in French, Dutch and English.

Artothèque MUSEUM
(☎065-40 53 12; www.artotheque.mons.be; Rue Claude de Bettignies; adult/child €6/2; ⏲10am-6pm Tue-Sun) Ever thought it was a pity that all those items sat in museum storerooms, never seeing the light of day? Well, this innovative space in a former convent chapel lets you examine a wide range of objects from various museum basements, with interactive screens (in French, but staff can arrange translation) allowing you to locate them and inform yourself about them. Items range from soldiers' wartime rations to ceramics to clothing to fine art. Original and entertaining.

Hôtel de Ville HISTORIC BUILDING
(Grand Place 22) Mons' splendid 15th-century city hall is the most visually arresting building on the photogenic, *café*-lined Grand Place. It has become customary among visitors to score a wish by stroking the head of an iron monkey (Singe du Grand Gard) on the front left flank of the building's gateway portal, though traditionally it was only supposed to work for women hoping to get pregnant. The gateway leads to a pretty courtyard garden.

Beffroi TOWER
(www.beffroi.mons.be; Parc du Château; ⏲10am-6pm Tue-Sun) The 80m-tall Unesco-listed baroque belfry is a 17th-century marvel billowing with black-and-gold mini-domes. Get the lift to the top for panoramic views. An interactive multilevel exhibition gives information on the history of the building and the town, and the surrounding garden (admission free) occupies the hilltop site of what was originally Mons' fortress. Admission includes a multilingual audio guide.

LE DOUDOU

Known locally as Le Doudou, Unesco-listed festival **La Ducasse** (www.ducassedemons.be) sees the remains of Ste Waudru (a 7th-century female miracle worker and Mons' patron) raucously paraded around town on Trinity Sunday (eight weeks after Easter Sunday) in the Procession du Car d'Or. At lunchtime on the Grand Place, drums and chanting accompany the Lumeçon, a mock battle pitting St George against a wickerwork dragon.

Lesser characters include the Chinchins (18th-century soldiers and St George's sidekicks) and a gang of devils helping out the dragon. If you dare, join the beer-boisterous crowd surging forward to grab hairs from the dragon's tail as it flails around. Purloining a dragon hair augurs good luck.

Get the full rundown at the Musée du Doudou.

Collégiale Ste-Waudru CHURCH
(www.waudru.be; Place du Chapitre; ⏲9am-6pm) Within this lofty, airy 15th-century Gothic church you'll find the golden reliquary of Ste-Waudru (hanging above the altar) and the fanciful 1782 Car d'Or, a gilded, cherub-festooned coach used to carry it during Ste-Waudru festival Le Doudou. The small **treasury** (www.tresorsaintewaudru.mons.be/; Collégiale Ste-Waudru, Place du Chapitre; adult/child €4/2; ⏲noon-6pm Tue-Sun) displays Ste-Waudru's shrouds and a sword-slashed skull in a reliquary – supposedly of sainted Merovingian king Dagobert II. Some conspiracy theorists consider that Dagobert's murder in 675 was an attempt to put an end to the 'Jesus bloodline'.

Musée François Duesberg MUSEUM
(☎065-36 31 64; www.duesberg.mons.be; Sq Franklin Roosevelt; admission €5; ⏲2-7pm Tue, Thu, Sat & Sun) If you're a fan of exotic gilded clocks, dazzling porcelain and silver coffeepots from 1775 to 1825, check out the rich

collection at this sumptuous three-room museum. It's in the former national-bank building between Collégiale Ste-Waudru and the train station.

BAM GALLERY
(Musée des Beaux-Arts; 065-40 53 24; www.bam.mons.be; Rue Neuve 8; adult/concession €8/5; 10am-6pm Tue-Sun) This modernist glass cube of a gallery is the product of a rebuild for the city's tenure as a European Capital of Culture in 2015. It hosts temporary exhibitions, with at least one high-profile display planned each year.

Silex's MUSEUM
(www.silexs.mons.be; Rue du Point du Jour, Spiennes; adult/child €9/2; 10am-6pm Tue-Sun Apr-Oct) Six kilometres southeast of Mons, a peaceful agricultural scene covers what was a major Neolithic flint-mining site. One of the most impressive shafts is covered by this lightweight metal museum, which gives decent information on how the flint was knapped and made into durable tools. Three daily visits descend to the mine – an atmospheric experience – but must be prebooked well in advance via Mons' tourist office (groupes@ville.mons.be).

There's access for travellers with disabilities, but otherwise you must park 1km away and stroll through pleasant farmland. There are buses to Spiennes from Mons.

Cimetière Saint-Symphorien CEMETERY
(Rue Nestor Dehon, St-Symphorien) Just 5.5km east of Mons, this small cemetery is one of the most peaceful and thought-provoking in Belgium. The resting place of roughly equal numbers of German and British soldiers from WWI, it includes the tombs of the first and last Commonwealth soldiers to die in the conflict.

Sleeping

Auberge de Jeunesse HOSTEL €
(065-87 55 70; www.lesaubergesdejeunesse.be; Rampe du Château 2; dm/s/d €28/46/68; P @) Just before the base of the belfry, this modern, well-equipped HI hostel has an attractive tiered design making good use of the sloping terrain. It's worth booking ahead. Prices drop significantly in quieter months. Rates are €2 less per person for those 26 and under; 10% HI discount.

★**Dream Hôtel** HOTEL €€
(065-32 97 20; www.dream-mons.be; Rue de la Grand Triperie 17; s/d €94/113; P @) Centrally located in a revamped 19th-century chapel, Dream Hôtel combines a good level of comfort with more than a dash of Belgian

CARNAVAL DE BINCHE

Binche lives for its Unesco-listed **Carnaval de Binche** (www.carnavaldebinche.be; Mardi Gras), which culminates on Shrove Tuesday. The undisputed stars are the Gilles, male figures dressed alike in clogs and straw-padded suits decorated with heraldic symbols. In the morning each 'brotherhood' of Gilles clomps to the town hall. Outside, they briefly don spooky green-eyed masks while shaking sticks to ward off evil spirits in a formalised stomp 'dance'.

After a lunchtime lull, up to 1000 Gilles march across town in one vast, shuffling, slow-motion parade, wearing their enormous ostrich-feather headdresses (weather permitting). Oranges are lobbed intermittently into the heaving crowd and at observers who cheer from those windows that haven't been protectively boarded up. Don't even think of hurling one back, however tempting it might be – the Gilles-thrown oranges are metaphorical blessings.

Despite appearances, the carnival is a serious celebration, taking months of preparation and involving strict rules of conduct. The rituals surrounding it date back hundreds of years and the Gilles' finery is thought to be an interpretation of the elaborate, Inca-inspired costumes worn by courtiers at a world-famous feast held here by Mary of Hungary to honour Emperor Charles V in 1549.

If you're in town at another time of year, get a feel for what the carnival's about at the **Musée International du Carnaval et du Masque** (064-33 57 41; www.museedumasque.be; Rue St-Moustier 10; adult/child €8/3.50; 9.30am-5pm Tue-Fri, 10.30am-5pm Sat & Sun).

Mons–Binche bus 22 (€3.20, 40 minutes) runs every 40 minutes or so. At carnival time, however, impossible traffic makes taking the train much more sensible. Brussels-bound trains run hourly (€9.40, 1¼ hours), with easy en-route connections to Charleroi or Mons.

eccentricity, including multilingual murals, bowler-hat lamps and side tables made from drums. Bathrooms, with separate toilet, are excellent, and noise insulation is relatively good. There's a lovely little spa to wallow in and free (valet) parking.

Hôtel St James HOTEL €€
(065-72 48 24; www.hotelstjames.be; Place de Flandre 8; s €83, d €90-120; P) This refined old brick-and-stone house has had a trendy two-tone makeover. Behind the main building, via a handkerchief of garden, a newer, equally fashionable rear section has less road noise. It's just across the ring-boulevard, 10 minutes' walk east of the Grand Place: follow Rue d'Havré, then cross the big junction.

Hôtel Infotel HOTEL €€
(065-40 18 30; www.hotelinfotel.be; Rue d'Havré 32; standard/superior d €90/110; P) This boxy hotel has pleasant if fairly generic furnishings, but the welcome is friendly, there's a kettle and coffee in the room, and parking is free. That's quite a plus given the location just steps from the Grand Place.

Eating

Mons is stuffed with good-value eateries and numerous gastronomic restaurants. A range of bistros and cafes lines the Grand Place.

Henri BELGIAN €
(065-35 23 06; Rue d'Havré 41; mains €9-18; noon-2.30pm & 6.30-9pm Tue-Sat, noon-2.30pm Sun & Mon;) Cheerful tavern-style restaurant crammed with local diners. For an authentic Mons dish go for *côtes de porc à l'berdouille:* pork in brown sauce.

La Vie est Belle BELGIAN €
(065-56 58 45; Rue d'Havré 39; mains €8-18; noon-3pm & 6-11pm Tue-Sat, noon-3pm Sun) This family-style restaurant is superb value for home-style Belgian food that's filling rather than gourmet (think meatballs, mashed potatoes, rabbit or mussels). The naive puppet models adorning the decorative mirrors add character.

L'Envers BISTRO €€
(065-35 45 10; www.lenvers-mons.be; Rue de la Coupe 20; mains €15-24; 11am-2.30pm & 6-10.30pm Mon-Sat;) Just above the pumping bar scene of the Marché aux Herbes, this bustling spot deals out classic bistro favourites complemented by a list of daily dishes with some innovative takes on traditional ingredients. It's all very tasty, service is friendly, and there's pleasant outdoor seating. Meals can take a while on busy nights.

Le Pastissou FRENCH €€
(065-31 92 60; Rue des Fripiers 14; mains €15-22; noon-3pm & 7-10pm Tue-Sat) Warmly lit and cosy, this little space is bossed by a bloke from southwestern France and, appropriately, the speciality here is cassoulet, which comes in a variety of delicious incarnations. A number of other regional dishes, with duck and spicy sausages featuring heavily, add to the authentic feel.

Salon des Lumières FRENCH €€
(0474 29 25 84; www.salondeslumieres.com; Rue du Mirroir 23; mains €18-23; 6.30-10pm Wed-Sun) Walk aesthetically and gastronomically into history. This is film set–style perfection, lit by old chandeliers with real candles. Downstairs it's the Louis XVI era in all its louche grandeur; upstairs the furniture is more Napoleon III but every bit as lavish. Food wise, the idea is to use field herbs and flowers to create the flavours of those ages.

The menu's obsession with pancakes is a convoluted reference to Louis XIV's sun symbolism. On Sundays there are occasional theatrical interludes.

★ **Vilaine Fille, Mauvais Garçon** MODERN FRENCH €€€
(Naughty Girl, Bad Boy; 065-66 67 62; www.vilainefillemauvaisgarcon.be; Rue de Nimy 55; mains €26-28, set meals €27-48; noon-3pm & 7-10.30pm Tue-Fri, 7-10.30pm Sat, noon-3pm Sun) Artful gastronomic takes on traditional plates, with familiar ingredients appearing in surprising ways, are the hallmarks of this enjoyable restaurant. The smart contemporary interior in a historic building makes for relaxed, quality dining. The menu is short, and there are various set meals depending on which day it is.

Drinking & Nightlife

Terrace cafes in the Grand Place are a grand place for a beer. Later, the bars on the Marché aux Herbes and adjacent Rue de la Clef get very lively.

La Lorgnette BAR
(www.facebook.com/lalorgnette; Rue des Clercs 2; 3pm-3am;) Just off the Grand Place, this hipster-ish two-level bar is decked out in blond wood and makes a pleasant, sociable spot for a beer, attracting a clientele of various ages. The house gimmick is a flambéed beer served in a bowl-style glass.

Information

Maison du Tourisme (065-33 55 80; www.visitmons.be; Grand Place 27; 9am-7pm daily;) On the main square, with lots of booklets and information, and bike rental.

Getting There & Around

Mons' **train station** (Place Léopold) (provisional until the new Calatrava design is finally finished) and neighbouring **TEC bus station** (065-38 88 15) are 700m west of the Grand Place. There are very regular services to the following destinations.

Brussels (€9.40, 50 minutes)

Charleroi (€6.50, 35 minutes)

Tournai (€7.30, 30 to 55 minutes)

Free public buses shuttle around, linking the train/bus station and the Grand Place.

Waterloo Battlefield

Tourists have been swarming to Waterloo ever since Napoleon's 1815 defeat, a seminal event in European history. The event's bicentenary saw a smart new underground museum pep up the site of the battlefield, which is, in this case, many fields: a vast, attractive patchwork of gently undulating cropland dotted with memorials and historically meaningful buildings. Re-enactments are usually held on the weekend nearest the battle's anniversary (18 June).

The main battlefield site is known as Hameau du Lion (Lion Hamlet), some 5km south of central Waterloo town. In Waterloo town the **tourist office** (02-352 09 10; www.waterloo-tourisme.be; Chaussée de Bruxelles 218; 9.30am-6pm Jun-Sep, 10am-5pm Oct-May;) rents out bicycles to explore the area.

Sights

Hameau du Lion (Lion Hamlet)

★Memorial 1815 MUSEUM

(02-385 19 12; www.waterloo1815.be; Rte du Lion; adult/child €16/13, with Wellington & Napoleon headquarters museums €19/15; 9.30am-6.30pm Apr-Sep, 10am-5pm Oct-Mar) Inaugurated for the 2015 bicentenary, this showpiece underground museum and visitor centre at the battlefield gives some detail on the background to Napoleon's rise, fills in information on key incidents, then describes the make-up of each side's forces. There's a detailed audio guide and some enjoyable technological effects. The climax is an impressive 3D film that sticks you right into the middle of the cavalry charges. There's surprisingly little detail on the battle itself, though. Includes admission to Panorama, Butte du Lion and Hougoumont.

Butte du Lion

(Lion Mound; 9.30am-6.30pm Apr-Sep, 10am-5pm Oct-Mar) Waterloo's most arresting sight is a steep, grassy cone topped by a massive bronze lion. It commemorates, incredibly, not victory nor the glorious dead but Prince William of Orange, wounded on this spot while co-commanding Allied troops. Building the mound took two years: women carted up soil in baskets. Climb 225 steps and survey the battlefield's deceptively minor undulations that so fooled Napoleon's infantry. Admission is included with admission to Memorial 1815, through whose visitor centre the hill is accessed.

Panorama

Included in admission to the Memorial 1815 visitor centre is the charmingly old-fashioned 1912 Panorama de la Bataille, a circular action-packed painting of the battle scenes. You view it from inside, across a 3D foreground littered with fallen helmets, broken-down fences, dead horses and the odd corpse. There's a rumbling soundtrack of battle cries, bagpipes, cannon fire and thundering hooves.

★Hougoumont

(www.projecthougoumont.com; 9.30am-6.30pm Apr-Sep, 10am-5pm Oct-Mar) This classic fortified farm is around 20 minutes' walk southwest of the Butte du Lion. Had Napoleon broken through here early in the battle, everything might have turned out very differently. Recently restored to its original appearance, this a peaceful rural spot: it's hard to imagine the desperate struggle of 1815, but a modern exhibition and impressive audiovisual display do their best to evoke it. Entry is included with Memorial 1815, from where free blue shuttle buses run to the farm.

A cottage in the complex houses a cosy **apartment** (in UK +44 1628 825 925; www.landmarktrust.org.uk; Ferme d'Hougoumont; 3/7 nights summer £1127/1928; P) decorated in period style that sleeps four and can be booked for stays of three days or more. Prices drop substantially in low season.

Other Battlefield Sites

Work is ongoing to upgrade attractions in the area and return the battlefield to roughly how it would have looked in 1815.

THE BATTLE OF WATERLOO

After a disastrous invasion of Russia and the 1813 loss at Leipzig, Napoleon Bonaparte seemed defeated and was imprisoned on the island of Elba. Yet on 1 March 1815 he escaped, landed in southern France and with remarkable speed managed to muster a huge army. The European powers promptly declared war and chose Brussels as the point at which to form a combined army. However, in those pre-rail days, that could take weeks. Napoleon knew that time was of the essence. If he could meet either army individually, Napoleon's 124,000 men would outnumber roughly 106,000 Anglo-Dutch-Hanoverian troops or 117,000 Prussians. But he had to strike fast before the two combined.

On 16 June Napoleon struck the Prussians at Ligny, where Blücher, the Prussian commander, was wounded and the Prussian army appeared to have been put to flight. Napoleon then turned his attention to British commander Wellington, whose troops were assembling at Waterloo, a carefully chosen defensive position just south of Brussels.

At sunrise on Sunday 18 June the two armies faced off, but the start of the battle was delayed due to soggy ground. The French attack started midmorning with an assault on Hougoumont farm, vital for the defence of Wellington's right. The doughty defence of it fatally slowed Napoleon's game plan. Meanwhile, by 1pm, the French had word that the Prussian army had regrouped and was moving in fast. Napoleon detached a force to meet it and for several hours battle raged at **Plancenoit**, depriving Napoleon of crucial manpower on the main battlefield.

At 2pm a massive wave of French infantry marched on Wellington's left flank. However, thousands of Allied musketeers, cleverly hidden in rows behind a ridge-top hedge, were invisible to the French infantry, slogging uphill through the mud – invisible, that is, until they rose row by row to unleash volleys of musket fire into the French ranks, whose close-knit formations compounded the difficulty of escape.

After this debacle, the French cavalry was sent in to charge Wellington's centre. However, the well-trained Allied infantrymen formed defensive squares in which their bayonets turned groups into impenetrable 'hedgehogs' of spikes. The musketeers couldn't reload and shoot, but the sabres of the cavalry were useless too: stalemate. For Napoleon the situation was becoming ever more urgent given the steady approach of the main Prussian force. Napoleon ordered his elite Imperial Guards to break through Wellington's centre. It was a desperate last-ditch effort through mud churned up by the cavalry's previous attempt; the soldiers were mown down by the opposing infantrymen from their protected high-ground position.

Around 8.15pm Wellington led a full-scale advance, the French fell into full retreat and Napoleon fled, abandoning his damaged carriage at Genappe with such haste that he left behind its cache of diamonds. He abdicated a week later and spent the rest of his life in exile on St Helena.

Musée Wellington MUSEUM
(Wellington's Headquarters; ☎02-357 28 60; www.museewellington.be; Chaussée de Bruxelles 147; adult/child €6.50/4; ⏰9.30am-6pm Apr-Sep, 10am-5pm Oct-Mar; 🚌W) Opposite the church and tourist office on the main road in Waterloo itself, this former inn is where Wellington stayed before the battle. The museum, accessible on the combined Memorial 1815 ticket, is old-fashioned but well put together and has a decent summary of the battle as well as items and sketches from the period. Temporary exhibitions are presented in the annexe behind.

Dernier Quartier Général de Napoléon MUSEUM
(Napoleon's Headquarters; ☎02-384 24 24; Chaussée de Bruxelles 66, Vieux-Genappe; adult/child €5/3; ⏰9.30am-6pm Apr-Sep, 10am-5pm Oct-Mar) The farmhouse complex where Napoleon breakfasted the morning of the battle now forms a small museum, accessible on the combined Memorial 1815 ticket. It's 4km south of the Hameau du Lion on the Waterloo–Genappe road, accessible by hourly Charleroi-bound bus 365a (the bus runs every two hours on Sunday).

ℹ Getting There & Around

TEC bus W runs every 30 minutes from Ave Fonsny at Brussels-Midi to Braine-l'Alleud train station, passing through Waterloo town and stopping near Hameau du Lion (€3.20). If coming by train, get off at Braine-l'Alleud rather than awkwardly located Waterloo station, then switch

CANAL LIFTS

The Canal Bruxelles–Charleroi was built in 1832 to carry coal to the capital, via 55 locks, two aqueducts and a tunnel – a journey of three days. It can now be done in one, thanks to various engineering marvels, which you can view, visit and appreciate by boat. The following are the two most spectacular.

Plan Incliné de Ronquières (http://voiesdeau.hainaut.be; Rte Baccara, Ronquières; lock adult/child €7.50/4.25, boat trip €4.50/4, both €10/7.25; 10am-7pm Apr-Oct, boat trips Sun May-Aug) This 1.4km-long slope, or 'sliding lock', at Ronquières is a curious 1968 contraption that lowers boats down a steepish gradient in a giant bathtub. It's strangely mesmerising to watch it trundling oh so slowly into action. The two-hour visit includes a 3D film and views from the top.

Strépy-Thieu Boat-Lift (Ascenseur Strépy-Thieu; 078-05 90 59; http://voiesdeau.hainaut.be; Rue Raymond Cordier, Thieu; lock adult/child €6/2.75, boat trip €6.50/4.25, both €10.50/6; 9.30am-6.30pm Apr-Oct, boat trips Sun May-Aug) The world's tallest ship lift (2002), raising or lowering gigantic 'baths' 73 vertical metres, is on a pharaonic scale, as was the €150 million it cost. Though you can watch the lift from outdoors, visits allow you to look down on the engine room, appreciate the construction via a 35-minute multilingual video, watch the action from the cafe, or take part in a quiz on Belgian genius. Boat trips take you through the lift, while a tourist train whizzes around the site.

Strépy-Thieu is just south of the Tournai–Brussels motorway, accessible on bus 30 from La Louvière.

to bus W to reach the battlefield. A hotel is under construction next to the visitor centre.

Nivelles

POP 26,800

Ancient Nivelles (Nijvel in Dutch) sports one of Belgium's most unusual and impressive churches, which looms powerfully over a pleasant town centre.

Sights

★Collégiale Ste-Gertrude CHURCH

(www.collegiale.be; Grand Place; tours adult/child €6/2; 9am-6pm Apr-Oct, to 5pm Nov-Mar, tours 2pm daily, plus 3.30pm Sat & Sun) FREE This 11th-century church was part of one of Europe's foremost abbeys, founded in 648. It's 102m long with a soaring multilevel western facade topped with a squat octagonal tower flanked by turrets. The interior's enormous Romanesque arches are unadorned, but notice the 15th-century chariot that's still used to carry Ste-Gertrude's silver *châsse* during Nivelles' principal procession. Fascinating and detailed two-hour guided tours in French get you access to the crypt, the tower gallery and the pretty cloister for photogenic views.

The pleasant cloisters are another highlight. Outside, watch the southern turret to see a 350kg gilt statue strike the hour with a hefty hammer. Tours also take in archaeological excavations and the grave of Charlemagne's lofty first wife, Himeltrude, whose 1.85m skeleton can be seen reflected by a well-placed mirror.

The abbey's first abbess, Gertrude, was a great-great aunt of Charlemagne's, and was later sainted for her miraculous abilities, including rat catching (which warded off plague) and devil snaring (which saved the mythical Knight of Masseik from losing a Faustian bargain).

Sleeping & Eating

Nivelles Sud HOTEL €€

(067-21 87 21; www.hotelnivellessud.be; Chaussée de Mons 22; r €88; P) On a roundabout 1.5km west of central Nivelles, this large motor inn–style hotel offers surprisingly decent rooms at attractive prices, as well as a restaurant and bar. Facilities are good, though it can get rowdy with weddings at weekends. Prices can halve at quiet times or if you book in advance.

Le Chant du Pain BAKERY €

(Rue du Géant 1b; snacks €1.50-4; 6am-7pm Mon-Sat) Nivelles' unique culinary speciality is *tarte al djote*, a creation that's somewhere between pizza and quiche but flavoured with fragrant green chard. Try a small takeaway one from this historic bakery-shop 150m east of the Grand Place via Rue de Namur.

★ **Le Cigalon** FRENCH €€

(☎0475 53 17 37; Rue de Bruxelles 32; mains €15-25; ⏲noon-2pm & 7-9.30pm Thu-Mon, noon-2pm Tue) This loveable spot has streetside seating and a sweet little garden area. It does a great line in regional French dishes – for sushi, head to its sister place a few doors down – with the odd Asian influence. House wines are remarkably tasty. It's in the street of eateries that exits the main square next to the turreted Palais de Justice.

Information

Tourist Office (☎067-22 04 44; www.tourisme-roman-pais.be; Rue de Saintes 48; ⏲9am-6pm Mon-Fri, to 5pm Sat & Sun) This helpful office is 250m uphill from the Grand Place and can organise English-language tours of the Collégiale. There's a smaller, mobile office often parked outside the entrance to the Collégiale.

Getting There & Away

The Grand Place is a 15-minute walk west from Nivelles' train station. There are regular trains to Brussels (€5.70, 25 to 35 minutes) and elsewhere.

Louvain-la-Neuve

POP 20,000

In the chaos of riot-filled 1968, the Francophone university faculties were violently driven out of Leuven. Louvain-la-Neuve was purpose built to give them a new home and thus most buildings here are archetypal 1970s collegiate.

Sights

★ **Musée Hergé** MUSEUM

(www.museeherge.com; Rue du Labrador 26; adult/child €9.50/5; ⏲10.30am-5.30pm Tue-Fri, 10am-6pm Sat & Sun) The inventive and touchingly nostalgic Hergé Museum celebrates the multitalented creator of comic-strip hero Tintin with an engaging, inventive and extensive display. Highlights include numerous models, pictures and source materials assembled by the artist to ensure the accuracy of his sketches. There's an entertaining audio guide. Note the original triptych portrait of Hergé by Andy Warhol, for whom Tintin was a cited influence. The gift shop is worth a peek too.

The museum's unique architecture alone is worth the visit: an abstract glass-and-concrete boat-shaped creation filled with multistorey geometrical forms slashed through with a central 'light chasm' filling the structure with intriguing angles and views.

Driving, you'll be funnelled into a weird underground space with pay parking available. The museum is a short walk from the bus and train stations.

Getting There & Away

Trains to Brussels (€5.30, 50 minutes) generally require a change at Ottignies. TEC bus 3 runs six times weekdays (€5.30, 35 minutes) to Braine-l'Alleud via Waterloo Mont-St-Jean, 1.5km from Waterloo's battlefield site. Bus 4 runs 10 times weekdays from Nivelles (€3.50, 30 minutes).

Villers-la-Ville

Abbaye de Villers RUINS

(☎071-88 09 80; www.villers.be; Rue de l'Abbaye 55; adult/child €6/2.50; ⏲10am-6pm Apr-Oct, 10am-5pm Wed-Mon Nov-Mar) Nestled in a pretty wooded dell are these extensive, ivy-clad ruins. Once one of Belgium's biggest monastic complexes, Villers was never rebuilt after the destructive onslaught of 1794, when, in the post–French Revolution fervour, virtually every such institution was sacked. To add insult to injury, a railway line was built through the site in the 1850s. It's an evocative, peaceful place with its gigantic, shattered church – an atmospheric venue for summer concerts and plays – grassy ruins and cute walled garden.

Across the road, **La Cave du Moulin** (☎071-87 68 65; www.moulindevillers.be; Rue de l'Abbaye 55;

TINTIN

Quiff-headed boy-reporter Tintin is, dare we say it, the most famous Belgian. Charming young and old alike, Tintin's adventures involve a beloved team of misfits, including dog Snowy, crusty old salt Captain Haddock and diva-with-a-heart-of-gold Bianca Castafiore. Tintin books have been translated into more than 50 languages and still sell more than two million copies a year. Blistering barnacles! Creator Georges Remi's pen name, Hergé, came from his reversed initials, RG, pronounced in French. His initial efforts featured some crude racial stereotypes, later regretted by him as he took a genuine interest in portraying other cultures.

mains €16-20; ⏲11am-7pm Wed & Sun, to 9pm Mon & Thu-Sat Apr-Oct; 📶👪) is mediocre food-wise but ideal for a drink in an old stone-vaulted mill house after you've visited the ruins.

Villers-la-Ville is on the Ottignies–Charleroi railway line. The train station is 1.6km south of the ruins.

Charleroi

POP 204,700

Until the 1960s this region's coalfields were the main force behind Belgium's economy. These days the main reason that travellers transit bedraggled Charleroi is to take budget flights from its international airport. However, there's a certain demonic grandeur in the rust-chimneyed steelworks, and a few art-deco beauties in the down-at-heel centre. A couple of great museums are on the city's outskirts.

Sights

★Musée de la Photographie MUSEUM
(☎071-43 58 10; www.museephoto.be; Ave Paul Pastur 11; adult/child €7/free; ⏲10am-6pm Tue-Sun) One of Europe's biggest and most impressive photography museums, it has an engrossing collection of historic, contemporary and artistic prints. Don't miss the area upstairs dealing with airbrushing, tricks of the trade and optical illusions. Particularly intriguing is a little curtained room in which you effectively stand within a giant pinhole camera. Although most labels are in French, the ideas are generally self-explanatory. It occupies a 19th-century convent at the centre of dreary Mont-sur-Marchienne, 3km south of Charleroi by regular bus 70.

Le Bois du Cazier MUSEUM
(☎071-88 08 56; www.leboisducazier.be; Rue du Cazier 80; adult/student €7/4.50; ⏲9am-5pm Tue-Fri, 10am-6pm Sat & Sun) This sizeable complex occupies a mine site where a horrific accident killed 262 miners in 1956. A gripping multilingual video commemorates that; admission also includes access to a museum celebrating Charleroi's heyday as a centre of steel, glass and coal industries. A glass collection has items dating back millennia, while workshops offer demonstrations of bronzeworking and glass-blowing. Allow at least two hours, or three including the landscaped walk up former slag heaps. Bus 52 runs hourly Monday to Saturday from Charleroi-Sud train station.

CHARLEROI ('BRUSSELS SOUTH') AIRPORT

Around 6km north of Charleroi, **Charleroi Airport** (www.charleroi-airport.com; 📶) is Belgium's main hub for budget airlines, notably Ryanair. Two or three **coaches** (www.brussels-city-shuttle.com; around €14; ⏲7.50am-midnight) per hour take 55 minutes to reach Brussels. Flibco (www.flibco.com) offers connections to Luxembourg, Bruges and Ghent. Bus A runs to/from Charleroi-Sud train station (€5, 20 minutes, free with train ticket, purchase bus-plus-rail ticket at airport).

The nearest of the generic airport accommodations is Ibis Budget, which, while physically close to the terminal, is actually 1.4km away by road.

Eating

Restaurant du Boulevard FRENCH €€
(Le Deauville; ☎071-31 40 21; Blvd Tirou 28; mains €15-26; ⏲noon-2.30pm & 7-10pm Mon & Wed-Sat, noon-10pm Sun) Wilfully old-fashioned, this place refuses to believe that Charleroi has fallen on hard times, though the blend of '20s, '70s and modern decor is curious on the eye. The menu, with a couple of Spanish quirks, doesn't shy away from brains and kidneys; it's all very tasty, if slightly overpriced, and service is polite.

Entertainment

Charleroi/Danses DANCE
(☎071-31 12 12; www.charleroi-danses.be; Les Écuries, Blvd Mayence 65c) Charleroi's cultural highpoint is its world-renowned avant-garde dance company, which performs here at Les Écuries theatre.

Information

Tourist Office (☎071-86 14 14; www.paysdecharleroi.be; Place Charles II 20; ⏲9am-6pm Mon-Sat, to 3pm Sun; 📶)

Getting There & Away

Charleroi-Sud train station is on the southern side of town. Trains run around half-hourly to the following destinations.

Brussels (€9.40, 55 minutes)
Mons (€6.50, 35 minutes)
Nivelles (€4.60, 25 minutes)

OFF THE BEATEN TRACK

CASTLE TOWNS

Back in the 13th century, the border between the County of Namur and the Duchy of Brabant lay close to Gembloux. The region's villages are still dotted with minor medieval castles.

Around 5km southwest of Gembloux, which has a Unesco-listed belfry, the pretty hamlet of **Corroy-le-Château** hides a seven-towered 13th-century castle in thick private woodlands. It opens for occasional weekend visits. The village of Sombreffe is less appealing than Corroy, but its **castle** (www.chateau-de-sombreffe.be; Chaussée de Chastre) has a particularly fine quiver of towers. If the gate's open, wander in for a peek at the courtyard.

At Ligny, against Blücher's Prussians, Napoleon won his last victory. Battle fans can visit the memorabilia-filled **Musée de la Bataille** (☎071-81 83 13; www.si-ligny.be; Rue Pont-Piraux 23, Ligny; adult/child €5/free; ⏰10am-5pm Thu-Mon Apr-Oct), with two floors of material relating to that and Wellington's nearby confrontation at Quatre Bras.

If you want to stay in the region, the lovely **Golf Hotel de Falnuée** (☎081-63 30 90; www.golf-hotel-falnuee.com; Rue Émile Pirson 55, Mazy; s/d/ste €80/90/150; P 📶) incorporates a 13th-century stone tower. Its dreamily verdant course is set in a rural valley. Above the vaulted restaurant in the stables are comfortable modern guest rooms decorated with contemporary art. Breakfast is €10.

Thuin

POP 14,600

One of central Wallonia's quainter towns, Thuin is a picturesque medieval huddle of ridge-top streets peering down on the wooded Sambre River. The centrepiece is its Unesco-listed **beffroi** (Place Albert Premier; adult/youth/child €3/1/free; ⏰10am-noon & 1-6pm Tue-Sun Apr-Sep, plus Mon Jul & Aug, to 5pm Oct), a 1639 stone bell tower topped with five slate spires and numerous gilded baubles. Apart from the (loud!) bells and old/new clock mechanisms, the tower is empty, and one climbs (with audio guide) up metal steps and steep ladders for the fine regional views. Enter via the **tourist office** (☎071-59 69 19; www.visitthudinie.be; Place Albert Premier 2; ⏰9am-6pm Apr-Sep, to 5pm Oct-Mar), which has free town maps suggesting a hilly 1¼-hour walk through the town's 'hanging' (ie steeply terraced) garden.

Thuin train station is across the river far below the old city. There are regular trains to Charleroi-Sud (€2.90, 20 minutes).

Aulne

With 7th-century origins, but destroyed post French Revolution in 1794, the atmospheric **monastery** (www.abbayedaulne.be; Rue Vandervelde, Aulne; adult/child €4/free; ⏰1-6pm Wed-Sun Apr-Sep, 1-5pm Sat & Sun Oct, opens daily Jul & Aug some years) in this river valley is a mixture of picturesque ruins, surviving 18th-century buildings and a later 19th-century convent church. Cistercians ran the place in its heyday, when a sophisticated watercourse system ran around the complex. The skeletal remains of the Gothic church and the ruined cloister attest to the scale of this once-thriving community. Signboards are in French, but you can grab an English guide from the kiosk.

Afterwards, walk around the rear wall to the timeless **brasserie-taverne** (☎071-56 20 73; www.valdesambre.be; Rue Vandervelde, Aulne; ⏰1pm-8pm daily summer, weekends only winter), whose Blonde des Pères beer, brewed here, is served in earthenware chalices. A tour including tasting costs €5.50.

In July and August, the ABBA special bus runs at weekends from Charleroi-Sud station to here, otherwise you'll need wheels. The surrounding wooded scenery of the Sambre valley appeals, and there's a happy waterside family scene here at weekends, with open-air cafe-restaurants and activity options.

Ragnies

Distillerie de Biercée DISTILLERY
(☎071-59 11 06; www.distilleriedebiercee.com; Rue de la Roquette 36, Ragnies; ⏰shop 9am-5pm Mon-Fri, plus noon-6pm Sat & Sun Apr-Nov) Around 6km south of Thuin, the Distillerie de Biercée is a great opportunity to see inside

one of Wallonia's classic fortified-farm complexes. This one is impressively renovated, the brick vaults hosting a spacious *café* decorated with historic enamel drink advertisements and winding copper piping. You can taste its local fruit brandies and gins, including classic P'tit Peket, or take a one-hour **distillery tour** (adult €7; 3pm Tue-Sun Apr-Sep, weekends only Oct & Nov) including samples.

The distillery is by tiny Ragnies, one of the region's most attractive hamlets. Schoolbus 194 runs here from Thuin, but driving or walking is more likely to be useful.

Botte du Hainaut

This undulating area is a mixture of farms, woodlands and castle villages that's very pretty but oddly undertouristed. Chimay makes a good base for exploration.

Philippeville

Souterrains TUNNEL

(adult/child €4/2, 1 person only €5; tours 1.30pm & 3pm Mon-Sat) Between 1659 and 1815 Philippeville was an ultra-fortified enclave of France, completely encircled within the Holy Roman (and later Habsburg) Empire. At the eastern end of the main square, the **tourist office** (071-66 23 00; www.tourismephilippeville.be; Rue de la Balance 2; 9am-5pm Mon-Fri year-round, 10am-3pm Sat Mar-Nov & 10am-3pm Sun Jul & Aug) organises fascinating 90-minute guided walks through sections of the fort's subterranean passageways, the *souterrains*, of which more than 10km remains. Philippeville is easily accessed by train (€5.70, 45 minutes) or bus (€3.20, one hour) from Charleroi-Sud.

The walks start with a useful introductory video and culminate at little **Chapelle des Remparts** (Blvd de l'Enseignement), a unique chapel fashioned from the citadel's former gunpowder store.

L'Eau de Heure

In wilderness-light Belgium, this series of forests and small reservoir lakes has cachet, and an enterprising series of outdoor activities make it a popular family destination. You can kayak, mountain bike, walk lakeside paths, skydive, sail, windsurf, zipline, waterski and much more. Starting points for most activities are around the **Plate Taille visitor centre** (071-50 92 92; www.lacsdeleaudheure.be; Rte de la Plate Taille 99, Boussu-lez-Walcourt; 10am-5pm Oct-Mar, to 6pm Apr-Jun & Sep, to 7pm Jul & Aug;) FREE.

Activities

Aquacentre WATER PARK

(www.lacsdeleaudheure.be; Rue du Bois du Four; adult/child €10/8) This new water park offers indoor and outdoor pools and a water slide.

Spin WATER SPORTS

(071-31 39 82; www.thespin.be; Rue Crossart 61, Boussu-lez-Walcourt; 1/2/4hr €20/30/40; daily Jul & Aug, Wed-Sun Apr-Jun, Sep & Oct) Offers a waterskiing experience pulled by overhead cables.

Tours

Dam Tours TOUR

(Centre d'Accueil de la Plate Taille; adult/child €7.50/6.50; 11.30am & 3.30pm Wed, Sat & Sun Sep-Jun, 11.30am, 1.30pm, 3.30pm & 5.30pm daily Jul & Aug) From the Plate Taille visitor centre in Boussu-lez-Walcourt, tours take you up the dam's brutalist concrete tower for a lake-wide panorama.

Le Crocodile Rouge BUS TOUR

(www.lecrocodilerouge.be; adult/child €17/15; 1-4pm Wed, 1-6pm Sat & Sun Apr-Jun, Sep & Oct, 1-6pm daily Jul & Aug) Le Crocodile Rouge runs an amphibious bus tour that drives off the shore and splashes straight into the lake. Other kid-friendly activities are grouped under the same name; all start from the Plate Taille visitor centre in Boussu-lez-Walcourt.

Mariembourg

Mariembourg was once a highly important citadel-fortress guarding the border of the Spanish Low Countries. Its capture by the French in 1555 was a major blow to the Spaniards, who hurriedly built Philippeville to replace it. Mariembourg retained its powerful wall bastions until 1852, when they were removed as proof of Belgium's pledged neutrality.

Activities

Chemin de Fer à Vapeur des 3 Vallées TRAIN RIDE

(060-31 24 40; http://cfv3v.in-site-out.com; Chaussée de Givet 49; adult/child €12.50/8.50; weekends Easter-Oct, daily Jul & Aug) Mariembourg's principal attractions are these trains running through charming scenery to Treignes (40 minutes) from a station 800m southeast of the centre. Check the website's timetables for steam *(vapeur)* trains, which usually leave at 2.20pm and 4.50pm on 'green' dates (mostly midsummer), returning 80 minutes later.

Sleeping

★**Château Tromcourt** B&B €€
(060-31 18 70; www.tromcourt.com; Hameau de Géronsart 15, N939; s/d €60/80, breakfast €10; P) Around 3km northwest of Mariembourg, near the N5, is this welcoming family-owned 1660 stone mansion with turret, banquet hall and lots of imitation old master paintings. The lounges are packed with re-gilded classic furniture and ceramic fireplaces. Rooms are well appointed and have soft beds. A great attraction is the chance to hand feed the wallabies, llamas and deer.

Drinking & Nightlife

Brasserie des Fagnes BREWERY
(060-31 15 70; www.fagnes.com; Rte de Nismes 26 (N939); 11am-8pm Tue-Thu, 10am-10pm Fri-Sun;) Around 1km south of Mariembourg towards Nismes, this tourist-oriented microbrewery creates four well-balanced Super des Fagnes beers (€2.70). Try them in a large part-timbered bar-*café* incorporating the working brewery equipment and a cute free museum of historic brewing paraphenalia. There's pleasant outdoor seating and decent-value food also.

Getting There & Away

Trains stop here en route between Charleroi (€7.30, 55 minutes) and Couvin (€2, seven minutes).

Nismes

A short detour from Mariembourg, the centre of Nismes sees a pretty river neatly dividing the old church from a fanciful neo-Gothic castle (now the town hall) set amid extensive public parkland. This contains a restored series of water gardens that you can tour by **motorboat** (060-31 16 35; www.viroinval.be; per 30min/1hr €12/23, plus deposit; 11am-6pm Wed-Fri, 10am-5pm Sat & Sun Easter-Oct, 10am-6pm daily Jul & Aug) rented from beside the flag-draped central bridge.

RURAL SLEEPING

Much of the rural accommodation here and elsewhere in Wallonia is in farmstays and *gîtes* (www.gitesdewallonie.be). These are great options that usually require advance bookings.

It's hard not to salivate at the aromas of butter and garlic wafting from **La Bonne Auberge** (060-31 10 90; www.bonneauberge.be; Rue Bassidaine 20; mains €15-20; 11am-3pm & 6-9pm Thu-Tue;). Despite the cosy country elegance, the delicious local food comes at unexpectedly affordable prices.

Bus 56 heads from Namur to Nismes (€5.30, 1½ hours) via Philippeville, Mariembourg and Couvin roughly hourly weekdays (every two hours on Saturday, one only on Sunday night).

Couvin

POP 14,000

A modest railway terminus, with a main street choked by trucks and traffic, Couvin is the Botte's biggest town. The old town's central knoll of austere grey-stone buildings has a passing appeal.

Sights

Bunker d'Hitler 1940 BUILDING
(http://tourisme.couvin.com; Place St-Méen, Brûly-de-Pesche; adult/child €6/5.50; 10.30am-6pm Tue-Sun Easter-Sep, plus 10.30am-5pm Sat & Sun Oct-early Nov) For 22 days in 1940 the Nazi leader commanded Western Front operations from deep forest here, 8km south of Couvin. The very modest concrete bunker can be visited, along with two pavilions that house some explanatory displays, but you'll need wheels.

Sleeping & Eating

Nulle Part Ailleurs FRENCH, BISTRO €€
(060-34 52 84; www.nulle-part-ailleurs.be; Rue de la Gare 10-12; mains €21-22, bistro mains €18-21; 11.30am-2.30pm & 7-9.30pm Wed-Sun;) A typical grey-stone building on Couvin's main road combines an excellent restaurant, specialising in carefully sourced French and local produce, and a characterful little bistro. Upstairs, five guest rooms (€80/90 per single/double) make a reasonable stab at country-cute decor, most successfully in 'Liseron'.

Getting There & Away

Trains run to Couvin from Charleroi-Sud (€8.10, one hour) every couple of hours. Bus 56 runs from Namur (€5.30, 1½ hours) via Philippeville and Mariembourg.

Chimay

POP 9900

Globally celebrated for its Trappist beer, Chimay is a classic castle town whose compact Grand Place is overshadowed by a looming, extravagantly spired 16th-century church. It's a good base for exploring the surrounding network of pretty lanes and rural villages.

Sights & Activities

Château de Chimay CASTLE
(060-21 45 31; www.chateaudechimay.be; Rue du Château 18; adult/child €9/7; tours 2.30pm & 3.45pm Tue-Sun mid-Mar–mid-Nov, plus 11am Thu-Sat & 2.30pm & 3.45pm Mon Jul & Aug) Off the Grand Place, a stone archway leads to this 15th-century castle, much damaged, altered and renovated over the years. It's the traditional home of the princes of Chimay and well worth a visit - self guided, with an iPad providing video and audio information; there's also a 3D film.

Espace Chimay MUSEUM
(Auberge de Poteaupré; www.chimay.com; Rte de Poteaupré 5; exhibition €6.50; bar-restaurant 10am-6pm Tue-Thu, 10am-10pm Fri-Sun Nov-Mar, plus 10am-6pm Mon Apr-Jun, Sep & Oct, 10am-10pm daily Jul & Aug) Chimay's world-famous Trappist beers have been brewed since the 1860s at austere **Abbaye de Scourmont** (www.scourmont.be; church 7am-8pm), 9km south of Chimay. There are no brewery visits, but 1km before the abbey, this visitor centre has a small interactive exhibition explaining the abbey's brewing, cheesemaking and spiritual life. The entry fee gets you one 25cL beer, but you might feel it's money better spent to simply sit in the excellent *café*-restaurant reading the menu's potted history.

Various beer-and-cheese taster combinations are available, as well as low-priced dishes from sandwiches to full meals (mains €9 to €16). This is the only place where you can drink the light Chimay Dorée on tap. The seven high-quality guest rooms (€80 per double) are handy if you find you've sipped too much to drive.

Sleeping

Camping Chimay CAMPGROUND €
(060-51 12 57, 0476 99 85 80; www.chimaycamping.be; Allée des Princes 1; car, tent & 2 adults €11; Apr-Oct; P) Chimay's cramped camping ground is central yet relatively peaceful.

★ **Petit Chapitre** B&B €€
(060-21 10 42; www.lepetitchapitre.be; Place du Chapitre 5; s €75, d €85-105; check-in 4-6pm; P) In Chimay's heart, this delightful place offers charming B&B in a turreted, wisteria-draped building full of antiques and flamboyant furnishings. Each room has a very distinct character. It's directly behind the church, with a tiny flower-decked front terrace.

Information

Tourist Information (060-21 98 84; www.butteduhainaut.com; Rue de Noailles 6; 9am-6pm Jul & Aug, 9.30am-5pm Mon-Fri, 10am-5pm Sat & Sun;) Just east of the Grand Place.

Getting There & Away

BUS

Couvin Bus 60/1 (€3.20, 50 minutes) runs six-plus times weekdays, twice Saturday and once Sunday.

Charleroi Bus 109a (€3.20, 1¾ hours) runs via Beaumont six to 14 times daily.

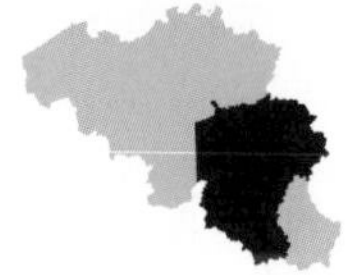

The Ardennes

LANGUAGES: FRENCH (& GERMAN AROUND EUPEN)

Includes ➡

Best Places to Eat

- ➡ La Calèche (p213)
- ➡ La Table des Sépulcrines (p217)
- ➡ Terra Terrae (p228)
- ➡ Maison Bouillon et Fils (p220)

Best Places to Stay

- ➡ La Malle Poste (p213)
- ➡ Ne5t (p208)
- ➡ Hôtel Neuvice (p228)
- ➡ Hôtel Beau Séjour (p218)
- ➡ Le Clos des Recollets (p221)

Why Go?

If you're looking for outdoor activities, fresh air and greenery, head for Belgium's southeastern corner. Here you'll find meandering rivers, dramatic cave systems, forested hills and deep valleys. There are some really special landscapes, with picture-perfect castle-topped medieval towns crowded into sweeping bends in a verdant-banked river. Eating is also great in the Ardennes, with pâtés, hams and other piggy products to the fore.

There's a wealth of things to see and do. It's Belgium's best zone for outdoor activities, while Stavelot, Malmedy and Eupen burst with revelry during their fabulous carnivals. Some of the Meuse Valley cities look dauntingly grimy, but they have plenty of attractions as well as lots of hidden history beneath the careworn exteriors.

Main towns are accessible by train and bus but to really appreciate the rural highlights you'll need a car or strong cycling legs.

Driving Distances

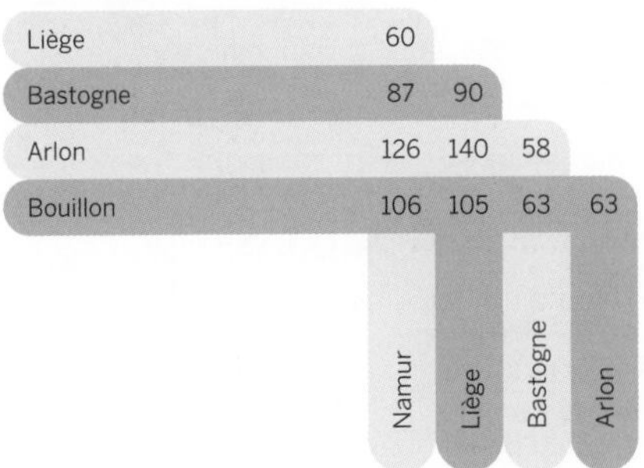

	Namur	Liège	Bastogne	Arlon
Liège	60			
Bastogne	87	90		
Arlon	126	140	58	
Bouillon	106	105	63	63

The Ardennes Highlights

1. Driving stunning riversides to Belgium's finest view at **Rochehaut** (p217)
2. Descending towards the centre of the earth at **Hotton** (p220) or **Rochefort** (p212)
3. Paddling picturesque rivers from pretty **La Roche-en-Ardenne** (p219)
4. Exploring the diverse attractions of **Liège** (p223), then enjoying its vibrant eating and nightlife scene
5. Visiting picturesque **Abbaye Notre Dame** (p218) in Orval, then sipping the monks' brews
6. Marching the ramparts of the atmospheric Crusader-era castle at **Bouillon** (p215)
7. Remembering the fallen at Bastogne's marvellous **war museum** (p239)
8. Hiking the moorland landscape of the **Hautes Fagnes** (p236)
9. Relaxing in rural perfection at sweet little **Crupet** (p210)
10. Celebrating Carnival at the **Laetare** (p237) in pretty Stavelot

Namur

POP 110,700

Despite its modest size, Namur (Namen in Dutch) is the 'capital' of Wallonia and hosts the region's decidedly undramatic parliament in a former hospice building. Historically the city's raison d'être has always been its location at the confluence of the Meuse and Sambre Rivers. It is commanded by a vast former military citadel that was one of Europe's mightiest fortresses until very recent times. Below the citadel, Namur's gently picturesque old-town core has much to discover if you look behind the slightly grubby exterior.

History

Namur's history is interwoven with that of its fortress. Celts and then Romans had military camps here, and in the Middle Ages the Counts of Namur built a well-protected castle on craggy rocks overlooking the river junction. Strengthened under Spanish rule in the 1640s, the castle was captured by the French in 1692, then redesigned as a textbook fortress by Louis XIV's renowned military engineer Vauban. Razed and rebuilt again thereafter, by WWI the fortress was considered impregnable, yet it fell within three days of the German invasion. In WWII Namur suffered again, with heavy bombing causing extensive damage. The citadel continued in military use right up until 1977.

Sights & Activities

The citadel is directly across the Sambre from the town centre. Comparatively upmarket Wépion straggles several kilometres southwest down the Meuse's western riverbank.

The Citadel

★Citadelle de Namur FORTRESS
(www.citadelle.namur.be) Dominating the town, Namur's mighty fortress covers a whole hilltop with ramparts, tunnels and grey walls. What you see now is more 19th and 20th century than medieval, and is compelling, great for strolling and offers terrific views. The best are from a section known as Château des Comtes and the *café* Le Panorama (p210), by the curious art deco sportsground Stade des Jeux. Most open areas, including the rampart footpaths, are accessible at any time.

Be careful not to get locked into the Terra Nova zone whose main gates lock at 6.30pm. Citadel access for pedestrians is on the steep sloping Rampe Verte from Rue des Moulins or via a stairway from Place St-Hilaire. By car use Rte Merveilleuse from behind the 1911 casino building.

Six shuttles (€2) run between the train station and Terra Nova, daily in July and August, weekends at other times. Alternatively take bus 3 (hourly) to the Château de Namur (p208) and stroll downhill from there.

Terra Nova MUSEUM, VISITOR CENTRE
(Rte Merveilleuse 64; adult/child €4/3; ⏲10am-6pm Apr-Sep, to 5pm Oct-Mar) The citadel's central section is a 19th-century former barracks with a new visitor centre exploring the history and architecture of this important military bastion. From here, various guided tours (adult/child €6/5) depart.

Souterrains FORTRESS
(Terra Nova; adult/child €6/5; ⏲3-5 visits daily Apr-Sep, Mon-Fri Oct-Mar) In its later guises, the fortress moved the majority of its key installations underground. Fascinating visits, by tour only, walk you through the citadel's web of dripping tunnels showing you never-tested 1939 gas-proof bunkers and clever Vauban architectural tricks. Be ready for 250 steps and temperatures of around 13°C. Ongoing renovations are to result in an updated experience by 2016 but might restrict access at times.

Parfumerie Guy Delforge PERFUMERY
(www.delforge.com; Château des Comtes; ⏲10am-5.30pm Mon-Sat, 2-6pm Sun) This specialist perfume-maker fills an old stone house with floral aromas and classical music. While it's mostly a shop, there are tours of the cavern-based perfume laboratory on Saturday at 3.30pm (€3.50), plus Monday to Friday during school holidays. Open until 6pm April to October.

La Médiévale WALKING TOUR
(Terra Nova; adult/child €6/5; ⏲10.30am Mon-Fri, 10.30am & 2pm Sat & Sun Apr-Sep) This walking tour explores the citadel's Château des Comtes area. You get to peep inside the small, otherwise closed dungeon museum area of the Logis Comtal and visit a 'medieval garden', though in reality there's little that's medieval about the buildings here, as most were rebuilt for 19th-century military needs.

> **CITADELLE PASS**
>
> A **Citadelle Pass** (adult/child €11/8) gives you entry to the Terra Nova visitor centre, and a tourist train visit to the Souterrains and medieval sections.

Namur

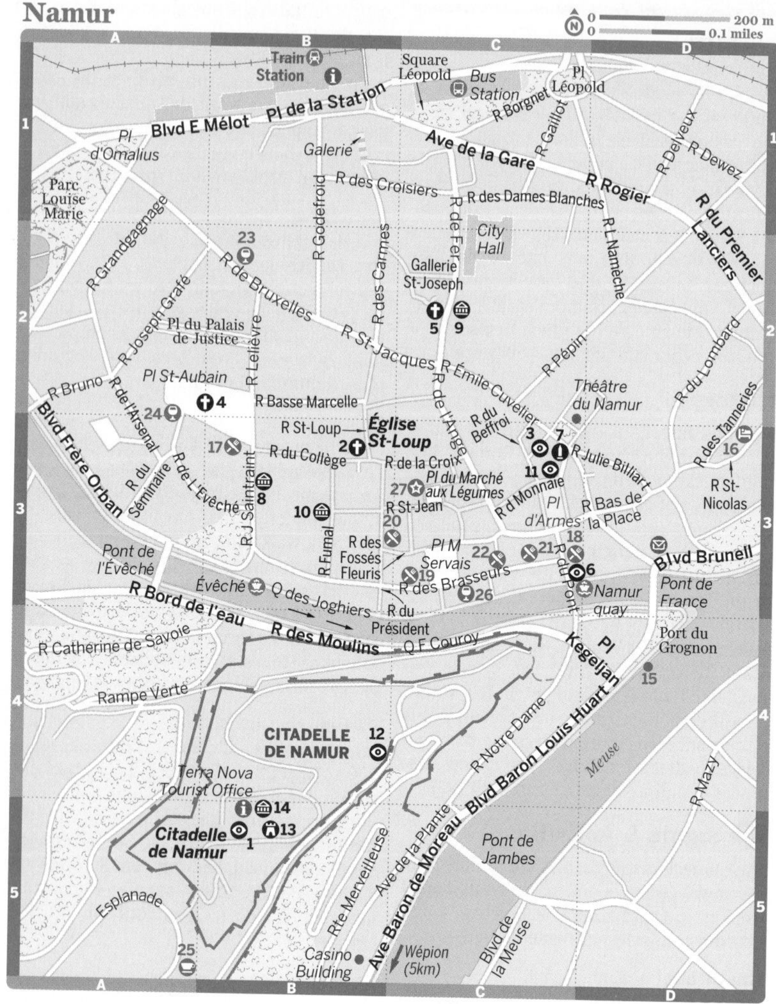

Tourist Train TRAIN

(adult/child €6/5; 10.30am-5.30pm Apr-Sep) This 25-minute ride (with commentary) saves boot leather when visiting the citadel's widely spread attractions. Departures are hourly from Terra Nova or the Esplanade car park.

City Centre

Place d'Armes SQUARE

Namur's central square has been marred by a 1980s department store yet still features the elegant stone-and-brick **Palais des Congrès** (www.namurcongres.be) conference centre, rebuilt in the 1930s with war reparations from Germany (the German army having torched the whole square in 1914). Behind lies the Unesco-listed **Beffroi** (Belfry; Rue du Beffroi), a medieval stone fortress tower with an 18th-century clock spire.

Just off the square, behind a statue of beloved local composer Nicolas Bosret, hides a tiny **stone seat**. This is where the Roi des Menteurs (King of the Liars) is crowned during September's amusingly drunken Fêtes de Wallonie festivities.

Musée de Groesbeeck-de-Croix MUSEUM

(081 24 87 20; www.lasan.be; Rue J Saintraint 3; adult/concession €3/1.50; 10am-5pm Tue-Sun) In a very fine 1753 former abbot's house are

Namur

Top Sights

1 Citadelle de Namur ... B5
2 Église St-Loup ... B3

Sights

3 Beffroi ... C3
4 Cathédrale St-Aubain ... B2
5 Église St-Joseph ... C2
6 Halle al'Chair ... C3
7 'King of Liars' Seat ... C3
8 Musée de Groesbeeck-de-Croix ... B3
9 Musée des Arts Anciens du Namurois ... C2
10 Musée Félicien Rops ... B3
11 Palais des Congrès ... C3
12 Parfumerie Guy Delforge ... B4
Place d'Armes ... (see 11)
13 Souterrains ... B5
14 Terra Nova ... B5

Activities, Courses & Tours

15 Bateaux Meuse ... D4
La Médiévale ... (see 14)

Sleeping

16 Hôtel Les Tanneurs ... D3

Eating

17 Brasserie François ... B3
18 Délices du Grognon ... C3
19 Entre Sambre et Mer ... C3
20 Fenêtre Sur Cour ... B3
21 Le Temps des Cerises ... C3
22 Parfums de Cuisine ... C3

Drinking & Nightlife

23 Le Bouffon du Roi ... B2
24 Le Chapître ... A2
25 Le Panorama ... A5
26 Vino Vino ... C3

Entertainment

27 Piano Bar ... C3

displays of decorative arts in 23 beautifully furnished rooms around a formal courtyard garden. Don't miss the 18th-century kitchen. At the time of research it was closed, as a building in the same complex was being adapted to hold the town's archaeological museum.

Musée des Arts Anciens du Namurois MUSEUM
(☎081 77 67 54; www.museedesartsanciens.be; Rue de Fer 24; adult/child €3/free, audio guide €2; ⏲10am-6pm Tue-Sun) In an 18th-century mansion, this interesting museum displays old artworks from the local region, paintings by 16th-century artist Henri Blès and many religious pieces, including a hoard of priceless Mosan chalices, crosses and reliquaries with a very colourful history. Entry fees rise during temporary exhibitions. Enter opposite the tall, red baroque frontage of the 1655 **Église St-Joseph** (Rue de Fer).

Musée Félicien Rops MUSEUM
(☎081 77 67 55; www.museerops.be; Rue Fumal 12; adult/child €3/free, audio guide €2; ⏲10am-6pm Tue-Sun, daily Jul & Aug) Celebrated local artist Félicien Rops (1833–98), born a few streets away at Rue du Président 33, had a penchant for illustrating erotic lifestyles and macabre scenes as you'll rapidly discover at this eponymous museum.

Halle al'Chair NOTABLE BUILDING
(☎081 23 16 31; www.lasan.be; Rue du Pont 21) Formerly the meat market, this 16th-century riverside building is one of few venerable structures to have survived Namur's history of continual wartime pummellings.

★ **Église St-Loup** CHURCH
(www.eglisesaintloup.be; Rue du Collège) Baudelaire reputedly described this remarkable baroque church as a 'sinister and gallant marvel'. From the purple marble columns, black stone arches, elaborately carved confessionals and complex ceiling tracery sculptured in white tufa, it's a curious and imposing sight. At the time of research, it was being opened by volunteers as often as possible, but hours were variable.

Cathédrale St-Aubain CATHEDRAL
(www.cana.be; Place St-Aubain; ⏲8.30am-4.45pm Tue-Fri, to 7.30pm Sat, 9.30am-7.30pm Sun) This vast Italianate neoclassical cathedral, finished in 1767, is undeniably impressive outside but has a rather remote, mausoleum-like off-white interior and feels a bit uncared for.

Bateaux Meuse BOAT TOUR
(☎082 22 23 15; www.bateaux-meuse.be; Blvd Baron Louis Huart; ⏲Apr-Sep) Offers three daily 50-minute river cruises around central Namur (adult/child €7.50/5.50) and, in July and August, a 3pm ride to Wépion, passing through the impressive lock of La Plante (adult/child return €13/11). Board at the jetty near the Walloon parliament building.

Wépion

Grand early-20th-century turreted homes give a sedate grandeur to this riverside suburb, synonymous with strawberries in any Belgian mind.

Musée de la Fraise MUSEUM
(☎081 46 20 07; www.museedelafraise.be; Chaussée de Dinant 1037; adult/concession €3.50/2.50; ⊙2-6pm Tue-Sun Apr & Sep, 2-6pm Tue-Fri, 11am-6pm Sat & Sun May-Aug) This little museum-cum-info-office in the Wépion area sells strawberry beer, strawberry liqueurs and strawberry jams. In summer it runs guided visits to a little strawberry plantation. The museum is 7km south of central Namur.

Sleeping

City centre accommodation is limited but if you've got wheels there's ample choice along the Meuse Valley and in country villages beyond.

Auberge de Jeunesse HOSTEL €
(☎081 22 36 88; www.lesaubergesdejeunesse.be; Ave Félicien Rops 8; dm €28, €2 off for under 26, HI members 10% discount; ⊙8am-11pm mid-Mar–mid-Oct; @) On a peaceful stretch of river happily away from the busy road, this modernised HI hostel partly occupies the attractive red-brick mansion that was artist Félicien Rops' studio. Good breakfast is included. It's 2.5km south of central Namur; bus 3 runs here from the train station and bus 4 stops nearby.

★**Le Beau Vallon** B&B €€
(☎081 41 15 91; www.lebeauvallonwepion.be; Chemin du Beau Vallon 38; d €70, s/d without bathroom €50/60; P) Set in well-kept lawns with a private chapel, these utterly charming rural *chambres d'hôtes* are within a 1650 stone farmstead maintaining original floorboards, banisters and fireplaces. Rooms have a cheerful cottagey decor and the host family is delightful. It's 11km south of central Namur, off the N92 beyond Wépion. Follow signs for Rougemont golf course.

Hôtel Les Tanneurs HOTEL €€
(☎081 24 00 24; www.tanneurs.com; Rue des Tanneries 13; s/d €85/100, with sauna €125/140; P@) Fashioned out of a renovated 17th-century tannery, this hotel unites modern comfort with historical charm. It's a complex warren of rooms, no two the same. Some are double-level affairs with Jacuzzis while others have rambling rooftop views. The cheapest rooms are very small and less atmospheric, but great value. Breakfast is €11.

Château de Namur HOTEL €€
(☎081 72 99 00; www.chateaudenamur.com; Ave de l'Ermitage; s/d from €105/135; P) Crowning lovely gardens at the top of the citadel park, this hotel looks, at first glance, like a believable tower-fronted castle. In fact the building is a 1930s caprice with rooms in various stages of renovation. You won't find baronial lounges or suits of armour, but the citadel-top location is peaceful and the price is fair.

★**Ne5t** BOUTIQUE HOTEL €€€
(☎081 58 88 88; www.ne5t.com; Ave Vauban 46; r €260-380; P) Tucked away on the shoulders of the citadel hill in an upmarket residential district, this discreet, genteel hotel makes a great spot for relaxation. Located in a venerable farmhouse with extensive, manicured grounds, it offers the full range of spa treatments (not cheap) and feels like a rural retreat. Staff bend over backwards to be helpful.

Royal Snail BOUTIQUE HOTEL €€€
(☎081 57 00 23; www.theroyalsnail.com; Ave de la Plante 23; s/d €150/195; P@) Boasting

MOSAN ART

While 'Mosan' could refer to anything from the Meuse Valley, Mosan art is generally associated with superb Romanesque chalices and crosses of copper, bronze, gold and brass made in the ancient Diocese of Liège. Eleventh-century Huy was initially at the forefront of such metallurgical developments, with a Huy goldsmith thought to be the creator of the fabulous Mosan font now displayed in Liège's Église Collégiale St-Barthélemy (p226). However, the craft soon became so firmly associated with Dinant that one form of fine copperwork remains known today as *Dinanderie*.

One of the last great exponents of Mosan metalwork was Brother Hugo d'Oignies, co-founder of a priory at Oignies, east of today's Charleroi. His late-12th-century masterpieces perfected the use of filigree for decorative features and was an early European experimenter with *niello*, in which a dark copper-alloy inlay highlights delicate lines etched onto a gold or brass background.

Fine examples are exhibited in Namur's Musée des Arts Anciens du Namurois (p207), with more Mosan art on display in Liège at both the Musée de la Vie Wallonne (p225) and Grand Curtius (p226).

plenty of character and a good mix of business and leisure travellers, this sassy, offbeat hotel offers plenty of facilities – though the see-through plunge pool is more visual gag than leisure option – including an enticing on-site restaurant, nifty urban garden and relaxing bar deck. Rooms vary substantially, but all are cheerfully modern. Prices are usually lower than these rack rates.

Eating

City Centre

Délices du Grognon CREPERIE €
(Rue du Pont 15; light meals €10-13; 11.30am-4.30pm Tue-Thu, to 9.30pm Fri & Sat;) Much-loved locally, this cheery choice near the bridge does a wide range of croques (toasted sandwiches) and crêpes, making it the perfect lunch or snack stop. Expect a genuine welcome.

★**Entre Sambre et Mer** SEAFOOD €€
(081 83 55 04; www.entresambreetmer.be; Rue des Brasseurs 110; mains €16-21; noon-2pm & 6-9pm Tue-Sat) Offering great value for quality seafood, this is a family-run restaurant with a warm, unpretentious feel. Daily specials complement a menu heavily weighted towards the sea with very fair prices; delicious oysters and other shellfish are highlights alongside full-of-flavour fish preparations. When the weather's fine, dining in the quiet courtyard alongside is a treat. Try a ceramic cup of Breton cider as an aperitif.

Le Temps des Cerises BELGIAN, FRENCH €€
(081 22 53 26; www.cerises.be; Rue des Brasseurs 22; mains €18-24; noon-2.30pm Tue-Wed, noon-2.30pm & 6-10.30pm Thu-Fri, 6-10.30pm Sat) The food is authentic Walloon and French, the cosy restaurant a slightly twee pastiche of gingham with scarlet-framed mirrors, and the wall graffiti comes courtesy of thespian-star customers including Charlotte Rampling and Benoît Poelvoorde.

Brasserie François BRASSERIE €€
(081 22 11 23; www.brasseriefrancois.be; Place St-Aubain 3; mains €17-24; 10am-11pm Mon-Fri, to 11.30pm Sat & Sun;) This stately 200-year-old building has an interior full of polished brass and waistcoated waiters, yet it remains curiously unpretentious and appeals for a casual drink or its typical range of brasserie meals.

Fenêtre Sur Cour BELGIAN, FRENCH €€
(081 23 09 08; www.fenetresurcour.be; Rue du Président 35; mains €15-22; noon-2.30pm & 6-10pm Mon-Sat, noon-2.30pm Sun) A high-ceilinged 1902 building with down-to-earth touches serves reliable Belgian dishes including *ris de veau* (sweetbreads), *gratinade St-Jacques* (scallops au gratin) and cheap weekday lunches. The restaurant interconnects with co-owned Exterieur Nuit bar: between the two hangs the world's most amusingly useless cable car.

Parfums de Cuisine MODERN FRENCH €€€
(0495 16 84 74; www.parfumsdecuisine.net; Rue de Bailly 10; lunch/dinner menu €26/65; noon-2pm & 7-9pm Tue-Sat) The homey candlelit interior here matches the fuss-free atmosphere and service. The cuisine, however, is rather more sophisticated, with plenty of innovation and subtle flavour combinations at a pretty generous price. Be prepared to take some time over the meal and go with the flow.

Wépion

Le Lodge BRASSERIE €€
(081 40 08 91; www.lodgewepion.be; Chaussée de Dinant 931; mains €16-25; noon-2.45pm & 6-10.30pm;) Riverside at Wépion's northern edge, Lodge's brasserie section turns out tasty, generous portions of Belgian standards, its log-faced walls dwarfed by big river-view windows. Service can be tardy, but the setting is marvellous and there are decent draught beers. Upstairs is the more sedate restaurant.

L'O à la Bouche FRENCH €€€
(081 58 34 83; www.restaurantloalabouche.be; Rue Armand de Wasseige 1; mains €26-34; noon-2pm & 7-9pm Tue-Fri, 7-9pm Sat) Chef Olivier Vanden Branden calls his cuisine 'artisanal' rather than gourmet, but the standards are very high and some French-Belgian classics get an exotic twist. It's just off the main road in the heart of Wépion.

Drinking & Nightlife

The cobbled streets around tree-lined Place du Marché aux Légumes make up the town's liveliest quarter.

★**Vino Vino** WINE BAR
(www.vinovino.be; Rue des Brasseurs 61; 5pm-midnight Tue-Wed, noon-midnight Thu-Sat) Marc runs this little haven of pleasure and he is excellent value for a chat about wine. There's always something interesting available by the glass, and he rustles up plates of absolutely delicious deli products – with standout rabbit or trout rillettes (plates €6 to €14).

LOCAL KNOWLEDGE

SUMMER FUN

Cap Estival (www.capestival.be; ⏲mid-May–late Sep) The open area at the confluence of the rivers Sambre and Meuse is transformed in summer into a sort of open-air Namur living room, centred around a casual outdoor brasserie, where people drop by to flirt, have a drink or meal, watch one of the regular arts performances or let their kids try out the sandpit or weekend bouncy castle.

Le Bouffon du Roi PUB
(www.facebook.com/lebouffonduroi; Rue de Bruxelles 60; ⏲11.30am-1am Mon-Fri, 6pm-2am Sat, 6pm-1am Sun; 📶) Reminiscent of a typical Euro-Irish bar but without the signposts to Killarney, this is popular with students from the nearby university and has a beer garden out the back. With several decent tap options supplemented by regularly switched guest barrels, it's a fine place to try a few brews. Look for the jester's hat in the window.

Le Chapître PUB
(Rue du Séminaire 4; ⏲5pm-1am Sun-Fri, to 2am Sat; 📶) At this convivial and charmingly rustic beer pub, available brews are listed on a lengthy blackboard menu. The Chapître 'house beer' (€3.30) is a highly drinkable blonde. The outdoor tables get lively with students either side of the summer break.

Le Panorama CAFE
(www.lepanorama.be; Esplanade; ⏲10am-last customer; 📶) High in the citadel, this airy, bell-spired pavilion has eagle's-perch views across the Meuse and the woodlands that extend attractively into the distance. Vistas from the spacious terrace are even better. It does a varied menu from snacks to brasserie-style dishes.

☆ Entertainment

Piano Bar LIVE MUSIC
(Place du Marché aux Légumes 10; ⏲9pm-1am or later Mon-Sat) The blandest bar on Namur's liveliest square makes amends by hosting free live music most weekends, and regular events midweek. Check its facebook page for the monthly agenda. Drink prices rise slightly during concerts.

ℹ Information

Tourist Office (☎081 24 64 49; www.namurtourisme.be; Square Léopold; ⏲9.30am-6pm; 📶) At the train station. Additional information booths at the citadel (Terra Nova; ⏲10am-6pm Apr-Sep, to 5pm Wed, Sat & Sun Oct-Mar).

ℹ Getting There & Away

The **train** and **bus stations** are adjacent on the northern edge of the centre. Some buses depart from around the train station.

The following fares are for trains from Namur:

DESTINATION	FARE (€)	DURATION (MIN)	FREQUENCY (PER HR WEEKDAYS)
Brussels	8.90	65	2
Charleroi	5.70	30-50	2-3
Liège	8.90	50	2
Luxembourg City	34.60	120	1
Mons	11.50	65 to 75	2

ℹ Getting Around

Bicycle For short-hop city rides use **Libiavelo** (www.libiavelo.be; membership per day/week/year €1/3/30), Namur's citybike scheme. For hires of over 30 minutes use **La Maison des Cyclistes** (☎081 81 38 48; www.maisonsdescyclistes.be; Place de la Station 1; annual membership €10, plus bike hire per day €3; ⏲11am-7pm Mon, Wed & Fri, 7am-7pm Tue & Thu, plus 9.30am-12.30pm & 1.30-6pm Sat & Sun mid-May–mid-Sep).

Bus From near the train station routes 4, 21, 30 and Dinant-bound 34 pass through Wépion. Convoluted bus route 3 links the youth hostel and the Château de Namur. An all-day city-bus ticket costs €5.

Ferry In summer **Namourette** (www.ville.namur.be; per stop €0.50; ⏲10am-5.30pm Jul & Aug, weekends only Jun & Sep) riverboats link five central jetties two or three times an hour.

Crupet

One of the region's loveliest villages, little Crupet is set in gloriously verdant rolling countryside east of Yvoir. It's locally famous for trout dishes, served in a handful of restaurants. Beside the stone church is an amusingly kitschy grotto shrine, and in the stream valley below is picturesque **Château des Carondelet**, a moated 13th-century tower house. It's private but photogenic from the outside, especially in morning light.

Sleeping

★Le Moulin des Ramiers B&B €€

(☎083 69 02 40; www.moulindesramiers.be; Rue Basse 31; r €125) Beautifully set in the valley below town, this is an oasis of peace in what was once the village mill. It's caringly run, and the host pays genuine attention to guests' needs. Rooms are spacious and very comfortable. You'll generally need to pre-arrange arrivals.

Château de la Poste HOTEL €€€

(☎081 41 14 05; www.chateaudelaposte.be; Ronchinne 25; d €99-300; P 📶) Contemporary colour and humorous twists bring life to this grand 19th-century castle-hotel set in 42 hectares of parkland. It's a spectacular sight, with postcard-perfect perspectives everywhere. Numerous activities are on offer, and there's a family-friendly atmosphere, though a personal touch is lacking. Discounted pricing usually available. Be aware that some rooms aren't in the main building. Around 3km west of Crupet, near Ivoy.

Getting There & Away

Bus 128 heads from Yvoir train station to Crupet (€2.10, 15 minutes) five times weekdays (morning and evening only) and twice on Saturday.

Dinant

POP 13,600

Though over-touristed and traffic-logged, Dinant has a striking setting, strung along a riverbank under spectacular cliffs. One of its claims to fame is as the birthplace of Adolphe Sax, who invented...yes, you guessed it.

Sights & Activities

Église Notre-Dame CHURCH

(Place Reine Astrid; ⏲9am-6pm Apr-Oct, to 5pm Nov-Mar) Imparting gravitas and Gothic grandeur amid the tour coaches, this sits right under the rock face. Indeed, the current church was built when part of the cliff fell away and destroyed the old one in 1227; only a beautiful Romanesque doorway (to the right as you enter) remains of the original. The distinctive bulbous spire was added in the 16th century.

Citadelle de Dinant FORTRESS

(☎082 22 36 70; www.citadellededinant.be; Le Prieuré 25; adult/child €8/6; ⏲10am-6pm Apr-Sep, to 4.30pm Oct-Mar, closed Fri mid-Nov–Mar, closed weekdays Jan) Though sparse on sights, this vast, unadorned 1818 citadel looms menacingly on its clifftop, offering toe-curling views high over town. The entrance price includes the cable car to the top, though you can take on the 408 steps if you need to work off lunch.

Jardins d'Annevoie GARDENS

(☎082 67 97 97; www.annevoie.be; Rue des Jardins 37, Annevoie; adult/child €7.80/5.20; ⏲9.30am-5.30pm Apr-Oct, to 6.30pm Jul & Aug) Laid out in 1758 around the manor house of Charles-Alexis de Montpellier, these gardens are a delightful mix of French, Italian and English styles, incorporating plenty of fountains and tree-lined waterways. Annevoie is 12km north of Dinant.

River Cruises

Several operators along the quay offer trips on the Meuse from April to October, ranging from 45-minute jaunts (adult/child €7.50/5.50) to longer trips to Anseremme or Freÿr. In Freÿr, the riverside Renaissance **château** (☎082 22 22 00; www.freyr.be; Freÿr 12, Hastière; adult/child €8/free; ⏲11am-5pm Tue-Sun Jul & Aug, to 5pm Sat & Sun Sep–mid-Nov & Apr-Jun) boasts very impressive formal gardens.

Bateaux Meuse BOAT TOUR

(Croisières Mosanes; ☎082 22 23 15; www.bateaux-meuse.be) A wide variety of summer river cruises around Dinant and beyond, including trips to Anseremme and Freÿr (adult/child €13/9, two hours return).

UNLUCKY DINANT

From the 12th century, Dinant was a major centre for a form of Mosan copper- and brasswork that's still known today as *Dinanderie* (p208). However, that ended in 1466, when the town was virtually destroyed by Burgundian King Charles the Bold. Why? Because some townsfolk had dared to call him a bastard. Naming the Bishop of Liège as Charles's illegitimate father certainly didn't help either. History repeated itself in WWI when around 10% of the population was executed and much of the town razed in retaliation for resisting the German occupation.

Adolphe Sax, born in Dinant in 1814, proved no luckier than his hometown. He invented a wide range of musical instruments including the saxophone, which he patented in 1846. Yet he died penniless in 1894 after a decade of legal wrangles.

Sleeping & Eating

There are no standout central hotels: head to Crupet with wheels or day-trip from Namur. Restaurants are abundant but also generally desultory, and aimed at package tourists.

Information

Maison de Tourisme (082 22 28 70; www.dinant-tourisme.com; Ave Cadoux 8; 9am-5pm Mon-Fri, 9.30am-5pm Sat, 10am-4pm Sun;) Just across the bridge from the church.

Getting There & Away

Namur is easily accessed by regular train (€4.70, 30 minutes) or bus (€3.20, 45 minutes). Flat riverside bike paths trace much of the route (28km), albeit sometimes joining the busy main road.

Han-sur-Lesse

The Lesse river winds through pretty oak woods, meadows and limestone hills. At Han-sur-Lesse the river tunnels underground forming magnificent caves – the famous **Grottes de Han** (084 37 72 13; www.grotte-de-han.be; Rue Lamotte 2; adult/teen/child €16/14/10; daily Apr–mid-Nov, days vary rest of year). Guided visits (English often available) start after a 10-minute ride in charmingly rickety open-sided tram cars. Stroll through a succession of impressive subterranean galleries, each well endowed with stalactites and especially fine draperies (beautiful translucent 'curtain' formations). The climax is a short sound-and-light show and a cave with stalactites that reflect beautifully in the water. Gradients and steps aren't especially challenging but dress appropriately (13°C) and allow around two hours. May to August departures are every half-hour, dropping to hourly off season. The ticket office is on the main square along with Han's grey-stone church and a **tourist office** (084 37 75 96; Place Théo Lannoy; mountain bikes 2hr/day €10/25; 10am-4.30pm;) that rents out bicycles.

PassHan (adult/teen/child €27/24/17) offers three other attractions with the cave visit. By far the most interesting is the enjoyable 75-minute ride through **Le Parc** (www.grotte-de-han.be; adult/teen/child €16/14/10; approximately half-hourly). Sitting on partly covered truck wagons, you're driven several kilometres past and through woodland and meadow enclosures stocked with wolf, lynx, bison, eagle owls, Przewalski's horses and other rare European fauna. The scenery is very pretty, however, commentary is not in English and summer queues can be annoying. A variant allows you to walk part of it and rejoin the wagon further along.

Regular bus 29 runs nine to 10 times daily from Han-sur-Lesse via Rochefort to the station at Jemelle, on the Brussels–Luxembourg line.

Rochefort

POP 12,500

A very pleasant regional base for exploring this part of Belgium, Rochefort also has a lesser-known gem of a cave system. Almost everything is strung along the main street, known variously as Rue de Behogne, Place Roi Albert 1er and Rue Jacquet. This rises gently from an imposing statue-fronted church, passes the tourist office and continues to the private Château Comtal. Many shops and *cafés* sell Rochefort's famous Trappist beer, but the Abbaye de St-Rémy, where it's brewed (3km north), is closed to the public.

Sights & Activities

★Grotte de Lorette CAVES
(084 21 20 80; www.grotte-de-lorette.be; Drève de Lorette; adult/child €8.50/5; visits 10.30am-noon & 2-3.30pm Sat & Sun Easter-Nov, every 45 minutes 10.30am-4.15pm daily Jul & Aug) This cave system has fewer stalactites than nearby Han, and handling the 626 relatively steep steps is more physical. However, the small-group visits give a vastly more personal experience. Half-lit stairways give a magical hint of the main cave's great vertical depth (65m) and there's a memorable revelation of its full majesty at the end of a visit during an atmospheric light show. It's 500m southeast of Rue Jacquet via Rue St-Gervais.

Malagne RUINS
(084 22 21 03; www.malagne.be; adult/child €6.50/5; 11am-6pm Sat, Sun & school holidays Apr-Oct) On the third Sunday of July, this Gallo-Roman archaeological site comes to life with a whole series of period demonstrations. At other times, the attractive rural ruins are less dynamic and you'll probably value the €3 audio guide to make sense of the excavations, reconstructed mill, experimental archaeological projects and Roman vegetable gardens. It's 2.5km east of Rochefort.

Cycle Sport BICYCLE RENTAL
(084 21 32 55; www.cyclesport.be; Rue de Behogne 59; rental per morning/afternoon/full day €15/20/25, electric bike €20/25/35; 9.30am-

noon & 1.30-6.30pm Tue-Sat, 9.30am-noon Sun) About 200m downhill from the church, Cycle Sport mends and rents bicycles. The tourist office sells useful cycling maps.

Sleeping

Le Vieux Moulin HOSTEL €
(084 21 46 04; www.giterochefort.be; Rue du Hableau 25; adult/under 26 €18/14, membership/sheets €1.55/4.10; P) Pleasant riverside hostel. Zigzag down from the square beside the tourist office, cross the park and it's the orangey-red building directly across the footbridge to the right. Rates include simple breakfast. Regularly booked out by groups.

Les Roches CAMPGROUND
(084 21 19 00; http://les-roches.blogspot.be; Rue du Hableau 26; sites per car, tent & 2 people €22; Apr-Oct; P @) Just below town by the river, this has grassy sites separated by hedges. You get free entry to a nearby outdoor pool.

Margot'L GUESTHOUSE €€
(084 34 51 79; www.margotl.be; Place Albert Premier 19; s/d €55/70;) On the main street, this modern bolthole is run by the excellent La Malle Poste hotel and features six cute rooms with comfortable modern design, softened by a few touches in typically rustic French style. No breakfast.

Le Vieux Logis HOTEL €€
(084 21 10 24; www.levieuxlogis.be; Rue Jacquet 71; s/d/tr/q €79/90/115/140; check-in to 6pm;) Facing the château, with shutters and window-boxes on its stone facade, this atmospheric old place has lashings of antique furniture and wooden panelling, plus an almost medieval courtyard garden. Up creaky stairs, rooms have period furniture but dated bathrooms. Wi-fi doesn't reach most of them. If you love character rather than facilities, you'll love it here.

Le Vieux Carmel B&B €€
(084 44 53 41; carogoethals@hotmail.com; Rue Jacquet 61; d €75-85; P) Once part of a 17th-century convent, the stone-floored guest lounge features a boar's head and a roaring fire in winter (the 'Ardennes TV'). Most intriguing of the five rooms is 'Denise' with its claw-foot bathtub on the old floorboards facing the bed. 'Charlotte' and smaller 'Helena' are less magical.

★ **La Malle Poste** HOTEL €€€
(084 21 09 86; www.malleposte.net; Rue de Behogne 46; s/d incl breakfast €130/170, small s/d €90/130; P) Enter through a 17th-century coaching inn that houses the indulgent restaurant, above which are two particularly impressive suites featuring metal four-poster beds. A stone tunnel, complete with 8000-bottle wine collection, links to a subterranean swimming pool and sauna; above, large modern rooms feature Jacuzzis. In the eaves, cheaper, smaller 'Cocher' rooms have Ardennaise decor. Lovely garden. Standout place.

Eating & Drinking

Croquant Caramel CAFE €
(Ave de Forest 2; light meals €5-9; 10.30am-6pm Fri-Wed;) This thoroughly modernised 1952 cafe serves pancakes, waffles, good coffee and great ice cream at Rochefort's main junction. It does a range of daily dishes which might feature quiche or raclette. Outdoor seating puts you in the heart of things.

La Gourmandise ARDENNAISE €€
(084 22 21 81; www.la-gourmandise.be; Rue de Behogne 24; mains €13-26; 10am-10pm;) It's a likeably casual eating scene at this main-street spot that combines a shop selling regional produce with a lounge bar and restaurant area. There's a wide-ranging menu served throughout the afternoon, though the charcoal grill is only fired up at mealtimes. Food is tasty, and generously proportioned: think slabs of pâté and charcuterie, Ardennes fry-ups but also several salad choices.

Couleur Basilique BISTRO €€
(084 46 85 36; www.couleurbasilic.be; Rue de Behogne 43; mains €16-24; noon-2pm & 7-11pm Thu-Mon;) Beside the basilica church, this fresh, youthful bistro has a secret weapon in its rear terrace, with views over the river valley. There's a bit of Asian fusion going on, as well as steaks, pork knuckle and tasty salads.

★ **La Calèche** FRENCH, ARDENNAISE €€€
(084 21 09 86; www.malleposte.net; Rue de Behogne 46; menus €35-70, mains €22-45; Fri-Tue;) In the beautifully re-appointed 17th-century building that forms the entrance to La Malle Poste hotel, La Calèche offers elegant fine dining on pressed tablecloths, with an open kitchen, decent-sized portions and friendly staff. In season, the menu often features game. There's an excellent if pricey wine list; make sure you see the cellar.

Information

Tourist Office (084 34 51 72; www.valdelesse.be; Rue de Behogne 5; 8am-5pm

Mon-Fri, 10am-5pm Sat, 10am-4pm Sun Oct-Mar, 8am-5pm Mon-Fri, 9.30am-5pm Sat & Sun Apr-Sep, to 6pm Mon-Fri Jul & Aug; ⓦ)

Getting There & Away

Regular bus 29 runs nine to 10 times daily from Rochefort to the nearby station at Jemelle (€2.10, 15 minutes), on the Brussels–Luxembourg line.

Lavaux-Sainte-Anne

The photogenic **Château Lavaux-Sainte-Anne** (www.chateau-lavaux.com; Rue du Château; adult/child €8/5; ⏲10am-6pm Wed-Sun, daily Jul & Aug) is a moated 1450 fortress converted into a lordly mansion in 1634. The four towers come with machicolations and bell-shaped domes, while furnished rooms display various exhibits from local crafts to hunting trophies. Tickets include entry to a three-pond wetland with attractive views back to the castle.

Attached to a brasserie-*café*, just above the castle, loveable **B&B 4 Lunes** (☎084 38 84 26; www.les4lunes.be; Rue du Chateau 1b; d one/two nights €80/125; ⏲Feb-Dec; ⓦ) combines modern decor and elements of exposed brickwork.

On the main square is renowned upmarket restaurant **Lemonnier** (☎084 38 88 83; www.lemonnier.be; Rue Lemonnier 82; mains €38-54, degustation €82; ⏲noon-2pm & 7-9pm Thu-Mon; ⓦ) with nine bright, fresh guest rooms (doubles from €130), a memorably contemporary garden and a super-stylish sitting room.

Bus 166a from Jemelle station via Rochefort reaches here one to two times weekdays, but not during school holidays.

Redu

At junction 23 of the E411, the **Euro Space Center** (☎061 65 64 65; www.eurospacecenter.be; adult/child €11/8; ⏲10am-7pm Jul & Aug, to 5pm or 6pm rest of year, last entry 2hr before closing; 👪) is a family-oriented mix of fun and education including a long series of movies and gadgets followed by a simulator ride. For €6 extra a bungee-style contraption offers the sensation of moon walking at one-sixth of Earth's gravity, and a planetarium show is another €4. Outside (no ticket necessary) there's a labyrinth quiz and a solar system built to scale.

Around 3km west, sweet little **Redu** (www.redu-villagedulivre.be) is a village full of secondhand and antiquarian bookshops. Redu's big bash is the **Nuit-du-livre** (⏲1st Sat of Aug) when bookstalls open all night and fireworks pop at midnight. Two of the village's tavern-restaurants offer inexpensive guest rooms.

Bus 61 runs to Redu two to four times weekdays from Libramont, where there's a train station.

St-Hubert

POP 5700

Cutting across country between Redu (or Rochefort) and Bastogne you'll pass through an area rich with deer and wild boar where the ancient abbey town of St-Hubert bills itself as 'European Capital of Hunting and Nature'.

Sights & Activities

Basilique des Saints-Pierre-et-Paul CHURCH
(www.basiliquesainthubert.be; Place de l'Abbaye; ⏲9am-6pm Apr-Oct, to 5pm Nov-Mar) The grey stone church is the town's main sight. Its netting-draped late-Gothic interior has fine 1733 oak choir stalls topped by cross-headed stags, reflecting the legend of St Hubert, whose grave here made the former abbey into a major pilgrimage site from the 9th century. Guided visits (several languages) cost €1.50, or €2.50 including the crypt.

On **St-Hubert's Day** (⏲early Nov), the square outside hosts one of Belgium's weirder religious ceremonies as priests bless a menagerie of dogs, along with their owners' bread!

Fourneau St-Michel MUSEUM
(☎084 21 08 90; www.fourneausaintmichel.be; adult/child €5/2; ⏲9.30am-5pm Tue-Sun Mar-Nov, to 5.30pm daily Jul & Aug; 👪) Around 10km north of St-Hubert towards Nassonge, Fourneau St-Michel is an open-air museum of 'Walloon life', with rustic old buildings stretching across 200 acres.

Walking

The thick forest north of town has several marked paths for day walks, including two of nine to 10 kilometres (Les Abanages and Plain de Saint Michel), the Roi Albert (11km) and Bilaude (20km). Ask at the tourist office that was due to open opposite the church at last visit; some information is at www.saint-hubert-tourisme.be

Sleeping & Eating

★**L'Ancien Hôpital** BOUTIQUE HOTEL €€
(☎084 41 69 65; www.ancienhopital.be; Rue de la Fontaine 23; s €65, d €99-120, chapelle €145;

P) St-Hubert's most appealing hotel, this six-roomer is a fully modernised 17th-century hospice and 19th-century royal hunting lodge with a fine restaurant. It's just downhill and around the corner from central Place du Marché.

Romain des Bois ARDENNAISE €€
(061 40 01 96; www.romaindesbois.be; Place du Marché 18; mains €13-18; noon-9.30pm Wed-Sun;) Facing the basilica, an all-wooden interior is festively decorated with furniture made from tree trunks, hats and wine bottles. Try the risotto with wild forest mushrooms.

Getting There & Away

St-Hubert is a ride (€3.20, 30 minutes) on bus 51 or 162b from Libramont station, on the main Brussels–Namur–Luxembourg City line. Bus 5 runs to closer but less useful Poix station. All run Monday to Friday only.

Bouillon

POP 5400

Dreamily arrayed around a tight loop of the Semois River, pretty Bouillon is protected by its gloriously medieval castle, gnarled and grim up on the hill. On a summer evening, limpid light and reflections in the water can make this one of Belgium's prettiest towns.

Sights

★Château de Bouillon CASTLE
(061 46 62 57; www.bouillon-initiative.be; Rue du Château; adult/child €7/5; 10am-7pm Jul & Aug, to 5pm or 6pm Feb-Jun & Sep-Dec, weekends only Jan; P) Slouching like a great grey dragon high on the central rocky ridge, Belgium's finest feudal castle, accessed by two stone bridges between crags, harks back to 988, but it is especially associated with Crusader knight Godefroid (Godefroy) de Bouillon, whose name you'll hear a lot in these parts (p216). The super-atmospheric castle still sums up everything you might wish for – dank dripping passageways tunnelling into the hillside, musty half-lit cell rooms, rough-hewn stairwells and many an eerie nook and cranny to discover.

It's worth investing in the audio guide (€2) or guidebook (€1.50) for background info. Daytime entry includes the open-air bird shows (11.30am, 2pm and 3.30pm March to October) when trained 'wig-snatching' owls, hawks and eagles swoop low over spectators' heads. To really get the heebie-jeebies, try the nighttime **torchlight tour** (adult/child/torch €10/7/2.50; 10pm Wed-Sun Jul & Aug). Book ahead.

> **COMBO TICKET**
>
> A **combination ticket** (adult/child €14.50/10) is available for the castle, Musée Ducal and Archéoscope, or just the first two (€9.50/6).

Musée Ducal MUSEUM
(061 46 41 89; www.museeducalbouillon.be; Rue du Petit 1; adult/child €4/2.50; 10am-6pm Easter-Sep, to 5pm Oct-Dec & Feb-Easter) Below the castle, this museum spreads over two historic houses and incorporates an antique smithy. Displays highlight Godefroid de Bouillon's life (p216), the First Crusade, the local metallurgy industry and local artist Albert Raty (1889–1970). The folklore section is only open in summer.

Archéoscope Godefroid de Bouillon MUSEUM
(061 46 83 03; www.archeoscopebouillon.be; Quai des Saulx 14; adult/child €6.25/4.95; 10am-5.30pm daily May-Aug, Tue-Sun Sep-Dec & Feb-Apr) On the eastern riverbank – enter via the tourist office – in a 17th-century former convent building, Bouillon's flashiest attraction is designed to bring Godefroid's story to life. Visits start every 35 minutes with a multilingual film, after which you walk through the screen into a darkened space moodily showing off a replica of Godefroid's Jerusalem tombstone.

Tombeau du Géant VIEWPOINT
(Rue Moulin du Rivage, Botassart) The Ardennes' most celebrated panoramic viewpoint, the 'Giant's Tomb' encompasses a perfect hoop of river valley around 5km north of Bouillon (but 10km by road), from which it's accessible on an interesting circular hike.

Activities

The tourist office sells excellent walking and cycling maps great for exploring the extensive oak and beech forests surrounding Bouillon. The gentle meanders of the Semois offer peaceful kayaking. As well as Bouillon operators, there are also kayak outfits in Alle (p217) and Vresse (p217).

Semois Kayaks KAYAKING
(0475 24 74 23; www.semois-kayaks.be; Blvd Vauban; Easter-Sep) Organises kayak trips

GODEFROID DE BOUILLON

This crusader knight is seen as one of Belgium's old heroes, though the actions of his army would receive few medals today.

Born around 1058, Godefroid (Godfrey) sold the ducal castle of Bouillon to the prince-bishop of Liège in 1096, using the money to lead one of three Crusader armies across Europe to the Holy Land. Well before meeting their Muslim foes, Godefroid's army seriously degenerated in both number and ethics, slaughtering thousands of Jews in towns across Germany soon after setting off.

It took three years to reach Jerusalem. The crusader soldiers breached the city walls on 15 July 1099 and proceeded to massacre an estimated 40,000 Muslims and Jews. According to a contemporary account, six months after the slaughter, the streets still reeked of rotting bodies. Victorious Godefroid was offered the title 'King of Jerusalem' but settled instead for 'Defender of the Holy Sepulchre'. He died, perhaps poisoned, a year later, but his brother Baudouin reigned on, keeping the Holy Land 'Belgian' for several more years.

around the Tombeau de Géant to Poupehan (€18 per person, 15km) and from Poupehan to Frahan-sur-Semois (€15 per person, 5km).

Les Epinoches KAYAKING
(061 25 68 78; www.kayak-lesepinoches.be; Faubourg de France 29; Easter-Oct) Takes you by minibus to Dohan (one-/two-person kayak €20/36, 14km east) and other destinations then lets you kayak back.

Sleeping

B&B Adam B&B €
(061 46 71 56; guyadam10@skynet.be; Rue du Brutz 10; tw without bathroom €33, breakfast €4) Two *chambres d'hôtes* rooms in an utterly charming antique cottage backing onto a green, art-filled little short cut up to the castle. The kitchen, replete with homemade jams, is almost a museum of rustic style. English-speaking host Guy brims with delight at explaining the region's fabulous hiking routes (laminated maps available to guests).

It also has two great-value cottages alongside. Les Miquelets, sleeping two to three adults, costs €273 per week, while larger Le Flores is €375 to €451. Various off-season deals, including shorter stays, are available.

Auberge de Jeunesse HOSTEL €
(061 46 81 37; www.lesaubergesdejeunesse.be; Rte du Christ 16; dm/tw €24/66, under 26 €2 off, HI members save 10%; closed Jan; P) Perched on a ridge, this homely HI hostel has breathtaking views over the castle, river and town. If walking from the bus station turn left, follow Rue des Champs to the T-junction, turn right and wind up into Rte du Christ. From central Bouillon, take a short cut up stairs near Place St-Arnould. Reserve ahead.

Camping Halliru CAMPGROUND €
(061 46 60 09; halliru@bouillon.be; Rte de Corbion 1; per adult/child/camp site €3.20/1.70/4.80; Apr-Sep; P) South of town 1.5km along the river. Go through the tunnel under the castle and turn left.

★**Hôtel Panorama** HOTEL €€
(061 46 61 38; www.panoramahotel.be; Rue au Dessus de la Ville 25; s/d €80/90, superior d €110-140; P) From outside it's a dated Swiss ski-lodge, but the inside decor is an attractive mix of russets and browns, art prints and the odd Indian cabinet. Nearly all rooms have fine views, there's a gastronomic restaurant (menu €45), spa featuring Jacuzzi (with view) and plunge pool, and four different 'flavours' of guest lounge. A very relaxing place to unwind.

La Ferronnière HOTEL €€
(061 23 07 50; www.laferronniere.be; Voie Jocquée 44; d incl breakfast €102-140; P) This charming ivy-clad mansion, 500m northeast of the centre, is decorated in a fresh, lightly classical style. The unique feature is a beautifully maintained little garden and dining terrace (menus €38 to €68) with a perfectly framed distant castle view. There's a pretty new spa annexe too.

Auberge du Moulin Hideux HOTEL €€€
(061 46 70 15; www.moulinhideux.be; Moulin Hideux 1, Noirefontaine; r/ste €205/255, breakfast €20; P@) Set in a lovely landscaped garden with ponds, ducks and tennis court in Ardennes forest around 8km from Bouillon, this upmarket former mill offers faultless rooms decorated in posh French country style, and an excellent restaurant. It's consummately relaxing and the welcome from the owners feels genuine.

Eating & Drinking

★La Table des Sépulcrines ARDENNAISE €€
(☎061 32 07 63; www.latabledessepulcrines.be; Quai des Saulx 10; mains €18-25; ⏲11am-10pm Fri-Tue, plus Wed Jun-Sep; 📶) A comfortable modern interior in part of the old convent complex on the riverside is Bouillon's best recent arrival. With a generous spirit and inventive eye, the chef creates some wonderfully satisfying dishes based on the surrounding region's produce. It falls between hearty traditional bistro and contemporary fine dining and offers remarkably good value for this quality.

Les Remparts ARDENNAISE €€
(☎061 28 74 76; Quai des Remparts; mains €16-23; ⏲11.30am-2.30pm & 6.30-9.30pm Thu-Tue) Tucked away in a strip of rather mediocre eateries by the river under the castle, this little place is a bit of a squeeze with its small square tables, but it is worth it for authentic local dishes, encompassing trout and plenty of offal, including tripe, sheep's tongue and sweetbreads. It's all very tasty.

La Vieille Ardenne PUB FOOD €€
(☎061 28 79 87; Grand Rue 9; mains €13-20; ⏲10am-midnight, closed Wed Sep-Jun; 📶) Beer flagons dangle from the beams of this compact, traditional Ardennes-style *café*-eatery, and summer tables overflow onto neighbouring pavements. Fair-priced trout and quail are served along with seasonal *gibier* (game) dishes in October and November. Sample *Brasserie de Bouillon's* local historically themed beers.

Information

Maison du Tourisme (☎061 46 52 11; www.bouillon-tourisme.be; Quai des Saulx 12; ⏲10am-6pm Mon-Sat, to 5pm Sun; 📶) By the river opposite the castle.

Getting There & Away

To reach Bouillon, train to Libramont, then take bus 8 (€3.20, 45 minutes, roughly hourly weekdays, twice-hourly weekends).

Bouillon to Vresse

The Semois River forms eccentric loops flanked by vividly green waterside meadows swiftly swallowed in steeply rising wooded valley sides. By car, follow winding roads that roller-coaster between streamside and plateau-top villages. Courbion to Vresse-sur-Semois via Rochehaut is one of Belgium's loveliest drives. Although some riverside meadows are marred by caravan sites, there are many lovely scenes to admire. The river around Vresse and Alle is ideal for kayaking. In autumn the colours here are spectacular.

Regional centre Vresse-sur-Semois has a fortress-like 1786 stone church-tower and an incongruous reconstruction of Belgium's first steam locomotive. Historically, it was a retreat for artists and thinkers, including surrealist poet Jean Cocteau; a gallery exhibits some of the works of the 'Vresse School'. Across its 18th-century bridge (Pont St-Lambert) is the pretty stone hamlet of Lafôret.

Sights & Activities

★Rochehaut VIEWPOINT, VILLAGE
The scenery west of Bouillon reaches a memorable climax at Rochehaut where a long balcony surveys a glorious view down across a perfect river curl enfolded in deep green forests. On the pastoral peninsula deep below is the attractive little hamlet of Frahan-sur-Semois, accessed by a steep footpath and pedestrian bridge.

Centre d'Interprétation d'Art GALLERY
(☎061 58 92 99; www.fondation-chaidron.com; Rue Albert Raty 112, Vresse-sur-Semois; adult/child €5/free; ⏲Apr–mid-Nov 2-5pm, to 6pm weekends Jul & Aug) In the centre of Vresse, this attractive gallery boosts its permanent collection (audio guide included) of painting and sculpture by artists with a connection to the town with a free annual exhibition.

Pont de Claies BRIDGE
(Lafôret; ⏲Jul & Aug) Installed every summer is Belgium's last seasonal footbridge. Originally designed to let tobacco harvesters reach their crops, it's made by placing hazel-weave onto log stilts embedded in the river. The bridge site is 500m down an unpaved track from the church.

Cap Semois KAYAKING, CYCLING
(☎061 50 13 54; http://kayak-capsemois.be; Rue du Perré 79-80, Vresse-sur-Semois; 1-/2-/full day bike rental €20/25, kayak hire & pick-up €28-34; ⏲Easter-Sep) Multisport agent with bike rental, kayaking, rafting and more. Kayak trips range from seven to 18 kilometres and include pick-up.

Récréalle KAYAKING, BICYCLE RENTAL
(☎061 50 03 81; www.recrealle.be; Rue Léon Henrard 16, Alle-sur-Semois; ⏲daily Apr-Sep, Fri-Sun Oct-Mar) This veritable village of activities at Alle, 20km west of Bouillon, has minigolf and winter skating as well as bike rental, kayaking and climbing.

Sleeping & Eating

There are hotels and *chambres d'hôtes* in virtually every village.

★Hôtel Beau Séjour HOTEL €€
(☎061 46 65 21; www.hotel-beausejour.be; Rue du Tabac, Frahan-sur-Semois; s €55, d €90-110; P 📶) Right in the middle of the classic Ardennes view, this valley hotel below Rochehaut is more than just a holiday-snap curiosity: it's worth the descent to discover an authentic village haven. It's not a luxury place, but it's comfortable, cordial and the sort of relaxing spot where you begin to think about jacking in your job and staying forever. Wi-fi doesn't reach most rooms.

B&B Del Campo B&B €€
(☎061 58 71 48; www.bbdelcampo.be; Rue Albert Raty 18, Vresse-sur-Semois; d incl breakfast €75-85; 📶) Opposite the bus stop in Vresse is this solid, foursquare stone house run by an extremely welcoming couple. Comfort and attention to detail are guaranteed aspects of a stay here, whichever of the four colourful contemporary-style rooms you end up in. Evening meals (€20) by arrangement.

Auberge de la Ferme HOTEL €€€
(☎061 46 10 00; www.aubergedelaferme.be; Rue de la Cense 12, Rochehaut; s/d from €105/150; P 📶) Occupying a large proportion of Rochehaut's cottages, this rambling auberge offers good-value rooms in such a wide variety of sizes and styles that they publish their own newspaper full of options. The restaurant-reception is decorated with carpentry tools and, off season, is one of the region's eateries most likely to be open. Rochehaut's very best views are just across the street.

Try the superb Cuvée de Rochehaut (8%, €3.50), a specially brewed double-fermented amber beer.

Mon Manège à Toi FRENCH €€
(☎061 50 21 49; www.monmanegeatoi.com; Mouzaine-sur-Semois; mains €17-22; ⏲noon-8.30pm Fri-Sun, to 3pm Mon, daily Jul-Aug; 📶👪) Amid pristine emerald meadows just west of Alle, a footbridge crosses Renoir-like water scenes to this punnily named village eatery whose centrepiece is a large rocking horse. There's plenty of fish on the menu, including local trout.

Information

Maison du Tourisme (☎061 29 28 27; www.ardenne-namuroise.be; Rue Albert Raty 83, Vresse-sur-Semois; ⏲9am-6pm daily Jul & Aug, 8.30am-5pm Mon-Fri, 10am-5pm or 6pm Sat & Sun Mar-Dec, shorter hours winter)

Getting There & Away

Useful buses are 9, connecting Gedinne train station with Vresse and sometimes Alle, and 43, connecting Vresse, Alle and Rochehaut with Menuchenet, connected with Bouillon by bus.

Orval

None of Belgium's famous beer abbeys is more photogenic than **Abbaye Notre Dame** (☎061 31 10 60; www.orval.be; adult/child €6/3; ⏲9.30am-6.30pm) when its golden sandstone is glowing in soft afternoon light. A Cistercian monastery since 1132, the complex had barely finished a total rebuild when, in 1793, it was wrecked by antireligious French Revolutionary soldiers. Rebuilding only restarted in the 1920s. The evocative ancient ruins were left to one side and can be visited along with an 18th-century pharmacy room, an audiovisual on monastic life (French/Dutch), a medicinal herb garden and a curious museum in the labyrinthine vaults. Visitors are welcome to attend offices in the modern monastery church; it's also possible to stay here (by arrangement) on a spiritual retreat (hotellerie@orval.be), during which you're encouraged to join in the daily cycle of prayers.

The abbey's famous brewery is normally closed to visitors, but 300m from the monastery is Orval's modern tavern, **À l'Ange Gardien** (☎061 31 18 86; www.alangegardien.be; Rte de Orval 3; ⏲11am-9pm daily Jul & Aug, to 9pm Thu-Tue Sep & Oct, to 6pm Mon, Tue & Thu, to 9pm Fri-Sun Nov-Jun; 📶). As well as 'normal' Orval it also serves draught 'Orval Vert', a lighter, hoppier monastery ale available nowhere else. Many meals incorporate Orval beer and/or cheese. Upstairs is an exhibition space and roof terrace with abbey views.

Bus 24 Florenville-Virton passes Orval three to five times weekdays.

La Roche-en-Ardenne

POP 4200

If you're arriving from the west, La Roche makes a sudden dramatic appearance, its evocative ancient fortress ruins crowning the town's central knoll above a tight curl of the verdant Ourthe Valley. At the castle's base, most of the town's facilities are closely huddled along 500m of main street. Locally, the town is well known for its smoked hams, kayaking and WWII decimation.

Sights

Château Féodal CASTLE
(☎084 41 13 42; www.chateaudelaroche.be; adult/child €5/3; ⏰10am-6pm Jul & Aug, 11am-5pm Apr-Jun, Sep & Oct, 1-4pm Mon-Fri, 11am-4.30pm Sat & Sun Nov-Apr) La Roche's picture-postcard 11th-century ruins look especially memorable floodlit on a foggy night and viewed from the Hotton road. There's not a great deal inside but the site makes for pleasant, steep strolls, and in July and August you could spot a ghost. At 10pm sharp! Sometimes closed in bad weather.

Musée de la Bataille des Ardennes MUSEUM
(☎084 41 17 25; www.batarden.be; Rue Châmont 5; adult/child €8/4; ⏰10am-6pm Tue-Sun Apr-Dec, plus Mon Jul & Aug, weekends only Jan-Mar) Waxwork scenes, maps and the odd video provide a competent, if unsophisticated, explanation of La Roche's involvement in the wintry Battle of the Bulge, when 114 villagers perished and 90% of La Roche's buildings were flattened. The personal remembrances of local women are especially poignant.

Grès de la Roche MUSEUM
(☎084 41 12 39; www.gresdelaroche.be; Rue Rompré 28; adult/child €5/3; ⏰11am-5pm Jul & Aug, plus selected weekends & holidays; 👪) Learn about La Roche's two main cottage industries in an imaginative half-hour audio-guided tour (no short cuts!). Press-and-sniff buttons add some fun as you're introduced to kiln-firing and ham-smoking methods. Pottery workshops for children are available in summer. The museum is 500m from Place du Bronze following the river east.

Moulin de la Strument MILL
(www.strument.com; Petite Strument 62; adult/child €4/3; ⏰10am-noon & 2-5pm Sat & Sun Feb-Dec, daily Jul & Aug) The meticulously restored original workings of this three-storey, 19th-century watermill are worth a visit; it's free for guests at the lovely attached hotel.

Parc à Gibier ZOO
(☎084 31 10 15; www.parcagibierlaroche.be; Plateau Deister; adult/child €5.50/3.50; ⏰10am-5pm Easter-Oct, to 7pm Jul & Aug, to 5pm Sat & Sun Nov-Easter; 👪) This is typical of several Ardennes animal parks designed to introduce children to local wildlife, notably deer, wolves and wild boars. It's around 2km northeast of La Roche, most interestingly reached on foot starting out along the path up to tiny Ste-Marguerite Chapel above the castle.

OFF THE BEATEN TRACK

HIKING THE TRANSARDENNAISE

One of the best ways to appreciate the Ardennes scenery is this 160km hiking or mountain-biking route between two of the region's prettiest towns, Bouillon and La Roche-en-Ardenne. It's easily divided into comfortable stages, with accommodation in villages on or close to the route. **Europ'aventure** (☎061 68 86 11; www.europaventure.be) can organise a package for you, with accommodation and baggage transfer.

Activities

The winding Ourthe passes through steep wooded valleys with lovely meadows, making for appealing kayaking (or rafting) when water is high enough (far from certain in summer). Most services drop you at Nisramont (25km, €21) or Maboge (12km, €16) to paddle back to La Roche.

Kayaking-cycling combos (€30) are also possible. Mountain bikes (VTT) can be hired and the tourist office (p220) sells maps detailing cycling and hiking routes.

Ardenne Aventures ADVENTURE SPORTS
(☎084 41 19 00; www.ardenne-aventures.be; Rue de l'Eglise 35) Kayaking, rafting, mountain bikes, horse-riding and more from their base on the main street.

Brandsport ADVENTURE SPORTS
(☎084 41 10 84; www.brandsport.be; Place du Marché 16) Kayaking, mountain bikes, shooting, caving, climbing and zip-lining on a forest 'rope course'. The main base is in Mierchamps village (with simple group accommodation), but at weekends and daily in July and August it opens an office on La Roche's main street.

Sleeping

Le Vieux La Roche B&B €
(☎084 41 25 86; www.levieuxlaroche.com; Rue du Chalet 45; s/d €35/48; 📶) Above a typical family home, five simple, unpretentious but great-value guest rooms share two toilets. Each has a private shower; rear rooms avoid road noise.

Moulin de la Strument HOTEL, CAMPGROUND €€
(☎084 41 13 80; www.strument.com; Petite Strument 62; s/d/ste €83/95/115, sites per person/tent €3.50/10; P📶) The town's most charming hotel (closed January) and camp site (Easter to

October) are nestled next to a babbling stream in a secluded, wooded valley 800m south of the main-street bridge. It's a wonderful rural retreat yet just a short stroll to the centre.

Le Corumont B&B €€
(084 41 14 53; www.lecorumont.be; Rue Corumont 13; d €80-95; P) There is simply no better view of La Roche than the exceptional panorama that's all yours from the private balconies of this warmly welcoming four-room B&B. Decor is colourful and furniture laid out according to feng shui ideas. In fine weather, take breakfast on a sheltered terrace with swing seat. Beds are rather small in the cheaper doubles. Check-in from 5pm.

Les Genêts HOTEL €€
(084 41 18 77; www.lesgenetshotel.com; Corniche de Deister 2; s/d €/86/99;) This loveable family-style hotel boasts sweeping views down towards the river and castle from its terrace, garden and suave yet cosily old-fashioned lounge. Cacti, a grandfather clock and a spurious antique stove add character. The bedrooms show their age a bit but are comfortable enough.

Villa le Monde B&B €€
(084 41 28 16; www.villalemonde.com; Rue du Nulay 9; s/d €68/78;) Run by a young well-travelled Dutch couple, this super little four-room B&B has an airy hostel-style bar lounge with fabulous castle views. It offers great mountain-biking advice and can arrange excursions.

Eating & Drinking

Numerous presentable but unremarkable eateries dot the main street and Place du Bronze.

★ **Maison Bouillon et Fils** DELI €
(084 41 18 80; www.maison-bouillon.be; Pl du Marché 9; light meals €3-12; salon 11.30am-3pm Wed-Sun, shop 8.30am-6.30pm Wed-Mon) This legendary charcuterie shop is packed to the beams with sausages, hams and smoked meats. Peckish? Head next door to the gingham-tableclothed tasting cafe, a local classic. The *tartines* (sandwiches) arrive with a dish of pickles, good washed down with a shot of Prunalet, the local plum liqueur.

L'Apéro ARDENNAISE €€
(084 41 18 31; Rue Clérue 5; mains €12-20; 11.30am-2pm & 6-9.30pm Tue-Sun, plus Mon Jul & Aug) Tight-packed, cosy and run with good humour, this is just down the road from the main bridge and does a decent-value line in local dishes with a dash of Portugal. Game features heavily, and the *civet de sanglier* (wild boar stew) is a favourite.

Information

Tourist Office (084 36 77 36; www.la-roche-tourisme.com; Place du Marché 15; 9am-7.30pm Jul & Aug, 9.30am-5pm Sep-Jun) On the main drag.

Getting There & Away

Bus 15 runs from Marloie on the Brussels–Namur–Luxembourg rail line, to La Roche (€3.20, 30 minutes to one hour) four to seven times daily.

Hotton

Hidden beneath partly-wooded hills 1.7km southwest of Hotton, the **Grottes de Hotton** (084 46 60 46; www.grottesdehotton.com; Chemin de Spéléoclub; adult/child €9/6; 10am-5pm Apr-Oct, to 6pm Jul & Aug, visits 12.30pm, 2pm, 3.30pm Sat & Sun Nov-Mar) are some of Belgium's most awesome caves. Sculpted grottoes sprout pretty stalagmites and weird 'eccentrics' – mini corkscrews or horizontal protrusions apparently defying logic. However, the real highlight is descending a former siphon through upturned vertical strata into a dramatically narrow, 37m-high subterranean chasm. Guided visits (around 80 minutes) can feel overly long and aren't necessarily in English. Tours depart roughly hourly in summer; otherwise call to check departure times. Dress for 12°C and prepare for 580 steps. Between here and town is an Allied war cemetery, with some 600 Commonwealth tombs.

Trains on the Jemelle–Esneux–Liège line stop at Melreux from which bus 11 and 13 runs the short, walkable hop to Hotton.

Durbuy

POP 400

Durbuy's photogenic cobblestone alleys, riverbanks and restaurants are understandably well filled with tourists from across Benelux. In fact, it can be almost unbearably crowded on summer weekends, so try and time your visit for midweek. The village is undeniably handsome, with cute craft shops and eateries housed in solid grey stone buildings in a sculpted river valley.

Sights & Activities

On the main square, the very professional tourist office (p222) has an ATM and plenty of suggestions for attractions to keep you in town (topiary garden, jam-maker, microbrewery, diamond museum, horse-cart rides, etc). Durbuy also has a wide selection of outdoor activities on offer. Activity companies rent mountain bikes, offer bike-kayak combos and have booths in central Durbuy during weekends and summer. Booking is wise at all times.

Château de Durbuy CASTLE
(closed to public) At the heart of Durbuy is this fairly modest riverside castle that dates from 1756, the medieval original having been destroyed under Louis XIV of France.

Le Labyrinthe AMUSEMENT PARK
(www.lelabyrinthe.be; Barvaux-sur-Ourthe; adult/child €13/10; 10am-7pm early Jul-early Oct) Humdrum nearby Barvaux is famous for an annually sculpted labyrinth cut into a maize field to a different design each summer. Allow a few hours. Avoid during or after heavy rain.

Durbuy Adventure ADVENTURE SPORTS
(086 21 28 15; www.durbuyadventure.be; Rue de Rome 1; 9am-6pm Apr-Oct;) Organises a bewildering range of outdoor activities – kayaking, canoeing, mountain biking and more – at several different locations around Durbuy, plus at Barvaux and Rome, a small settlement in between, where they have a karting course, climbing adventures and a lake offering 'waterballs', where kids get 10 hilarious minutes in a walk-on-water plastic bubble.

La Petite Merveille ADVENTURE SPORTS
(086 21 16 08; www.lpm.be) Offers kayaking, mountain biking and a range of climbing activities.

Sleeping

There are numerous hotels and rooms for rent.

La Petite Maison GUESTHOUSE €
(086 21 49 00; www.durbuy-info.com; Rue des Récollects 4; r €50;) Three charming rooms to rent from a gregarious English-speaking owner in the loveliest quarter of town. The Petite Maison itself is just that: a little cubic building that feels like an oversized doll's house. Each well-loved room comes with microwave, toaster, coffee and kettle so you can make your own breakfast. It's phenomenal value, especially for those doing the €150 four-night deal (check in Monday, check out Friday). Prices are for up to three guests.

Camping Le Vedeur CAMPGROUND €
(086 84 11 27; www.durbuyinfo.be; Rue Fond de Vedeur 1; per person €5.50, per tent €5-10; mid-Apr–mid-Oct;) Riverside camping ground with simple facilities an easy stroll from town.

★ **Le Clos des Recollets** BOUTIQUE HOTEL €€
(086 21 29 69; www.closdesrecollets.be; Rue de la Prévôté 9; s/d €108/135;) Harmoniously refurbished rooms are scattered around three delightful interconnecting half-timbered houses above a recommendable upmarket restaurant (Thursday to Monday, menus €34 to €68) that's close to the best in town. Summer diners can spread outside onto an intimate tree-lined square.

Hôtel Victoria GUESTHOUSE €€
(086 21 23 00; www.hotel-victoria.be; Rue des Recollectines 4; d Mon-Thu from €100, Fri-Sun from €120;) A confident melange of old and new, this hotel couldn't be more central. Rooms up the time-worn wooden stairs are inviting and well priced for this quality. Some retain exposed timber beams. There's a modern spa complex and decent bar-restaurant.

Le Sanglier des Ardennes HOTEL €€
(086 213 262; www.sanglier-des-ardennes.be; Rue Comte d'Ursel 14; d €100-140;) Durbuy's classic address showcases a very contemporary sense of urban chic while retaining its enviable site overlooking the river. The 'wellness' spa is an attractive highlight, though the restaurant isn't quite of the same standard.

Eating

Le Louca's Bar TAPAS €
(Rue Recollectines 15; light meals €8-14; 11am-10pm Thu-Tue) This cute little spot has a sweet terrace and an interesting selection of wines from different nations – including Belgium. They do a selection of tapas-sized dishes, as well as cheese platters, salads and daily hot specials.

Le Fou du Roy FRENCH, BELGIAN €€
(086 21 08 68; www.fouduroy.be; Rue Comte d'Ursel 4; mains €16-25; 10am-2.30pm & 6.30-10pm Wed-Sun) A cosy, well-run restaurant in the castle's former concierge quarters, featuring a decor of clocks in one room, modern-meets-farmyard in another, and a tiny triangular handkerchief of garden terrace. Meals run around daily specials, set menus and a short menu of bistro classics.

Aux 10 Clefs BELGIAN €€
(www.aux10clefs.be; Rue Comte d'Ursel 41; mains €11-17; 11am-9pm Thu-Mon) Farmhouse-style place in a 300-year-old building serving

WORTH A TRIP

ACHOUFFE BREWERY

Despite the silly gnomes on the labels, some of the Ardennes' best beers are brewed by **La Chouffe** (☎061 23 04 44; www.achouffe.be; Achouffe; adult/teen/child €9/5/free; ⏰2pm Mon, Wed, Sun or by appointment). The name is a mild pun on Achouffe, the pretty Ourthe Valley village where it's brewed. Brewery visits are mostly by appointment (sign up online) and the three weekly drop-in tours are in Dutch. But if you miss out, there are three appealingly rustic taverns where you can taste their fine brews in driver-friendly *galopin* (180ml) glasses; notably **La Grange** (www.lagrangeachouffe.be; ⏰10.30am-8pm), a friendly pub just across the stream-bridge, with pleasant outdoor tables overlooking a stocked trout pond. The **Chouffe-Shop** (⏰9am-midday & 1-5pm Mon-Fri, 10am-6pm Sat & Sun) sells beer and brewery merchandise.

Achouffe is 4km off the E25 motorway, west of junction 51. There's no useful public transport.

comparatively inexpensive Belgian home cooking along with trout, sandwiches, ice creams and more.

Information

Tourist Office (☎086 21 24 28; www.durbuy-info.be; Place aux Foires 25; ⏰9am-5pm Mon-Fri, 10am-6pm Sat & Sun Sep-Jun, 9am-6pm daily Jul & Aug)

Getting There & Away

The nearest train station to Durbuy is 4km east at Barvaux on the Liège–Jemelle line. Taxi, walk or cycle from there, or catch a bus (lines 10/2, 99), though timetables vary widely. Bus 11/5 goes to Melreux station.

Petite Somme

About 4km west of Durbuy, this attractive hamlet sports photogenic **Château de Petite Somme** behind an open floral lawn. The 13th-century structure has neo-Gothic additions, while the interior mixes beautifully restored gilt mouldings with vividly coloured wall paintings of Vedic deities watched over by enthroned Prabhupada statues. The decor makes sense since this is home to **Radhadesh** (☎086 32 29 26; www.radhadesh.com; Petite Somme 5), headquarters of Belgium's Hare Krishna community. All-comers can drop in at the **vegetarian restaurant** (dishes €5-14; ⏰11am-8pm Apr–mid-Nov, noon-6pm Tue-Sun mid-Nov–Mar; 🌿) that fronts the castle, but to get inside you'll need to join somewhat long **guided tours** (adult/child €6/3; ⏰Dutch & French several daily, English 4pm Sat & Sun) that take in the temple room, climb the tower and watch a 15-minute video on Krishna consciousness.

Buses 11/5 and 99 run here schooldays only from Durbuy.

Huy

POP 21,200

Straddling the Meuse between Namur and Liège, Huy (pronounced 'wee') was one of northern Europe's first chartered cities (1066) and a metallurgical centre within the Prince-Bishopric of Liège. Today, sights that survived WWII are intriguing without being really beautiful. Don't be intimidated by the gigantic, doomsday cooling towers of Tihange nuclear power station 3km east of town. Central Huy is 1.5km south of its train station; wandering its knot of central alleys is rewarding.

Sights & Activities

Collégiale Notre-Dame CHURCH
(treasury adult/child €3/2; ⏰9am-noon & 1-6pm Tue-Sun Apr-Oct, to 4pm Nov-Mar) A bit drab from outside, this Gothic church is rather lovely once you enter, with floor-to-ceiling (almost) stained glass behind the altar and a rose window. The **treasury museum** (admission €3; ⏰2-5pm Wed-Mon Jul & Aug, 2-5pm Sat & Sun Apr-Jun & first half Sep) is focused on four fabulous Mosan chest-reliquaries dating from the 12th and 13th centuries.

Musée Communal MUSEUM
(☎085 23 24 35; Rue Vankeerberghen 20; ⏰2-5pm Tue-Sun Apr-Oct) FREE A tiny alley beside the attractive 1766 town hall leads into cobbled Place Verte, where you'll find sharp-spired Église St-Mengold and the 16th-century Maison Nokin. Mysterious Rue des Frères Mineurs continues east between high, ancient walls, emerging beside the town's main museum. Exhibition rooms are set around an atmospheric 1669 cloister, worth a look even when the museum is shut.

Fort de Huy FORTRESS

(www.huy.be; Chaussée Napoléon; adult/child €4/2; ⌚9.30am-5pm Mon-Fri, 10am-6pm Sat & Sun Apr-Jun & Sep-Oct, 10am-6pm daily Jul & Aug) The centre of Huy is overshadowed by this indomitable stone fortress, an oppressively dour structure that dates from 1818 and was used by German forces in WWII as an interrogation centre. It's reached via a zigzag path starting on the riverside beyond the church. Don't expect views if you don't enter.

Cruises BOAT TRIP

(adult/child €4/3; ⌚2pm, 3pm & 4.30pm Tue-Sun Easter-Oct) Running from opposite the tourist office (where you book and pay) on the riverfront, these cruises last for about an hour. Don't rely on it running outside of high season.

Sleeping & Eating

For a selection of restaurants, wander pedestrianised Rue Griange directly south from Grand Place.

Le Temps Passe B&B €€

(☎085 24 00 28; www.letempspasse.be; Rue Vierset-Godin 10; s/d incl breakfast €80/100; 📶) Three lovely rooms run out of a gift and design shop place you right in the heart of things in Huy, in its most attractive quarter.

Information

Tourist Office (☎085 21 29 15; www.pays-de-huy.be; Quai de Namur 1; ⌚8.30am-6pm Mon-Fri, 10am-6pm Sat & Sun) Beside Collégiale Notre-Dame in the turreted former Hospice d'Oultremont building.

Getting There & Away

Trains run to Namur (€5.30, 25 minutes) and Liège (€4.90, 35 minutes) at least twice-hourly.

Modave

Few of Belgium's numerous castles have an interior to beat memorable **Château de Modave** (☎085 41 13 69; www.modave-castle.be; adult/child €7.50/free; ⌚10am-6pm Tue-Sun Apr–mid-Nov; 👪). The most arresting of the well-preserved 1673 stucco ceilings is the heraldic relief that covers the entrance hall. But the audio-guided visit shows you another 20 majestically furnished rooms plus a lead-lined stone-cut bath, remarkable bed-alcove and balcony from which you can suddenly appreciate the castle's strategic perch on a 60m cliff above a pretty rural stream. There's no hint of this topography from the castle's level main frontage, which comprises classical French gardens, an extensive grey-stone fortified farm and grand avenues leading from Modave village.

Modave is 13km south from Huy via the N641, accessed on bus 126a (€2,10, 20 minutes, nine to 10 weekdays, three Saturday). By car, numerous attractive rural lanes invite further exploration en route to Hamoir and Durbuy.

Jehay

In the golden glow of late afternoon, **Château de Jehay** (www.chateaujehay.be; Rue du Parc; adult/child €5/3; ⌚2-6pm Tue-Fri, 11am-6pm Sat & Sun Apr-Oct) is one of Wallonia's most photogenic sights. Like a gingerbread fantasy, this turret-spiked 1550 castle is a fabulous confection of alternating brick and stone rising from a tree-ringed moat. The less-spectacular interior consists of elegant furnished rooms, while outbuildings house changing exhibitions.

Jehay is around 6km north of Amay, a mostly humdrum town whose partly 11th-century church, Église Saint-Georges et Sainte-Ode, has an unusual triple-spired portal tower.

Bus 85 stops three to eight times daily nearby between Liège (€3.20, 55 minutes) and Huy (€3.20, 30 minutes).

Liège (Luik)

POP 197,000

Wallonia's largest city has a bit of a downbeat feel at first glance, but don't be deceived. It doesn't take much scratching to discover an entirely different Liège, a living architectural onion with layer upon layer of history lying just beneath the disfigured surface. Proudly free-spirited citizens are disarmingly friendly and no Belgian city bubbles with more *joie de vivre*. With an excellent eating scene and lively nightlife, Liège is quirky, urban and oddly compulsive.

History

Bishop of Tongeren-Maastricht, St-Lambert was praying at a chapel here in 705 when he was murdered by enemies from an opposing clan. Miracles and pilgrimage ensued; donations from visitors such as Frankish emperor Charlemagne allowed the development by 1015 of St-Lambert's Cathedral, then one of the greatest in northern Europe.

Liège

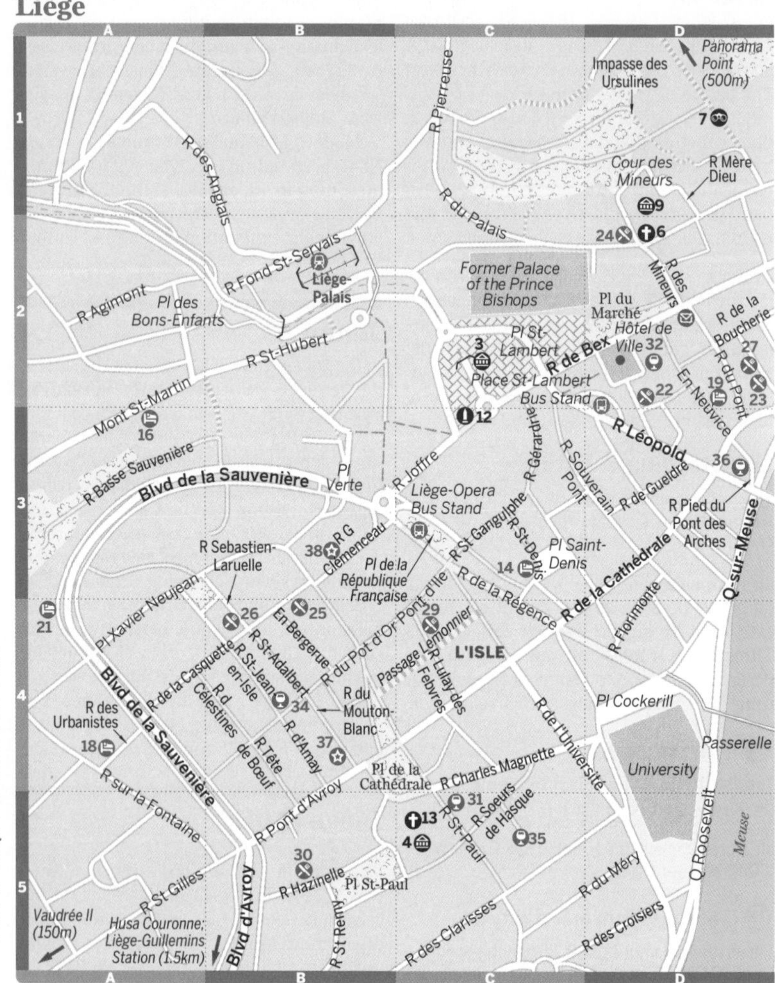

Wielding both religious and secular powers, the prince-bishops of Liège ('mini-popes') managed to maintain their territory's independence for almost eight centuries, endowing the city with numerous religious architectural masterpieces. Initially the bishops' rule was remarkably enlightened. Personal liberties were enshrined here centuries before such freedoms were accepted in surrounding feudal Europe. Comparative broad-mindedness plus access to Crusader-purloined monastic translations of Arabic scientific texts gave the region a technological edge in the development of local industries from metallurgy to distillation. However, by the late 18th century the prince-bishopric had become a clumsy anachronism and economic gripes led to the 1789 Révolution Liégeoise. Liège townsfolk ousted the prince-bishop and voted in 1793 to demolish the city's fabulous St-Lambert's Cathedral, a symbol of the hated rulers. Swiftly thereafter Liège was occupied and annexed by revolutionary France.

Post-Waterloo (1815), the territory passed to the Dutch king, then English-influenced large-scale steel production swept Liège into a new industrial age that only really ended in the 1970s.

Liège

Top Sights

1 Grand Curtius F1
2 Musée des Beaux-Arts de Liège E2

Sights

3 Archéoforum C2
4 Cathédrale St-Paul C5
5 Église Collégiale St-Barthélemy F1
6 Former Church of St-Antoine D2
7 Montagne de Bueren D1
8 Musée d'Ansembourg F1
9 Musée de la Vie Wallonne D1
10 Musée Tchantchès F5
11 Outremeuse F4
12 Tchantchès Pilot Sculpture C3
13 Trésor C5

Sleeping

14 Amosa Liège C3
15 Auberge de Jeunesse F4
16 Crowne Plaza A3
17 Hôtel Hors Château E1
18 Hôtel Les Acteurs A4
19 Hôtel Neuvice D2
20 Nº 5 Bed & Breakfast F1
21 Pentahôtel Liège A4

Eating

22 Amon Nanesse D2
23 Chez Nathalie D2
24 Dix-Huitième D2
25 Enoteca B4
26 Histoire Sans Faim B4
27 Le Bistrot d'en Face D2
28 Le Thème E1
29 Leblanc C4
30 Terra Terrae B5

Drinking & Nightlife

31 Au Tableau Qui Dit des Bêtises C5
32 Beer Lovers D2
33 Café Le Petit Bougnat F5
34 La Cour St-Jean B4
35 Le Pot au Lait C5
36 Les Olivettes D3

Entertainment

37 Cinema Churchill B4
38 Opéra Royal de Wallonie B3

Shopping

39 La Batte E3

WWI saw Liège become the world's first city to suffer a campaign of aerial bombing, courtesy of new-fangled Zeppelin airships. However, by holding out for 12 days, Liège's brave defenders gave the rest of Europe just enough time to prepare a defence from Germany's westward march.

Sights & Activities

Musée de la Vie Wallonne MUSEUM
(www.viewallonne.be; Cour des Mineurs; adult/child €5/3; ⌚9.30am-6pm Tue-Sun) In an adapted convent-cloister building, this curious display takes visitors on an amble through the region's past, exploring everything from 12th-century Mosan metalwork to 1960s room interiors. Notable is the watercolour of the rooster that's now Wallonia's symbol, but the highlight for the ghoulish is an original guillotine and the embalmed head of the last

man to feel her kiss. Stereoscope black-and-white photos of Liège are also intriguing. Temporary exhibitions are housed in the former church of **St-Antoine**.

★**Musée des Beaux-Arts de Liège** GALLERY
(http://beauxartsliege.be; Féronstrée 86; adult/youth €5/3; ⏲10am-6pm Tue-Sun) From outside, this museum is a 1980s concrete travesty. Within, however, clever design creates a spiral of gallery spaces ideal for viewing the excellent collection of paintings by French-speaking Belgians. The scope ranges from fine medieval canvases by Lambert Lombard and Pierre Paulus to surrealist works by Paul Delvaux. Particular strengths are century-old images of industrial Wallonia. Constantin Meunier's *La Coulée à Ougrée* has an almost Soviet-realist feel, while Cécile Douard's inspired *Le Terril* portrays worker women struggling up a metaphorical slag heap.

★**Grand Curtius** MUSEUM
(☎04-221 94 04; www.grandcurtiusliege.be; Féronstrée 136; adult/child €9/free; ⏲10am-6pm Wed-Mon) The splendid Grand Curtius uses the thoroughly renovated mansion of a 17th-century Liège entrepreneur to unite four discrete museum collections. It then makes a very ambitious stab at explaining the whole history of art from prehistoric stone chippings to art-nouveau pianos, while interweaving tales of Liège artists and industries. The result is somewhat bewildering, but there's an incredible wealth of treasures to discover; you'll need a couple of hours to do it justice, more with the detailed audio guide (included) and temporary exhibitions (extra).

Musée d'Ansembourg HISTORIC BUILDING
(☎04-221 9402; www.liegemuseum.be; Féronstrée 114; adult/teen/child €5/3/free; ⏲10am-6pm Thu-Sun) Less a museum than a magnificently furnished 1755 Regency mansion with original stucco ceilings and some gilded leather 'wallpaper', highlights include four original 17th-century Oudenaarde tapestries. Explanations are very cursory so you could easily see all 18 rooms in around 20 minutes.

Église Collégiale St-Barthélemy CHURCH
(Place St-Barthélemy; adult/child €2/free; ⏲10am-noon & 2-5pm Mon-Sat, 2-5pm Sun) This large Rhenish-style church has twin Saxon-style towers and a cream-and-cerise exterior. It houses a famous 1118 baptismal font that's one of the world's most celebrated pieces of Mosan art; the great brass bowl was rescued from St-Lambert's Cathedral when it was demolished in 1793. It rests on oxen figures and is adorned with five baptismal scenes, elaborately described in a video screened nearby. To glimpse the font for free, peer through the long, narrow slit window in the church's western end.

Cathédrale St-Paul CHURCH
(www.cathedraledeliege.be; Place de la Cathédrale; ⏲8am-5pm) FREE The central cathedral has soaring Gothic vaults, an elaborate neo-Gothic pulpit, colourfully patterned ceiling and fine stained-glass windows. Off the closed-in cloister, its slickly presented three-level **Trésor** (Treasury; ☎04-232 61 32; http://tresordeliege.be; adult/child €5/free; ⏲2-5pm Tue-Sun) guards many artworks, vestments and chalices rescued from St-Lambert's Cathedral in 1793, most notably the jewel-studded gold-and-silver reliquary of St Lambert. In the form of a life-sized bust, the reliquary supposedly contains Lambert's skull (though six other Lambert skulls also apparently exist!) and is encrusted with intricate tales from the saint's life.

Archéoforum MUSEUM
(☎04-250 93 70; www.archeoforumdeliege.be; Place St-Lambert; adult/concession €6/5, combined ticket with the cathedral Trésor €8/7; ⏲9am-5pm Tue-Fri, 10am-5pm Sat during termtime, 10am-5pm Tue-Fri school holidays) Once one of the greatest churches in northern Europe, St-Lambert's Cathedral was demolished from 1793 in the aftermath of the Revolution Liégeoise, very decidedly marking the end to the independent prince-bishopric of Liège. All that now remains is a mere scattering of foundation stones hidden beneath Place St-Lambert. These archaeological diggings, along with remnants of an earlier Roman villa, can be seen in the atmospherically (if sometimes impractically) underlit Archéoforum.

Visits include a 15-minute computer-simulated 'tour' of the original cathedral plus a video documenting the farcical 20th-century history of the site (both in English).

Montagne de Bueren VIEWPOINT
Several tiny medieval passageways burrow beneath the house fronts of Rue Hors Chateau, most disappearing into picturesque hidden yards, but well worth exploring. However, the Montagne de Bueren continues steeply up all the way to the top of the former citadel hill in 373 steps. At the top is a war memorial and city panorama point behind which are the grassy 5m-tall brick fortress bastions. The summit is a hospital.

It's less strenuous to climb the narrow side stairways that lead past Nun's restaurant-bar into the gated Terraces des Minimes. Formerly the terraced fruit gardens of a series of religious orders, this is now a lovely hillside park-garden with great views that survey the incredible chaos of Liège's rooftops.

★Liège-Guillemins Station ARCHITECTURE
Around 2km south of central Liège, the city's main train station is an incredible 2009 icon designed by Santiago Calatrava (no, it didn't come in on time or under budget). Its bold white sweeping curves create a unique modernist structure that looks like a vast glass-and-concrete manta ray.

Outremeuse AREA
(www.fgfw.be/rlom) Across the Meuse River from the city centre is the island of Outremeuse, whose working-class residents consider it a 'Free Republic', a freedom that is chaotically celebrated on 15 August.

Festivals

★Festival Outremeuse FIESTA
(mid-Aug) A week of raucously drunken celebrations in Outremeuse culminates on 15 August when sermons are read in Walloon dialect, then everyone gets tipsy on *pékèt* (local gin). Expect firecrackers, puppets, traditional dances, a procession of giants and vast unruly crowds. Next day from 5pm the surreal cremation and burial of a bone symbolically marks the end of festivities.

A 'mourning' parade shuffles around the Outremeuse district, its brass band interspersing up-tempo carnivalesque music with sombre dirges accompanied by hammy weeping. Hilarious. Dress in black and bring celery!

Nocturne des Coteaux CULTURAL
(www.lanocturnedescoteaux.eu; 1st Sat of Oct) Liège comes alive at dusk with 20,000 candles forming beautiful patterns on the vertiginous Montagne de Bueren. Historic buildings (many usually closed) open their doors, there are numerous free concerts and at 11.30pm fireworks cap things off.

Sleeping

Auberge de Jeunesse HOSTEL €
(04-344 56 89; www.lesaubergesdejeunesse.be; Rue Georges Simenon 2; dm/s/d incl breakfast €28/46/68, €2 cheaper for under 26, 10% off for HI members; @ wi-fi) This friendly, modern HI hostel in Outremeuse makes a great base, with attractive public areas and good facilities. It's a short stroll from the centre of town across the Meuse.

★Pentahôtel Liège HOTEL €€
(04-221 77 11; www.pentahotels.com; Blvd de la Sauvenière 100; r €95-145; P @ wi-fi) Styled along contemporary urban lines, this is an upbeat place above an attractively modish bar-restaurant: in fact, the bar staff double as receptionists. Rooms are large, and there are a lot of pleasing little features in them that will appeal to the frequent traveller. Another big benefit of staying here is that you can't see the ugly facade once you're inside.

Amosa Liège HOTEL €€
(04-331 93 35; www.amosaliege.be; Rue St-Denis 4; r €129-185; wi-fi) Confident and modern, this has an enviable central location, a can-do attitude and very commodious rooms. Colour schemes are modern beiges and greys, and bathrooms are excellent, though you may need a degree to work the taps and lights. A vivaciously modish bar and restaurant enlivens downstairs and reasonably priced parking is available just across the square.

Nº 5 Bed & Breakfast B&B €€
(0494 30 58 73; www.n5bednbreakfast.be; Pl St-Barthélémy 5; r €115-135; wi-fi) Right in the museum zone, this super-elegant and highly original B&B is actually two characterful

GEORGES SIMENON – A FULL LIFE

Liège-born author Georges Simenon (1903–89) did nothing by halves. His famous character Inspector Maigret appeared in no less than 76 different crime-busting novels yet that's barely a quarter of Simenon's astoundingly prolific tally. He could churn out a book, on average, every 120 days, still had time to move house 33 times and to bed an incredible 10,000 women. Well, the latter is his own immodest estimate. His second wife claims it was 'only' 1200.

Diehard Simenon fans can visit 28 places loosely related to the writer's youth and career using the tourist office's multilingual brochure *Sur les traces de Simenon* (downloadable) and/or an audio-guide tour (€6, two hours). One of few tangible visible references to Simenon is his birthplace at Rue Léopold 24, which is marked by a brass plaque.

houses linked by a pleasant and rather surprising courtyard. Five rooms are all decorated a little differently, with stylish modern fabrics and attractive bathrooms. Readers rave about the breakfasts, featuring homemade produce. There's even a sauna and massage treatments available.

Hôtel Hors Château GUESTHOUSE €€
(☎04-250 60 68; www.hors-chateau.be; Rue Hors Château 62; s/d/ste €78/95/125;) Brilliantly located in the city's historical quarter, the nine rooms combine contemporary design with bare antique brickwork and old beams. Call ahead to arrange arrival times as reception isn't permanently attended, and there's gated access. Breakfast costs €12.

Husa Couronne HOTEL €€
(☎04-340 30 00; www.hotelhusadelacouronne.be; Place des Guillemins 11; r €95-135;) Entered via a narrow corridor in the insalubrious area facing Liège-Guillemins station, the Couronne is unexpectedly stylish with design features worthy of a top hotel. Room sizes vary considerably without affecting the price, which, climbs steeply with demand. The location is far from central, but ideal if you're catching an early train. Breakfast €16.

Hôtel Les Acteurs HOTEL €€
(☎04-223 00 80; www.lesacteurs.be; Rue des Urbanistes 10; s €54-68, d €76-84;) This basic but personable 16-room hotel has 24-hour reception in its congenial, inexpensive *café*. En suite toilet-shower booths are tiny in some rooms, very cramped singles lack natural light and 'double' beds are narrow. Nonetheless the triple rooms are generously sized and the overall atmosphere is pleasant. Relatively central; breakfast included.

★ **Hôtel Neuvice** BOUTIQUE HOTEL €€€
(☎04-375 97 40; www.hotelneuvice.be; En Neuvice 45; r €140-170;) A superb conversion of a pair of historic houses, this stylish choice places you right on a characterful alleyway in the heart of central Liège. Service is personable, while rooms offer enough character for the holidaymaker and enough facilities for the business traveller. The breakfast chamber is atmospherically vaulted, and the central atrium is pleasant while browsing a book from the library.

Crowne Plaza HOTEL €€€
(☎04-222 94 94; www.crowneplazaliege.be; Mont St-Martin 9; r €159;) Two of Liège's finest ridge-top historic town house mansions form the jaw-dropping centrepiece of this attractive redevelopment. A modernist lobby-bar stretches out onto the rooftop of the main accommodation block. Upper rooms there share superb views over town or back towards the Sélys Longchamps tower, home to the posher suites. Standard rooms tend to be low down looking, only at the cliff front.

Eating

There's plenty of midrange choice around the Place du Marché and a curious variety on the boisterous little pedestrianised streets leading off Rue Pont d'Avroy. In Outremeuse, Rue Roture is an old cobbled alley lined with sweet little restaurants.

★ **Terra Terrae** FRENCH, FUSION €€
(☎0495 32 16 43; www.terraterrae.be; Rue Hazinelle 4; mains €24, 3-course menu €34; noon-2.30pm & 6.30-9.30pm Mon & Thu, noon-2.30pm & 6.30-10pm Fri & Sat) Confident contemporary cuisine with a variety of influences makes this eatery on a quiet street near the cathedral a pleasure – but not one you can expect to bag a table for without a reservation. Influences from 'the south' include Provence, Italy and northern Spain. Presentation and service are excellent. At weekends, the menu takes on a more 'gastronomic' air.

Le Bistrot d'en Face FRENCH €€
(☎04-223 15 84; www.lebistrotdenface.be; Rue de la Goffe 10; mains €15-20; noon-2.30pm & 7-9.30pm Wed-Sun, closed lunch Sat) Excellent quality rural French food served in a candlelit 16th-century building whose traditional gingham-and-beams interior is enlivened by some bold contemporary portraiture. Vegetarians should look elsewhere. Carnivores, choose carefully if you're squeamish about head, bone marrow or *andouillette* (pork intestine sausage). Staff could be friendlier, but that's life. Reservations recommended.

Leblanc GRILL HOUSE €€
(☎04-223 31 43; www.maisonleblanc.be; Rue Lulay des Fèbvres 5; mains €19-29; 6.30-10pm Tue, noon-1.30pm & 6.30-10pm Wed-Sat) Given that you walk through a butcher's shop to these simple but enticing tables, don't expect vegetable medleys from the tablet-based menu. Steaks come from various provenances (there's the inevitable wagyu option if the company's paying). Scallop carpaccio with truffles is a standout starter. Service is a bit curt at times, but they listen to how you want the meat.

Enoteca ITALIAN €€

(☎04-222 24 64; www.enoteca.be; Rue de la Casquette 5; 2-/3-/4-course menu €25/27/30; ⏲noon-2.30pm & 7-9pm Mon-Fri, 7-9pm Sat) Widely respected for serving top-quality Italian food using fresh ingredients, all prepared before your eyes in the white-tiled open kitchen. Five-course dinners (€39) on Friday and Saturday evenings.

Histoire Sans Faim BARBECUE €€

(☎04-222 00 34; Rue Sébastien Laruelle 3; mains €14-24; ⏲noon-2.30pm & 6.30-10pm Mon & Wed-Fri, 6.30-10pm Sat & Sun) On the northern edge of the bar district, the speciality of this friendly, intimate restaurant is *pierrade* – cook-it-yourself barbecues on hot stones. Meat or seafood, away you go: it's delicious. The name is a pun on the *NeverEnding Story* (don't let on that Tom Cruise wasn't in it) and menu items are named after films.

Le Thème FRENCH €€

(☎04-222 02 02; www.letheme.com; Impasse de la Couronne 9; 3-/5-course menus €35/40, with wine €55/60; ⏲from 7pm Mon-Sat) This cosy restaurant, tucked away in a hidden yet central alley – worth a wander at any time – serves up menus that are eccentrically designed around a regularly changing theme. Think Alice in Wonderland or The Avengers; reliably good.

Chez Nathalie FRENCH €€

(☎04-222 16 57; Rue de la Goffe 12; mains €13-23; ⏲6.30-9.30pm Tue-Sat) With your needs overseen with a motherly concern, it's difficult not to sink into Parisian-style bliss in this loveable spot. It could audition for the role of bistro in any mid-20th-century movie but the food is vibrant and tasty enough to banish any clichés.

Amon Nanesse BELGIAN €€

(La Maison du Pékèt; ☎04-250 67 83; www.maison-dupeket.be; Rue de l'Épée 4; mains €13-20; ⏲noon-2.30pm & 6-10.30pm; 📶) Just behind Place du Marché, this rambling antique house with bare-brick walls and heavy beams combines a lively bar (open until 2am) specialising in *pékèt* shots with a restaurant serving satisfying pub meals including *boulets a la liègeoise* (meatballs in raisin-sweetened gravy) and *café liégeois* (coffee and ice-cream sweet) for dessert.

Dix-Huitième MODERN BELGIAN €€€

(XVIIIème; ☎04-250 58 00; www.ledixhuitieme.be; Rue du Palais 2; mains €22-39, menu €35; ⏲noon-2pm & 7-9.30pm Tue-Thu, noon-2pm & 7-10pm Fri, 7-10pm Sat) Despite occupying a prominent corner in old Liège, it's easy to miss this gourmet option, but make sure you don't. The quality of the beautifully presented dishes could justify a much loftier price. Best, though, is a table on the terrace on a fine evening, with historic Liège around you and the prospect of a memorable meal imminent.

🍷 Drinking & Nightlife

Tiny lanes around the Rue du Pot d'Or are the nightlife centre. The Place du Marché is the place for a quieter drink.

★**Le Pot au Lait** PUB

(www.potaulait.be; Rue Soeurs-de-Hasque; ⏲10am-4am Mon-Fri, noon-4am Sat & Sun; 📶) Down a private cul-de-sac of psychedelic murals and lamps like radioactive triffids lies Liège's wackiest pub-*café*. Watch UFOs landing while lobsters wear dentures and mannequins show off their scars in a colour-overload masterpiece. Regular live music. An alternative classic.

La Cour St-Jean PUB

(www.lacourstjean.be; Rue St-Jean-en-Isle 23; ⏲11am-6am Mon-Fri, 2pm-6am Sat, 7pm-6am Sun; 📶) Small and cosy, with dark, characterful ambience, this pub is popular with Liège 20-somethings and has excellent Mort Subite beers on tap. It's right in the heart of the nightlife zone so there are plenty of options around if it's not your scene.

Les Olivettes PUB

(☎0498 47 04 50; Rue Pied du Pont des Arches 6; ⏲from 8pm Fri & Sat, from 11am Sun) In the days of Jacques Brel *cafés chantants* were common – simple pubs where crooner, pianist and accordionist sang for their beer. Today Les Olivettes is a rare, authentic survivor, its *pékèt*-supping audience even more geriatric than the performers. Unique, no cover, expect plenty of interaction. Closed for renovation at time of research: let's hope it doesn't change.

Beer Lovers BAR

(www.beer-lovers.be; Rue de la Violette 9; ⏲11am-10pm or later Tue-Sun) The modern lines of this central bar-cafe sometimes clash with the tradition-laden Belgian beer labels, but it's a pleasing place to try them nonetheless. There's a changing list of a dozen or more on tap, and hundreds of bottles available, with a shop alongside for take-homes. Food

TCHANTCHÈS

Liège's mascot and oldest 'citizen' is a big-nosed wooden puppet called Tchantchès, supposedly born between cobblestones in the city's 'free' Outremeuse quarter on 15 August 760. His miraculous arrival is an oft-retold humourous tale that's a thinly disguised biblical satire. However, unlike the baby Jesus, Tchantchès has a penchant for getting riotously drunk on *pékèt* (Walloon gin) and head-butting people. Still, beneath such minor flaws, he's good-hearted and much loved, typifying the free spirit of the Liègois. His 'life story' is retold in thickly accented Walloon-French through puppet shows at the **Musée Tchantchès** (☎04-342 75 75; www.tchantches.be; Rue Surlet 56; admission with show €3.50; ⏲8am-5pm Mon-Thu, to 12.30pm Fri). On Place St-Lambert there's a cartoonesque **statue** of Tchantchès piloting a little metal aeroplane.

is limited to croques (toasted sandwiches), saucisson and cheese.

Vaudrée II BAR
(www.vaudree.be; Rue St-Gilles 149; ⏲8am-1am Mon-Thu, 9am-3am Fri & Sat, 9am-midnight Sun) With all the ambience of a municipal funeral parlour and a bit of a walk from the centre, this is a venue whose worth may be questioned. Yet, with 24 – some of them not commonly found – beers on tap and very friendly staff, it's worth the pilgrimage for beer aficionados. Bring your own atmosphere. Shop opposite.

Café Le Petit Bougnat BAR
(Rue Roture 17; ⏲5pm-late Tue-Sun) Wonderfully genuine local rustic *café* with rough floors, candles in bottles and the perfect terrace on Outremeuse's sweetest square. Expect mayhem all around here during the Festival Outremeuse (p227).

Au Tableau Qui Dit des Bêtises WINE BAR
(Rue Charles Magnette 23; ⏲2pm-close Wed-Sun; 📶) With a tree-shaded terrace by the cathedral, this place is popular with arty young professionals and hipsters. It makes a fine friendly place to sip a glass of wine, and the attached bistro does decent food, with a regularly changing menu.

☆ Entertainment

Opéra Royal de Wallonie OPERA
(☎04-221 47 22; www.operaliege.be; Rue des Dominicains 1; ⏲box office noon-6pm Mon-Sat) This restored main opera house, the 1820 Théatre Royal, is a centrepiece of the town. Book tickets at the box office or online.

Cinema Churchill CINEMA
(☎04-222 27 28; www.grignoux.be; Rue du Mouton-Blanc 18) Three-screen art deco cinema with a grand stained-glass facade. Most films in their original language with French subtitles.

Shopping

★**La Batte** MARKET
(⏲8am-2.30pm Sun) One of Belgium's most vibrant markets, this multicultural affair encompasses cheap designer rip-offs, second-hand gear, food stalls and more along the riverside in the centre of town.

ℹ Information

Office du Tourisme (☎04-221 92 21; www.liege.be/tourisme; Rue de Féronstrée 92; ⏲9am-5pm Oct-May, to 6pm Jun-Sep)

ℹ Getting There & Away

BUS

Eurolines (☎02-274 13 50; www.eurolines.be) international buses leave from near the Liège-Guillemins train station.

Bus services to the surrounding area mostly depart from stops on Place St-Lambert or Liège-Opera, outside the opera house.

TRAIN

Long-distance trains arrive 2km south of the centre at dazzling Liège-Guillemins station. Switch onto a local train to reach Liège-Palais for the city centre.

From Liège-Guillemins, international destinations include:

Cologne (€38, one hour, six daily)
Aachen (€19, 25 minutes, six daily) Change in Welkenraedt for a cheaper but longer service.
Maastricht (€5.30, 35 minutes, hourly)
Paris (€102, 2¼ hours, five direct daily)
Frankfurt (€103, 2¼ hours, four direct daily)
Luxembourg City (€45, 2½ hours, six direct daily)

Destinations in Belgium:

Brussels (€14.80, one hour) Half-hourly via Leuven (€10.80, 35 minutes).
Bruges (€21.10, two hours, hourly)
Namur (€8.90, 45 minutes, twice-hourly)

Getting Around

Buses 1 or 4 (which does a useful circuit of the whole centre) link Liège-Guillemins to central Place St-Lambert.

La Maison des Cyclistes (☎04-222 20 46; www.maisondescyclistes.be; Place des Guillemins 2; per 2hr/day/weekend €6/14/20; ⊙1-6pm Mon, 7am-noon & 1-6pm Tue & Thu, 11am-noon & 1-6pm Wed & Fri) Bike rental at Liège-Guillemins train station. Turn left as you exit at ground level.

Around Liège

Blégny Mine

For one of the best industrial experience tours you'll find anywhere, don a hard hat, jump in the cage lift and descend through a pitch-black moment into the life of a 20th-century Belgian miner. The two-hour guided tour of Unesco-listed **Blégny Mine** (www.blegnymine.be; Rue Lambert Marlet 23, Trembleur; mine adult/child €9.80/6.90, museum €4/2.80) starts with a 20-minute film (English subtitles) before setting off to soak up the sounds and smells of the pit. For non-French speakers there's an audio guide, but it's well worth trying to understand the human guide too, or you risk missing some memorable demonstrations – and the two sets of information are complementary.

The mining museum fills you in on the bigger picture of coal and charcoal, while a playground and small zoo, as well as a tourist train, mean that there's plenty here to keep the family busy for much of the day.

Note that the mine is at Trembleur not Blegny. Some (not all) daily route 67 buses pass within 300m between Liège Gare-Léopold (50 minutes) and Vise (25 minutes).

Seraing

POP 64,000

If you thought Charleroi was Belgium's ugliest city, you haven't seen Seraing. Once at the forefront of Belgium's industrial revolution, its rusty steel plants and time-warp brick tenements now have a fascinating ghastliness amid which the former summer palace of the prince-bishops still stands most incongruously. This became the headquarters of the region's original steelworks, founded in 1817 by English entrepreneur John Cockerill, whose statue now fronts the nearby Georgian-style town hall. Some 4km west along the quay, the Seraing's one compelling attraction is the world-famous **Val St-Lambert Glassworks** (Cristal Discovery; ☎04-330 36 20; www.cristal-discovery.be; Esplanade du Val; adult/child €6/4; ⊙10am-5pm Apr-Oct), which has occupied a former monastery site since 1826. Once the planet's leading glassmaker, its workforce has dwindled from 5000 in 1900 to a few dozen today, but it still manages to create lead-crystal masterpieces with almost 19th-century tools. Visits start in the former abbot's 1751 'chateau' with a 20-minute film. You can peruse some extraordinary glass sculptures and learn about the history of glass-making. It's well worth experiencing while the opportunity lasts. Access is by bus 9 from Liège-Opéra bus stands via Liège-Guillemins train station.

Spa

POP 10,600

Europe's oldest health resort, Spa is *the* original spa from which the English word derives. The healing properties of Spa's warm spring waters were recognised as far back as the 1st century AD. Henry VIII of England, in need of a relaxing 16th-century bath after occupying Tournai, praised the waters' curative powers. By the 18th century Spa had become a luxurious retreat for European royalty and intellectuals. Tsars, politicians and writers including Victor Hugo and Alexandre Du-

CRYSTAL CREATIONS

In much of Asia, Belgium's fame relies far less on its beer and chocolate than its glassware. Nineteenth-century maharajahs loved the stuff, and barely an Indian palace exists that doesn't sport at least a couple of Belgian crystal chandeliers. The most famous name is **Val St-Lambert** from Seraing, whose production peaked before WWI. Although some 90% of its production was sent for export, distinctive two-colour cut-glass pieces remain prized possessions in many a Belgian home. These days, however, most such manufacture has shifted to places with lower labour costs, while changing tastes have also posed a challenge for surviving designers. Should you want pieces of classic Belgian glassware it's ironically often cheaper to buy antique items, especially if you don't need a full set. (Some Brussels shops are specialists.)

mas came to what became nicknamed the 'cafe of Europe'. In the later 19th century its popularity waned, but it has seen a certain rejuvenation with the modern Thermes spa complex on a hilltop directly above town.

Sights

Casino HISTORIC BUILDING
(087 77 20 52; www.casinodespa.be; Rue Royale 4; 11am-4am Sun-Thu, to 5am Fri & Sat) The 'world's first' casino, originally built in 1770, is one of a trio of grand neoclassical buildings at the centre of town, along with the original 1862 bathhouse (not currently in use) and the 1908 Exhibition Halls. To gamble or simply to admire the casino's muralled ceilings you'll need to be over 21 years of age and have your passport handy.

Parc de Sept Heures PARK
With a picturesque Léopold II–era pavilion and wrought-iron marketplace hosting Sunday morning flea markets, this charming park features minigolf, *pétanque* and pony rides in summer. The park's northern side slopes very steeply up through splendid beech woods to the Thermes spa complex.

Villa Royale Marie-Henriette MUSEUM
(Ave Reine Astrid 77; adult/child €4/1; 2-6pm Mar–mid-Nov) While Belgium's King Léopold II was playing colonial domination in Congo, his feisty Hungarian-born queen avoided the boredom of Brussels by moving to Spa and riding her horses across the Ardennes. The 1862 Napoleon III–style former hotel where she stayed is now a minor museum.

WORTH A TRIP

SPA-FRANCORCHAMPS, GRAND-PRIX CIRCUIT

Circuit Spa-Francorchamps (www.spa-francorchamps.be; Rte du Circuit 55) is Belgium's foremost motor-racing circuit, cited by many F1 drivers as their favourite course. Set in hilly part-woodland it includes climbs and a dramatic 150-degree bend near the main paddock, 500m west of Francorchamps village between Spa and Stavelot. Hotels book out way in advance for Belgium's Formula 1 Grand Prix. At that time traffic can be gridlocked as far away as Liège. But the circuit also hosts lower profile races most weekends between April and mid-October, some free. See website for dates.

The stables include a series of horsey exhibits and an old forge, while the main building features old Spa water bottles and laquerware boxes produced as early souvenirs to sell to spa-goers.

It's 500m west of the tourist office, opposite the short diagonal spur road that heads southwest to the train station.

Spa Monopole FACTORY
(087 79 41 11; www.eaudysseedespa.be; Rue Auguste Laporte 34; adult/child €5/2.50; 9.30am-5pm Mon-Fri) Selling the waters of Spa remains big business, with millions of bottles filled annually at this plant behind the train station. A visit is self-guided and includes a view over the factory's production floor. Book online.

Thermes de Spa SPA
(087 77 25 60; www.thermesdespa.com; Colline d'Annette et Lubin; 10am-9pm Mon-Fri, to 10pm Sat, to 8pm Sun) Fronted by a circular glass facade, this top-rate spa offers a wide variety of saunas, hammams, hydrotherapy pools and beauty treatments with a wide range of packages. Access is by steep woodland footpath or glass cube pod-funicular (€1.50 one-way) from the Parc de Sept Heures, or by a very circuitous road.

Sleeping & Eating

Spa has several hotels and lots of B&Bs. A series of central *café*-brasseries with terraced tables beneath fine shady trees face the casino complex, a scene slightly marred by endless clogging on Rue Royale.

★ **Villa des Fleurs** BOUTIQUE HOTEL €€
(087 79 50 50; www.villadesfleurs.be; Rue Albin Body 31; r €109-159; P) Entering this Napoleon III–style villa feels like there should be a butler awaiting you as you pass the grand framed paintings and trickling wall fountains. Rooms are elegant and spacious, without descending into period style. There's an attractive garden too. It's three minutes' walk up Place du Monument from the funicular area.

Radisson Blu Palace Hôtel HOTEL €€€
(087 27 97 00; www.radissonblu.com; Place Royale 39; s/d midweek €120/140, weekend €180/200; P) If you've come for spa soaks, this modern, upmarket place is the obvious choice, with discounts at the Thermes and a dedicated funicular so you can get there in your dressing gown. Confusingly, Spa has a

second Radisson Blu, the manorial-style Balmoral 2km east of town.

La Tonnellerie BELGIAN €€€
(☎087 77 22 84; www.latonnellerie.be; Parc des Sept Heures; mains €25-29; ⊙noon-2.30pm & 7-9.30pm Thu-Tue) Tucked delightfully into the central park, this relatively sophisticated chalet-style half-timbered restaurant offers well-prepared upmarket fare with lovely outdoor tables overlooking the park. There are also fair-priced guest rooms (€85 to €120) with modern colour schemes and a wine theme.

Information

Pouhon Pierre-le-Grand (☎087 79 53 53; www.spatourisme.be; Rue du Marché 1a ; ⊙9am-6pm Mon-Wed & Fri, 10am-6pm Thu, Sat & Sun Apr-Sep, to 5pm Oct-Mar;) The restored octagonal-fronted stone building hosting the tourist office was the site of Spa's original springs. It was renamed for Russian tsar Peter the Great whose visit to Spa in 1717 helped popularise the resort. Photo exhibition and free water tastings.

Getting There & Away

Spa is on a spur off the Liège–Aachen line. Hourly trains from Verviers-Central (€3.10, 30 minutes) run via Theux, which sports a medieval castle. To/from Liège (€5.30, 55 minutes) change trains in Pepinster.

Verviers

POP 56,000

Nestled into the Vesdre River valley, 20km east of Liège, sprawling Verviers was already a cloth town in the 15th-century but became an international centre for wool processing in the early 1800s. Amid post-industrial decline the town retains some patchily genteel corners. It's perversely likeable and a base from which to venture into the Haute Fagnes.

Sights

Centre Touristique de la Laine et de la Mode MUSEUM
(☎087 30 79 20; www.aqualaine.be; Rue de la Chapelle 30; adult/child €6/4; ⊙10am-5pm Tue-Sun) Within an 1803 former wool-processing mill, this audio-guided visit details the rise and fall of Verviers' cloth industry and explains the well-preserved industrial equipment, from old wool combs to mechanical spinners to local technological inventions. You'll find other large pieces of historical textile-factory equipment dotted around Verviers, repurposed as street art.

Place du Marché ARCHITECTURE
At the centre's eastern end, Vervier's most attractive little square is dominated by a stately town hall, with cobbled Mont du Moulin descending photogenically past ivy-draped and half-timbered buildings to the north. A road sign points incongruously to Bradford (775km), and other traditional textile towns.

Musée des Beaux-Arts et de la Céramique GALLERY
(☎087 33 16 95; http://musees.verviers.be; Rue Renier 17; adult/concession/child €2/1/free; ⊙2-5pm Mon, Wed & Sat, 3-6pm Sun) If you can catch it open, pop in to see this small but high-quality collection of 14th- to 19th-century paintings and remarkable ceramics.

Limbourg VILLAGE
If you're driving to Eupen, detour from Dolhain to this unusually well-preserved hill-citadel village (9km from Verviers) with its oversized church and extraordinarily uneven cobblestones in its long, picturesque main square.

Sleeping

Hôtel des Ardennes HOTEL €
(☎087 22 39 25; www.hotelverviers.com; Place de la Victoire 15; d €70, s/d without bathroom €45/55; P) Above a small 1896 brasserie that stocks over 70 beers, this hotel has a combination of basic rooms with shared bathroom and cheaply renovated but rather attractive doubles with bathrooms and gold-painted walls. Friendly, inexpensive and handily right beside Verviers-Central train station.

Rêver d'Art B&B €€
(☎0477 73 59 20; www.reverdart.be; Rue Henri François Grandjean 16; r €90;) Behind a proud 1884 facade, this is an artistic B&B where you can choose to take breakfast in the 1st-floor gallery or instead receive a voucher to use in town at Jean-Philippe Darcis (p234).

Hôtel Verviers HOTEL €€€
(☎087 30 56 56; www.hotelverviers.be; Rue de la Station 4; d standard/superior €148/158; P) This landmark 100-room hotel occupies a beautifully repurposed 1891 former station, whose grand brick structure is stylishly lit at night. The restaurant and bustling brasserie have a fashionable feel but aren't dauntingly exclusive, while guest rooms strike a fine balance between modern design and functionality. Superior rooms are duplexes. Prices are usually lower than these rack rates.

Eating & Drinking

Jean-Philippe Darcis SWEETS, CAFE €
(☎087 33 98 15; www.darcis.com; Rue Crapaurue 121; sweets from €1.50; 7am-6pm Tue-Sat;) The tea room of one of Belgium's foremost *chocolatiers,* famed particularly for his macarons (a gift box of 24 will set you back €35). It's between Place Verte and Place du Marché on Verviers' central shopping street.

La Boule Rouge PUB FOOD €
(☎087 33 39 50; Pont St-Laurent 10; mains €9-18; kitchen 11am-11pm Mon-Sat, 5-11pm Sun) Popular rustic-style *café* with a half-timbered frontage, people-watching terrace, a wide range of beers and food that's good and inexpensive. It's between Place Verte and Place du Martyr.

La Seigneurie INTERNATIONAL €€
(☎087 33 48 05; Pont St-Laurent 11; mains €15-24; noon-2pm & 6-11pm;) Quite a few Verviers restaurants deal in no-frills Greek/Belgian/North African combinations, with couscous royal alongside pork skewers and steak frites. This modishly redecorated spot sees the boss benevolently greeting diners, who are all regulars. The menu is long but basically a few plates with different sauces. Meat quality is surprisingly good and portions very generous.

Eau 1725 GREEK €€
(☎087 30 15 25; www.eau1725.com; Rue Cerexhe 96; meals €17-20; noon-2pm & 6pm-midnight Thu-Sun, 6pm-midnight Mon & Wed;) Flavours are Greek but with a French twist here; stews are particularly tasty. There's no hint of faux-Hellenic statuary in this tastefully updated 18th-century town house with extra seating in an atmospheric brick-vaulted cellar. It's one of a strip of appealing river-facing choices by the tourist office, a great area to dine on a summer evening.

Le Quai des Artistes BELGIAN €€
(☎087 78 50 13; Rue Xhavée 92; mains €14-22; 11.30am-2.30pm Mon, 6-9.30pm Wed & Thu, 11.30am-2.30pm & 6-10.30pm Sat, 6-10pm Sun;) This classic corner brasserie facing the theatre has had a suave makeover and offers an impressive range of Belgo-French food. Good for a calm drink too.

Entertainment

Spirit of 66 LIVE MUSIC
(☎087 35 24 24; www.spiritof66.be; Place du Martyr 16) One of Belgium's foremost venues for blues-rock gigs, with a knack for finding and re-presenting half-forgotten former greats whose stars have passed...rather like Verviers itself. There's something on more days than not.

Information

Office du Tourisme (☎087 30 79 26; www.paysdevesdre.be; Rue Jules Cerexhe 86; 9am-5pm Apr-Oct, closed Mon Nov-Mar) Two blocks south of the wool museum in a fine, century-old town house with temporary exhibitions and a video explaining why Verviers was the 'City of Water'.

Getting There & Away

From Verviers-Central train/bus station (500m west of central Place Verte, 600m southeast of the wool museum):

Stavelot Bus 294 (€3.20, five to seven daily) via Malmedy.

Botrange Nature Centre Rocherath-bound bus 390 (€3.20, three to five daily).

Aachen, Germany Six direct trains daily (€6.10, 30 minutes).

Liège-Guillemins Trains thrice hourly (€4.20, fast/slow 17/28 minutes).

Local trains stop at Verviers-Central and at marginally more central Verviers-Palais.

The Eastern Cantons

The 854 sq km Eastern Cantons (Cantons de l'Est in French, Ost Kantonen in German; www.eastbelgium.com) is Belgium's officially German-speaking area with its own Germanophone parliament. Its greatest attraction is the Haute Fagnes area of moorlands between Eupen and Malmedy. Both towns hold excellent carnivals, and the area's history is intriguing. Stavelot-Malmedy had been semi-independent since AD 650 and remained so, albeit later co-ruled with Liège, until 1795. After Waterloo (1815), Stavelot stayed within the Netherlands but Malmedy, Eupen and St-Vith were given to Prussia, subsequently becoming part of Germany. The Netherlands and Prussia couldn't agree who'd get a then-valuable zinc mining settlement now known as Kelmis, so that became 'Neutral Moresnet' and remarkably survived as one of Europe's least-known semi-independent states until invaded by Germany in 1915.

In 1863, Bismarck declared the speaking of French illegal. Eupen became thoroughly Germanised, but the citizens of Malmedy maintained their various forms of Walloon dialect as a kind of resistance (it remains essentially Francophone today). After WWI, the whole Eastern Cantons became Belgian but was claimed back again by Germany 20 years later. Men from these towns were forced to fight alongside soldiers of the Third Reich throughout WWII. In 1945, Americans liberated the towns, which were handed to Belgium once again.

Eupen

Eupen is by far Belgium's most Germanic town and makes a useful staging post for reaching the Haute Fagnes. Its Rosenmontag carnival, the day before Mardi Gras, lacks the weird characters of the Stavelot or Binche equivalents but is one of Belgium's most joyously colourful. Eupen houses the **parliament** (www.dgparlament.be; Platz des Parlements 1) for Belgium's German-speaking region in an 1812 mansion.

Sleeping & Eating

Gîte d'Étape HOSTEL €

(Eupener Jugendherberge; ☎087 55 31 26; www.gitesdetape.be/eupen; Judenstrasse 79; dm youth/adult €20/22.60; ⏲reception 5-10pm; P 📶) A hilltop location at the southern edge of town gives this hostel some lovely sweeping views over rolling forested hills. It was closed for renovations last time we passed by but should be open by the time you read this. Breakfast included; other meals available.

★ **Julévi** B&B €€

(☎0478 49 32 36; www.julevi.be; Heidberg 4; s/d €80/100; 📶) A charming, English-speaking couple have transformed this 1869 linen merchant's house into a stylishly comfortable retreat featuring quality box-spring mattresses, fluffy monogrammed towels and a delightful guest lounge with honesty bar. It trumps most hotels and there's even a little verandah, garden and library. It's on the steps that rise from Werthplatz, two blocks south of the station, to leafy Heidbergpark.

Puzzled by the name? It's an acronym of their children's names.

Getting There & Away

Eupen's train station (*bahnhof* in German) is served by hourly trains from Liège-Guillemins (€6.90, 45 minutes) and Verviers (€3.50, 20 minutes).

Hautes Fagnes

These 'High Fens' constitute Belgium's country's largest nationally protected reserve, an environmentally unique upland plateau of swampy heath and sphagnum peat bogs surrounded by considerable stands of woodland. The region is often wet, misty and shrouded in low cloud. But if you're suitably prepared this can add to its mesmerising quality. The area is criss-crossed with trails for bracing day hikes and cross-country skiing routes. There are four main trailheads on the N676, each around 1.5km apart. Each has a restaurant, ski-hire facilities in season and limited information on walking routes.

Sights & Activities

Botrange Nature Centre VISITOR CENTRE

(☎080 44 03 00; www.botrange.be; Rte de Botrange 31; visitor centre free, museum adult/child €6/3; ⏲10am-6pm Apr-Oct, to 5pm Nov-Mar) Hidden 300m west of the Eupen–Bütenbach road (1km south of Signal de Botrange and 2.5km north of Ovifat), this information centre has a museum that explains the Hautes Fagnes' evolution through a geological 'time tunnel' and examines the long-term effects of sheep grazing, logging and peat extraction (peat heated local houses right up until the 1960s). Sadly the audio guide is far too slow and the 25-minute movie isn't in English. You can access Hautes Fagnes trails from here also.

Signal de Botrange TOWER

(⏲10am-6pm Wed-Sun) FREE This, 5km north of Ovifat, is Belgium's highest point. But at 694m that's not saying much. Indeed the domed plateau landscape looks almost flat and the only eye-catching feature here is a 1954 stone tower with all the charm of a fire-station lookout. To climb it, find the door within the attached restaurant building. Across the road you can access a network of trails. There's also a **tourist office** (☎080-44 73 00; www.facebook.com/waimestourisme; Rte de Botrange 133; ⏲10am-3pm Mon-Fri, to 4pm Sat & Sun) here.

Mt Rigi HIKING

(www.mont-rigi.be; Rte de Botrange 135; ⏲information office 9am-4pm) By a pub-restaurant that's open for food all afternoon is a trailhead for the Fagne de la Polleur loop trail (4km or 6km), as well as an information office. At the junction of the Eupen–Malmedy and Eupen–Bütenbach roads.

Baraque Michel HIKING

(www.ski-baraquemichel.be) Beside a typical Ardennes-style restaurant, a marked path past tiny Chapel Fischbach then links with the

WALKING THE FAGNES

A particular attraction for short walks are the boardwalk sections, allowing you to observe the Fagnes' boggy environment without causing damage or sinking into it. The well-signed **Fagne de la Polleûr** loop is a 4km circuit, mostly boardwalked, with useful interpretive panels (French/Dutch/German) introducing relevant wildlife and plants, and an interesting weather station. It's accessed from Mt Rigi or Baraque Michel, and has an extension that takes it to 6km.

For most other hikes, a rambler's first purchase should be the 1:25,000 *Hautes Fagnes Carte des Promenades* map, which shows dozens of other routes. At the time of research, curiously, it was €7 in some places and €12.95 in others. The reserve has some restricted zones, clearly marked.

The 4000-hectare reserve is a haven for wild boar, roe deer, hen harriers and black grouse, though you're far from certain to see any. Indeed, some trails close during the grouse's nesting period (April to July). Hard to spot botanical curiosities include *Drosera rotundifolia* (a carnivorous sundew plant) and *Trientales europaea* (Wintergreen Chickweed), a rare seven-petalled flowering plant.

Fagne de la Polleûr loop. Across the road starts a 22km cross-moor hike to Eupen. Only walk for three minutes to see a curious 1839 stone pillar marking what was then the Belgian-Prussian border. Baraque Michel is 8km north of Ovifat, and 15km south of Eupen.

Getting There & Away

Buses 390 from Verviers (€3.20, 30 minutes, three to five daily) and 394 from Eupen (€3.20, 20 minutes, three to eight daily) run past all of these.

Ovifat

Ovifat is the first village south of the Hautes Fagnes. On snowy days, it becomes one of Belgium's modest **ski centres** (080 44 67 74; www.skialpin-ovifat.com; access/lift/parking/ski-set rental €1.50/1/2/10; 9.30am-4.30pm when snow allows) with three grades of piste.

On the southernmost edge of Ovifat, an idyllic little streamside lane descends 500m from a small car park to the very picturesque **Château de Reinhardstein** (080 44 68 68; www.reinhardstein.net; Chemin du Cheneux 50; adult/child €7/5.50; visits 11.15am & 2.30pm Sat & Sun, plus 2.30pm Tue & Thu Jul & Aug). Originally built in 1354 and restored to archetypal fortress appearance in 1969, the castle can only be visited by guided tour. But even when closed, it's well worth the short stroll to admire the sturdy exterior framed by mature trees.

You could alternatively walk up to Reinhardstein 800m from the northern edge of the dam that forms a forest-rimmed reservoir lake near Robertville.

At the northern edge of Ofivat, just 2km from Botrange Nature Centre, is a **Gîte d'Étape** (080 44 44 67; www.giteovifat.org; Rue des Charmilles 69; dm incl breakfast €18.10-22.60, under 26 €16-20, plus per person per stay €3.50;) hostel, in pleasant grassy grounds. It's tucked away behind the **Domaine des Hautes Fagnes** (080 44 69 87; www.dhf.be; Rue des Charmilles 67; d/f €129/170;), a 1970s architectural blooper but a godsend for families given the range of activities (pool, saunas, sports) all included in the accommodation price. There are some great midweek deals.

Buses 390 from Verviers (€3.20, 35 minutes, three to five daily) and 394 from Eupen (€3.20, 25 minutes, three to eight daily) run to adjacent Sourbrodt, a short stroll away.

Malmedy

Malmedy grew rich as a tanning centre from the 16th century. The historic city centre was heavily bombed in 1944 but castle-like **Lang Villa** and 1901 **Hôtel de Ville** survived, forming a knot of attractive buildings around the twin-towered 1784 **cathedral**. Attached, in its covered cloisters, the **Malmundarium** (www.malmundarium.be; Place du Châtelet 9; adult/child €6/3; 10am-6pm Tue-Sun Apr-Oct, daily Jul & Aug, to 5pm Nov-Mar) is a cultural centre and museum where temporary exhibitions pad out permanent features on city history, carnival and the former tanning and paper-making industries. The last tannery went bankrupt in 1994. It also offers tourist information.

Malmedy's big event is **Cwarmê** (Sun 7 weeks before Easter), four days of carnival festivities whose high-point is on the Sunday before Mardi Gras – handy if you want to head to Eupen for Rosen Montag the next day. Amid a confusing cast of characters, the luridly colourful *Haguètes* dance and parade with their *hape-tchâr* (flesh-snatcher) articulated tongs. If grabbed by such tongs, the correct response is to kneel and mutter a special Walloon 'apology'.

Sleeping & Eating

Auberge de Jeunesse HOSTEL €

(080 33 83 86; www.lesaubergesdejeunesse.be; Rte d'Eupen 36, Bévercé; dm/tw €21/54, €2 off for under 26, 10% off for HI members; reception 4-10pm; P) Around 2km towards Eupen (bus route 397), Malmedy's HI hostel overlooks a camping ground from an unusually comfortable lounge and games room set around a central fireplace.

L'Espirit Sain HOTEL €€

(080 33 03 14; www.espritsain.be; Chemin-Rue 46; s/d €80/98;) Eleven suitably stylish rooms above a contemporary design restaurant that serves straightforward honest food – salads, trout and simple meat dishes – at very reasonable prices (mains €10 to €18).

Getting There & Away

The nearest train station is Trois Ponts, near Stavelot, on the Liège–Luxembourg line. From there bus 745 runs roughly hourly (two-hourly Sunday) to Malmedy (€3.20, 20 minutes), arriving at Rue de la Gare, a few minutes' walk from Malmedy's central Place Albert Ier.

Stavelot

POP 6900

Set amid gentle slopes with appealing glimpses of surrounding lush green hills, little Stavelot is the Amblève Valley's most attractive and historic town. The town's turbulent history long revolved around the scheming prince-abbots who ruled the territory of Stavelot-Malmédy, which enjoyed long periods of virtual independence like Liège. Architecturally Stavelot offers a loveable mix of grey-stone, tile-fronted and half-timbered 18th-century houses on the narrow lanes around the cobblestoned central square.

Sights & Activities

Hanging amid Stavelot's flower baskets you might be alarmed to notice many a decapitated head. With their long, red, up-turned noses, these represent the *Blancs Moussis*, white-caped figures who are the mainstay of Stavelot's unique carnival, Laetare.

Abbaye de Stavelot MUSEUM

(080 88 08 78; www.abbayedestavelot.be; Cour de l'Abbaye 1; adult/concession incl temporary exhibition €9.50/8; 10am-6pm) The once gigantic church of the Stavelot-Malmédy prince-bishops was destroyed in the aftermath of the French Revolution. But behind the archaeological fragments that remain is a similarly large abbey building painted a vibrant crab-red. Its museums, videos and audio guide introduce the historical intrigues of the prince-bishopric. There's also an interesting series of temporary exhibitions and an impressive collection of racing cars and motorbikes illustrating 100 years of motor racing. Not so strange, given the proximity of Spa-Francorchamps (p232).

Upstairs, a two-room sub-museum introduces Guillaume Apollinaire (1880–1919), the French poet, art critic and champion of Picasso. Youthful Apollinaire summered here one year while his mum gambled in Spa. Presumably she lost, as they slipped away without paying their hotel bill.

Festivals

Laetare CARNIVAL

(www.laetare-stavelot.be; 3 Sundays before Easter) One of eastern Wallonia's most celebrated pageants, Laetare is one of the last festivals in Belgium's busy Lenten calendar. Stars of the show are the eerie 'Blanc Moussis' wearing distinctive masks like sneering, blank-eyed Pinocchios. These disguises reputedly date back to the 16th century when the prince-abbot forbade local monks from taking part in the town's festivities.

Sleeping

Camping de Challes CAMPGROUND €

(080 86 23 31; Rte de Challes 5; site per adult/child/tent/car €5.50/3/2.50/3; Apr-Oct; P) About 1.5km east of Stavelot in a lovely meadow by the river, this camp site has plenty of trees providing shade and is well-kept, though simple.

★ **Dufays** B&B €€

(080 54 80 08; www.bbb-dufays.be; Rue Neuve 115; d midweek/weekend €115/125;) This exquisitely restored 200-year-old stone building offers six lavish B&B rooms, each with a special character. All are delightful but the art deco decadence of 'Années 30' and the tasteful on-safari brilliance of the 'Africa Room' (great balcony views) are particularly memorable. The 'China Room' sleeps four,

not counting two full-sized terracotta warriors who watch you sleep.

★Bel Natura B&B €€
(0476 49 37 40; www.belnatura.be; Ave Ferdinand Nicolay 18; s/d €72/80;) Behind an upmarket Italian grocery, this fabulous 1869 tannery-owner's mansion has vast high-ceilinged, fully equipped rooms. The fine breakfast is blessed by a wooden Buddha in a grand drawing room with baronial-style ceiling and an alluring terrace facing trees and hills. It's remarkable value. Organise arrival times as the charming English-speaking owners don't live on-site.

Auberge St-Remacle GUESTHOUSE €€
(080 86 20 47; www.stavelot-auberge.be; Ave Ferdinand Nicolay 9; s/d €65/80;) Above a very central bar-restaurant facing the abbey, this has okay recently renovated rooms and a decent wi-fi connection. The bar and street can make for a bit of noise, but the location is perfect. Breakfast is €9.

La Maison/L'Espion B&B €€
(080 88 08 91; www.hotellamaison.info; Place St-Remacle 19; s/d from €75/110;) In a distinguished town house above a classy restaurant (mains €21 to €25) on Stavelot's pretty main square, La Maison's rooms come with old-board floors, period furniture and original fireplaces. Rooms in the L'Espion section are bigger and grander, and have better, newer bathrooms. But by far the most memorable features are the lavish chandelier-draped breakfast rooms complete with original Italian fabric walls.

Eating

Au Coin de ma Bulle CAFE €
(www.aucoindemabulle.be; Rue Massange 11; light meals €7-16; 11.30am-6.30pm Tue-Thu, to 10.30pm Fri & Sat;) Cheerful and central, this main-street cafe does a range of light meals – we're talking croques, quiche and the like – supplemented by daily lunch specials and weekend dinners.

★Mal-Aimé BELGIAN €€
(080 86 20 01; www.omalaime.be; Rue Neuve 12; 3-courses €30; 7-9.30pm Fri & Sat, noon-3pm & 7-9.30pm Sun) This eccentric delight is a special place to eat that also offers comfortable, if ultra-minimalist modern rooms (single/double €85/95). Despite absurdly slow service, the three-course meals are feats of top cuisine at bargain prices. Sunday meals are four-course 'surprises'. The dining room is smothered in bohemian quotes, poems and massed pictorials relevant to Apollinaire who did a runner from this very place in 1909.

The remarkable stained-glass frontage looks best at breakfast (included).

Le Loup Gourmand BELGIAN €€
(www.le-loup-gourmand.be; Ave Ferdinand Nicolay 19; mains €14-23; noon-2.30pm & 6-10pm Thu-Tue;) With a terrace on the main street and courteous, if a trifle slow, service, this place presents a wide-ranging menu of everything from steaks to salads to mussels. It's all well presented and fairly priced. Straight-up and likeable. The name refers to a wolf that killed a donkey carrying stones for the abbey but was then forced to take its place by St-Remacle.

Information

Tourist Office (080 86 27 06; www.stavelot.be/tourisme; 10am-1pm & 1.30-5pm) The abbey's cash desk doubles as a tourist office, with a useful selection of maps and guides for cycling and hiking sold from the abbey's gift shop.

Getting There & Away

From Trois Ponts train station, bus 745 runs roughly hourly (two-hourly on Sunday) to Stavelot (€2.10, 10 minutes), continuing to Malmedy. Bus 294 runs Trois Ponts–Stavelot–Verviers (€3.20, 70 minutes, five to seven daily) via Francorchamps and Tiège, where you can change for Spa.

Coo

In the 18th century, monks from Stavelot's abbey created an oxbow lake on the Amblève by digging a short-cut river channel at the tiny hamlet of Coo (pronounced 'Koe'). Cascading 15m this forms Belgium's tallest 'waterfall'. It's no Niagara, but cupped in a pretty woodland valley, the scene is charming at dusk once the hordes of day trippers have gone home. Meanwhile, by day, if you can stand the summer crowds, Coo makes a useful starting point for all manner of outdoors activities.

Activities

Coo Adventure ADVENTURE SPORTS
(080 68 91 33; www.coo-adventure.com; Petit-Coo 4) Offers mountain-bike rental, kayaking, paintball, shooting, abseiling, archery, zip-lining, caving, quad-biking, a tourist train to a game park and 'dropping', an orienteering exercise where you're dumped at a random location with a map. White-water rafting is water-level dependent, often best

WORTH A TRIP

BOATING UNDERGROUND AT REMOUCHAMPS

The famous **Grottes du Remouchamps** (☎04-360 9070; www.mondesauvage.be; Rue de Louveigné 3; adult/child €14/9; ⏰10am daily Feb-Nov, weekends only Dec-Jan, last entry 5.30pm) cave system lacks the dramatic depth of Rochefort, and its stalactites aren't a patch on those of Han-sur-Lesse. Nonetheless, the reward of an 85-minute tour is its culmination in a remarkable 700m punt down a half-lit underground river. Mind your head, bring a plastic bag to cover wet seats and dress for 12°C; nothing too smart as you'll descend a narrow 1912 spiral staircase that can be a little muddy. Tours depart once a group of around 20 has assembled. That can be very fast in high season but might take an hour or two in winter. Whatever official timings might indicate, the last tour is demand-dependent, so better go earlier.

The cave entrance is beside the tourist office on Remouchamps' main street, near the river bridge which is overlooked by the **Hôtel Bonhomme** (☎04-384 40 06; www.hotelbonhomme.be; Rue de la Reffe 26; s/d €65/99, superior €85/125; 📶). This nostalgically old-fashioned post hotel dates from 1768 and has been in the same family for eight generations. There's a tree-hugged, white-washed stone facade, the *café* is a wood-panelled classic, and rooms have semi-antique furniture. Four have been fully upgraded keeping the historic effect but adding designer bathrooms with Jacuzzi. The restaurant serves local trout and the terrace is pretty, albeit suffering from road noise. Just ignore those stairs with clashing pink paintwork.

from November to February. You can even test drive a Ferrari (€85 for 15 minutes). It's well worth phoning ahead to check availability of any activity.

Plopsa Coo AMUSEMENT PARK
(☎080 68 42 65; www.plopsa.be; Coo 4; per person over/under 1m €25/10; ⏰daily Apr-Aug, plus weekends Sep–mid-Nov) This mid-sized amusement park has over 20 summer activities including a bob-luge, labyrinth, bumper cars, minigolf and cable car that rumbles up the hillside for pleasant views. An attraction is the pretty rural setting and parents (and teenagers) can nip across to other activity providers for a whole series of adrenaline activities while the kids are occupied.

Sleeping

There are sleeping options in town, but better choices in Stavelot (there's a pleasant 7km walk between these villages) or at nearby La Gleize.

Aux Ecuries de la Reine HOTEL €€
(☎080 78 57 99; http://auxecuriesdelareine.be; La Gleize 23; s/d €80/110; P 📶 🏊) The best choice near Coo, 5km north, is this repurposed stable once used by bored Belgian Queen Marie-Henriette. It now features a lovely sloping garden, outdoor swimming pool and a range of fully modernised rooms with rustic beams. There is a two-night minimum stay most weekends. Check-in is across the road at the appealing cafe-restaurant Le Vert de Pommier.

Getting There & Away

Coo's train station is on the Liège–Luxembourg line with trains every two hours. Bus 142 runs to Remouchamps two to six times daily (€3.20, 30 minutes)

Bastogne

POP 15,100

During WWII's Battle of the Bulge, Bastogne was encircled and heavily bombarded by German forces but refused to capitulate. Nearly 70 years later, the town's tourist industry still revolves around its valiant wartime history and it's a place where the US army are unambiguously heroes. The marvellous museum of the conflict is well worth a trip.

Sights & Activities

Bastogne's main square – a car park adorned with a Sherman tank – is named Place McAuliffe for the famous general. From here, Bastogne's main drag, Rue du Vivier/Rue du Sablon, leads 800m northeast to the stone church, Église Saint-Pierre, behind which the lonely little Porte de Trèves gate-tower is the last remnant of a long-gone city wall.

★**Bastogne War Museum** MUSEUM
(☎061 21 02 20; www.bastognewarmuseum.be; Colline du Mardasson, 5; adult/child €12/8; ⏰10am-6pm Tue-Sun Sep-Jun, to 7pm daily Jul & Aug) This marvellous modern museum takes you into the heart of WWII, audio-guided by imagined

voices of civilian and military participants. The entrance level focuses on the lead-up to the war, then covers key events. It's a useful summary, with well-presented snippets and a short 3D film. Downstairs is the Battle of the Bulge and defence of Bastogne. It has two brilliantly realised theatrical audiovisuals among well-displayed memorabilia and information. Near the end, don't miss two TVs with survivors of atrocities recounting their shattering experiences.

Though the automatic audio guide can be clunky and won't suit everyone, it's a minor fault. Serious war buffs won't find much that they didn't know here, but the change in focus from a worldwide perspective to the fate of this small Belgian town is an affecting one. There's a decent cafe with outdoor seating. The museum is 1.5km northeast of Place St-Pièrre

Mardasson American War Memorial MEMORIAL

(Colline du Mardasson) A gentle hill is topped by a large memorial shaped as a circle within a five-pointed star. Its sombre grey pillars are inscribed with the names of the American states and a narrative of the battle. A cave-like chapel-crypt beneath features Protestant-, Catholic- and Jewish-themed mosaics by Fernand Léger. It's 1.5km northeast of Place St-Pièrre, next to the Bastogne War Museum.

Bastogne Barracks BARRACKS

(Camp Heinz; ☎061 24 21 24; Rte de la Roche 40; ⏲10am-4pm Tue-Sun) FREE These active barracks were once HQ of General MacAuliffe's 101st Airborne Division. To look inside, sign up here to join one of the enthusiastic and excellent free guided visits, which peruse the reconstruction centre for WWII vehicles and the 'Nuts' room explaining key parts of the Battle of the Bulge. It's 500m north of Place St-Pièrre: follow 'Autre Directions' signs at the defunct Bastogne Nord station building.

Reg Jans Battlefield Experience BATTLEFIELD TOUR

(www.regjans.com) Personalised, small-group English language tours led by the grandson of a WWII veteran. Tours typically visit sites associated with the Battle of the Bulge, often seeking out still extant bullet holes and bunkers. Book well ahead.

Sleeping

Hôtel Léo at Home HOTEL €€

(☎061 21 14 41; www.hotel-leo.com; Place McAuliffe; s/d incl breakfast €69/89; P 📶) Handily located right on the main square, this compact hotel is run by the famous Léo restaurant a few doors down. Though the building doesn't have all mod-cons, the rooms are modernised, with particularly good contemporary bathrooms. Larger superior rooms are in a separate building.

BATTLE OF THE BULGE

Widely nicknamed the Battle of the Bulge, the Battle of the Ardennes (not to be confused with the WWI battle) was one of the fiercest land confrontations of WWII. In September 1944, both Belgium and Luxembourg had been liberated by American troops after four years of German occupation. However, the Allies then pushed on into the Netherlands and France, leaving relatively few soldiers to defend the forested Ardennes. Hitler, sensing this weakness, ordered a counter-attack in the depths of winter. The offensive ploughed through the hills and valleys of northern Luxembourg and into Belgium forming a 'bulge' in the Allied line. It was a desperate attempt to capture Antwerp and the Meuse River ports to block supplies and paralyse the Allied advance. Hitler's army got within sight of Dinant but failed to break through.

During this invasion, the town of Bastogne was surrounded, but its defenders, the American 101st Airborne Division, kept fighting. When offered an opportunity to surrender, their commander General Anthony McAuliffe gave the curt, much-quoted response: 'Nuts!' His troops held out until early January, when Allied reinforcements managed to drive Nazi forces back through snowy Luxembourg into Germany. By the end of the battle in January 1945, over 20,000 troops on each side had died, along with numerous civilians as many Ardennes villages including La Roche-en-Ardenne, Houffalize and St-Vith had been bombed to rubble. Memorials to this tragic Christmas are numerous across the region. Bastogne and Luxembourg City have large military cemeteries and there are dozens of poignant museums, most memorably in Bastogne and Diekirch.

Eating & Drinking

Wagon Léo BRASSERIE €€

(☎061 21 14 41; www.wagon-leo.com; Rue du Vivier 4; mains €9.90-27; ⏰11.30am-9.30pm Tue-Sun) Open since 1946, this genteel and renowned spot is fronted by a 1940s tram carriage with wooden-inlay walls. With a bistro and a restaurant section, it's a reliable, value-packed venue for anything from spaghetti bolognese to some quite elaborate French-style meat dishes.

Brasserie Lamborelle BAR

(☎061 21 80 55; www.brasserielamborelle.be; Rue Lamborelle 19; ⏰11am-11.30pm Wed-Thu, to midnight Fri & Sat, to 10pm Sun; 📶) This small cosy pub with bottle lamps and enamel signboards serves raclette and *pierrades* (hot-stone on-the-table barbecues; €18.50 to €23.50), along with tasty, inexpensive pub meals. A remarkable range of beers includes the 'house brew' Airborne (€4.50), a brown ale served in a novel helmet-shaped ceramic cup. It's off Rue Viver not far from the square. Real fire in winter.

Information

Maison du Tourisme (☎061 21 27 11; www.paysdebastogne.be; Place McAuliffe; ⏰9.30am-12.30pm & 1-5.30pm) By the tank in the square. Rent normal (€17/25 for a half-/full day) and electric (€25/35) bikes.

Getting There & Away

Bus 163b runs roughly hourly (two-hourly at weekends) to Libramont (€3.20, 45 minutes) station on the Brussels–Arlon–Luxembourg train line.

Arlon

POP 28,300

If you're driving to Luxembourg, the south Ardennes' regional capital Arlon (Aarlen in Dutch) makes a good pit stop. First settled as a Roman trading post, the town's small central core retains a medieval street plan (but not appearance), spiralling almost imperceptibly up to a central hilltop, crowned by a church where once a powerful fortress stood.

Sights

Musée Archéologique MUSEUM

(☎063 21 28 49; www.ial.be; Rue des Martyrs 13; adult/child €4/2; ⏰9am-noon & 1-5.30pm Tue-Sat, plus Sun Apr-Sep) Mementoes of Arlon's Roman and Merovingian history are displayed in the rich, but rather static, Musée Archéologique. A combination ticket (€6) also allows you to visit the attractively furnished **Maison Gaspar** (www.ial.be; Rue des Martyrs 16; adult/child €4/free; ⏰9.30am-noon & 1.30-5.30pm Tue-Sat year-round, plus Sun Apr-Sep) across the road, with sculptures, photos and a notable 15th-century altarpiece.

Sleeping & Eating

Hôtel Trulli HOTEL €€

(☎063 21 81 79; www.trulli.be; Ave Nothomb 2; s/d incl breakfast €45/65; 📶) A short stroll downhill from the central square, Place Léopold, these rooms above an Italian restaurant have tiny bathrooms but have been renovated sufficiently to make them rather a good deal.

Le Fils de Paul BELGIAN €€

(☎063 57 01 03; www.lefilsdepaul.be; Rue de Diekirch 25; mains €18-25; ⏰noon-1.30pm & 7-9.30pm Tue-Fri, 7-9.30pm Sat) Decked out in gastropub style with dark wooden furniture, a black banquette and floorboards, this upbeat central eatery offers an intriguing range of dishes, including reliably good fish and absolutely delicious *cocottes* (stews served in the pot), as well as a range of wines by the glass or *pichet* (carafe).

Drinking & Nightlife

Taverne La Forum PUB

(Rue des Capucins 8; ⏰6pm-late Mon-Sat; 📶) For a beer, head to this cosy stone-roofed cellar pub, which has several fine brews on tap and many lambics by the bottle. No food is served.

Information

Maison du Tourisme (☎063 21 63 60; www.ot-arlon.be; Rue des Faubourgs 2; ⏰8.30am-5pm Mon-Fri, 9am-5pm Sat & Sun) A block northwest of Arlon's main square, Place Léopold. Ask about guided visits to the Tour Romaine, a small but curious subterranean fragment of Roman stonework reached by a little tunnel.

Getting There & Away

Arlon's train/bus station is 600m southwest of Place Léopold.

Bastogne Bus 1011 runs three times daily (€5.30, 45 minutes), otherwise take bus 3 to Martelange then bus 2.

Brussels (Train, €21.10, 2¾ hours, hourly)

Libramont One to two hourly express (IC) trains (€7.30, 30 minutes). 'L' trains take an hour longer.

Luxembourg (Train, €10.80, 20 to 30 minutes, half-hourly)

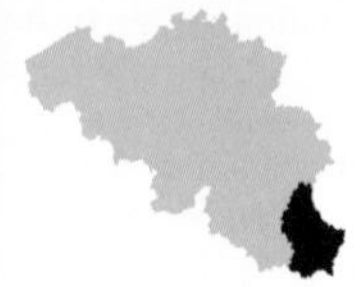

Luxembourg

Includes ➡

Best Places to Eat

- ➡ Le Sud (p251)
- ➡ La Cristallerie (p251)
- ➡ La Distillerie (p256)
- ➡ Restaurant au Vieux Château (p264)
- ➡ Grimougi (p259)

Best Places to Stay

- ➡ Hôtel Parc Beaux-Arts (p250)
- ➡ La Pipistrelle (p250)
- ➡ Hôtel Simoncini (p250)
- ➡ Hostellerie de la Basilique (p259)
- ➡ Auberge Aal Veinen (p262)

Why Go?

Consistently ranked among the world's top-three nations in both wealth and wine consumption, life in little Luxembourg seems good. But all the lax taxation and bank headquarters conceal an absolutely charming slice of northern Europe. The capital has a fairy-tale quality to its Unesco-listed historic core, memorably perched along a dramatic clifftop. Beyond, you'll rapidly find yourself in rolling part-forested hills where a string of beguiling villages each form attractive huddles beneath stunning medieval castles. Then there's all the fun of the fizz in Moselle wine country and some loveable walks to take in the pretty micro-gorges of Müllerthal. All in all, this little country has plenty of surprises. That's some achievement given its wholesale destruction during WWII, a sad history remembered in war museums across the country.

Driving Distances

	Luxembourg City	Clervaux	Vianden	Echternach
Clervaux	64			
Viaden	45	37		
Echternach	33	54	32	
Bastogne (Belgium)	63	27	43	72

Luxembourg Highlights

❶ Pacing Europe's 'most beautiful balcony', Luxembourg City's **Chemin de la Corniche** (p244) and the scenic descent to the Grund

❷ Staying the night in the gorgeous historic village of **Vianden** (p261)

❸ Tucking in to traditional and avant-garde cuisine in the lively **restaurants** (p250) and **bars** (p252) of Luxembourg City

❹ Hiking into the enchanting **Müllerthal** woodlands and rocky microcanyons from historic **Echternach** (p257)

❺ Visiting the spectacular, distinct castles at **Beaufort** (p259), **Bourscheid** (p260) and **Larochette** (p257)

❻ Seeing where General Patton is buried with his troops at the moving **US Military Cemetery** (p249)

❼ Tasting sparkling wines amid the groomed vineyards of the **Moselle Valley** (p255)

❽ Resting and strolling around the picturesque village of **Esch-sur-Sûre** (p263)

LUXEMBOURG CITY

POP 111,300

If you thought that the Grand Duchy's capital was nothing more than banks and EU offices, you'll be delighted to discover the attractive reality. The Unesco-listed Old Town is one of Europe's most scenic capitals, thanks largely to its unusual setting, draped across the deep gorges of the Alzette and Pétrusse rivers. It's full of weird spaces, tunnels and surprising nooks to explore. Good museums and a great dining scene makes this a top city to visit. It's worth visiting on a weekend, when hotel prices drop and on-street parking is free.

History

The foundations of today's city took root in 963 when Sigefroi (Siegfried), Count of the Ardennes, built a castle. From 1354 the region was an independent duchy; conquered by Burgundy in 1443, it was later incorporated into the Habsburg empire. The city's remarkable fortifications proved particularly impressive during the French revolutionary wars, although not quite good enough to survive a seven-month French siege in 1792–93. After Waterloo in 1815, Luxembourg was declared a Grand Duchy under the Dutch king, though eventually split in two after Belgian independence.

When the Dutch King William III died in 1890, his daughter Wilhelmina became queen of the Netherlands. However, by Luxembourg's then-current rules of succession, only males could rule the Grand Duchy. This quirk resulted in Luxembourg's previously nominal independence actually becoming a reality, and thus Luxembourg City emerged as a fully fledged European capital.

Germany occupied the city during both world wars. Luxembourg City's shiny glass Kirchberg area is now host to several major EU organisations, including the European Investment Bank and European Court of Justice.

Sights

The Old Town counterpoints some fine old buildings with modern museums and an offering of high-end restaurants. The picturesque Grund area lies riverside, way below at the base of a dramatic fortified escarpment.

Old Town

Much of Luxembourg's charm is gained from simply strolling the Chemin de la Corniche and Old Town. Buzzing Place Guillaume II, surveyed by the neoclassical Hôtel de Ville, is the city's heart.

Two state-of-the art museums offer imaginative exhibitions with multilevel spaces extended by digging deep into the rocky ground beneath.

★Chemin de la Corniche AREA

This pedestrian promenade has been hailed as Europe's 'most beautiful balcony'. It winds along the course of the 17th-century city ramparts with views across the river canyon towards the hefty fortifications of the Wenzelsmauer (Wenceslas Wall). The rampart-top walk continues along Blvd Victor Thorn to the Dräi Tier (Triple Gate) tower.

★Bock Casemates FORTRESS

(Montée de Clausen; adult/child €4/2; ⏲10am-5.30pm Mar-Oct, last entry 5pm) Beneath the Montée de Clausen, the clifftop site of Count Sigefroi's once-mighty fort, the Bock Casemates are a picturesque, atmospheric honeycomb of rock galleries and passages – yes, kids will love it – initially carved by the Spaniards between 1737 and 1746. Over the years the casemates have housed everything from gar-

LUXEMBOURG'S ROYALS

Dutch monarchs wore a second crown as Grand Dukes of Luxembourg from 1815 until 1890. When King William III died, his only surviving child became Queen Wilhelmina. However, by Luxembourg's then laws, its crown could not pass to a woman. Thus Adolph of Nassau took over as duke. His descendants rule to this day. Changes to the hereditary rules allowed Marie Adélaïde to become grand duchess, but perceptions of her pro-German stance in WWI meant she was persuaded to abdicate after the war. Remarkably, the Grand Duchy put its royal family up for referendum in 1919. The result was a resounding 'yes' and Marie Adélaïde's younger sister Charlotte took the throne.

The current Grand Duke Henri met his wife María Teresa, a Cuban-born commoner, at university in Geneva. Although they live in a castle (the 1911 Château Colmar-Berg), their kids were sent to ordinary schools, and it's quite possible to bump into royals at the shops or cinema. Compared with some royals, they remain much respected.

risons to bakeries to slaughterhouses; during WWI and WWII they sheltered 35,000 locals.

Royal Palace PALACE
(www.lcto.lu; 17 Rue du Marché-aux-Herbes; tours adult/child €10/5; 10am-5pm Thu-Tue mid-Jul–early Sep) Photogenically punctuated with little pointy turrets, this 1573 palace has been much extended over the years. It now houses the Grand Duke's office with parliament using its 1859 annexe. In summer the palace opens for gently humorous 45-minute guided tours, dealing mostly with family history. From the medieval-Gothic dining room, the palace's interior style morphs into sumptuous gilded romanticism upstairs.

Tours must be pre-booked via the Luxembourg City Tourist Office (p254). With only 40 tickets available per tour, you'd be well advised to book ahead, especially for English-language ones (at time of research, 3.30pm and 5pm). Other tours (Letzeburgesch, French, German and Dutch) are somewhat less-heavily subscribed.

MNHA MUSEUM
(Musée National d'Histoire et d'Art; www.mnha.lu; Marché-aux-Poissons; adult/under 26 €7/free; 10am-6pm Tue-Sun, to 8pm Thu) Startlingly modern for its Old Town setting, this unusual museum offers a fascinating coverage of art and history. It starts deep in an excavated rocky basement with exhibits of Neolithic flints, then sweeps you somewhat unevenly through Gallic tomb chambers, Roman mosaics and Napoleonic medals to an excellent if small art gallery. Cézanne and Picasso get a look-in while Luxembourg's Expressionist artist Joseph Kutter (1894–1941) gets a whole floor.

★ **Musée d'Histoire de la Ville de Luxembourg** MUSEUM
(Luxembourg City History Museum; 47 96 45 00; www.mhvl.lu; 14 Rue du St-Esprit; adult/under 21 €5/free; 10am-6pm Tue-Sun, to 8pm Thu) This remarkably engrossing and interactive museum hides within a series of 17th-century houses, including a former 'holiday home' of the Bishop of Orval. A lovely garden and open terrace offers great views.

Cathédrale Notre-Dame CATHEDRAL
(Rue Notre-Dame; 10am-noon & 2-5.30pm) Most memorable for its distinctively elongated black spires, sumptuously carved Renaissance portal inside the main doorway and attractive stained glass, the 17th-century cathedral contains a tiny but highly revered Madonna-and-child idol (above the altar) and the graves of the royal family (in the rather atmospheric 1930s crypt).

LUXEMBOURG CARD

The worthwhile **Luxembourg Card** (www.visitluxembourg.com; 1-/2-/3-day adult €13/20/28, family €28/48/68) gives free admission to over 50 of the country's top attractions, discounts on some others, plus unlimited use of public transport. You'll save money if visiting more than two museums or castles a day. Purchase online, from tourist offices, train stations or major hotels. The website details what's included.

Place de la Constitution PLAZA
Towering above this leafy triangular 'square' is a monolith topped by a wreath-bearing golden maiden commemorating Luxembourg's WWI dead. Beyond, the valley falls away to the Pétrusse River; several viewpoints overlook the scene.

Casino Luxembourg GALLERY
(Forum d'Art Contemporain; 22 50 45; www.casino-luxembourg.lu; 41 Rue Notre-Dame; adult/under 26/child €5/3/free; 11am-7pm Mon, Wed & Fri, to 8pm Thu, to 6pm Sat & Sun) This grand onetime society mansion saw the great Hungarian composer-virtuoso Franz Liszt give his last concert. Now the building is used as an interesting exhibition space for contemporary art.

Grund

You may find that this idyllically pretty little waterside district down in the valley is your favourite part of Luxembourg. The main joy is cafe-hopping while strolling the pedestrian lanes down from the Old Town and on over to Clausen.

Natur Musée MUSEUM
(46 22 33 1; www.mnhn.lu; 25 Rue Münster; adult/under 21 €4.50/free; 10am-6pm Tue-Sun;) This family-oriented, interactive museum covers all the natural history bases with stuffed animals and lifesized dinosaurs.

Abbaye de Neumünster ARTS CENTRE
(26 20 52 1; www.neimenster.lu; 28 Rue Münster; 8am-7pm Mon-Fri, 10am-6pm Sat & Sun) Dominating the Grund riverbank, this large complex is a renovated abbey turned cultural centre. Around the cloister is a permanent display of sculpture by local Lucien Wercollier,

Luxembourg City

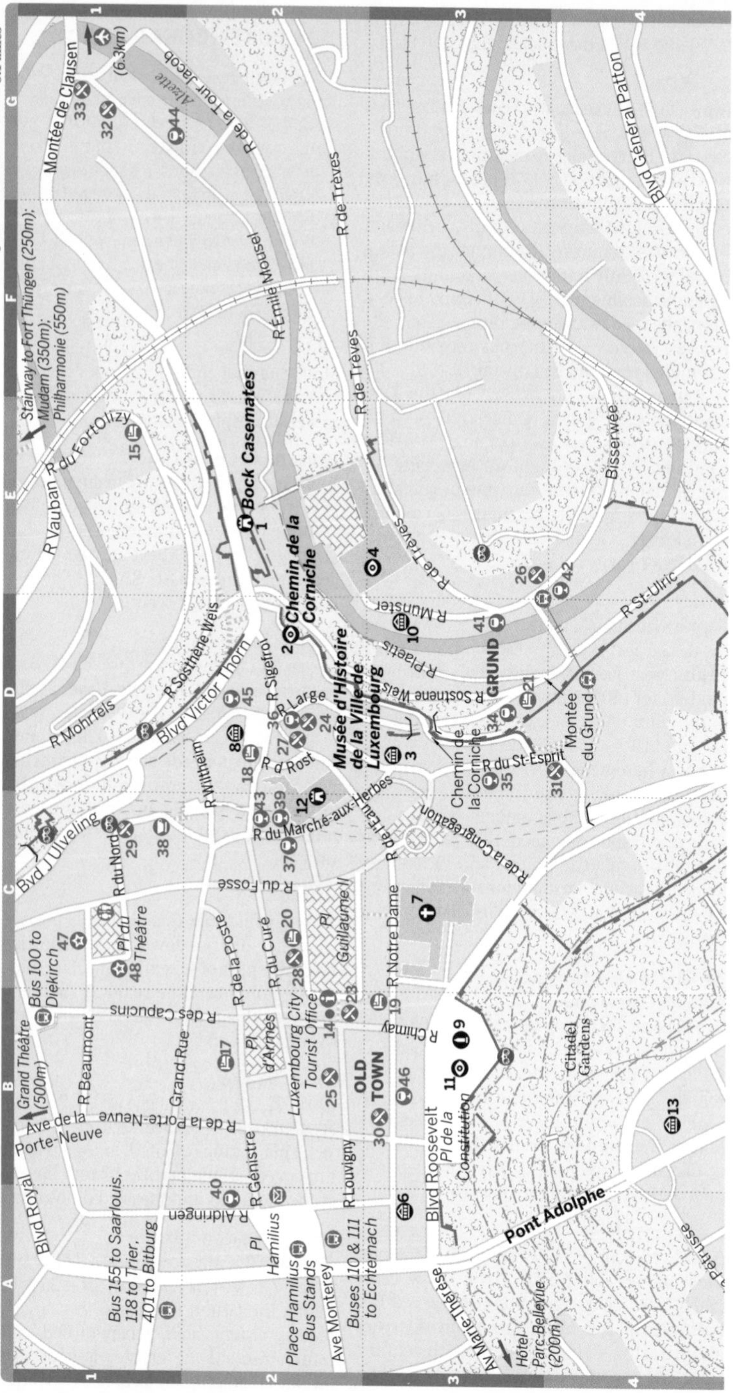

0 — 200 m
0 — 0.1 miles

A B C D E F G
1 2 3 4

Blvd Royal
Grand Théâtre (500m)
Ave de la Porte-Neuve
Bus 100 to Diekirch
47
R Beaumont
Bus 155 to Saarlouis, 118 to Trier, 401 to Bitburg
48
Pl du Théâtre
R du Nord
29
38
Blvd J Ulveling
R Mohrfels
R Vauban
R du Fort Olizy
Stairway to Fort Thüngen (250m); Mudam (350m); Philharmonie (550m)
15
Montée de Clausen
33
32
(6.3km)
44
Alzette
R de la Tour Jacob
Grand Rue
R de la Porte-Neuve
R des Capucins
R Aldringen
40
17
R de la Poste
R Wiltheim
Blvd Victor Thorn
R Sosthène Weis
8
18
45
Bock Casemates
1
Pl Hamilius
R Génistre
Pl d'Armes
R du Curé
R du Fossé
43
39
R Sigefroi
36
R Large
27
24
R Émile Mousel
Place Hamilius Bus Stands
Luxembourg City Tourist Office
28
20
37
12
R du Marché-aux-Herbes
R d Rost
2
Chemin de la Corniche
Ave Monterey
25
14
Pl Guillaume II
23
Musée d'Histoire de la Ville de Luxembourg
R de Trèves
R de Trèves
Buses 110 & 111 to Echternach
R Louvigny
OLD TOWN
30
19
R Notre Dame
R de l'Eau
3
R Plaetis
10
R Münster
4
6
46
R Chimay
7
R de Trèves
Blvd Roosevelt
Pl de la Constitution
11
9
R de la Congrégation
Chemin de la Corniche
R Sosthène Weis
GRUND
41
Av Marie-Thérèse
Hôtel Parc-Bellevue (200m)
Pont Adolphe
35
R du St-Esprit
34
21
26
31
Montée du Grund
42
Citadel Gardens
Bisserwée
R St-Ulric
Blvd Général Patton
13
Pétrusse

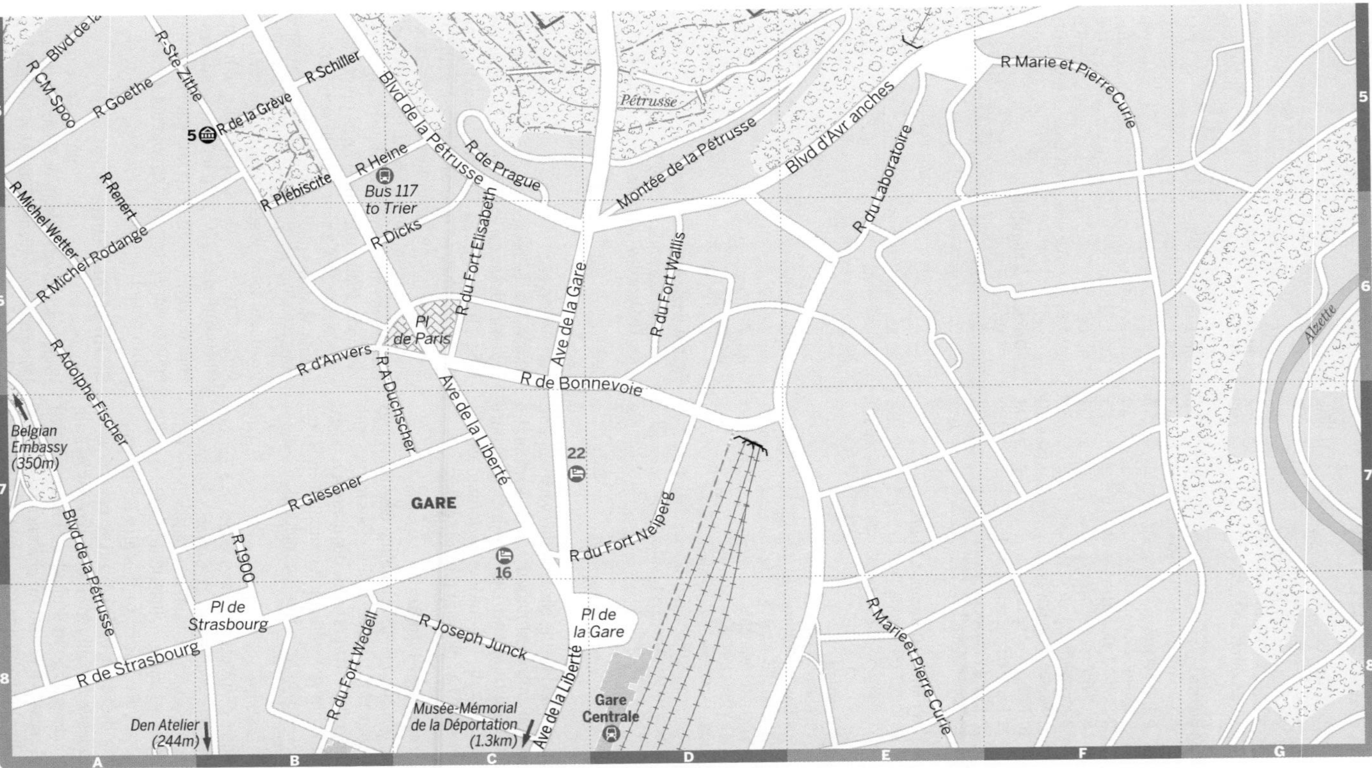
Blvd de la
R CM Spoo
R Goethe
R-Ste Zithe
5
R de la Grève
R Schiller
Blvd de la Pétrusse
R de Prague
Pétrusse
Montée de la Pétrusse
Blvd d'Avr anches
R Marie et Pierre Curie
R Heine
Bus 117 to Trier
R Plébiscite
R Renert
R Michel Wetter
R Michel Rodange
R Dicks
R du Fort Elisabeth
Ave de la Gare
R du Fort Wallis
R du Laboratoire
Alzette
Pl de Paris
R d'Anvers
R A Duchscher
R de Bonnevoie
R Adolphe Fischer
Belgian Embassy (350m)
Ave de la Liberté
22
R Glesener
GARE
Blvd de la Pétrusse
R 1900
16
R du Fort Neipperg
Pl de Strasbourg
Pl de la Gare
R de Strasbourg
R du Fort Wedell
R Joseph Junck
R Marie et Pierre Curie
Gare Centrale
Den Atelier (244m)
Musée-Mémorial de la Déportation (1.3km)
A
B
C
D
E
F
G
5
6
7
8

Luxembourg City

Top Sights
1 Bock Casemates E2
2 Chemin de la Corniche D2
3 Musée d'Histoire de la Ville de Luxembourg D3

Sights
4 Abbaye de Neumünster E3
5 Am Tunnel B5
6 Casino Luxembourg A3
7 Cathédrale Notre-Dame C3
8 MNHA D2
9 Monolith B3
Musée de la Banque .... (see 13)
10 Natur Musée D3
11 Place de la Constitution B3
12 Royal Palace C2
13 Spuerkeess B4

Activities, Courses & Tours
14 City Promenade Tour B2
Wenzel Walk .... (see 14)

Sleeping
15 Auberge de Jeunesse E1
16 Carlton Hôtel C7
Hôtel Bristol .... (see 16)
Hôtel Français .... (see 17)
17 Hôtel Le Place d'Armes B2
18 Hôtel Parc Beaux-Arts D2
19 Hôtel Simoncini B3
20 Hôtel Vauban C2
21 La Pipistrelle D3
22 Park Inn C7

Eating
23 Á la Soupe B2
24 Am Tiirmschen D2
25 Basta Così B2
26 Bosso E3
27 Bouquet Garni D2
28 Brasserie Guillaume C2
29 Chiggeri C1
La Cristallerie .... (see 17)
30 L'Adresse B3
31 L'Annexe D4
32 Le Sud G1
33 Mousel's Cantine G1

Drinking & Nightlife
Brauerei .... (see 32)
34 Café des Artistes D3
35 De Gudde Wëllen D3
36 Dipso D2
37 Go Ten C2
38 Konrad Cafe C1
39 Le Palais C2
40 L'Interview A2
41 LiquID D3
42 Scott's E4
43 Urban Bar C2
44 Verso G1
45 Vinoteca D2
46 Zanzen B3

Entertainment
47 Cinémathèque C1
48 Théâtre des Capucins C1

imprisoned by the Nazis in this very building. Several other exhibition spaces surround a central atrium and large river-facing courtyard, a venue for outdoor performances. The brasserie has pleasant terrace seating.

Kirchberg Plateau

EU institutions sit on a hilltop new-town area in impersonal modern blue-glass towers with harsh steel-strut art. But the plateau is edged with chunky fortification remnants and there are several fine cultural attractions.

★ Mudam GALLERY

(Musée d'Art Moderne; www.mudam.lu; 3 Parc Dräi Eechelen; adult/under 21 €7/free; 11am-8pm Wed-Fri, to 6pm Sat-Mon) Groundbreaking exhibitions of modern, installation and experiential art are hosted in this airy architectural icon designed by IM Pei. The collection includes everything from photography to fashion, design and multimedia. The glass-roofed cafe makes a decent lunch/snack spot.

To reach Mudam, take bus 1, 8 or 16.

Fort Thüngen MUSEUM, FORT

(Musée Dräi Eechelen; www.m3e.lu; 5 Parc Dräi Eechelen; adult/under 26 €5/free; 10am-8pm Wed, to 6pm Thu-Sun) FREE This squat building is a 1730 twin-towered extension of the plateau's vast complex of Vauban fortifications. It has an interesting museum about Luxembourg's historic defences and also hosts changing exhibitions. If the relevant door is open, climb up onto the roof for an original view back towards Mudam's glass-roofed wings.

From here it's possible to return downtown on foot. Walk steeply downhill between further bastions, tunnel through Fort Obergrünwald, then turn left (easily missed) and descend a long zigzag stairway. You emerge across the railway viaduct from the youth hostel.

South of the Centre

Spuerkeess MUSEUM, ARCHITECTURE

(Banque et Caisse d'Épargne de l'État; www.bcee.lu; 1 Place de Metz; 9am-5.30pm Mon-Fri) FREE In a dramatic, century-old, castle-style building,

Spuerkeess is the state savings bank, and hosts an intriguing **Bank Museum** (9am-5.30pm Mon-Fri) FREE tracing 150 years of tradition and innovation in banking, from piggy banks to ATMs and bank robbers.

Am Tunnel GALLERY
(40 15 24 50; www.bcee.lu; 16 Rue Ste-Zithe; 9am-5.30pm Mon-Fri, 2-6pm Sun) FREE Deep beneath the Spuerkeess bank is a permanent exhibition on photographer Edward Steichen, the man behind Clervaux's Family of Man (p264). Access, however, is via an entirely separate building and tunnel carved 350m through the Bourbon plateau. The tunnel walls are used for changing collections of excellent photographic art.

Musée-Mémorial de la Déportation MUSEUM
(24 78 81 91; 3a Rue de la Déportation, Gare de Hollerich; 9am-noon & 2-5pm Mon-Fri) FREE Thousands of Luxembourgers were deported during Germany's WWII occupation of Luxembourg, and 1200 of the country's 3700 Jewish population perished. The train station where their harrowing journey began is now a small museum. Take bus 18.

Hamm

★**US Military Cemetery** CEMETERY
(www.abmc.gov; 50 Val du Scheid; 9am-5pm) In a beautifully maintained graveyard near Hamm lie over 5000 US WWII war dead, including George Patton, the audacious general of the US Third Army who played a large part in Luxembourg's 1944 liberation. It's a humbling sight, with its long rows of white crosses (and the odd Star of David). It's just near the airport off the N2; bus 15 gets you close. Take it to the second-last stop, Käschtewee.

Tours

The Luxembourg City Tourist Office (p254) runs excellent guided walks.

City Promenade Tour WALKING TOUR
(adult/child €12/6; German & French noon, German & English 2pm) Two-hour guided walk around the old town. Run by the tourist office.

Wenzel Walk WALKING TOUR
(adult/child €15/7.50; French/German/English 3pm Wed & Sat) Winds 2½ hours through the upper and lower towns, through fortifications and along nature trails. If you miss the weekly guided walk, lead yourself using a brochure from the tourist office, also downloadable from the www.lcto.lu website.

Sleeping

Many (but by no means all) accommodation options range from dated to distinctly dowdy. Midweek, many seem dauntingly overpriced, but prices drop substantially at weekends. Accommodation is marginally cheaper around the train station, a slightly sleazy area by Luxembourg standards.

There's only one city youth hostel, but rural HI hostels are relatively accessible at Bourglinster (17km) and Larochette (28km), both on Luxembourg–Diekirch bus route 100.

Auberge de Jeunesse HOSTEL €
(22 68 89; www.youthhostels.lu; 5 Rue du Fort Olisy; dm/s/d €25/40/60, HI members €3 off; P@) This state-of-the-art hostel has very comfortable, gender-segregated dorms with electronic entry. There are good-sized lockers (bring your own padlock), laundry facilities and masses of space including a great terrace from which to admire views to the old city. En suite dorms cost €1 more.

It's a short but steep walking descent from the Casemates area down stairs near the 'Clausen Plateau Altmunster' bus stop. The cafe does a decent two-course dinner for €10.90.

Carlton Hôtel HOTEL €€
(29 96 60; www.carlton.lu; 9 Rue de Strasbourg; s/d Mon-Thu €105/138, Fri-Sun €80/115;) Despite attempts to disfigure its grand facade with modern red signage, this remains an atmospheric 1920 building with original staircases and floral stained glass in the old-fashioned foyer. Rooms have been upgraded and corridors are striking with conical torch-style lamps. Very close to the train station; breakfast included.

Hôtel Vauban HOTEL €€
(22 04 93; www.hotelvauban.lu; 10 Place Guillaume II; s/d €95/140;) The location in the heart of town here is fabulously central and the 16 rooms have been modernised, though smaller singles are rather claustrophobic. Parking around here is very expensive, so it's a better option for those on public transport.

Hôtel Bristol HOTEL €€
(48 58 30; www.hotel-bristol.lu; 11 Rue de Strasbourg; s €65, d €75-95;) While you shouldn't expect luxury, the Bristol's rooms are fair value for the relative bargain price; the cheapest doubles share a bathroom. The front desk is friendly and staffed 24 hours and there's a bar stocked with local characters downstairs. Very handy for the train station.

★Hôtel Parc Beaux-Arts BOUTIQUE HOTEL €€€
(☎26 86 76 1; www.parcbeauxarts.lu; 1 Rue Sigefroi; ste Mon-Thu advance/rack rates €190/405, Fri-Sun from €145; @ 📶) Exuding understated luxury, this charming little hotel comprises a trio of 18th-century houses containing 10 gorgeous suites. Each features original artworks by contemporary artists, oak floors, Murano crystal lamps and a fresh rose daily. Seek out the 'secret' lounge hidden away in the original timber eaves. It's in the heart of the bar and restaurant zone, so expect some street noise at weekends.

★La Pipistrelle BOUTIQUE B&B €€€
(☎621 300 351; www.lapipistrelle.lu; 26 Montée du Grund; r €170-220; 📶) Just four sumptuous rooms in a charming location mean you'll have to book early to enjoy this standout choice. It's located in an historic house with plenty of interesting features but the rooms are stylishly rendered with modern fabrics and open bathrooms. Breakfast is an extra €16; there are lots of appealing bars and restaurants very close by.

The nearby lift can zip you up to the Old Town, saving your legs.

★Hôtel Simoncini HOTEL €€€
(☎22 28 44; www.hotelsimoncini.lu; 6 Rue Notre-Dame; s/d incl breakfast Mon-Thu from €155/175, Fri-Sun €125/145; @ 📶) A delightful contemporary option in the city centre, the Simoncini's foyer is a modern art gallery and the smart, bright rooms have slight touches of retro-cool. As it's not very big, and prices are pretty low for central Luxembourg, it gets booked up midweek well ahead.

Hôtel Le Place d'Armes BOUTIQUE HOTEL €€€
(☎27 47 37; www.hotel-leplacedarmes.com; 18 Place d'Armes; r €230-550; P @ 📶) Right on the busiest central square, history, art and style meld perfectly in this gorgeous five-star package that has combined seven antique buildings into an enchanting labyrinth incorporating part-cave stone-wall meeting rooms, light-touch modern lounges and inner courtyards. Each luxurious room is different, some with fireplaces, beams or old wooden ceilings. Staff are assiduously courteous without pretension.

Park Inn HOTEL €€€
(☎26 89 18 1; www.parkinn.com; 45 Ave de la Gare; r Fri-Sun from €125, Mon-Thu from €244; 📶) Above a shoe store/shopping centre, this is a selection of modernist rooms that glow in their themed colours. It has good business-standard facilities and is handily close to the station. Good value at weekends, when you're in market central, but the weekday rate can rise vertiginously according to demand.

Hôtel Parc-Bellevue HOTEL €€€
(☎45 61 411; www.parcbellevue.lu; 5 Ave Marie-Thérèse; r Mon-Thu €145-185, Fri-Sun €80-100; P 📶) A handy stroll to the centre, this complex offers decent rooms decked out in Scandinavian-style blond wood, with pleasing beds and showers. It's expensive midweek but a bargain (for Luxembourg) at weekends. Otherwise, extras like parking and breakfast are pricey. Wi-fi is free and works well.

Hôtel Français HOTEL €€€
(☎47 45 34; www.hotelfrancais.lu; 14 Place d'Armes; s/d Mon-Fri €110/148, Sat & Sun €99/125; @ 📶) Handily central hotel offering 24 somewhat small but presentable rooms above a popular brasserie on this busily social square.

Eating

Eating is expensive in Luxembourg, but there's a lively dining scene. For characterful dining options, hunt around in the alleys and passages collectively nicknamed 'Ilôt Gourmand' directly behind the Royal Palace. There are interesting alternatives in Grund and the Clausen area. Daily in summer, tables spill merrily onto leafy Place d'Armes, with everything from burger chains to classy seafood on offer. Inexpensive but mostly characterless places for Asian food are in the train station area.

Bosso ALSATIAN, GERMAN €
(www.bosso.lu; 7 Bisserwée; mains €9-17; ⏰5.30-11.30pm Tue-Thu, 11.30am-11.30pm Fri-Sun; 📶) In summer, the biggest attraction of this good-value Grund restaurant is the hidden courtyard garden where seating is attractively tree-shaded. Try the *flammeküeche*, wafer-thin Alsatian 'pizzas' or various takes on potato rösti, or just linger over a drink.

Á la Soupe CAFE €
(www.alasoupe.net; 9 Rue Chimay; breakfast €3.50-7, soup €4.90-7.30; ⏰10am-7pm Mon-Fri, to 6pm Sat) Central and minimally stylish soup station serving Moroccan and detox soups, as well as classic chicken.

L'Annexe BRASSERIE €€
(☎26 26 25 07; www.lannexe.lu; 7 Rue de St-Esprit; mains €17-24; ⏰noon-2pm & 6.30-10pm Mon-Fri, 6.30-10pm Sat; 📶) Central but tucked away, this pleasing modern brasserie offers just

the right blend of tradition and modernity in its good-value, constantly changing menu. It's popular with lawyers from the adjacent courts, but nobody will frown if you turn up in shorts and flip-flops either. The *plat du jour* is cheap at €13, but you're often better off going à la carte.

Am Tiirmschen LUXEMBOURG €€
(☎26 27 07 33; www.amtiirmschen.lu; 32 Rue de l'Eau, Ilôt Gourmand; mains €18-25; ⊙noon-2pm Tue-Fri, 7-10.30pm Mon-Sat) This is a great place to sample typical Luxembourg dishes, but it also serves good fish and French options in case your companions don't fancy *kniddelen* (dumplings) or smoked pork. It has a semi-successful mix of old and pseudo-old decor, with heavy, bowed beams.

L'Adresse FRENCH €€
(☎66 16 81 40 5; www.ladresse-restaurant.com; 32 Rue Notre-Dame; mains €19-29; ⊙noon-2.30pm Mon & Tue, noon-2.30pm & 7-9.30pm Wed-Sat) Small and cosy, with its little wooden tables and placemats, and posters with classic French designs, this place tries to recreate a Parisian bistro in the Grand Duchy. And it succeeds: the intimate atmosphere is backed up by the daily-changing blackboard menu, which features classics like steaks, chops and salads, all well-prepared.

Bouquet Garni FRENCH €€
(☎26 20 06 20; www.lebouquetgarni.lu; 32 Rue de l'Eau; mains €15-32, lunch/dinner menus from €15/35; ⊙noon-2pm & 7-10pm Mon-Fri, 7-10pm Sat) Service here is slipshod to say the least, but the attractive dining areas – a cute covered terrace and interior spaces with ancient masonry and weathered exposed beams – add character. The food isn't quite gourmet, but it's of decent quality, and the €42 three-course menu is excellent dinnertime value for Luxembourg.

Chiggeri INTERNATIONAL €€
(☎22 99 36; www.chiggeri.lu; 15 Rue du Nord; restaurant mains €28-35, café mains €20-28; ⊙restaurant noon-2pm & 7.30-10pm, brasserie noon-3pm & 7pm-1am or later; 📶) In a historic turreted building or on its super summer terrace, Chiggeri offers a whole range of dining experiences. Downstairs there's a boisterous astrally-decorated brasserie-*café* and Moroccan-themed lantern room. Up a ragged staircase, a classy yet congenially relaxed restaurant with Afro-Aboriginal decor elements has an extraordinary wine list. Food is a bit hit-and-miss, but the place has bags of character.

Sunday brunch is a big event here.

LOCAL KNOWLEDGE

LOCAL LINGO

Though it's long been an everyday language, Letzeburgesch was only proclaimed Luxembourg's national tongue in 1984. Meanwhile almost all Luxembourgers also speak French and German, the two other official languages, with many also fluent in English. Useful Letzeburgesch vocabulary includes *moiem* (hello), *eddi* (goodbye), *gudd* (good/delicious) and *schein* (beautiful). Thank you is '*merci*', but with a stressed first syllable unlike in French.

Another language you'll hear widely is Portuguese: there's a huge immigrant community making up over 15% of the population. These 'Lusobourgers' first arrived as migrant labour in the 1960s.

Mousel's Cantine BRASSERIE €€
(☎47 01 98; www.mouselscantine.lu; 46 Montée de Clausen; mains €22-28; ⊙noon-2pm & 6-10pm Mon-Fri, 6-10pm Sat; 📶) This very authentic wood-panelled brasserie is owned by the Mousel brewery and has upped its prices to cash in upon its uniquely nostalgic appeal. Steaks, lamb chops and garlic horse supplement typical Luxembourg mainstays. Wash it down with a ceramic tankard of unique Gezwickelte unfiltered beer.

Basta Così ITALIAN €€
(☎26 26 85 85; www.bastacosi.lu; 10 Rue Louvigny; mains €14-27; ⊙noon-2.30pm & 7-10.30pm Mon-Sat; 📶) Lamps on pikes, old beams and wall drapes create a romantic old-meets-new atmosphere in this inviting, relatively spacious restaurant serving interesting twists on classic Italian cuisine.

★**Le Sud** MODERN FRENCH €€€
(☎26 47 87 50; www.le-sud.lu; 8 Rives de Clausen; degustation €78, mains €32-38, 1-/2-/3-course lunch €24/32/39; ⊙kitchen noon-2pm & 7.30-10pm Tue-Fri, 7.30-10pm Sat, noon-3pm Sun; 📶) Walk through a copper brewing still, then jump in the elevator to find some of Luxembourg's finest French food, served with an elegant smile. It's especially renowned for pigeon and truffles, and offers great value for this quality. If you decide not to eat here, it's still worth visiting the panoramic bar (open until 1am).

★**La Cristallerie** MODERN FRENCH €€€
(☎27 47 37 42 1; www.hotel-leplacedarmes.com; 18 Place d'Armes; menus €58-175; ⊙noon-2pm &

LUXEMBOURG'S ECONOMY

Little Luxembourg is famous for its 150-plus banks. But it also has a business-friendly tax regime that encourages inward investment. A little too business-friendly, perhaps: in late 2014, the Luxleaks scandal revealed the duchy to be a haven of legal tax avoidance, with many multinational companies basing their operations here and paying minimal taxes for their entire European operations. Ironically, one of the key figures in any enforcement of tighter control will be European Commission president Jean-Claude Juncker, who was actually Luxembourg's prime minister when many of these liberal laws were introduced.

Although the duchy's coal and iron industries declined in the 20th century, Luxembourg City is still a metallurgical heavyweight as HQ of ArcelorMittal, the world's largest steel company. And lots of people come daily from neighbouring countries just to fill up with cheaper petrol. Petrol taxes are low, but they're far from insignificant and provide another big earner for the treasury.

7-9.30pm Tue-Fri, 7-9.30pm Sat;) This indulgent gastronomic restaurant is hidden on the 1st floor of the Place d'Armes Hotel, lit with original stained glass and decor decked out in relatively subtle gilt. One of the degustation menus is vegetarian, and wine flights are available for all.

Brasserie Guillaume SEAFOOD €€€
(26 20 20 20; www.brasserieguillaume.lu; 12 Place Guillaume II; mains €18-40; 11.30am-midnight;) With tables on this emblematic square, this could be another tourist trap eatery. But far from it: so seriously do they take their seafood here, they drive over to Paris's famed Rungis wholesale market. Cake stand–like seafood platters are popular and delicious, but the beef carpaccios and fish dishes are also sublime. Service is busy and competent, and the kitchen's open later than most.

Drinking & Nightlife

The Old Town, Grund and the Clausen area are the top drinking spots. *The* nightclub scene is in the repurposed former Mousel brewery complex at Rives de Clausen, where half-a-dozen themed bar-resto-clubs stand shoulder to shoulder. A handy night bus runs back to the centre.

There's a second set of clubs and late-night bars along Rue des Bains, and many more along unprepossessing Rue de Hollerich around four blocks south of the train station.

★**Dipso** WINE BAR
(www.dipso.lu; 4 Rue de la Loge; 3pm-midnight or 1am Tue-Sun;) This has genuine atmosphere under its vaulted ceiling and on its tiny, fight-for-a-seat terrace. With 20-something wines by the glass, you might need the platters of cold cuts, sushi etc (€18 to €25) to soak it all up. Beware expensive bottles: it's the sort of place that, after quaffing a few looseners, the three-figure burgundy might seem like a sound plan.

Café des Artistes PUB, BAR
(22 Montée du Grund; 5pm-1am Tue-Sun;) In this loveable, atmospheric *café,* every inch of wall and ceiling is covered with posters old and new. The old candlelit piano usually bursts into life with folk tunes Wednesday to Saturday nights.

Konrad Cafe CAFE, BAR
(www.facebook.com/Konradcafe; 7 Rue du Nord; 10am-midnight Mon-Thu, 10am-1am Fri-Sat, 11am-midnight Sun;) Relaxed and happily bohemian, this sweet cafe is a cordial spot to drop in at any time of day for juices, light meals (€4 to €10) or a coffee and something sweet. At night it becomes more of a bar, with a downstairs space hosting regular comedy and live music.

De Gudde Wëllen BAR, CLUB
(www.deguddewellen.lu; 17 Rue du St-Esprit; 5pm-1am Wed-Thu, to 3am Fri & Sat;) This small, graffiti-chic, Old Town bar has a varying program of DJ nights, parties and concerts (predominantly electro), usually without cover charge.

L'Interview PUB
(21 Rue Aldringen; 7.30am-1am Mon-Fri, 10am-1am Sat, 3pm-midnight Sun;) Mirrors and wood panelling make this wonderfully unpretentious *café* look like an old-timers' hangout, but the evening's pumping, well-chosen music caters predominantly for a pre-party, student-age crowd.

Vinoteca WINE BAR
(www.vinoteca.lu; 6 Rue Wiltheim; noon-3pm & 6pm-1am Tue-Fri, 6pm-1am Sat;) Though its at-

mospheric interior and dozens of wines by the glass are praiseworthy, the principal virtue of this wine bar is its sublime terrace looking out over the ramparts of the Old Town.

Zanzen BAR

(www.zanzen.lu; 27 Rue Notre-Dame; ⌚noon-1am Mon-Sat) With a fashionably dark interior, this well-established spot is central but a little away from the more boisterous action. It does reasonable food, but appeals most for a romantic after-dinner digestif, with candle-lit tables and decent mixed drinks.

LiquID PUB, CLUB

(http://liquid.canalblog.com; 17 Rue Münster; ⌚5pm-1am Mon-Fri, 7pm-1am Sat; 📶) Atmospheric Grund pub-*café* where two rough-walled antique houses have been knocked together and straddled by a central horseshoe of bar. Live jazz Tuesday, blues gigs Thursday.

Le Palais BAR

(www.lepalais.lu; 13 Rue Marché-aux-Herbes; ⌚11am-1am Tue-Thu, 11am-3am Fri, 1pm-3am Sat; 📶) The happy crowd out on the street, flowing rum and fake tropical vegetation could have you believe that you were in some Caribbean beach club, until you venture into the sleek, dark interior (or get the bill). There are decent DJs in every night, spinning everything from jazz (Tuesday) to house (weekends).

Go Ten BAR

(www.goten.lu; 10 Rue du Marché-aux-Herbes; ⌚noon-1am Mon-Thu, noon-3am Fri, 2pm-3am Sat, 5pm-midnight Sun; 📶) One of the current darlings of the central Luxembourg bar zone, this has a curious green lichen wall, an east Asian feel to some of the decor and indeed does some Japanese food during the day. It's as a cocktail bar that it excels though, with its tasty G&Ts and mojitos seeing crowds spilling right across the street.

Urban Bar BAR

(www.urban.lu; 2 Rue de la Boucherie; ⌚11am-1am Sun-Thu, to 2am Fri & Sat; 📶) One of several closely huddled hip bar-*cafés* in the Old Town drawing cosmopolitan crowds with lots of English spoken. The waves of 1970s-retro foam panelling look like ceilings for a *Star Trek* space pod, while the sociable picnic tables on the street are where the action is in summer. It does a menu of burgers and similar.

Brauerei BAR

(www.bigbeercompany.lu; 12 Rives de Clausen; ⌚10am-2pm & 4.30pm-1am Mon-Thu, 10am-2pm & 4.30pm-3am Fri, 10am-3am Sat; 📶) The huge main brewhall of a former brewery retains giant flywheels and brewing vessels but now reverberates with music and chatter. It does a popular line in food, and the beer is pretty good.

Scott's PUB

(www.scotts.lu; 4 Bisserwée; ⌚noon-1am; 📶) One of several appealing options for a beer in the heart of Grund. Inside it's a British-style pub, outside seating is perched right above the river.

Verso CLUB

(www.verso.lu; 17 Rives de Clausen; ⌚8pm-1am Wed-Thu, to 3am Fri & Sat; 📶) One of the liveliest dance floors in the Rives de Clausen bar, restaurant and nightclub precinct.

☆ Entertainment

Summer weekends blur into what feels like one long festival (www.summerinthecity.lu) of which a great highlight is the merry **Blues & Jazz Rallye** (http://festivals.lcto.lu; ⌚mid-Jul) FREE. Tickets for a vast range of other concerts and events are available through **Luxembourg Ticket** (☎47 08 95 1; www.luxembourg-ticket.lu).

Cinema

For mainstream movies, **Cinenews** (www.cinenews.lu) tells you what's on where.

Cinémathèque CINEMA

(☎47 96 26 44; www.cinematheque.lu; 17 Place du Théâtre; adult/child €3.70/2.40) Golden oldies, cult classics and 'world' movies screened at reasonable prices, plus 10pm open-air summer specials in the courtyard of nearby Théâtre des Capucins.

Live Music

Many big-name acts perform at either **Kulturfabrik** (www.kulturfabrik.lu) or **Rockhal** (www.rockhal.lu), both in Esch-sur-Alzette, 25 minutes away by train.

Den Atelier LIVE MUSIC

(☎49 54 85 1; www.atelier.lu; 54 Rue de Hollerich) This industrial-cool venue for local and touring groups welcomes big names on a regular basis. It's on an unpromising-looking main road about 500m west of Gare Centrale. There's a gaggle of unexpectedly stylish bars hidden nearby at number 42.

Theatre, Opera & Dance

For an easy overview, consult www.theatres.lu.

Philharmonie CONCERT HALL
(☎26 32 26 32; www.philharmonie.lu; 1 Place de l'Europe) Stunning modernist glass oval across the Red Bridge in Kirchberg that hosts jazz, classical and opera. Take bus 1, 8 or 16.

Grand Théâtre PERFORMING ARTS
(☎47 96 39 00; www.theatres.lu; 1 Rond-Point Schuman) Performing-arts complex featuring an impressive line-up of international dance, opera and theatre.

Théâtre des Capucins THEATRE
(☎47 96 39 00; www.theatres.lu; 9 Place du Théâtre) A small venue with an open-air courtyard for revues and summer film screenings.

Information

HotCity (www.hotcity.lu; per day/week €4.90/12.90; wi-fi) Public wi-fi through much of the city giving free access to official Luxembourg sites. However, surfing requires payment.

Luggage Lockers (Gare Centrale; per day €3; 6am-9.30pm) Turn left on platform 3 and go to the end.

Luxembourg City Tourist Office (LCTO; ☎22 28 09; www.lcto.lu; Place Guillaume II; 9am-6pm Mon-Sat, 10am-6pm Sun) Sells city guides (€2), and has maps, walking-tour pamphlets and event guides.

Main Post Office (www.post.lu; 25 Rue Aldringen; 7am-7pm Mon-Fri, to 5pm Sat)

Zitha Klinik (Ste-Thérèse; ☎49 77 61; www.zithaklinik.lu; 36 Rue Ste-Zithe; 7am-7pm Mon-Fri) Central clinic. For emergencies, this and two other hospitals are on rotation at night and weekends: call ☎112.

Getting There & Away

BUS

Long-distance – the term is relative – buses pick up from a variety of central points. Several routes head into Germany and France, where you can connect with local networks. Consult timetables at www.mobiliteit.lu. Useful connections:

Echternach (bus 110 & 111, €2, 45 minutes)

Bitburg via Echternach (bus 401, €2, 1¼ hours)

Saarlouis (bus 155, €2, 1½ hours)

Trier (bus 117 & 118, €2, one hour)

Diekirch via Larochette (bus 100, €2, one hour)

TRAIN

Trains are run by **CFL** (p302), with good connections all through northern Europe. Sample fares from Gare Centrale, 1km south of the old city:

Brussels (€39, three hours, hourly) Via Arlon and Namur.

Diekirch (€2, 45 minutes, half-hourly) Via Ettelbrück.

Liège (€36 to €45, 2½ hours, hourly) Some direct, others changing in Namur or Marloie.

Paris (€82-104, 2¼ hours,) Direct five to six times daily via Metz.

Trier (€18, one hour, hourly) Continuing to Koblenz (€46.20, 2½ hours).

> **PUBLIC TRANSPORT IN LUXEMBOURG**
>
> Luxembourg has a one-price domestic ticket system. Wherever you go by public transport within Luxembourg the price is the same, €2 for up to two hours, €4 for the day. With the Luxembourg Card (p245), it's entirely free, as is entry to many sights throughout the country.

Getting Around

There's a handy **elevator** (6.30am-2am) from river-level in Grund up to Rue Saint-Esprit in the old town.

TO/FROM THE AIRPORTS

For Luxembourg Airport, take city bus 16 from Gare Centrale (€2, every 10 minutes Monday to Saturday, half-hourly Sunday, 25 minutes) via Place Hamilius and Kirchberg or bus 29 that heads eastwards from Gare Centrale (€2, 20 minutes, every 15 minutes Monday to Friday, half-hourly Saturday, none on Sunday).

For airports Frankfurt-Hahn (two hours), Frankfurt Airport (four hours) and Charleroi (2¾ hours), book **Flibco** (www.flibco.com) buses online for savings.

BICYCLE

Velóh (☎800 611 00; www.en.veloh.lu; subscription per week/year €1/15, plus €1 per hr; 24hr) Short-hop bike rental scheme. Rides of under 30 minutes are free. The initial subscription is payable by bank card at one of 25 special stands.

Vélo en Ville (☎47 96 23 83; 8 Bisserwée; per half-/full day/weekend/week €12.50/20/37.50/100; 8am-noon & 1-8pm Mon-Fri, 10am-noon & 1-8pm Sat & Sun Apr-Sep, 7am-3pm Mon-Fri Oct-Mar) Hires mountain bikes and city bikes; helmets extra. Free cycle-routes pamphlet available. Groups and under 26ers get a 20% discount.

BUS

Detailed maps of bus routes are available (in French) at www.autobus.lu. Most routes run often, stopping at the train station and Place Hamilius. Purchase tickets at the Gare Centrale, vending machines at major stops, or from the driver. Tickets (€2/4 for two hours/full day) are good for all city and national transport. Most buses operate 5.30am to 10pm, but on Friday and Saturday nights there's also a limited night bus service.

CAR

The cheapest open-air car park is Glacis, 800m northwest of Place d'Armes. Street parking is free at weekends, or €1 per hour 8am to 6pm Monday to Friday.

MOSELLE VALLEY

A great way to spend a day, Luxembourg's wine region isn't huge but is well set-up for visits. The wide Moselle River forms the border with Germany, its steeply rising banks covered with seemingly endless vineyards. All along the scenic riverside from Schengen to Wasserbillig you'll find a succession of villages and wineries.

Getting There & Away

BICYCLE

A good alternative for visiting the Wine Route is renting a bicycle with **Rentabike Miselerland** (entente-moselle.lu/rentabike-miselerland; per day €10), free if you have a Luxembourg Card. Pick-up at one of numerous points and drop-off at another: just make sure that you check closing times and take ID.

BOAT

Princess Marie-Astrid (75 82 75; www.marie-astrid.lu) This river-boat cruises different Moselle routes on different summer days (see website), with eating options on board. Sample fares are Schengen–Remich €6.50, Schengen–Trier €21.

BUS

Routes (at least hourly with few or no Sunday departures):

160, 175 Luxembourg City–Remich (€2, 40 to 45 minutes)

185 Remich–Remerschen–Schengen–Mondorf (€2, 35 minutes)

450 Remich–Ehnen–Grevenmacher (€2, 25 minutes)

474, 475, 485 Grevenmacher–Echternach (€2, 40 minutes)

Schengen & Remerschen

If the name Schengen sounds familiar it's probably because of the 1985 and 1990 treaties signed here that led to the border-free travel regime across large parts of Europe – the Schengen Area. Actually the signing was in a boat moored off Schengen at a midriver point where, very symbolically, France, Germany and Benelux meet. Commemorating these agreements and the European project, the **Musée Européen** (www.schengen-tourist.lu; Rue Robert Goebbels, Schengen; 10am-6pm Mon-Fri, 11am-6pm Sat & Sun) FREE has not-terribly thrilling displays including hats from customs officers of all the EU's member states. There's a pleasant cafe with terrace seating.

Opposite, in a mini–Sydney Opera House in the river, is a **tourist office** (23 60 93 11; www.schengen-tourist.lu; Rue Robert Goebbels, Schengen; 10am-6pm Mon-Fri, 11am-6pm Sat & Sun) that hires bikes as well as containing a gift shop selling a range of pro-European souvenirs.

Goethe and Victor Hugo both once stayed in Schengen's ivy-draped 1779 castle-tower, next to the museum. That's now flanked by a bigger 19th-century castle that's now a hotel.

At Remerschen, 3km north of Schengen, there's an excellent modern **youth hostel** (26 27 66 700; www.youthhostels.lu; 31 Wäistrooss/Route du Vin, Remerschen; dm/s/d €24/39/59, HI members €3 off; check-in 5-10pm; @) where dorms and rooms come with private bathroom. It's easy stumbling distance from **Caves du Sud** (www.vinsmoselle.lu; 32 Wäistrooss/Route du Vin; 10am-9pm Tue-Sun May-Oct), a vast 1940s winery building

WINE TASTING

Excellent *crémants* from the Moselle vineyards give Luxembourg the fizz and pop that keeps it buzzing throughout the summer. But the region also produces fruity Rivaners, lush Pinot Blancs and balanced Rieslings, not to mention Pinot Gris, Gewürztraminer and Auxerrois. You can taste many of these along Luxembourg's 'Wine Route', where several wineries (large companies and co-operatives rather than family châteaux) offer visits. Most take over an hour and won't always start the moment you arrive, so allow plenty of time to see a video of production techniques, then walk through the vast stainless-steel fermentation and storage tanks. Each visit explains the *méthode traditionelle* by which Champagne-style wines get fizzy; visits end with a glass or three. Alternatively, you can cut to the chase, forgo the tour and head straight to each winery's tasting room.

containing a boat-shaped bar. Tasting local wines is good value (white/bubbles from €1.70/3.50) and there's a restaurant.

Remich

Some 23km southeast of the capital, Remich is the Wine Route's main transport hub. It's a pleasant town with a bridge to Germany and an old-fashioned feel; it's favoured by locals for indulgent lunches, picnics and riverside promenades. A line of stately hotels are all on the wrong side of the very busy riverside road. One-hour pleasure cruises, plus further options with buffet meals or shows, are operated by **Navitours** (☎75 84 89; www.navitours.lu; adult/child €9/4.50; ⏱3-6 tours daily Mar-Oct).

Wine fans should head to the northern edge of town where, behind a popular restaurant, **Caves St-Martin** (☎23 69 97 74; www.cavesstmartin.lu; 53 Route de Stadtbredimus; tour incl one taster €5.20; ⏱1.30-5pm Tue, 10-11.30am & 1.30-5pm Wed-Sun Apr-Oct) really are caves – time blackened and hewn directly into a cliff. St-Martin's excellent *crémant* is actually produced elsewhere but the creation process is explained inside the cool of the tunnels (bring a sweater). Despite stated opening times, tours depart based on groups so individuals are advised to book via the website. Bus 450 Remich–Grevenmacher stops out front.

Wormeldange

Wormeldange is an attractive small town with a bridge crossing to Germany.

Caves à Crémant Poll-Fabaire WINERY
(☎23 69 66 1; www.vinsmoselle.lu; 115 Wäistrooss/Route du Vin; tour €4; ⏱tours 1-6pm Mon-Sat, tasting room 8am-8pm Mon-Fri, 9am-8pm Sat, 9am-9pm Sun May-Oct, reduced hours winter) Arguably Luxembourg's best *crémants* come from this large art deco block at Wormeldange's northern edge. It's best to call ahead, but spontaneous tours might be possible. See vast bottle spinners and bottle-laying robots in action. You can sample a hefty wine selection in the tasting room (five glasses of still or sparkling wine €6), elegantly presented on a wrought-iron 'vine'.

Grevenmacher

Workaday Grevenmacher is the Wine Route's largest town. On the riverside just by the bridge to Germany, **Caves Bernard-Massard** (☎75 05 45 1; www.bernard-massard.lu; 8 Rue du Pont; tour €6-9; ⏱tours 10am-5.30pm Tue-Sun Apr-Oct) is an especially upmarket establishment that feels more like a grand hotel. Probably Luxembourg's best-known producer of sparkling wines, the slick, humorously presented tours take only 20 minutes, departing with great frequency and led by smartly dressed guides. The delightfully genteel tasting cafe has a summer terrace with river views, albeit across a busy road.

MÜLLERTHAL

This scenic area is Luxembourg's best for outdoor activities. Müllerthal's intriguing corners are cut with narrow, mossy ravines, crystal-clear creeks and strange rock formations. A great network of hiking trails is the best way to reach these hidden areas, largely located in the sighing woodlands west of historic Echternach. Pedal there through castle villages or paddle down the Sûre.

Though the Müllerthal area is nicknamed Little Switzerland, that's for the patchwork of forests and grassy fields: there's not the vaguest hint of an Alpine peak.

Bourglinster

POP 650

Worth a quick stop en route to Larochette, Bourglinster's 18th-century **castle** (Rue du Château) FREE sits within the shattered ruins of a bigger 12th-century fortress destroyed by a 1684 French attack. The main building hosts exhibitions and the courtyard is used for occasional performances. Side wings contain two classy restaurants.

La Distillerie (☎78 78 78 1; www.bourglinster.lu; Château de Bourglinster; degustation menus €80-125, with wine €130-200; ⏱noon-3pm Wed, noon-3pm & 7-9.30pm Thu-Sun) is a full-blown gastronomic extravaganza. Set in a pillared stone chamber, elegantly warmed by comfortable colours and furnishings, it is firmly upmarket yet feels approachably comfortable by the standards of many exclusive fine-dining establishments. Part of the same set-up and based firmly on local produce, **Brasserie Côté Cour** (mains €26 to €34, same hours) is excellent value.

Down in the village, on a street of handsome houses leading up into romantic woodland, **Bourglinster Youth Hostel** (☎26 27

66 35; www.youthhostels.lu; 2 Rue du Gonderange; dm/s/d €24/39/59, HI members €3 off; check-in 5-10pm;) occupies an outwardly classical salmon-hued 1761 house whose interior has one historic staircase but is otherwise fully contemporary, with mostly six- and eight-bed dorms. It makes a tranquil budget base for exploring by bike.

Bus 100 stops here on its Luxembourg–Larochette–Diekirch route hourly; there are few Sunday services.

Larochette

POP 2100

Two modest rivers cut a dramatic gash in a woodland plateau and little Larochette fell in. Hemmed between their banks and the rapidly narrowing rock walls, the village's sturdy slate-roofed houses cluster beneath the dramatic clifftop ruins of its medieval castle.

Sights

Château de Larochette CASTLE

(83 74 97; Route de Mersch; adult/child €3/1; 10am-6pm mid-Mar–May & Sep-Oct, to 7pm Jun-Aug) Larochette's dominantly positioned castle is accessed from the centre by steep paths or by a longer, gentler 2km road (start off towards Mersch then double back). Up close, the site is less complete than it appears from below, but exploring the castle lawns, wall stubs and stairways is nonetheless compelling. The four-storey 1385 keep is especially worth climbing for the vertiginous view from its box window.

You can also peep into the dungeon or deep well shaft. There's often an art exhibition on show.

Sleeping

Auberge de Jeunesse HOSTEL €

(26 27 66 550; www.youthhostels.lu; 45 Rue Osterbour; dm/s/d €24/39/59, HI members €3 off; Mar-Dec;) At the northern end of town, turn left just before the Esso petrol station and cross the bridge to find a three-storey blue house that makes a sound budget base. This is a regional bike-hire pick-up and drop-off point.

Hôtel de la Poste HOTEL €€

(87 81 78; www.hotelposte.lu; 11 Pl Bleiche; s/d €85/105;) Better than Larochette's largely lacklustre options, this historic central hotel has genuinely welcoming staff and decent rooms, including one in which US General Patton reputedly once slept.

Getting There & Away

Hourly bus 100 stops in Larochette between Diekirch (€2, 20 minutes) and Luxembourg City (one hour). There are fewer Sunday services.

Echternach

POP 4900

A fine base for hiking and biking and one of Luxembourg's prettiest towns, Echternach boasts a strikingly beautiful central square and a long history as a monastery settlement. It makes a great base for exploring this part of the country and is the sort of place everyone descends on for a lazy afternoon's stroll on a sunny weekend.

History

Site of a 1st-century Roman villa, Echternach passed to the Merovingian kings, who in turn presented the area to Northumbrian missionary St-Willibrord who, as Bishop of Utrecht, founded a church here in AD 698. Among Ripon-born Willibrord's many miracles was the fact he wasn't beaten to death by the angry guardians of pagan temples that he vandalised in the name of his God.

By the time of Willibrord's death in 739, Echternach had become a thriving monastery. Its scriptorium became one of northern Europe's most influential and its basilica-church was rebuilt in fine Romanesque style in 1031. A vast Benedictine abbey developed around the basilica and a town around that. After the French invasion of 1794, however, the church was sacked and the abbey used as a porcelain factory.

Sights

Echternach's main sights are around Place du Marché, reached from the bus station by strolling along the cafe-filled Rue de la Gare.

Dënzelt ARCHITECTURE

(Place du Marché) The delightful town square's pinched waist is given character by this distinctive, modestly sized former law-court building that has 14th- and 15th-century origins, though the arcade, statues and corner turrets that give it its current neo-Gothic appearance date from an 1895 rebuild.

St-Willibrord Basilica CHURCH

(www.willibrord.lu; 9.30am-6.30pm) The abbey that was Echternach's raison d'être was rebuilt in 1862 but bombed to rubble during WWII, when much of the town was severely damaged. Nonetheless, Willibrord's relics

WORTH A TRIP

HIKING THE MÜLLERTHAL TRAILS

West of Echternach, highlights of hiking the well-signposted **Müllerthal trails** (www.mullerthal-trail.lu) are squeezing through shoulder-wide micro-gorges, crossing trickling streams with mossy banks, and passing distinctively eroded sandstone formations. This is hardly Bryce Canyon but quaintness trumps grandeur.

Three distinct but connected loop trails (37 to 38km each) form the backbone of the network, but various connected local walks, designated as 'Extra Tours', mean that you could happily spend a week or more hiking the whole circuit. Echternach is a trailhead for trails 1 and 2, while trail 3 passes through both Beaufort and Larochette. Trail 2 is the prettiest, has the most rock formations and is also the most up-and-down. The website suggests a six-day grand circuit of the three loops, which is easily accomplished either overnighting along the trail, or bussing back to Echternach each day. The trails are very well signposted.

Shorter walks include the E1 (11.7km), a well-marked circular path that starts up Rue Charly from Echternach bus station and winds through the intriguing **Gorge du Loup** (Wolfsschlucht).

slept peacefully in the crypt and today the complex has been rebuilt. The new incarnation is a dark and sombre affair with 1950s stained-glass windows, but the vaulted crypt still contains the highly venerated relics of St Willibrord in a primitive stone coffin covered by an elaborate white-marble canopy.

★ **Abbaye d'Echternach** MONASTERY, MUSEUM
(adult/child €3/1.50; museum 10am-noon & 2-5pm Easter-May & Oct, to 6pm Jun & Sep, 10am-6pm Jul & Aug) Reconstructed 18th-century abbey buildings spread back from the basilica towards the tree-lined banks of the Sûre. Tucked away just north of the main church, the atmospheric museum occupies the vaulted basement that once formed the famous scriptorium. You'll see facsimiles of beautiful pages from classic illuminated manuscripts, the stunning cover of the Codex Aureus, a copy of a Celtic high cross, Merovingian sarcophagi and a video of the Sprinprozession (St-Willibrord Pageant) through the ages.

Stroll through the gateway in the abbey's northern arcade to peek through wrought-iron gates at the splendid 1736 Orangery in formal French-style gardens, or head east between tennis courts to find a 1761 rococo pavilion.

Villa Romaine RUIN
(26 72 09 74; www.mullerthal.lu; 47 Rue des Romains; 10am-noon & 1-5pm Tue-Sun Easter-Oct) FREE Excavated during the creation of the reservoir lake, today a popular boating and recreation area, this Roman villa has sparse remains but was obviously an impressively large, hacienda-style set-up. It's about 1km from town in pleasant parkland.

Activities

Marked hiking trails start from near Echternach's bus station. Flat riverside bicycle paths trace the Sûre River all the way to Diekirch (27km), south into the Moselle Valley and along a former railway line to Luxembourg City. The Echternach Youth Hostel rents bicycles (per day city/mountain bike €8/15) and has a 14m indoor **climbing wall** (26 27 66 400; guest/nonguest €5/6; 7-10pm Tue & Fri, 4-7pm Sun). Kayakers could take bus 500 to Dillingen and paddle back with **Outdoor Freizeit** (86 91 39; www.outdoorfreizeit.lu; 10 Rue de la Sûre; 1-/2-person canoe rental €20/30; 9am-4pm).

Festivals

Sprinprozession CULTURAL
(http://tinyurl.com/ozkmjg7) On Whit Tuesday, the Sprinprozession sees many townsfolk and pilgrims whipping out their hankies as thousands dance in formation through the streets of Echternach. It's the culmination of the St-Willibrord pilgrimage, and some suggest that the dance was originally designed to mimic the writhing of plague-sufferers and in so doing provide protection.

Sleeping

Echternach Youth Hostel HOSTEL €
(Auberge de Jeunesse; 26 27 66 400; www.youthhostels.lu; Chemin vers Rodenhof; dm/s/d €24/39/59, HI members €3 off; check-in 4-10pm; P) Set by the lake two kilometres south of the centre, this hostel has great scope for activities, with bike hire, a climbing wall and adventure park. Facilities are modern and comfortable.

Camping Officiel CAMPGROUND €
(☎72 02 72; www.echternach-tourist.lu; 5 Route de Diekirch; camp site per adult/child/small tent/large tent €5.30/3/2.50/6.50; ⏰Apr–mid-Oct; P) Just 200m from the bus station, this camping ground has tennis courts, pool and a children's playground.

★**Hostellerie de la Basilique** HOTEL €€
(☎72 94 83; www.hotel-basilique.lu; 7 Place du Marché; s/d/tr incl breakfast €95/122/168; ⏰late Mar-early Nov; P@) With a perfect location right on the central square, this place, despite some fairly bland interior decor, offers smart, well-equipped modern rooms with comfortable beds and has staff that seem like they want to be there. A great base for this part of Luxembourg, with parking available and a downstairs cafe-restaurant (mains €12 to €22).

Tours Medievales APARTMENT €€
(www.echternach-tourist.lu; per 3 nights/week from €375/750;) Small sections of Echternach's former city walls are still visible incongruously set amid suburban houses. Four of the wall's medieval towers have been imaginatively converted into modern, upmarket accommodation, each sleeping four to six. However, they're only available for stays of three nights or more and should be booked way ahead via the tourist office.

Hôtel Le Pavillon HOTEL €€
(☎72 98 09; www.lepavillon.lu; 2 Rue de la Gare; s/d/q €72/88/146;) On a central pedestrian corner just off Echternach's main square, the Pavillon has warm colours, lantern lamps and a taste for Macke prints. There's a French-Luxembourgish brasserie (mains €15 to €27) on the ground floor.

Hôtel de la Sûre HOTEL €€
(☎61 26 64 77; www.hoteldelasure.lu; 49 Rue de la Gare; s/d €65/80, comfort d €120;) Above a steakhouse and popular street *café*, this hotel, behind a classic facade, supplements its mixed bag of standard offerings with better, modern rooms featuring pale fabrics and subtle wall decor lightly signed with a gilded hummingbird motif. Some have a Jacuzzi.

Eating

Gelateria Venezia ICE CREAM €
(3 Rue de la Gare; double scoop €2.40; ⏰10am-1am mid-Feb–Nov;) As soon as the temperatures soar above 15°C, queues start forming at this central ice-cream parlour and cafe. Pistachio and coconut flavours were given the thumbs-up in an enthusiastic vox pop conducted at last visit. The coffee is also decent.

★**Grimougi** MEDITERRANEAN €€
(☎72 00 26; www.grimougi.com; 34 Rue du Pont; mains €17-27; ⏰11.30am-2pm & 6-10pm Sun-Mon & Wed-Fri, 6-10pm Sat) Just off the tourist beat and much more interesting than the restaurants around the square, this offers innovative, beautifully presented fare with French, Italian, Portuguese and other influences. Delicious salad combinations and meats with succulent sauces are highlights. It's essential to book at weekends, when locals pack it out.

Oktav Amadeus ITALIAN €€
(www.oktav-amadeus.lu; 56 Rue de la Gare; pizza & pasta €10-16, mains €21-30; ⏰11.30am-4.30pm & 6-10.30pm) This comfortably fashionable black-and-white decor restaurant has wise-cracking, waistcoated waiters bringing forth well-cooked Italian food and scrumptious thin-crust pizzas. There's a street terrace too, though the main-drag side is more interesting than the views of the bus station.

Information

Tourist Office (☎72 02 30; www.echternach-tourist.lu; 10 Parvis de la Basilique; ⏰10am-6pm Mon-Sat, to noon Sun) Very helpful office facing the basilica. The website has a useful town map you can download.

Getting There & Away

Bitburg, Germany (bus 401, €2, 25 minutes, every hour or two Monday to Saturday)

Larochette (bus 414, €2, 40 minutes, eight to nine per day Monday to Saturday) Via Beaufort.

Luxembourg City (bus 110 & 111, €2, 45 minutes, several per hour Monday to Saturday)

Beaufort

POP 2400

Across a pretty, part-wooded valley behind Beaufort village is a ruinous but very imposing five-storey medieval **castle** (www.chateau-beaufort.lu; adult/under 26 €5/free; ⏰9am-5.30pm Apr-early Nov). Once the site of a Roman camp, the sandstone fortress expanded from 12th-century origins but never recovered from WWII bombing during the Battle of the Ardennes. There's no 'interior' or decor but there are many levels to climb and explore. The ticket desk sells locally-made plum and blackcurrant liqueurs.

There's plenty of scope for hiking and cycling. Walking suggestions and bicycle rental are available from reception at **Camping Plage** (☎83 60 99 300; www.campingplage.lu; 87 Grand Rue; camp site for 2 people, car & small tent €17.50, tipis per person €15, chalet d €60; P 📶 ≋), which doubles as a tourist office. Nonguests can use its heated outdoor pool (adult/child €4.50/2.50) or winter ice rink (adult/child €4/2.50). It's 700m north of the church beside the road to Reisdorf/Eppeldorf.

The newly built **Beaufort Youth Hostel** (☎26 27 66 300; www.youthhostels.lu; 55 Route de Dillngen; dm/s/d €24/39/59, HI members €3 off; ⏲check-in 5-10pm; P @ 📶) has excellent facilities including smart en suite rooms, bowling and a decent cafe-restaurant.

Vine-draped **Auberge Rustique** (☎83 60 86; www.aubergerustique.lu; 55 Rue du Château; s/d €55/70; ⏲food noon-8.30pm; P 📶) would overlook the castle, but for a curtain of trees. It offers eight rooms with bright new bathrooms above a loveable country pub-restaurant whose speciality is trout. A five-course vegetarian dinner costs €36.

Beaufort has bus links to Diekirch/Ettelbrück (502), Echternach (414), Larochette (414) and Luxembourg City (107).

NORTHERN LUXEMBOURG

The Grand Duchy's northernmost region is an extension of Belgium's Ardennes, with winding, fast-flowing rivers cut deep through green tablelands. Main draws are pretty Esch-sur-Sûre, Bourscheid's dramatic castle ruins and the charming getaway village of Vianden. Between here and Luxembourg City is Gutland (literally 'Goodland'), a heavily farmed area whose towns are relatively nondescript. The main rail hubs are Diekirch and forgettable Ettelbrück.

Ettelbrück

POP 8300

The main square in Ettelbrück is called Place Patton in honour of US Third Army General George S Patton who led a liberating US force into town on Christmas Day 1944. He famously noted: 'No bastard ever won a war by dying for his country. He won it by making the other poor dumb bastard die for his'. However, by December 1945 Patton himself was dead following a car accident in Germany. In an unlikely residential street, little **General Patton Museum** (☎81 03 22; www.patton.lu; 5 Rue Dr Klein; adult/child €5/3; ⏲10am-5pm Jun–mid-Sep, 1-5pm Sun mid-Sep–May) displays some interesting chunks of WWII aircraft and plays a half-hour black-and-white video about Patton's exploits. Otherwise, its selection of wartime photos, ammunition and helmets is considerably less impressive than the museum in Diekirch.

Château de Bourscheid

Viewed from the N27 or CR438, 8km north of Ettelbrück, this splendid **castle ruin** (www.bourscheid.lu; adult/youth/child €5/4/3; ⏲9.30am-5.30pm Apr–mid-Oct, 11am-3.30pm mid-Oct–Mar) is surely the nation's most dramatic. As you get closer, the degree of degradation is much clearer but it's still very interesting to clamber about the wall stubs. Admission includes a remarkably extensive audio guide and there's a trio of somewhat odd 'visuella' slide presentations to ponder en route. Don't miss climbing the rather squat, 12th-century, square keep for classic turret-framed views over the forested river bend below.

Bus 545 from Ettelbrück stops in Bourscheid village, from where the lonely castle is a steep 1.8km descent to the southwest. On the way down is the snack-bar-cafe Panorama (attached to a camping ground), from which views down towards the castle are especially impressive.

After visiting the castle you could descend another winding 2km to the N27 and return to Ettelbrück on bus 550. While awaiting the bus consider a snack, beer or Germanic local dish at the **Brasserie de Vieux Moulin** (www.amkeller.lu; snacks €3-9, mains €16-24; ⏲kitchen 11.30am-2pm & 6-9.30pm; 📶), a former watermill near the junction behind a lonely hotel.

Diekirch

POP 6200

One of northern Luxembourg's major towns, Diekirch gives its name to the nation's most famous beer and has a worthwhile war museum.

Sights

Musée National d'Histoire Militaire MUSEUM

(www.mnhm.lu; 110 Rue Bamertal; adult/child €5/3; ⏲10am-6pm) Luxembourg's most comprehensive war museum, Diekirch's Musée National d'Histoire Militaire, set in a former brewery in the town centre, is packed full of WWII equipment, vehicles and memorabilia. Numerous well-executed mannequin scenes illustrate the suffering and hardships of the battles fought in the thick snows of Christmas 1944.

Musée d'Histoire(s) Diekirch MUSEUM
(MHsD; www.mhsd.lu; 13 Rue du Curé; adult/under 21 €5/free; ⏲10am-6pm Tue-Sun) In the pedestrian zone, the modern city museum has exhibits that include a Roman mosaic floor from a villa site nearby.

Musée d'Histoire de la Brasserie Diekirch & Conservatoire National de Véhicules Historiques MUSEUM
(☎26 80 04 68; www.cnvh.lu; 20 Rue de Stavelot; adult/child €5/free; ⏲10am-6pm Tue-Sun) Centrally located, the one-room Brewery Museum celebrates Diekirch Beer, the Grand Duchy's best-known lager. The ticket price also allows you to peruse a modest car collection.

Sleeping & Eating

Hôtel Au Beau Séjour HOTEL €€
(☎26 80 47 15; www.hotel-beausejour.lu; 12 Rue Esplanade; s/d incl breakfast €85/95; P 📶) On the main road through town, this offers rooms recently renovated in stylish black, white and grey. Downstairs is a good restaurant (mains €19 to €28). Get a room at the back as the traffic gets growly pretty early.

Restaurant du Commerce BRASSERIE €€
(☎80 95 50; 1 Rue du Marché; mains €18-24; ⏲noon-2pm & 6-10pm Tue-Sun; 📶) A few eating options cluster around the square, pleasantly removed from the busy main road. This is the best of them, with decent-value grilled meats that you cook yourself on a hot stone, outdoor seating and, on the day we visited, an enormous pasta special.

Information

Tourist Office (☎80 30 23; http://tourisme.diekirch.lu; 3 Place de la Libération; ⏲10am-12.30pm & 1-6pm Mon-Fri, 10am-12.30pm & 1-5pm Sat) On the square in the small pedestrian centre.

Getting There & Around

It's 700m from the co-habiting train and bus stations to Place de la Libération. Trains arrive regularly from Luxembourg City (€2, 45 minutes, half-hourly) via Ettelbrück. Or catch bus 100, which does the journey in an hour via Larochette.

Nordstad Rent-a-Bike (☎26 80 33 76; www.rentabike.lu; 27 Rue Jean l'Aveugle; per day city/mountain bike €10/15; ⏲10am-5pm Apr-Sep, by arrangement Oct-Mar)

Vianden

POP 1800

Palace, citadel, fortified cathedral? At first glance it's hard to tell just what it is towering so grandly amid the mists and wooded hills above historic Vianden. In fact it's a vast slate-roofed castle complex whose impregnable white stone walls glow golden in the evening's floodlights, creating one of Luxembourg's most photogenic scenes. Vianden's appealing old town is essentially one road, cobbled Grand Rue that rises 700m to the castle gates from a bridge across the River Our. Newer sections of town follow the riverbanks.

On weekend afternoons in summer, Vianden can get overloaded with tourists and traffic. But get up early and you'll have the whole town largely to yourself.

History

One of the region's first 'cities', Vianden (Veianen in Letzeburgesch) gained its charter way back in 1308 and developed as a major leather and crafts centre. Its craftspeople had formed their own guilds by the late 15th century, by which stage the county of Vianden had become part of the greater Nassau lands. In the 1790s, like the rest of Luxembourg, Vianden was swallowed by revolutionary France, but after 1815 when the French withdrew, a large part of the county was given to Prussia. Vianden itself was left an impoverished backwater cut off from its traditional hinterland. Trade died off and many townsfolk were forced to seek work as travelling minstrels. Meanwhile, the Dutch king who'd been handed the town saw little use in its gigantic, hard-to-heat castle. In 1820 he sold it to a scrap merchant who stripped out and flogged any marketable building materials. What remained of the castle fell into ruin despite occasional attempts to shore up the walls. It was not until 1977, when the Grand Ducal family formally gave the castle to the Luxembourg state, that long-term restoration finally went ahead. The result was spectacular and the castle has since been not only a tourist magnet but also the backdrop set for several movies.

Sights & Activities

★**Château de Vianden** CASTLE
(☎83 41 08 1; www.castle-vianden.lu; adult/child €6/2; ⏲10am-4pm Nov-Feb, to 5pm Mar & Oct, to 6pm Apr-Sep) This château's extraordinary outline is the result of an almost-total 20th-century restoration after the original,

built from the 11th to 14th centuries, had fallen into complete ruin. Walkways in the bowels of the edifice display different layers of occupation, from Roman onwards. Open to the air, the 'Byzantine Hall' is a marvellous space, while the Gothic polygonal chapel is built around a central well. Plusher halls display fine Flanders tapestries, while photo galleries show the reconstruction process and snaps of famous visitors.

There's not much info in English, so grab an audio guide (€2). The appealingly vaulted, barrel-strewn Keller bar opens occasionally for jazz concerts.

Grand Rue STREET

Grand Rue's most attractive section is around Place Victor Abens, where the town hall stands astride a small spring. There's an attractive church and an easily missed alley beside Hotel Heintz leading to a pretty cloister that was once at the heart of the 1248 Trinitarian Monastery.

The stairway between Grand Rue 58/60 (also the alley between 106/108) takes you towards an isolated 1603 belfry standing on a ridge outcrop. It's closed to visitors, but it's a nice view from here.

Musée d'Histoire de la Ville de Vianden MUSEUM

(☎83 45 91; 96-98 Grand Rue; adult/child €3/1.50; ⏲11am-5pm Tue-Sun Easter-Oct, plus Mon Jun-Aug) This inspiring little museum is formed from two knocked together old Vianden houses. One maintains its full 19th-century decor, the other partly retains equipment from its 1950s incarnation as a bakery. Upstairs, historical and cultural exhibits are brought to life by human cut-out mannequins and push-button music. It's all in German, but a well-presented English-language accompanying text is available on request at the ticket desk.

Musée Littéraire Victor Hugo HISTORIC SITE

(www.victor-hugo.lu; 37 Rue de la Gare; adult/youth/child €4/3.50/2.50; ⏲noon-6pm Tue-Sun) Across a historic bridge from Grand Rue is a replica Rodin bust of French writer Victor Hugo. In 1871 Hugo stayed for three months in the house facing this point, part of his 19-year exile from France. Those three months were long enough for him to get the Vianden castle architect fired for substandard reconstruction work. Even if you're not excited by Victor Hugo's manuscripts and sketches, the house's windows offer some of the very best castle views available.

Télésiège CHAIRLIFT

(www.vianden.lu; 39 Rue du Sanatorium; adult/child one way €3.90/2.30, return €5.30/2.80; ⏲10am-5pm Easter–mid-Oct, closed Mon Easter-May & Oct) The *télésiège* takes 11 minutes to swing across the river and up through oak woods to a snack bar whose terrace offers lovely sweeping views across town and oblique glimpses of the castle (to which it's around 15 minutes' downhill forest walk). Photos of you with the town as a backdrop are snapped as you come up and can be bought.

Indian Forest ADVENTURE SPORTS

(www.vianden-info.lu; adult/child €18/13; ⏲10am-6pm Apr-Oct, closed Mon early and late in season) Between the castle and the top of the chairlift, this adventure park has various routes through the forest using zip lines, skywalks and similar.

Sleeping & Eating

In season there's ample choice along both Grand Rue and the riverbanks. When things are quiet, restaurants tend to close very early.

Vianden Youth Hostel HOSTEL €

(Auberge de Jeunesse; ☎26 27 66 800; www.youthhostels.lu; 3 Montée du Château; dm/s/d €22/37/55, HI members €3 off; ⏲Feb–mid-Dec, check-in 5-10pm; 📶) Within an archetypal shutter-fronted Vianden mansion close to the château entrance, this isn't quite as well equipped as some other Luxembourg hostels but makes a more-than-adequate budget base.

★ **Auberge Aal Veinen** INN €€

(☎83 43 68; http://vianden.beimhunn.lu; 114 Grand Rue; s/d €60/80; ⏲closed mid-Dec–mid-Jan; 📶) Rooms in this highly recommended spot manage to feel remarkably stylish and well appointed considering they've been seamlessly inserted into an ultra-quaint barrage of ancient dark-wooden beamwork. There's a good on-site restaurant.

Hôtel Heintz HOTEL €€

(☎83 41 55; www.hotel-heintz.lu; 55 Grand Rue; s €55-85, d €65-95; ⏲closed Oct-Easter; 🅿📶) The old-fashioned elegance of the Heintz occupies what was once the brewery-inn of the Trinitarian monks. Grandfather clocks, top hats and other historical knick-knacks decorate landings flanking a fine old staircase. Guest rooms are fresh, sometimes brightly coloured, and sport watercolours or paintings of Vianden. Despite the sober front, the back is a riot of creepers and foliage.

WORTH A TRIP

WESTERN LUXEMBOURG

If you're driving between Arlon and Ettelbrück, consider following the Eisch Valley. Peaceful lanes wind through thick woodlands, passing several castles, both crumblies and mansion-style châteaux. Sturdy ruins peep out between the trees above the pretty village of **Septfontaines**. The grand château at **Ansemborg** allows visitors to admire the statuary and geometric topiary in its attractive **formal gardens** (www.gcansembourg.eu; 10am-1pm & 3-7pm) FREE. At a sharp bend just beyond, a steep, narrow lane climbs 1.5km to the mighty medieval castle of **Hollenfels** across the moat bridge of which lies the dramatically located **Hollenfels Youth Hostel** (26 27 66 500; www.youthhostels.lu; 2 Rue du Château, Hollenfels; dm/s/d €22/37/55, HI members €3 off; check-in 5-10pm; P).

The route emerges onto Luxembourg's central north–south highway near **Mersch**, whose main street, Place St-Michel, has a rather stately air with pastel-coloured house-fronts, a twin-towered Italianate church, dragon statue and modest four-storey castle whose peach-walled gatehouse hosts the tourist office.

Hôtel-Restaurant Petry HOTEL €€
(83 41 22; www.hotel-petry.com; 15 Rue de la Gare; s/d incl breakfast €73/93, superior €79/99;) Halfway between the bus stand and tourist office, the Petry's rooms are comfy if fairly standard – the superior rooms are worth the small upgrade – but the beamed walls of an ancient house give it a little more atmosphere than other co-owned hotels in the village. There's an excellent pool/spa annexe, riverside views and a great terrace.

There's lots of eating choice here, including pizzas from a real oven.

Auberge Aal Veinen GRILL HOUSE €€
(Beim Hunn; 83 43 68; http://vianden.beimhunn.lu; 114 Grand Rue; mains €14-26; noon-3pm & 6-10pm Wed-Mon;) Snugly carved into the rock, this warm and welcoming two-level restaurant is a haven for marinated grilled meats, charcuterie platters and general good cheer. Quality is good, and quantities are very generous: it's all too easy to overorder.

Lajolla Lounge CAFE, RESTAURANT €€
(www.aubergevianden.lu; 35 Rue de la Gare; pizzas €11-14, mains €13-26; 10am-last customer) This outdoor terrace arrayed along the riverfront promenade has about the best view of the castle you can hope for from a cafe. It serves anything from drinks to duck liver, bready pizza to shrimp croquettes, but its opening hours are irregular. Find it behind the Victor Hugo house beneath the Auberge de l'Our.

Information

Tourist Office (83 42 57; www.vianden-info.lu; 1a Rue du Vieux Marché; 10am-noon & 1-6pm Mon-Fri, 10am-3pm Sat & Sun, closed Mon Oct-Mar) Just off Grand Rue facing the main bridge.

Getting There & Around

Vianden-Bréck bus stop is right outside the tourist office.

Clervaux (bus 663, €2, 45 minutes, three to four daily)

Ettelbrück via Diekirch (bus 570, €2, 25 minutes, half-hourly, hourly on Sunday).

Esch-sur-Sûre

POP 300

This tiny village wraps around a knoll virtually surrounded by an emerald-green loop of the Sûre River. Topped by a modest AD 927 castle tower, the scene is one of Luxembourg's prettiest, though there's not a great deal to do here except potter about and relax. All the better, many would say. An annual night market, held on a Saturday in July or August, brings the place to vibrant life.

Sights & Activities

Duch vum Séi MUSEUM
(Musée de Draperie; 89 93 31 1; www.naturpark-sure.lu; 15 Route de Lultzhausen; adult/under 21 €3/free; 10am-noon & 2-6pm Mon, Tue, Thu & Fri, 2-6pm Sat & Sun) This old cloth factory 700m west of the village is now a museum whose displays include an impressive collection of old textile looms. It doubles as an information centre for the Parc Naturel de la Haute Sûre, promoting local produce and environmentally aware leisure in the attractive surrounding region (www.vumsei.lu).

Sleeping & Eating

Camping Im Aal CAMPGROUND €
(83 95 14; www.camping-im-aal.lu; 1 Rue Camping Aal; camp site €7, plus per adult/child €7/4;

(⌚Feb-Dec; P 📶) This camp site has a lovely riverside position beneath a forested slope about 800m east of Esch. It gets very busy in summer. Mountain-bike hire available.

Hôtel-Restaurant de la Sûre HOTEL €€
(☎83 91 10; www.hotel-de-la-sure.lu; 1 Rue du Pont; d €77-160; 📶) Occupying a decent percentage of the village's cottages, this has a wide variety of rooms dotted here and there. Though some are in quainter settings than others, all are relatively modern and polished; some feature steam room or Jacuzzi. The central building features a gourmet restaurant, and offers numerous services like bike hire and baggage forwarding.

Getting There & Away

Bus 535 from Ettelbrück (€2, 25 minutes) runs hourly or more (two-hourly on Sunday). From Wiltz, bus 618 (€2, 20 minutes) runs eight to 10 times daily Monday to Saturday.

Wiltz

POP 5500

Sweeping up a partly wooded hill, Wiltz's limited historic centre is largely hidden behind trees, and from below the whole town looks pretty banal. However, those trees hide a Renaissance town hall and a rather stately château, whose grounds and open-air theatre come to life during the impressive, month-long **Wiltz Festival** (www.festivalwiltz.lu; ⌚Jul).

Sights

Château de Wiltz CASTLE, MUSEUM
(☎95 74 44; www.touristinfowiltz.lu; Grand Rue; combined museum ticket adult/under 21 €3.50/free; ⌚9am-noon & 2-5pm Mon-Fri, 10am-noon & 2-5pm Sat Sep-Jun, 9am-6pm daily Jul & Aug) The château hosts a helpful tourist office as well as three museums: a tannery, an exhibition on the Battle of the Ardennes, and, best of the three, a brewing museum, with an attractive oversized bottle collection, an authentic if relocated classic bar and a working minibrewery (tastings cost €2 extra).

Sleeping & Eating

Hôtel au Vieux Château HOTEL €€
(☎95 80 18; www.hotelvchateau.com; 1 Grand Rue; d/ste €80/130; P 📶) Superbly handy for the château, this tastefully modernised 19th-century mansion has seven luminously bright rooms as well as an excellent restaurant. Breakfast is €15.

★Restaurant au Vieux Château FRENCH €€€
(☎95 80 18; www.hotelvchateau.com; 1 Grand Rue; lunch 2/3 courses €14/16.50, menus €36-63; ⌚noon-2pm & 7-9pm Wed-Sun; 📶) Right by the castle, this offers divine French-influenced meals in an excellent if sedate restaurant which spills out onto a tree-shaded garden terrace.

Getting There & Away

Wiltz–Luxembourg City trains (one hour) run hourly via Ettelbrück. For Clervaux, take hourly bus 642 (40 minutes) or the slightly slower 645; there are no services on Sunday.

Clervaux

POP 1300

Attractive Clervaux, not to be confused with the famous abbey of Clairvaux in eastern France, is a sloping tongue of land wrapped into a deep wooded curl of the Clerve river. Dominating are a curious patchwork-style 1913 neo-Romanesque church and a very distinctive whitewashed castle. The latter is a fully rebuilt replica of the 12th-century original, razed in WWII. Although it contains two other minor **museums** (one museum adult/child €3.50/free, two museums €5/free; ⌚10am-6pm Tue-Sun May-Sep, weekends only Oct-Apr) – one on Luxembourg's castles, the other on the Battle of the Ardennes – the castle's primary attraction is Edward Steichen's world-famous photography exhibition, **Family of Man** (www.steichencollections.lu; Château de Clervaux; adult/under 21 €6/free; ⌚noon-6pm Wed-Sun Mar-Dec). Gifted to Clervaux in 1964, the collection comprises 273 black-and-white, mid-20th-century photos from 68 countries, interspersed with sayings and quotations. It was conceived as a thought-provoking 'mirror of the essential oneness of mankind'. Clervaux has several central hotels but lacks a bit of charm for an overnight stay.

Getting There & Away

BUS

Vianden (bus 663, €2, 45 minutes, three to four daily)

Wiltz (bus 642, 40 minutes, hourly except Sunday) Or take the slightly slower 645.

TRAIN

Liège (€24.60, 1½ hours, every two hours)

Luxembourg City (€2, one hour, hourly) Via Ettelbrück (30 minutes).

Understand Belgium & Luxembourg

Belgium & Luxembourg Today

Belgium's unique and tumultuous history has bequeathed its citizens a multilingual state. While this is a source of great cultural richness, and a two-destinations-for-the-price-of-one bonus for travellers, it's also increasingly the cause of tension and political rifts within the country. Luxembourg, the world's only remaining grand duchy *and* it's most wealthy (it has the highest GDP per capita of any nation), has had its genteel wrist slapped for its controversial taxation regime; it also finally fell into step with its European neighbours by legalising same-sex marriage in 2014.

Best in Film

Two Days, One Night (2014) Factory life in Wallonia's industrial heartland.
Rust and Bone (2012) A gritty tale split between the Côte d'Azur and Belgium.
L'Enfant (2005) A petty crook coming to grips with fatherhood in Liège.
Reste Bien Mec! (2008) Unlikely hip-hop comedy from Luxembourg.
Les Barons (2009) Comedy set in Brussels' North African community.
Girl with a Pearl Earring (2003) Belgian and Luxembourgian cities stand in for Vermeer's Delft.
Man Bites Dog (1992) Cult crime mockumentary.

Best in Print

A Tall Man in a Low Land (Harry Pearson; 1998) A decade or so old but still the funniest, most insightful Belgian travelogue.
The Belgians: An Unexpected Fashion Story (Oscar van den Boogaard; 2015) From the 2015 exhibition of the same name, the ultimate overview of the country's fashion industry.
King Leopold's Ghost (Adam Hochschild; 1998) Both biography and comprehensive account of Belgium's Congo history.
Flanders: A Cultural History (André de Vries; 2007) An anecdote-packed cultural history of Flander's cities and countryside.

Wilderness Days

Belgians went to the polls to elect a new government in what proved to be a historic election in 2010. With no grouping of parties managing to form a workable coalition, the country coasted along with only a caretaker leader for a record-smashing 541 days. The final compromise was extraordinary (and extraordinarily Belgian). The greatest number of votes (17.4%) had gone to the N-VA, a conservative, Dutch-speaking party with Flemish nationalist leanings. Yet after a year and a half of talking, the eventual choice for prime minister was Elio Di Rupo, neither right wing nor Flemish but a socialist, openly gay French speaker.

On paper the main reason behind this was the seemingly arcane issue of splitting the Brussels-Hal-Vilvoorde electoral/juridical district. But at a deeper level this was seen as a possible 'last straw' in Belgium's apparent drift towards an eventual split along linguistic lines. In the end the BHV division went ahead in July 2012 along with a raft of constitutional reforms

Let's Stay Together

For a while, a split felt almost inevitable, with political debate no longer centring on the degree of autonomy but rather around the concept of confederalism, but ever-surprising Belgium failed to explode. That said, the threat of 'bye-bye-Belgium', as Francophone satirists have dubbed a possible Flanders-Wallonia divorce, has not disappeared.

State reforms put into place from 2012, leading up to the 2014 election, gave more autonomy to regions and communities, making Belgium one of the most decentralised countries in Europe. This, along with a new five-year term and simultaneous elections at all levels of government, made the 2014 elections particularly high stakes, the losers facing five long years in opposition. No more was this so than in the highly volatile, splintering world of Flemish politics.

The election, though fraught, again brought no signs of immanent rupture. After new monarch King Phillipe nominated Bart de Wever of the N-VA to form a coalition, a mere five months of discussions elapsed before four parties came to an agreement and installed Walloon Charles Michel as prime minister. The N-VA certainly did well out of a widespread desire for change, but its confederalist ideas appear to be pragmatically put on hold, and the party players more interested in being able to form a centre-right ruling government.

Meanwhile Belgium's economic picture is mixed. Heavy industry continues to be battered despite extremely high productivity. Renault closed its Vilvoorde plant in 2007, the Voorst VW factory in Brussels was severely downsized when switched to Audi A1 production in 2009–10, and in 2012 Ford announced the closure by 2014 of their production unit in Genk. Still, the country has been outperforming the Eurozone average according to OECD reports, and its heavy fiscal deficit is slowly being cut.

Cultural Boom

While Belgium still talks of economic decline, the region hardly seems in the grip of austerity. Cultural life appears to be as healthy as ever and for visitors there continues to be a surge of new possibilities in terms of attractions, including a slew of new museums, and endless new restaurant and bar openings. The opening of the MAS museum tower in Antwerp in 2011 not only provided that city with a major new attraction but also kick-started the massive redevelopment and steady gentrification of the once-ragged docklands area of 't Eilandje. This pushes onwards with Zaha Hadid's ambitious design for the Port Authority. Ghent's own inner docklands continue to be refurbished, huge plans for its St Pieters train station are afoot and its greater port area remains a remarkable economic success, while Mons opened a number of new museums and basked in its role of European City of Culture in 2015.

Meanwhile in Luxembourg...

Contented, wealthy Luxembourg had its genteel wrist duly slapped in late 2014 with the eruption of the catchily titled LuxLeaks scandal. The Duchy's low 'business-friendly' tax regime has long attracted global giants like Amazon and ArcelorMittal to set up Luxembourg bases. A consortium of journalists, working from confidential PricewaterhouseCoopers reports, uncovered a huge number of sweetheart deals, or 'comfort letters', that absolved over 300 multinational companies from billions of dollars in tax commitments at the very time when the EU's economic outlook was at its worst.

The level of controversy has only been heightened by the fact that the European Commission chief Jean-Claude Juncker was Luxembourg's long time prime minister when the tax deals were implemented. However, the EU's investigation led to at least one victory: from mid-2015, Amazon ceased to channel all its European sales revenue through Luxembourg.

POPULATION: **11.2 MILLION/553,000 (BELGIUM/LUXEMBOURG)**

AREA: **30,528/2586 SQ KM**

GDP: **US$434 BILLION/53.1 BILLION**

INFLATION: **0.45%/0.7%**

UNEMPLOYMENT: **8.6%/6.9%**

if Belgium & Luxembourg were 100 people

56 would be Dutch-speaking
39 would be French-speaking
3 would be Luxembourgeois-speaking
1 would be German-speaking
1 other

belief systems

(% of population)

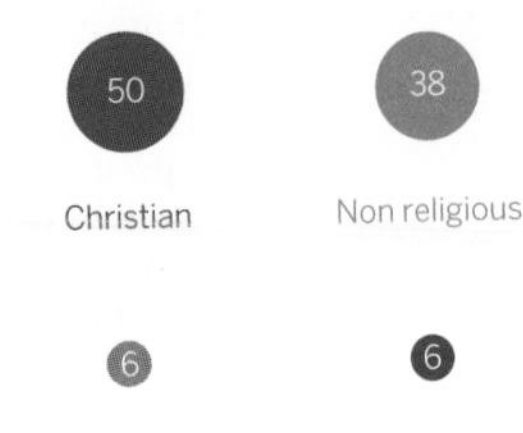

population per sq km

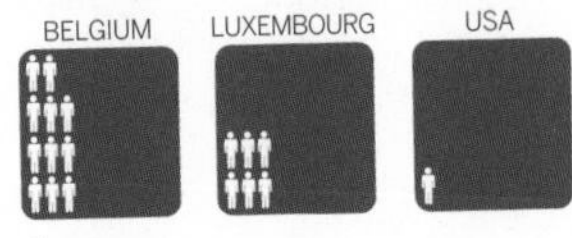

History

The current nation states of Belgium and Luxembourg first appeared on the political map of Europe rather haphazardly in the 19th century. Little Luxembourg only emerged from under the Dutch umbrella due to a quirk in royal inheritance rules. And when an opera kick-started Belgium's independence in 1830, nobody thought that the country would last. Some still doubt that it will. However, the fascinatingly tangled history of the 'Low Countries' goes back way before such shenanigans.

Overview

Belgian talent for industry and trade was already apparent 6000 years ago, when Neolithic miners dug extensively to create high-quality flint tools at Spiennes near Mons. Aubechies' Archeosite is a recreated village showing how these and later eras of early 'Belgians' might have lived.

The region had a rich Roman history but really came to prominence in the 13th and 14th centuries, when the cloth trade brought Bruges, Ghent and Ypres international stature. When Protestantism swept Europe in the 16th century, the Low Countries (present-day Belgium, the Netherlands and Luxembourg) initially embraced it, mainly in the form of Calvinism, much to the chagrin of their ruler, who was, by this stage, the fanatically Catholic Spanish king Philip II. From 1568 a series of wars lasting 80 years resulted in Holland and its allied provinces claiming independence under Protestantism, while Belgium and Luxembourg stayed under Catholic rule – first Spanish, then Austrian Habsburg. A short but destructive period of French rule following the French Revolution resulted in the desecration of the great monasteries, which had long been major players in the rural economy, and notably in Liège, which had been ruled by prince-bishops for over 800 years. After Napoleon's defeat in 1815 (at Waterloo near Brussels), the Dutch took over for 15 years. Catholic Belgium split from Protestant Holland in 1830, grabbing half of Luxembourg, the other half staying Dutch until 1890.

By this time Belgium was growing rapidly wealthy through impressive industrialisation, helped by King Léopold II's brutal asset-stripping from his 'personal' colony – the Congo.

In WWI Belgium was officially neutral, but the Germans invaded anyway. Western Flanders became a blood-soaked killing field, and whole towns, including historic Ypres, were bombarded into the mud. In WWII the countries took another pasting as Allied bombing raids tried to dis-

TIMELINE

57–51 BC

Julius Caesar's invading Roman legions find unexpectedly stiff resistance from brave Belgae warriors around Tongeren.

AD 466

Clovis, the uniting king of the Frankish clans, is born near Tournai. His conversion to Catholicism has lasting effects throughout the region.

980

Liège becomes an independent prince-bishopric, a status it keeps for over 800 years.

lodge Nazi German occupiers. The Ardennes (including Luxembourg) were the scene of Hitler's last-gasp offensive around Christmas 1944. After two such devastating wars, Benelux countries understandably became leaders in the drive for European security and integration, and Brussels now hosts the headquarters of both the EU and NATO.

Top Gallo-Roman Sites

- *Malagne, Rochefort*
- *Gallo-Roman Museum, Tongeren*
- *Villa Romaine, Echternach*
- *Musée Archéologique, Arlon*
- *Archéoforum, Liège*
- *Archeosite, Aubechies*

Romans, Vikings & Bishops

As any Belgian schoolkid will proudly tell you, Belgae warriors were the 'bravest' opponents of Julius Caesar during the Roman conquests of Gaul (57–50 BC). Students elsewhere might be less familiar with these Germano-Celtic heroes and their leader Ambiorix, who was essentially resurrected as a national icon once Belgium became independent in 1830. Of course, this being Belgium, he soon gained a slightly self-mocking Asterix-style comic-book persona.

Having shrugged off the Belgae, the Romans stayed on in Gallia Belgica for 500 years. Perhaps they liked the beer. They founded Tournai and Tongeren and built many a *castrum* (fortified camp) and villa, notably at Arlon and Echternach. In the 5th century, with the Roman Empire collapsing, Germanic Franks took control of Flanders, while in the south, Merovingian kings set up a kingdom based around Tournai that eventually controlled much of northern France. The south thus moved into a Latin linguistic orbit, creating a division with the Germanic north that remains to this day.

In the 9th and early 10th centuries, parties of raiding Vikings wreaked havoc, looting churches and pillaging villages. In reaction, a jigsaw of feudal domains developed, with locals offered the protection of increasingly powerful counts and dukes in exchange for funding. In the middle of all this was a curious patchwork of church territories ruled autonomously by the prince-abbots of Stavelot-Malmédy and the prince-bishops of Liège, entities that would retain autonomy right through to the late 18th century. Among other factors, tax advantages in the prince-bishopric led to the flourishing of metal crafts at Huy and brewing in Hoegaarden.

A statue in Brussels' Place Royale depicts Crusader knight Godefroid (Godefroy) de Bouillon, who sold up his Ardennes estates at Bouillon to lead an army in the First Crusade in 1096. While their men were away crusading, many women of the Low Countries joined religious-based self-help communities called *begijnhoven*.

The Rise of Flanders

Flanders lacked much in the way of natural resources, but once Viking threats had receded its citizens grew rich turning imported wool into top-quality textiles. As the cloth cities Ypres, Bruges and Ghent boomed over the 12th to 14th centuries, merchants exchanged not just goods but also cosmopolitan ideas. Craftsmen and traders joined forces to form guilds, setting standards for their craft and establishing local trade monopolies. But the aspirations of these burghers – a historically significant manifestation of non-aristocratic, non-clerical power – often clashed with those of their overlord counts in terms of rights, privileges and taxes. To confuse matters further, there were also conflicts between the lords and their kings.

1196

The counties of Namur and Hainaut go to war in one of many regional battles over inheritance rights.

1302

Flemish guildsmen defeat a far superior French cavalry force. They celebrate by hacking off defeated knights' gilded spurs and displaying them in Kortrijk's main church.

Early 14th century

Ghent becomes one of Europe's biggest cities.

1339–41

Plague kills huge numbers of people. Those who survive often turn to superstitious religion, the distant basis for several odd Belgian folkloric parades.

Flanders was in a particularly tricky situation. The Count of Flanders was vassal to the French king. However, Flanders' weaving economy relied on a steady supply of high-quality wool from England. So when Flanders sided with its English trading partners during Anglo-French conflicts, the French army showed up to teach it a lesson. In 1302 bloody confrontations known as the Bruges Matins kicked off a famous anti-French revolt that culminated at the Battle of the Golden Spurs at Kortrijk/Courtrai, where the French knights were dramatically (if temporarily) defeated. Since 1830 the battle has become romanticised as a symbol of Belgian (and more recently Flemish) pride. However, the revolt actually resulted in a humiliating 1305 treaty that forced Flanders to pay huge indemnities and give France a large tract of its territory.

The 'glorious entry' of Philip II into Brussels in 1549 was so grand that it is now recreated every July as the Ommegang.

The Burgundian Empire

The region's political landscape changed significantly under Philip the Bold (r 1363–1404), who had been 'given' Burgundy by his father the French king and went on to acquire Flanders by tactical marriage. His grandson, extraordinary Philip the Good (Phillipe-le-Bon, or Philip III) of Burgundy (r 1419–67), continued playing off France and England while collecting counties much as a philatelist collects stamps. By the end of his reign most of proto-Belgium (except Liège) had joined northeastern France and the Netherlands in what would be remembered as the Valois Burgundian Empire. Remarkable prosperity saw Ghent become northern Europe's largest city after Paris, and many Flemish towns built magnificently ornate belfries, market houses and town halls as symbols of wealth and hard-won civil liberties. Bruges-born Philip was the richest man in Europe and his Brussels court the height of culture and fashion. The arts flourished, particularly tapestry-making and painting, with the emergence of the artists known now as the Flemish Primitives.

When Philip's successor died in battle in 1477, his only offspring was the as-yet-unmarried 19-year-old Mary of Burgundy. Guided by her wily British-born stepmother, Margaret of York, Mary married Maximilian of Austria, yanking the Burgundian lands into a rapidly expanding Habsburg empire. Her son became Philip I (the Fair), the first Habsburg king of Castile in Spain. But her daughter, Margaret of Austria, remained in Mechelen as the de-facto ruler of the Low Countries. Her rule ushered in Mechelen's massive cultural blossoming, while Margaret also acted as guardian to her nephew, Philip I's son, the future Charles Quint.

Medieval cities each needed a royal charter before they could build belfries, which thus became a symbol of civil freedoms. The construction of belfries started in Tournai in 1188; Aalst was not permitted one until 1460.

Habsburg Rule

Habsburg/Holy Roman Emperor Charles Quint ruled an empire on which the sun never set three centuries before Queen Victoria could claim the same. Born in Ghent, Charles grew up in Mechelen and, before

1346–60

Continuing Anglo-French war leads England's Edward III to cut off wool exports. Numerous Flemish weavers forced out of work emigrate to Britain.

From the 1420s

Duke Philip the Good of Burgundy sponsors classic Flemish Primitive artists including Jan van Eyck and Hans Memling.

1425

Belgium's first university is established at Leuven. It will later educate the famous map-maker Gerardus Mercator, born 1512.

1429–67

The formerly antagonistic duchies and counties of proto-Benelux are brought together within the Burgundian empire.

CHARLES QUINT OR KEIZER KAREL?

What do Charles Quint, Keizer Karel, Charles V, Carlos I and Kaiser Karl all have in common? Answer: they were all the same person. Born in Ghent in 1500, Charles was arguably the most powerful teenager in human history. Once you've learnt the various possible alternative renderings, you'll notice his name turning up in all sorts of Belgian contexts, from beer labels to historical tours to the Brussels Ommegang.

By the ripe old age of 15 Charles already ruled the Low Countries (as Charles II of Burgundy). The next year he also became king of Spain (as Carlos I), a position of extraordinary wealth in the 16th century given Spain's brutal seizure of the New World (ie Mexico, Peru and the Caribbean) and its hoards of Inca and Aztec gold. Then in 1519 he was crowned king of Habsburg Austria and the Germanic 'Holy Roman Empire' as Emperor Charles/Karel/Karl V. He wasn't yet 20. As if that weren't enough, his good fortune continued in 1522 when his tutor and closest friend and adviser, Adrian of Utrecht, was elected Pope.

moving to Spain, ruled from the splendid Coudenberg Palace in Brussels, where he was advised by the great humanist Desiderius Erasmus.

Suffering increasing competition from manufacturers in England, the great Flemish cloth towns were feeling an economic pinch. So when Charles imposed a series of taxes to finance his foreign wars, the burghers of Ghent planned an uprising. Charles returned to suppress the revolt in 1540, making the defeated ringleaders walk around town wearing nooses, source of a nickname for Ghent folk that's used even today. Thereafter Charles made conscious efforts to encourage Antwerp's growth rather than rely on the troublesome West Flemish towns. In 1555 Charles abdicated, leaving his Germanic territories to one son (Ferdinand) and his western empire, including the Low Countries, to another son (Philip II), whose conservatively Catholic Spanish education would prove very significant.

In Mechelen, Margaret of York's palace is now a theatre, while Margaret of Austria's place has become the courthouse. Of the Hof ten Walle in Ghent where Charles V was born, only a gatehouse now remains, though the area is still called Prinsenhof in his honour.

Religious Revolt

From the mid-15th century, the development of semi-mechanised printing caused a blooming of education, with humanist thinkers including Erasmus and Thomas More attracted to the vibrant intellectual centres of Mechelen and Brussels. However, printing also made it easier for literate 'ordinary' people to read the Bible. Suddenly priests who had grown wealthy by 'selling' indulgences (reduced punishments for sins) could no longer claim such practices were God's will. The result was a wave of revolutionary Protestantism, the Reformation. Charles Quint's son Philip II tried the techniques of the Spanish Inquisition to stifle dissent, but in raising taxes to pay his Spanish mercenaries he stirred up local resentment all the more. In 1566 many Protestants ran riot, ransacking churches in an 'Iconoclastic Fury' and destroying religious icons, which they considered idolatrous. Philip retaliated

1500
The future Holy Roman Emperor Charles V, who will become one of the most powerful rulers in European history, is born in Ghent.

1562
Although faithful servants of the Spanish crown, Counts Egmont and Hoorn vocally oppose the introduction of the Inquisition in the Low Countries.

1566
Iconoclastic riots and Protestant idealism set off decades of fighting, leading to the 'Dutch Revolts' against the rule of Catholic Spain.

1604
After a devastating four-year siege, Ostend becomes the last major Benelux town to be recaptured by the Spaniards.

Ransacked Religious Sites

Abbaye d'Aulne, near Charleroi

Abbaye de Villers, Villers-la-Ville

Abbaye Notre Dame, Orval

Archéoforum (underground remnants of Liège's St-Lambert cathedral)

with a force of over 10,000 troops led by the Duke of Alba (Alva). Alba's tenure as governor of the Low Countries, infamous for its cruelty, kicked off 80 years of turbulence known variously as the Dutch Revolt, the Wars of Religion and the Eighty Years' War. British involvement was blatant, with England's Protestant Elizabeth I actively supporting the revolutionaries against Philip, her brother-in-law. It was to punish English meddling in Flanders that Spain sent the ill-fated Armada in 1588.

The Spanish Netherlands

After decades of destruction, the Netherlands expelled the Spaniards and emerged as an independent Protestant entity. However, Spain steadily recaptured Belgium and Luxembourg (the 'Spanish Netherlands'). In the regained territories, the population was fed a heavy dose of Catholicism. Many Protestants and anti-Spanish free thinkers (including much of the merchant class) moved to the Netherlands or England. The economy thus stagnated, though Liège, as a large independent prince-bishopric, had been spared the worst convulsions and its businessmen prospered around this time.

In 1598 Philip II handed the Spanish Netherlands to his daughter Infanta Isabella and her husband (and nephew), Archduke Albert of Austria. While wars rumbled on sporadically, their flamboyant court sponsored new industries such as lace making and diamond processing. Bombastic baroque churches were built to underline the Catholic Church's power and were filled with magnificent artworks stressing a religion where the faithful were offered the hope of magical redemption.

The only church whose interior has remained intact from before the Iconoclastic Fury is the splendid St-Leonarduskerk at Zoutleeuw.

In 1648 the Peace of Westphalia treaties finally recognised the independence of the Netherlands from both Spain and the Holy Roman Empire. However, this newly confirmed 'peace' was an economic disaster for the Spanish Netherlands, as a clause of the treaty demanded that part of the Scheldt River be closed to all non-Dutch ships. As a result, Antwerp's trade collapsed, while a golden age dawned for Amsterdam, the region's new premier port. The 'peace' proved very short-lived. France had already helped itself to parts of Flanders and southern Wallonia in the 1650s. Then, in 1667, with Spain fighting Portugal and Holland battling England, the way lay open for Louis XIV to grab much more. The Dutch and British patched things up to prevent further French advances. Indeed the countries became strong allies after England's return to Protestantism, with Dutchman William of Orange becoming England's William III (as co-monarch with Mary II). Nonetheless, Franco-Dutch wars continued to sweep proto-Belgium for much of the following decades, reaching a climax in 1695, when Louis XIV bombarded Brussels to splinters. Once again France occupied much of the area, sending in military engineer Vauban to fortify military strongholds such as Namur, Ypres, Philippeville and Luxembourg.

1609

Rubens' arrival in Antwerp coincides with a 12-year ceasefire in the Eighty Years' War between Spain and the proto-Netherlands.

1659

The Treaty of the Pyrenees makes Philippeville a French fort within the Spanish lowlands and also formalises Flanders' loss of Artois.

1695

Louis XIV's French troops bombard and largely destroy Brussels. Miraculously, the magnificent city hall survives.

1713–14

After decades of war with France, a Europe-wide peace deal splits the Spanish Empire, with its Southern Netherlands given to the Austrian Habsburgs.

Austrian Rule & French Occupation

When Charles II of Spain died childless in 1700, his will passed the Spanish Netherlands to a French prince. This implied that the French and Spanish empires would eventually be joined into one superpower. The prospect horrified Britain and Holland and resulted in the War of the Spanish Succession (1701–13). French and English forces skirmished for a decade until the Treaty of Utrecht forced a curious compromise in which Spain handed over proto-Belgium (as well as much of Italy) to the Habsburg Austrians, who ruled from 1713 to 1794. Influenced by the Enlightenment, the Austrians relaxed censorship and encouraged significant development.

In 1789 the French Revolution threw European politics into a new maelstrom. Anti-religious and anti-monarchic events in Paris reverberated in proto-Belgium, where the Brabantine Revolution created the short-lived United States of Belgium and the Révolution Liégeoise ousted the prince-bishops of Liège. The Austrians swiftly restored the old order, but in 1794 French armies marched into the Austrian Netherlands and introduced French revolutionary laws including the repression of the Catholic Church. The independence of Liège's prince-bishopric was definitively ended, many churches were ransacked, and Belgium's once-magnificent monasteries were looted, their lands nationalised and many abbey churches demolished as a source of building stone.

Napoleon Bonaparte's French Empire came crashing down with his ill-advised 1812 attempts to conquer Russia. But 'Boney' made a remarkable last-gasp return in 1815, during which the whole future of Europe was decided by mud, rain and a few hours of fighting near Brussels at the pivotal Battle of Waterloo. After Napoleon's defeat, the Congress of Vienna created the United Kingdom of the Netherlands. This incorporated what are today the Netherlands and Belgium. Meanwhile, the newly restored Grand Duchy of Luxembourg (then twice its current size) was declared the personal property of the Dutch king, who concurrently became Grand Duke.

The United Kingdom of the Netherlands

The United Kingdom of the Netherlands was created largely to preserve the balance of power in Europe and to create a buffer state should France have any northward ambitions. That people of different religions and customs were being forced together was of little consequence. William of Orange-Nassau, crowned William I in Brussels, made enemies quickly after refusing to give southern Belgium fair political representation and trying to impose Dutch as the national language. The latter angered not only Francophones but also Flemish speakers, who regarded their language as distinct from Dutch. Few would have imagined a Brussels

Among Catholic Brits who joined anti-Protestant Spanish forces in the Low Countries was one Guy Fawkes, later infamous for his botched British gunpowder plot (1605).

Great Museums for Regional History

- *Grand Curtius, Liège*
- *Musée BELvue, Brussels*
- *Musée d'Histoire de la Ville de Luxembourg, Luxembourg City*
- *Bastogne War Museum, Bastogne*
- *Abbaye de Stavelot, Stavelot*
- *STAM, Ghent*

1789–96

Proto-Belgium is swallowed by the ideas and then the troops of revolutionary France, resulting in the looting, destruction and privatisation of its once-magnificent abbeys.

1815

Napoleon's surprise comeback is quashed at Waterloo, just south of Brussels. Luxembourg is designated a Grand Duchy under the Dutch crown.

1830

An opera in Brussels sparks revolution against 15-year-old Dutch rule. Belgium is born, much to its own surprise.

1885

Belgium's Léopold II personally acquires the Congo, ultimately leading to the fabulous regeneration of Brussels but the death of millions of Africans.

REVOLUTIONARY PERFORMANCE

An enchanting if highly simplified story of Belgium's foundation starts on 25 August 1830, with the Brussels premiere of French composer Daniel Auber's new opera, *La Muette de Portici*, at La Monnaie in Brussels. The story, sung in French, centres on a 1647 Naples uprising against the Spanish, featuring large crowd scenes and dramatic effects. Fired up by the duet 'Amour sacré de la patrie' (Sacred Love of the Homeland), the mainly bourgeois Francophone audience poured into the streets to join workers already demonstrating outside the theatre against their Dutch rulers. Together they stormed the Palais de Justice, chased out the Dutch troops and, in a glorious crowning moment, raised the flag of Brabant over Brussels' City Hall. Belgium was born.

opera performance to be the spark to set off a revolution, yet that's what happened on 25 August 1830.

Independence

The January 1831 Conference of London recognised the independence of Belgium (initially incorporating Luxembourg) and the country was officially declared a neutral state. Unemployed royal wannabe Léopold of Saxe-Coburg Gotha, who had been married to the Princess of Wales and was the uncle of Prince Albert, was bundled out of the British court to be crowned Léopold I of Belgium. However, Belgium's independence was only accepted by the Netherlands in 1839, once Belgium agreed to 'give back' the eastern half of Luxembourg (the section that's now independent Luxembourg) over which the Dutch king was recognised as Grand Duke.

A monument on Brussels' Place des Martyrs commemorates the 467 people who died in the 1830 revolution, and a statue at De Panne marks the spot where Léopold I came ashore to become the new country's king.

The Industrial Revolution got off to a roaring start, with coal mines developed in the Borinage (around Mons and Charleroi) and iron making in Liège and later in Luxembourg. But Luxembourg's membership of a German customs union led to tensions between France and Prussia. Eventually, to stop a war breaking out, the 1867 Second Treaty of London enforced Luxembourg's neutrality by tearing down Luxembourg City's main fortifications. The Grand Duchy nonetheless remained under the Dutch crown until 1890, when a quirk in the rules of royal succession meant that its previously notional independence suddenly became a reality.

Léopold II

Coming to the throne in 1865, Léopold II was committed to transforming his father's little kingdom into a world-class nation. He put great effort into bolstering Brussels, commissioning the construction of monumental buildings such as the daunting Palais de Justice.

Then, in 1885, mainly through a series of dubious treaties and contracts, Léopold personally acquired a huge slice of central Africa that

1890
Different succession laws lead to the independence of modern Luxembourg from the Netherlands.

Early 20th century
Wallonia's steel and glass manufacturers put Belgium at the forefront of modern technology.

1905–14
Booming Belgian cities embrace the sinuous aesthetics of art nouveau. Brussels (1911) and Ghent (1913) host major World Fairs.

1914–18
WWI makes Flanders Fields synonymous with mud, blood and poppies. Ypres, Nieuwpoort and Diksmuide are wiped off the map, albeit eventually reconstructed.

was 70 times larger than Belgium. This he disingenuously named the 'Congo Free State'. While he appeared to be setting up schemes to 'protest' the slave trade, 'his' Congolese people were anything but free. The rubber plantations proved extremely lucrative for Léopold (tyres had been developed in the mid-1890s), but Congo army manuals from that time describe women and children kept hostage to force men to fulfil rubber quotas. Reports suggest that, over the next 25 years, huge numbers – perhaps up to half of the Congolese population – perished, directly or indirectly, due to Léopold's rule. Writers including Mark Twain and Sir Arthur Conan Doyle were vocal campaigners for Congolese reforms, and Joseph Conrad's novel *Heart of Darkness,* the inspiration for the movie *Apocalypse Now,* was set in Léopold's Congo. Finally, in 1908, the king was stripped of his possession by the Belgian state, embarrassed by the terrible reputation it had brought the nation. Congo nonetheless remained an important Belgian colony until 1960.

It is unknown how many Congolese people died in Léopold II's 'private garden'. According to Adam Hochschild's fascinating book *King Leopold's Ghost*, the furnaces in the Congo offices in Brussels burnt for over a week to destroy the archives after he forfeited the territory.

WWI

When Léopold II died in 1909 he was succeeded by his 21-year-old nephew Albert I (r 1909–34). Five years later the whole world changed as WWI broke out and Germany occupied neutral Belgium. However, fast as it was, the German advance was crucially slowed by the plucky defence of Liège. And in the far north at Nieuwpoort, it was halted altogether by the old defensive trick of flooding low-lying fields. This required the opening of the canal sluice gates, a dicey operation undertaken by brave volunteers under daily fire. Thus protected, a tiny triangle of Belgian land around Veurne remained unoccupied, and Albert took up residence here to personally lead the Belgian army. Further German advances towards the strategic French coastal towns were prevented. 'Brave Little Belgium' was born, and 'Remember Belgium' was used on recruitment posters in Great Britain. But Allied counter-attacks proved futile. The armies dug trenches and became bogged down for four years of futile sorties that killed hundreds of thousands and devastated Western Flanders.

After WWI the Treaty of Versailles abolished Belgium's neutral status and the country was given reparations from Germany, including an area known today as the Eastern Cantons, along with Germany's former colonies of Burundi and Rwanda in central Africa. In 1934 much-loved Albert I died in a mysterious rock-climbing accident and was succeeded by his son, Léopold III.

There are royal websites (www.monarchie.be and www.monarchie.lu) for Belgium and Luxembourg, respectively.

WWII

On 10 May 1940 the Germans launched a surprise attack and rapidly occupied the Netherlands, Belgium and Luxembourg. Unlike his father, Belgian king Léopold III put up little resistance and quickly surrendered to

1939–44

Germany again invades both Belgium and Luxembourg, which remain occupied for most of WWII. Jewish and Roma populations are decimated.

Christmas 1944

In a last-gasp German counter-offensive, the 'Battle of the Bulge' devastates many towns and villages across Luxembourg and the Belgian Ardennes.

1951

King Léopold III abdicates following the complex 'Royal Question' over his supposed wartime collaboration with the Nazi occupation regime.

1958

The Atomium is built as the centrepiece for the last Brussels World Fair, celebrating the nation's remarkable postwar economic resurgence.

the Germans, leaving the Allies in a precarious state. This appearance of appeasement would eventually force Léopold's abdication in 1951. The Belgian government, opposing the king's decision, fled to London, where it operated in exile throughout WWII. A strong resistance movement developed during the Nazi occupation, but there was also collaboration from fascist elements of Belgian society, notably Léon Degrelle's Francophone Rexists and parts of the Flemish nationalist movement. The German occupation regime deliberately played up long-festering tensions between the linguistic groups for divide-and-rule purposes, Belgium's Jewish population fared terribly, and the small Roma (gypsy) minority was all but wiped out.

When Belgium was liberated in 1944, Léopold's brother Charles was appointed as regent, a duty he carried out until Léopold's abdication.

Sites Commemorating WWII

- *Bastogne War Museum, Bastogne*
- *Atlantikwall, Ostend (Oostende)*
- *Mons Memorial Museum, Mons*
- *Musée National d'Histoire Militaire, Diekirch*
- *US Military Cemetery, Luxembourg City*
- *Fort Breendonk, near Mechelen*

After WWII

Despite their serious wartime beatings, both Luxembourg and Belgium rebounded rapidly, fuelled by the coal and iron industries. In 1958, Brussels' World Fair showcased Belgium's great industrial advances, a message driven home by the unique architecture of the Atomium. The same year Brussels became the provisional seat of the European Commission and in 1967 NATO moved its headquarters to Brussels from France, the French having withdrawn from NATO's military wing.

But linguistic tensions remained and a 'language frontier' was officially delineated in 1963, creating four language areas (Dutch-, French- and German-speaking communities plus bilingual Brussels). As in many Western nations, the peace-and-love attitude of the Flower Power era was shaken in 1968 by violent student-led demonstrations. In Belgium these riots took a particular intercommunal turn at Leuven, where the Francophone part of the city's world-famous university was effectively forced to leave the stridently Flemish city, decamping eventually to Louvain-la-Neuve.

During the 1970s the global economy was hard hit by an overnight quadrupling of oil prices. The 'old' heavy industries (mining, glass and iron) slumped, and with them the formerly prosperous steel and mining cities in Wallonia and Luxembourg. Luxembourg circumvented these economic woes by introducing favourable banking and taxation laws that encouraged a new raft of investors and financial institutions. For bigger Belgium such solutions were not possible, and well-intentioned attempts to shore up its moribund factories with subsidies and socialist rhetoric proved futile. But while the post-industrial Walloon economy stagnated, the more diversified, smaller-scale industries of Flanders were less affected, and in later years the Flemish economy surged ahead as investment in newer technologies bore fruit. Increasingly an economic angle was added to the disputes between linguistic communities. State reforms of

1960

Belgian Congo (later Zaire) gains independence after major anti-colonial demonstrations. Civil war follows as Katanga province attempts to secede, with suspected Belgian connivance.

1968

The Western world is rocked by student-led popular civil disobedience, most famously in Paris. In Leuven the troubles turn violently intercommunal.

1970s

Economic stagnation sets in as heavy industry becomes uncompetitive in Wallonia and Luxembourg.

1974

Belgian cycling champion Eddy Merckx wins the Tour de France for a remarkable fifth time.

BELGIUM'S ROYALS

- Léopold I (r 1831–65) – became Belgium's first king in 1831 almost by accident. He narrowly missed the British throne when his wife, Princess Charlotte (the British heir apparent), died in childbirth. He then turned down the throne of newly reborn Greece, thinking Greek independence had little future.
- Léopold II (r 1865–1909) – bearded 'brute' with controversies in Congo.
- Albert I (r 1909–34) – brave, tin-hatted 'soldier king' of WWI.
- Léopold III (r 1934–51) – questions over his dealings with Hitler caused the 'Royal Question'; abdicated.
- Charles – acted as regent (not officially king) during Léopold III's Swiss exile (1944–50), then retired to Ostend, where he became an artist.
- Baudouin (r 1951–93) – popular, bespectacled 'priestly' king.
- Albert II (r 1993–2013) – Baudouin's younger brother; abdicated in favour of his son in 2013.
- Philippe/Filip (r 2013–) – Belgium's current monarch.

the 1980s and '90s gave parliaments to both the linguistic communities and the three regions (Flanders, Wallonia and Brussels-Capital), overlaid within a newly federalised state. Numerous powers were devolved to regional level, with such devolution further extended in 2012.

Into the 21st Century

Towards the end of the 20th century Belgium was rocked by infamous paedophile scandals and rising racism. The 1999 elections booted out the Christian Democrat party after 40 years in power. The political scene this century has largely been one of party-political gridlock, reflecting an increasing polarisation of politics along linguistic lines. A series of uncomfortable coalitions – taking months to form, and fully 1½ years in the case of the 2010 election – has made government a tense, tetchy affair. In the 2014 election a centre-right coalition was formed on an austerity platform.

Luxembourg's long-serving Prime Minister Jean-Claude Juncker, a master of realpolitik in power from 1995 to 2013, is now President of the European Commission. One of his early tasks will be to manage something of a crisis in his homeland, as the full scale of Luxembourg's over-friendly tax regime for businesses has incurred the wrath of its EU partners. Nevertheless, the Grand Duchy's economy remains one of the world's strongest per capita.

For those born into a world of on-demand downloads, it's hard to conceive just how much 1960s teenagers relied on Radio Luxembourg as the only non-pirate radio station broadcasting new 'pop' music into the UK, years before Radio 1 and way before MTV.

1993

Belgium becomes a three-part federal state comprising Flanders, Wallonia and Brussels-Capital. Further regional autonomy is granted in 2012.

2010–11

Elections leave Belgian politicians unable to form a coalition government for nearly 18 months.

2013

King Philippe/Filip accedes to the throne after his father's abdication.

2014

The 'Luxleaks' scandal focuses attention on Luxembourg's lax taxation of big business and prompts demands for change from other European countries.

The Belgian People

The Linguistic Divide

Dutch spoken in Flanders is very similar to that spoken in the Netherlands. Belgian and French French are as close as American and British English. Some Walloon dialects, though little spoken these days, are essentially distinct languages. Bruxellois is a unique Brussels pidgin adding in words from Dutch, French, Walloon, Spanish and Yiddish.

For Luxembourgers, French-Letzeburgesch bilingualism is a day-to-day necessity that's worn very lightly. But in Belgium, language is a defining issue. Belgium's population is basically split in two, a split that can, broadly speaking, be traced back to the break-up of Europe after the decline of the Roman empire. Dutch-speaking Flemish make up about 60% of the population, mostly in the country's north – predominantly flat Flanders (Vlaanderen). In southern Belgium – Wallonia (La Wallonie) – the population mostly speaks French, albeit a variant that sounds slightly comical to Parisians. To complicate matters, in Wallonia's Eastern Cantons (Ost Kantonen) live around 70,000 German speakers. And then there's Brussels: officially bilingual but predominantly French-speaking and geographically surrounded by Flanders.

French-speaking locals describe themselves as Belgians and only rarely as 'Walloons', which would imply speaking one of the almost-folkloric Walloon languages. However, most people in Flanders consider themselves primarily Flemish in a way that is equivalent psychologically, though not linguistically, to the self-image of Scots within the UK. Everything from the media to political parties is divided along language lines. And the result is a remarkable and growing lack of communication between Wallonia and Flanders. Francophones tend to stereotype the Flemish as arrogant and humourless; the Flemish see Francophone Belgians as corrupt, lazy or feckless, an exaggerated image jocularly accepted by some southerners. A century ago, Wallonia was Belgium's wealthier half, but its heavy industries slumped in the 1970s. Meanwhile, Flanders invested in 'new' businesses and its massive ports boomed from increasing global trade. Many in Flanders resent financially propping up the now poorer south, a tendency only increased by global economic woes. Flemish nationalists increasingly call for greater autonomy or even Flemish independence. Contrastingly, Walloon nationalism is virtually unknown and, while TV immerses most Francophone Belgians in French popular culture, very few would actually consider joining France in the event of a national split. Indeed Francophone Belgians are far more disparaging of the French than of their Flemish cousins.

More than 400 mosques now dot Belgium, with Brussels and Antwerp having the most sizeable Muslim populations – mostly immigrants from Morocco, Turkey, Algeria and Pakistan, and their descendents.

Multiculturalism

Curiously, on paper, Luxembourg is by far the EU's most multicultural country, with 43% of the population having been born elsewhere. However, as such foreigners are mostly Italian, Portuguese and other predominantly Catholic Western Europeans, you shouldn't expect a radical ethnic melting pot. Statistically, Belgium's main immigrant communities are Moroccan, French, Turkish and Italian. There's also a sizeable population

THE RED DEVILS

The Belgian football (soccer) team is one of the few things that unify sentiment across the linguistic divide between Wallonia and Flanders. Thanks partly to a total rethink of training methods, particularly for younger age groups, the current Belgian team is probably the best in its history. A sackful of players of flair and finesse grace teams in the top leagues across Europe, and at time of writing the national team, nicknamed the 'Red Devils', were ranked number three in the world, with star players such as Eden Hazard and Thibaut Courtois to the fore.

originating from Belgium's former African colonies (Congo, Rwanda and Burundi). Many immigrants arrived in the 1960s to work in the mines.

As in many European countries, attitudes to immigration seem to be hardening, and the Vlaams Belang far-right party has won votes actively opposing it. Perceptions of Islamic extremism haven't helped the cause: though the suspect arrested in the 2014 Jewish Museum shooting was a French national, Belgium produces more Islamic State recruits per capita than any other EU nation, and places like Verviers are often cited by Western intelligence sources as hotbeds of radicalism. As always, however, behind the sensational headlines is an overwhelming majority of peacefully coexisting citizens.

Religion

Christianity was established early in the Low Countries, with powerful abbeys and monasteries the main politico-administrative force in some areas (notably Liège) for centuries. A wave of Protestantism hit during the 16th century, and when the Low Countries were divided, Holland adopted a predominantly Protestant faith while proto-Belgium was force-fed a heavy dose of Roman Catholicism. Despite a wave of anti-religious desecration in the wake of the French Revolution, Catholicism has remained a defining strand of national identity in both Belgium and Luxembourg. However, church attendance has plummeted since the 1970s, with only 3% of the Flemish population now going to church weekly. Nonetheless, roughly 75% of Belgians (and 87% of Luxembourgers) still consider themselves Catholic, at least as a badge of social status and politically enlightened conservatism.

Belgium's strong Catholic background once kept women's issues on the back burner; when abortion was legalised in Belgium in 1990, it caused a national drama as the pious Baudouin I temporarily stood down rather than sign the law. However, over the last decades attitudes have changed radically; Belgium was the second European country after the Netherlands to legally recognise same-sex unions (2003) and euthanasia (2002).

The historically vibrant Jewish community was decimated in WWII during occupation by German forces. Many were sent to concentration camps from a barracks in Mechelen, restored as a sombre memorial. Today Antwerp has a small but visible Orthodox Jewish community concentrated on the diamond district.

Sport

After football, cycling is Belgium's great sporting passion, with champions such as Tom Boonen, and especially Eddy Merckx, seen as national heroes. Two of the five 'Monument' one-day classic road races are held in Belgium: the part-cobbled Tour of Flanders (www.rondevanvlaanderen.be) has its finish line in Oudenaarde, where there's a major cycling museum, and the Liège-Bastogne-Liège (www.letour.fr/liege-bastogne-liege) takes in some glorious Ardennes scenery.

Curious local sports include pigeon racing, finch sitting *(vinkenzettingen)* and *balle-pelotte* (aka *kaatsen, jeu-de-balle* or *jeu-de-paume*). The last is a team game batting a hard ball using gloved hands, often played on village squares accompanied by the boozy oompah of local trumpeters, though there are also leagues.

Creative Cuisine

Belgium's multilayered identity is seen nowhere more strongly than in its cuisine. Upmarket restaurants in Belgium or Luxembourg once served straightforward French-influenced cooking, and many still do, but they've been joined by a new wave of globally influenced gastronomes who often draw on French technique but riff on Flemish traditions and reference flavours from their latest trip to Spain or Japan.

Flemish favourites are far from neglected, but Belgium's big cities also sport an incredible array of cuisines, both in dedicated restaurants and on pub and cafe menus. Italian food is ubiquitous and joined by many Thai and Vietnamese dishes that are more and more likely to be authentically spiced and sauced.

Don't be too shy to order a 'hot goat' *(chèvre chaud)*. What you'll get is a delicious starter plate of salad topped with warm goat's cheese.

Getting Local

The most iconic Belgian meal must be that hearty portion of mussels and chips, *moules-frites* (or, in Dutch, *mosselen-friet*). Forget forks – eat them local-style using an empty mussel shell as a pair of tweezers and remember that fresh mussels open spontaneously during cooking, so if you find one hasn't opened, don't force it as it might be off. Less recognised but every bit as archetypically Belgian is *waterzooi,* a cream-based, soupy stew traditionally made with chicken or fish, and incorporating potatoes and vegetables so you won't need a side dish.

Paling in 't groen/anguilles-au-vert is eel in a bright-green sorrel or spinach sauce. Another Flemish standard is *konijn met pruimen/lapin aux pruneaux,* rabbit meat cooked until tender in a sauce that's sweetened with prunes. The rich meaty stew known as *carbonade flamande* in French is variously called *stoverij, stoofvlees* or *Vlaamse stoofkarbonade* in Dutch. Recipes vary, but essentially you'll get a thick beer-based hot pot using chunks of tasty but usually low-quality stewing steak (usually beef, but sometimes horse). Look for pâtés and other pork products in the Ardennes – it is justifiably famous for them.

In most European Catholic countries, the scallop shell is instantly recognised as the symbol of pilgrims heading off on the ancient cross-continent trek to Santiago di Compostela – so much so, in fact, that the words in both Dutch and French for the scallop incorporate the name of St James *(St-Jacobsschelpen/ coquilles St-Jacques)*.

Luxembourg's cuisine adds a Germanic element. The national dish is *judd mat gaardebounen* – slabs of smoked pork served in a thick, cream-based sauce with chunks of potato and broad beans. Another Luxembourg speciality is *liewekniddelen mat sauerkraut,* liver meatballs with sauerkraut.

Belgian meatballs *(ballekes/boulettes)* in tomato sauce have traditionally been sneered at as something a 1950s homemaker might have served when the pantry was bare. However, the larger (tennis ball–sized) Liège version, served in fruity meat gravy, is making a gourmet resurgence, especially in Wallonia.

You might expect Brussels sprouts to be common here. But a far more archetypically Belgian vegetable is the endive, commonly served wrapped in ham and smothered in cheesy white sauce as *gegratineerde witloof/chicons au gratin.*

Another home-cooking classic is *stoemp,* essentially boiled potatoes mashed together with vegetables and served as a side dish or as a basic meal topped with sausage or ham.

Frites – Non-French Fries

The Belgians swear they invented *frieten/frites,* so don't think of calling them French fries here. At a proper *frituur/friture* (chip stand), *frieten/frites* are given a to-order second crisping before being served in a paper cone, smothered with large blobs of thick mayonnaise or another sauce. There are dozens of sauces – if you're overwhelmed by the choice, try Andalouse, which tastes like a mildly spiced thousand-island dressing.

On French-language menus don't confuse a *cassolette* with a *cassoulet* (silent 't'). The former refers to a little cooking pot holding virtually anything the chef might have dreamt up; a *cassoulet* is a rich bean-and-meat casserole originally from southern France.

Seasonal Foods

In autumn, especially in the Ardennes, menus will be full of *gibier* – a general term for seasonal game meats (pheasant, wild boar etc). In spring it's time for white asparagus *(asperges)*, most famously hailing from Mechelen. The official mussels season is usually September to February, although Belgium's signature Zeeland mussels are succulent and conspicuously larger than the French equivalents and available year-round.

Vegetarians & Vegans

Bigger cities (especially in Flanders) have growing numbers of vegetarian restaurants, though oddly many open only at lunchtime. Ghent is especially veg-friendly. There's also a growing availability of organic *(bio)* ingredients in shops and eateries. In rural areas, especially in Wallonia, however, vegetarians will find relatively slim pickings. While salads appear on most standard menus, many contain some form of cheese or meat. If you're stuck for dinner, a useful standby is the sensibly priced nonmeat fare at one of the ubiquitous Chinese, Vietnamese or Thai restaurants.

Chocolate

Chocolate is fundamentally a mix of cocoa paste, sugar and cocoa butter in varying proportions. Dark chocolate uses the most cocoa paste, milk chocolate mixes in milk powder, and white chocolate uses cocoa butter but no cocoa paste at all. Belgian chocolate is arguably the world's best because it sticks religiously to these pure ingredients, while other countries allow cheaper vegetable fats to replace some of the cocoa butter (EU regulations allow up to 5%).

Extensive listings of vegetarian and organic options in Flanders and Brussels are available (in Dutch) through EVA (www.evavzw.be).

The essential Belgian variety is pralines and creamy *manons,* filled bite-size chocolates sold from an astonishing range of specialist *chocolaterie* shops. Here glove-clad assistants patiently wrap whatever you select from the enchanting display – it's perfectly fine to buy a single chocolate. Or you can opt for a packaged selection (125g to 1kg) in a ribbon-wrapped *ballotin* (top-folded cardboard box).

If you're not a connoisseur it's hard to go wrong with ubiquitous chain Leonidas. However, many locals regard Leonidas with a snobby condescension, preferring pricier Neuhaus, Corné or Galler (the latter, though, can also be found in bar form in Carrefour supermarkets). Stylish black-box presentation, specialist bean sources and innovative flavours (think oolong tea) make Pierre Marcolini the brand of choice for gourmands. 'Boutique' *chocolatiers* with special reputations include Chocolate Line, which created its nasally ingested choco-shot for the Rolling Stones, and

GETTING RAW

If you see the term *filet* on a menu it generally implies a steak of some type. But *filet américain* is quite different: it's Belgium's equivalent of steak tartare, ie a blob of high-grade, raw minced beef, prepared with small quantities of onion, seasoning and a raw egg yolk. Meanwhile, the Italian import *carpaccio* is a popular starter dish of raw meat strips served with olive oil, lemon and Parmesan.

Verviers-based Jean-Philippe Darcis, known for his use of pure-origin beans (he's also Belgium's *macaron* king).

If you want eel *(anguille)* be careful not to order *andouille* by mistake. The latter is a super-strongly flavoured sausage made with intestines and stomach parts that rarely suits the squeamish.

Waffles

The waffle *(wafel/gaufre)*, Belgium's signature snack, is often heaped with cream, fruit or chocolate sauce for tourists, but traditionally it should be just lightly dusted with icing sugar and eaten hot off the griddle. Brussels' waffles are light, crispy, rectangular and deeply indented. The *gaufre de Liège* has rounder edges and a breadier dough made with a hint of cinnamon. For recipes of several lesser-known versions, see www.gaufresbelges.com.

Coffee & Tea

Throughout much of Belgium, order a coffee and you'll generally get something approximating an Americano in strength and style (even though it's frequently called an espresso). Such coffee usually comes accompanied by a biscuit or chocolate and, unlike in France, you don't normally pay extra for milk (real or evaporated). Be aware that in traditional Belgian cafes a '*cappuccino*' is a regular coffee topped with sweetened whipped cream.

If that thought strikes fear into your caffeine-addicted heart, rest assured that change is afoot. In Brussels, Antwerp, Ghent and many other small cities in Flanders, global coffee culture has found a stronghold. Baristas at these places know their stuff, use high-quality roasts and offer your standard choices of espresso, *macchiato,* flat white, *cortardo* and the like. Frédéric Nicolay, of cafes Belga, Walvis and Barbeton, specialises in finding unloved spaces in Brussels and revamping them with reclaimed materials. Antwerp's Caffènation got the ball rolling back in 2006 and is now joined by Normo, Kolonal Koffie, Broer Bretel and a host of others. Even tea is being treated with a newfound respect: a number of places (Antwerp's Jane and Buchbar, to name two) going as far as weighing the leaves and timing the brew before serving.

Recognising that livestock production contributes up to 20% of Earth's greenhouse gases, Ghent has declared Thursday to be Veggie Day for the city's councillors, civil servants and schoolkids.

Wine & Spirits

Beer may be king in Belgium, but wine *(wijn/vin)* is the standard accompaniment to a meal, and large and respectable wine lists are increasingly found in bars and pubs, especially in the large cities. While French wine dominates, many places also serve Spanish, Italian and New World wines, the latter often having a mark-up that doesn't quite reflect its quality.

If you're keen to drink local, Luxembourg's Moselle Valley, a 42km strip along the left bank of the Moselle River designated the AC Moselle Luxembourgeoise, produces essentially the same varieties as the nearby Alsace: Pinot Blanc, Pinot Gris, Auxerrois, Riesling, Gewürztraminer and Pinot Noir. Apart from the high-yield Riverner (Müller-Thurgau), these are usually elegant, dry and good value. There is also a Crémant de Luxembourg, a well-respected sparkling *méthode traditionnelle.*

Jenever (*genièvre* in French, *pékèt* in Walloon) is an archetypal Dutch-Flemish spirit flavoured with juniper berries. It's the historical precursor to modern gin, but it's sipped straight and never diluted with tonic. For beginners the most palatable choices are sweetened fruit versions. However, ask for a *witteke* (literally a 'little white one') to get a classic *jenever,* which is almost colourless when *jonge* (young) or yellow-tinged (*oude*) when barrel matured. Hasselt boasts a *jenever* museum and an annual *jenever* festival, while seemingly endless mini-shots of *pékèt* are *de rigueur* during Liège's chaotic 15 August celebrations.

Belgium's star biscuit is the *speculaas/speculoos,* a cinnamon-flavoured gingerbread often served with coffee. They're shaped into the form of St Nicholas for 6 December festivities.

Belgian tap water *(kraantjeswater/eau du robinet)* is perfectly drinkable. However, dare to ask for some in a restaurant and you can expect at least a very contemptuous look and more likely a flat refusal. Mineral water comes *plat/plate* (flat) or *bruisend/pétillante* (sparkling).

Belgian Beer

No other country has a brewing tradition as richly diverse as that of Belgium, with beers ranging from pleasant pale lagers to wild, wine-like Flemish reds and lambics. But its the 'angels and demons' that draw the connoisseurs: these big bold brews often derive from monastery recipes and conjure the diabolical with names like Forbidden Fruit, Judas and Duvel (devil).

The most famous of all, six Trappist beers, are still brewed in active abbeys. With alcohol levels coming in at between 7% and 11% alcohol by volume, such brews are designed to be sipped slowly and savoured, certainly not chugged by the pint. For that, you have the standard Belgian lagers, notably Jupiler, Maes and Stella Artois – what you'll get at any *café* (pub/bar) if you just ask for a *pintje/bière* – which perhaps can't rival their German or Czech counterparts, but are deliciously drinkable none the less.

First Sips

When the Black Death came to the low lands in the 11th century, Arnold, the abbot of Oudenburg, convinced his parishioners to drink beer instead of water. Part of the process of medieval beer making involved boiling the water, and this trick proved rather, well, miraculous. Arnold became patron saint of brewers, and beer became an everyday drink. Early beer may have been little more than spontaneously fermented barley soup, but over the next few centuries beer-mad monks developed sophisticated brewing methods, as well as ways to enhance the flavour, adding honey and spices.

The great era of abbey beer production did not, in fact, begin until the early 19th century. Monasteries that had been ravaged in the anti-religious convulsions of the French Revolution were in need of funds to rebuild their shattered communities and their numbers swelled with those from French orders. Old monastic beer recipes were revived and improved upon, and the monks realised they were onto a nice little earner.

BEER FESTIVALS

Belgium's many beer festivals are a fabulous place to meet brewers, taste unusual brews and meet other beer lovers. They range from meet-the-microbrewer events to large international showcases.

Bruges Beer Festival (www.brugsbierfestival.be) Early February.

Zythos Beer Festival (www.zbf.be) Leuven; late April.

Belgian Beer Weekend (www.belgianbrewers.be) Brussels; early September.

Modeste Bierfestival (www.modestebierfestival.be) Antwerp; early October.

Poperinge Beer Festival (www.poperingebierfestival.be) Late October.

Kerstbierfestival (Christmas beers; www.kerstbierfestival.be) Essen; December.

Trappist & Abbey Beers

Based in Leuven, AB.InBev (www.ab-inbev.com) is the world's biggest brewer with a 25% global market share. It owns brands from Budweiser to Boddingtons, Labatt to Löwenbräu and Belgo-Luxembourg trademarks including Stella Artois, Leffe, Hoegaarden, Jupiler, Diekirch and Mousel. The giant conglomerate's Belgian origins stretch back to 1366.

Today many top Belgian brews remain 'abbey beers' in name only, the monks having outsourced the brewing in return for royalties. Examples include excellent Grimbergen, Maredsous and Leffe, originally linked with a monastery in Dinant but now brewed by the giant multinational AB-InBev. Some local producers have named brews for ruined abbeys, as with Oudenaarde's recommended Ename and Val de Sambre's Abbaye d'Aulne, created in a microbrewery beside the ruins of Aulne Abbey. Almost all the abbey beers are available in at least two styles: Bruin/Dubbel/Double beers are dark, while Blonde/Tripel/Triple are golden.

Six abbeys of the strict Cistercian order still brew within the monastery walls and these rich, smooth and intriguingly complex Trappist beers are considered the epitome of the Belgian beer experience. 'Trappist' is a controlled term of origin, rather than a style, and come in varying colours and strengths. Chimay, Orval and Westmalle are now ubiquitous and each has a beer-tasting *café* near its respective abbey. It takes a little more effort to seek out excellent Rochefort or 'newcomer' Achel from the rural Sint Benedictus Monastery (www.achelsekluis.org), where brewing was only revived in 1999. But the Holy Grail for Belgian beer fans is Westvleteren, whose beers bear no labels and can only be identified by the colour of their caps. The yellow cap Westvleteren 12 (10.8% alcohol) is a dark, unfiltered, malty beer whose intense complexity sees it regularly voted among the world's very best. But with supply incredibly limited, your best hope of tasting it is to visit the abbey *café* in person. Even there, if you want to buy more than a six pack, you'll need an appointment. It all adds to the thrill and mystique. If you can't find a bar serving Westvleteren, consider sipping St-Bernardus from nearby Watou, based on recipes and techniques originally guided by a Westvleteren master brewer.

White Beers

Known as *witbier/bière blanche* in Dutch/French, white beers are thirst-quenching wheat beers, typically cloudy, flavoured with hints of orange peel and cardamon and drunk ice cold with a twist of lemon on summer afternoons. Best known is from Hoegaarden, which has an interesting brewery museum. Brugs Tarwebier (from Bruges) is also a good choice.

Lambics & Fruit Beers

In the Senne Valley southwest of Brussels, mysterious airborne microorganisms allow the spontaneous fermentation of archetypal lambic

UNUSUAL BREWS

Oerbier A stealthy dark ale from Esen near Diksmuide.

Pannepot Tasting like liquid, alcoholised black chocolate, Struise Brewers' signature beer is often sold in Woesten, or seek out their experimental draughts at Gainsbar in Kortrijk.

Garre A floral-headed 11% marvel unique to the eponymous bar in Bruges.

Airman Served in a helmet at Bastogne.

Alpaïde stout Proves that Hoegaarden can go beyond white beer.

Brugse Zot Bruges' merry jester.

Moinette Bio Organic ale.

Lupulus Excellent hoppy ale from eastern Ardennes.

La Chouffe Achouffe's blond, elf-branded beer.

Vaudrée Blonde Powerful but great-tasting.

Liefmans Goudenband Strong Flemish sour brown, care of the first female brewmaster of Belgium.

CHARGE YOUR GLASSES

One of the adjunct pleasures of drinking beer in Belgium is the branded glass that each beer is served in. You'll find them for sale at specialist beer shops as well as at flea markets, where you can pick them up for around €2 to €4 each, with some dealers also stocking vintage versions and special editions. Each style of beer has a particular shaped glass, which supposed highlights its flavour and other characteristics.

Bowls The archetypal Belgian bowls are large stemmed vessels designed especially for sipping heavy ales. Some are solidly goblet like, while others can be as dainty as a wine glass. Orval's chunky faceted glass chalice evokes its monastic past, although its design dates only from the 1930s.

Tulip A bulbous body and gently flaring lip makes the most of aromatic beers and is also designed to enhance the head. The blond Duvel's is possibly the most elegant, both in its classical form and in its yearly artist editions and high-tech unbreakable version designed to take the punishment that Belgium's many summer festivals can dish out. La Chouffe's gnomes also grace a pretty tulip.

Flutes The wine-like fruit beers and lambics are, fittingly, often served in what looks like a bloated champagne flute, which aides carbonation and aroma.

beers (*lambiek* in Dutch). The idea is magical. However, the taste of pure lambic is uncomfortably sharp and acidic. It's rendered more palatable by barrel-maturing for up to three years, then blending (to make *gueuze*), sweetening with sugar/caramel (for *faro*) or by adding fresh soft fruit, notably cherries (for *kriek*) and raspberries (for *framboise*). You can discover a whole range of *geuze, kriek* and lambic flavours and learn more about their production at De Lambiek in Alsemberg near Brussels. Several commercial fruit beers are over-sweetened, but Boon Kriek is better than most, richly fruity and tart without heavy acidity.

Category Busters

Not all beers fit into neat categories, and not all abbey-style brews are abbey beers. Mechelen produces the splendid Gouden Carolus range. Refreshing, hoppy golden ales are brewed by La Chouffe, Brasserie des Fagnes and many more. Antwerp's trademark beer, de Koninck, is a brown ale. A plethora of small-production artisan breweries craft special beers, sometimes experimenting with curious vegetable additions, historic recipes or coming up with 'seasonal' beers as at the historic steam-brewery at Pipaix (p189).

Curiousities

Set in pleasantly rolling hills, the relatively ordinary Hainaut village of Ellezelles (www.ellezelles.be) makes valiant efforts to attract tourists with tales of witches, celebrating in carnival style the Sabbat des Sorcières (www.sorcieres.eu) on the last weekend of June. It also makes comically preposterous claims of being Hercule Poirot's 'birthplace'. But its most appealing feature is its **Brasserie Ellezelleoise** (Rue Guinaumont 75; beer €3; ⌚11am-8pm), an endearing brewery-pub creating and serving Quintine 'witch' beer and 'Hercule' stout, playing on the Poirot theme.

Beer Tours

Many breweries offer visits by arrangement for groups. Drop in opportunities are possible at Bruges' De Halve Maan (p91), the brilliantly old-fashioned Cantillon lambic-works (p59) in Brussels and at Pipaix's steam brewery (p189). With a little planning it's easy to join group tours of Stella Artois (p174) in Leuven or La Chouffe (p222) in Achouffe. You can just drop in to Antwerp's city brewery, De Koninck (p152); for a self-guided tour of the brewery hall and museum, along with tastings, while Hoegaarden (p179) and Chimay (p202) offer 'beer experience' visits.

Beer Resources

Belgian Brewers Association *(www.beerparadise.be)*

Confederation of Belgian Beertasters *(www.zythos.be)*

Beer-drinkers' opinions *(www.ratebeer.com)*

Beer Tourism *(belgium.beertourism.com)*

Podge's Beer Tours *(www.podgebeer.co.uk)*

Belgian Smaak *(www.belgiansmaak.com)*

Arts & Architecture

Although Belgium has only been Belgium since 1830, the region's cities have been at the forefront of the arts for much of the last seven centuries. Bruges was the centre for the 'Flemish Primitives', Antwerp the base of superstar Pieter Paul Rubens, and Brussels an early centre for both art nouveau and surrealism. The country continues to have a vibrant cultural life, with globally recognised contemporary-art stars, a flourishing electronic-music scene, great modern dance and an endearing devotion to the 'ninth art': the comic strip.

Art

Primitives & Hellraisers

Blossoming in 15th-century Bruges was a group of groundbreaking painters who pioneered a technique of painting in oil on oak boards, adding thin layers of paint to produce jewel-bright colours and exquisite detail.

They became known collectively as the Flemish Primitives. Not all were Flemish and their work was anything but primitive: the name derives from the Latin *primus,* meaning first, an indication of their innovative and experimental approach. Perhaps the greatest such work still extant is the world-famous *Adoration of the Mystic Lamb,* a multi-panelled altarpiece in Ghent's cathedral by one or both of the Van Eyck brothers.

Particularly significant was the decision to use oil-painting techniques to achieve a new degree of realism and to then use this realism to depict secular subjects in place of religious themes. Bruges' Groeningemuseum has some particularly superb works, including an intimate portrait of his wife by Jan van Eyck (c 1390–1441). In his wake came Tournai-born Rogier van der Weyden (c 1400–64), who at one time was even considered to outshine the master. Judge for yourself at Tournai's main gallery.

Possibly trained in Brussels under Rogier van der Weyden, German-born Hans Memling (c 1440–94) arrived in Bruges aged around 25 and swiftly became a favourite among the city's merchant patrons. His association with St John's Hospital resulted in the commissioning of the glowing religious works now displayed in the Museum St-Janshospitaal (Memlingmuseum), where his St Ursula reliquary counts among Bruges' most important treasures.

Get an idea of Jan van Eyck's intricate masterpieces from the comfort of home at www.jan-van-eyck.org.

Another significant Flemish Primitive figure was Leuven's Quentin Matsys (1466–1529), who painted a set of grotesque portraits so timeless that they could have jumped out of a Lewis Carroll fairy tale. These hinted at the chaotic horrors to follow in the works of Dutchman Hieronymus Bosch (c 1450–1516). Bosch's most fascinating paintings are nightmarish scenes, visual parables filled with gruesome beasts and devilish creatures often devouring or torturing agonised humans. Bosch's work had obvious influences on the great 16th-century Flemish painter Pieter Bruegel the Elder, whose studies of peasant life remain as collectable as Bosch's apocalyptic canvases. You can peruse a fine selection of Bruegel's work in Lier and might visit his grave in Brussels' Kapellekerk. Bruegel's sons continued the family craft, though Jan Bruegel would turn away from his father's depiction of crowd scenes towards an obsession with the floral still life. The world was changing.

Baroque Counter-Reformation

Styles changed dramatically following the Counter-Reformation of the 17th century. Suddenly huge, powerful canvases full of chubby cherubs and ecstatic biblical figures were just the thing to remind a wavering population of a Catholic God's mystical power. Few artists proved so good at delivering such dazzling, seductive spectacle as Antwerp-based Pieter Paul Rubens. His most celebrated altarpieces were painted for Antwerp's delightful Onze-Lieve-Vrouwekathedraal. Rubens was so prolific that after you've spent some time in Antwerp, it's almost a relief to find a museum that *doesn't* feature his works.

Rubens' studio nurtured artists such as Anthony van Dyck (1599–1641), who focused on religious and mythical subjects, as well as portraits of European aristocrats. In 1632 he was appointed court painter by Charles I of England, and knighted. His contemporary Jacob Jordaens (1593–1678) specialised in depicting everyday Flemish life and merrymaking.

If you believe Karl Hammer's 2010 art-detective mystery thriller *The Secret of the Sacred Panel*, the Van Eyck Ghent altarpiece is not just a glorious example of 1420s art but the key to unraveling sacred mysteries surrounding Jesus' crucifixion that held occult significance for WWII Nazi Heinrich Himmler.

Modern Movements

Three Belgian names dominate in the latter 19th century, each taking art in notably different directions. In mid-career Constantin Meunier (1831–1905), Belgium's most famous sculptor, took the morally brave step of giving up lucrative bourgeois commissions to concentrate on painting social-realist scenes depicting the lives and difficulties of workers in industrial Belgium. James Ensor (1860–1949), celebrated in his hometown Ostend, pioneered expressionism way ahead of his time. And Fernand Khnopff (1858–1921) developed a beguiling 'symbolist' style reminiscent of contemporary pre-Raphaelites Gabriel Rossetti and Edward Burne-Jones. Khnopff's work decorates part of the St-Gilles town hall, and his (largely rebuilt) childhood home is now the Hotel Ter Reien in Bruges.

As Argenteuil was to French impressionism, rural St-Martens-Latem was the creative crucible of Belgian expressionism after 1904, with two formative groups of painters setting up home in the village. The best-known artist of the set was Constant Permeke (1886–1952), whose bold portraits of rural Flemish life blended cubism, expressionism and social realism. Meanwhile Mechelen-born Rik Wouters (1882–1916), a prime figure of Brabant Fauvism, sought the vibration of light in sun-drenched landscapes, bright interiors and still-life canvases. His work can be seen at Mechelen's Schepenhuis.

Emerging in Paris in the 1920s as a response to the horror of WWI and the rapid technological changes of the early 20th century, surrealism worked with the neglected associations and omnipotent dream world of the subconscious. It found fertile ground in Belgium: artists had grown up with the likes of Bosch and Bruegel, and the country had a front-row seat to the carnage of the trenches. Best known is René Magritte, now celebrated with his own Brussels gallery-museum, along with Paul Delvaux whose St-Idesbald house-studio gives a curious set of insights.

Contemporary Scene

Belgium's contemporary art scene is booming, with a strong base of local collectors, proximity to art-fair hubs Cologne and Basel, and a network of respected art schools and museums.

One of Europe's best known, and often most controversial, painters, is Luc Tuymans (1958–), who lives and works in Antwerp. Based on photographic source material, his washed-out, haunting canvases toggle between historical events – the Holocaust, Belgian Congo controversies, child-abuse scandals – and the absolutely banal, acknowledging the long Belgian realist tradition while displaying a dark mistrust of the image itself. Tuymans' work was among the first to be exhibited in Brussels' cutting-edge Wiels gallery after its 2007 inauguration.

Like Tuymans, Ghent-based Michaël Borremans also works from photographic images, although his work is far more invested in the technique of oil painting. His precise but ever-elusive work is known for its emotional, but far from romantic, depiction of human subjects.

Back in Antwerp, the now (supposedly) retired 'assemblagist' Henri Van Herwegen (1940–), aka Panamarenko, a pseudonym conjured from a bastardised abbreviation of 'Pan American Airlines Company', spent much of his career creating bizarre sculptures and installations that typically fuse authentic and imaginary flying contraptions. Also from Antwerp, Jan Fabre is a huge creative and intellectual presence in his hometown. A stage designer and playwright as well as an artist, he is best known for reworking the ceiling of the Africa Room in Brussels' Royal Palace, which he turned iridescent using the wing cases of thousands of exotic beetles.

Every country needs at least one arch-provocateur, and neo-conceptual Wim Delvoye gleefully fulfills this roll. A penchant for tattooing pigs and making stained glass from x-rated x-rays has made him famous, but his creation of *Cloaca,* an installation that's a gustatory production line, turning food into faeces without human intervention, has also made him wealthy.

The late Jan Hoet (1936–2014) – a curator rather than an artist – was perhaps the Belgian art world's most influential figure (along with its most charismatic: he was often dubbed Belgium's 'sexiest man'). Among his many achievements at home and on the broader European stage was the establishment of the SMAK gallery in his adopted home of Ghent.

Film

Belgium's best-known film star is 'Muscles from Brussels' Jean-Claude Van Damme, hardly known for his high-brow performances. However, the local movie scene tends to be contrastingly thought provoking. Its hard-hitting classics include *L'Enfant* (2005), about a petty crook coming to grips with fatherhood, and *Rosetta* (1999), about a girl searching for work and meaning to her life. Both are gritty affairs filmed in miserable suburbs of Liège. Neither do much for that city's tourism image.

Low-budget 2008 hip-hop comedy *Reste Bien Mec!* showed an alternative side of Luxembourg, while *Les Barons* (2009) offers a fascinating look at attitudes in Brussels' North African community. Before that, *Man Bites Dog* (1992), a cult crime mockumentary written, produced and directed by Rémy Belvaux, André Bonzel and Benoît Poelvoorde, the film's co-editor, cinematographer and lead actor respectively, helped cement the country's reputation for black comedy.

In 1929, *My Fair Lady* screen superstar Audrey Hepburn was born to a Dutch mother in Brussels. Their home at Rue Keyenveld 46 has a commemorative plaque.

Animation fans will admire the work of Raoul Servais, whose sublime linework has its roots in the 1960s, although he remains prolific to this day, with a fan base across Europe and in Japan.

Ghent and Bruges both have film festivals, while Brussels has two: the International Fantastic Film Festival, and Anima, focusing on cartoons.

Dance

Until the 1980s, Belgian ballet was dominated by Swiss choreographer Maurice Béjart and his Mudra school in Brussels. Mechelen-born Anne Teresa De Keersmaeker changed that, with her experimental dance school PARTS and her group Rosas (www.rosas.be) putting Belgium on the international dance map. In her elegant, if sometimes extreme, wake have been a number of Belgian experimentalists, including Wim Vandekeybus, Jan Fabre, Alain Platel and current international darling Sidi Larbi Cherkaoui. Belgian dance companies, including the venerable, Antwerp-based Flemish Royal Ballet (www.koninklijkballetvanvlaanderen.be), enjoy fruitful relationships with the fashion scene: the likes of Dries van Noten and Walter Van Beirendonck are regular costume designers.

Music

Belgium has produced fine but unsung musicians for hundreds of years, but during the 20th century the country finally had global impact. Romani guitarist Django Reinhardt is known as the first European-born jazz musician and became one of the most loved guitarists in the world. His fame is possibly only matched by thoughtful *chansonnier* Jacques Brel, of Flemish background but born in Brussels and who sang almost exclusively in French.

Belgium has been a huge if rather self-deprecating player in the world of electronic music, known throughout Europe for being a hotbed of experimentation. With no legislation limiting club hours, the scene went wild with newbeat and EBM (electronic body music) in the late '80s (Technotronic's *Pump Up the Jam* foreshadowing what was to come). From the early '90s onwards, Ghent's R&S label unleashed a stream of 'cutting-edge techno gold'. As well as signing and mixing the likes of international stars Aphex Twin and Derrick May, it also championed local acts such as CJ Bolland. Another Ghent export, Soulwax and its later incarnation 2manydjs, shot to global fame in the mid-2000s, while Brussels-based The Magician, best known for his 2014 single 'Sunlight' as well as his famous remixes for Norwegian Lykke Li, is a current star.

Jozef Devillé's 2012 film *The Sound of Belgium* explores the scene in loving detail as well as proposing that its roots can be found in the electronic organ–fuelled country dance halls of the '50s, the slowed-down-soul 'Popcorn' dance nights of the '70s and the region's far more ancient but no less exuberant carnival traditions.

DJ mad as Belgium might be, the last few years have seen a growing indie scene as well, with bands such as Intergalactic Lovers, Goose and Amatorski being firm festival-circuit favourites. Classical music thrives, too, and the country is proud to have several opera houses, with active companies in Ghent (p140) and Liège (p230).

Major Writers

- *Guido Gezelle (1830–99)*
- *Hendrik Conscience (1812–83)*
- *Georges Simenon (1903–1989)*
- *Hugo Claus (1929–2008)*
- *Chika Unigwe (b 1974)*

Comic Strips

Belgian comic series and characters will more than likely have played a part in your childhood, no matter where you grew up. Belgium has a consuming passion for comic strips (*stripverhalen/bandes dessinées* in Dutch/French), which are considered the 'ninth art' and spawned a major publishing industry throughout the 20th century. Les Schtroumpfs, De Smurfen or, yes, the Smurfs began life as an in-joke by comic artist Peyo (the pen name of Pierre Culliford) in 1958 and are now a worldwide franchise. Asterix may have been drawn and written by the French duo René Goscinny and Albert Uderzo, but it was first published and made famous by the Franco-Belgian magazine *Pilote*.

Before them, though, was Tintin, first created by the great Hergé (the pseudonym of Georges Remi) in the late 1920s as a pullout section in a newspaper. Tintin books have been translated into dozens of languages and have sold hundreds of millions of copies. The series has also survived long enough to encounter charges of colonialism and racism, although it's defended by most fans as simply a product of its time. Hergé is celebrated at a fine museum in Louvain-la-Neuve. Other cartoon stars include Philippe Geluck's thought-provoking fat cat Le Chat, Willy Vandersteen's Suske and Wiske (Bob and Bobette in French) and Morris' Lucky Luke.

In Brussels many house ends are painted with cartoon-character scenes. In Ghent there are several places where graffiti artists express themselves, including one very central 'graffiti alley', Werregarensteeg.

Architecture

Belgium is endowed with a fine legacy of architectural delights, though with much restoration along the way, given a succession of wars. Unesco's World Heritage list includes a large selection of Belgian buildings, plus the whole old-town centres of Luxembourg City and Bruges.

Some of Belgium's finest cathedrals and most of its great abbey churches were ripped down during the anti-religious turmoil of the 1790s; the once-grand abbeys at Aulne and Villers-la-Ville still lie in atmospheric ruins from that time. However, a great many splendid religious structures did survive, including the sturdy Romanesque Collégiale Ste-Gertrude in Nivelles. Romanesque architecture, characterised by very hefty columns and semicircular arches, disappeared gradually over the 12th and 13th centuries once new understandings of building technology allowed the introduction of light, pointed arches and the development of soaring Gothic vaulting. Tournai's cathedral, built in three clearly discernible sections, offers a vivid example of that architectural progression.

Between Durbuy and Liège, peeping through trees on a ridgetop in Esneux, is the remarkable 1905 Château de Fy (no public access). Some locals believe that a photo of Fy snapped in WWII was the inspiration for Walt Disney's Sleeping Beauty Castle. Most mainstream reports cite Neuschwanstein in Germany as a far more likely candidate.

In the cloth-trading towns of the medieval Low Countries, wealth and education led to precocious ideas about personal rights. These notions are embodied in the grand guildhouses on market squares and, particularly, in the construction of secular belfries (Bruges' is particularly incredible) and ornate city halls, most memorably in Brussels and Leuven. Another architectural innovation unique to the Low Countries was the *begijnhof/béguinage,* a protected semi-religious enclosed village-settlement.

The Counter-Reformation's Italian influence can be seen at its peak in Antwerp's St-Carolus-Borromeuskerk, although the church's high Baroque style, incorporating Rubens' lavish sculptural and painterly decoration, is uniquely Flemish.

For most of the 18th century, architecture took on a cold, rational, neoclassical style, typified by Brussels' Place Royale. After independence, but especially under its second king, Léopold II (r 1865–1909), Belgium focused on urban redevelopment. Léopold realised that making Brussels more aesthetically appealing would boost its economic potential. Partly using personal riches he'd gained through exploitation of the Congo, he funded gigantic public buildings including the Palais de Justice, created the monumental Cinquantenaire, and laid out vast suburban parks linked to the city by splendidly wide thoroughfares such as Ave Louise and Ave Tervuren. Much of this expansion coincided with a late-19th-century industrial boom that saw Belgian architects experimenting with new materials.

From the early 1890s, Brussels was at the forefront of art nouveau design, using sinuous lines, organic tendrils and floral motifs to create a genuinely new architectural aesthetic. One of the best examples, the Old England Building, combines wrought-iron frames, round windows, frescoes and *sgraffito,* a distinctive incised-mural technique of which a stunning example graces the facade of Brussels' Maison Cauchie. Antwerp also has some excellent art nouveau facades, especially in Zurenborg.

After WWI, the harder rectilinear lines of art deco came to dominate, presaged by buildings such as Ghent's 1912 Vooruit and Brussels' 1911 Palais Stoclet.

Tragically, earlier 20th-century styles were largely undervalued during the 1960s and 1970s and some of Belgium's finest art nouveau buildings were torn down. Worldwide protests over the 1965 destruction of Victor Horta's Maison du Peuple helped bring about laws protecting Brussels' heritage, and the Atelier de Recherche et d'Action Urbaines (ARAU) was formed to save and renovate city treasures. The former Belgian radio and TV building, Flagey, was one art deco landmark to be rescued, but other swathes of cityscape have gone under the demolition ball, notably in Brussels to make way for the bland glass buildings that typify the EU quarter.

Despite some public acclaim, Belgium's 21st-century architecture has mostly proved less than majestic. Antwerp's sail-topped Justitiepaleis is certainly memorable but fails to offer the wow factor and Bruges' white-elephant Concertgebouw feels like a modernist token. That said, Santiago Calatrava's Guillemins train station in Liège is truly astonishing.

Survival Guide

Directory A-Z

Accommodation

Accommodation ranges from camping grounds and budget hostels through B&Bs, rural options and midrange hotels to top-end hotels.

Availability varies markedly by season and area. May to September occupancy is very high (especially at weekends) along the coast, in Bruges and in popular villages of rural Luxembourg and the Ardennes. However, those same weekends you'll find hotels cutting prices in business cities like Brussels, Liège, Mechelen and Luxembourg City.

National taxes are invariably included, but several towns add a small additional *stadsbelasting/taxe de séjour* (city tourist tax), which might add a euro or two to the tally.

At most B&Bs and some hotels, reductions for longer stays are fairly common, while some places demand a minimum two- or three-day stay, especially at key times of the year.

Many options include breakfast. Many hotels (especially in rural areas) offer *demi-pension* (half-board) deals including breakfast and a set lunch or dinner. Some popular places in touristy areas of the Ardennes will only rent rooms on a *demi-pension* or *pension complète* (full board) basis during key summer weekends. Grander rural getaways increasingly offer *séjour gastronomique* options: accommodation plus various meals that are often high-end, four-course affairs.

Many hotels accept pets, usually charging around €3 to €8 per night for the service.

B&Bs

B&Bs (*gastenkamers* in Dutch, *chambres d'hôtes* in French) are prevalent in both rural and urban Belgium, but thinner on the ground in Luxembourg.

B&B standards can vary from unpretentious homestays to luxury boutique hotels. Many are run by vibrant hosts whose enthusiasm for the job can be seen in characterful interiors and thoughtful decor. The best B&Bs offer a level of charm and refinement that trumps all but the very finest top-end hotels.

You'll generally need to book ahead and arrange a mutually agreeable arrival time. Check-in is often not available until 5pm. Be prepared for stairs, as lifts are usually nonexistent.

Official B&Bs are listed by local tourist offices, but website www.airbnb.com has more informal homestay-style addresses.

Camping, Caravan Parks & Hikers' Huts

Camping and caravan facilities are plentiful, especially in the Belgian and Luxembourg Ardennes. Booking ahead is wise as space can be limited. Typical rates are compounded from per person, per car and per site fees. For those with small tents, it is sometimes cheaper to arrive without reservation, assuming space remains.

Useful websites:

Camping Flanders (www.camping.be) Camping-ground finder for Flanders.

Camping Key Europe (www.campingkeyeurope.com) This useful card gives discounts at lots of camping grounds across the region, streamlines the check-in process and provides insurance. You can buy it via campsite association websites (€16) or at selected camping grounds.

Camping Wallonia (www.campingbelgique.be) Extensive by-commune camping-ground listings for Wallonia.

Camprilux (www.camping.lu) Luxembourg camping grounds.

BOOK YOUR STAY ONLINE

For more accommodation reviews by Lonely Planet authors, check out http://lonelyplanet.com/hotels/. You'll find independent reviews, as well as recommendations on the best places to stay. Best of all, you can book online.

Hikers' Huts

Known as *trekkershutten* in Flanders and *wanderhütten* in Luxembourg, these small four-person wooden cabins come with basic cooking facilities but charge extra for electricity or heating usage. Maximum stay is four nights. They're mostly attached to camping grounds or provincial recreation parks, with many along Flanders Cycle Route. Many are mapped on the Dutch site www.trekkershutten.nl.

Gîtes & Apartments

A great family option, especially in rural areas, is to rent an apartment or especially a holiday home known as a *gîte* (*landelijk verblijf* in Dutch, *gîte rural* in French).

While rentals are often by the week, many also allow shorter stays. Some *gîtes* are also available for rental by the room, with one-night stays possible.

Prices vary significantly by season, number of occupants and house standards. Some are on farms, others in castles, converted stables or historic buildings.

There is often a significant extra cleaning charge. Don't confuse a *gîte* with a *gîte d'étape*, which in Belgium is essentially a hostel, albeit sometimes limited to group bookings.

Useful *gîte* websites:

Gîtes de Wallonie (www.gitesdewallonie.be) The website's map feature is especially helpful and also shows rural B&Bs in Wallonia.

Logeren in Vlaanderen (www.logereninvlaanderen.be) *Gîtes* in Flanders.

Tourisme Rurale Luxembourg (www.gites.lu) *Gîtes* in Luxembourg.

Hostels & Gîtes d'Étapes

Hostels (*jeugdherbergen* in Dutch, *auberges de jeunesse* in French) generally charge from €18 to €28 for a dorm bed, including sheets and basic breakfast. Neither towels nor soap are usually included.

A few of the cheapest hostels charge extra for sheets.

If you're planning to stay at several Hostelling International (HI) hostels (www.lesaubergesdejeunesse.be, www.youthhostels.be, http://youthhostels.lu), it's worth joining your local hostel association. Members save €2 to €3 per night. Alternatively, if you keep proof of six nights' worth of stays in Flanders, Wallonia or Luxembourg (but not a mixture) you qualify for a membership card.

Rates are cheaper for under-30s in Flanders, or under-26s in Wallonia.

Membership is also required for some hostel-style **Gîtes d'Étape** (☎02-209 03 00; www.gitesdetape.be) where bed charges are low and meals available.

A few hostels are summer only; some others close during midwinter. Many have a lock-out policy, typically between around 11am and 5pm and almost all are unstaffed at night.

Bring your own padlock to use hostel lockers.

Hotels

The classification system awards stars for facilities (lifts, room service, dogs allowed etc) so don't assume that such classification necessarily reflects quality or price.

It's unlikely that you'll find a hotel room (*kamer* in Dutch, *chambre* in French) for under €40/50 per single/double, even with shared bathroom facilities. Midrange hotels typically charge between €70 and €130 for a double room. Check-in time is rarely before 2pm, with check-out around 11am.

Prices vary somewhat to fit demand. At weekends and in summer, prices fall (sometimes dramatically) in business cities like Brussels and Luxembourg. However, they rise in tourist places like Bruges, the coastal towns and the Ardennes resorts. It's well worth checking hotel websites for last-minute and advance-purchase deals.

Some smaller hotels are effectively just rooms above a restaurant and, when the restaurant's closed, there will be no receptionist unless you arrange an arrival time.

Motels

If you're driving and don't mind drearily banal locations in outer suburbs, industrial parks or at motorway junctions, you can often get a comparatively inexpensive bed in motor-inns or motels.

Campanile (www.campanile.com) Branches off motorways near Bruges, Ghent, Liège and Brussels Airport.

HOSPITALITY WEBSITES

Organisations such as Couchsurfing (www.couchsurfing.org) or Hospitality Club (www.hospitalityclub.org) put people in contact for informal free accommodation offers. Even if you're not comfortable crashing in a stranger's house, these sites are a great way to meet and socialise with locals. Airbnb (www.airbnb.com) is a popular system for organising paid homestays and rentals, from private rooms in people's flats to top-value holiday rentals and almost anything else you can think of.

PRICE RANGES

Ranges are based on the cost of a double room in high season.

€ under €60

€€ from €60 to €140

€€€ over €140

Activities

Cycling

Cycling is a major local passion whether as transport, speed-sport or off-road trek by mountain bike (*terreinfiets* in Dutch, *VTT* in French). For the less physically fit, many bike rental shops hire out electric bikes (with power-assistance that reduces the strain on harder climbs). Bike helmets are not a legal requirement. Secure your bicycle carefully as theft flourishes, especially in Flanders. Mopeds are also allowed on bike paths.

BELGIUM

In flat Flanders bikes are an everyday means of travel, so dedicated cycle lanes are commonplace on roadsides and drivers are (relatively) accommodating, though strong winds can prove discouraging. Cycle Network Flanders (www.fietsroute.org) is an incredibly extensive and well-marked web of bicycle routes using cycle paths and minor lanes for which keyed maps and booklets are available in local tourist offices. A multilingual book *Topogids Vlaanderen Fietsroute* compiles over 60 detailed 1:50,000 route maps and relevant accommodation options. There are downloadable versions.

Wallonia's networks of cycle paths, RAVel (http://ravel.wallonie.be) and Randovelo (www.randovelo.org) often use canal or river towpaths and former railway tracks rebuilt with hard surfaces. Rando-Vélo sells a range of guide maps.

Bikes can be taken on a Belgian train on payment of a supplement (€5/8 one trip/all day) to the passenger fare. Bicycle hire is available from agencies that are often at or very close to major train stations. Most bike-rental shops also do repairs.

LUXEMBOURG

Luxembourg is criss-crossed by numbered bicycle paths (*pistes cyclables*). Some cross hilly country and require considerable fitness, others are more sedate. Locally available guidebook *40 Cycle Routes*, published by Éditions Guy Binsfield, describes 40 selected cycle tours with topographical maps and track descriptions. Bikes can be rented in most major tourist centres, helmets are not compulsory and you can bring your bicycle on a Luxembourg train, space permitting, for free.

Hiking

Crossing Belgium you'll find various long-distance footpaths called **Sentiers de Grande Randonnée** (GR; www.grsentiers.org), along with countless shorter trails for afternoon rambles. Most are well signposted and keyed to topographical hiking maps sold by tourist offices, which can offer plenty of advice to walkers. In flat Flanders, hiking routes typically follow countryside bicycle paths where you must be careful to give way to cyclists.

Simple accommodation for ramblers is available in much of Luxembourg and Flanders in specially conceived hikers' huts (p293).

Golf

Finding one of Belgium's numerous golf courses is easy through the Royal Belgian Golf Federation (www.golfbelgium.be). Look for '*cherchez un club*' in the French version of the page.

Rock Climbing

BelClimb (http://en.belclimb.be) is a superb resource for climbers offering exhaustive links to climbing guides, a searchable map of Belgium's indoor-climbing practice

Climate

Brussels

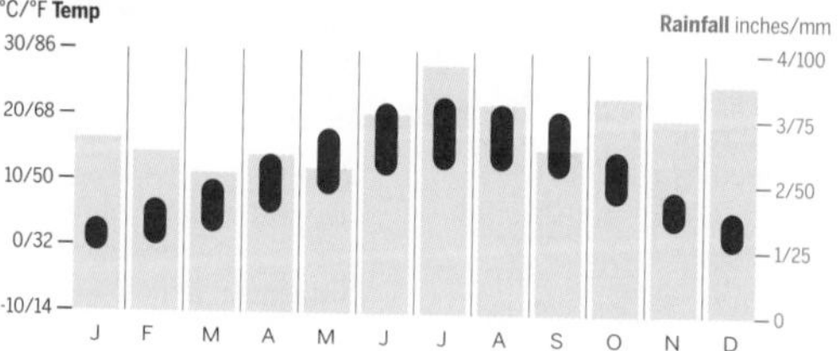

Luxembourg City

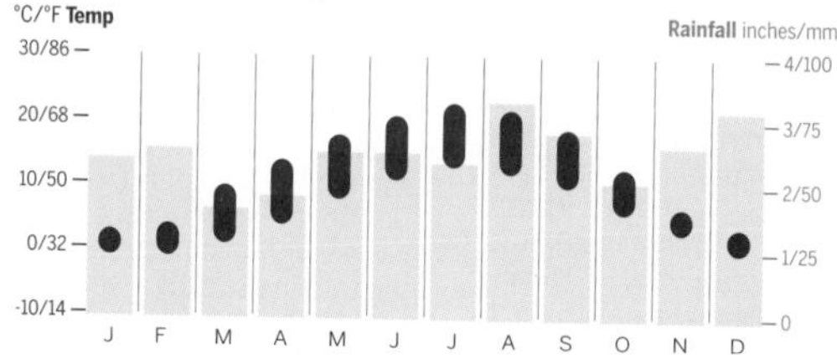

Ostend

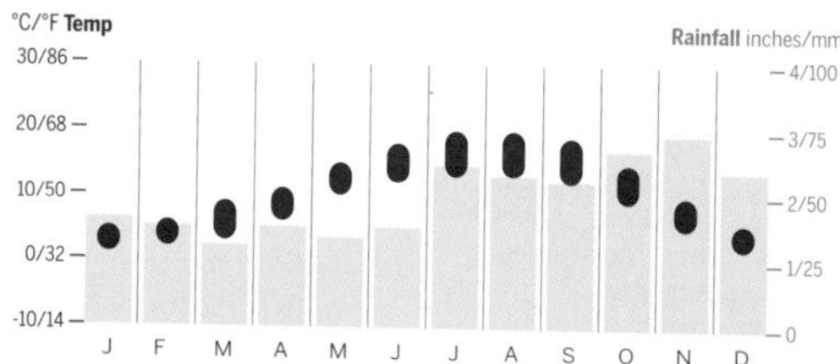

gyms and details of local competitions.

Skiing

This isn't the Alps. There are few major slopes and no ski resorts. Nonetheless, when the Ardennes gets sufficient snowfall, Belgian TV stations give detailed reports and the E411 rapidly fills up with wannabe skiers hurrying south before it all melts again. Most such skiing is cross-country *(langlaufen)* on woodland tracks around Eupen. Dutch-language site Ardennen Sneeuw (www.ardennen-sneeuw.be) gives snow conditions at all the major Ardennes ski areas. There's a handful of downhill pistes.

Customs Regulations

For goods purchased *outside* the EU, the following duty-free allowances apply:

Tobacco 200 cigarettes, 50 cigars or 250g of loose tobacco

Alcohol 1L of spirits (more than 22% alcohol by volume) or 2L light liquor (less than 22% abv); 4L of wine; 16L of beer

Perfume 50g of perfume and 0.25L of eau de toilette

Coming from within the EU, you can bring unlimited quantities for personal use. Nevertheless, expect to be asked questions if you are carrying more than: 800 cigarettes, 200 cigars or 1kg of loose tobacco; 10L of spirits, 20L of fortified wine or aperitif, 90L of wine or 110L of beer.

Discount Cards

Museums and sights typically offer small discounts to seniors (those over 65, sometimes over 60) and often give bigger discounts to those under 26. Accompanied children (under 12) generally pay even less or go free. Students with an ISIC (International Student Identity Card) might, but won't always, qualify for the 'concession rate' (usually the same as seniors). Bigger Belgian cities offer discounted passes to a selection of municipally owned sights and many have one day a month when key museums are free. The **Luxembourg Card** (www.visitluxembourg.com; 1-/2-/3-day adult €13/20/28, family €28/48/68) offers value for visits to the Grand Duchy.

Electricity

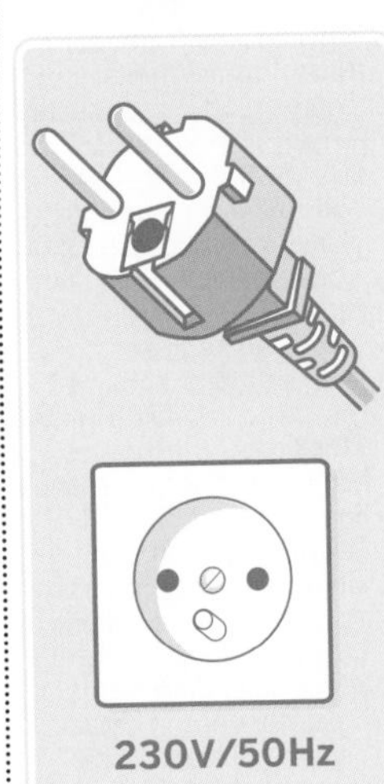

230V/50Hz

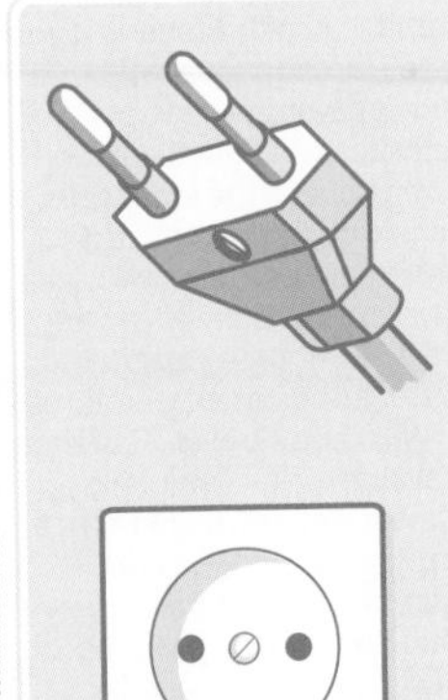

220V/50Hz

EATING PRICE RANGES

The following price ranges are based on the cost of a typical main course.

€ under €15

€€ from €15 to €25

€€€ over €25

Food

For more on food, see Creative Cuisine (p280).

Gay & Lesbian Travellers

Attitudes to homosexuality are pretty laid-back in both Belgium and Luxembourg. Same-sex couples have been able to wed legally in Belgium since 2003, and since 2006 have had the same rights enjoyed by heterosexual couples, including inheritance and adoption. Luxembourg legalised same-sex marriage in 2015, and prime minister Xavier Bettel soon took advantage to tie the knot himself.

Health

Travel in Belgium and Luxembourg presents very few health problems. The standard of care is extremely high; English is widely spoken by doctors and medical clinic staff and tap water is safe to drink.

Specific travel vaccinations are not required for visitors to the region.

Citizens of the European Economic Area (EEA) are covered for emergency medical treatment on presentation of a European Health Insurance Card (EHIC), though they will be liable to pay a per-appointment fee as a local would. You can then take the official receipt to claim a reimbursement of up to 75% through a Belgian

PRACTICALITIES

News

Keep up to date with the Bulletin (www.thebulletin.be), Belgium's invaluable English-language news weekly.

Weights & Measures

Use the metric system for weights and measures. Decimals are indicated with commas, while thousands are separated with dots (full stops).

mutual health-fund office (Ziekenfond/Mutualité).

Enquire about EHICs at your health centre, travel agency or (in some countries) post office well in advance of travel.

Citizens from other countries should find out if there is a reciprocal arrangement for free medical care between their country and Belgium or Luxembourg. If not, health insurance is recommended.

Doctors' bills are generally payable immediately in cash, so visit an ATM beforehand. At a hospital (*ziekenhuis/hôpital* in Dutch/French), you are more likely to be able to pay your bills with plastic.

Pharmacies

For minor self-limiting illnesses you might save a doctor's fee by asking advice at a pharmacy (*apotheek/pharmacie* in Dutch/French).

Most are open from about 8.30am to 7pm Monday to Friday, plus Saturday mornings.

At night or weekends 'duty' (*wachtdienst/de garde*) pharmacies charge higher prices. Use these websites to check which is open when:

Belgium Pharmacies (www.pharmacie.be in French) Search Pharmacie de Garde (French) or Apotheek van Wacht (Dutch).

Luxembourg Pharmacies (www.pharmacie.lu/service_de_garde)

Insurance

A travel insurance policy to cover theft, personal liability, loss and medical problems is recommended. There's a variety of policies available. Travel insurance also usually covers cancellation or delays in travel arrangements; for example, if you fall seriously ill two days before departure.

Buy insurance as early as possible. If you buy it the week before you are due to fly, you may find that you're not covered for delays to your flight caused by strikes or other industrial actions that may have been in force before you took out the insurance.

Browse extensively online to find the best rates.

Paying for your airline ticket with a credit card often provides limited travel accident insurance, and you may be able to reclaim the payment if the operator doesn't deliver.

Certain bank accounts offer their holders automatic travel insurance.

Make sure you get a policy that covers you for the worst possible health scenario if you aren't already covered. Make sure it covers you for any activities you plan to do. Be sure to check the small print. Also find out in advance if your insurance plan will make payments directly to providers or reimburse you later for overseas health expenditures.

Worldwide travel insurance is available at www.lonelyplanet.com/travel-insurance. You can buy, extend and claim online anytime – even if you're already on the road.

Internet Access

Internet cafes – often doubling as call-shops – exist, but are comparatively ephemeral; ask at the tourist office.

Wireless internet access is very widespread; several cities have extensive networks and nearly all hotels, as well as many restaurants, cafes and bars, offer free access to customers and guests.

Data is very cheap. If you've got an unlocked smartphone, you can pick up a local SIM card for a few euros and charge it with a month's worth of data at a decent speed for under €20.

Money

See Need to Know (p16) for costs and First Time (p19) for tipping.

Belgium and Luxembourg adopted the euro (€) in 2002. Euro notes come in five, 10, 20, 50, 100, 200 and 500 denominations and coins in one, two, five, 10, 20, 50 cents and €1 and €2.

Credit cards are widely accepted. ATMs are very common and are the best way of accessing cash.

Opening Hours

Restaurants generally open for lunch from noon until 2.30pm, while dinner is typically served from 6.30pm to 10pm. Gastronomic restaurants with multicourse menus might have only one sitting, while brasseries have more fluid hours, usually serving until 11pm and possibly staying open until midnight or 1am with at least a limited menu.

Bars and *cafés* in some cases close only when the last barfly drops.

Shops in both countries usually open from 10am to 6.30pm Monday to Saturday, some closing for lunch, especially in smaller towns. Tourist-oriented shops often open Sundays then close Mondays. Sunday trading is also common among chains of convenience stores, while night stores (*nachtwinkel* or *magasin de nuit*) work dusk till dawn.

Banks open from 8.30am or 9am and close between

3.30pm and 5pm Monday to Friday. Some close for an hour at lunch, and many also open Saturday mornings.

Larger post offices open at 9am, closing at 6pm or 7pm Monday to Friday, and noon Saturday. Smaller branches close at 5pm, have a lunch break and are closed Saturdays.

Public Holidays

New Year's Day 1 January

Easter Monday March/April

Labour Day 1 May

Iris Day 8 May (Brussels region only)

Ascension Day 39 days after Easter Sunday (always a Thursday)

Pentecost Monday 50 days after Easter Sunday

Luxembourg National Day 23 June (Luxembourg only)

Flemish Community Day 11 July (Flanders only)

Belgium National Day 21 July (Belgium only)

Assumption Day 15 August

Francophone Community Day 27 September (Wallonia only)

All Saints' Day 1 November

Armistice Day 11 November (Belgium only)

Christmas Day 25 December

Telephone

International country codes +32 for Belgium, +352 for Luxembourg. When calling Belgium from abroad, drop the initial 0 from the number.

International dial-out access code ☎00

In Belgium and Luxembourg dial the full number without an extra area code.

The cheapest and most practical solution for making calls and using data is to purchase a local SIM card and pop it in your own phone. First make sure your phone isn't blocked from doing this by your home network. There are several providers: check current offers. Some are online only.

Time

Both countries run on Central European Time. Clocks move forward one hour for daylight-saving time on the last Sunday in March, and revert again on the last Sunday in October. The 24-hour clock is used.

Brussels and Luxembourg are an hour ahead of London and usually six hours ahead of New York.

Tourist Information

Almost every town and village has its own tourist office – *dienst voor toerisme*, *toeristische dienst* or simply *toerisme* (in Flanders), *maison du tourisme*, *office du tourisme* or *syndicat d'initiative* (in Wallonia and Luxembourg).

Offices are marked with an easily identifiable white-on-green 'i' symbol.

Most give away brochures, sell detailed walking/cycling maps and can usually book accommodation and arrange guided tours on your behalf.

Useful contacts:

Visit Wallonia (www.belgiumtheplaceto.be) Wallonia and Brussels

Visit Flanders (www.visitflanders.com) Flanders

Visit Luxembourg (www.visitluxembourg.com) Luxembourg

Travellers With Disabilities

New buildings, including hotels and shops, are required to be constructed in a 'disabled-friendly' way. Slowly increasing numbers of public buildings are thus sprouting lifts and/or ramps, but with numerous buildings that are centuries old, such additions are not always easy to incorporate.

Access to public transport is rapidly improving and information about facilities is decent.

Trains have wheelchair spaces, but it's important to contact the departure station at least a day before.

In all cities and many big towns, larger hotels can usually accommodate travellers in wheelchairs, as can many official HI hostels.

Some useful resources:

Accessible Travel Info Point (☎070 23 30 50; www.accessinfo.be; Grasmarkt 61, Brussels) You can download the ever-expanding brochure, which has masses of detail on the accessibility of attractions and accommodation in Flanders and Brussels with a graded rating system.

Bruxelles Pour Tous (www.bruxellespourtous.be) Valuable online 'guidebook' for Brussels, giving good information about facilities and attractions for disabled visitors.

Welcome.lu (☎36 64 66 1; www.welcome.lu; 65 Ave de la Gare) Luxembourg accessibility site with useful information, mostly in French.

Visas

A valid passport or EU identity card is required to enter. Most Western nationals don't need a tourist visa for stays of less than three months. South Africans, Indians and Chinese, however, are among those who need a Schengen visa. For more information contact the nearest Belgian or Luxembourg embassy or consulate, or check the websites http://diplomatie.belgium.be or www.gouvernement.lu.

Australian and New Zealand citizens aged between 18 and 30 can apply for a 12-month working holiday visa under a reciprocal agreement – contact the Belgian embassy in your home country.

Transport

GETTING THERE & AWAY

Belgium and Luxembourg are easily accessed from Europe and beyond. There are direct flights from numerous destinations, cross-Channel ferries and a comprehensive rail network connecting all across the continent.

Flights, cars and tours can be booked online at lonelyplanet.com/bookings.

Air

Brussels is the major airport for the two countries and is pretty well connected. Charleroi airport is a budget hub, and Luxembourg has its own airport. Other airports like Liège are almost exclusively used by summer charter flights.

You may find it cheaper or more convenient to fly into one of the major airports in neighbouring countries – in Frankfurt, Amsterdam or Paris, for example – and continue into Belgium or Luxembourg by train. Airport websites give up-to-date listings of the airlines that operate from them. The biggest Belgian carrier is Brussels Airlines (www.brusselsairlines.com).

Airports

Antwerp Airport (www.antwerpairport.be) Daily flights on CityJet to London, some seasonal Jetairfly services to Spanish and other European destinations. VLM serves Geneva, and Southampton in the UK.

Brussels Airport (www.brusselsairport.be) Belgium's main international airport. Well connected to Europe and Africa, plus some direct flights to North America and Asia.

Charleroi 'Brussels-South' (www.charleroi-airport.com) Belgium's main hub for low-cost airlines is 55km south of Brussels near Charleroi.

Luxembourg Airport (www.lux-airport.lu) Luxembourg's international airport. Flights mostly limited to European hops. EasyJet links to/from London Gatwick.

Land

Trains are generally faster but more expensive than coaches, though price wise much depends on how early you book.

If driving from the southeast, fill your petrol tank in Luxembourg for low prices. Only in exceptional circumstances are there border controls at crossings into or between Belgium and Luxembourg.

Bus

LONG DISTANCE

Long-distance international buses almost always require advance booking. Book two months ahead for the best fares.

Eurolines (www.eurolines.eu) Large international bus network; usually cheaper than equivalent train tickets. Useful routes served at least daily include London–Brussels (seven to eight hours), London–Bruges/Ghent (six to seven hours), Brussels–Paris (four hours), Brussels–Amsterdam (three to four hours)

CLIMATE CHANGE & TRAVEL

Every form of transport that relies on carbon-based fuel generates CO_2, the main cause of human-induced climate change. Modern travel is dependent on aeroplanes, which might use less fuel per kilometre per person than most cars but travel much greater distances. The altitude at which aircraft emit gases (including CO_2) and particles also contributes to their climate change impact. Many websites offer 'carbon calculators' that allow people to estimate the carbon emissions generated by their journey and, for those who wish to do so, to offset the impact of the greenhouse gases emitted with contributions to portfolios of climate-friendly initiatives throughout the world. Lonely Planet offsets the carbon footprint of all staff and author travel.

and Brussels–Berlin (10 hours). Liège and Antwerp also served.

Ecolines (www.ecolines.net) Consortium of mostly Baltic or Eastern European coach lines.

REGIONAL

A few local and city bus companies operate cross-border services, such as between De Panne/Adinkerke and Dunkerque, and between Luxembourg and Trier. Used mostly by locals, these are rarely well publicised to visitors.

Car/Motorcycle

- Northern Europe is one vast web of motorways, so Belgium and Luxembourg are easily accessed from anywhere.
- There's no problem bringing foreign vehicles into Belgium or Luxembourg, provided you have registration papers and valid insurance ('Green Card').
- Most car-hire companies in the Netherlands, France, Germany or other EU nations won't have a problem with your taking their car into Belgium or Luxembourg, but check rental conditions before you do so.

Train

Reaching Belgium and Luxembourg by train is very easy from most of northern Europe, with high-speed links running regularly between major cities, and easy connections to the broader French, Dutch and German networks.

High-speed trains require seat reservations, and advance-purchase discounts can prove massive, though you'll usually forfeit the right to changes.

Travellers under 26/seniors get discounts of 50/30%, but only on full-price fares.

Ordinary trains are mostly fixed price and without assigned seating.

Internet bookings save you a few euros over Belgian pay-and-go tickets for most international tickets. Check out www.b-europe.com and www.cfl.lu or operator websites of the country of origin.

www.seat61.com An invaluable compendium of advice when planning European train trips.

www.loco2.com A useful website for comparing routes and times and buying tickets.

HIGH-SPEED TRAINS

- Thalys (www.thalys.com) operates on the following routes:

Brussels Midi–Liège–Aachen–Cologne (1¾ hours, five daily)

Brussels Midi–Paris Nord (82 minutes, 16 daily)

Brussels Midi–Antwerp–Rotterdam–Schiphol–Amsterdam (110 minutes, 11 daily)

- Eurostar (www.eurostar.com) runs Brussels Midi–Lille–London (two hours) seven to 10 times daily.
- Deutsche Bahn (www.bahn.com) has ICE trains running Brussels Midi–Liège–Aachen–Frankfurt (three hours, four daily) via Cologne (1¾ hours) and Frankfurt airport.
- SNCF (http://voyages-sncf.com), the French rail operator, runs TGV trains Bruxelles Midi–Paris CDG Airport (1½ hours) and direct to several other French cities. TGV also runs several daily Luxembourg–Paris-Est trains (2¼ hours).

Ordinary Trains

With European railcards, high-speed trains incur a surcharge. For cheaper travel or more flexible travel (no need to prebook) there are alternative slower trains:

Aachen Hourly local trains take 55 minutes from Liège-Guillemins, changing in Welkenraedt.

Amsterdam Hourly IC trains run Brussels Central–Amsterdam (3¼ hours).

Frankfurt Can be reached from Luxembourg in around four hours, changing at Koblenz (2½ hours).

Lille Hourly local lines from Kortrijk and Tournai.

Maastricht Hourly local trains take 33 minutes from Liège-Guillemins.

Paris There's no easy option without reservations.

Trier Served regularly from Luxembourg City (one hour).

Sea

At the time of research, there was only one ferry service operating from Belgium: the P&O (www.poferries.com) service Zeebrugge–Hull (14 hours, overnight).

The quickest way across the Channel is to travel via the French port of Calais, around an hour's drive west of Ostend. Fastest and generally most frequent are the drive-on tunnel trains of Eurotunnel (www.eurotunnel.com), taking 35 minutes around twice an hour to Folkestone.

Usually less expensive are the ferry services linking Calais with Dover run by P&O and cheaper DFDS (www.dfds seaways.co.uk), which take 60 to 90 minutes to Dover depending on the boat. DFDS also has boats sailing Dover–Dunkerque (two hours), but though Dunkerque is nearer Belgium, the port is awkwardly located so total times are about the same.

Tips for travel include:

- Same-day returns, sometimes valid for one night and two days, can be vastly cheaper than one-way tickets. However, you MUST use the return section as planned or else you become liable for a hefty supplement that gets charged to your credit card.
- Fares can vary enormously but usually include up to five passengers per car.
- Websites like www.directferries.com are useful for comparing the prices of different operators.

GETTING AROUND

Air

The speedy train network and short distances mean there are essentially no domestic flights within Belgium and Luxembourg.

LOOK RIGHT!

In towns and villages, if a junction is not regulated by a stop or give-way sign (although most, in practice, are), cars darting out from right-hand side streets have right of way over vehicles. It's easy to get caught out, so always look right.

Bicycle

Bicycle on train Ticket required in Belgium. Costs €5/8 for one journey/whole day. Free in Luxembourg.

Bike helmets Not a legal requirement for cyclists and generally not worn by adults.

Short-Hop Bicycle Hire

➡ Brilliant short-term bicycle-rental schemes operate in several cities. Grab a bike to go from point A to point B, then drop it off and pick up a new one for the next hop. As long as you return the bike to any automated station within 30 minutes, hire charges are minimal or nil, but keep the bike longer and the fee rises.

➡ Use a credit card to buy a membership or day pass, usually online. You get a swipe card or PIN code that releases a bike when you need one. Double-check online that your returned bike has been registered as such to avoid charges.

➡ The schemes work pretty well, except if you're heading, say, to a popular nightlife area late on Saturday evening, when finding anywhere to drop the bike can prove problematic. Be sure to pick up or download a bike-station map.

Longer-Term Bicycle Hire

Bikes can easily be hired in many cities, typically at or near a train station.

Bus

Bus frequency is highest on school days. Fewer operate on Saturday, while Sunday services are often scant to nonexistent. Some rural buses don't operate at all during school holidays (including the whole of July and August). Rural journeys are often slow and circuitous; in some areas buses are on-demand only, so you must phone ahead (details vary).

The route planner at www.belgianrail.be gives useful bus suggestions if that's the logical choice for your route. In Luxembourg, use www.mobiliteit.lu.

Flanders

Bus and tram networks are operated by **De Lijn** (☎high toll 070-22 02 00; www.delijn.be). A single ticket is €3 for up to an hour and can be purchased on board or from a ticket machine or kiosk. A €7/12/18 pass (€5/10/15 pre-purchased) allows one/three/five days' bus and tram travel anywhere in Flanders.

Wallonia

TEC (www.infotec.be) buses charge according to the number of zones travelled (€2.10 for a short trip, €3.20 for longer ones, €5.30 on Express buses). Various one-day (€10) and multijourney passes are available. Tickets are slightly cheaper bought beforehand than on board.

Luxembourg

Luxembourg is served by a comprehensive bus network. A ticket for all domestic transport costs €2 for up to two hours, or €4 for the whole day.

Car & Motorcycle

A car can prove an encumbrance in Bruges, Ghent, Antwerp and Brussels: you'll spend more time finding parking than actually driving anywhere. However, in the country having a car will transform your experience, as many rural attractions are hard to reach by public transport.

Belgium's motorway system is extensive, toll free and mostly illuminated at night – an expensive source of national pride. However, traffic often grinds to a halt, especially on the ring roads around Brussels and Antwerp at rush hour and on the coastal roads at weekends. Constant repairs result in frequent diversions and long traffic jams. Roads in Luxembourg are contrastingly excellent.

Bring Your Own Vehicle

Drivers should have the following with them.

➡ passport and driving licence

➡ vehicle registration (proof of ownership)

➡ insurance documents, plus emergency-assistance numbers for Belgium and Luxembourg

All cars should also carry:

➡ warning triangle

➡ reflective jacket

➡ fire extinguisher (compulsory for Belgian-registered vehicles only)

Winter tyres are not mandatory in Belgium but are recommended. UK and Irish cars must have their headlamps adjusted.

Driving Licence

Be aware that if you're under 18 you can't drive legally in Belgium even if you have a valid licence in your home country. Otherwise, visitors from EU countries and many non-EU countries (there's a list at http://tinyurl.com/p2nrusq) can use their home licences. A few countries need an International Driving Permit to drive in Belgium.

Fuel

➡ Luxembourg has some of the cheapest petrol in Western Europe, with fixed prices that are typically €0.20 to €0.30 less than in Belgium.

- Diesel is around €0.30 per litre cheaper than petrol in Belgium. Note that diesel is *diesel* in Belgian French, not *gazole* as in France.
- Many petrol stations are automated, so you'll need a PIN-coded credit/debit card.

Car Hire

For renting, foreign drivers will need to show their passport or ID card as well as their driving licence and a credit card. Most rental companies require drivers to be aged 23 or over and to have been driving for at least one year. Generally, hire agencies allow you to visit any of the other Benelux (or even European Economic Area countries) without insurance worries, but check conditions.

Renting tips:

- Compare rates online.
- Check whether there's an extra per-kilometre charge.
- When comparing rates, factor in insurance costs and excess liability.
- Weekly rentals are generally vastly better value than rates for one or two days.
- Beware of hefty surcharges when renting from airports or stations.
- Quoting frequent-flyer airline memberships can accumulate points.
- A free 'upgrade' isn't always an advantage, as bigger cars are often less fuel efficient.
- Travellers have reported issues renting with Hertz/Dollar/Thrifty at Brussels Airport, so we'd advise steering clear.

Road Rules & Hazards

- Remember the 'give way to the right' rule.
- Speed limits: 30km/h school zones, 50km/h built-up areas, 90km/h open road, 120km/h Belgian motorways, 130km/h Luxembourg motorways.
- Blood-alcohol limit 0.5 grams per litre of blood.
- Seat belts are compulsory front and rear.
- City centres are devilishly laced with frustratingly complex one-way systems.
- Trams have priority.
- Be conscious of bicycles approaching the 'wrong way' via cycle paths.

Hitching & Ride Sharing

Hitching can be a good way of meeting locals and, while not that popular, is still relatively common.

Hitching is never entirely safe, and Lonely Planet does not recommend it. Travellers who hitch should understand that they are taking a small but potentially serious risk.

Ride sharing is widespread in Northern Europe: www.blablacar.com is probably the most popular website for posting and searching for rides.

Local Transport

The major cities in both countries have efficient and reliable bus networks. Trams are also used in some Belgian cities, and Brussels and Antwerp also have metro systems. Public-transport services generally run until about 11pm or midnight in major cities, or until 9pm or 10pm in towns.

Taxis are metered and tips are not required. While you'll often find taxis waiting outside airports and major train stations, elsewhere you'll usually need to phone for one (ideally an hour or so ahead). Trying to flag down passing taxis is next to fruitless.

PLACE NAMES

Frequently, road signs in Belgium give only the Dutch or French rendering of town names. This can be very confusing for foreigners. Some key ones to be aware of:

ENGLISH	DUTCH	FRENCH
Aachen* (G)	Aken	Aix-la-Chapelle
Antwerp	Antwerpen*	Anvers
Bruges	Brugge*	Bruges
Brussels	Brussel*	Bruxelles*
Courtrai	Kortrijk*	Courtrai
Jodoigne	Geldenaken	Jodoigne*
Köln*/Cologne (G)	Keulen	Cologne
Leuven/Louvain	Leuven*	Louvain
Lille* (F)	Rijsel	Lille
Mechelen/Mechlin	Mechelen*	Malines
Mons	Bergen	Mons*
Namur	Namen	Namur*
Nivelles	Nijvel	Nivelles*
Paris* (F)	Parijs	Paris
Roeselare	Roeselare*	Roulers
The Hague (N)	Den Haag*	La Haye
Tournai	Doornik	Tournai*
Trier* (G)	Trier	Trèves
Veurne	Veurne*	Furnes
Ypres	Ieper*	Ypres

* name as used locally; (F) place is in France; (G) place is in Germany; (N) place is in the Netherlands

Train

Belgium's trains are run by **SNCB** (Belgian Railways; ☎02-528 28 28; www.belgianrail.be (domestic trains)), while in Luxembourg it's **CFL** (☎24 89 24 89; www.cfl.lu).

Belgium

TICKET TIPS

- Tickets should be purchased at ticket offices, ticket machines, or online.
- Check online first for advance-purchase specials.
- If you board a train with no ticket, buying once aboard will incur a €7 surcharge.
- Single tickets are priced by kilometre, but there's a higher fee for Thalys trains.
- Under-26s can buy a Go-Pass 1, which costs €6 and is valid for any one-way trip within Belgium.
- Return tickets are normally twice the price of singles except:

On weekends from 7pm Friday, when a return ticket getting back by Sunday night costs 75% of the price of two singles or less.

For seniors (over 65), who pay just €6 for a return 2nd-class day trip anywhere in Belgium. Valid for travel after 9am weekdays or any weekend except mid-July to mid-August.

CHILDREN

Kids under 12 travel for free when accompanied by an adult. Families travelling with three kids or more pay half price for over-12s (including adults) too.

PETS

Pets need a €2.30 ticket unless carried in a basket or cage.

BICYCLES

Bikes cost €5 on top of a single ticket fee (folding bikes are free). If you pay €8 you can take one on any number of train trips during one day.

MULTI-TICKET PASSES

- **Go Pass 10/Rail Pass** Ten one-way trips anywhere in Belgium (except to/from border stations) for those under/over 26 years cost €51/76. Transfers en route are permitted, but not stopovers (ie you're supposed to take the first feasible connection). Before getting aboard you must write into the space provided the start and end stations plus the date. Valid for one year, the pass is not limited to one person, so you could, for example, write in the same details four times over and use the ticket for a group of four people.
- **Key Card** A similar card allowing 10 short-hop rides (typically 15km maximum) for €20. All of the following options would be valid: Antwerp–Lier, Lier–Mechelen, Brussels–Waterloo and Waterloo–Nivelles. As with the Rail Pass you must fill in the date, starting station and end station for each ride before boarding. However, no transfers are permitted, so if you change trains you'll need to fill in a second line on the pass, effectively doubling the price of the trip.

Luxembourg

Luxembourg's joint railway-bus network is coordinated by **CFL** (☎24 89 24 89; www.cfl.lu). There are just two main ticket types, both allowing unlimited travel on any public transport within the country (except to/from border crossings). From the time you date-stamp it, a €2 *kuurzzäitbilljee (billet courte durée)* ticket is valid for two hours, while a €4 *dagesbilljee (billet longue durée)* is valid all day and until 4am the next morning. Purchase your ticket at an office or train station or pay a €1 supplement once aboard. Upgrading to 1st class costs just €1 per journey extra.

Train Passes

Various passes cover single European countries or a combination of them. For purposes of Interail and Eurail, Belgium, Luxembourg and the Netherlands are considered one nation: Benelux.

While these passes can offer value, their elevated prices mean they aren't always a great option. There are cheaper passes for students, people aged under 26 and seniors. Supplements (eg for high-speed services) and reservation costs are not covered, and terms and conditions change – check carefully before buying. Always carry your passport when using the pass.

EURAIL

Eurail (www.eurail.com) offers a good selection of passes available to residents of non-European countries. Passes should be purchased before arriving in Europe.

The Eurail Benelux pass gives a number of days in a one-month period, and is valid for travel in Belgium, Luxembourg and the Netherlands. It costs €157/189/217/292 for three/four/five/eight days. Regional passes allow you to combine Benelux with France or Germany, while a Select pass allows you to select four neighbouring countries. The Global Pass offers travel in 28 European countries, either five days in 10, 10 or 15 days in a two-month period, or unlimited travel from 15 days up to three months. The Global Passes are much better value for under-26s, as those older have to buy a 1st-class pass.

On most Eurail passes, children aged between four and 11 get a 50% discount on the full adult fare.

INTERRAIL

If you've lived in Europe for more than six months, you're eligible for an InterRail pass (www.interrail.eu). The InterRail Benelux pass offers travel in Belgium, Luxembourg and the Netherlands for three/four/six/eight days in a one-month period, costing €118/149/199/239 in 2nd class. The Global Pass offers travel in 30 European countries and costs from €264 for five days' travel in any 10-day period, to €626 for a month's unlimited train travel. On both passes, there's a roughly 30% discount for under-26s.

Language

Belgium's population is split between Dutch-speaking Flanders in the north, French-speaking Wallonia in the south, and the small German-speaking region, known as the Eastern Cantons, based around the towns of Eupen and St Vith in the east. Brussels is officially bilingual though French has long been the city's dominant language.

The Dutch spoken in Belgium is also called 'Flemish', underlining the cultural identity of the Flemish people. The grammar and spelling rules of Dutch in Belgium and in the Netherlands are the same, and 'Flemish' *(Vlaams)* is not a separate language in itself.

Visitors' attempts to speak French in Flanders are generally considered culturally insensitive and ill-informed, especially in less tourist-oriented cities such as Leuven and Hasselt. English, on the other hand, is considered neutral and quite acceptable – many Flemish speak English fluently.

Luxembourg has three official languages: French, German and Letzeburgesch. Most people are fluent in all three as well as in English, which is widely spoken in the capital and by younger people around the countryside.

Letzeburgesch is most closely related to German and was proclaimed the national tongue in 1984. Luxembourgers speak Letzeburgesch to each other but generally switch to French when talking to foreigners. A couple of Letzeburgesch words often overheard are *moien* (good morning/hello), *äddi* (goodbye) and *wann ech gelifft* (please). Like French speakers, Luxembourgers say *merci* for 'thank you'. A phrase that might come in useful is *Schwatzt dir Englesch?* (pronounced 'schwetz dear anglish') meaning 'Do you speak English?'

WANT MORE?

For in-depth language information and handy phrases, check out Lonely Planet's *Western Europe Phrasebook*. You'll find it at **shop.lonelyplanet.com**, or you can buy Lonely Planet's Fast Talk app at the Apple App Store.

DUTCH

The pronunciation of Dutch is fairly straightforward. The language does distinguish between long and short vowels, which can affect the meaning of words; for example, man (man) and maan (moon). Also note that aw is pronounced as in 'law', eu as the 'u' in 'nurse', ew as the 'ee' in 'see' (with rounded lips), oh as the 'o' in 'note', öy as the 'er y' (without the 'r') in 'her year', and uh as in 'ago'.

The consonants are pretty simple to pronounce too. Note that kh is a throaty sound, similar to the 'ch' in the Scottish loch, r is trilled – both may require a bit of practice – and zh is pronounced as the 's' in 'pleasure'.

If you read our coloured pronunciation guides as if they were English, you'll be understood just fine. The stressed syllables are indicated with italics.

Where relevant, both polite and informal options in Dutch are included, indicated with 'pol' and 'inf' respectively.

Basics

Hello.	*Dag./Hallo.*	dakh/ha·*loh*
Goodbye.	*Dag.*	dakh
Yes.	*Ja.*	yaa
No.	*Nee.*	ney
Please.	*Alstublieft.* (pol) *Alsjeblieft.* (inf)	al·stew·*bleeft* a·shuh·*bleeft*
Thank you.	*Dank u/je.* (pol/inf)	dangk ew/yuh
You're welcome.	*Graag gedaan.*	khraakh khuh·*daan*
Excuse me.	*Excuseer mij.*	eks·kew·*zeyr* mey

How are you?
Hoe gaat het met u/jou? (pol/inf) — hoo khaat huht met ew/yaw

Fine. And you?
Goed. khoot
En met u/jou? (pol/inf) en met ew/yaw

What's your name?
Hoe heet u/je? (pol/inf) hoo heyt ew/yuh

My name is ...
Ik heet ... ik heyt ...

Do you speak English?
Spreekt u Engels? spreykt ew *eng*·uhls

I don't understand.
Ik begrijp het niet. ik buh·*khreyp* huht neet

Accommodation

Do you have a ... room?	*Heeft u een ...?*	heyft ew uhn ...
double	*tweepersoons-kamer met een dubbel bed*	*twey*·puhr·sohns·kaa·muhr met uhn *du*·buhl bet
single	*éénpersoons-kamer*	*eyn*·puhr·sohns·kaa·muhr
twin	*tweepersoons-kamer met lits jumeaux*	*twey*·puhr·sohns·kaa·muhr met lee zhew·*moh*

How much is it per ...?	*Hoeveel kost het per ...?*	hoo·*veyl* kost huht puhr ...
night	*nacht*	nakht
person	*persoon*	puhr·*sohn*

Is breakfast included?
Is het ontbijt inbegrepen? is huht ont·*beyt* *in*·buh·khrey·puhn

bathroom	*badkamer*	*bat*·kaa·muhr
bed and breakfast	*gasten-kamer*	*khas*·tuhn·kaa·muhr
campsite	*camping*	*kem*·ping
guesthouse	*pension*	pen·*syon*
hotel	*hotel*	hoh·*tel*
window	*raam*	raam
youth hostel	*jeugdherberg*	*yeukht*·her·berkh

Directions

Where's the ...?
Waar is ...? waar is ...

How far is it?
Hoe ver is het? hoo ver is huht

What's the address?
Wat is het adres? wat is huht a·*dres*

Can you please write it down?
Kunt u dat alstublieft opschrijven? kunt ew dat al·stew·*bleeft* *op*·skhrey·vuhn

Can you show me (on the map)?
Kunt u het mij tonen (op de kaart)? kunt ew huht mey *toh*·nuhn (op duh kaart)

Eating & Drinking

What would you recommend?
Wat kan u aanbevelen? wat kan ew *aan*·buh·vey·luhn

What's in that dish?
Wat zit er in dat gerecht? wat zit uhr in dat khuh·*rekht*

I'd like the menu, please.
Ik wil graag een menu. ik wil khraakh uhn me·*new*

Delicious!
Heerlijk!/Lekker! *heyr*·luhk/*le*·kuhr

Cheers!
Proost! prohst

Please bring the bill.
Mag ik de rekening alstublieft? makh ik duh *rey*·kuh·ning al·stew·*bleeft*

I'd like to reserve a table for ...	*Ik wil graag een tafel voor ... reserveren.*	ik wil khraakh uhn *taa*·fuhl vohr ... rey·ser·*vey*·ruhn
(eight) o'clock	*(acht) uur*	(akht) ewr
(two) people	*(twee) personen*	(twey) puhr·*soh*·nuhn

I don't eat ...	*Ik eet geen ...*	ik eyt kheyn ...
eggs	*eieren*	*ey*·yuh·ruhn
fish	*vis*	vis
(red) meat	*(rood) vlees*	(roht) vleys
nuts	*noten*	*noh*·tuhn

bar	*bar*	bar
beer	*bier*	beer
bottle	*fles*	fles
bread	*brood*	broht
breakfast	*ontbijt*	ont·*beyt*
cafe	*café*	ka·*fey*
cheese	*kaas*	kaas

Question Words – Dutch

How?	*Hoe?*	hoo
What?	*Wat?*	wat
When?	*Wanneer?*	wa·*neyr*
Where?	*Waar?*	waar
Who?	*Wie?*	wee
Why?	*Waarom?*	waa·*rom*

Numbers – Dutch

1	*één*	eyn
2	*twee*	twey
3	*drie*	dree
4	*vier*	veer
5	*vijf*	veyf
6	*zes*	zes
7	*zeven*	*zey*·vuhn
8	*acht*	akht
9	*negen*	*ney*·khuhn
10	*tien*	teen
20	*twintig*	*twin*·tikh
30	*dertig*	*der*·tikh
40	*veertig*	*feyr*·tikh
50	*vijftig*	*feyf*·tikh
60	*zestig*	*ses*·tikh
70	*zeventig*	*sey*·vuhn·tikh
80	*tachtig*	*takh*·tikh
90	*negentig*	*ney*·khuhn·tikh
100	*honderd*	*hon*·duhrt
1000	*duizend*	*döy*·zuhnt

coffee	*koffie*	*ko*·fee
cold	*koud*	kawt
dinner	*avondmaal*	*aa*·vont·maal
drink list	*drankkaart*	*drang*·kaart
eggs	*eieren*	*ey*·yuh·ruhn
fish	*vis*	vis
fork	*vork*	vork
fruit	*fruit*	fröyt
glass	*glas*	khlas
grocery store	*kruidenier*	kröy·duh·*neer*
hot	*heet*	heyt
juice	*sap*	sap
knife	*mes*	mes
lunch	*middagmaal*	*mi*·dakh·maal
market	*markt*	markt
meat	*vlees*	vleys
menu	*menu*	me·*new*
milk	*melk*	melk
plate	*bord*	bort
pub	*kroeg*	krookh
restaurant	*restaurant*	res·toh·*rant*
rice	*rijst*	reyst
salt	*zout*	zawt
spicy	*pikant*	pee·*kant*
spoon	*lepel*	*ley*·puhl
sugar	*suiker*	*söy*·kuhr
tea	*thee*	tey
vegetables	*groenten*	*khroon*·tuhn
vegetarian	*vegetarisch*	vey·khey·*taa*·ris
water	*water*	*waa*·tuhr
wine	*wijn*	weyn
with	*met*	met
without	*zonder*	*zon*·duhr

Emergencies

Help!
Help! — help

Leave me alone!
Laat me met rust! — laat muh met rust

I'm lost.
Ik ben verdwaald. — ik ben vuhr·*dwaalt*

There's been an accident.
Er is een ongeluk gebeurd. — uhr is uhn *on*·khuh·luk khuh·*beurt*

Call a doctor!
Bel een dokter! — bel uhn *dok*·tuhr

Call the police!
Bel de politie! — bel duh poh·*leet*·see

I'm sick.
Ik ben ziek. — ik ben zeek

Where are the toilets?
Waar zijn de toiletten? — waar zeyn duh twa·*le*·tuhn

I'm allergic to (antibiotics).
Ik ben allergisch voor (antibiotica). — ik ben a·*ler*·khees vohr (an·tee·bee·*yoh*·tee·ka)

Shopping & Services

I'd like to buy ...
Ik wil graag ... kopen. — ik wil khraakh ... *koh*·puhn

I'm just looking.
Ik kijk alleen maar. — ik keyk a·*leyn* maar

Can I look at it?
Kan ik het even zien? — kan ik huht *ey*·vuhn zeen

Do you have any others?
Heeft u nog andere? — heyft ew nokh *an*·duh·ruh

How much is it?
Hoeveel kost het? — hoo·*veyl* kost huht

That's too expensive.
Dat is te duur. — dat is tuh dewr

Can you lower the price?
Kunt u wat van de prijs afdoen? — kunt ew wat van duh preys *af*·doon

There's a mistake in the bill.
Er zit een fout in de rekening. — uhr zit uhn fawt in duh *rey*·kuh·ning

ATM	*pin-automaat*	*pin*·aw·toh·maat

foreign exchange	*wisselkantoor*	*wi*·suhl·kan·tohr
post office	*postkantoor*	*post*·kan·tohr
shopping centre	*winkel-centrum*	*wing*·kuhl·sen·trum
tourist office	*VVV*	vey·vey·*vey*

Time & Dates

What time is it?
Hoe laat is het? — hoo laat is huht

It's (10) o'clock.
Het is (tien) uur. — huht is (teen) ewr

Half past (10).
Half (elf). (lit: half eleven) — half (elf)

am (morning)	*'s ochtends*	*sokh*·tuhns
pm (afternoon)	*'s middags*	*smi*·dakhs
pm (evening)	*'s avonds*	*saa*·vonts
yesterday	*gisteren*	*khis*·tuh·ruhn
today	*vandaag*	van·*daakh*
tomorrow	*morgen*	*mor*·khuhn

Monday	*maandag*	*maan*·dakh
Tuesday	*dinsdag*	*dins*·dakh
Wednesday	*woensdag*	*woons*·dakh
Thursday	*donderdag*	*don*·duhr·dakh
Friday	*vrijdag*	*vrey*·dakh
Saturday	*zaterdag*	*zaa*·tuhr·dakh
Sunday	*zondag*	*zon*·dakh

Transport

Is this the ... to (the left bank)?	*Is dit de ... naar (de linker-oever)?*	is dit duh ... naar (duh *ling*·kuhr·*oo*·vuhr)
ferry	*veerboot*	*veyr*·boht
metro	*metro*	*mey*·troh
tram	*tram*	trem
platform	*perron*	pe·*ron*
timetable	*dienst-regeling*	*deenst*·rey·khuh·ling

When's the ... (bus)?	*Hoe laat gaat de ... (bus)?*	hoo laat khaat duh ... (bus)
first	*eerste*	*eyr*·stuh
last	*laatste*	*laat*·stuh
next	*volgende*	*vol*·khun·duh

A ticket to ..., please.
Een kaartje naar ... graag. — uhn *kaar*·chuh naar ... khraakh

Signs – Dutch

Dames	Women
Gesloten	Closed
Heren	Men
Ingang	Entrance
Inlichtingen	Information
Open	Open
Toiletten	Toilets
Uitgang	Exit
Verboden	Prohibited

What time does it leave?
Hoe laat vertrekt het? — hoo laat vuhr·*trekt* huht

Does it stop at ...?
Stopt het in ...? — stopt huht in ...

What's the next stop?
Welk is de volgende halte? — welk is duh *vol*·khuhn·duh *hal*·tuh

I'd like to get off at ...
Ik wil graag in ... uitstappen. — ik wil khraak in ... *öyt*·sta·puhn

Is this taxi available?
Is deze taxi vrij? — is *dey*·zuh *tak*·see vrey

Please take me to ...
Breng me alstublieft naar ... — breng muh al·stew·*bleeft* naar ...

I'd like ...	*Ik wil graag ...*	ik wil khraakh ...
my bicycle repaired	*mijn fiets laten herstellen*	meyn feets *laa*·tuhn her·*ste*·luhn
to hire a bicycle	*een fiets huren*	uhn feets *hew*·ruhn

I'd like to hire a ...	*Ik wil graag een ... huren.*	ik wil khraakh uhn ... *hew*·ruhn
basket	*mandje*	*man*·chuh
child seat	*kinderzitje*	*kin*·duhr·zi·chuh
helmet	*helm*	helm

Do you have bicycle parking?
Heeft u parking voor fietsen? — heyft ew *par*·king vohr *feet*·suhn

Can we get there by bike?
Kunnen we er met de fiets heen? — *ku*·nuhn wuh uhr met duh feets heyn

I have a puncture.
Ik heb een lekke band. — ik hep uhn *le*·kuh bant

bicycle path	*fietspad*	*feets*·pat
bicycle repairman	*fietsen-maker*	feet·suhn·*maa*·kuhr
bicycle stand	*fietsenrek*	feet·suhn·*rek*

FRENCH

The sounds used in spoken French can almost all be found in English. There are a couple of exceptions: nasal vowels (represented in our pronunciation guides by o or u followed by an almost inaudible nasal consonant sound m, n or ng), the 'funny' u (ew in our guides) and the deep-in-the-throat r. Bearing these few points in mind and reading our pronunciation guides below as if they were English, you won't have problems being understood. Note that syllables are for the most part equally stressed in French.

In this chapter both masculine and femine forms are provided where necessary, separated by a slash and indicated with 'm/f'.

Basics

Hello.	*Bonjour.*	bon·zhoor
Goodbye.	*Au revoir.*	o·rer·vwa
Excuse me.	*Excusez-moi.*	ek·skew·zay·mwa
Sorry.	*Pardon.*	par·don
Yes.	*Oui.*	wee
No.	*Non.*	non
Please.	*S'il vous plaît.*	seel voo play
Thank you.	*Merci.*	mair·see
You're welcome.	*De rien.*	der ree·en

How are you?
Comment allez-vous? ko·mon ta·lay·voo

Fine, and you?
Bien, merci. Et vous? byun mair·see ay voo

You're welcome.
De rien. der ree·en

My name is ...
Je m'appelle ... zher ma·pel ...

What's your name?
Comment vous appelez-vous? ko·mon voo·za·play voo

Do you speak English?
Parlez-vous anglais? par·lay·voo ong·glay

Question Words – French

How?	*Comment?*	ko·mon
What?	*Quoi?*	kwa
When?	*Quand?*	kon
Where?	*Où?*	oo
Who?	*Qui?*	kee
Why?	*Pourquoi?*	poor·kwa

I don't understand.
Je ne comprends pas. zher ner kom·pron pa

Accommodation

Do you have any rooms available?
Est-ce que vous avez des chambres libres? es·ker voo za·vay day shom·brer lee·brer

How much is it per night/person?
Quel est le prix par nuit/personne? kel ay ler pree par nwee/per·son

Is breakfast included?
Est-ce que le petit déjeuner est inclus? es·ker ler per·tee day·zher·nay ayt en·klew

campsite	*camping*	kom·peeng
dorm	*dortoir*	dor·twar
guesthouse	*pension*	pon·syon
hotel	*hôtel*	o·tel
youth hostel	*auberge de jeunesse*	o·berzh der zher·nes

a ... room	*une chambre ...*	ewn shom·brer ...
double	*avec un grand lit*	a·vek un gron lee
single	*à un lit*	a un lee
twin	*avec des lits jumeaux*	a·vek day lee zhew·mo

with (a)...	*avec ...*	a·vek ...
air-con	*climatiseur*	klee·ma·tee·zer
bathroom	*une salle de bains*	ewn sal der bun
window	*fenêtre*	fer·nay·trer

Directions

Where's ...?
Où est ...? oo ay ...

What's the address?
Quelle est l'adresse? kel ay la·dres

Could you write the address, please?
Est-ce que vous pourriez écrire l'adresse, s'il vous plaît? es·ker voo poo·ryay ay·kreer la·dres seel voo play

Can you show me (on the map)?
Pouvez-vous m'indiquer (sur la carte)? poo·vay·voo mun·dee·kay (sewr la kart)

Eating & Drinking

What would you recommend?
Qu'est-ce que vous conseillez? kes·ker voo kon·say·yay

What's in that dish?
Quels sont les ingrédients? kel son lay zun·gray·dyon

I'm a vegetarian.
Je suis végétarien/ végétarienne. (m/f) zher swee vay·zhay·ta·ryun/ vay·zhay·ta·ryen

I don't eat ...
Je ne mange pas ... zher ner monzh pa ...

Cheers!
Santé! son·tay

That was delicious.
C'était délicieux! say·tay day·lee·syer

Please bring the bill.
Apportez-moi l'addition, s'il vous plaît. a·por·tay·mwa la·dee·syon seel voo play

I'd like to reserve a table for ...	*Je voudrais réserver une table pour ...*	zher voo·dray ray·zair·vay ewn ta·bler poor ...
(eight) o'clock	*(vingt) heures*	(vungt) er
(two) people	*(deux) personnes*	(der) pair·son

appetiser	*entrée*	on·tray
beer	*bière*	bee·yair
bottle	*bouteille*	boo·tay
bread	*pain*	pun
breakfast	*petit déjeuner*	per·tee day·zher·nay
cheese	*fromage*	fro·mazh
children's menu	*menu pour enfants*	mer·new poor on·fon
coffee	*café*	ka·fay
cold	*froid*	frwa
delicatessen	*traiteur*	tray·ter
dinner	*dîner*	dee·nay
dish	*plat*	pla
egg	*œuf*	erf
food	*nourriture*	noo·ree·tewr
fork	*fourchette*	foor·shet
glass	*verre*	vair
grocery store	*épicerie*	ay·pees·ree
highchair	*chaise haute*	shay zot
hot	*chaud*	sho
(orange) juice	*jus (d'orange)*	zhew (do·ronzh)
knife	*couteau*	koo·to
local speciality	*spécialité locale*	spay·sya·lee·tay lo·kal
lunch	*déjeuner*	day·zher·nay
main course	*plat principal*	pla prun·see·pal

Numbers – French

1	*un*	un
2	*deux*	der
3	*trois*	trwa
4	*quatre*	ka·trer
5	*cinq*	sungk
6	*six*	sees
7	*sept*	set
8	*huit*	weet
9	*neuf*	nerf
10	*dix*	dees
20	*vingt*	vung
30	*trente*	tront
40	*quarante*	ka·ront
50	*cinquante*	sung·kont
60	*soixante*	swa·sont
70	*soixante-dix*	swa·son·dees
80	*quatre-vingts*	ka·trer·vung
90	*quatre-vingt-dix*	ka·trer·vung·dees
100	*cent*	son
1000	*mille*	meel

In Francophone Belgium, though not in Luxembourg, the numbers 70 and 90 are *septante* and *nonante* respectively.

market	*marché*	mar·shay
menu (in English)	*carte (en anglais)*	kart (on ong·glay)
milk	*lait*	lay
plate	*assiette*	a·syet
red wine	*vin rouge*	vun roozh
rice	*riz*	ree
salt	*sel*	sel
spoon	*cuillère*	kwee·yair
sugar	*sucre*	sew·krer
tea	*thé*	tay
vegetable	*légume*	lay·gewm
(mineral) water	*eau (minérale)*	o (mee·nay·ral)
white wine	*vin blanc*	vun blong
wine list	*carte des vins*	kart day vun
with	*avec*	a·vek
without	*sans*	son

Emergencies

Help!
Au secours! o skoor

I'm lost.
Je suis perdu/ perdue. (m/f) — zhe swee·pair·dew

Leave me alone!
Fichez-moi la paix! — fee·shay·mwa la pay

There's been an accident.
Il y a eu un accident. — eel ya ew un ak·see·don

Call a doctor.
Appelez un médecin. — a·play un mayd·sun

Call the police.
Appelez la police. — a·play la po·lees

I'm ill.
Je suis malade. — zher swee ma·lad

It hurts here.
J'ai une douleur ici. — zhay ewn doo·ler ee·see

I'm allergic to ...
Je suis allergique à ... — zher swee za·lair·zheek a ...

Shopping & Services

I'd like to buy ...
Je voudrais acheter ... — zher voo·dray ash·tay ...

May I look at it?
Est-ce que je peux le voir? — es·ker zher per ler vwar

I'm just looking.
Je regarde. — zher rer·gard

I don't like it.
Cela ne me plaît pas. — ser·la ner mer play pa

How much is it?
C'est combien? — say kom·byun

It's too expensive.
C'est trop cher. — say tro shair

Can you lower the price?
Vous pouvez baisser le prix? — voo poo·vay bay·say ler pree

There's a mistake in the bill.
Il y a une erreur dans la note. — eel ya ewn ay·rer don la not

ATM	*guichet automatique de banque*	gee·shay o·to·ma·teek der bonk
credit card	*carte de crédit*	kart der kray·dee
internet cafe	*cybercafé*	see·bair·ka·fay
post office	*bureau de poste*	bew·ro der post
tourist office	*office de tourisme*	o·fees der too·rees·mer

Signs – French

Entrée	Entrance
Femmes	Women
Fermé	Closed
Hommes	Men
Interdit	Prohibited
Ouvert	Open
Renseignements	Information
Sortie	Exit
Toilettes/WC	Toilets

Time & Dates

What time is it?
Quelle heure est-il? — kel er ay til

It's (eight) o'clock.
Il est (huit) heures. — il ay (weet) er

It's half past (10).
Il est (dix) heures et demie. — il ay (deez) er ay day·mee

morning	*matin*	ma·tun
afternoon	*après-midi*	a·pray·mee·dee
evening	*soir*	swar
yesterday	*hier*	yair
today	*aujourd'hui*	o·zhoor·dwee
tomorrow	*demain*	der·mun

Monday	*lundi*	lun·dee
Tuesday	*mardi*	mar·dee
Wednesday	*mercredi*	mair·krer·dee
Thursday	*jeudi*	zher·dee
Friday	*vendredi*	von·drer·dee
Saturday	*samedi*	sam·dee
Sunday	*dimanche*	dee·monsh

Transport

boat	*bateau*	ba·to
bus	*bus*	bews
plane	*avion*	a·vyon
train	*train*	trun

I want to go to ...
Je voudrais aller à ... — zher voo·dray a·lay a ...

Does it stop at ...?
Est-ce qu'il s'arrête à ...? — es·kil sa·ret a ...

At what time does it leave/arrive?
À quelle heure est-ce qu'il part/arrive? — a kel er es kil par/a·reev

Can you tell me when we get to ...?
Pouvez-vous me dire quand nous arrivons à ...? — poo·vay·voo mer deer kon noo za·ree·von a ...

I want to get off here.
Je veux descendre ici. — zher ver day·son·drer ee·see

first	*premier*	prer·myay
last	*dernier*	dair·nyay
next	*prochain*	pro·shun

a ... ticket	*un billet ...*	un bee·yay ...
1st-class	*de première classe*	der prem·yair klas
2nd-class	*de deuxième classe*	der der·zyem las
one-way	*simple*	sum·pler
return	*aller et retour*	a·lay ay rer·toor

aisle seat	*côté couloir*	ko·tay kool·war
cancelled	*annulé*	a·new·lay
delayed	*en retard*	on rer·tar
platform	*quai*	kay
ticket office	*guichet*	gee·shay
timetable	*horaire*	o·rair
train station	*gare*	gar
window seat	*côté fenêtre*	ko·tay fe·ne·trer

I'd like to hire a ...	*Je voudrais louer ...*	zher voo·dray loo·way ...
4WD	*un quatre-quatre*	un kat·kat
bicycle	*un vélo*	un vay·lo
car	*une voiture*	ewn vwa·tewr
motorcycle	*une moto*	ewn mo·to

child seat	*siège-enfant*	syezh·on·fon
diesel	*diesel*	dyay·zel
helmet	*casque*	kask
mechanic	*mécanicien*	may·ka·nee·syun
petrol	*essence*	ay·sons
service station	*station-service*	sta·syon·ser·vees

Is this the road to ...?
C'est la route pour ...? say la root poor ...

(How long) Can I park here?
(Combien de temps) Est-ce que je peux stationner ici? (kom·byun der tom) es·ker zher per sta·syo·nay ee·see

The car/motorbike has broken down (at ...).
La voiture/moto est tombée en panne (à ...). la vwa·tewr/mo·to ay tom·bay on pan (a ...)

I have a flat tyre.
Mon pneu est à plat. mom pner ay ta pla

I've run out of petrol.
Je suis en panne d'essence. zher swee zon pan day·sons

I've lost my car keys.
J'ai perdu les clés de ma voiture. zhay per·dew lay klay der ma vwa·tewr

GLOSSARY

Nl/Fr after a term signifies Dutch/French.

abdij/abbaye (Nl/Fr) – abbey
apotheek (Nl) – pharmacy
ARAU (Fr) – Atelier de Recherche et d'Action Urbaine (Urban Research & Action Group)
auberge de jeunesse (Fr) – youth hostel

bakker/bakkerij (Nl) – baker/bakery
balle-pelotte – Belgian ball game
begijn/béguine (Nl/Fr) – inhabitant of a *begijnhof*
begijnhof/béguinage (Nl/Fr) – community of *begijnen/béguines*; cluster of cottages, often around a central garden
Belasting Toegevoegde Waarde (BTW) (Nl) – value-added tax, VAT
Belgische Spoorwegen (Nl) – Belgian Railways
Benelux – Belgium, the Netherlands and Luxembourg
benzine (Nl) – petrol
betalend parkeren (Nl) – paid street parking
biljart/billard (Nl/Fr) – billiards
billet (Fr) – ticket
boulangerie (Fr) – bakery
BP (boîte postale) (Fr) – post office box
brasserie (Fr) – brewery; café/restaurant often serving food all day
brocante (Fr) – bric-a-brac
brouwerij (Nl) – brewery
brown café – small, old-fashioned pub with wooden-panelled interior
bruine kroeg (Nl) – *brown café*
Brusselaar (Nl) – inhabitant of Brussels
Bruxellois (Fr) – inhabitant of Brussels; name of the city's old dialect
bureau d'échange (Fr) – foreign-exchange bureau

café – pub, bar
carte (Fr) – menu
centrum (Nl) – centre
chambre (Fr) – room
chambre d'hôte (Fr) – B&B guesthouse
Charles Quint – Holy Roman Emperor Charles V
château (Fr) – castle, country mansion
chocolatier (Fr) – chocolate-maker
commune (Fr) – municipality
couvent (Fr) – convent
cuistax – see *kwistax*

dagschotel (Nl) – dish of the day
demi-pension (Fr) – half board (ie accommodation, breakfast and dinner)
dentelle (Fr) – lace
dienst voor toerisme (Nl) – tourist office

église (Fr) – church
entrée (Fr) – entry
estaminet (Fr) – tavern
étang (Fr) – pond
EU – European Union
Eurocrat – EU administrative official
Europese Instellingen (Nl) – EU Institutions

fiets (Nl) – bicycle
frieten/frites (Nl/Fr) – chips or fries
frituur/friture/friterie (Nl/Fr/Fr) – chip shop

galerij/galerie (Nl/Fr) – covered shopping centre/arcade
gare (Fr) – train station
gastenkamer (Nl) – B&B/guesthouse
gaufres (Fr) – waffles
gemeente (Nl) – municipality
Gille (Fr) – folkloric character typical of the Binche carnival
gîtes d'étapes (Fr) – rural group accommodation, sometimes also a hostel
gîtes ruraux (Fr) – countryside guesthouses
godshuis (Nl) – almshouse
GR (Fr) – long-distance footpaths
grand café (Fr) – opulent historic *café*
gratis/gratuit (Nl/Fr) – free
grotte (Fr) – cave, grotto

hallen/halles (Nl/Fr) – covered market
herberg (Nl) – old-style Flemish pub
hof (Nl) – garden
holebi – LGBT (*ho*mosexual-*le*sbian-*bi*sexual)
Holy Roman Empire – Germanic empire (962–1806) that was confusingly neither theocratic nor predominantly Italian/Roman for most of its history
hôpital (Fr) – hospital
horeca (Fr/Nl) – the hospitality (*ho*tel-*re*staurant-*ca*fe) industry
hôtel (Fr) – hotel, historic town house
hôtel de ville (Fr) – town hall

Institutions Européennes (Fr) – EU Institutions
ISIC – International Student Identity Card

jardin (Fr) – garden
jenever – (Nl) Flemish/Dutch gin
jeu-de-balle (F) – see *balle-pelotte*
jeugdherberg (Nl) – youth hostel

kaartje (Nl) – ticket
kamer (Nl) – room
kant (Nl) – lace
kasteel (Nl) – castle
kerk (Nl) – church
kwistax – pedal-carts popular on Belgian beaches

magasin de nuit (Fr) – 24-hour shop
marché aux puces (Fr) – flea market
markt/marché (Nl/Fr) – market
menu (Nl & Fr) – fixed-price meal with two or more courses (what is called the menu in English is the *kaart/la carte*)

menu du jour (Fr) – fixed-price, multicourse meal of the day

molen/moulin (Nl/Fr) – windmill

Mosan – from the Meuse River valley

musée (Fr) – museum

nachtwinkel (Nl) – 24-hour shop

NATO – North Atlantic Treaty Organisation military alliance headquartered in Brussels (NAVO/OTAN in Dutch/French)

NMBS (Nl) – Belgian National Railways

office de tourisme (Fr) – tourist office

oude (Nl) – old

OV (originele versie) (Nl) – nondubbed (ie movie shown in its original language)

pâtisserie (Fr) – cakes and pastries; shop selling them

pékèt – Walloon for *jenever*

pension complète (Fr) – full board

pharmacie (Fr) – pharmacy

pitas (Fr) – stuffed pitta bread

place (Fr) – square

plat du jour (Fr) – dish of the day

plein (Nl) – square

poort/porte (Nl/Fr) – gate in city wall

premetro – trams that go underground for part of their journey (found in Brussels and Antwerp)

prior[itaire] (Fr) – priority mail

priorité à droite (Fr) – priority-to-the-right traffic rule

RACB (Fr) – Royal Automobile Club de Belgique

routier (Fr) – trucker (also truckers' restaurant)

SHAPE – NATO's 'Supreme HQ Allied Powers Europe' near Mons

slijterij (Nl) – shop selling strong alcohol

SNCB (Fr) – Belgian National Railways

sortie (Fr) – exit

stad (Nl) – town

stadhuis (Nl) – town hall

stadsbelasting (Nl) – city tax

stationnement payant (Fr) – paid parking

STIB (Fr) – Société des Transports Intercommunaux de Bruxelles (Brussels Public Transport Company)

syndicat d'initiative (Fr) – tourist office

taxe de séjour (Fr) – visitors' tax

terreinfiets (Nl) – mountain bike

toeristische dienst (Nl) – tourist office

toneel/théâtre (Nl/Fr) – theatre

toren/tour (Nl/Fr) – tower

trekkershut (Nl) – hikers' hut

tuin (Nl) – garden

TVA (Fr) – value-added tax, VAT

vélo (Fr) – bicycle

VO (version originale) (Fr) – nondubbed film

voorrang van rechts (Nl) – priority-to-the-right traffic rule

VTT (vélo tout-terrain) (Fr) – mountain bike

wassalon (Nl) – laundrette

weekend gastronomique (Fr) – accommodation plus breakfast and some meals

ziekenhuis (Nl) – hospital

Behind the Scenes

SEND US YOUR FEEDBACK

We love to hear from travellers – your comments keep us on our toes and help make our books better. Our well-travelled team reads every word on what you loved or loathed about this book. Although we cannot reply individually to your submissions, we always guarantee that your feedback goes straight to the appropriate authors, in time for the next edition. Each person who sends us information is thanked in the next edition – the most useful submissions are rewarded with a selection of digital PDF chapters.

Visit **lonelyplanet.com/contact** to submit your updates and suggestions or to ask for help. Our award-winning website also features inspirational travel stories, news and discussions.

Note: We may edit, reproduce and incorporate your comments in Lonely Planet products such as guidebooks, websites and digital products, so let us know if you don't want your comments reproduced or your name acknowledged. For a copy of our privacy policy visit lonelyplanet.com/privacy.

OUR READERS

Many thanks to the travellers who used the last edition and wrote to us with helpful hints, useful advice and interesting anecdotes: Fabio Baldi, Laura Cavatorta, Paul Finn, John Hodges, Mikael Kirkensgaard, David MacBryde, Koulla Moore, Charlotte Stevens, Deb Williams and Julie Woods.

AUTHOR THANKS

Helena Smith

Continued thanks to Anne Ponslet, Kristof Buntinx and the USE-It gang. Also to Karel for the hospitality, and Alex for his company at Ypres and for helping me find the Matonge party.

Andy Symington

As always, I owe many thanks to helpful people across Belgium and Luxembourg, particularly in tourist offices. Specific thanks for various favours go to Nathalie Van Waeyenberge, Jean Dubois and Sandrine Rousseau. Reinhard Sahre uncomplainingly drove a very long way for a beer in Liège and Eduardo Cuadrado Diago and José Eliseo Vázquez Rodríguez generously kept things running smoothly at home during my frequent absences. Thanks also to my family for their support and to the LP team, particularly Mark Elliott for a great previous edition to work with.

Donna Wheeler

Many thanks to the ever-fabulous Antwerpers who made my stay a delight, including Nele, Dries and Nadine and the very generous and knowledgable Philippe d'Hoore. In Mechelin, thanks to Tim and Linda for the great tips, to Leuven's Bar Stan boys for such sweetness and to Karien in Ghent. Much gratitude, too, to Daniel Nettheim for your wonderful company, Darryn Devlin for your soothing voice from afar and Joe Guario for the constant love and support.

ACKNOWLEDGEMENTS

Climate map data adapted from Peel MC, Finlayson BL & McMahon TA (2007) 'Updated World Map of the Köppen-Geiger Climate Classification', Hydrology and Earth System Sciences, 11, 163344.

Cover photograph: Sunset over the Belfry, Bruges; Alyaksandr Stzhalkouski/Alamy ©

THIS BOOK

This 6th edition of Lonely Planet's *Belgium & Luxembourg* guidebook was researched and written by Helena Smith, Andy Symington and Donna Wheeler. The previous edition was written by Mark Elliott and Helena Smith. This guidebook was produced by the following:

Destination Editor Kate Morgan

Product Editors Kate Mathews, Kathryn Rowan

Senior Cartographer David Kemp

Book Designer Wendy Wright

Assisting Editors Sarah Bailey, Pete Cruttenden, Carly Hall, Victoria Harrison, Gabby Innes

Cover Researcher Naomi Parker

Thanks to Neill Coen, Ryan Evans, Elizabeth Jones, Darren O'Connell, Kirsten Rawlings, Diana Saengkham, Ellie Simpson, Lauren Wellicome

Index

Map Pages **000**
Photo Pages **000**

Map Pages **000**
Photo Pages **000**

Map Legend

Sights
- Beach
- Bird Sanctuary
- Buddhist
- Castle/Palace
- Christian
- Confucian
- Hindu
- Islamic
- Jain
- Jewish
- Monument
- Museum/Gallery/Historic Building
- Ruin
- Shinto
- Sikh
- Taoist
- Winery/Vineyard
- Zoo/Wildlife Sanctuary
- Other Sight

Activities, Courses & Tours
- Bodysurfing
- Diving
- Canoeing/Kayaking
- Course/Tour
- Sento Hot Baths/Onsen
- Skiing
- Snorkelling
- Surfing
- Swimming/Pool
- Walking
- Windsurfing
- Other Activity

Sleeping
- Sleeping
- Camping

Eating
- Eating

Drinking & Nightlife
- Drinking & Nightlife
- Cafe

Entertainment
- Entertainment

Shopping
- Shopping

Information
- Bank
- Embassy/Consulate
- Hospital/Medical
- Internet
- Police
- Post Office
- Telephone
- Toilet
- Tourist Information
- Other Information

Geographic
- Beach
- Gate
- Hut/Shelter
- Lighthouse
- Lookout
- Mountain/Volcano
- Oasis
- Park
- Pass
- Picnic Area
- Waterfall

Population
- Capital (National)
- Capital (State/Province)
- City/Large Town
- Town/Village

Transport
- Airport
- Border crossing
- Bus
- Cable car/Funicular
- Cycling
- Ferry
- Metro station
- Monorail
- Parking
- Petrol station
- S-Bahn/S-train/Subway station
- Taxi
- T-bane/Tunnelbana station
- Train station/Railway
- Tram
- Tube station
- U-Bahn/Underground station
- Other Transport

Note: Not all symbols displayed above appear on the maps in this book

Routes
- Tollway
- Freeway
- Primary
- Secondary
- Tertiary
- Lane
- Unsealed road
- Road under construction
- Plaza/Mall
- Steps
- Tunnel
- Pedestrian overpass
- Walking Tour
- Walking Tour detour
- Path/Walking Trail

Boundaries
- International
- State/Province
- Disputed
- Regional/Suburb
- Marine Park
- Cliff
- Wall

Hydrography
- River, Creek
- Intermittent River
- Canal
- Water
- Dry/Salt/Intermittent Lake
- Reef

Areas
- Airport/Runway
- Beach/Desert
- Cemetery (Christian)
- Cemetery (Other)
- Glacier
- Mudflat
- Park/Forest
- Sight (Building)
- Sportsground
- Swamp/Mangrove

OUR STORY

A beat-up old car, a few dollars in the pocket and a sense of adventure. In 1972 that's all Tony and Maureen Wheeler needed for the trip of a lifetime – across Europe and Asia overland to Australia. It took several months, and at the end – broke but inspired – they sat at their kitchen table writing and stapling together their first travel guide, *Across Asia on the Cheap*. Within a week they'd sold 1500 copies. Lonely Planet was born.

Today, Lonely Planet has offices in Franklin, London, Melbourne, Oakland, Beijing and Delhi, with more than 600 staff and writers. We share Tony's belief that 'a great guidebook should do three things: inform, educate and amuse'.

OUR WRITERS

Helena Smith

Brussels, Bruges & Western Flanders Helena fell for Brussels on a drunken/architecture weekend with a great friend; she goes back for the live music, the chocolate and the vampires. A travel writer and photographer, Helena blogs about food and community at eathackney.com.

Andy Symington

Western Wallonia, The Ardennes, Luxembourg Andy first visited Belgium and Luxembourg as a backpacking youngster and was immediately impressed by this under-the-radar destination's historic towns and marvellous beer. Having returned several times over the years, he relished this opportunity to get to know the south in more depth and was blown away by the springtime beauty of the Ardennes' rivers. Based in Spain, Andy is an experienced travel writer who has authored and co-authored numerous Lonely Planet and other guidebooks. Andy also wrote Need to Know, First Time, Itineraries, History, Belgian People and the Survival Guide.

Read more about Andy at: https://auth.lonelyplanet.com/profiles/andy_symington

Donna Wheeler

Antwerp & Eastern Flanders Fuelled by a love of Flemish painting and the Antwerp Six, Donna had a crush on Belgium long before first venturing there over a decade ago. Since then, the country's quiet culturedness and relaxed charm has made it one of her favourite destinations. Her writing on art, architecture, history and food appears on LP.com, BBC.com Travel, National Geographic Traveler and My Art Guides, she's authored guidebooks to Italy, France, Tunisia, Algeria and Norway and is the creative director of travel magazine *She Came to Stay*. Donna also wrote Welcome to, Top 15, If You Like, Month by Month, Travel with Children, Belgium & Luxembourg Today, Creative Cuisine, Belgian Beer, and Art & Architecture.

Read more about Donna at: https://auth.lonelyplanet.com/profiles/donnawheeler

Published by Lonely Planet Publications Pty Ltd
ABN 36 005 607 983
6th edition – April 2016
ISBN 978 1 74321 391 9

10 9 8 7 6 5 4 3 2 1
Printed in China